Praise for *Tripping*

"A fascinating journey through the wonders and terrors of psychedelic life."
—*Elle*

"Balancing seriousness with a great sense of adventure, this terrifically engaging compendium avoids all of the expected cultural and psychological cliches. Hayes has not only assembled a group of highly literate testimonies, but has placed them in a broader historical, social, and religious context. Hayes clearly intends to demystify the use of psychedelics."
—*Publishers Weekly*

"Both informative and highly moving. A responsible approach to documenting profound experiences with drugs."
—*Lancet*

"Intriguing. Traverses the lines between reality and expanded consciousness, detailing how psychotropics affect the creative process and their underlying chemical and physiological effects. The narratives are informative, cautionary, hilarious and spooky."
—*San Francisco Chronicle*

"Hayes is such a bristling and intelligent writer that one almost wishes he had written the whole book himself. In the McKenna interview, and in Hayes's introduction, the free flow of ideas about these *verboten* substances and their anthropological/psychological possibilities is exhilarating."
—*The Oxford American*

"Hayes has done his research well. His introductory chapters are riveting, unique, and challenge many of the commonly held beliefs about psychotropic drug use."
—*Santa Fe New Mexican*

"A brilliant collection without a dud in the lot. Hayes is a superior editor precisely because he understands that generic conventions are no more than a scaffolding for creation. Accordingly, he has included only those [stories] that possess the greatest novelty—in the best Terence McKenna sense of the word. Speaking of McKenna, the cherry on this cake is a new 'conversation' with Terence. In the rich treasury of McKenna interviews, this one stands out as one of the most panoramic. Hayes, besides being a fine editor and interviewer, is a serious scholar in his own right. With its many and various virtues, *Tripping* will appeal to all kinds of readers, from researchers to sensation-seekers."
—*Relix*

"An excellent travel guide that demystifies the shrill and long-standing propaganda of the Drug Enforcement Agency, Nancy Reagan, and the Hollywood studio system."
—*Flaunt*

"For seriously treating what is often characterized as nihilistic and destructive enterainment, [*Tripping*] deserves its place in the literature of psychoactive substances. The concluding conversation with Terence McKenna is entirely fitting."
—*Booklist*

"Exciting and very personal tales about the transforming effects of drugs. A feast of recognition and inspiration." —*Soft Secrets* (Holland)

"Along with serious essays, [*Tripping*] takes an objective, well-rounded look at altered states." —*State Press* (Arizona)

"We can theorize about psychedelics till the cow patties come home, but there's nothing as poignant, perplexing, and funny as a well-told trip report. Charles Hayes has gathered together some great ones. *Tripping* is instructive, hilarious and—let's face it—enticing. I *loved* it."
—R.U. Sirius, founder of *Mondo 2000*

"Exhilarating and alarming. Does more to capture the 'heaven and hell' aspects of the psychedelic experience than any other book of our generation." —Rick Strassman, M.D., author of *DMT: The Spirit Molecule*

"A fascinating collection of accounts from behind the veil. Can we really put into words that of which we can not speak? The best efforts so far can be found here."
—Karl Jansen, M.D., Ph.D., author of *Ketamine: Dreams and Realities*

"This richly rewarding book takes the reader into uncharted domains of consciousness and creativity. The stories told, the reflections given reveal the phenomenal landscapes of innerspace."
—Jean Houston, Ph.D., author of *A Mystic Life*

"An important contribution to countercultural history."
—Paul Krassner, author of *Psychedelic Trips for the Mind*

"Here's life from the trenches of consciousness, psychedelic style. *Tripping* presents a dipperful of dreams as seen and recounted by the users of hallucinogens. It may not be 1968, but you'd never know it after reading this diary-like collection. Things are as psychedelic as ever, and here's why." —Thomas Lyttle, author of *Psychedelics ReImagined*

TRIPPING

Charles Hayes (b. 1955) has been a writer/editor for a variety of businesses and organizations, a communications manager for a marketing firm, and a journalist whose work has appeared in *The Oxford American*, *High Times*, *Heads*, *The Earth Times*, and *E* magazine. A resident of Westchester County, New York, Charles can be contacted by e-mail at *Trippingtales@aol.com* and at his Website, *www.psychedelicadventures.com*.

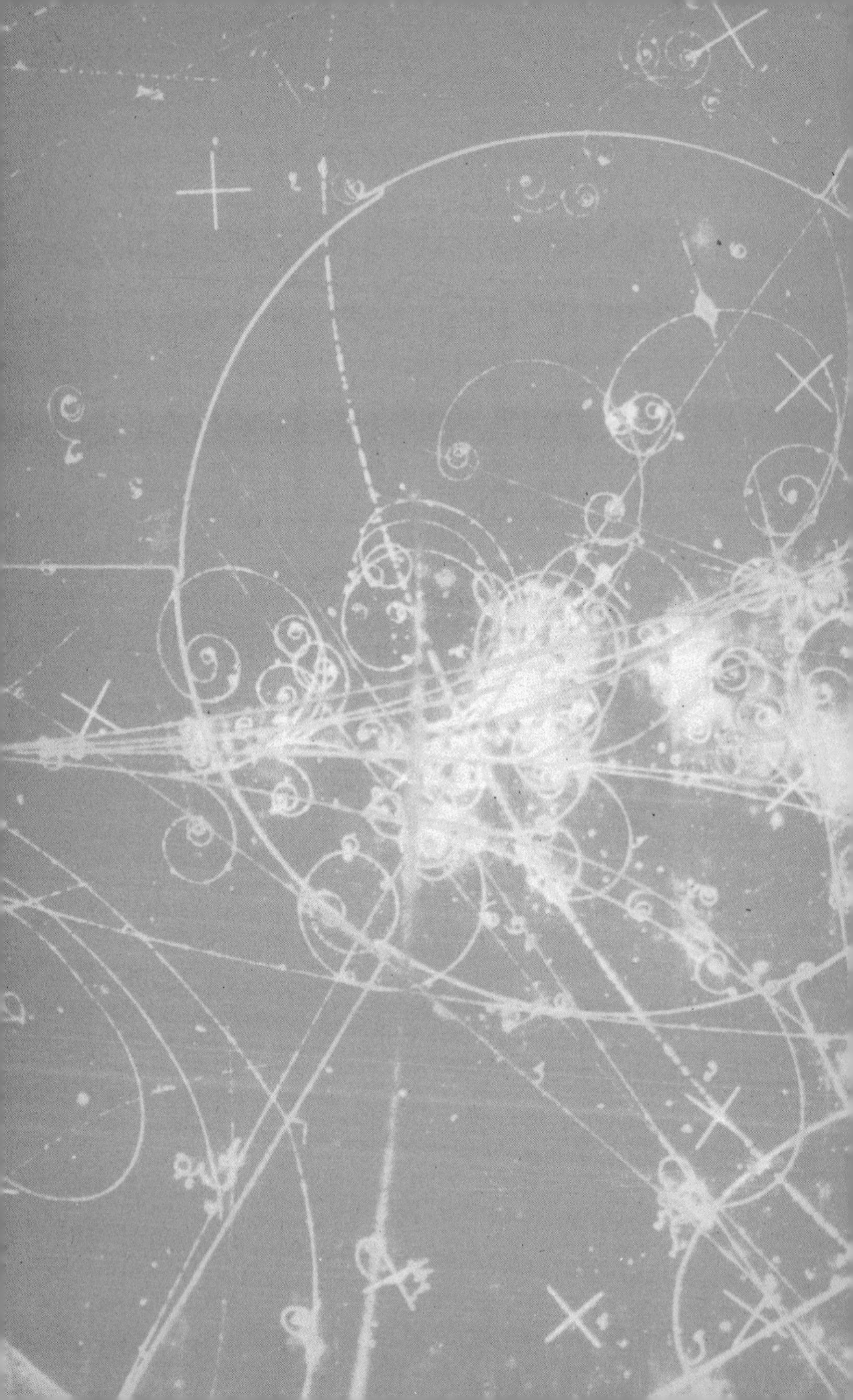

TRIPPING

An Anthology of True-Life Psychedelic Adventures

Edited and with an Introduction and Other Texts by Charles Hayes

PENGUIN COMPASS

PENGUIN BOOKS
Published by the Penguin Group
Penguin Group (USA) Inc., 375 Hudson Street, New York, New York 10014, U.S.A.
Penguin Books Ltd, 80 Strand, London WC2R 0RL, England
Penguin Books Australia Ltd, 250 Camberwell Road, Camberwell, Victoria 3124, Australia
Penguin Books Canada Ltd, 10 Alcorn Avenue, Toronto, Ontario, Canada M4V 3B2
Penguin Books India (P) Ltd, 11 Community Centre, Panchsheel Park, New Delhi – 110 017, India
Penguin Books (N.Z.) Ltd, Cnr Rosedale and Airborne Roads, Albany, Auckland, New Zealand
Penguin Books (South Africa) (Pty) Ltd, 24 Sturdee Avenue,
Rosebank, Johannesburg 2196, South Africa

Penguin Books Ltd, Registered Offices: 80 Strand, London WC2R 0RL, England

First Published in Penguin Compass 2000

10 9 8 7 6 5

Background art for title page spread and part title pages adapted from a bubble chamber photograph depicting a spray of subatomic particle tracks, courtesy of the European Organization for Nuclear Research (CERN)

LIBRARY OF CONGRESS CATALOGING-IN-PUBLICATION DATA
Tripping : an anthology of true-life psychedelic adventures / edited and with an introduction by Charles Hayes.
p. cm.
Includes bibliographical references and index.
ISBN 0 14 01.9574 2
1. Hallucinogenic drugs and religious experience. I. Hayes, Charles, 1955–

BL65.D7 T752000
154.4—dc21 00-035633

Printed in the United States of America
Set in Trump Mediaeval
Designed by Jessica Shatan

for all who had the courage to share for this book some of the most private, intimate, and momentous details of their lives,

for the spirit of the late Terence McKenna, a true Magellan of the imagination and Copernicus of the hyperreal, who braved the alien otherness of it all and sighted myriad new heavenly bodies in the cosmos of consciousness,

for my mother, that she may finally understand some of the things that had her so worried back in my student years,

for Mark, Fred, and Iris, who were there when I made my first glimpses through the wall and on such occasions helped to spark the ineffable,

and

for Doug and Andy, who didn't make it back from the longest trip of all.

Vision Crystal by Alex Grey, oil on wood panel, © 2000, courtesy of the artist.

A vision [is] not, as the modern philosophy supposes, a cloudy vapor or a nothing, but [is] organized and minutely articulated beyond all that the mortal and perishing nature can produce. He who does not imagine in stronger and better lineaments, and in stronger and better light than his perishing eye can see, does not imagine at all.

—William Blake

Note to the Reader

The reader should be advised that, in some instances, the consumption of psychotropic substances can lead to physiological and/or psychological harm. Many of the substances discussed in this book, or their sources or by-products, can be toxic or otherwise injurious. Moreover, most of the substances mentioned are illegal in the United States and/or other countries, where possession or use can be punishable by imprisonment for a significant period of time. In publishing this book, the author and publisher intend only to provide readers with a factual, insightful report on the physical and psychological experiences of those who have experimented with psychotropic substances. Neither the author nor the publisher endorses or encourages their use, and neither shall be liable or responsible for any loss, injury, or damage allegedly arising from any information or suggestion in this book.

Preface

One of the things that prompted this book was the tale of a real Celt of a fellow I knew who worked as a pressman in the inky bowels of one of New York City's dailies, where the paper was printed. One night at a smoky, old-time saloon for "newspapermen," he relayed how he'd taken acid one evening and witnessed his own conception by way of catching his parents in the act of making him. There they were on the living-room sofa, enjoined at the loins, making tender love in the supple skins they wore the night they brought him into this world. He said that he'd just sat there and wept at the shuddering beauty of the scene, the roseate gleam on the lovers' bodies, and the sweet desire that moved them to merge so moistly and meaningfully.

The story amazed me. It was as if he'd been granted a glimpse of his own genesis through a sort of umbilical telescope, a once-in-a-lifetime cruise through the sap of the family tree. Still, I wondered about the rules that govern such screenings. Of course, you're really not supposed to see these things, I thought. It must have been the action of some powerful agent that had pulled some strings to broadcast such a sacred moment.

Visions of this sort are naturally considered forbidden, a violation of the sanctity of parental privacy, akin to unveiling the face of Jehovah Himself—not to mention the whole rap sheet of Oedipal transgressions inherent in peeking through the keyhole of your parents' love chamber when they're getting it on. It's just not done. If you get caught, you're in trouble, right? But who was there to catch him? Only his conscience, perhaps, but he didn't feel guilty about what he was seeing. Far from it. He was so overcome with joy and tenderness—and gratitude for being hatched in such a loving, orgasmic reverie—that he was weeping for the sheer conjugal majesty of it all.

I wondered, Is there a legitimate spiritual, psychological, or emotional purpose for his being shown this vision? Will he be a better person for having spied on his parents in the act of coitus, even if they were doing it to beget him? Well, spying may not be the word for this, but the sort of act he'd just taken in is not your standard spectator sport. Should his peeping be chalked up to chemical tomfoolery and summarily tossed back into the iridescent spume of the psychedelic sea as so much indigestible Freudian detritus?

Other questions arose. Could there have been any authenticity to the vision? Could it actually have occurred the way he saw it? Or was it a sort of multimedia Jungian-style merging of the yin and yang hemispheres of his subconscious into one orgone-suffused ball of wholesome regenerative energy by which he effectively gave birth to himself? Clearly, the vision had worked its "intended" effect. He was in total rapture and later considered the vision a grace. Still, I wondered, isn't there a damn good reason for the erection of the curtain he'd peeked through? And why was *he* allowed to part the curtain? What made *him* special? Was it who he was or what he ate? How do you get hold of the metaphysical View-Master that holds such phantasmal celluloid in its image wheels? Is it conceivable that a psychoactive drug could be sanctioned for such purposes by the powers that govern human consciousness and our relations with our progenitors?

The (generic) psychedelic, of course, can also open the hatch at the other end of a life span, when the wick first licked by the flame of creation finally wavers, flickers down, and poof!—blows out altogether. According to Terence McKenna, one of history's most compelling champions of psychedelic consciousness (who, sadly, died of brain cancer in April 2000, when this book was in production), psychedelic states anticipate the dying process, which can be an inward journey to explore celestial, paradisal, and infernal realms. In revealing that the emperor wears no clothes and that things fall apart, the psychedelic experience decrypts the death bound into all things. (Feeling that death was close, McKenna told a group gathered at the Esalen Institute in December 1999, "If psychedelics don't ready you for the great beyond, then I don't know what really does.")

Death is therefore a succinct term for the process of undoing to which all our doings must and do lead. Showing us brief, resonant images of aging and decay (e.g., one's own mug on that of a car-crash victim lying on the road, a hallucination one tripper reported to me), and dissolving the boundaries that separate us from the knowledge of life in the next room (the next skin, the next eon, the next incarnation . . .), the psychedelic is most surely concerned with death, with endings that, if we could only see, become beginnings in other forms.

When the psychedelic first rocked me in my early twenties with shimmering new sensibilities that shook my petty mortal concerns like so many scales from my skin, it struck me that I was being offered a friendly glimpse into the grave. For the first time I had the distinct notion that death was not some stationary finish line or exit door off in the hopefully distant future, but a body of revelation that even now arced back toward the beginning, reaching back to inform, to ready, to greet, and to welcome. I saw that my own death could be a lyric *memory,* that the circular river of time was like a gently flowing menstrual stream from the mind of God, a pregnancy with death the child.

Naturally, there are more terrifying guises of death that the psychedelic can conjure, but these are likely tied to the latent guilt that knowledge of death is a sort of transgression—along the lines of Jehovah's grave *warning* that no mortal shall ever see His face. In the frightfully ratiocinative short story by the prerevolutionary Russian writer Leonid Andreyev, after Lazarus has a taste of the Other World, the salt in this one loses its savor. In the film *Raiders of the Lost Ark* (1981), Indiana Jones (Harrison Ford) is forbidden to open his eyes to behold the power and mystery of Creation unleashed when the Ark of the Covenant is unduly sprung open by the Nazis. There is invariably at least one story in each of the world's mythologies that admonishes us not to poke around in such realms or crowd the Creator Himself.

Perhaps there are some cosmological scenes that are set off limits to human awareness by the powers of the universe, authorities senior by far to those of family and state. There could be good reason to keep a lid on the cask that holds the mysteries of the Great Beyond, but then again, maybe that's too much to ask of mere mortals. If such a cache can be found, perhaps we owe it to ourselves to open it and have a look. If the voices of the Sirens are so sweet, can't we hear just a verse or two? Maybe the force that forbids us is only fear and not some imperative moral authority after all.

In the belief that glimpses into alternative realities can shed light on this one, and that no encounter with the ineffable is so otherworldly as to be justly forbidden or void of some correlative (if not yet determined) meaning for this life, I set out in 1994 to document psychedelic experiences that were transformational, awe-provoking, or otherwise indelible to their subjects. After several years spent digging up willing voices for the project in locations across the globe, and then transcribing their stories, the product of my quest is the compilation of narratives that this book comprises.

My intent in assembling these unusual, often unsettling tales is to create a work not so much of literature but one of *document.* By rendering into print the astonishing phenomena of psychedelic drugs—as well as their impact on the human psyche—they can be rescued from the stream of ephemera, dried off in the prosaic light of reading lamps, and then ruminated over by a larger population of fellow and vicarious travelers.

The contents of this book are in many ways the stuff of dreams, in this case chemically induced ones: phantasms seen with eyes that were opened by a foreign agent, a force often so subversive as to undermine one's faith in the reality of things as they generally appear. If dreams conjured in sleep should have any meaning for those awakened by them, then these gathered here, spun out of some keen yet alien wakefulness, might have even more.

Universal Mind Lattice from *Sacred Mirrors* series by Alex Grey, acrylic on canvas, © 2000, courtesy of the artist.

Contents

Void/Clear Light from *Sacred Mirrors* series by Alex Grey, acrylic on canvas, © 2000, courtesy of the artist.

PART I

Introduction

The Psychedelic [in] Society: A Brief Cultural History of Tripping

Psychedelics are notorious today because of the rude splash they made in the Sixties and Seventies, when the tidal wave of altered consciousness they unleashed billowed across the social landscape, upsetting many an apple cart, Newtonian and otherwise, along the way. During the course of this insurrectional drive to expand the human mind, millions of students, artists, and other seekers were ushered by chemical agents toward—and, hopefully, through—the Doors of Perception, a term borrowed from William Blake by Aldous Huxley to describe, in his 1954 book of the same title, the expansive universe to which drugs such as LSD can open up the mortal brain—a realm in which everything appears, in Blake's words, "as it is, infinite."

Timothy Leary's calls to "tune in" psychedelically, and Ken Kesey's Electric Kool-Aid Acid Tests, the multimedia LSD extravaganzas immortalized by Tom Wolfe, steered untold legions through these portals into a molten state of being which is all but smothered today beneath the buttoned-down collars of straitlaced yuppie composure. Because most psychedelic drugs have been illegal since 1966, there are no accurate polls to determine the numbers of people who experimented. But many at least temporarily heeded Leary's clarion call to abandon middle-class security and catch the wave of revelation by gulping down psychotropic chemicals. Leary's death in 1996 has sparked a burst of introspection on the impact of the drugs he proselytized, and the high numbers of Baby Boomers who stormed heaven with them now have the stature to contemplate the fruits of their rebellions.

The demographics of tripping are actually much broader than one might suspect. You needn't be a hippie to have a psychedelic background. The corporate and civic leaders who are running the country today are likely to have once been experimental longhairs in their school days. We know that President Bill Clinton and both major-party candidates vying to succeed him, Vice President Al Gore and Texas governor George W. Bush, have all admitted or intimated that they've used illegal drugs in the past. Indeed, many in high places today have been in even higher ones in their youth, touring the outer galaxies of their own minds on acid and other psychedelics. Millions have a unique lens embedded in their minds composed of the rarefled fibers of their hallucinogenic experiences. Meanwhile, many who didn't "turn on" are wondering, "What did I miss?" Still others, psychedelic veterans among them, find "recreational" drugs and the culture of their "indulgence" disquieting, and for good reason from their perspective. Trips, after all, were known to go awry.

As the new millennium begins, the use of psychedelics is again on the rise after tapering off in the 1980s. How could this be happening? Wasn't the first time around, the convulsive Sixties and Seventies, too unsettling for anybody to want to go back? Well, the fact is that human beings will always want to suspend everyday reality, be it by legal means or otherwise, and they will always be at least curious about alternate states of consciousness, especially those that are consecrated in many of the world's ancient traditions.

Veneration for the induced visionary experience has roots in virtually every culture on earth, however sublimated or repressed it is today. In fact, one could argue that the use of visionary plants and hallowed drafts has been seminal to the development of civilization. Two of the most pervasive and influential cultures the planet has ever seen, that of Hellenistic Greece and Aryan India, contained at their very core inspirations derived from the ingestion of psychedelic concoctions.

For two thousand years before its eradication by Christians in the fourth century A.D., the celebration of the Eleusinian Mysteries was the peak-experience of the ancient Greeks, a "holy institution," according to religion historian Huston Smith, for regularly opening "a space in the human psyche for God to enter." After a half year of rites, the pilgrimage to Eleusis just west of Athens climaxed with the reenactment of a sacred drama that was enhanced by the drinking of *kykeon,* a grainy beverage believed to contain barley ergot. Among notable initiates were Socrates, Plato, Sophocles, Aristotle, Aeschylus, Cicero, Pindar, and possibly Homer. A communion between gods and men, between the living and the dead, the ceremony at Eleusis was a symbolic journey to the underworld to claim back from death Persephone, the daughter of the grain goddess Demeter. The setting for this ur-psychedelic experience was a *telesterion* (initiation hall) at the very site where Persephone is said to have emerged from Hades with the newborn son she'd conceived there. A series of breathtaking, masterfully orchestrated special effects enthralled the senses and conjured the specter of deliverance from the forces of darkness through a ritualized resurrection. The whirlpool of stimuli that washed over initiates involved an Oz-like chimera of voices, music, perfumes, mists, light, and shadows. According to Carl A. P. Ruck, co-author with R. Gordon Wasson of *The Road to Eleusis* (1978), at the peak of the crescendo, the "bellowing roar of a gong-like instrument that outdid . . . the mightiest thunderclap, coming from the bowels of the earth" announced the arrival of the queen of the netherworld.

All were forbidden by penalty of death to tell what they'd seen. "Even a poet could only say that he had seen the beginning and the end of life and known that they were one, something given by God," writes Ruck. "The division between earth and sky melted into a pillar of light." Of course, some couldn't hold their tongues about such a marvel. A scandal ensued when some aristocratic Athenians began celebrating the Mysteries at dinner parties in their homes with groups of "drunken" revelers. Ruck believes that it may have been for the crime of using the sacred brew recreationally that Socrates was tried and condemned. (Such a profanation of the holy potion might have a modern-day parallel in the spilling of LSD into the well water of the mass media and youth culture during the early Sixties.)

Notably, the Mysteries were not freely conjured by anyone who could get their hands on the *kykeon.* They were the exclusive charge of two families who served as hierophants for two thousand years. Clearly, the indoctrination and rites leading up to the swigging of the mash were at least as influential as the concoction itself in weaving the phantasm that stole over the pilgrims' senses. Such congregational participation and extensive preparation for a psychedelic experience is almost unheard of in the modern West. If anything like the Eleusinian Mysteries had survived the high-tech world of today, it would almost certainly be diluted and profaned, taking the form of a commercialized adventure-tourism attraction involving a multimedia circus of light and sound somewhat akin to the group-mind experience of a Trips Festival or a rave. Re-creation of the *kykeon* brew has proved elusive, however, even to such consummate ergot specialists as Albert Hofmann, who used the fungus in his 1938 invention of LSD.

The earliest known religious texts are a collection of hymns called *The Rig Veda,* written by Aryans who swept down into India from Siberia. Among the 1,028 verses, considered the foundation of the Hindu religion, 120 are devoted to praise for the rootless, leafless plant called Soma, which is deified for conferring immortality and divine inspiration. "We have drunk the Soma; we have become immortal; we have gone to the light; we have found the gods." (*Rig Veda* 8.48.1–15)

Wasson conjectured that Soma was *Amanita muscaria,* the red-capped Fly Agaric mushroom depicted ubiquitously to this day in European folktale literature and used ritualistically by Siberian and some Native American tribes. This conclusion was based, in part, on the *Amanita*'s unique ability to inebriate people who drink the user's urine, which is corroborated by a reference in *The Rig Veda* to ceremonial urine drinking. Wasson tried *Amanita* several times himself, but never really got off. Terence McKenna believed that Soma is actually the *Psilocybe cubensis* mushroom, in part because of the generally weak and erratic performance of the *Amanita* mushroom in modern trials. In this volume, however, I've included an *Amanita* trip tale that corroborates Wasson's theory, an excerpt (page 114) from Clark Heinrich's book *Strange Fruit* (1995), which has not yet been published in the United States. Uncovering the ancient ethnobotanical truth about Soma is an ongoing endeavor, but there is little doubt that the very ether of Indian religion is a psychotropic, probably mycelial, plant.

The average American today still has little if any inkling of the traditions for the sacramental use of mushrooms and other plants by cultures across the globe, lumping all drugs into one Baggie-ful of stupefying intoxicants that will turn you into a sick, lazy lowlife bound for jail or an early death. Unlikely as it may seem, however, an appreciation for the induced visionary experience is apparent not so far beneath the surface of mainstream modern culture. For me this remnant sensibility is epitomized in the vision of Walt Disney (a known cocaine user), whose *imagineered*™ re-creations of classic fables often alluded to the fruitful alterability of consciousness.

The pivotal scene in *Dumbo* (1941), for instance, is the transformation of consciousness and augmentation of capacity—in this case, the big-eared elephant's motor skills—via a hallucinatory delirium brought on when the dejected pachyderm drinks a barrelful of water into which, unbeknownst to him, a bottle of spirits had been accidentally spilled. To the foreboding lyrics and serpentine melody of "Pink Elephants on Parade," Dumbo begins seeing things "you know that ain't" (a succession of fractals and geometrical patterns, forms morphing into new ones, and scenes of Oriental mystery and erotica), then passes into oblivion, from which he wakes up in the highest branches of a tree. Thus Dumbo earns his wings not through an act of obeisance to the Ten Commandments but in the throes of a psychotropic-induced visionary state.

Fantasia (1940) features scenes that portray synesthesia ("See the music, hear the pictures," reads the video's promotional copy) and other phantasmic phenomena that make it one of the most beloved of all films to view while tripping. Disney's chief visualist for the project was the subject of mescaline experiments by Kurt Beninger (an associate of Carl Jung and Herman Hesse), whose groundbreaking work *The Mescaline Inebriation,* was published in 1927. In the early decades of Disneyland, a pink elixir was served upon entry in the Enchanted Tiki Room to accentuate the pleasure of the tropical respite and render the bird songs that much sweeter. The psychoactive element of the potion was make-believe, of course, but today, in deference to stricter notions of "family values" now in vogue, the suggestive little cocktail is no longer offered to visitors.

Since the cataclysms of the Sixties and Seventies, a more tenacious if less overtly messianic subculture has grown up around the psychedelic. Nowhere in the industrial world is psychedelic consciousness more aboveboard and appreciated than in the computer software business, where it is regarded as the inspiration for cybernetics—the very definition of twenty-first century communications efficiency—by many of its most illustrious practitioners. According to Jaron Lanier, a pioneer in the virtual reality industry, "almost to a person, the founders of the [personal] computer industry were psychedelic-style hippies. . . . Within the computer science community there's a very strong connection with the '60s psychedelic tradition, absolutely no question about it."

In the TNT docudrama *Pirates of Silicon Valley* (1999), Apple founder Steve Jobs is depicted on an acid trip in which he conceives himself as the conductor of his own cosmic symphony. Bob Wallace, one of the early developers of Microsoft, who now runs Mind Books, the on-line purveyor of tomes devoted to psychedelic and alternative consciousness, has said that his conception of shareware as a formal business application was psychedelically inspired. Lotus spreadsheet designer Mitchell Kapor, cofounder with Grateful Dead lyricist John Perry Barlow (see page 212) of the Electronic Frontier Foundation, an Internet advocacy organization, has attributed certain "recreational chemicals" to sharpening his business acumen. Bob Jesse left his position as vice president of business development at Oracle, the world's second-largest software company after Microsoft, to head the Council on Spiritual Practices, a nonprofit organization that advocates (among other things) the responsible use of *entheogens* (divine-manifesting drugs) for religious purposes. Such a marriage of technology and psychedelic consciousness—and a resoundingly profitable and influential one at that—might have been foretold by Marshall McLuhan's 1968 observation that "the computer is the LSD of the business world."

The possibility that industrial success might in any way be attributed to the psychedelic is not overtly bantered about in Wall Street boardrooms, where psychedelic acuity is not yet measured out in lucre as an asset or variable in a company's fortunes. But according to author and media theorist Douglas Rushkoff, firms "such as Sun Microsystems that lead the Valley of the Nerds [Silicon Valley] recognize the popularity of psychedelics among their employees." You need only look at the covers of the cyber-age magazines *Wired* and *Mondo 2000* to conclude that the computer cognoscenti have had at least some contact with the whirring currents of the psychedelic mainframe.

The phrase "We're all connected," often exclaimed during a psychedelic experience, might just as well be uttered by a PC user tapping into the mycelium-like World Wide Web for the first time. Cyberspace is, in many respects, an electronic mirror of the hyperspatial web of synaptic nerves running through the Universal Mind, the Indra's Net of impulses and receptor sites that some say they've accessed by psychedelics. (According to the ancient myth, Indra, the king of the Hindu pantheon, created a vast web comprising strings of jewels. Each jewel both reflected and was reflected by all the others, thus revealing both its uniqueness and its universality.) A sort of invisible yet real medium of contact between any and all points, cyberspace is a habitat for the mitosis-like proliferation of the idea germs called *memes,* and an endless mind field on which to explode the fractal equations that portray the parallel orders of controlled chaos in the universe.

Much of what I unearthed about contemporary psychedelic culture would be considered elementary or passé to the many who tune into recordings of McKenna's incandescent rants; travel hundreds of miles to raves, Rainbow Gatherings, or neo-pagan festivals like Starwood and Burning Man; subscribe to hyperspatial mind rags like *TRP*, *Head Magazine,* and *Magical Blend*; and log on to the homepage for the *Salvia divinorum* Research and Information Center and other psychedelic Websites. But I uncovered a great deal of information about the subject that I wish I'd known back when I was a teenage tripper in the 1970s. My research revealed how much I and others were in the dark—and still are—in regard to maximum safety and security issues, the history of psychedelic substance usage, and the wisest methods of navigating the various hazards and hassles of the psychedelic experience. Although there have been many new developments since I started out (new substances, resources, methods), much of the apparent change that I perceive in psychedelic culture is only a function of my earlier ignorance. When I started tripping at age fifteen, I'd barely boned up on the subject. There was information and guidance available, of course, but I was aware of very little of it.

I have since learned that the modern psychedelic revolution first germinated in the time and place that I was born, in mid-Fifties Los Angeles, unofficially inaugurated on a brilliant morning in May 1953, when Huxley threw back four hundred milligrams of "mescalin" sulfate in the tawny, then-unspoiled Hollywood Hills. The psychedelic then enjoyed a decade of expansive development before generating so much heat that the law was provoked to come down harshly on it. (The state of California's ban on LSD took effect on October 6, 1966, and the other states soon followed suit.) Many might be astonished that "mind-blowing" psychedelics once enjoyed an age of relative freedom of proliferation and experimentation, during which one worried not about getting busted and only minimally about "freaking out." During that window of opportunity, psychologists, Beats and artists, and various members of the intelligentsia, including some pillars of the ruling class, experimented quietly and not so quietly with mescaline sulfate, psilocybin tablets, and LSD-25 to mostly rave reviews.

Cary Grant, the very emblem of debonair Forties-era class, admitted taking acid over a hundred times under psychiatric supervision in the 1950s. Thrilled with the results, he credited LSD with helping him control his boozing and come to terms with unresolved conflicts involving his parents. (I recall a circa 1970 article in a Chicago daily in which Grant described how, during an early acid experience, he was so overwhelmed with the expurgatorial power of the drug that he felt he was about to let loose with a terrific, system-wide, psychical bowel movement.) Time/Life publisher Henry Luce described "chatting up God" on a golf course during an LSD session, while his wife, Clare Boothe Luce, cleaned her psychical house with the medicine. A right-wing ideologue, Mrs. Luce believed that LSD was fine for the elite, but not advisable for the masses. "We wouldn't want everyone doing too much of a good thing," she is reported as saying.

Before the ban, psychedelic research focused on the use of LSD in treating alcoholism, depression, sexual neuroses, autism, compulsive syndromes, and criminal psychopathology. By 1965 there were more than two thousand scientific papers describing the treatment of up to forty thousand patients with psychedelic drugs. Success was commonplace. Among the more stunning results were from studies in which LSD was used in the treatment of autistic children at UCLA Neuropsychiatric Institute and of chronic alcoholics at Hollwood Hospital in British Columbia and Spring Grove State Hospital in Baltimore. In a 1961 letter to Leary, Alcoholics Anonymous founder William Wilson waxed glowingly about the "immense and growing value" of "LSD and some kindred alkaloids," having personally experienced their ability to break down barriers within the self.

By the time I boarded the psychedelic bus in 1970, the commotion over LSD had already spawned a backlash against the dispersal of the chemicals far beyond the enclaves of the elite to the teenyboppers of a mass media–fed youth culture. Leary is held largely responsible for this debacle. After conducting several laudable studies as a Harvard psychologist, and pioneering and then road-mapping the psychedelic landscape in highly serviceable books used as bibles by trippers in the know during the Sixties—*The Psychedelic Experience: A Manual Based on the Tibetan Book of the Dead* (1964) and *Psychedelic Prayers after the Tao Te Ching* (1966)—the zealous pie-eyed piper actually helped ruin the name—and hence the experience of LSD as well as other psychedelics—by his puerile jingoism and shenanigans. (The rise and fall of the psychedelic revolution is chronicled brilliantly in *Storming Heaven: LSD and the American Dream* [1987] by Jay Stevens, which depicts the social factors and cumulative events that led to the national hysteria over LSD, which overtook the country and finally led to the drug's criminalization.)

The dark age of the Leary hangover may now be giving way to new light on the psychedelic horizon, visible through some cracks in the wall of proscription. Thirty-four state legislatures and the District of Columbia have passed laws—though in conflict with federal law—recognizing marijuana's medical value. The FDA has recently ended its decades-long ban on clinical psychedelic use and approved new trials for LSD, psilocybin, DMT, MDMA, and ibogaine. In Brazil the Uniao do Vegetal (UDV), a religious order that uses ayahuasca as a sacrament, got the legal right to do so by the national government in 1992. According to Curtis Wright, director of the addictive drugs division at the FDA, "It's clear that these agents have a role in understanding how the mind works, and there's also a role for them as potential ways to help people."

Back when I did most of my tripping, there were basically five psychedelic substances in use among my circles: LSD, so-called mescaline (usually inferior acid), peyote, psilocybin mushrooms, and MDA, the more potent and hallucinogenic precursor to MDMA or Ecstasy. Today there's a whole galaxy of new choices, including an apparently infinite string of synthetic analogs banned automatically by the Analog Act of 1986. Alexander (Sasha) Shulgin, the former research scientist at Dow Chemical affectionately dubbed "the Godfather of MDMA," has annexed an extensive archipelago of new territory to the psychedelic continent by creating—and then self-testing—new potions with the flick of a molecule. In *PiHKAL* (1991), an acronym for "phenethylamines I have known and loved," Shulgin and his wife, Ann, document his laboratory inventions and their psychoactive properties in the context of "A Chemical Love Story," a tale describing the courtship between these two now august and beloved figures in the psychedelic community.

In 1997 I sat in on a DMT cell group in Manhattan, the likes of which, according to one member, have propagated as a response to McKenna's irresistible endorsements. A cluster of fellows smoked the high-octane tryptamine in a dark room, then soared off internally for twenty minutes or so, returning to their senses to compare notes. The experience is so intense and otherworldly that it can take a while to piece together just a fraction of what has happened. "If only I could remember the last thing I saw before I came out . . . ," stammered one of the psychonauts, struggling to reassemble the bolt of truth that had just laid siege to his mind.

No longer a mere trend, rave (or dance) culture has swept the world since the late 1980s, a pacific movement by a mycelial network of MDMA-fueled Techno music revelers from Manchester, England, to Koh Phangan, Thailand. In the U.K., where rave took off and where youth culture burns fiercest perhaps, it is believed that the number of MDMA "pills" taken every week has increased steadily from one million in 1992. The ravers I met in London in 1997 gave me to believe that their legions, along with their defiant temperament, are growing. In the working-class district of Brixton, I talked to a laser technician for rave shows who predicts an apocalyptic confrontation between the British government and the increasingly Ecstatic youth. (It remains to be seen whether the commercialism and pop-star iconoclasm that have most recently crept into rave events, once notable for their sporelike spontaneity and the diffuse anonymity of the music, will numb the nerve ends of the movement and render it increasingly harmless from the perspective of authorities.)

The organic counterpart to Shulgin's artificial pharmacopeia is the burgeoning field of ethnobotany, led by intrepid, rainforest-trekking scholars such as McKenna, Wallace, and *Pharmacotheon* (1993) author Jonathan Ott, all intent on cataloging Mother Nature's psychotropic tools and their use in shamanic rites by traditional cultures across the globe. There's an ample and growing body of scholarship devoted to indigenous practices related to sacred plants, with passages on psychedelic seeds, snuffs, brews, and other preparations that read like accounts of occult fetish worship in James Frazier's *The Golden Bough* (1890) or Margaret Mead's *Coming of Age in Samoa* (1928). The adventure-travel circuit is riddled with mystical-magical locales where one can participate in authentic tribal rites with ayahuasca or the San Pedro cactus, take mushrooms or Ecstasy on a tropical beach under the full moon, or eat legal hash from a government shop. For the armchair traveler, Paul Devereux's *The Long Trip: A Prehistory of Psychedelia* (1997) charts the use of sacred plants all over the world from the beginning of recorded history.

The ancient Mayan civilization, whose shamans apparently made ample use of the psilocybin mushroom, figures heavily in the mythology of today's psychedelic culture. One of my participants, the London laser specialist I'll call Stan, was keen to this, while also embodying several matrices of contemporary psychedelic sophistication. Coming of age in what might be called "old wave" psychedelia—dropping acid at free festivals during the Seventies—his trade involves synchronizing beams of light to the rhythms of Goa Trance and Drum 'N Bass music for throngs of MDMA-popping twenty-somethings. But

Stan's real cup of tea is a fascination with both the anthropology and the headspace of the tryptamines.

A few years ago Stan was studying the Mayan codices in the British Museum Library when he spotted a glyph that a Christian scholar had identified as a "night light" (i.e., the artificial light of candles or paraffin), but which he believed was actually a cross section of the *yage* vine, a component of ayahuasca. Finding it curious that there were carvings of kings from separate generations sitting together eating, he translated a codex that gave what he interpreted as a recipe for time travel, using the *yage.* To celebrate the discovery, he and his brother-in-law, a mycologist, undertook a risky regime of psilocybin in combination with harmaline, an MAO inhibitor meant to potentiate the tryptamine in the mushrooms, over a period of several days.

In the course of their visioneering expedition, they encountered a network through time constructed by Mayan psychedelic shamans, who, Stan believes, set dates when they'd meet up with ancestors or progeny. When they knew that cosmological conditions were aligned for them to contact a royal figure from another age, the shamans would drink a tryptamine brew and use a form of psychical telekinesis to time-travel to meet up with him. Meanwhile, the long-departed or distant-future king would, in turn, be looking back because he knew that the shamans were looking for him. Disintegrating into the biospheric mesh of the planet, Stan recalls, "we immediately saw them and they saw us." After upping the dose of harmaline to dangerous levels, they had visions of the last scenes of the Mayan civilization, people dying of Old World diseases such as smallpox, diphtheria, and cholera. However accurate his archaeological findings and historical notions, Stan's experiences bespeak the transtemporal and cosmopolitan sensibility of the contemporary psychedelic scene.

Oral ingestion of DMT with beta-carboline MAO inhibitors is now a sort of totem among many of today's trippers, a way to both encounter and embody the Archaic Revival: the return to pure, autochthonic theology, often via modern chemistry, extolled in McKenna's 1991 compilation volume of that name. These days there's many an amateur ethnopharmacologist and psychedelic brewmeister out there, calculating the tryptamine to MAOI ratios just so. (Indeed, MAOIs can be dicey admixtures that can cause blackouts when taken in combination with tryptamines and possibly death when mixed with MDMA. Prescription MAOIs carry a slew of warnings about dangerous combinations.) Writes R. U. Sirius, cofounder of *Mondo 2000* (which *Time* calls "the cyberculture mindstyle manual-magazine"), "You can find it [the independence and erudition of the new counterculture] on the Net, where millions of youths log on to psychedelic bulletin boards. Read through the public conversations, and you'll start to wonder how many young psychedelic chemists conversant in biotechnology, comparative religion and visionary literature, are hiding in the American heartland."

There is no doubt that, with the advent of the new millennium, the use of psychedelics will continue to rise, both responsibly and otherwise, as they are increasingly seen as tools for penetrating the veils of quotidian *maya* and mass-media illusion spun by corporate greed. According to the best hopes of the new psychedelic vanguard, the expanded intelligent use of these plants and chemicals will usher in an eon of shamanic vistas and stronger definitions true to primordial forms: a pagan, aboriginal order in which the spirit will reign preeminent.

Early rave party invitation, London, 1987, artist unknown.

Basic Features of the Psychedelic Experience

One of the most remarkable features of the psychedelic experience I discerned in the course of my research was a cycle of contraction and relaxation, culminating in a kind of oceanic release. The subject begins to feel closed in—as if some ethereal sphincter is cutting him off from the realm of light and life, sometimes seemingly to the point of strangulation or death, only to open up, usually as a result of his conscious surrendering to the experience, to reveal a world that sparkles anew or alludes to the infinite expanse of the All (or the Shining Void, depending on one's terminology).

Is it a coincidence that ergot, the grain fungus used in the manufacture of LSD and, possibly, the psychedelic brew quaffed at Eleusis by the ancient Greeks, contains the same alkaloids that are used in obstetrics to induce labor contractions? It seems consistent with natural biorhythms that there is a contraction before the opening up. In 1981 I took a good quantity of mushrooms at a Halloween party at a Long Island bar. The place was hopping with a mischievous, autumnal Celtic energy emanating from the young, largely Irish-American crowd, which was gyrating to the rock-'n'-roll beat in grim reaper, red devil, and wicked witch costumes. As the drug came on, I began to feel psychically throttled, as though I were in the stiff clench of Satan, who bloody wanted to extinguish me. My friend Neal noted my agitation and said, "Hey, let's go outside for some air." I followed him out, leaned against a car, and took in some deep breaths. Almost instantly, the fiendish clamp melted away and I began to masticate madly on the harvest-charged air.

So many trippers get caught in such jaws, which have natural echoes in the constriction and trepidation of the birthing and dying processes. The contracting agent could be many things, but perhaps the common denominator is the feeling of the wall of time moving in, delineating the all-to-slim confines of a lifetime. In defense, the ego strains to reaffirm its customary sense of scale, but finally gives in to some compelling force in the swell washing over, and surrenders—often out of a real back-to-the-wall lack of any other choice—thereby enabling the tripper to catch the cosmic wave and ride it in.

Throughout this book are tales of harrowing struggles between "staying cool" and "losing it," with surprising results when the latter occurred. Perhaps a universal mechanism is at work, though each tripper has his or her own way of explaining how it works. The psychedelic can render ever so palpably the titan struggle between Thanatos, the death instinct, and Eros, the regenerative impulse that bears the germ of love, should it ever break free of death's constricting grip. For a short and indelible time, the terrible combat is framed in time as a gladiator clash, so it's possible to see who's winning and cheer on a favorite—that is until the entire amphitheater is blown away in one gust of empyrean wind.

The too-sudden opening up of the universe can, in turn, induce an onslaught of panic at what Aldous Huxley called the "horror of infinity," a terror of the vastness of the void within or without, of the utter minuteness and aloneness of the soul in the cosmos. A clenching reflex is, after all, a natural response to the floor and ceiling flying out of your mind. One subject in the mid-Sixties psychedelic research of Robert Masters and Jean Houston was so spooked by the sheer enormity of space that she was afraid of falling through the "vast spaces between atoms."

An eschatological theme is recurrent throughout many a trip. A sense of finality comes over the subject, who feels that he's just spent his last chance to fulfill a required regimen before vaporizing into nothing, that he's moving at increasing velocity toward the end of his temporal cell, the current mode or pattern he's in, or of life itself. But as the aperture narrows and the walls move in, a whirlwind of epistemological revisionism can happen as your life flashes before you. Many new resolutions are made under such duress. Often, though not always, the taut clutch of the clock hands is pried loose by a surge of expansive relief that rides through, revealing time's true nature as more surfboard or mattress stuffing than vise or reaper's scythe.

Observing this phenomenon in so many of the subjects I talked to, I'm not surprised that Terence McKenna formulated an entire scheme for the End of History, a culmination of synchronistic eventfulness within an ever-tightening spiral of time. When the experience flows well, this buildup of anticipation or dread empties out into an almost comic lightness. This dynamic is captured musically in the transition between the first two sections of the Beatles' "A Day in the Life" (1967), in which the orchestra rises to a screechy crescendo, only to bounce into a reverie about waking up on an ordinary morning—life goes on.

But the going can be rough. If you don't have smooth passage over that bump, the ultimate climax or *eschaton* that sits like a giant period (full stop) at the end of a life's sentence—or aren't held in a good grip by the angels on the Other Side who can pull you over, you may run into a wall or pass through it as only a ghost of your former self. When there is no such bridge, usually furnished by a "high-enough" dose to propel you all the way through the cycle, panic ensues. Your voice loses its harmonic grounding in your core and chatters whitely as your legs pump furiously, treading air, going nowhere, your nose pressed painfully to the windscreen of your ditched and motionless vehicle, as you gaze into the marrow of entropy and death. But once the invisible spring is sprung, you can feel as though you're sitting in a paradisal garden, your senses caressed by the glad hand of creation, your entire being anointed with the sacred secretion, the very ooze of Time itself. In other words, reprieve: reprieve from the timorous vigil of watching the minutes of your life mount the stairs to your attic retreat, when, through a brief window of opportunity, you can see that the quantity of time in the world is absolutely ample and just.

A trip can work as a sort of exorcism. You can feel as if you've evicted some haunting living entity—that demon bastard that's been vexing you or holding you back. But you can also feel as though you've taken one aboard, absorbed some spectral pneumatic spook, which, unpurged by the full flowering of the trip dynamic, remains chained in an abysmal *bardo* cell, trapped between death and rebirth. Worse, you can even feel as though you've given up *the* ghost, fallen dead to the world: become a chill, unanchored wad of refuse consciousness floating just out of reach above the glowing orange coils of mortal commerce. You can see wraiths in the faces of companions too. I took a farewell dose of acid with a girlfriend at the end of our ill-fated affair, and saw the specter of a black hog inlaid in her face, an omen that the love had died. Another time, I saw the two heads of Janus over the one of an undosed reveler at a wedding party—a sign to me that he (or was it me?) was stuck in the Roman realm of the unredeemed.

Haunting images and presences can abound, some that ravage you enough to dissuade you from entering the psychedelic realm again, and some that linger until the mind can break them down and finally pass them out. The notion frequently instilled by the psychedelic, that one is not alone, can have an impact ranging from terror to comfort, depending on the perceived nature of the visitor, and the disposition and hospitality of the host.

Even a bad trip can be illuminating, particularly when experienced in a psychiatric or similarly supportive setting. With some measure of success, LSD therapists of the late Fifties and early Sixties urged their subjects to explore the internal abysses they confronted in order to flush deep-seated hatreds and fears to the surface and to help undo psychic knots that had been tied by the hands of fate. In the belief that "bummers can be productive and liberating," the Mexican doctor Salvador Roquet went so far as to *induce* bad trips, encouraging his patients to "go toward the pain." Jewish patients, for instance, were forced to listen to speeches by Hitler. (Roquet was a mentor to Richard Yensen, Ph.D., who successfully treated alcoholics in the early Sixties at the Maryland Psychiatric Research Center. In 1997 Yensen had acquired the largest legal supply of LSD in America [499 doses] after receiving FDA approval to use it to treat drug addicts at his Baltimore clinic, the Orenda Institute, provided that he revise his research and safety protocols.)

Accepting the "one danger of the mystical path: there is no way back without doing oneself harm," Peter Matthiessen's girlfriend in *The Snow Leopard* (1978) "saw that she might free herself by living out the fear of death, the demoniac rage at one's own helplessness that drug hallucinations represent, and in that way let go of a life-killing accumulation of defenses." While it's no mean feat to benefit from and then wax sanguinely about a freak-out, the sudden exposition of a nagging neurosis is often a psychiatric breakthrough in itself, as well as a marked leap forward in the subject's personal development. Heaven help the rare tripper for whom the negativity conjured by the psychedelic seems so utterly inexplicable as to become a brand-new vexation and burden.

But trips needn't be so utterly otherworldly and unfamiliar. Stanislav Grof, one of the world's premier authorities on psychedelic research and therapy, describes the psychedelic experience as a "catalyst or amplifier of mental processes." Instead of inducing "drug-specific" states, he says, psychedelics "seem to activate preexisting matrices or potentials of the human mind," working as an "inner radar that scans the system and detects contents with the strongest emotional charge." A psychedelic experience can force parcels of emotional content to the surface where they can interact with the light of day in a way that can lead to catharsis.

Interestingly, on his maiden mescaline sulfate voyage, Huxley was not as taken with the change to his personal constitution or perceptions as he was with his sudden access to the "realm of objective fact." Today we know that just as the psychedelic can evince what the Christian mystic Meister Eckehart called the *Istigkeit,* the *isness* or *suchness* of things in the objective realm, it can also flush out emotional stores from deep within the psyche. Thus it can appear to illuminate the true nature of both the observer and the observed.

At the end of a romance that seemed to have the promise of eternity but lasted but a single summer, I bought some acid in Washington Square Park in Manhattan and dropped it with my girlfriend in the middle of the night. As the day broke, we ended up strolling up Fifth Avenue, the city's main artery, to its heart, Central Park. The walk logically concluded at the northeast corner of Fifth and 59th Street, where we leaned on the mailbox there and convulsed calmly and elegiacally about the anguish of our stricken affair. All the shouting, tears, emotional violence, and recrimination were rolled up into a throbbing ball of feeling that we could handle and touch and look upon in wonder: "*What have* we been crying about?" I was able to disentangle myself and step back. Gesticulating earnestly, I told her I was sorry it had been so hard on her. I had no reluctance setting my own demands aside and acknowledging her pain. Her tears had found my eyes.

The acid had literally wrung the feelings from our guts, instilling the entire turgid drama of our relationship with perspective. It was a relief that it was out of us, that we could see it as a third entity. We lay down on the patch of lawn beneath the statue of William Tecumseh Sherman and laughed at all our whining and wailing, all the time we'd wasted grasping for what we didn't have. When we got home from the park, it was startlingly apparent that an affirmation had taken place. As she took in her image in the mirror, she was immediately struck with how much she liked what she saw. She set to kissing herself, cooing in a narcissistic lust that made me jealous—jealous that I didn't love myself so wholeheartedly and unabashedly, and that she didn't love me so much as she did herself. I've never seen anyone on earth get on so well with a mirror—with or without LSD. Considering the stream of often alienating reflections that creep across a looking glass during a trip, this was indeed an exceptional interaction between tripper and mirror.

As it can congeal dull pangs of emotion into sharp, expressive definition, the psychedelic can similarly accentuate the underlying character of a multifarious social environment, drawing out a unified theme from a jumble of diverse and disparate elements. In *Amazing Dope Tales* (1980), Stephen Gaskin (a contender for the 2000 Green Party presidential nomination) describes the unspoken interplay between musician Ravi Shankar and his concert audience, illustrating the cycle of the crowd's acceptance and resistance to his performance. Gaskin depicts a distinct aural and visual tableau woven by Shankar's sitar playing, which billows over the seated listeners until they mount an unconscious revolt against the turbulent sensuality of the Indian maestro's "sexual raga." At the clashing point, Gaskin perceived a thud like two solid objects meeting underwater, and then a barrage of phantom fruit thrown in outrage against the stage, before the music again subdued and overwhelmed the crowd. The LSD had thus provided a sort of telepathic notation for the dialogue of energy between the active Shankar and his passive but silently recalcitrant audience.

The psychedelic can proffer intense dawnings of awareness, flashes of supernal insight, wisdom and inspiration, moments when it is clear there is something going on beyond the mortal ken, some ethereal tide that swells behind the concrete wall of apparent fact. For a few months after a watershed vision in 1980, I felt alchemically changed, blessed for being shown proof of the Divine and a peek behind the Wizard's Curtain at the invisible light behind all things. It became unmistakably obvious to me that my workaday mind was only the tip of the consciousness iceberg. On a 1982 mushroom trip at a farm in upstate New York, I became aware of a gurgling brook in my chest, the sense that there was a visceral Atlantis with rich, loamy psychical soil that went way down deep beneath my heart, connecting me chthonically to the body of humankind and the spirit that runs through it.

At the outset of an MDMA experience with a girlfriend in 1983, we emerged from a mild slumber, making love. At that moment, I felt the intense magnetic pull of a well of love bliss, and the air I expired with rich yawny groans of pleasure came from deep within the core of a dreamy earthen consciousness. I was convinced that I was using only a fraction of my sensorium, and that the psychedelic had expanded this limited awareness and opened up my mind like a can opener. You could practically hear the gush of stale air rushing out of my cranium.

The iceberg/tip analogy is often apt in descriptions of the vastness of the universe as perceived on the psychedelic, relative to the meager measurements registered on the stubby dipsticks we commonly use to gauge reality. In *The Long Trip*, Paul Devereux describes an acid trip (his first) in which "sound was encased in silence . . . [and] time was suspended within the great medium of eternity. . . . Eternity was always present; time was merely a glowing reflection off its surface like the sparkle of sunlight in the waters of a stream." When asked about the issue of time during his maiden mescaline experiment, Huxley replies, "There seems to be plenty of it," a line full of subtle mirth that evokes for me the image of a child at play with abundance, as though the contents of the hourglass had overrun into a gamesome sandbox.

After several MDA excursions over a two-month period in 1979, I was convinced that the universe was more verb than noun and much less fixed and solid than it had been purported to be. Time had slowed down to the point that I could perceive the excruciating bliss of a flower opening up to the sun, and hear the gentle, subaural creaking of petals emitting sylphlike groans of ecstasy. Love itself seemed to flow through the veins of time. As Huxley wrote, "I was seeing what Adam had seen on the morning of his creation—the miracle, moment by moment, of creation . . . The Being of Platonic philosophy," with the added dimension of becoming.

The psychedelic can thus offer a chance to capture—or recover—the rapture of union, to snap out of the trance that sustains the illusion of our separation from everything around us. Sensory stimuli often play a part in dispelling this rumor of disparateness. There's a certain diaphanous quality to things seen on the psychedelic, a sympathetic blurring of the lines, an overdrape of molecular fabric that suggests that we are all a bit of everything. The magnification of inherent colors and essences can become so intense that common boundaries are dissolved, as adjacent forms bleed into one another, revealing the delicate underlying web that links all forms.

But hallucinations are hardly the only feature of the psychedelic experience to induce such a sense of connection or oneness. Deep within the whirring internal engines of the psyche, in a domain of consciousness quite independent from but not unrelated to the five senses, a process of hyperidentification can be weaving an entire network of new and powerful associations. As documented by Masters and Houston, during "depersonalization" and "ego dissolution," the psychedelic subject can identify with an external entity to the point of seeming to *become* that entity.

Obviously this has potentially fearsome ramifications. For instance, what if you identified with the wrong entity, like a heinous serial killer, or something closer to home, say, the "dark side" or "shadow self" of your own personality? Such concerns are usually allayed with the same sort of retort given to the worry over what a hypnotist might impel someone in his spell to do: You never do anything significant that you don't really want to do.

But the psychedelic has a way of breaking you down before it builds you up again. When your defenses are low, even when you're sober, the boundaries separating you from elements in the immediate environment, for instance, the crowd noise in a room, fall away. Once your armor is off, the world just floods in on you. Such kinetics are common enough in the mundane moments of everyday life. For example, one night out to dinner with my family, uninebriated, I was feeling a bit run-down and vulnerable, and found myself mindlessly parroting a phrase I'd just overheard from a nearby table, even though it had absolutely nothing to do with the conversation at my table or anything at all. I'd temporarily lost my moorings enough to involuntarily "identify" with an impertinent utterance by a complete stranger. If you're exposed to certain elements in the environment long enough, they can break down your defenses and burrow into you.

As a kid I spent so much time in the summer surf at Crescent Beach on Block Island that in the evenings I could literally feel the movement of the tides inside my body. The rhythmical motion of the sea had gotten under my skin and into my psychic viscera.

The psychedelic, of course, can magnify this process to cosmic proportions. Whatever you subject yourself to during a psychedelic experience can have a way of registering somewhere within you before the effects of the drug completely evaporate. In that sense, the maxim that you are what you eat can have psychedelic relevance. Consider the case (recounted to me) of the youth who dropped acid with a group that just hung out and watched *Helter Skelter* (1976), the made-for-TV movie that depicts the grisly crimes of the homicidal Manson family. When he got home and went to bed, the lightbulb in the hall outside his room began to ooze big drops of blood that fell in a pool on the floor.

So too the power of transference is expanded a thousandfold. By dissolving the ego and other psycho-emotional boundaries, the psychedelic accelerates and amplifies the process of internalizing elements of the external world, enabling the tripper to effectively consummate a process of identification by "dissolving into" or "becoming" the object of focus. A bisexual fellow I spoke to related two occasions, once on hashish and once on peyote, during which he "merged" identities with a woman whose gender-specific facial features melted away before his eyes. Another chap I interviewed reported that the corduroy Levi's worn by a girl he fancied during a teenage acid trip suddenly spread to every other surface of the room. The LSD had magnified the object of his desire macroscopically, indicating that she was "the whole world" to him, at least at that moment. Still another participant described a tremendous, acid-induced mutual orgasm with his girlfriend that he was sure had flooded his bed with bodily fluids, only to find, once the mist had cleared, that no penetration had occurred at all and that the two of them were, in fact, still clothed.

A trip can function as a crack of lightning, an explosion of light so brilliant that it scorches the emotional flesh and casts deep saturnine shadows in the cavern of the soul. Many trippers feel as if their psyches were opened up by a bolt from above or from within, as a roiling wave of stimuli floods their sensorium to the point of overflow. When the opening doesn't close up entirely, one might see and feel more than one wants, leaving at trip's end a gaping raw nerve where there once was nothing but smooth visceral skin. Writes Huxley, "The literature of religious experience abounds in references to the pains and terrors overwhelming those who have come, too suddenly, face to face with some manifestation of the *Mysterium tremendum.*"

Usually, the surge of light portrays the spectrum of the human soul in sympathetically bright colors, but the heightened definitions can accentuate one's sense of polarity, duality, and schism. The flash may be so bright and hard as to be virtually blinding, whereby the shadow winds up being the sustained legacy of the trip. Indeed, the divine light may seem like some dim star until seen on the psychedelic—though even then, the "gratuitous grace" might not be received so gracefully. It all depends on how infinity is met, whether the overgrown ivy of social conditioning and the hard-gripped ego have been sufficiently burned away. Without supple psychical retinas and the intuitive grace to receive, the brilliance of "heaven" can be too much of a good thing. In fact, all that "lit-upness" as Huxley called it, can feel hellish: intrusive, relentless, and anything but restful.

There is often the sense on psychedelics of seeing the true colors of people. Indeed, auras are often visible to some trippers. During a black period in my own life (a spell during the morbid twenties), I prayed that at least somebody would be able to see the faithful chromatics of my soul. I imagined that if and when the physiological house that contained my being could be looked into (perhaps not until death), angels or other heavenly inspectors would be able to open up the skin to reveal a network of luminous bands of tissue that accurately depicted the true character of my inner life, all the sweet and noble yearnings, even those unachieved or poorly expressed. Then they would set about to untangle sinews of brilliant, diaphanous sapphire blue, rainforest green, and fiery orange from the darker strands that had been laying siege to them, tissues corroded by psychic rust, the pathetic vanity of redemption yearnings, and the blind reflex of revenge and self-hatred for failing to break through. All these colorless weeds would be pared away, leaving only the blazing hues of the enduring spirit. The immortal emberlike radiance of these gemlike tissues I envisaged was drawn directly from my psychedelic-inflected intuition.

In my experience, these refulgent jewels I imagined were hyperlinks to supranatural entities, including godhead, as well as the numinous attributes of the human biospiritual life force—e.g., valor, pathos, mercy, and the regenerative energy that the visionary psychologist Wilhelm Reich called orgone. "In vision," wrote Huxley, "men see a profusion of what Ezekiel in the Old Testament calls 'stones of fire,' and what Weir Mitchell . . . [the physician and novelist, who in 1897 published the first known report on peyote inebriation by a white person] calls 'translucent fruit.' " Huxley argues that the aesthetic and associated pecuniary value ascribed to jewels comes from their likeness within the Mind at Large to images of the splendor seen in visions: "The landscapes, the architectures, the clustering gems, the brilliant and intricate patterns—these in their atmosphere of preternatural light, preternatural color and preternatural significance, are the stuff of which the mind's antipodes are made. . . . The causal chain . . . begins in the psychological Other World of visionary experience, descends to earth and mounts again to the theological Other World of heaven."

In *True Hallucinations* (1993), McKenna describes a mushroom-enabled vision of the ultimate gem, the Philosopher's Stone, the alchemical grail of the ages: a "hyperdimensional jewel, a polyhedron each side of which is a window into another time, place or world." The psychedelic hints that the provenance of such supernal beauty is in the smithies of the divine mind, the beholder of all things. The uncanny suspicion that the radiance in visions is drawn from a source beyond the visible world forever robs the more homespun interplay of earth and light of its ultimacy—or so the psychedelic would have you believe.

In the long term, the psychedelic wields a double edge that can dig a schism, an ontological gash between the blindingly bright flash of exaltation and the dank limbo of mundanity—or worse: the punitive hell of shame for falling short of the brilliance. Much of what a trip imparts is not integrated because it isn't "real," though it still prods the psyche's interior walls in search of somewhere to persist and to expiate. Many nascent revelations are snagged on the tendrils of fear or brushed away by gotta-get-to-work pragmatism, so many little still-birth spirits running in circles between cloying materialism and the taste of eternity just out of reach.

Tripping is a volatile and potentially excruciating endeavor under any circumstances, regardless of set and setting. Even clinical researchers don't know enough about the kinetics of psychedelics, according to Oscar Janiger, the LSD therapist (and cousin to the late Allen Ginsberg) who administered the drug to L.A. cognoscenti in the Fifties and Sixties. "You can't manipulate it [LSD] as skillfully as you would like," he says. "It's like atomic energy—it's relatively easy to make a bomb, but much harder to safely drive an engine and make light." "The LSD experience is an enormous event for those who can integrate it into their subsequent existence, but those who are unprepared may be fragmented by it," says Sidney Cohen, a contemporary of Janiger's, who did similar work with largely the same crowd and later became director of the substance abuse program at the National Institutes of Health.

In my opinion, reassimilation of the experience is an important and largely unrecognized issue among the psychedelic community. As the feeling of being "tuned in" fades away, you can empathize with the fate of the mentally challenged protagonist (Cliff Robertson) in the movie *Charly* (1968), whose cognitive potential is awakened by a medical intervention, only to experience a relapse. My main dismay about LSD was over the turbulence that developed when the cool-air heights of the trip met the tepid doldrums of ordinary consciousness.

As Devereux writes, "I did not understand how one could come back from such mental vastness, and drop into one's identity again. . . . Over the following days [after his first acid trip], however, my ego boundaries hardened again, and my exposed psyche grew protective layers to insulate it from the world. But these layers were to be forever thinner than before."

If there are treasures to bring back from these mad dashes into the psychical wilderness (like the hasty gathering of bounty off the floor of a rolled-back ocean before the tide returns), where do you pay the duty demanded for their importation into the prosaic realm of weekday responsibilities to which we're all sentenced to life? All too often the resplendent jewel you've snatched in hyperspace begins to melt in your hand upon reentry, fading like a fleeting hypnagogic image. Now you see it, now you don't. The French Symbolist poet Charles Baudelaire has a beautifully incisive and bittersweet poem called "The Double Room," in which he bemoans the landlord's knock on the door while he's swimming in an opium reverie. This short work of prose from *Paris Spleen* (1869) is as eloquent an expression as any I've read of the heartbreak and devastation of coming down from a trip.

One's psychedelic regimen may begin with the darning of a metaphysical tear that comes apart later at another seam. At the outset of the main psychedelic flowering of my consciousness back in 1979, I felt I was curing a lifelong fissure (the schism of birth, the cleft consciousness of the mortal condition) and beginning to tap into a unified cosmology. But after a while, the transitory nature of my psychedelically heightened emotional well-being seemed mischievous, even malicious. It was unnerving to fluctuate between solid, electric cheer and stale dissolution. During the 1982 psilocybin trip in upstate New York, I alternated between quiet, surging confidence and blubbering despair that left me gasping for answers. I took in great gulps of mercurial oxygen and coagulated into a whole, confident spirit, then in the next turn of the Earth, dissolved into nothing, all my inspired fortitude dissipating through some invisible aperture in the burst-balloon void of my ego. I set about to build myself up again, only to have the whole thing collapse like a castle made of so much entropic sand in the surf of an untamable and unfathomable inner cosmos. Bafflingly, the same power that re-created me could knock me flat. I was utterly stumped and brokenhearted.

When you come down from a trip, you have to contend with the psychedelic bends and reassimilate your "new" mind or reborn spirit with your former identity and the shapes of things in the "real" world. You can feel like some cold discarnate mind: pure vigilance, like the eye, a tissue never touched. Alienation from what ought to be familiar terra firma isn't the only hazard, however. You might encounter something so aberrant or abject about yourself as to be unspeakable, so it sits in your psychic colon, forever undigested. Especially for the frail and unprepared, a bad trip can be a violent rap upon the tender life-force, springing a trapdoor to the rank sewer of despair and the specter of chaos.

Whenever it seemed I'd lost the struggle with the psychedelic, I felt like a chastised child, like Mickey's Sorcerer's Apprentice in *Fantasia*, admonished for the hubris of appropriating powers much larger than my petty stature could effectively wield. Frankly, I think that quite a lot of us Baby Boomers got our asses whupped by acid and other psychedelics. The message at times, if you cared to admit it to yourself or anyone else, seemed to be that you didn't belong here, that you were trespassing on territory you'd have to be a mystic samurai to understand. After a freak-out, you don't necessarily rush back out into hyperspace, so you run loops around the hole in yourself, furtively skirting the scar on your youthful psyche, terrified of reconstructing the same pattern of brain cells as the psychedelic's bruise, afraid that if the dots were connected again, they might spell INSANITY.

Indeed, the psychedelic can pull the old switcheroo, turning on you after starting out on a soft and beatific note. Such an about-face may seem like a trick or something more sinister, a function of some hellish private twilight zone. (Aptly enough, Rod Serling himself, in a circa 1970 public-service spot, warned youngsters that the LSD capsule he held up between thumb and forefinger could be an express ticket to the sort of turmoil and alienation he immortalized in his classic television show.)

Just as you might feel baptized and cleansed by a beatific archetype, so too can you feel charred and singed by a negative one, as if the mark of Cain has been branded into you. In the film version of Paddy Chayefsky's *Altered States* (1980), the sensory-deprived protagonist Eddie Jessup (William Hurt) has a horrifying hallucination of himself nailed to a cross with a satanic goat's head over his own—flailing vainly to break out of the damnation and the suffocation, as he drifts off through the infinity of the cosmos. Although the vision was not drug-induced, it echoed one of my own that had been, and thus had my heart pounding when I first saw it on the big screen.

The sublime side of the psychedelic experience is amply extolled in stories that relay the soaring joys of kissing the creatures of the sun, copulating with the galaxy, cleansing one's callused heart in the clear blue stream of the Redeemer's gaze, and other elations. For sure, the psychedelic can offer glimpses of heavenly radiance, but also of its shadows: awful plummets through flaming caves of pain, the moral vertigo that rips through your soul like some heinous phallic-vine out of *Alien* (1979) and tries to snuff you out. ". . . I came loose from the sky," writes Ken Kesey in a story from *Demon Box* (1986), describing a steep fall he took from a chemical high, vexed by "the chilly hiss of decaying energy." The psychedelic can fray the tissues that hold your ego and self-esteem together, allowing you to sink into the loneliest, most inhospitable hole in your being, where you may find yourself cascading helplessly into the unholy depths of the human mind.

Sometimes there's hell to pay, and the bill can seem terrifically high. The torment is often related to the sense that you've been through all of this before, that you're stuck in a loop that keeps dragging you round and round to the same meat-locker prison in time and space. It seems you've got to pay to avoid going through all this again and again, and it's up to you to locate the elusive Station Master and cough up the required fees to get home. It is telling that so many who soared through the psychedelic stratosphere, notably rock musicians Jim Morrison and Jerry Garcia, later craved the opiate gravity of alcohol and/or narcotics to bring them home to their bones again. It was a rough road to travel sometimes, to put it mildly. Too often a trip can feel like the mental equivalent of careening randomly through cyberspace, sans mouse, on a browser that could jam on the damnedest of sites. I've often bemoaned the fact that I was unaware of how to prepare for the tumult that could ensue, and lacked the skills with which to chart the stormy psychedelic seas when I really needed them.

The complaint is often voiced that there is no true shamanic tradition in modern industrial culture to guide us through the psychical headspace, no board-certified metaphysical safari leaders in the yellow pages to hold our hands through the rocky straits and precipitous mountain passes of the psychedelic encounter with Self and Other and Death and all their merry consorts. It's no easy thing to find an Elder of the Way to embolden and support you as you face the soul-specific manifestations of that ultimate power that the psychedelic can unleash. A less than enabling environment for such quests is created by the Godzilla called the War on Drugs, a campaign of misinformation and terror (the threat and harsh vengeance of prison sentences) that strikes indiscriminately, just as brutally at cannabis as it does against crack cocaine. In a society where virtually no distinction is made between addictive narcotics and visionary plants that are sacred to indigenous peoples, one of the first casualties is an aboveboard safehouse of knowledge and support for the psychedelic pursuit.

But in reality, the knowledge base for reverential psychedelic usage is definitely there to be found, for instance, in the extensive psychedelic bibliographies and Websites, and among Native American users of peyote and the psychedelically sage Buddhists who are the spiritual offspring of the original Zen tripmaster, Alan Watts. Such guidance, unfortunately, is just not pervasive enough to meet the needs of the legions of trippers who go running out into hyperspace without any road maps at all.

In my research, there was some initial queasiness at the prospect of seeing the odd skull worm crawl out, arcane, private stuff that had been locked away for a long time, and maybe for good reason. But whenever I felt quaky about delving into the inner rooms of the psychedelic, I kept coming back to a cosmic refrain that reverberates through my life like a pedal-steel guitar chord: the twang of joy and gratitude I felt for the feral bliss of living that roared through me, along with a titanic empathy for humankind and a buoyant reverence for the heart that beat at the core of Creation. It was a feeling akin to what Huxley described as "an unspeakable sense of gratitude for the privilege of being born in the universe," citing Blake's observation that "gratitude is heaven itself." In my life, there has been nothing so comforting as this state, *rocked* by LSD or MDA, in which I felt immensely grateful to the Lord for the breath in my body and the gift of life. The sense of belonging was consummate. It was as though I'd attained the deceptively modest goal that Huxley ascribes to all of us: "to discover that we have always been where we ought to be."

The validity of using a psychotropic substance to achieve mystical states is a matter of continuing controversy, of course. Can you really get "there" by drugs? And even if you can, does a rapture induced by a chemical have any enduring effect after the symptoms wear off? Some maintain that we could use an occasional lift out of everyday consciousness, however brief, to get an aerial perspective of the forest we're wandering through, and to reinstill the impulsiveness and joy that's been drained away by flatline thinking.

In *Religions, Values, and Peak-experiences* (1964), the humanist psychologist Abraham Maslow asserts that transcendental states are the very gist of religion, conferring the vital meanings of values and life itself. Sadly, the shimmering meanings of religion are lost in boring sermons, symbols, and concretizations, but the shock of a peak-experience, like the "gratuitous graces" of Catholic theology that Huxley cites, can restore the orgasmic dynamic of joy and rapture, and jolt the sleeper awake from the nightmare of pursuing goals not lit from within. With just one glimpse of heaven, one can reconcile oneself with the presence of evil and the specter of death, and see that living is an end unto itself.

Although he corresponded with Leary and (according to his daughter Ann Kaplan) supported his wife's undergoing a single, apparently uneventful, psychedelic session with Grof, Maslow never took the psychedelic himself and came short of actually endorsing its use as a potentiator of peak-experiences, but it's been well documented that the psychedelic tends to raise deep religious issues and prompt reflection on ultimate values. In the early Sixties, clinical experiments with prison convicts and others in the Leary-directed Harvard Psilocybin Project (among other studies) demonstrated the power of the psychedelic to lead subjects to consider what Maslow calls "final values" that help answer fundamental questions such as: What are my obligations to society? What are truth, justice, and virtue? What must I be ready to die for?

One of the most compelling cases for the religious potential of the psychedelic is Walter Pahnke's famed Good Friday Experiment at

Boston University's Marsh Chapel in 1962, which involved twenty divinity students from Andover-Newton Seminary School. Leary supplied psilocybin against the ruling of the Harvard administration, which had been trying to scrap the Psilocybin Project. Dubbed "the miracle of Marsh Chapel," the experiment—in which half the students were given psilocybin tablets and the other half were given placebos—conclusively demonstrated the capacity of the psychedelic to induce religious ideation, as nine of the ten given the psilocybin reported having mystical experiences. In spite of its success, the experiment was the last straw for the Harvard administration and the beginning of the end of Leary's career there.

There is certainly merit in the principle of reaching the mountaintop just for a minute rather than not at all—for the sheer exhilaration of reaching the top. But there are still unresolved issues regarding the ephemeral nature of the psychedelic-abetted revelatory experience and whether lasting value can be gleaned from such a short burst of neurological activity induced by external agents. It's possible that the nature of the psychedelic experience is such that its enduring meaning is more slippery to the grasp than revelations attained over time and through arduous discipline. Most formal religions would have you build up spirituality over a lifetime, so that the knowledge is tempered with instruction on how to live with it.

William James, however, points out that *all* mystical experiences have an ephemeral yet indelible quality. In *The Varieties of Religious Experience* (1902), he delineates four "marks" of the mystical experience: ineffability, transiency, a noetic (intellectual) quality, and passivity. Mystical states, he writes (be they Christian, Sufi, yogic or, as James himself underwent, nitrous oxide–inspired), put the individual will in temporary abeyance, as if the subject were "grasped and held by a superior power." They are difficult if not impossible to convey in words and are rarely sustained for longer than a half-hour before fading into the "light of common day. Often, when faded, their quality can but imperfectly be reproduced in memory; but when they recur it is recognized; and from one recurrence to another it is susceptible of continuous development in what is felt as inner richness and importance." Often one is struck with the familiarity of the revelation, as though he is now revisiting an inherent, buried truth, having "been here before" at some indefinite time in the past.

Inconclusive as a fleeting glimpse of the ineffable may be, such phenomena impressed upon James that

> our normal waking consciousness . . . is but one special type of consciousness, whilst all about it, parted from it by the filmiest of screens, there lie potential forms of consciousness entirely different. We may go through life without suspecting their existence, but apply the requisite stimulus, and at a touch they are there in all the com-

> pleteness. . . . No account of the universe in its totality can be final which leaves these other forms of consciousness quite disregarded. How to regard them is the question—for they are so discontinuous with ordinary consciousness. Yet they may determine attitudes though they cannot furnish formulas, and open a region though they fail to give a map. At any rate, they forbid a premature closing of our accounts with reality. Looking back at my open experiences, they all converge towards a kind of insight to which I cannot help ascribing some metaphysical significance. The keynote of it is invariably a reconciliation. It is as if the opposites of the world, whose contrariness and conflict make all our difficulties and troubles, were melted into unity. . . . Those who have ears, let them hear; to me the living sense of reality only comes in the artificial mystic state of mind.

Those who crave a mystical breakthrough, either with or without the psychedelic, should be prepared to come up empty. A tripper can inflame his senses but lack the mental or spiritual framework for his discoveries, winding up like the monkey in the Buddhist allegory, which hops from window to window, knowing nothing new or binding. "Lacking the temper of ascetic discipline," Matthiessen writes, "the drug vision remains a sort of dream that cannot be brought over into daily life. Old mists may be banished, that is true, but the alien chemical agent forms another mist, maintaining the separation of the 'I' from the experience of the Other."

The Buddhist scholar Jack Kornfield cautions would-be nirvana seekers that going after an instant *satori*, a flash of illumination prior to full enlightenment, is largely futile, like trying to win the lottery, and that moral discipline should be used to condition the mind for the highest spiritual states. In traditional Buddhist societies, he points out, instruction starts with *sila*, virtue, which builds *ahimsa:* caring, a nonviolent relationship toward living beings, which expands the heart and quiets the "monkey mind." The inner realms are explored through yoga concentration practices aimed at *samadhi*, attunement to the unity of life. The third domain is *prajna*, wisdom through higher insights built on the basis of virtue and discipline. Kornfield stresses that especially arduous training is required to resist attachment to states of rapture, expanded awareness, and light, which are actually only the first openings of consciousness. To progress spiritually, the Buddhist must recognize that these states too dissolve, as exalted as they seem. Naturally, this is daunting to many a seeker, who might then be beset by fear and despair over the impermanence of life. One craves deliverance, but one must let even that go.

Both psychology and religion lay claim to the territory of psychedelic consciousness. Notes *Storming Heaven* author Jay Stevens, the "self-shattering point" where one "merges with the world," so common to the psychedelic, is "known to the Buddhists as *satori,* to the Hindus as *samadhi,* and to the psychological community as 'temporary loss of differentiation of the self and the other world.' " Kornfield asserts that the heaven, hell, and archetypal realms brought to light by modern psychedelic research have "already been charted by the breadth of Buddhist psychology." But I think that a good psychological cartography of the human mind under the influence of the psychedelic can provide, in spite of being somewhat mechanistic, an ecumenical *lingua franca* and a useful framework for discussing the dynamics of tripping—a set of terms that doesn't require a religious leap of faith and can speak to the rational in all of us.

Although each trip, like the tripper, is unique to itself, there is some measure of universality to the psychedelic experience. In the 1920s the German-born psychologist Heinrich Kluver documented "form constants" in the visuals of mescaline subjects, dividing them into essentially three types: weblike filigree structures such as honeycombs; the tunnel; and the spiral, in "descending" order (my quotation marks), as the subject moves deeper into the unconscious. Some of the geometrical motifs may reflect the inner architecture of the retina, while the tunnel and spiral are common with near-death and rebirth experiences, both of which have psychedelic parallels. The spiral has shown up as the mise-en-scène for portrayals of hypnosis, time travel, and mental transformation in films, TV shows, and animated cartoons (e.g., transport via the Wayback Machine featured on the *Rocky and Bullwinkle Show*). The subject falls through space while twirling in a spiral (or against a twirling-spiral background), reemerging in the next scene in another reality altogether. Those silly hypnotic gizmos that look like big electric lollipops employ a spinning circle with a spiral optical effect to mesmerize their victims.

Sasha Shulgin's popular six-level system for rating the "perceived strength" of psychedelic experiences—Minus (baseline), Plus-minus (indeterminate), then Plus-one through four—was designed to refer only to intensity, not content. To help map the latter, my research uncovered two "atlases" of the psychedelic landscape: that produced by Stanislav Grof's decades of research in Czechoslovakia and the United States with some six thousand subjects of psychedelic sessions; and that formulated by Robert Masters and Jean Houston during the course of their work with 206 subjects. Unlike the circa 120 participants in my project, who ingested a wide range of psychedelics in mostly informal and illegal settings, the subjects of these scientists were dosed mostly on legal LSD in comfortably controlled, clinical settings in the company of a sympathetic psychologist and/or other guide.

While set and setting have a profound influence on the outcome of an individual trip, the spectrum of perceptual phenomena in the psychedelic experience is, by and large, the same. Between Grof's "formal characteristics of nonordinary consciousness" and Masters and Houston's "psychological effects" of the psychedelic experience, just about anything can happen during a trip, including: identification with external things microcosmic, macroscopic, and both at once—with or without loss of personal identity; visions of archetypal forms, deities and demons, and complex mythological sequences that seem to have a life of their own; time travel; oceanic and volcanic (explosive) ecstasy; and clairvoyance and clairaudience (the ability to perceive sounds beyond the range of hearing).

In *The Varieties of Psychedelic Experience* (1966), Robert Masters and Jean Houston (the latter a noted author and human capabilities scholar and onetime editorial consultant to First Lady Hillary Rodham Clinton) denoted four successive levels of psychedelic experience: the *sensory,* the *recollective-analytical,* the *symbolic,* and the *integral.* Each leads the subject deeper into his own psyche toward integration with disparate elements of the self as well as with the universe at large. Grof's four levels of psychedelic experience are largely parallel with Masters and Houston's: the *abstract or aesthetic* (sensory enhancement); the *psychodynamic, biographical, or recollective* (in which one relives emotionally relevant memories and symbolic experiences similar to dreams); the *perinatal* (the activation of repositories or matrices within the subconscious mind); and the *transpersonal* (in which consciousness has expanded beyond ego boundaries and transcended the limits of time and space). The only major point of divergence between the two cartographies is with Grof's emphasis on the perinatal dimension, which entails profound encounters with the trauma of one's own birth as well as confrontations with death. Grof is very big on the reliving of *biological* birth itself. Some of his research subjects have reported accurate details about their births that they could not have known without being told.

Tracing the four steps, in less clinical terms, you begin the psychedelic journey with the world coming in on you ever so much closer, pulsing or flashing here and there and waving at you to grab your attention. *This is your world. Notice these things.* As the definitions of the external world gain strength, the details of your own life and personality are summoned to the fore, as if to answer the first wave of stimuli. *This is who and what you are.* Once the self is up on the screen, it's only a matter of time before one is immersed in scenes of intimate and profound biographical significance, which take on new and instructive spins and dimensions that implode into elaborate dramas, displaying the vastness of internal psychical space. *There are few limits to what you thought was your finite little self.* Finally, that immensity symbiotically reflects the vastness of the entire universe, and the frontiers that separate you from the external world are obliterated, leaving you free to merge with an environment that no longer punctuates itself with seemingly random isolated details but now presents itself as a holistic unity. *You see, you are everything.* At the deepest level of transpersonal states, writes Grof, the "universe is seen as an infinite web of adventures in consciousness, and the dichotomies between the experiencer and the experienced, form and emptiness, time and timelessness, determinism and free will, or existence and nonexistence have been transcended."

Among the people I interviewed, I discerned several "types" of psychedelic experiences, though inevitable overlapping occurred, and some were completely off the map. Many subjects had profound experiences in which they encountered God, the All, the true path of righteousness, or simply an ultra-vivid definition of their own values, identity, and life force, the character of the revelation varying with the theology of the tripper. Several of my subjects described out-of-body, "I know what it's like to be dead" phenomena. Some related encounters with discarnate entities or other mysterious presences. There were reports of divination and telepathy, as well as acts or events of apparent magic or miracle that defy the mechanistic model of physics. No catalog of trips would be complete without a few freak-outs: incidences of bum trip, panic attack, and even apparent psychosis, momentary and otherwise. Consistent with the often cavalier spirit of the times, there were a good number of "accidental" revelations, visionary experiences that flowed out of a kicks-motivated trip, often a result of the all-too-common unintentional double-dose, when the tripper felt he wasn't getting off on the first hit and went ahead and dropped another. A not unlikely scenario that resulted: youth-run-amok trips and stumbles upon a revelation or two. Included here as well are a few accounts of states that induced the subject to actions while tripping that he would not normally take—usually *not* a good idea, as the psychedelic state is better spent passively, in my opinion, in watch, listen, and learn mode.

Jason's encounters (page 180) with the "shining ones" on an astral plane, and a "luminous being" in the Arizona desert underscore the psychedelic's inclination to show us that we've got company. Marcel's story (page 283) depicts how the psychedelic can take the tripper by the hand and usher him toward an audience with godhead. The understanding and forgiveness transmitted by the deity the drug conjured for him would seem to flow directly from the wellspring of aboriginal religion. On another trip, Marcel believes he has literally folded a 45-RPM record to fit into his pocket. The sincerity of his belief that the laws of physics were successfully transgressed gives shelter to the very idea of miracle.

The narrative of Leonard Gibson, president of the Association of Holotropic Breathwork International (page 257), illustrates the dual nature of the psychedelic as both light and heat. When an eerily numinous flame suddenly combusts to announce the spirit of a departed friend, Leonard's dome is lit, but his psyche is singed by the otherness of the vision. As the flame evolves, over the course of a months-long regimen of pure LSD, into the Burning Bush, the discord between the spirit and the flesh is aggravated, resulting in psychological turmoil.

Daniel's story (page 120) of seeming to go up in smoke along with the tinsel talisman he'd tossed onto a burning yule log illustrates the importance of choosing your material fetishes carefully. They may vaporize in the flames—and "you" along with it. Fortunately, he found a cozy and supportive place to "die" and get an overview of his life. Similarly carried away by LSD, Kevin's sense of impending death or orgasm—he can't tell which—reveals the mighty and seemingly conflicting crosscurrents that can flow simultaneously through the psyche of one human being (page 247).

On the day of the Human Be-In of January 1967, San Francisco rock scene photographer Herbie Greene (page 152) underwent a breakthrough via a hallucination comprised of imagery from two of his phobias at the time, snakes and car crashes, respectively. Could anything but the psychedelic, at the speed of a veritable smart bomb, so quickly find these emotional flashpoints, forge an instant link between them, and then implode in a liberating psychodramatic event?

The award-winning science fiction writer Robert Charles Wilson tells (page 351) how he took heart from testimonials such as Peter Stafford's *LSD: The Problem-Solving Psychedelic* (1967) and overcame his writer's block with the help of a well-focused acid trip. His ego pared away, he realized that he wasn't the writer so much as the messenger. The experience enabled him to effectively step out of the self-absorption that was drowning his talent. He goes on, however, to relate the old switcheroo properties of the psychedelic in a cautionary story of a bad turnabout.

The ability of MDMA to instill a powerful sense of self-affirmation is portrayed in Megan's tale (page 307) of achieving vaginal orgasm through intercourse for the first time, as she is united with a real-life animus figure via a vivid hallucination that is atypical of the drug. The story demonstrates how MDMA (and its chemical brethren) can instill a sense of entitlement to what's yours, the sense of belonging to one's own pleasure, the realization that there is a fair portion of this world that one should righteously and dutifully claim. The fleeting image of rabbit fur that flickers throughout her erotic episode evokes the flavor of *Alice in Wonderland* (1865) and matters sylvan and carnal.

Ruth's narrative (page 357) takes an ironic turn in that the very institutions she had been rebelling against, home and the Church, became places of sanctuary after she sees each in the new light of LSD. (Imagine Christian clergy, inspired by such a tale, dabbing a little acid on communion wafers before pressing them on the tongues of waverers.) Advised by her high-school classmate not to look into the mirror, she does so anyway and sees herself as "God" herself. As is borne out in a few stories included here, when you look into the mirror on the psychedelic, you've got to be ready for the entire menagerie, the thousand and one clowns that emerge from a single face. The parade of images may seem to reveal the alpha and the omega, as though a seed has been exploded into all of its generations and incarnations.

When trips are taken in places saturated with history, energies latent in the landscape, real or attributed, can be unleashed. Aaron relates (page 57) how, when he and his girlfriend looked into each other's faces at an ancient windswept temple in India, each saw a series of apparitions snag their forms on the other like newspapers blown against a street lamp on a gusty day. All the more remarkable is the sort of shared operating platform the two were using as the acid conjured myriad masks and guises of each other.

The odyssey recounted by writer/translator Stephen Kessler (page 366) is a harrowing yet hilarious tale of long-term madness kicked off by a psychedelic goofball consumed at the fateful Altamont concert in 1969. After tracing Stephen's travails as an "angelic revolutionary" through the institutional maze of a prison and a hospital, readers may be amazed at his enduring belief today that there was a strong dose of truth in his delusions.

A stunning medical discovery may be at the heart of the story by *Wired* staff writer Steve Silberman, who recounts (page 380) how he accessed, via psilocybin, a secret biological control panel on which he could view his own physiological processes and regulate them in the manner of biofeedback. The health-care possibilities of this "organismic display monitor" would seem to be fantastic.

The eschatology of the psychedelic is demonstrated in several stories included here. In the course of Kenny's excursions on *Salvia divinorum* and 5-MeO DMT, respectively, (page 240), he encounters an alien birthing chamber and flashes to the moment of his death, worried that he might be missing the boat if his psyche, catapulted free of his body by the drug, has not yet returned.

Lena's (page 250) is the tale of a true psychonaut bent on plumbing the depths of her mind to answer the riddle of a troubling thirty-minute gap on her memory tape she experienced during a 5-MeO-DMT trip. The notion that the human mind may have secrets that must be ferreted out, some Seventh Seal to be opened to get to the bottom of things, bespeaks the intrepidness of this tripper.

Another brave soul is Jeremy (page 199), who is still on a decades-long search for peace and sanctuary from a devastating acid trip that has, on occasion, been revisited in flashbacks. The trip had begun innocently enough when he experienced a déjà vu of divine joy and understanding, as though stumbling upon a golden trove of submerged knowledge. But then the fragile state of godliness is underscored when Jeremy plunges into a pit of Nietzchean eternal recurrence and it dawns upon him that he is waking up from a good dream only to return to a nightmare. After going through both these types of flashing back *within* the trip, he must then endure the ongoing specter of real flashbacks that perversely reconstruct the worst moments of the bad déjà vu. Excoriating himself for faltering in his faith, branding himself guilty of the sin of doubt, Jeremy courageously seeks to confront his nemesis face-to-face.

Does it require a strained leap of faith to take the alleged fantastical properties of the psychedelic seriously? Maybe not. Ironically, the products of empirical, rationalist thinking confirm some of the cosmological principles of the psychedelic, e.g., the plasticity of time, and the notion of matter as energy. Although most of our minds still ride on linear, Newtonian-Cartesian rails, the high tide of human understanding of our place in the universe is embodied in quantum physics, which actually *embraces* the discrepancy of subatomic particles alternately appearing as particles and waves. For the last half century, the emphasis in physics has been on *process:* not the wheels but their spin.

Materialist psychology holds that the nature of consciousness is purely sensorial, echoing John Locke's Enlightenment Age axiom that there is nothing in the intellect that has not first been processed by the senses. Grof, who has done perhaps more than anyone to demonstrate that the psychedelic state is not a "toxic psychosis" but a "journey into the unconscious or superconcious mind," maintains that consciousness is much more than mere cellular activity in the brain, but rather a chain of reactions along a continuum of mindfulness distributed throughout the universe. The most direct challenge to the principles of mechanistic science is phenomena from transpersonal experiences, such as "the relativity and arbitrary nature of physical boundaries, nonlocal connections in the universe, memory without a material substrate, nonlinearity of time, [and] consciousness associated with inorganic matter." Many of his LSD patients reported identification with plants, stones, or lightning, with surprising insight into photosynthesis and other natural processes. Like McKenna, Grof uses the hologram analogy for the encryption of the veritable *Spiritus Mundi* itself in our DNA molecules, which may be accessed by the chemical reaction of the psychedelic. "Each of us," he says, "contains information about the entire universe or all of existence, has potential experiential access to all its parts, and in a sense is the whole cosmic network."

Grof calls for an entire paradigm shift to accommodate the full potential of reality. The Newtonian-Cartesian model is largely inadequate, he says, because it rejects the great steps forward in twentieth-century science as well as data from parapsychology, near-death experiences, psychedelic research, shamanic practices, ancient and Oriental religion, and aboriginal rituals. He maintains that a broader and more accurate paradigm of reality can be seen through the prisms of quantum-relativistic physics, information and systems theory, cybernetics, and recent discoveries in neurophysiology and biology.

Grof hails the new science of *becoming* rather than mere being, in which humans are not the passive object but agents in evolution, in fact, evolution itself. (Recall that Huxley chastised Plato for his parochial concern for "being" rather than "becoming.") The old mechanistic view of the universe is thus supplanted by a view of the universe as a unified, invisible web of events and relationships—the *holomovement,* to use the word coined by Einstein colleague David Bohm—in which any describable entity or event is derivative of an indefinable totality too immense to be seen in true parallax. Solid matter has thus disappeared, leaving energy and archetypal patterns of perpetual becomingness. If we follow Grof's thinking, consciousness, which he contends pervades both mind *and* matter, is the connecting principle in this cosmic web, the glue that holds it together.

Grof's model is plausible. Building upon the notion that the subatomic structure of the universe is not absolutely static or solid, it's conceivable that the psychedelic can alter the perception of energy, matter, and time in such as way as to enable select random access of the spatial and temporal dimensions and make it possible to inhabit the skins of a variety of forms and entities. For a brief time that may seem like a sliver of eternity, the subject may be able to grok on any or all sensory and consciousness levels, other matrices of reality along the space-time continuum—and even a supramatrix into which all manner of reality may be contained—before the subatomic structure of the brain/consciousness interface hardens back up into relative solidity, and the cosmic chariot turns back into a pumpkin, as the drug's effects wane. The mechanics of such physics may become more evident and comprehendible to us later, just as the apparently magical power of electricity did subsequent to Ben Franklin's launching his kite up into the heavens to be struck by lightning.

No examination of the impacts of psychedelic drugs would be complete without addressing the worst fears about them, those related to concerns that they might cause neurological damage or make a person insane, if only for a moment. Indeed, this book contains several accounts of distinct departures from reality, some of which had long-term repercussions.

In any discussion of altered states such as madness and the psychedelic experience, terms of reference will vary depending on one's perspective. For instance, an LSD subject may interpret a hallucination as a "cosmic vision," while a traditional psychiatrist might deem it a symptom of "toxic psychosis." "Enlightenment" to one may appear as "insanity" to another, though, interestingly, in 1994 the psychiatrists' resource, *The Diagnostic and Statistical Manual of Mental Disorders* (DSM), adopted a new diagnostic category: "the religious or spiritual problem," thus punching a hole in the antiseptic wall of clinical psychiatry to accommodate yearnings of the spirit. The term *ego dissolution,* a temporary melting away of personality frontiers, a feature of some psychedelic and some mystical states, may thus gain currency in the domain of medical psychology.

Clinically speaking, *psychosis* is a state marked by mental impairment and the loss of reality in sensory perception and/or cognitive process. The two most common types of psychosis are that associated with *schizophrenia,* a chronic illness, one of the symptoms of which is a waxing and waning psychosis, and that associated with *mania,* one of the two phases of bipolar disorder (formerly called manic depression), another chronic illness, the other phase being acute depression. In schizophrenic psychosis, which often features auditory hallucinations, the break with reality and mental dysfunction is more pronounced, while mania tends to be marked by an expansive, elevated mood with somewhat less severe mental impairment. The most acute psychoses are those in which there is a clear break with reality marked by a lack of insight into one's condition.

Psychosis and the psychedelic state can indeed share some discrete symptoms—hallucinations, delusions, and flight of ideas, to name a few—but it is extremely rare that such symptoms would be present as a result of a psychedelic, without at least some critical measure of insight into the fact that the abnormal phenomena are ephemeral features of consciousness. Hence, the mentally sound tripper who hallucinates a clown riding a bicycle through a wall (as was related to me) almost invariably recognizes the perceptual illusion as such and does not believe that what he or she is seeing is "real." It's worth noting that etymologically, the meaning of the word *hallucinate,* from the Latin *hallucinari,* has less to do with perceptual dysfunction or seeing things "you know that ain't" than with "dreaming or wandering in the mind."

Ideas of reference, the illusion, sometimes of a paranoid nature, that events or elements in the environment are intended specifically for the subject's perception, can occur during some psychedelic states, though rarely without an attendant objectivity about them, which furnishes cognitive reassurance that there is reason to suspend judgment and action based on their content. According to Dr. Julie Holland, attending psychiatrist at Bellevue Hospital in New York City, delusions of reference are much more likely to be a symptom of the dissociative anesthetics PCP and ketamine than most other psychedelic drugs. Emotional lability, or instability—a state in which one cries and/or laughs very easily—is characteristic of both mania and the psychedelic state, as is the ecstatic, epiphanous state marked by profound feelings of everything fitting together. Thus, Holland argues, the state of mind generated by classic psychedelics, such as LSD, mescaline, and psilocybin, may serve as a useful model for mania, while PCP and high-dose ketamine, producing a more definitive break with reality, are *psychotomimetic* for the more delusional aspects of schizophrenia.

Like a horse, the psychedelic is capable of giving you a good workout and a great if wild ride, but also, on the odd turn, of tossing you from your saddle. If anything experiential is going to tip the balance of your cranial fruit basket, it's going to be feelings of an intense or *otherly* nature. For that reason alone, the psychedelic is as capable as any external agent of triggering a psychosis in a given individual. But it is extremely rare, given the population of users, that the break with reality it effects is so severe as to be characterized as psychotic after the drug has worn off. At the peak of what *Time* called an LSD "epidemic" in the months preceding its ban in 1966, the research community estimated that the incidence of psychotic breakdown during an acid trip was approximately seven in every one thousand users, most of whom already had a history of psychiatric disorder. Notes Holland, a full two percent of the general population is already either manic or schizophrenic, irrespective of drug ingestion, which might aggravate the condition.

A wholesome anxiety about going mad during a trip can appropriate the dynamics of the experience and spin the subject into a bad trip, which, in turn, can be a self-fulfilling prophecy caused by overexposure to the mere concept. As the media hammered away about the dangers of psychedelics during the late Sixties, the number and frequency of related panic attacks multiplied drastically. One way to convince a person on a bad trip that he has not lost his mind or gone "psycho"—that is, in the likely case that he truly hasn't—is to underscore the fact that his insight into his condition has not been suspended. In that respect, Holland says, "freaking out" itself is evidence that the tripper has not gone psychotic. The alarm response is a function of one's inherent awareness of the state he's in. One cause of a bad trip and/or trip-associated somatic discomfort, such as nausea, is the attitude of rejecting the psychedelic headspace. In as much as possible, she suggests to those who happen to be tripping, "You should embrace your altered state" to wipe away the dynamics of conflict. A calm, supportive, and beautiful or tabula-rasa neutral environment is the best set and setting for a trip and hence the best therapy for a bad one—and one best applied preventively from the trip's outset. A person in bad straits is urged to void his mind through meditation, visualization, or concentration exercises, or to simply take a few deep breaths and remember that the off-baseline state is only temporary, over in but a few hours.

To treat most "hallucinogen-induced" panic or anxiety attacks in emergency rooms, medical staff use Ativan, an injectable drug from the benzodiazepine family, which also includes Valium, Xanax, and Klonipin. The antipsychotic Haldol, which has largely supplanted the notoriously stupefying Thorazine, is generally not effective for two to fourteen days after injection and may have some adverse side effects.

The cause and impact of so-called psychedelic flashbacks are still somewhat unclear. The DSM's term for the phenomenon is "hallucinogen persisting perception disorder" (HPPD), the "re-experiencing following cessation of use of a hallucinogen of one or more of the perceptual symptoms that were experienced while intoxicated with the hallucinogen." Dr. H. D. Abraham claims that "structural damage" occurred in a number of flashback patients he has treated. In *Visual Disturbances in a Population of LSD Users* (1981), he describes several adverse neurological effects, including "acquired color confusion; difficulty reading; flashes of color; geometric pseudo-hallucinations; geometric phosphenes [subjective images generated by the internal structure of the eye]; halos around objects; imagistic phosphenes; intensified color; macropsia [a condition in which objects are abnormally increased in size], . . . and trailing phenomena."

According to Dr. Katherine R. Bonson, a pharmacologist at the National Institute on Drug Abuse, "post-hallucinogen perceptual disorder clearly exists in some individuals who have taken hallucinogens, but the frequency of these reactions in the population of users is extremely rare." Flashbacks, she says, "have not been shown to be caused by a chemical insult to the brain, nor are they brought about by the lingering presence of the psychedelic drug in the nervous system," since the body quickly processes the microgram quantities in which such substances are ingested. Rather they may occur because the psyche can have a hard time shedding the experience, just as a Vietnam War veteran may suffer from post-traumatic stress disorder and experience a reemergence of the sensory manifestations of the trauma during his waking consciousness or dream life. "Any powerful experience has the capacity to intrude on normal waking consciousness at any time," says Holland. "With psychedelics, one exposes oneself to powerful emotional bandwidths that may be traumatic and later intrude on normal waking consciousness. Such reemergences do not require a new trauma to trigger it."

Some of the fearsome rumors about the dangers of psychedelics have been put to rest—that LSD causes chromosomal damage, and that MDMA remains in or destroys the cerebrospinal fluid. As it turns out, according to Jeremy Weir Alderson, a leftist radio personality on WEOS in Geneva, New York, there is no known evidentiary basis for the most notorious and high-profile scare story ever about psychedelic drugs—that entertainer Art Linkletter's daughter Diane leapt to her death while tripping on LSD. Citing a 1990 letter he received from

Linkletter himself, Alderson says that the television celebrity, most famous for hosting the original *Kids Say the Darndest Things* show, wrote that he had no reason to believe that Diane was under the influence of LSD at the time she defenestrated and fell to her death from an L.A. apartment building in 1969.

But alarming findings have also been made. According to Bonson, the combination of MDMA and an MAO inhibitor can lead to a life-threatening increase in blood pressure known as hypertensive crisis. Incidents of tragedy stemming from MDMA-related dehydration exacerbated by dance exertion have made sensational headlines, especially in the United Kingdom. MDMA has also been found to cause a reversible damage to serotonin-containing nerve terminals in some laboratory animals exposed to repeated injections of large doses. Whether this amounts to neurotoxicity or neural plasticity is a matter of debate.

In a paper posted on Lycaeum, "the world's largest entheogenic library and community," lay researcher William E. White warns that "all dissociatives," even prescription dextromethorphan (DXM), are "extremely toxic to developing fetuses." Basing his conclusions on published animal studies, White claims that dissociatives "carry a real risk of permanent brain damage," in particular Olney's lesions or NNMA Antagonist Neurotoxicity, which can cause memory and other cognitive disturbances. Because it is prone to repeated use, ketamine, which Holland calls "the crack cocaine of psychedelics," may be especially worrisome in this regard, especially in higher doses. Ironically, before his untimely ketamine-related death on New Year's Eve, 1996, D. M. Turner, the pseudonymous, now-canonized figure of the psychedelic community, who'd championed the drug as the "ultimate . . . journey" in his *Essential Psychedelic Guide* (1994), had grown troubled by its "psychedelic heroin" properties, branding it a "Frankenstein molecule" that doesn't "obey the shamanic rules."

It is perhaps a literal pipe dream to imagine that the ingestion of a psychedelic and the attendant catalyzation of intense experiences would leave no lasting biochemical impact on the subject at all. "Emotions and sensations don't exist in 'the ether,' but are mediated by the brain, a physical substrate," stresses Dr. Jake Falk, attending psychiatrist at Mount Sinai Hospital in New York City, who has a private practice with a specialization in psychopharmacology. "Since the brain may create new neural pathways in response to experiences, perceptions, traumas, and substances ingested, the psychedelic experience can indeed induce a change in brain structure or function, which may be transient or permanent. No matter how it is derived—as a product of either natural or chemically induced experiences—a newly acquired response pattern, ranging from the fearful to the euphoric, has physiological underpinnings in the network of synapses that comprise the brain."

Because of the exposure to intense emotions and upsurges from the unconscious brought about by psychedelic drugs, experts recommend that those who suffer from a mental disorder or lack a firm emotional and psychological constitution abstain from using them without medical supervision.

Methodology and Perspectives Used in the Making of This Book

To give credit where it is due, the beauty and terror of the material related in this book really come more from the experiential viscera of human beings than from the substances that conjured them. The psychedelic is, after all, only a catalyst. When seen in this light especially, the extraordinary phenomena of psychedelic experiences arouse a sense of wonder at the radiance and intricacy of the human mind. Using this perspective, it might be more instructive to consider the agents that induce altered states as more messenger than message.

The attributed catalysts for the trips described in this book are the following psychoactive substances:

LSD
Hawaiian baby woodrose
Morning glory seeds
DMT/5-MeO DMT
DPT
Ayahuasca/pharmahuasca
Psilocybin mushrooms
Amanita muscaria (Fly Agaric) mushroom
Peyote/mescaline
San Pedro cactus
MDA/MDMA (Ecstasy)

Nutmeg
2C-B
Cannabis (hashish, marijuana)
Opium
Datura
Ketamine
PCP
DXM
Salvia divinorum
Calea zacatechichi (Mexican bitter grass)

See Appendix: A Concise Index of Psychedelic Substances (page 451), for basic chemical and botanical descriptions.

I use the term *psychedelic* for the whole lot. The word, coined in 1956 by Aldous Huxley's Canadian colleague psychiatrist Humphrey Osmond, means "soul [or "mind," as Osmond preferred] manifesting" from the Greek *psyche* (soul or mind) and *delos* (to reveal). Some of the drugs in this broad category, particularly the sacred plants used by indigenous peoples since antiquity, are referred to as *entheogens*, a term coined in 1979 by scholars R. Gordon Wasson, Carl A. P. Ruck, Jonathan Ott, Jeremy Bigwood, and Danny Staples, which means "generating the god or the divine within." MDMA and the reportedly skin-sensitizing and aphrodisiacal 2C-B (Venus) are called *entactogens* (creating a sense of the "touch within" or "generating touch"—a word coined by Heffter Research Institute cofounder Dave Nichols). MDMA, often referred to as an *empathogen* ("generating empathy," coinage attributed to psychologist and Leary collaborator Ralph Metzner), is often discounted as a true psychedelic because it doesn't break down the final frontier, the ego. But since it dissolves internal barriers to feeling and insight, and lives up to the soul-manifesting definition, I choose to include it in the category.

I'm most comfortable with the term *psychedelic,* because it has the broadest applications, not being a precise medical term. Some atheists and others object to the term *entheogen,* because they don't believe in "God" or the divine per se, whereas they do acknowledge the human psyche and the power of substances categorized as psychedelic to amplify and catalyze it. The term *hallucinogen,* which *is* used in the medical community, raises objection, because it implies that the sole function of the drug is to conjure false or chimerical images. Among some, especially those given to the sacred plants, the very term *drug* is offensive because it connotes that the substance is artificial, soporific, stuporous, deliriant, or anesthetic, and prone to recreational abuse—thus dismissing its potential revelatory value.

This book is a compilation of narratives drawn mostly from taped interviews conducted between October 1994 and October 1998. The selection of stories included here was based on the strength of their psychic resonance and literary merit and not by any predetermined agenda. My only criterion for recruiting the confidences in the first place was that the experiences described be "unforgettable" to the narrator, ranging in character "from the sublime to the terrifying." With few exceptions, the trips described in these pages were taken in informal and illegal settings.

I recruited several dozen participants through word of mouth and the posting of an author's query on the psychedelic-related Websites of the Multidisciplinary Association for Psychedelic Studies (MAPS), the Island Group, and Lycaeum; an author's query in the *New York Times Book Review* (which was most fruitful); and through the placement of classified ads in the *New York Review of Books*, the *Village Voice*, and the *San Francisco Bay Guardian*. I also did a mailing to about thirty-five notable and accomplished figures involved in psychedelics, a few of whom graciously agreed to participate. Setting up appointments to meet respondents at various locales around the world was made immeasurably easier by the relatively new communications technologies of e-mail and the laptop computer.

A collection of psychedelic narratives from people in every culture of the world has required a great deal more time, resources, and effort than I could muster. The demographics of the circa 120 participants (50 of whose narratives are presented in this book) are primarily of European extraction, with plenty of Jewish folk and a handful of Latinos and African-Americans. They are citizens of the United States, Canada, the United Kingdom of Great Britain *and* Northern Ireland, Sweden, Denmark, Germany, Holland, France, Italy, Hungary, and Australia. Almost all are viably employed denizens of the greater middle class (not poor, not rich) or students with a similar background, with a few exceptions. Men outnumbered women three to one. The heterosexual/gay ratio was about the same as in society at large, though revealing one's sexual orientation (or income, for that matter) was not required. The age range ran from eighteen to over seventy.

I did my own transcribing and then edited the verbatim transcripts, making appropriate modifications to maintain the story line, the anonymity of persons cited (where appropriate), and the truth and accuracy of claims and details (where appropriate), while remaining faithful to the essence of the narrative as originally relayed. The results were sent to the participants for corrections and last-minute embellishments. A few of the narratives were submitted by the participants as written texts, which I edited. A legal agreement signed by both parties guaranteed the anonymity of the interview subject, if he or she so wished, and gave me the rights to the interview or submitted material. The names of people and places have been changed to maintain anonymity where appropriate. In the biographical data that appear at the top of each narrative, all complete-name and a minority of single-name designations are authentic, with the balance of the latter being fictitious. All other data are true, if not specific. Narratives are presented in alphabetical order by first name, an arbitrary sequence intended to offer no hint as to what type of story will follow and thus permit random-access reading.

In one sense, the tales here are fleshed-out versions of the "trip reports" seen on Websites, which, instructive as they are, tend to be somewhat clinical, truncated, and disembodied. I tried to make the stories full-bodied narratives by and about real people whom readers might feel they have gotten to know a little by story's end. The accounts are presented mainly within the framework of discrete trip events or episodic narratives, though anecdotes and details about the surrounding time and environment and the subject's mind-set, lifestyle, and patterns of experience are incorporated to provide context, set the scene, explain motives, and heighten drama and color. Some of the stories, those by individuals highly committed to or otherwise taken up with the psychedelic, encompass several months or years in an individual's ongoing relationship with it. Where notable, some exposition is given to explain how the psychedelic experience has been integrated into the narrator's life.

The gathering of these voices in one place provides an opportunity for psychonauts to compare notes with one another, to see the similarities as well as the differences in the themes and the minutiae of their trips, from the first "body rushes" through the "trails" and other visual marvels, the "peaking" hours and soul-shaking revelations of transcendent being. The book also offers a chance for the uninitiated to vicariously experience the thrills and traumas of the trip, which can entail soaring states of bliss, heightened spirituality, and a titanic sense of drama and suspense. Many readers for whom psychedelics were only a phase may still wax nostalgic for the shimmering days of yore when they scored a few hits of Orange Sunshine or Purple Microdot, "dropped" them under their tongues, and kicked back to enjoy the fireworks that ensued. Of course, one strapped on a metaphysical seat belt with the hope that the experience wouldn't backfire into a bad trip. This happened often enough, though it might have been almost as enlightening as a positive experience: a bitter lesson in the dark light it shed upon the tripper's tender, underexamined psyche.

For the subjects themselves, the book is a unique forum to lift the lid on some of their most intense experiences and secrets. For many, the process of relaying their tale touched a raw nerve, arousing jitters, tears, or a visible or audible sense of cathartic relief. This confessional dimension gives the book an intensely personal character, making it a sort of *vox populi* of peak-experiences and coming-outs. Participants were able to go back and excavate key experiences in their lives and reclaim them. I wanted the book to be a refuge for those who saw "God" and were dismissed, and also for those who *didn't* attain the

Ultimate as advertised but encountered something else that shook them. Their experiences then become liberated from the no-sayers who contend that such altered states are self-indulgent fancy at best and mentally debilitating at worst, and from the self-appointed psychedelic clergy who wag their fingers and say that if you didn't see the White Light, you hadn't arrived. I see the project as a mining expedition or an archaeological dig to retrieve a storehouse of psych-bytes and memories that might have otherwise been deleted from the hard drive, swept away in time and buried in shame, neglect, or political correctness.

At the beginning, waves of fear came over me at the thought of looking under these rocks again. The things that scamper out can pose queasy, immense, or unreconciliable issues. But then I realized that that was the whole point—to let the sun shine under the stones of repression, to set the leper-crazies free. So I tried to furnish a safe haven for the weird, the agonizing, the exhilarating, and the transgressional—with no judgment rendered. Rather than run from such phantasms or hide them in a drawer, both narrators and readers can now hold them up to the light and scan them through a sort of impartial View-Master or home-movie screen, as which this book is intended to function. (Check this one out . . . Now, click to the next . . .)

At the peak of popular psychedelic usage, from 1966 to 1973, a large number of young people, high school and university students mostly, ingested a lot of pills and substances. Among many of these trippers, the use of psychedelics was a sort of competitive sport, like mountain climbing or sailing around the world. Bragging and one-upmanship was common, and victory could be claimed in a variety of guises, since only the tripper knew what he or she had and hadn't seen. In an effort to portray how the trips really went down in the heads of the people who took them, I tried to exert an ecumenical emphasis on honesty and realism, taking care not to delegitimize any person's experience, for example, because he or she took "street acid" from Detroit as opposed to LSD-25 conferred by legendary alchemist Augustus Owsley Stanley himself.

I've attempted to make an even playing field for all experiences, whether the tripper was spinning his own karmic wheel, stuck on it, or flung off of it altogether. Some trippers did it "right" and used the substances with ritual and respect, looking for higher values both within and beyond themselves, and their trips paid off accordingly. It's clear to me that the most successful experiences were built upon a foundation of knowledge and, at the very least, respect. But to give the Devil his due, a lot of revealing phenomena occurred when the psychedelic was taken without a thought but for the sparkling, hedonistic kick of it all. Some did it right and had bum trips anyway, while others tripped just for the thrill and *still* experienced transcendence or learned something valuable. Tripping is much more than a matter of boiling up a pot of vegetation and uttering the right incantations. It's a synergistic reaction between a vulnerable, idiosyncratic personality, a time and a place, and the whole cosmos. No matter how you prepared, a trip's outcome was determined by your temperament and how it interacted with the set and setting, the "head trips" of your companions, and the elements of fate and luck.

Psychotropic substances have been both glamorized and demonized, but what really happens when you trip? Do you feel the urge to fly or stare into the sun? The answers may be surprising. I tried to tear away all the Peter Max pop iconography and get down to the real substance of psychedelic experiences. No doubt there will be tenders of the sacred gardens and other fundamentalists who will say I betrayed "the cause" by not presenting only testimony that sanctifies the various "medicines" ingested. And there will be shrill protests from the mothers of the pharmaceutically disappeared, who will say I haven't made it clear enough that drugs can destroy lives. Actually, in presenting a variety of both negatively and positively received experiences, I believe I have offered a balanced perspective on the subject.

To compile the stories was a "trip" in itself. Throughout most of the project, from April 1995 to June 1998, I was living in Bangkok, Thailand, where my wife, an international civil servant, was stationed on assignment. From my base there, I circled the globe twice, traveling geographically over several continents, temporally over three decades of memories from psychedelic times, and psychically over the varied terrain of the subconscious. To get "the story," I traveled to Kathmandu, Delhi, Copenhagen, London, New York, Chicago, San Francisco, Los Angeles, Phoenix, and Kona, Hawaii, trekking over old stomping grounds as well as exotic foreign locales, looking up old friends and making new ones.

In Bangkok I was part of an expatriate community of North Americans, Europeans, and Australasians, which lent an appropriate sense of displacement to the project, a time- (and place-) out-of-mind character to the proceedings. Those who have left their homeland often have a good tale to tell, sometimes of a psychedelic nature, and a few such stories are included here. In Nepal I saw the Himalaya for the first time, taking in the soaring heights that served as the setting for some of the trips related to me, and grabbing the opportunity to reread Peter Matthiessen's *The Snow Leopard*, a literary inspiration for the project that includes several superb descriptions of the psychedelic experience in the context of his ruminations about Eastern mysticism.

India holds a special place in the imagination of the psychedelic movement, given the compelling spirituality of the ancient Hindu creeds, the tradition of sacred cannabis use, and the perennial appeal of the yogic *babas* or masters. In 1998 I attended the Kumbh Mela, a spiritual gathering held since antiquity every three years at one of four cities. That year it took place in Haridwar, a holy city where meat and liquor are outlawed, situated where the Ganges emerges from the Himalaya. The event attracted plenty of young Westerners on the adventure circuit, one of whom I interviewed about his experience in Ecuador with the San Pedro cactus (see page 328).

On Shiva Ratri, the most auspicious day of the festival, my friend Jonathan and I ate two *charas* biscuits filled with a sort of handmade hash and marijuana pesto (purchased legally at a government shop in Rajastan) and joined the throngs by the river and the parades in the streets. This day would be as psychedelic as any I'd spent in a long while. *Om nama Shivia:* praise to Shiva. Rumor had it that Ram Dass had come for the occasion, so we kept our eyes peeled in hopes of scoring an interview with this central figure in psychedelic history. We never found the famed American *baba* (who, alas, was still home in California recovering from a 1997 stroke), but as we walked through the sadhu camps, I saw one of the most profoundly stirring sights I've ever seen: Hindu renunciates—some naked, some loinclothed, some fancifully robed—sitting at their fires, seemingly levitated, looking like creatures of heavenly saffron-orange flame, smoldering coals of God's holy fire burning brightly. I stood transfixed as aural rivulets of warm, streaming devotion curled through the air, making quarter-tone turns at harsh crossroads of experience before blending into pungent, harmonic verses in the continuous hymn to the pain of being human.

My stay in India was enriched by meeting a European woman who had come there several years earlier to recover from a terrible depression brought on by the end of her marriage. She recounted an unorthodox, all-woman peyote ritual in the American Southwest she had taken part in, but her interest in the psychedelic was secondary to her regard for a spontaneous experience of kundalini energy ignition and cosmic oneness that occurred without inducement or warning. She told of a sudden explosion of pure heavenly fire that went off inside her as she emptied herself of all thoughts and desires at the very nadir of her life. The unexpected spiritual awakening left her trembling and weeping in gratitude for days afterward. After this, she saw the mighty *Ganga* as her salvation. Vowing to give herself to God, she served as the personal assistant to a swami until his death. Her story underscored the provenance of India as the motherland for the mystical quest, predating the psychedelic movement in the West by several millennia.

One place I came up dry—to my surprise, given its tolerant and progressive reputation—was my wife's native Denmark. During a visit there I tried to scare up some trippers to interview, but they teach their kids so effectively that drugs are harmful in this homogeneous Nordic kingdom that it's very hard to find a person outside Christiania, the hippie separatist ghetto in the middle of Copenhagen, who has tripped or has any positive regard for such a thing. I got some inkling of the background for the apparent national antipathy to psychedelics when I contacted Alex Frank Larsen, the award-winning journalist who filled me in on Denmark's notorious "LSD scandal," which he exposed in the mid-Eighties.

In a bizarre course of treatment administered by neurologist Einar Geert-Jørgensenan from 1960 to 1974, Larsen related, LSD was given—without their knowledge or consent—to more than five hundred people suffering from mental maladies ranging from mild depression to schizophrenia. The experiment spun out of control when many of the patients, some of whom had been given their "medicine" forcefully and were left unattended in basement cells, were overcome with upsurges from their troubled subconscious. According to Larsen, one reacted by stabbing her boyfriend to death, some committed suicide in the wake of the treatment, and many remained stricken and haunted for years, some permanently addled. After looking into U.S. government archives in Washington, D.C., Larsen learned that Geert-Jørgensenan's work was "closely followed and secretly supported by the CIA." Needless to say, the scandal did nothing to enhance the luster of psychedelics in this wholesome society that seems very content with beer and aquavit, *tak* you very much.

In London I was briefed on various dimensions of rave culture by several grad students, a journalist, and a laser technician (see page 11) involved in it. I also met briefly with the late Nicholas Saunders, the entrepreneur and author of several books on MDMA and "alternative" culture, who had made a crusade of making accurate, reliable information about MDMA available. (See Bibliography and Resources, page 461). I came away from these meetings with the impression that the culture that has grown up around MDMA in Britain is considerably more strident and cohesive than its counterpart across the Atlantic. This might have something to do with the feisty, insistent nature of the young over there. I was told that the organization and stealth that go into impromptu raves at unadvertised sites in the British countryside grew out of the so-called convoy or travelers movement that began in the Seventies. One of the great galvanizing events in the history of British youth culture took place on June 1, 1985, when thousands of alternative types intent on throwing a free festival descended upon Stonehenge in an orderly motor convoy only to be brutally turned away by the police. The confrontation, dubbed the Battle of the Beanfield, launched a new renegade society of music- and psychedelic-inspired youth that evolved, with the help of MDMA, into the rave culture that blossomed during the Manchester-based Madchester Summer of Love in 1988.

While I was stateside I felt that a trip to peyote country—home to that other race of Indians who are spiritual mentors for the psychedelic movement—was essential in order to document the fact that a viable, aboveground culture has grown up around the ancient tradition of psychoactive plant use in North America. With the aid of a guide named Mark, I made on-site visits to two institutions in Arizona that are focal points for the sacramental use of the cactus: the Peyote Way Church of God (PWCOG) in Klondyke, and the Peyote Foundation in Kearny. I interviewed the directors about the origins and administration of their respective institutions and the personal experiences that led to their becoming point men in the peyote way. Their narratives are included in this book (see pages 298 and 266, respectively).

Any trip to the American Southwest conjures the specter of the Indian's exile in their own land, what writer Jon Savage calls the "shadowy absence that's always present in America, the exterminated native race." En route from Tempe to Klondyke at five in the morning, Mark and I got out of the car in the old frontier outpost of Fort Thomas to check the road signs by a group of small mobile home–like installations near the rail crossing. As I stood in the dark, I heard the most eerily anguished utterance I've ever heard in my life. It sounded like some neutered, slaughtered soul, stricken with utter resignation and loss, so unearthly that I couldn't tell if it was the voice of a ghost warbling on the wind or a real person braying in eternal torment. Even if it was only the voice of the desert trickster, the coyote, for me the ethereal wail vocalized the mortal wound that whites have dealt the Native Americans by ripping their heartland away from them. In the context of my mission to encounter the peyote religion on its own soil, this seemed especially poignant to me. Mark took in one faint earful and we drove off in a hurry.

Incorporated in 1977, the PWCOG—"the oldest tax-exempt all-race peyotist church in the United States"—is situated on 160 acres in the isolated Aravaipa Valley on the "back side" of Mount Graham, a sacred site of the Apaches. Mark and I were welcomed warmly by church founder Immanuel Trujillo (Mana), whom Timothy Leary once called an American hero. Mana responded to my request for an interview by saying that he couldn't possibly have learned enough to begin talking about his peyote experiences, because "I ain't dead yet." Nearly everyone in Arizona I talked to about peyote, including a road man and three families of practitioners, said that it was a place to go, not a story to tell, a continuous journey of discovery, with the accent on "continuous."

Exempt from taxes, the church is financed by a cottage industry, Mana's trademarked ceramics enterprise. Members exercise "ritual labor" to produce the decorative ceramics which are sold at museums around the country. According to president Matthew Kent, who, along with his wife, Annie Zapf, helped Mana launch the Church, their guideposts were "the Mormons—a homegrown American church—and a little pamphlet that Tim Leary and Ralph Metzner put out called 'Start Your Own Religion,' a 1964 classic." The PWCOG requires members to adhere to some dietary rules (no alcohol, caffeine, sugar, or white flour) drawn from the Mormons' Word of Wisdom, which declares, among other things, that "strong" and "hot drinks" are "not for the belly," while "all wholesome herbs God hath ordained for the constitution, nature, and use of man."

As for the sacrament itself, church practice is the spirit walk, which involves fasting for two days prior to drinking a brew of peyote-button tea and sitting down quietly alone in the wilderness. Mana decided that the open-air solo rite was the best way for individuals to connect with peyote, especially for non-Indians who do not share the culture of songs, drums, and pipes that comprise the communal road meeting held inside a tepee. An Apache-French "half-breed," Mana has long championed the opening up of peyote to non-natives, in part to confer the legal right to the sacrament of his own grandchildren, who have less than twenty-five percent Indian blood, once a uniform requirement for legal exemption from prosecution. The belief that "no one should have to adopt someone else's culture to partake in the sacrament" is a key impetus for the church's creation.

To visit the Peyote Foundation near the Superstition Mountains, you have to call ahead to Leonard Mercado so he can raise the bridge gate over the Gila River to let you across. Leo, a former deacon in the PWCOG, launched the foundation in 1996 after his peyote plants were confiscated in a SWAT team–style raid by Pinal County authorities acting on an errant suspicion of marijuana plantation. The foundation holds NAC (Native American Church) road meetings and serves as a clearinghouse for information about the cultivation, practice, and legal status of peyote. Leo often faxes judges around the country to explain legal procedures for handling confiscated cacti.

"Something told me that if there was any microphone I could use to ask God a question, it was peyote," he says, by way of explaining, in part, his ordeal-tested commitment to the peyote way. Apart from a sincerity of purpose, there is no demanding protocol for participation in road meetings held at the foundation, where, for instance, an alcoholic coming off a binge is welcome to seek solace and guidance. "It's the medicine, not the rules, that confers the healing," Leo affirms.

Prior to moving back to the United States in 1998, the final stop in my Bangkok-based West-East itinerary was on the volcanic terrain of the Big Island of Hawaii, where I met with an affable and hilarious Terence McKenna at his home on the verdant slopes of Mauna Loa. The results of our discussions over two days are presented in this book (page 412).

The issue of whether I condone the ingestion of scheduled substances must inevitably be addressed. I should state, by way of elaborating on the disclaimer in the Note to the Reader (page ix), that I could never sit here and say that with all the variables in the respective chemistries of the individual human body and the psychoactive substances themselves, the medical uncertainties that persist about long-term use, the cultural and ethical taboos and legal proscriptions, the potentially mortal perils of black-market sources for illegal contraband, and the lack of reliable identification, dosage, and quality control and regulation for illicit substances, it is a good idea to go out there and take a banned substance like it's your birthright. But I could also never say that what some of these drugs do in ideal, informed and appropriately "controlled" circumstances, and even sometimes in less than ideal conditions, is inevitably and invariably "bad" or "harmful" or "wrong," because the record simply doesn't bear that out.

The aim of this book is to report *what really happened* within a fascinating, psychically resonant domain, to see what it suggests about the human mind and spirit as magnified in the funhouse mirror of the psychedelic state. That many of the stories are colored by the fact that a criminalized substance was ingested is not to glorify or condone the breaking of the law, but simply to make known what was not known previously, to shed light on an underreported reality, as well as the ineffable itself. That any law was broken is purely *incidental* to the story.

It is my belief that psychedelic drugs should *not* be ingested in an illegal, uninformed setting. They should *not* be taken outside an enabling environment that can proffer the benefit of medical, psychiatric, spiritual, or shamanic guidance by learned figures schooled in the dynamics and practice of the psychedelic voyage and even accredited as such. Furthermore, the chemical hygiene and appropriate, medically determined dosage of any substance consumed should be confirmed by authorities on such matters. Far from being a libertarian on the issue, I believe that almost all potentially useful psychotropic drugs should be legal but intensively controlled and regulated, so as to be administered in constructive, medicinal, and healing ways.

In the age of Prozac, there is demonstrated medicinal value in psychotropic drugs—for tightening or loosening screws in the mind, where appropriate, and for fine-tuning a biochemical balance in the brain. Such psychopharmacological progress was based upon unmistakable scientific evidence that the performance and mood of the mind can be influenced by subtle changes in its chemistry. Of course, there's a fine line between use and misuse of chemical interventions. The potential for abuse, mischief, and even evil is monstrous. There has to be some regulation to keep the stuff out of wicked hands, like those of military/spy organizations, for instance. Martin Lee and Bruce Shlain's *Acid Dreams: The Complete Social History of LSD: The CIA, the Sixties, and Beyond* (1992) documents how the U.S. government co-opted a drug it would ban for psychiatric, spiritual, or recreational use, in order to test its potential as a mind-control tool, with civilians and military personnel—some unsuspecting—as guinea pigs. The murderous cults of Aum Shinrikyo in Japan and Charles Manson in California reportedly used a regimen of LSD to warp the minds of their followers into compliance with evil edicts. Human history is rife with instances of the misuse of magic and technology. We ought to take care that psychedelics are used wisely, with retribution for those who don't.

To wipe away the grime of criminality associated with some psychedelic usage, and to formalize practices that might otherwise be naive and even dangerous, knowledgeable figures might be recruited to indoctrinate trippers in the subtle skills of navigating hyperspace. Virtually every responsible tripping expert recommends advance preparation and "basic training" for a psychedelic experience, through meditation and/or study, and, after that, guidance through at least the initial experiences by a responsible psychiatric or shamanic figure. Such a secure and instructive context was largely missing when the kids of the Sixties and Seventies took to the psychedelic skies and singed their wings in the flames of the Other World. "In an effort to integrate the yearning for spiritual exploration with present-day society concerns," the Council on Spiritual Practices in San Francisco has formulated a "Code of Ethics for Spiritual Guides," which outlines the responsibilities of those who might serve as "facilitators" of entheogenic and other encounters with the divine in light of the "risks" attendant with certain "primary religious practices."

Of course, one might question the whole idea of "preparing" for a psychedelic experience at all, a process that can be likened to gearing up for a tornado to rip through your home. The punch line of a trip is often enough that you can't take it with you. Still, the storm is more likely to be appreciated by the person who builds his own house than by the one who just lives in it. There are volumes of lessons about life's dynamics worth incorporating before you watch the cosmos engulf your puny, insignificant self and wash across your windscreen during the ensuing metaphysical twister. There's no sense in submitting yourself to an experience that can strip you down to your "nothing" unless you know it can happen and that you can fill the void imploded into you with something more life-enriching than it held before. Of that there are no guarantees, so who you are going into the experience—how supple and healthy your spirit and sense of self—makes all the difference in how you come out.

OverSoul by Alex Grey, oil on linen,
© 2000, courtesy of the artist.

PART II

The Narratives

Aaron

_B. 1967_

Author who writes about technology and the fringes of the spirit

Resides in San Francisco

Raised in Southern California

Trawling the Ghost Stream

During my travels through India with my girlfriend Janine in January 1995, we went to a place called Hampi, a small Hindu city that had been abandoned in the sixteenth century when marauding Moguls invaded from the north. It's situated in a dry, desert-like environment in Karnataka, about three hundred kilometers east of Goa. Today there's a small village in the midst of the ruins, nestled alongside the river that winds through the area.

The town is a big spot on the freak circuit, a refuge where Goa hippies go to chill out. Across the river from the village there are huge boulders which are very striking, like some of the formations you can see in northern Mexico, weird piles of strange rock like Antonin Artaud describes in his book *The Peyote Dance.* Many sadhus live around these outcroppings, a good number of them hash smokers. There's a nice interchange between the freaks and these smiling, cannabis-imbibing Shiva worshipers. Sometimes it's hard to tell the difference between them.

On the night before the full moon, Janine and I climbed up a small mountain near the village, taking a rather treacherous trail. On the peak was a very simple temple, a whitewashed building, where a whole bunch of freaks were hanging out for the sunset, smoking hash and chatting in many European tongues. Reaching this scene, we sat down and dropped some Black Microdot acid.

We couldn't tell if the temple was abandoned or still actively used. While people were still lounging on the roof, we poked around inside the temple and found that there was indeed still a god image deep within the inner sanctum. We had to shine a flashlight to see it, but the deity had a fresh strand of marigolds around its neck, which meant that it was still being "fed" and kept alive through worship. So it was still a living temple, though very primitive and run-down and probably not frequented much, except by freaks from the West.

After the sun went down, the freaks gradually disappeared. It got darker and darker. Finally, we looked around and noticed that we were the last ones, except for an old Indian man who came up and stood very near us. He didn't say anything, but was clearly checking us out. After a few minutes we started to get a bit apprehensive. We were coming on to the acid, wondering, "What's going on? Are we not supposed to be here?" He just stood there, and we just sat there, breathing, staying relaxed. Finally, he nodded to us and then left. Perhaps he was the guardian of the place, just making sure that nobody, with no one watching, turned to mischief and screwed around with the sacred site.

Janine and I climbed up to the roof of the temple and sat there. As the moon rose, we really came on. Then a warm wind picked up from the east, and something I'd read in some Tibetan meditation manual popped into my head, an admonition about the danger of meditating on top of windy mountains, because of all the spirits about. It was certainly a powerful place to be tripping on a psychedelic.

Typical for me in the early stages of an acid trip, I experienced big rushes that took me out of my body and put me in a different visual space. Often at this point I'll consciously settle back down to get a basic sense of where I am in the real world, and then go in and out of the onrushing psychedelic space through a sort of hyperspatial wormhole. But this orientation process produced a very amusing result on this occasion. *Okay, where am I? Oh yeah. I'm on top of a temple in India with a god inside and this ancient ruined city splayed before me in the glimmering light of the full moon.* It was like trying to ground yourself in a place that was already imaginary.

As the trip got more and more strange and intense, Janine and I had a shared hallucination, which went on for quite some time. We were sitting at the eastern ledge of the temple roof, on the edge of a cliff, facing the rising moon and the oncoming wind. We turned to look at each other. As every tripper knows, when you look at a face for a long-enough spell, it invariably melts and changes and takes on various personas. Something somewhat more phantasmagorical occurred this time.

It was as if we'd become skeletons and the wind carried spirits like sheets of loose newspapers on a windy day. Myriad specters and apparitions were blowing through us, getting caught on our material forms and then blowing away again, like a page of newsprint that tumbles along and clings to a bush or telephone pole a moment, before being swooshed away. Some of these beings were very hellish, hungry ghosts chattering in endless flight, slowly disintegrating in the winds of time. They'd cling to Janine's form, struggling to hold on, and then be whisked away again by the wind. We watched each other's faces silently for quite some time, maybe an hour.

It was very frightening. I switched into virtual reality mode, which is sometimes required when I reach the scarier parts of trips. Basically

I try to engage the arising phenomena as if I were operating a flight simulator of the bardo realms, doing my best to just perceive what comes up as insubstantial creations of the mind and resist being overcome by the attendant emotions. As one might expect, this only works some of the time.

At one point, Janine transformed into a chthonic snake goddess, which had far more graphic reality and force of presence than most of the other phantasms, and a wicked hunger in her eyes. When this image took over, I couldn't deal with it. I had to turn my head away. I was trying to stay with the frightening stuff, but this was just too much.

Janine later described her side of our mutual stare: "I saw in Aaron a whole life process, from a baby all the way to a very skeletal old man. Then the skin and the life force blew off, first the skin, and then the spirit, leaving him like smoke blowing away in the wind. There were some dark, sexually ravenous man-spirits that appeared, inevitably appealing in some limited way, very much a magnification of the erotically predatory male gaze. There were many images of old age, skeletal figures close to and even after death. I also saw the face of a very wise old man, suggested, no doubt, by the wizened guru omnipresent at least mythically in India. The wise man transformed into a death's head, and moved off into the space of death. All these different spirits were blowing around and when one landed on him, it was like a sheet of newspaper was stuck on his face. The personality would hold for a moment, and then it would drip off the way plastic melts."

Inevitably for me, a slice of cornball science fiction slipped into my trip. Deciding to try the staring game somewhere else, I looked up at the moon and had one of my more hilarious though frightening hallucinations. I thought to myself, "If I keep staring at this moon, something really freaky is going to happen, and it might not be that pleasant." But I'd signed up, so I kept staring at the moon, which was about forty-five degrees in the eastern sky. Suddenly and very viscerally, my entire sense of space changed.

I saw that the moon was actually a flashlight being beamed down onto us by some mischievous alien scientists, as though the plains of Karnataka were inside a petri dish under a microscope. Then I got a more distinct sense of the nature of these unseen beings. "Oh, the little creature notices us now. Isn't this amusing? Let's play with him a little bit." The moon began to shake. At this juncture, I consciously drew my eyes away. I didn't want to go down that tunnel anymore.

As we came down from the peak of the acid, we reached a familiar stage, when you're basically back in your body and the main ride is over, but you're still very high. Often this is a time of annoying restlessness: "Should I move? Should I stay here? Do I want to go somewhere else?" I was thinking how unfortunate it was to have hit the restless stage just then, because the trip had been incredibly wondrous so far. Just at that moment, around midnight or so, a crew of British freaks climbed up to the top of the temple, bringing blankets and whiskey and cigarettes and hash and fruit and candles. They laid out their stuff and we joined them. We weren't ready to climb down the mountain anyway, in the state we were in.

It was incredibly excellent timing, because we had a very grounding, human experience with these hilarious Brits. Unlike most of the freaks on the Goa/India circuit, they were wry and witty, and they reflected on the bizarre experiences of India—the filth, the sluggish trains, the colorful beggars with knives in their cheeks—in a very amusing and slightly cynical way. This was very refreshing. Most of the freaks were so humorless and pious—"I am on the psychedelic path, man, hanging out with authentic sadhus"—which can be lugubriously heavy and delusional, not to mention pretentious. At the end of the day, they're really just smoking a lot of dope and having a good time—as are a lot of the sadhus themselves.

After hanging out with these delightful folk for a few hours, we decided to go back to the village, where we'd let a room in a woman's house. We climbed down into the abandoned ruins, which were very spooky in the dark, and made our way back. In the village we came upon hundreds of people sleeping in the streets, so densely packed that we had to step gingerly between their corpselike bodies to make our way. Presumably some of them had vacated their homes so that they could rent them out to tourists like us who'd come just to have a trippy time.

Alice Dee

B. 1962

Financial adviser

Resides in San Francisco

Raised somewhere east of California, resided for a while in New York City

Highway to the Sky: The Road Seen Only by the Dreamer

The experience that attracted me to the psychedelic path was my maiden voyage, which took place in Jamaica in the early Nineties, when I was thirty. I was nearing the end of a wonderful vacation from my banker job in New York. On the bus returning to my hotel in Montego Bay from Rick's Cave in Negril, the tour guide asked us if we wanted to stop at Jenny's Cafe to get some Jenny cake. I asked her what it was and she told me it had ganja in it. Baked goods with real Jamaican ganja in it sounded exotic, so we stopped and my traveling companion Ruth and I bought a slice of chocolate Jenny cake at the roadside shack. The piece was about the size of a quarter of a single-layer round cake, and we split it between us. If I'd realized that the proper dosage was probably around half the size of my thumb, I would have eaten much less.

As the bus rolled along, I closed my eyes and saw forms morph into cartoon images, an entirely new visual phenomenon for me. When we arrived at the hotel, I was rather disoriented and staggered up to my room on the top floor. I lay down on the bed and noticed that my mouth was getting very dry, almost sticking to itself inside. I was concerned about choking, so I got up to get a glass of water. When I came back to the bed, I noticed a tremendous expansion in the range of my audio sensitivity. I was hearing sounds from far away as well as the voices of people in rooms below me very clearly, almost as if they were in the same room with me. Then a dramatic tolling sound rang into my room, the clanky tone of an anchor on its chain and then the taut, creaking sound of mooring ropes tied to the dock being pulled by the movement of the boat. The harbor was several hundred meters away, so I realized that there was something extraordinary going on, that this was not a common cannabis high. My curiosity was piqued.

I'd been reading Carlos Castañeda and was beginning to understand the process of acting with intent, so I asked myself, "What have you always wanted to do in this sort of state?" and the answer was to see proof of divinity, something I'd demanded since adolescence, when I'd turned away from religion in favor of a scientific purview of reality. In my studies of chemistry, finance, and other disciplines, it took more than an abstract doctrine to convince me of a theorem or formula's veracity. I required evidentiary or experiential *proof.* So with all my intent, I sent out to the universe the thought that I wanted to see God, if there was one. Almost immediately, a speck of bright light appeared in my closed-eye visual field, like a little star in the distance.

Growing in size and speed, the light moved from the left to the right. Soon everything was white but for some thin, crystalline rays, which were a source of particularly powerful brilliance. In the presence of this intense luminosity, there was no passage of time. It was as if all moments and all space coalesced into the light. As the light streamed toward me, engulfing me, I experienced a wave of extraordinary bliss, like a full-body orgasm, and the sense I was in the presence of something absolutely awesome. Sex is nothing compared to the ecstasy I felt at that moment. I had no awareness of body or ego or time, only a profound sensation of illumination and the feeling I was in the presence of All That Is, Eternity, God, whatever you might call something all-encompassing. I found words for the experience later, when I read a description of the "Clear Light of the Shining Void" in *The Tantric Mysticism of Tibet.* I thought, "Wow, that's just where I was." I'd apparently taken a sort of accidental shortcut to a place that many spiritual practitioners strive through ardent discipline to achieve, some for their entire lives.

Leary once referred to the mystic experience as a total reimprinting of the nervous system. When I came back from Jamaica, I felt totally new, as though I'd just been born. Having had so much ego burned away had cleansed and refreshed my spirit. It was a grace that profoundly changed my life by giving me a reason to override my scientific skepticism and accept the validity of the spirit. So I set out to explore this realm through sacred plants and other chemical gateways.

A few months later, I met a woman from Peru at a workshop whom I told about my experience. She said, "You know, you may want to take ayahuasca." She described its properties as a medicine and a teacher and put me in touch with an apprentice to an *ayahuascero* shaman in Peru, who led a ceremony in the New York City area, which I attended. When I took the medicine, I experienced being the mother of all, including myself, and even went through a sequence in which I birthed myself. Two weeks later, I flew down to Peru with a group for a full-fledged ayahuasca ceremony.

We trundled up the Amazon for a couple of hours out of Iquitos until we came to a little town with a special compound for ayahuasca initiations. The *ayahuascero* spoke only Spanish, which I didn't understand, but fortunately there were translators, and we also used sign language to communicate, which was fun. The people in charge of the ceremonies appeared to have a mixture of Spanish and Indian blood. Though some wore native garb with swirly patterned embroidery, they didn't seem to be the indigenous people with whom the practice originated.

I drank the medicine at about seven ceremonies, which I tend to merge in my memory into one weeklong experience. About twelve of us North Americans as well as a few visitors from neighboring villages sat around in a circle in the straw-roofed temple, which was open at the sides. An altar with a lit candle at one end served as the focal point. During the ceremonies, the shaman sang special songs called *icaros* and played some evocative twangy music. He waved a candle or a special flashlight through the air so that we could observe the especially long trails that ayahuasca manifests, ribbons of light that trail far behind the light source like stars with tails. It was usually quite dark during the sessions, though the moon came out at times, casting silvery shadows.

We did one session under a big, beautiful tree in the middle of the jungle. Moonlight came down through the trees onto a collection of leaves by the great tree. I looked at this spot for a while and it changed into a little doe, one of my power animals, all curled up. I looked away and then back again, and a different animal was there. I kept repeating this process, seeing a different animal in the same spot each time. It was as though I were cycling through a series of animal spirits within my own psyche.

I encountered the spirit of ayahuasca at various intervals. A fantastic morphing creature with a beak, like the faces depicted on shamanic masks, appeared, announcing, "I am the spirit of ayahuasca." An inner dialogue then ensued in which the voice of the medicine told me what my visions represented.

Most people in the North who know about ayahuasca think the DMT in the leaf component of the brew is the essential element and that the vine is added just as a monoamine oxidase inhibitor to potentiate and sustain the effects of orally ingested DMT. But I believe that it's the vine that brings the voice and the teacher to the medicine, and that the DMT within the leaf component contributes only the color and the pictorials. The contrast between traditional ayahuasca and the pharma (synthetic) variety I did later—which is long on visuals and short on guidance—made it very clear to me where the teaching, and hence the power of the medicine, was coming from.

One experience in particular taught me to listen to the voice. We were all on a special diet which we were supposed to observe during our stay at the compound, a very bland fare of white rice and boiled plantains with no oil, sugar, or salt. The nonvegetarians ate a type of fish without teeth called *boca chica.* I was eating the vegetarian diet, but didn't feel I was getting enough energy from it. I was very lethargic. With my eyes closed, I saw a vision of a pineapple, very clear and very colorful, hovering before me. Then the voice came in, saying, "Eat pineapple and you will feel better." Since it wasn't part of the strict diet, I thought the voice was teasing me. I broached this to the shaman and he gestured for me to follow him. He took me up to the temple, where he chopped up two huge pineapples with his machete and nodded, instructing me to eat. They were delicious. I felt much better almost immediately. The shaman said through an interpreter that the medicine had shown me the food I needed to eat to make me well, and that I could now include it in my diet.

For most of that week, ayahuasca was like an intentional "bad" or at least uncomfortable trip. It usually involves nausea, vomiting, and also diarrhea for some people. It's a heavy, sedentary kind of experience with some distinctly dark sides. Most of my imagery consisted of very spooky things, such as demons and goblins and skeletons. I'm not a very fearful person, so I was just observing it, saying, "Okay, if that's what you want to show me." But after the fifth or sixth session of the same sort of macabre material, I got a bit sick of it, so I said to the medicine, "Can't you show me anything positive?" and it was like a light was turned on. All of a sudden there was this beautiful scene in my inner eye: a river winding through a green pasture with a majestic tree, some horses grazing, and a beautiful couple making love in the middle of it all. It was stunningly gorgeous, all in brilliant Technicolor. I said, "Oh, thank you!" and then the visions went back to the demons and goblins. It was so funny!

I finally did have visions that were purely inspirational. In one session, I got very dizzy after thirty minutes of ingestion, but decided not to fight it and allowed myself to just keep spinning. After a while, my astral body began to spin, and then it spiraled upward, disassociating from my physical body altogether. I looked down and saw my body and the roof of the temple, and then I continued to fly up high in the air. I looked up and saw a beautiful full moon from which a moonbeam came toward me. Out of this ray of light came the apparition of a beautiful woman about my age with very pale skin and long silvery-blond hair. Dressed in a shimmery silver dress, she was the closest thing to a goddess I'd ever seen!

As she approached, she started to dance, and then gestured for me to dance with her. I love to dance. I've been a dancer since I was a very young child, and always enjoy the opportunity to express dance at raves and Grateful Dead shows. She taught me a beautiful swirling dance, a cross between a Deadhead-style space dance, a belly dance, and Tai Chi movements. So we performed this lovely flowing choreography together while I was in my astral body up in the sky.

I felt a call from my body that it needed me, so I nodded to the silvery goddess and then slipped back down to my physical form. As I opened my eyes, the shaman was standing before me, making gestures for me to come forward. This was very unusual because on ayahuasca, you never stand up unless you want to go vomit or have your diarrhea. "What on earth is he asking me to get up for?" I wondered. He'd never done that to anybody else in the group.

Then he began to make movements that mirrored those of the dance I'd just been taught by the goddess. I was totally blown away! He told me afterward through translators that he'd telepathically picked up on my desire to dance. My body had been slumped, so my movements were entirely on the astral plane and not echoed in my body. Others confirmed that I hadn't been moving during my trance. I declined his invitation to stand up and dance physically, since I'd just been dancing out of body, free of gravity. Ever since this vision, I often experience spiritual ecstasy while performing the dance bodily. I think of it as my own personal dance, as it was specially shown to me by the goddess in my vision. A friend observed that its movements are like sorcery motions that move Chi energy, much like the tensegrity movements that Castañeda promotes.

In another session, I had a vision of myself dead lying on a table in a morgue. I looked okay for being dead, with short silver-white hair. I asked the spirit how old I was as a corpse, and it responded, "Seventy-four." I watched as the body began to decompose and turn to dust. Then a wind came up and the pile of dust blew away until there was nothing left. This transpiration gave me a profound sense of peace. From then on, I've never had even a remote fear of death. There's a difference between an irrational, emotionally debilitating fear of death, and a justifiable concern about a potentially life terminating force. I'll get out of the way of a bus, but I don't fret neurotically about leaving this mortal coil. My death vision, like my maiden psychedelic voyage six months before, totally refreshed my perspective of life.

Within the domain of visionary travel, I'd now gone all the way toward the beginning, to my conception, and all the way toward the end, to my death. Like Scrooge's ghosts, the medicine had treated me to visions of the two most important transitions in my life cycle.

Ayahuasca is also known to enhance dreams even a few days after it's out of your system. One night, after all the sessions were over and I was relaxing, I had a dream of looking up in the sky and seeing an asphalt road with a dividing line. The sky was a beautiful blue and the road looked really odd in it, fading at each end.

I said to a friend, "Look at the strange road up there."

"What road?" he replied.

"You don't see anything up there?"

"No."

I realized that I was having a vision within my dream and that the road represented a spiritual path that is not necessarily seen by anyone else.

Since that trip to Peru, I've taken a wide variety of psychedelics, including both the traditional organic and the modern synthetic varieties. One mushroom trip is particularly memorable. I took about nine grams, a rather heavy dose for anybody. After blacking in and out of consciousness, I focused on my sweetheart lying next to me. While my eyes were closed, I kneaded his stomach like a cat does with her paws. Slowly, I felt the physical and energetic resistance between us give way. There will still a solid form, but it was now somewhat fluid, like mercury. Then I felt the boundary between what was me and what was him dissipate, and I merged totally into him. I felt a complete oneness with him and his spirit, as though I'd gone right into his body. I call this sort of experience "mushroom merging" and it's been a very meaningful highlight in my explorations.

I've explored some relatively unknown chemicals and new combinations of substances. I do my research first to see if anyone else has reported results and I ask doctors if there's a possible negative interaction. Recently I took ten tablets of Drexoral cough tablets in order to ingest 300 milligrams of DXM (dextromethorphan), which has some very trippy properties. I waited a while and didn't feel much, so I took two hits of my favorite acid to see what the combination would do.

I'm used to seeing wigglies on psychedelics, but soon the walls were warping like the surface of the ocean. Amazingly, I could cause the lava lamp and other features of the bedroom to warp when my mind ordered it to. "Move to the left. Okay, move to the right . . ." I'd never been able to manipulate open-eyed visuals with my mind before. After an hour of this, I closed my eyes and almost instantaneously, I went out of body to a place of power and shamanic possibility. It was an ethereal room with a network of energy strings that were connections to events past, present, and future. I plucked them, strumming them like you might the strings of a piano when the top is open. It was like playing God's pinball game, though there was no sound. After a while, I began to worry that I was fiddling around in a sacred, off-limits sort of place. "Maybe I shouldn't be playing with this stuff," I thought. So I backed off, feeling a sense of trepidation about tampering with things I shouldn't have touched.

As it dawned outside, I came back into my body and went to the mirror, which I love to look in while tripping. My reflection was short and fat, which I'm not in real life. It was if my looking glass had been replaced with a funhouse mirror. Then I held up a bracelet and it too was misshapenly short and fat. I looked at my cat and *she* was short and fat. Everything was short and fat. Even my car out on the street looked squat and obese. I'd never had a persistent visual distortion that rendered everything asymmetrical relative to two axes. Gradually, as I came down, the shapes of things reassumed normalcy.

I have a meditation I like to do at the end of a trip, when the sun is often rising. I live on a hill and can look out the window and see all of the lights of the city (San Francisco) slowly turn off. For about an hour and a half, I sit and gaze out my window and watch all the lights go out, one by one. It's very peaceful and relaxing, a great way to get insights, do some analysis, and recollect my thoughts.

This morning had one of the most beautiful sunrises I'd ever seen. There were strips of clouds across the sky, a full moon opposite the sun, and across the whole horizon, all the way up to the middle of the heavens, was a rainbow—and none of this was a hallucination. My visiting (undosed) mother had gotten up, and she joined me at the window and also appreciated it deeply.

A week after the trip, I discovered there were repercussions to my trespassing in the Room of Strings. Several unusual occurrences took place within a very short period of time. At the time, I was involved in an E-mail discussion group, which had just held a conference about the politics of consciousness, among other themes. The guy who'd been running the list suddenly decided to shut it down. Somebody died. Odd things happened to some of my friends. The synchronicity of strangeness seemed like a totally improbable excess of novelty. I sometimes wonder whether plucking those strings had pulled a few things out of whack in my life and in the lives of my friends—if I'd actually tweaked the strings of fate.

I place a great deal of stock in my psychedelic forays, which I consider essential to my spiritual growth, even though it is extremely difficult to reconcile my discoveries with consensus reality or—I should say—*current* consensus reality, as I entertain the hope that as the path proves fruitful for more and more people, increasing numbers will explore these realms and revise their narrow paradigms of reality.

Anne Waldman

B. 1945

Poet, performer, editor, teacher, translator, cofounder with Allen Ginsberg of the Jack Kerouac School of Disembodied Poetics at the Naropa Institute in Boulder, Colorado; author of Fast Speaking Woman, Kill or Cure, *and* Iovis, Books I & II*; editor of* The Beat Book *and* Out Of This World: the Poetry Project at St. Mark's Church in-the-Bowery*; co-editor with Andrew Schelling of* Disembodied Poetics: Annals of the Jack Kerouac School, *among over thirty published books*

Resides in Boulder, Colorado, and Greenwich Village, New York City

Raised in Greenwich Village, New York City

Point and Click: Icons in the Window to the Ancestral Manse

My first experience with lysergic acid, in the summer of 1965, conjured an archetypal vision that illuminated both my past history and my future development.

I was twenty, a student at Bennington College in Vermont, and had decided to travel out West to the now-celebrated Berkeley Poetry Conference. A great number of poets in what I refer to as "the outrider tradition"—major visionaries and mavericks, including Charles Olson, Robert Duncan, Robert Creeley, and Allen Ginsberg—were gathering to hold panels, present their work in public readings, and interact with students and passionate readers of poetry. The atmosphere surrounding the event was highly charged and magical. The conference was a major congregation for disparate avant-garde literary artists—including the Beats, the San Francisco Renaissance, the New York School, and Black Mountain—to come together and feed off of each other's energy. The aggregate voltage of their nexus sent shock waves through the literary establishment.

Those who convened at Berkeley were poets and writers in the prophetic tradition, many of whom were experimenting with psychedelics. There was a legend about the night when Charles Olson, who'd been head of the Black Mountain College, gave a very shamanic poetry reading during which he literally came apart on stage. The story was that he'd taken some psychedelic the week before and it had had this effect on him. His wife had just died. On acid, as I would soon learn myself, things come apart and then reforge.

I had friends at Harvard who were involved in some of Leary and Alpert's early acid experiments and turning toward the dharma. Poetry and Buddhism both stretched one's sense of relative and absolute reality and challenged the status quo, as well as one's own habitual patterns. Things were never what they "seemed." How could they be?

I drove out West with my brother and a Bennington friend. The journey itself was mind-expanding, as it was my first American sojourn beyond the confines of the restrictive intellectual mentality of the East Coast, the sort of elitism that harks back to Europe as a reference point for everything of consequence. Now I was headed toward the Orient! It was the proverbial "other" for me: the wild, unknown, and uncharted, where anything was possible. The landscapes and the continent's span were formidable, breathtaking, majestic. I had no idea how liberating—both metaphysically and symbolically—this venture was to be.

A high-school buddy of mine, Jonathan Cott, now a well-known writer, provided some hospitality on our arrival and hooked us up with other like-minded friends of his. He was attending Berkeley and involved in the Free Speech Movement and other on-the-edge endeavors. The people we met were friendly, excited, talkative and expansively open—and just getting "into" LSD, which did not yet have the cloud of legal proscription hanging over it. We were lighthearted, not just soulful and pious, but we carried along a copy of Leary's book based on *The Tibetan Book of the Dead* as a safety measure.

A few of us stayed on Nob Hill in the apartment of a well-heeled friend, which was spare and elegant and surrounded by an attractive landscaped yard. The irony of the night we dropped the potion was that we couldn't get across the bridge back to Berkeley for Allen Ginsberg's poetry reading, which promised to be one of the high points of the conference. Yet the sense of simultaneity and concentric worlds was strong. I instantly gravitated toward and bonded with a new friend, poet Lewis Warsh.

At the core of the trip was a very elaborate panoramic vision which inhabits and informs my genetic makeup still, a vision I return to in Buddhist practice and in dreams, which provides a kind of mental fortitude against the icy, sterile void. I visualized, witnessed, and encountered every person I'd ever known, even some with whom I'd had only remote contact, in a sort of rainbow gathering or holy convocation that brought the various strands of my own personal world together. I was the thread through which these folk gathered, which, in turn, conjured great responsibility for me, of care, attendance, and witness. I felt a duty to these sentient beings I'd been touched by or touched. The vision was not just a tableau, but interactive. When I looked at all these creatures, they returned the gaze and communicated in a new way to me.

All the lineages I could conjure were present: all the grandparents, siblings, offspring, extended family members, lovers, friends, teachers, and parents and relatives of friends. Every contact in my life was there, glowing, yearning, and empty, looking with curiosity toward the vast unknown void. Everyone I'd known since birth appeared, even the scoundrels and the family skeletons. I felt older than my years during this vision, and younger too, as if I'd lived countless lifetimes before and after relative "birth." There were some unfamiliar faces that manifested, but they were presences I trusted and somehow, intrinsically, knew. I underwent a series of brief encounters with other living, breathing "hairy bags of water" that locked me into a net of interconnectedness. All these beings were related through their touching my life, forming a shimmering Indra's Net, an endless web of relationship between karmas, between people and animals and everything else that moves and breathes in our pulsing, expansive universe. The Buddhist term for it is *pratitya-samutpada.*

My visions arrived with closed eyes. I knew enough to just sit still throughout the entire chimera. I needed to be alone for this part of the trip, though some passages were too powerful, those with a "low ego threshold," which were capable of sucking my entire being through their own void. There was some panic when I thought of pain I'd caused to others. I had overwhelming feelings of guilt toward those with whom I'd had unfinished business, conversations, and tendernesses never actualized. I was weeping during some of the encounters.

I saw my grandfather, a taciturn, soft-spoken man, a glass blower by trade, who'd died when I was five years old. There he was alive, luminous, sitting in a wooden lawn chair with peeling paint, beside Union Lake in south Jersey, asking me to sit in his lap. Years later, I worked with letters he wrote to my grandmother in the early decades of the century, incorporating them into my long epic poem *Iovis,* which takes on male energy in its various guises.

It was like a computer screen on which you can click on an image or word and it expands endlessly with infinite associations. I saw each person as an infant and in all his or her aspects. I felt very tender and open-hearted toward them. Each face prompted a feeling of great love—and also accountability, as though I might wake up and want to call or write to those I'd fallen out of touch with, to reconnect, even beyond the grave. All the beings I conjured wanted to be happy. They all wanted to be liberated from samsara. In every one of these instances, especially when there was a high level of power in the relationship, it led to something, a deeper understanding of our vulnerability. This pulsating, palpable vision had a sort of archetypal or mythic quality, like the peaceable kingdom or Noah's Ark. It was a paradigm for a vow that was uncannily recapitulated when I first took Tibetan Buddhist "refugee vows."

In early Buddhist practice you become a refugee. You give up all hope of salvation. Nothing out there but your own mind (which can be anywhere) is going to save you. You take a vow to perform a certain number of practices, that you will give your body, speech, and mind to the endeavor. You also take a vow toward egolessness, so it's not just "you" up against the whole world. You take the Bodhisattva vow that you will work tirelessly for the benefit of all sentient beings who were once your very own parents. This is beyond "idiot compassion," where anything goes. In fact, you must often be fierce with people, with friends, with family. It's a deep commitment to unsentimental honesty and work.

A Tree of Life is central to this vow. You begin with a visualization of this Tree to which you make your first prostration, which is really to your own luminous mind—not to some external godhead, Buddha, or other figure. You, in effect, *are* a tree, a part of that which holds every branch of life. You even visualize your own worst enemy. By necessity, that too must be included in the sacred vow to liberate all sentient beings.

It was as though my acid vision of the Tree was a sort of preliminary training for this commitment. So many moments of this first trip were like runes or seed syllables that would come to fruition later. Worlds were dissolving and reconstituting, moment to moment. The Dharmic axiom was in full sensory flower: *Nothing is solid. You are impermanent. Life is precious. You can't hold on. You will die. You are connected up with everything that breathes—the trees and the birds and the fish and so on, not to mention the inanimate beauties. Thought forms evolve upon thought forms, endless concentric wheels of aspiration.* I was shivering as the terms of the refugee vow were inscribed in my psyche, because they resonated so closely to the acid vision, which itself felt revelatory at the time. The Buddhist vow was a confirmation and gave direction to the molecular thrust of that initial vision.

After my vision played itself out, we all went rambling about in the mythical city of seven hills until we came to water, a stream in a nearby park. We folded and crumbled into the earth and into each other's bodies and minds. We were speechless and then defending our very existence out on a battlefield of life-and-death proportions. Words hung in the air. Time stood still. Infinities passed. And then a word or thought could take us into a next universe.

We believed, in spite of the Holocaust, the war raging in Vietnam, the suffering of people everywhere, that life was basically good. That belief was unconditional. It didn't depend on semblances of "good" and "bad." The darkness was someone else's evil version of reality, not reality itself. Nothing was that solid or insurmountable. The destruction was, in nature, organic; in humans, psychotic—the underpinning of the lords of materialism, of ego, of greed. We were changed forever, because we were experiencing these inspiring truths. And we could laugh at ourselves as well, as we saw through our various ego-trips and guises. Lewis said I looked like Christ, then saw me mutate through all stages of human and animal existence, from infancy to old age, howling as an embryo, then as a babe, and finally wretching as an old crone.

We attempted to cross the Bay Bridge to get to the conference, but our bodies were on another vector, dissolving into currents where the physical barriers were cumbersome. Why walk when you could fly without a body? On the other hand, one could be a lowly worm and sink into the ground to get to where one needed to be. Humble like the dust, exalted through the possession of indomitable powers—we flashed through these psychical phases—and all the stations in between—at speeds of light.

My vision of a great gathering or powwow within my own being had implanted a root of the divine universal Tree. The most immediate branch I extended was to the comrades with whom I'd traveled that night. I saw that we were part of an enormous sinewy archetype, a monstrous rooted and branching phenomenon, the primordial life force. I could see the buds opening constantly to new existences and whole colorful worlds. We were in it for the long run, the whole ride.

A few weeks later, Lewis and I did some Owsley acid in Mexico. Neither of us was twenty-one yet, so we had to borrow IDs from people older than us to get over the border. We had limited resources, staying in a run-down hotel in a red light district, living off of saltines and peanut butter. The place had cockroaches, a bare lightbulb and bright, ultramarine walls, which were pulsating wildly. Suddenly, the place was shaking, I thought, a function of our own minds and this fabulous drug. We felt we were experiencing the subterranean Aztec, ur-civilization energy, the volcanic aspirations and violence of primordial Mexico. It was hilarious to read in the paper the next day that there'd been an earthquake and people were evacuating town.

Lewis and I were later to marry, in 1967, and although the marriage didn't survive, we've remained close friends and artistic collaborators on many projects. Our offspring—his three and my one—are warmly acquainted. I would posit that this intensified connection through LSD at the advent of our relationship resulted in a permanent bond that has transcended certain all-too-familiar pitfalls of dissolution, neurotic anger, and despair.

I almost always did psychedelics as a sacred ritual. Once, when Bill Burroughs Jr. was lying in a coma, a group of us went out and ingested peyote in the mountains as a kind of healing rite. He did come out of the coma. Not that we had anything to do with it, but the fact that everyone was working with this intent helped us all.

My perspective now is that my first LSD experience was a partial blueprint or paradigm for the actions and karma of my life so far. Not that I've been saintly or holier than anybody else. The inspiration from that first vision—and its fantastic and historic milieu—did much to forge my commitment to *Sangha,* community, both Buddhist and poetic.

This has been borne out in my web of folk increasing a thousandfold through the activities of the St. Mark's Poetry Project, the Kerouac School at Naropa, through travels to Indonesia, India, Italy, Austria, and other "tours of duty," and through poetry and political events and convocations all over the world. That commitment also brought my life intimate with the activities and life of Allen Ginsberg, dear mentor and friend, also an "activity demon," whose historic reading I missed that same fateful night I was summoned to a sacred primordial vision, so seminal to my life and work.

Brendan

B. 1966

Postgraduate psychology student

Resides in Australia

Raised in Canberra and Sydney, Australia

PEALING FACES

When I was eighteen, trying to finish off my final year of high school after a period of homelessness during which I slept on floors at friends' houses, I was sharing a house with a guy named David, who was in a similar situation. I worked when I could, went to school, and, on some days, just stayed home and drank beers with David and other friends.

One night David told me how his father had been a practitioner of ritual magic who'd gone into trances and "channeled" beings to David even when the latter was just a young lad in his early teens. This had clearly freaked him out, even though he hadn't seen his dad in several years. I was raised an atheist and didn't believe a word about his father's purported powers, but I listened and talked to David about it anyway, enjoying the conversation. It was late evening, and I was lying back on the lounge as we chatted. Somewhere along the line I became aware of the fact that David's voice had changed and no longer sounded like him. I guess this was about the time he began to ask me some strange questions.

I sat up and looked over at him, and was absolutely flabbergasted. There was another face superimposed on his that melded into and changed it. A deep European voice spoke from David, and one face in particular made regular appearances. I'd consumed absolutely no drugs all day but for a few cigarettes, so there was no chemical explanation for what I was seeing.

"Who are you?" I asked.

"We are not one, we are many."

"Where is David?"

"He is asleep now."

I bolted upright in my chair, electrified, trying to come to terms with what was going on. I rubbed my eyes, but all my faculties confirmed that this was "real," though I didn't understand any of it. I asked a few lame questions:

"Is there God?"

"If you mean the God that judges, he is of no concern."

"What about drugs and alcohol? Are they really bad?"

"They are of this world." The voice laughed. "They are neither here nor there. If you want to make the most of life, don't give them too much of your energy."

The conversation went on for several hours until dawn, though I was acutely self-conscious about my inability to come up with intelligent questions, simultaneously wondering if I was going mad or if David had slipped some powerful hypnotic into my cup of tea. The spirit-being or whatever it was eventually departed, and when my friend came to, he said he remembered none of it, although he said he had just been trying to "channel" as his father had taught him. I was disturbed by the whole thing for a day or two, but quickly pushed it down and let it go. I couldn't assimilate the experience, so I discarded it.

Two or three weeks later, it was the night of the school dance. A friend named Glen who'd gone off to score some hash for me, came back with a bonus: two trips (hits) of Pink Panther acid. I was delighted. He had one under his belt already, though it hadn't kicked in yet. We went to the school dance, and I hung outside waiting for Peter, a friend who I was keen to do acid with. We hadn't known each other long and were very different from one another in many ways, but we got on really well and seemed to be very much alike on a deeper level.

Growing impatient, I took my trip and got a half-hour start on Peter by the time he arrived. He made me split the remaining one with him, so I ended up taking one and a half, while he did only a half. He was considerably larger than me, so my dose relative to body weight was much more than his. We quit the dance soon after, along with Glen, and walked to a nearby lake, where we climbed into the back of a lorry that was parked there, mulled up some hashish with tobacco, and smoked a joint.

At this point, the acid symptoms were minor. We were mellow, relaxed, and our night vision had deteriorated, so we decided to head back to my place, which involved Glen doubling each of us in turn on his 100 cc Suzuki. He took Peter first, then came back for me. As we drove, Glen sang awful Welsh songs from his childhood, and I laughed to the point I almost cried.

We all sat in my lounge room, Peter opposite me, Glen to one side. We began to talk, and the conversation quickly escalated in intensity. At one point, Glen, ever the thespian, said, "My God, you two sound like Rosencrantz and Guildenstern." Then he seemed to be overwhelmed by it all and promptly fell asleep. Peter and I laughed at how

Glen's Welsh-miner heritage was so pronounced, and turned back to our conversation. Then something took over that transcended both of us.

We were talking at a hundred miles an hour, but thinking the same thoughts. If one of us paused, the other spoke *exactly* the words that the silent one would have said had he continued. We both knew it was happening and took on the role of mere spectators as the secrets of the universe rolled off our lips, understandings beyond the grasp of our normal consciousness. This part of the trip was saturated with that "Aha!" feeling that accompanies genuine insight.

We made a play of the dialogue for a while, each pausing for a time and opening his eyes in wonder as the other spoke his thoughts even though he'd never uttered them before. We entered into a shared realm of superintelligence, thinking like gods and seeing the truths that were hidden beneath everyday reality. Revelation.

I turned to ash my cigarette, and when I looked back *that face* was suddenly there: the same face I'd seen on David a few weeks earlier. "Don't do that!" I cried, turning away, suddenly terrified. I looked back and the superimposed face looked at me, smiled and nodded to indicate it was indeed him. Peter was oblivious to what I was saying. I looked away again, becoming anxious. I hadn't mentioned what had happened with David. I hadn't told anyone, lest they think me mad.

"Do what?" Peter asked.

I responded by turning fiercely at him, catching his eye, and saying, *"This!"* He saw it immediately, a series of faces superimposed on mine. I'd somehow projected the specter to him. I turned away again.

"Now you know, so stop it," I said. But Peter was not one to back off, even when straight. "Look at me," he said, but I would not. Then I felt a powerful force, like a tractor beam, that came out of Peter and literally twisted my head back toward him. He was a fast learner! The face was there. I was tense, but Peter told me to stay cool and go with it. I knew he could see the faces. We both could.

For the next few hours we sat transfixed, staring at each other's "face," as myriad personas passed before us. Even the rate of change of the bizarre imagery seemed to synchronize between us. As we both commented on the strange procession, each of us saw shifts at precisely the same time. The depth of this phenomenon was driven home when the peripheral areas of my vision were suddenly filled with a bright paisley pattern. At the same instant, Peter pulled back in his chair, saying, "Wow . . . it's . . . it's . . ." He couldn't find the word. "It's electric orange paisley," I stated, and he agreed that that was exactly what it was. This incredible synchronicity became so obvious that our comments to each other were abbreviated to short phrases like "color change" or "face change," or maybe a comment on an especially notable face.

The faces were of all types, male, female, black, yellow, white, coarse, fine—a sad-faced clown with green hair, a Zulu warrior, a Japanese woman with a powdered white face: the complete range of humanity. The paisley pattern was consistent, though the colors shifted through reds, yellows, oranges, bright greens, and other intense hues. There was an implicit recognition that somehow we were all these people, maybe in past lives, or perhaps we were all of them simultaneously, so our apparent individuality was the true illusion. Like the face-spirit, we are many, like Krishna showing his God-nature to Arjuna, a million eyes, ears, and limbs, and we are all of them.

As dawn approached we tired. Peter went home and I went to sleep. For weeks afterward, there was a psychic link between us. If one of us wanted the other to phone us, he could will it. The other would do so, but without being aware of the link working. If we were in a large room, such as the school cafeteria, even with many other people, we were instantly aware of the presence of the other, almost as one is always subconsciously aware of the position of one's limbs in space.

Needless to say, this experience shattered my atheistic worldview and set me on a quest for understanding on which I still continue today.

Bruce Eisner

B. 1948

***Director of the Island Foundation, president of Mind Media Incorporated, author of* Ecstasy: The MDMA Story**

Resides in Santa Cruz, California

Born in Brooklyn, raised in Los Angeles

Dazed in the Desert at the End of Time

I underwent a sort of addled odyssey at my first Burning Man event, in 1995. Held every Labor Day for the last dozen years, Burning Man is like a combination Mardi Gras, circus, carnival, rave, performance-art happening, and outdoor costume party. I don't think anybody in attendance was straight that year. The crowd is an interesting demographic. There are people in the performing arts, oddball car collectors and rig-constructors more straight than "long-hair," an ex-hippie contingent, and then the young ravers and the pagans. Survival is key. You have to come prepared with your own shelter, food, and water.

The site is different each year, so as not to overuse the land for which the Bureau of Land Management grants the rights. In 1995 it was held on a dry lake bed north of Pyramid Lake in northwest Nevada, where they do the world land-speed records. My then-business partner Joe and I packed up my white Ford Escort and headed off on the eight-hour drive from Santa Cruz. We stopped for directions at one of the two casinos in Gearlock, the last vestige of "civilization" before we arrived at Sodom and Gomorrah. "You go out eleven miles and then you head towards the lights," we were told. So we did this trek through the desert, circling around the Burning Man headquarters and ending up at the rave camp.

When we arrived at one in the morning, it was a very chaotic scene. There were no law enforcement officers and little organization outside the central camp. I think there was one ranger throughout the entire Burning Man site. We couldn't find where to pay our money to get in, so we just entered and tried to find a place to set up our tent. There were mountains in the distance that appeared to be about five miles away but were actually about twenty-five, with nothing but flat desert floor between them and the site of the festivities. They tell you to bring a compass, but I don't know how to take sightings. Nowadays, they have streets and avenues at the Burning Man, so as long as you're not out in the desert, you're not lost.

The main camp featured a stage with nonstop burlesque shows, a camera obscura, a coffeehouse, and a lot of funny cars made up like dolphins and other animals, which were like small floats. About a mile away, there were a couple of different raves set up with scaffolding and massive sound systems.

We camped next to a guy in his forties who had a couch. Some younger people were gathered around, tripping out on 2C-B. I'd brought an exotic compound with me, a combination of four different phenethylamines, which was supposed to be great for sex. I was saving it to do it with Stacy, a woman friend, when I met up with her, but I couldn't find her the first night, so, after sharing stories by the sofa, I went to sleep.

When I woke up the next day, I found Stacy and a mutual friend, Roxanna, at the SF Raves camp, which had an Ambient tent with three motor homes covered by a giant parachute that provided shade in the 102-degree heat. It was so hot, you had to walk around with a parasol or a large hat. The three of us hung out there for a bit and then walked over to the main Burning Man camp.

I realized that all my friends—and all the drugs—were in a different campground than where Joe and I had set up, halfway between the main camp and the raves. So I went back to Joe and told him we should move our tent. But he said, "No, no, we spent two and a half hours pounding in stakes last night. We should stay right here." But then, a few minutes later he said, "Pull up everything," and we yanked out all the stakes and threw everything in the car. Just as we got in, a giant thunderstorm hit, with thunder, lightning, and rain, which went on for a half hour. "How did you know that was going to happen?" I asked him. "Well, there's something to being raised in El Centro [central California, east of San Diego]. You know when there's going to be a desert storm from the way it looks." When the rain stopped, it left a giant double rainbow. We drove over to the area where all our friends were. The wind was blowing pretty hard, so we helped them secure their tents and finally put up our own nearby.

As Saturday evening approached, some friends in a Volkswagen van were sitting around looking at some sugar cubes that belonged to a guy named Peter. They were saturated with a special kind of LSD from a stash twenty-five years old that had been stored away. I'd taken it previously and knew that it was very pure. Peter had made up a concentration of the acid called "thick doses," about six hundred micrograms each, which he'd droppered into the cubes. I asked Stacy if she wanted to take the other drug I'd brought with me.

"No, I think I'd rather wait till tomorrow night."

"But tonight Wicked (a group of rave deejays, Garth, Marky, Simon, Rayno) is playing."

"I want to do it when the Manbirds play," she said.

That was Sunday, the following night. So I went over to Peter and asked him for some of the acid. He took some of the liquid and put one big drop on my hand and I licked most of it up. I'd already taken about ten milligrams of prescription Ritalin. Joe asked me if I wanted to go with him and Peter to the main camp, but I said, "No, I'm going over to the raves." I wanted to share what was left on my hand with a guy I'd met near our first campsite. Ever since the early Seventies, I've been on a crusade to tell people that the acid that's around isn't very good. (I wrote "LSD Purity" for *High Times* back in 1977 and will soon publish a piece called "LSD Purity Revisited.")

On the way to the rave camp, some people sitting around a fire spotted me. "Hey, Bruce Eisner, Bruce Eisner. Come on over here and smoke some hashish." It was a big group of different kinds of people, a guy from Atlanta with really long blond hair, a New York drug dealer. Along came another rainstorm, so we all went in their tent and smoked the hash. Then they laid these little packages on me, psychoactive things they wanted me to try out, which I stashed away in my pocket.

When the rainstorm was over, I didn't really feel much besides the mild hash buzz. With really pure LSD you don't get any advance signals before it hits. That's how you can tell if it's pure or not. If it's impure, you'll get various tremors and vibrations as you're going up. I continued on toward the rave camp. When I reached there, I don't know how it happened, but after a short while I was totally naked. (My friends teased me later that I'd done a striptease and was dancing bare-assed on top of one of the speakers.) At one point I was dancing with five fire dancers, who were holding flames in their hands and gyrating to the "five elements." There was a lot of erotic energy going on.

I glanced at Joe, who'd apparently decided to go to the rave after all. He was sitting off to the side, shaking his head like he was a little disgusted at my antics. Then I found myself backing away from the rave, walking out toward the desert to take in the entire spectacle. Everything started changing rapidly. The whole planet started evolving and metamorphosing. The mountains rose and fell. A variety of terrains sprung out of the desert floor. I seemed to move between several different planets. The only constant on the landscape was a pyramidal canopy at the rave camp, a prominent landmark.

The whole event took on the character of a pagan ritual to end the universe, after which there'd be some transition to a higher plane. This perception was corroborated by a procession of geometric patterns and things in the external world, like the funny cars, which were coming at me, zooming in in a continuous flow. At one point, a beautiful girl whom I knew from other events came up and hugged me. The end of everything seemed to be coming. This feeling, along with the rapid parade of changing landscapes and incoming visual meteorites, persisted until around five in the morning.

Then I looked down and noticed that I was naked in the middle of the desert. I felt shy about my nudity, and a little cold. I needed something to get me warm. I saw a fire made from a few chunks of wood and gravitated toward it, circling around it for a while in hesitant uncertainty. Finally I sat down by the fire with a group of people, who started cooking something. A couple of them were from England.

"Cup o' coffee?"

"Sure, that sounds good."

"Cream and sugar?"

"Sure." So they brewed me up a cup.

Captain Crunch, the godfather of computer hacking, was circling around on a bicycle. He drove over and said hello to me. Some of the folks in this group were doing enormous doses of 2C-B, about 120 milligrams, which is way too much, so I assumed it was cut ten to one. A young guy who'd recognized me from other raves offered me a line, but I turned him down. I never really liked 2C-B. Then he offered me to come into his tent and smoke some weed. After that, he offered me some 5-methoxy DMT. I said, "No, I'm not going to do that. I'm still too high. Can I just hang out here?" He agreed and I tried to sleep when he left, but couldn't. I looked around and borrowed a pair of his pants, which were khaki with a tear on one side, pretty tight on me.

I wandered out of the tent. Everywhere I turned it was a mad circus, a phantasmagoria of weirdness. People were squatting around naked in mud. There were groups of people doing all kinds of strange performance art. In my heightened state and freshness to the scene, everything looked very odd indeed. During a break between rave music sets, Orb, an Ambient Techno group from England, came over the sound system. A voice-over from their album *Ultra World* sounded like Jehovah himself—"I am your god"—so my eschatological mood turned biblical.

I wandered out in the desert and saw what I perceived as a procession of cars leaving the event. "Oh, it's Monday morning, and everybody's going home," I thought. I kept searching for my camp. Finally, after walking way out without any water, I spotted something that looked like my tent. I went inside and saw immediately that it wasn't. I was despondent and dehydrated. At this point I didn't know the difference between good and evil. As I wandered out in the desert, away from all the cars and tents, I wondered if I should go out to the mountains, where there were civilizations and real people. So I headed for the hills.

As I walked past one guy, he called out, "Bruce Eisner. Come on over here." I ambled over and he gave me water and popsicles out of his freezer, all kinds of stuff. "Boy, you shouldn't be heading out that way," he said. "Your friends are probably camped back over there in one of the campsites." He suggested I turn around and go back in toward a big cluster of tents. So I trudged on and the first thing I saw was a big tent and a woman who looked like Stacy. I went in and started talking to her, but she didn't recognize me. I thought it was Stacy trying to fool me for some reason.

"Oh, you're Stacy."

"Oh, no, no, I'm not." Finally she asked, "Are you on acid?"

"Yeah, I took some yesterday."

"Go next door to the coffeehouse, where there's a ranger, and tell him you're on acid." So I walked into that tent.

I sat down next to the ranger and told him, "I'd like to get out of here tonight. My friends have all left." He said, "God, you look like I feel. Nobody's getting out of here tonight." I was kind of worried. It sounded ominous. (There's a photograph of me at this juncture that is in the Burning Man book published by *Wired* magazine. It's hard to recognize me, because I'm wearing a toupee, but it's me sitting on a couch looking a little bit lost.)

I walked out and looked at the camp. Outside it was Hell Year. There were Satan's instead of McDonald's, Starfucks instead of Starbucks, all this good and evil stuff, Marlboros with skull and crossbones. At a giant lingam, people were yelling, "Ling 'em, ling 'em, ling 'em!" Others were yelling, "Burn the man, burn the man." People were assembling for a procession.

I bumped into a giant bale of straw in which people were embedded like human sculptures. There was a little dwarf climbing about, giving cunnilingus to some of the females. Startled, I scurried away from this bizarre apparition. I jumped onto one of the cars in the procession, hoping to catch a ride, but they shooed me off, which made me very scared. I ran away and then boarded one of the RVs. I walked in the back and saw an alien in a big display case, a glowing thing like you'd see in a flying saucer movie. I disembarked and hopped up on an odd rig that looked like the starship *Enterprise*. Still hallucinating a full day after I'd licked the acid off my hand, I thought I was flying through space.

When they started burning the man, I hid out from the mania. I found an old camper that was open in the back. Inside was a mattress, so I curled in, closed it up and drifted off to sleep for an hour, waking up at two in the morning. It was cold, too cold, I decided, so I got out and walked out. The stars were awesome. I saw some people around a fire. An older guy who was wearing a big tall hat was staring at me. I must have looked like a down-and-out figure, wearing only a pair of pants with no shirt or shoes.

"Need some spare change, buddy?"

"No, but I could use a blanket or a jacket or something." He brought out a sheet and I wrapped it around me, which kept my body heat in. I wandered away from the fire and found an old army blanket on one of the performance structures, wrapping it around me. Then I found a pair of old tennis shoes, and with that, I was able to walk around freely. By now my feet were pretty cut up by the desert floor, which in some places looked as rough as the surface of the moon. I decided to go right to the raves. By now it was about four in the morning.

It was hard to sustain any real contact with anybody. People would ask me, "How's it going?" I'd say, "I'm okay." Then they'd say, "Are you on acid?" I'd say, "Yeah," and that was as deep as most of the conversations went. I'd lost my glasses, which had fallen off somewhere, so it was hard to make out where I was going. I finally reached the raves.

"You okay?" asked a guy sitting in the back of a pickup truck.

"No, not really. I lost my friends. They're gone. I'm really lost."

"Come on up here. What's your name, buddy?"

I told him and he was very excited.

"Your book [*Ecstasy: The MDMA Story*] changed my life. Here, have a can of beer." Then he gave me a sleeping bag to slide into, so I was finally snug and warm.

"It's Monday night, and my friends already left," I said.

"It's not Monday. It's *Sunday* night. Your friends are probably still here. We could go out and look for them."

I don't know how I'd lost a day. It just seemed like a long time. We talked for a while. I told him what I'd been doing, and he said, "I do MDMA, but I don't do that LSD stuff. Let's crash here and find your friends first thing in the morning." So I lay down and went to sleep. In the morning, his little sister came by, waking us up with a sweet "Good morning." It was all bright out. It had been a restful sleep.

"Okay, let's go find your friends now," he said, and we started walking around. He asked me if my car was two-door or four-door, because there were so many white coupes parked all over the area. I told him the wrong number of doors, but we finally found my camp anyway. He delivered me to my tent and we exchanged phone numbers. "Call me sometime," I told him. "You were really great to help me out." I parted the flaps of the tent and there was Joe asleep.

"Shut up," he said. "I'm trying to sleep."

"Aren't you glad to see me? I've been gone for two days."

"Just shut up. I've only had two hours sleep. I've been up on acid for two nights."

"Okay."

I got in the car and looked for the keys, but they weren't there. I went back to the tent. "Hey, Joe, the keys are gone."

"You had them in your pants."

"Oh, my God!"

I started talking to the folks around our tent. "We heard a radio broadcast that there's a bunch of keys that people had found at the ranger station," someone reported. So I walked all the way over to the ranger station at the central camp and asked if there was a lost and found. I located that and there were zillions of keys there, but none of them were mine. So I went back to my camp, where I bumped into a guy from Czechoslovakia who'd been given the same acid I'd had and had also been lost for two days. He said it had been like heaven and hell, but he'd wound up at a camp where everybody spoke Czechoslovakian. He thought he'd gone crazy. "This was the strongest stuff I'd ever had," he said.

I went back to Joe. By now he realized there was a serious problem. He said, "You threw your pants off at the rave."

"Oh, that's right!"

"They're probably still there. Why don't you go over there and check it out."

So I went over to the rave area, where they were packing up all the sound equipment into trucks and taking down the scaffolding.

"Is there a lost and found here?"

"Oh yeah. Over there." I looked through a bunch of shirts and shoes and jackets, but found no pants.

"Did you guys find a pair of pants?"

They were English guys. One of them said, "Oh, the guy with the pants, the guy with the pants," and he pulled out my pants. There they were with my belt and my wallet, my keys, and all the little packets of special substances that people had given me on Saturday night. It was all together.

I returned to my tent. Joe and I were very relieved that we didn't have to call a tow truck, which would have cost two hundred dollars to go the seventy miles from the nearest town. We packed everything up and drove back to Santa Cruz.

It was about a week before I fully reintegrated from that experience to the point that I was back in touch with everyday affairs in a normal sort of way. It usually takes me much quicker. The full wave of the trip lasted about thirty-six hours, though the acute part kicked out, as normal, after about eight hours. Being a psychedelic veteran who has tripped hundreds of times, it was a little surprising to be thrown for such a loop, but Peter's "thick dose" was the first really good acid I'd had since the late Sixties, the only material that enabled me to have eyes-open visuals. Only three other times in my life have I had LSD as strong and pure. I've had dozens of major trips, including a few journeys, via different substances, to a future world, and a sort of after-death experience, where I saw a city of light filled with light beings. Although many of my earlier trips were powerful and spiritual in nature, I hadn't had the experience to contextualize them. I was almost fifty at the time of this Burning Man trip.

I came away from that trek in the desert with three precepts. I decided that I didn't want to take LSD again until I'd worked on these things. One was that I needed to become more organized. When I got back home, everything seemed especially unruly in both my office and in my home. Second, I needed to simplify my life, and third, I wanted to treat people with more love and compassion.

Long ago I was a hippie and hitchhiked to India and done all the wild things, but now I felt I'd gone back into the parent culture and become a part of the Establishment. Ironically, even with all the status and comfort of that lifestyle, I'd stumbled upon what it was like to be a homeless person, lost and bumped around from one place to the next. I vowed to extend a helping hand to people who don't have anything, just as when I was wandering disoriented at the mercy of the crowd, people had stepped forward and helped me out.

Since the 1995 Burning Man, I haven't become as organized as I would like, but I have acted upon my compassion more often, for instance by helping out an alcoholic friend by having him stay in my home for a while, and giving support to some people who were mentally unhinged. Order and simplicity can come in time, but I've decided to let the empathy flow now.

Carl

B. 1953

Biochemistry Ph.D., consultant for major multinational corporation in Southeast Asia

Resides in Southeast Asia

Born and raised in the American Southwest

WAT OF THE WORLD

When I was twenty, I had a profound near-death experience in the Grand Canyon on peyote. I was attending Northern Arizona University, living in Flagstaff, doing a lot of wilderness hiking and button eating on weekends. I had connections with a highwayman who (legally) transported buttons from west Texas to the NAC (Native American Church) in Arizona. He considered it a public service to give the medicine to white people to make them heal their ways. Every weekend, he'd pull up in my driveway in his cacti-laden pickup truck.

To meet up with friends who were doing a long cross-canyon hike, I did a solo hike in a remote area of the canyon. We'd arranged to rendezvous at the top of a high ridge on the North Rim. Many of the canyon's geological features are named for religious figures, e.g., Buddha Cloister, Cheops Pyramid, the Temples of Isis, Mentius, and Confucius; the Towers of Set, Ra, and Osiris. I had to get to a ridge above Shiva Temple, about seven miles from the rim, which involved hiking through a creek bed, climbing over boulders, wading through creeks, some bushwhacking, and scaling a few steep cliffs. I was using a topographical map to help me find the indentations called "keys" by which I could climb from one vertical level to the next. (The map I used that day is now framed and on display in my home.)

It was a sunny day, about fifty-five degrees, in the autumn of 1973. I ate a token amount of peyote buttons that morning, just a third of what I'd usually take, because I had to do some pathfinding and didn't want to be confused and get lost or have an accident. I had a daypack with two quarts of water, some dried fruit and nuts, a length of rope, and a pocketknife. I was wearing a pair of old Levi's, a pullover sweatshirt, a flannel shirt, and hiking boots. Since I was meeting my friends for only the day, I made a temporary base camp down below, on the floor of Phantom Canyon.

In that part of the Grand Canyon, there were two-thousand-foot cliffs with only a few places broken down enough to permit passage on foot. Once you get off the trail, it's all route finding, like mountaineering work, which was especially difficult where I was. There were all these long, narrow plateaus and only a scant few locations where you can punch through to the next higher strata. I hiked up the drainage of Phantom Canyon all the way to the head wall. It was vertical all around me, with no path up. I was told that if I could get up on this first shelf, I could contour along it, staying at roughly the same elevation for a ways, until at some point, I'd find a way up to the top of the saddle between Shiva Temple and the North Rim.

I had to get off the trail and bushwhack in order to climb up. I wound up less than a hundred feet from where I was supposed to be, but on the wrong ridge, apparently a blind one. I was on a ledge between Tiyo Point and Shiva Temple on Shiva's Saddle slightly below the top, on a very crumbly vertical face. The geological composition of the Grand Canyon is very old, and often loose. Where I was, you could carefully pull yourself up on a rock, but you couldn't put too much of your weight on it until you had a feel for how much it could sustain.

I clambered up to a point where the rock was too flaky for me to continue up and even more difficult to climb down. I'd trapped myself on the face without a secure foothold, with a two-thousand-foot vertical drop. I was about twenty feet up a sheer cliff from a narrow three-meter shelf. I considered jumping to the shelf, but had to rule it out, because even if I landed on it, I'd probably bounce over the edge.

The rock I was holding on to with my right hand pulled right out of the face of the mountain. I released it, letting it go crashing down to the canyon floor, thinking, "That could have been me." My left hand had a grip on another rock, but I wasn't sure if that one too wouldn't pull out of the substrate it was lodged in. I had a tenuous foothold on a tiny ledge, but the other foot didn't have a good place to set, so I could only tuck it behind the other one. I held all my weight on my right foot, keeping balance with the rock in my left hand, which I didn't want to yank too hard for fear it would come out. I got sewing machine legs, a palsylike tremor you get when your pins lack the strength to support you.

I panicked. I was exhausted, sweating like mad, stuck in an awkward position, my legs giving out. I couldn't conceive of any way out. I saw nowhere else to climb, and if I lost my grip, I would surely die. There was no other possible fate. *If only there was a root to grab on to.* My heart was beating heavily. I sized up my condition and realized I had no hope. So I gave up my desire to control the situation. I surrendered to whatever would happen, realizing that it was beyond my capability to get out of this predicament. At the moment I consigned myself, I was hit with a jolt of light like a bolt of lightning.

In that instant, my entire perspective changed. My fear of dying evaporated, and everything I could see seemed alive and immensely beautiful and meaningful. Trees, rocks, cacti, the entire landscape was radiating with relevance. From a stunning bird's-eye view I could see the gorge of the Colorado River, the big, red-walled cliffs on the sides of the canyon I was in, and the ones adjacent to it. It was as if everything were backlit or lit from underneath and not just by the sun from above. Everything was glowing with an abundant, bright white light.

I realized that if indeed I was going to fall, it wouldn't be nearly so serious as I'd thought, that nothing really important would be lost, because my essence transcended my physical being and would be maintained if my body ceased living. I no longer felt separate from anything. There was no "I" reflecting on myself or my situation. A curtain was lifted and I saw the magnitude of life and was totally absorbed by it. The moment lasted just a minute or two, but it embraced a lifetime. I suddenly understood the cliché of Oneness, that everything in the world is connected and part of a Whole, and that that interlinkage is a truer characterization of the relationship of things than that of me and my body being separate from all the other mes and their bodies. Amazingly, my uniqueness was not lost in the whole. I felt that what was good or noble or salient about me as an individual was more essentially present among the One. I saw that one's life made a permanent record, just as a tape or a notebook survives as a statement or expression. My twenty years from infancy to that moment on the face of the cliff would survive independently of major works, having children, or the usual ways we think of continuing ourselves. My life was etched on something. It was always going to be there.

I was calmed by these revelations, which enabled me to get back the strength I'd used up in my fright. I got my legs to stop shaking, and simply climbed down the twenty feet to a safe platform. Getting off the cliffside was a feat that required good hand-eye coordination, agility, timing, and reflexes, but I have no clue how I actually did it. Perhaps I was so consumed with cosmic consciousness that the mechanics of climbing down were automatic. When I got to safety, I wept for joy uncontrollably for several hours. Then I hiked back to my base camp, laid down on my mat, drank some water and ate some fruit, and tried to figure out what it meant. (I didn't have to worry about being missed. My friends would just figure I wasn't able to make it.)

I was probably directing myself toward such an experience. I was reading books about Zen Buddhism by Alan Watts and other writers. I was looking for something, and I surely found it—by accident. It was worth a lifetime of trouble. The thrill was not so much relief that I was alive, but that I was *blessed. Now I know what I only suspected before.* In those very concentrated few seconds I felt the strongest emotions, the most intense fear, and then the most powerful joy I've ever felt in my life. What I learned was not a new set of rules to jot down, but a new embracing attitude toward life.

The treasure of this revelation superseded what was previously most important to me, which was being alive. It wasn't that I wasn't glad to be alive. I was. But getting myself to safety was secondary to the knowledge—and not just the belief—that there was a connection between me and the rest of the universe, that I was more than what's within the envelope of my skin.

"Why me?" I asked myself. "Why was I spared?" My life was over, and I got it back. I've got twenty-five years and counting since this reprieve. You don't take things for granted after a near-death experience of any kind. Every day is a unique gift and a new opportunity for which I feel immensely grateful and obligated to contribute something worthwhile to humanity. I still wonder if there was an intervention. *Maybe I have an important job to do.* But that question is a small, incidental, mechanical consideration. It doesn't keep me up nights. What I wonder about is the depth of my obligation. It's not that I foresee taking some dramatic or heroic action that will compensate for getting my life back. I just want to pitch in in terms of right livelihood (one of the eight paths of Buddhist righteousness). In my scientific field, I can help to make food more accessible to poorer nations. I want to be as mutualistic as I can be. It's not enough to just be an individual taking responsibility for yourself and no more, the game I call "pig in the trough," where the object is to get your snout down in the slop and to elbow all the other pigs so they don't get as much as you. That's the game that most people feel they have to play. It's totally incompatible with what I learned on the mountainside and since.

I've had about six revisits of the experience in which I felt I was up there beholding the canyon and the empyreal mystery again, though not as intensely as during the original event. Positive developments trigger these episodes, events that make me feel I'm going where I wanted to go or that I've accomplished something meaningful.

About a dozen times since the event, I've met people who've had similar experiences, and it's like a homecoming to compare notes. In most of them, interestingly enough, drugs did not play a role. I'd probably feel better if I could say that mine was not drug-related, but I believe it was the small dose of buttons I'd eaten that morning, combined with the residual mescaline in my bloodstream due to my regular use, which was hyperactivated by the adrenaline of my panic to launch my visionary state. Without the peyote, I don't believe I would have had a so-called near-death experience or at least one so luminous and full-bodied.

I do landscape photography and am always looking for a representation of nature that reflects the experience. I often look at Japanese and Chinese landscape paintings and think, "This guy knows!" When I was in Rome in 1978, I visited the Sistine Chapel and saw some tapestries by Raphael depicting the life of Jesus. The story of Christ was never that compelling to me, but when I saw the luminosity of these works, I knew that the artist was galvanized by something quite like what I'd experienced. I felt a connection to him. The peyote-inspired Huichol Indian yarn paintings from central Mexico also remind me of the radiance I saw in the landscape that day. The figures are outlined with red and yellow yarn, which gives the impression of a light glowing from behind, and they're arranged randomly in space, which suggests an interrelationship that's not based on a vertical or horizontal hierarchy.

There *is* no hierarchy in the cosmology of Oneness. You might think you're better than a frog or a mouse or an earthworm, but in the midst of my revelation, I got the feeling that I wasn't any better than anything. The only thing that made me special was my awareness of my connection to the whole, a knowledge more valuable than status or being some so-called important individual.

There seemed to be two different ways to view things afterward. One came out of the feeling I was a fly on the wall with grandeur all around me, that whatever my petty little story was, it was insignificant in the vast scheme of creation. So one approach is to minimize your ego and yield to the flow. The other way is just the opposite, to expand the ego to encompass the world of which you're a part and to take some measure of responsibility for everything—not that you can control what happens—but to put yourself in the game and to do, within the natural limitations of one human life, what you think is right and consistent with your principles, and to take on goals beyond your own personal ambitions. The two approaches seem to be on opposite ends of the spectrum, but somehow they're not. They complement each other.

If I think I can push someone over the edge of his consciousness into a greater awareness, I give him a Zen Buddhist whack of the cane to help cleanse his perceptions. Waking people up could very well be part of my obligation, one of the reasons for telling my story. I go out of my way to recharge that knowledge for myself. Meditation, beautiful natural surroundings, good music, and artworks all enhance this part of me, serving as reminders and helping me refocus. And every year, I try to go hiking in the Grand Canyon, the wat of the world.

Charles Hayes (author of this book)

B. 1955

Journalist, freelance writer, marketing consultant

Resides near New York City

Born near Los Angeles and raised near Chicago

First Flights: Orville and Icarus

My first experience with LSD was on April 28, 1971. I was a fifteen-year-old high-school sophomore living in Wilmette, Illinois, on Chicago's illustrious North Shore. I'd already smoked plenty of pot and taken "mescaline" a couple of times, but acid was the big one. I'd been hesitant at first, waiting for the "right" moment. In spite of its being a Wednesday with school the next day, this balmy spring day seemed to have all the foundations for a positive experience. So my best friend, Reed, and I took a hit each of Blue Blotter after school and rode our bicycles to a favorite intersection in neighboring Evanston.

We made frequent pilgrimages to this corner of Dempster Street, which had a Hear Here record store (to buy albums by the likes of Procul Harum, Blodwyn Pig, and Firesign Theater), the Whole Earth Bookstore (to browse hippie lifestyle manuals), the Khaki clothing store (for flannel shirts and work boots), and the Spectacle, a head shop (to procure hash pipes, rolling papers, and underground comics). It was a few days after the second annual Earth Day and it was essential that we refuse bags wherever we shopped, a policy I enforce to this day.

We started getting off on the ride home, so we dismounted our bikes at a dune by Lake Michigan. The acid took me directly to my lucid, "higher self." It was as though I'd arrived at my true nature: sincere, clean of purpose, and more useful and worthwhile than I'd ever felt in my life. I can't fathom what it was that made me feel so "perfect" and "enlightened" or what specific obstacle the chemical had overcome to enable me to feel so wholesomely fabulous. I felt a sweeping reassurance that everything was all right after all, that I was on the right track, with decent morals, sensitive perceptions, and worthy intellectual interests in music, philosophy, politics, and yes, even mind-expanding drugs. It was as though everything had clicked into place and I was able to see the proverbial glass as *more* than half-full and was eagerly drinking of it.

I was grateful for this flash of inspiration and called out, "Right on, acid!" in appreciation. We stayed until after dark, conversing eye to eye with a strong, even sense of excitement, as though the fuse to our true-blue selves had been lit and was blazing steadily away. We planned to furnish our parents the excuse that we'd ridden our bikes too far and couldn't make it back in time for dinner. The acid was so worthwhile, we weren't even that nervous about getting in trouble. I knew I'd have to face a stern dressing down from my parents, who'd be pissed off I was out so late, but I was going to meet that challenge with my innocent lie and by not really arguing. Reed and I wanted to stay together for the duration, and since his parents had nine other kids to think about, we decided that he'd come home with me.

When I walked up the back porch around 7:30 and saw my father's reproachful face, I felt a surge of sympathy and affection for him. He was wearing a dark, patterned shirt I'd seen since childhood, which was very characteristic of him and his time. He was angry, but I felt big enough to understand instead of being angry myself or afraid. It was the first time I ever felt so grown up as to confer such compassion on my own parents, a breakthrough I noted silently with pride. Of course, it also helped that Reed was there to ease the sting of their reproof. It couldn't have gone smoother, and we all went out for an all-you-can-eat seafood dinner at a nearby Howard Johnson's.

When I got home, I stayed up and watched an NBA basketball game on TV, noting how removed I now felt from the world of jocks and athletic competition. Basketball had been a favorite pastime sport in my "youth" just a few months earlier. I also felt perplexed and disappointed that the buoyant, upright feeling of the acid had evaporated and apparently could not be sustained. I'd returned to my same old timorous adolescent self.

The very next time I tripped I encountered the shadow side of "enlightenment." It was during the summer of 1971, after sophomore year. My new friend Frank had been eager to see what I was like on the stuff, since I hadn't taken any with him yet. Our mutual friend Reed, his usual tripping partner, was away on a cycling tour, so we made arrangements to get together so that I could trip with him, only this time he wasn't taking any himself; he was just going to monitor me. We decided to do it early in the morning in order to have the whole day to discombobulate, a wise decision, as it turned out. So I got up very early and was out of the house by eight o'clock, a suspicious move from my parents' perspective, as they were used to my getting up much later during the summer.

It was a beautiful morning and stayed that way all day. I rode my bicycle over to meet Frank at the Plaza del Lago. I dropped a tiny silver tablet of LSD and we rode over to Gilson Park to wait for it to kick in. After a while, I felt very high and we went over by the harbor, to the Bahai Temple, the famous orange-juice-squeezer profile on the North Shore skyline. We'd never been inside the place, which is the only such cathedral in North America, an architectural novelty and a serene tourist attraction for visitors of all nationalities.

We went inside and walked around with a crowd of sightseers and then went to sit in the auditorium to watch a promotional film on the Bahai faith. This production seemed quite corny to me from my acid altitude and adolescent, know-better cleverness. The religion seemed too ecumenical and all-embracing at the expense of intensity and integrity of principle. The film showed scenes of smiling folk from all continents celebrating this mosaic religion that combines the teachings of Christianity, Judaism, Islam, Buddhism, Hinduism, and a few other popular creeds. Fortunately, there were only about ten other people scattered throughout the sizable theater, because I was doing a lot of hyper acid-giggling that might have offended some of the "devout." The quivery, electric LSD energy poured out of me a kind of giddy contempt for community, to which my nose was turned up by a teenage idolatry of the rebel maverick.

The walls of the theater were breathing in and out and there were glowing, pulsing lines along the architectural joints from ceiling to floor, my first hallucinations ever. After we emerged from the auditorium, we looked at a panel depicting the various religions that comprised the melting pot of the Bahai faith. Even more dubious than I was, Frank challenged the Bahais' claim to be truly ecumenical while excluding a sort of Blakean/Miltonic Satan from their pantheon. I shrugged, finding this theological question, like others posed that morning, far too abstruse to ponder fruitfully.

We rode back to the park, where we sat on a bench by the lake and talked. I asked myself, "What's the date?" but couldn't determine what it was within the few seconds I'd expected the answer to come. I was then jolted with a sharp pang of panic and a horrific case of vertigo as I fell headlong through my own inner space. I'd just heard about a guy who "didn't know who or where he was," a cautionary *Twilight Zone* sort of tale about an acid trip gone wrong, and I was testing my own faculties against this drastic model. There was a faint physical pain in my brain as I plunged through a void in my mind. I felt like a kite in the sky, helpless before the whims of the wind, with no power of my own to get down to terra firma. I got extremely agitated and, in a brittle, trebly tone, implored Frank that we get moving.

I hadn't divulged the extent of my discomfort, but I was completely frantic, in utter mortal dread that I'd permanently rearranged my brain cells into a whole new schematic that would prevent me from ever reassuming my original mind and self. Sweating a metallic smell, I was careening on the terror that all the original flavors and textures of existence, including my own personality, had been permanently knocked askew by this LSD I'd stupidly taken. I truly thought I might have blown it, lost it completely. No matter how much I tried to let things drift and think of "something else," I couldn't resolve the frightful question "How am I going to get down?"

We rode vaguely toward home on our bikes. I pulled up at the house of a neighbor and hurried up the porch steps. Alarmed that I might be turning myself in to the authorities, Frank nervously called out, "You're going to get in trouble!" as I rang the doorbell. But it was the residence of Ruth and Marshall, a hippie couple in their mid-thirties who flew a peace flag and had three boys for whom I often baby-sat, a detail I hadn't had time to share with Frank in my urgency to get help.

It was the perfect refuge for me to go, just around the corner from home but still concealed from the eyes of my parents, a place where I could be cared for by adults who weren't hostile to my condition and had even been there themselves. I told them I was too high and needed to come down. Sweet Ruth, a skinny, Jewish hippie-housewife, braless in bell-bottoms and tank top, rushed out immediately to get some downers or tranquilizers from a "freak" doctor they knew.

Marshall smiled and consoled me by confiding that he'd recently "freaked out" on acid himself, writhing around on the kitchen floor in agony over the sort of father he was, tripping out on drugs with all his responsibilities. This cheered me up somewhat. If an adult could flip out on acid, it was okay for a fifteen-year-old kid. When Ruth returned, I downed the pills and anxiously anticipated a somnolent blanket of relief. I just sat on their living room sofa and in a lawn chair in their backyard, quiet and forlorn, staring at their beatific young children, who were yet unspoiled by the terrors of psychedelics.

The downs helped calm me, but they didn't exactly clear my head. To purge all the toxins from my bloodstream, Frank and I took a long walk through south Wilmette, the nearest faraway place I wouldn't likely be seen by anyone who knew me. We got back to my house as the sun began to change from yellow to late-day orange, in time to be reminded of my weekly duty to mow the lawn. Frank obviously had greener pastures to get to, so after he took off I revved up the power mower. Pushing the noisy machine over my tedious but familiar cutting course, the satisfying smell of oil combustion in my nostrils, I felt blanched and depleted but glad to be back home.

Just before dinner, my cousin Pat, who was visiting from California, looked into my face and asked, "What's with *you?* You look like you've seen a ghost." When we all sat down, my father asked me what kind of dope I'd fled the house so early to take that day, pointing his paternal finger at the queer hour I'd slipped out, and that I'd come back wan and pale. At that point, I was coasting on downers or tranquilizers and the remnants of a once-powerful acid buzz. It took a great effort just to eat a favorite meal of baked chicken. But I didn't confess to anything. The pressure wasn't that bad. I was relieved to be somewhat myself again.

A few months later, I learned that my father himself had "freaked out" while high on grass. At the invitation of Ruth and Marshall, my parents acceded to "just trying it" once. Dad took a few tokes of the communal joint and just didn't feel himself anymore, which set him into a dither. After a long late-night walk with Ruth, he'd calmed down and vowed never to touch the stuff again.

Eat the Moment

MDA was the first great drug twang to my psyche. It rocked me with a triumphal jounce of vitality, joy, and gratitude to the Maker for making it all happen: "Wake up! Be glad! Sing the song of your body and your being. Love yourself and your human brethren. And thank you, Lord, for creating all this."

I'd graduated from the University of Michigan at Ann Arbor the previous spring and was spending the winter working in Key West, Florida. I was far away from my family and friends in suburban Chicago, out on my own for the first time in the "real world"—if you can call the southernmost point in the United States and sybaritic haven for hippies, gays, bikers, and smugglers "real." I'd moved down there on a lark, picking up a ride with a fisherman I'd met on a New England island where I'd spent the summer and fall after school. One night, he'd handed me a pole out on a breakwater and said, "Try your luck." I promptly hauled in a huge bluefish, which felt like a bright omen indeed.

It had been a profoundly fruitful winter in Key West. I'd begun to write in my own singular voice and had just met Eliza, a woman who seemed to satisfy all of my romantic longings, at the famous Sloppy Joe's saloon by the wharf during her spring break from Guilford College in North Carolina. Later that month, March 1979, after she'd driven back to school, I took my first MDA with Tom and Jeffrey, friends who'd come south on their spring break from Ann Arbor. The three of us ingested the potion one night when I was done with my evening shift as a service bartender at the Casa Marina, a refurbished waterfront hotel built in the 1930s.

We got off around midnight, sitting by the ocean, which felt hugely alive with the waves crashing and the wind blowing around. In relation to the sea, I felt as tiny and tossable as the cigarette burning in my hand. "I'm glad we found each other," I declared, the first of several voluptuously sentimental pronouncements I would make that night. I was brimming with affection and felt it was a fortunate accident that we scattered, sundry kindred souls had had the fortune of converging. "Ah, we *found* each other," registered Jeffrey. So opened up did he feel too, he confided, "I feel like a woman." Not to differ with Jeffrey, I replied, "I feel like a man." For the first time in my life, I felt sexually confident, and the drug had kicked in some animal urgency and a mythical and mystical dimension to the whole dynamic.

After a while we went home to hang out for the rest of the night. I lived in an apartment in a single-story house on Eisenhower Street, by a small cove. The entry was on the side, from a porch that wound around the building. We'd left the front door open to get the vitality of the weather and the texture of nature flowing into the room. A cat wandered in, piqued with curiosity at the energy within. Palm fronds rustled. The sky grew light with the dawn. It was extremely beatific and easygoing, like the welcome, familiar sound of a creaking country door opening on a sunlit room.

Tom was enjoying the trip but had this wolflike jaw spasm, as though there were some carnivore deep within this wondrous energy gnawing to break free, that would yet be cuddly and peaceful if it emerged. I felt that the demon within was smiling in placation, its evil in check.

We drank Miller High Life and smoked Camel Filters, which had, in part because of their packaging, a tawny, sweat-salty, humane aura about them, like work-hewn skin lightly singe-kissed by the sun. The drug eliminated all the pain of inhaling tobacco smoke. Each drag was full of briny delicious taste. My lungs seemed to open up to a great reception of oxygen. All air became truly vital and pure pleasure to draw in. ("Breathe like the ocean" I would tell an MDMA partner some four years later, enraptured with the deep satiation I felt ingesting and expiring air.) MDA enabled me to breathe in long, drawn-out groans of animal ecstasy. I never felt such respiratory bliss or uttered so many long-breathed, full-voiced moans and sighs of genuine pleasure as I did on this drug. My larynx seemed to be transformed so I could make beastly growling sounds naturally, without feeling contorted or pretentious. I could never replicate the ease of these feral noises when sober.

We listened to rock music from a south Florida radio station on a clock radio. The Loggins and Messina song "Sailin' the Wind" came on and it sounded like one of the most gorgeous hymns I'd ever heard. The swelling saxophone solo put me over. This was all the more surprising because I'd never thought much of the duo. I was struck with a new sense of possibility out there, that I could be awakened to dozens of wondrous phenomena, some embedded in things I already "knew."

We also listened, on a tiny portable deck, to Jeffrey's dub mix, which included tracks from George Harrison's *Wonderwall Music.* I remarked that some of the Indian-inflected passages sounded like wailing Palestinian babies or the heat-withered moos of sacred Asian cows, and that an angry discontented drone conjured the image of a mob marching Jesus off for crucifixion. The MDA had activated a matrix of my imagination that resonanted with biblical and other lands saturated with (T. S. Eliot's) "significant soil."

Throughout the episode, I uttered extemporaneous lines such as "Skim across time like a skipping stone" to express new takes on my relationship to the fourth dimension. As we began to come down, I urged the reluctant Jeffrey to "eat the moment" and share his portion of the remaining powder *now* in order to keep us moving through this birth canal of magical immediacy and connection with life. He lay back and stared off into space, murmuring something about "lions in Aladdin's lamp," which sounded like a magnificent vision, full of exoticism and magic. (Years later, he would say that MDA, which he took several more times, had "ripped my soul raw." He eventually killed himself, for all I knew still haunted by the acute vulnerability he'd felt on MDA. Because the drug had been such a spectacular affirmation for me, I was never troubled by the suspicion that it might have been "drugs" that drove him over the edge.)

The MDA seemed to augment the surging, affirmative developments in my life, my newfound poeticism and the passionate, erotic love for Eliza. The drug fanned the flame in my loins while melding it to a godly feeling of devotion. I felt a new molten order within me, a unity of flesh and conscious fire. Consistent with this fiery theme, another physical reaction was intense heat flashes in my lower arms, which I felt sporadically even while sober in the years to come. I always wondered if my cells had been altered by what I called the drug's "hard fire."

Just before Easter, I left Key West for the sleepy southern college town of Greensboro in the Carolina Piedmont to reunite with Eliza for three weeks, en route to New York City, where we would live together that summer. On the first MDA trip with Eliza, she sank into a soporific stupor. It was as though the drug had caused a gravitational sag in her psyche. This threw me off. I'd assumed "a splendid time is guaranteed for all" on the stuff. She felt alternately hot and cold and would crawl over and lie on me for warmth during the cold spells.

It was then that I first glimpsed her childish selfishness, the yawning, hungry narcissism that seductively implored, "Give me." She was so beautiful and desirable to me that I *wanted* to give, but this initial reaction of hers to MDA was a sign that portended the problems that would intensify to mythic proportions later on. "It's time for you to give and share," I told her, a bit wounded by her antiresponse to the magical powder I'd so sanguinely shared with her.

As we recovered our good graces, she grew enraptured with the drowsy depths of her consciousness, immersing herself in Baudelaire's "bath of indolence." As we closed our eyes toward slumber for the night, I became aware of a brilliant sun rising from the center of my being, a new dawn and a ripening of my soul, which brought a smile and its equivalent in a humming sound.

A few days later, she agreed to give it another go and we took MDA with her roommate Maria, her neighbor Chet, and her classmate Sue. After getting off, we lay out on the lawn behind their apartment building, looking up at the moon over a Piedmont forest. From time to time, I gave a long moan of pleasure, which fortunately had a reassuring ring to the others. I told Eliza to whisper, "It's mine," because I wanted her to have "it" and stop worrying about getting more. All four of them wanted to be near me, to touch me, to feel my warmth and vitality, and to exchange this beautiful, affectionate vibe between us. While we lay there, there was a gentle overlap of limbs punctuated by warm clasps of hands. When we stood up, we reached over and hugged each other.

At one point, I felt the earth "nibbling" at me in a friendly, inviting way. I turned to Eliza and said, "Thank you for letting me roam through the chambers of your heart." I felt like a lion that had captured the freedom of the wild in the sanctuary of her love. Turning to God above the pine trees, I said, "Stick your tongue down my throat, Lord," craving even more of His loving presence than I could feel in the luscious air I was drinking in. The five of us were like a pride of lions sprawled on a loamy, grassy hillside, digesting the hunt.

When the others went home around four in the morning, Eliza, Maria, and I went inside their ground-floor apartment, lit candles, and listened to two LPs I'd brought: *Music from Big Pink* by The Band and Van Morrison's *Moondance.* I'll never forget the stirring, folk-hymnal sound of "The Weight," those opening strums of acoustic guitar joined by crackling drum whacks, a revival-hall piano, then Levon Helm's Ozark Mountain bray: "Pulled in from Nazareth . . ." The song was saturated with the psalms and industries of experience and it suffused my chest with the same. The sound of Van Morrison harmonizing with himself in the soulful chorus waves of "Caravan"—"Nah na na na, Nah na na na"—brought a gasp of ecstasy out of Eliza. He sounded like the mythic sated lion the drug kept conjuring.

The three of us were completely at home with each other, as though we'd known each other for years, though I'd only spent a total of less than a week with either of them. The feelings engendered by this mystic elixir had enfolded us into a loving family. I later came to view this sojourn to North Carolina as "the best three weeks of my life."

My MDA experiences formed a core of sensibilities that informed everything that came afterward. I expressed the numinosity of the Lordly presence I'd felt in some lines of a poem I wrote later:

Your presence brushes in me even as you hover
High amid the pine in the silver waters of the moon.
As I lie here at your feet, gravity's arm
'Round my waist, the hunt digesting,
My temples and jaws course hard and bright
With the livid ripe red blood of my life renewed
For having dined on your deft silence.

This Flesh Does Not Know How to Burn

In June 1980, at my friend Dirk's wedding in St. Charles, Missouri, I finally cracked the membrane of reality. Most of the previous trips had been just an excuse to act wild. Now, at age twenty-four, came deliverance to a transcendent realm.

The occasion was a sensational wedding affair at which everything felt symbolic, allegorical, even scriptural. The Noah's Ark Motel, where many of us in the younger set were lodging, had a biblical animal motif, and the name of the town ringed my own with a halo, a portent of transfigurations to come.

Just after the marriage ceremony, I took a jaunt through the church graveyard with Michael, a Canadian friend of the bride I'd struck up a friendship with. When he recited some Baudelairean line about a poet's best friend being the grave, it felt like a natural segue to step out from the matrimonial to the funereal. (As it happened, two years later, Dirk was killed in a motorcycle accident and we all returned to the Ark on a pilgrimage from Chicago to lay his ashes to rest.)

We "dropped" in the evening after the reception. The acid was Red Blotter, procured in the Pacific Northwest. In the designated party room at the motel was a Russian samovar I'd brought as a wedding gift, and a *Time* magazine featuring a report on the Soviet Union with a predominantly red cover. Everything was coming up red that night.

A couple of others tripped too, but Michael and I were the fun boys, acting the most electric. I started sputtering souped-up Dada phrases such as "Throw me out a Roman window," as Blondie sang "Dreaming Is Free" on *Saturday Night Live*. Someone asked Michael, "When's this guy going to shut up?" So we left the group and wandered out into the halls around one A.M.

Michael urged me to stare at the ceiling to see if any visions came. He'd told me earlier that on his most recent trip he kept looking into the void until he encountered a vivid archetypal face, which divided into light and dark hemispheres representing the sacred and the pro-fane or some such dichotomy. While staring at the hall ceiling, I seemed to feel the pace and hear the sound of the earth turning. Then I saw the face of Johanna, Dirk's former girlfriend, who'd flown from California for the wedding. In the image, she looked beautiful, but her lips were parched, which imbued her face with a shade of spiritual pathos. Just then, Johanna herself appeared from around the corner and the three of us felt a rush of synchronicity.

Back in our room, Michael suggested I stare again at the bumpy plaster ceiling, confident that I, as he had, would break through to a new dimension. I lay back on my bed and stared overhead into what looked like small-curd cottage cheese. After a few minutes, the eyes of the Devil materialized out of a goat face that converted, with just the slightest, most delicate adjustment of spatial particles, into a lamb's, and then back again. The goat appeared hungry and discontent, while the lamb had these beautiful eyes, moist and soft and open and filled with a deep compassionate soulfulness that could only have been forged by suffering. For the rest of the night, Michael's face too seemed to be a site where the two archetypes played out their eternal struggle, each vying for control.

Then the Devil visage on the ceiling exuded a territorial imperative. The specter of Satan asserting himself provoked a fuck-you rage in me which drove softer features back into the spectral mask that was now completely transfixing me. I growled in hatred at the Fiend and soon he wept tears of ash from his right eye, while his left (on my right) yielded into a glowing ember of magnificent orange-red light. Rimmed by a thin ring of blue luminescence, it seemed to go on and on into infinity.

The tears seemed to be Satan's concession of defeat, that he was made only of perishable mortal substance. "This flesh does not know how to burn," I heard myself say in shuddering awe for the power of the "Unifire" to vaporize all matter and flesh, especially that void of spirit. I felt a strong, definitive sense that this gorgeous, enthralling berry star or "blood light" (an image I attribute to poet Gerard Manley Hopkins) was the light of the Father shining down to me through the blood of Christ. It was clearly an A.D. light. I felt a profoundly warm sense of being cradled in the love of the Father and a confidence that this love would ultimately be revealed to all in myriad resplendent dimensions. Then I watched as a procession of angel faces drifted across the ceiling. Michael, who was somehow—almost telepathically—completely tuned in to this vision, remarked that it was the light of Pentecost I'd seen.

Later that night I opened up a local directory at random to the page with the local Pentecostal Church, prompting him to nod, knowingly. "You see, there's something going on." I told him I was distracted by the last four letters of the word Pentecost, which sounded vaguely ominous, for some reason, though when I learned the true meaning of the word a few days later—the spirit of the resurrected Christ beaming down to his disciples, filling their hearts with comfort, love, and confidence—it seemed an apt term for my epiphany.

I was subliminally aware that there was a price to pay for such mad dashes into sacred, revelatory territory. One always had to scramble back before daybreak on these trips, and not before being stopped at a checkpoint by a border guard before the dawn. There you paid a customs duty on the psychic treasure you'd acquired, before scampering on to slip back into your skin. But the "price of experience" as William Blake called it, was high. You generally couldn't manage to bring it all over. Only a trace of the mercurially got inspiration stayed with you, usually. And then there was the question of whether you'd truly "earned" it.

Around three in the morning, I returned to the original party room, where the remaining wakeful revelers were sitting cross-legged on the floor in quiet conversation. After my vision, there was a clear demarcation between Michael and me, and the others. Wearing a bedspread cape over my naked upper body as I came in to get more beers from the ice-filled bathtub, I remember feeling very different from my brother who was there, that there had been some kind of change in me and a division between us, that I had moved on to a "higher" plane. The apparent cleft between us would aggravate my conscience in the years to come.

The night went on into the wee hours. The visions had ceased, but it was impossible to feel sleepy. Michael and I went outside to take a walk around the motel grounds. I had a bottle of red wine, but lacked a corkscrew, so I cracked the neck on the parking-lot asphalt, producing a jagged edge. I hastily tipped the bottle to get some wine in my throat, by this time in need of a warm tonic for my vision-addled brain. The motel security guard appeared and I lost a heartbeat thinking I was in trouble. But he was genuinely concerned and asked to look inside my mouth to see if I'd cut myself. He told me to go back inside, and I eagerly obliged him.

I felt very grateful for his letting me go and not calling the police or hauling me off somewhere. I was amazed at how stupid and desperate I was to open the wine so violently, which seemed an apt metaphor for the nagging suspicion that I'd bitten off more than I could chew that night. I thanked the security guard with a firm handshake and a long sympathetic look from my simmering, dilated eyes. Then I went in to lie down, to wrestle with the acid, tequila, and beer in my bloodstream, the venereal agony in my loins that came from a longing to touch, and the mind-blowing revelation I'd had a few hours earlier.

As the new day dawned, I felt as though I were on a psychic collision course, trapped in some eternal conflict or dialectic, which was embodied in the difficulty in deciding whether "Let it Be" or "Across the Universe" should be the final chime of the night before it was finally over—whenever that might be. By now it was morning. I went out to the pool for a dip in my jeans, talking to Jim and his wife, Laurie, about bringing children into the world, which, on this of all days, they pronounced as a cruel, wrong idea. I was freaked that the verdict from their cozy matrimonial quarter was thumbs down.

I went back to the room and started chirping manically to Michael, who was alarmed and annoyed at the twittering discomfort I'd brought in the door. He was trying to ease down from the acid himself, of course. I was literally at my wit's end, a runaway train running on empty, burning up the ashes at the base of the furnace. A violent panic was billowing.

When the wedding party finally dispersed, I holed up an extra night at the Ark before returning to my job in New York, where I then began the struggle to understand what had just struck me. The visions had been so compelling that I now felt convinced of life's, and perhaps even my own, "divinity." I felt assured of the Resurrection and the pervasive truth of Christ's love, yet in the months to come, all of this proved too hard for me to incorporate into my practical, everyday consciousness. Gradually, the specter of doubt—and its punitive repercussions—seeped into my thoughts. Moreover, I began to wonder if the apparitions I'd seen had been some kind of malicious farce or, more ambiguously, a projection of my own naive dreams of transcendence and absolution, utterly meaningless and inconsequential outside the experiential theater within which they'd appeared.

Having trouble adjusting to postcollegiate adulthood, I was dirt-poor and "underemployed" as a clerk in an audio-publishing firm. My personal life was in turmoil. To my growing horror over the year after my Christly vision, I built up an intense anger for two people I loved, Ray, a friend from my youth I looked up to, and Julia, a woman to whom I'd given the most elaborate surge of passion in my life. Compounding my social and professional troubles, six days before my twenty-fifth birthday I was shocked and stricken by the murder of John Lennon, a figure I'd venerated since childhood. When I received no birthday greeting from Julia, it felt like the world was crashing. A horrific solstice gloom descended over me as the year came to an end.

The trip in St. Charles had commenced my final psychedelic passage, a series of trips extending from that summer to the next, which was drawn from the sheet of fifty hits I'd brought back from the wedding.

On one dose, with my dear friends Jay and Marilyn, late in the summer of 1980, I struck through to the ground spring of my grief. It was Marilyn's first time and while we waited in her cozy studio apartment in Chelsea for Jay to get off work at *Newsweek*, I played her some Beethoven and Doors, which sounded like acoustical manifestations of some immense orgasmic tension prolonged to Promethean dimensions. At one point, Marilyn wept in amazement as the door to her bathroom started to "melt." When Jay arrived, we all took each other in in a very open and approving way and talked about all the great times we'd had together since we'd met in college.

I'd gone home from this glowingly congenial evening and lay down to sleep, only to be surprised by a tumbling soft urgency in my chest. I began to cry and the crying kept on coming and coming. I wept in waves of sweet, sinewy grief, for what seemed like about four hours. I was very sad about Julia's absence, but the anguish was still fluid and malleable; I wasn't yet frozen into the painful paralysis that came over me months later, when I realized that her love, like Lennon's life, was really gone.

To trigger new crying jags and turn over barnacled old stones in my psyche, I'd think about myself and my own heartbreak and disappointments, then about Julia, previous girlfriends, and other friends and loved ones. I'd conjure an exquisitely endearing image of each person, a fusion of his or her frailty and compassion as lit from within by the rising breath of love's whimsy. Switching channels from person to person, I went through the various characteristic loves I felt for each one. The sobbing came in long, rhythmic torrents and the sound of the tears and the throat grief pouring out of me was like gushes of rain or music. It was the most protracted cathartic experience I've ever had.

By the time of my final LSD experience, in July 1981, a year after St. Charles, I was overcome with alienation and despair, no longer capable of working through my emotions. In the bleak final hours of that last trip, I took a long nocturnal walk from the Upper West Side to the Village and back. At one point I felt a jolt to my heart when I thought about a passage in *The Urantia Book*, a volume of esoteric Christian cosmology I was reading at the time, in which Jesus destroys all his writings, among other personal effects, to eradicate all physical remnants of his life in the flesh. In my stricken state, this struck me as a morbid act and a terrible sacrifice. As a budding poet, as I fancied myself, the idea of annihilating the few works I'd produced terrified me on a strange primordial level. I'm still not sure why. No one was asking *me* to make that sacrifice.

Then, on a dimly lit block of Broadway, between 103rd and 104th Streets, I saw that a woman I'd dated briefly some months back was ambling toward me with a female friend. I didn't slow down or stop to say hello, but instead faintheartedly leaned over as I passed right next to her and touched her left shoulder with my right forefinger, muttering, "Hey." She just kept walking. It gave me a start that I'd been so ignored and that I hadn't had the guts to make a formal encounter of it. I felt like a ghost.

When I arrived home in my minuscule basement apartment on 108th Street, I lay down and sensed the presence of a terrible angel hovering in judgment over me. I had the dank, fatalistic sense of being ruined with the stamp of damnation. This was perhaps the culmination of the guilt I felt for the sin of harboring what I feared might become a killer rage. Feeling betrayed for a variety of reasons, some petty and narcissistic, some legitimate and long overdue, the fury I'd been nurturing became utterly at odds with my newfound divine consciousness. It was so perpendicular to being a seer of Christ and a believer in his mercy that under the strain, I felt I was turning to ash and fading from the land of the living.

A few days later, upon my return from a party where I'd consumed an abundance of Greek red wine served with a fiendishly rich lamb stew, I hallucinated a beastly countenance in my mirrored reflection, with eyes in the nipples staring back at me. Something burst in my mind, and the blood of pandemonium flooded into it. It was the advent of a black night of the soul that would last several months and affect my life for years to come.

Now, the ironic thing about this whopping bummer of a final acid voyage was that during its peak hours I could have had the human communion I'd needed if I'd simply enfolded myself in the life of the flesh.

Marilyn and Jay and I had dropped the last of the Red Blotter at her apartment on a cloying summer night at a time when my heartbreak over losing Julia was the most acute. It had just become irrevocably clear to me that she'd kept me hanging for a year and was now completely done with me. To retaliate, I'd just mailed off a poison-pen letter filled with several acrid sentiments, impelling her with a sort of demonic menace to think of *me* at the most intimate and doubt-plagued moments of her life. This letter so immortalized my ire that I eventually had to put a match to a copy I'd kept, in order to break myself free of the hate-beam it was sending out.

By contrast, Jay and Marilyn were in smooth, sprightly spirits. After an hour of flirtatious banter, Marilyn slipped out of her clothes and crawled like a lithe lioness onto her bed, wordlessly inviting Jay and me to make love with her. We started to. I kissed her and licked her nipples and fingered her deeply with a middle digit much longer than she'd been accustomed. She reacted with immense pleasure, but I was feeling too hurt and vulnerable to take up her wordless invitation to dig in deeper. It felt like dangerously fragile territory to cross into, a new "relationship" to which, however frivolously it had been conceived, I would have to stay "true"—a word that had taken on a frightening tone of finality.

Both Jay and Marilyn were quite willing to share her squirming, hungry body with me, but I wasn't all up to it. I took only my shirt off, leaving my jeans on, symbolically conferring a "higher" sort of love, while Jay delivered the "lower" kind, tonguing her most tender flesh, then screwing her in furious, rapid thrusts. While doing so, he took on a satyr's grimace, as faint red flames leapt off his back.

We slowed down and pulled apart for a while and then I watched as she got down on her knees between Jay's legs while he sat on the sofa, and slowly, after some playful nudges and murmurs, licked and sucked his penis while he lay his head back and moaned, bare-teethed, with intense satisfaction. She ran her hands over his knees and thighs, while her mane of tousled, streaked-blond curls bobbed over his crown. The sight of this stunning erotic pose from just a few feet across the room put me in a icy trance.

I was so consumed with the fact that Julia would never be back to kiss any part of me with such delicious devotion that I did not pick up on the fact that I could have joined in the sensuous rapture before me. I could have slipped out of my pants, grabbed Marilyn's rump cheeks, and plunged right into her luscious rear crevice, or sat back in the big armchair and received the ministrations of her pulp-warm lips and wet-tongue graces. Jay told me later that she'd been all the more flushed with excitement while I was watching and that she was hot to have both of us inside her for the next few hours. But I was zonked in the zone of deprivation and exile and soon left the apartment with the sight of Marilyn rocking and moaning on Jay's lap plastered to my mindscreen.

To this day, I believe my decision to leave at this juncture was a fateful one that determined the depth and severity of my semi-suicidal depression over the next year. If I'd relaxed just a little more, disrobed completely and participated full- instead of half-bodily, I might not have felt so accursed and erased as I did after leaving Marilyn's apartment and taking my long march through the city in a vain attempt to exorcise my despair. The lysergic had heightened the tension, aesthetics, and skin sensitivity of the erotic drama unfolding before me, while paradoxically underscoring my role as mere spectator to the pageant of connubial union, which I felt had passed me by while cruelly grazing me with its exquisite touch.

In the latter half of the Eighties, I finally emerged from the sterile morbidity of this period, but I never took LSD again. Acid can bring such stunning revelations, but you can hardly plan their arrival or accommodate the terrific magnitude of the meanings that your psyche, in its naïveté or twisted reasoning, ascribes to them. If you're one to believe that LSD has a mind of its own, you might suspect it was being a bit sly with you sometimes.

Ideally, it informs you of unity and connectedness, that there's no true division between matter and energy, God and humanity, time and experience. But sometimes it tricks you into believing you're set apart or worse, cast out, which is surely *maya* magnified a thousandfold. You can kick yourself for forgetting once again the native truths you stumble upon early on in the psychedelic journey. But what makes us forget, and why are these apparently genetic memories so difficult to explode into the full flower of consciousness, decrypted once and for all to set us free?

Charlie

B. 1971

Staff member at a humanist psychology institution

Resides in San Francisco

Raised in Aspen, Colorado

THAT'S WHEN I REALIZED I WAS OUT OF MY SENSES

My first experience with psychedelics took place in 1986 in Aspen, Colorado. I was fifteen years old, pretty young in retrospect. I'd been smoking a lot of pot since junior high school. I kept hearing rave reviews about LSD's mind-expanding properties, so I couldn't resist.

I had a lot of freedom, too much really. My mother was very liberal, having come of age in the Seventies, doing plenty of drugs. My stepfather was still a hippie at heart. Sometimes he'd discreetly smoke a couple of bowls to relax when he came home from work. In fact, I got most of the dope I smoked from his drawer. He never missed any of it. I had enough to supply me and all my friends with the best pot you could buy.

We lived in an upper-middle-class neighborhood with a nice car and a lot of other toys. My stepfather is a real estate broker and investor who'd moved to the Aspen area and started investing in the early Seventies. He'd had a notion that it was going to be big and he was right. We lived in a big house on the side of Snowmass Mountain, the site of the famous ski resort. I could ski from the resort to my house. Deer roamed through our backyard.

It was the beginning of the summer after freshman year. One evening around sunset, I took a hit of Zodiac, a blotter acid with an astrological chart on the back, with four friends: three guys and a girl. All four of them had tripped before. Another guy, Peter, met up with us later, though we didn't have enough acid for him. We had plenty of pot, so we went to Wagner Park in the center of town to enhance our psychedelic high by smoking a doobie.

We sat in a circle under an aspen tree. Peter, being straight, rolled us a very big joint, which we passed around. It was rumored that the pot was laced with opium, but I couldn't tell. After I smoked this stuff, I really started to feel the effects of the LSD. We sat cross-legged in the circle, laughing at nothing in particular, just being high and feeling connected with each other. Though its source was not specific, there was a great deal of deeply felt joy and mirth circulating between us. As I laughed, I began to feel vibrations throughout my body. Everything below my head became increasingly numb the more I laughed until I was completely unconscious of any part of my body but my head. I felt as though I were just a head floating above the ground. As soon as that notion took hold, everyone else became just a head as well.

Then I saw vibrant electric illuminated arrows passing clockwise between us in the circle. They looked like cartoon arrows in a diagram, moving and pulsing between us in a definite rhythm. My friends' faces became caricatures often associated with cartoon characters. I told Peter he resembled Donald Duck, which was cause for a good laugh all around. I realized that the band of arrows illustrated the field of energy between us, and that the acid had made it manifest. When I meditated on that idea, I felt a profound harmony with my friends. There were larger arrows of red, purple, and green, which marked the main artery between us, and smaller ones, which were gray, in the secondary channels between us.

Apprehending the interconnectedness of our energies and the dissipation of boundaries, I exclaimed something totally absurd, like "This is the meaning of life!" I was thunderstruck: "I get it! This is what it's all about!" I saw that we were bonded beyond the realms of corporeality and intellectual articulation. Aside from our heads, we were totally united. It was a direct experience of oneness with others, a total novelty in my life at the time.

After a while, my mind started to wander away from the circle. I was distracted by cars passing by, the lights in the town, becoming less sanguine. I heard sirens and started to panic. I kept hearing them again and again and brought it up to the group.

"Did you guys hear that?"

"No, I don't hear anything. What are you talking about?"

They convinced me I was hearing things. That's when I realized I was out of my senses. I got scared and started wondering, "What if the police catch me? I'm doing something illegal." I was suddenly overcome with diffidence. Once I ventured out of our cozy little circle into my own head, the trip started to go sour. The germ of fear had entered me. I wanted to leave and go somewhere else.

I continued to hear sirens, very loud, over and over, so I convinced myself it was only a hallucination. I looked to Peter, the sober one, for guidance. Even though he was a year younger than I was, he'd already tripped and was proud of it. "Sure, I know what you're going through," he reassured me. "I wish I had some!" When the sirens went off, I looked at him for any sign they were real. If he panicked, then I knew that I would have reason to. That's how I got through the anxious moments. He never registered an alarming sound.

After I came down, I thought the trip had been the coolest experience I'd ever known. I was convinced that my life would never be the same. I felt I'd had a religious epiphany, even though I'd started the trip recreationally. It deepened my sense of reality. In fact, it blew it out of the water. I knew now that there was so much I'd been taking for granted. In a romantic, teenage way, I went into a sort of existential angst. *What does all this mean? Is this really the way life is? How can I get deeper into it?* I became a psychedelic diehard.

On my last major acid trip, in November 1986, I had a heaven-and-hell experience and went a little berserk. By then, in spite of its clearly spiritual initial tone, LSD had become almost overtly recreational for me. My friends and I decided to take some acid in honor of the homecoming parties. I was a sophomore and played basketball for the school team, but I didn't give a shit about the football team or sports in general, really. It was party time. There was a homecoming dance at a nightclub called Andre's. Upstairs there was a bar and disco with mirrors and lights and everything else. It was the perfect opportunity to trip out and have a great time.

I was with my friends Russell, a tripping partner my age, and Mark, a senior two years older than us, who got the acid for us: Zodiac again. We were psyched he'd been able to find some, because it was considered the heavy stuff. I always wanted to relive the intensity of my first experience. Mark gave us two hits each and said to take only one and save the other for later, in case it wasn't as powerful as we'd expected. There were supposed to be six regular doses in each hit.

Russell and I took one hit each in an alley. A minute after I'd put it in my mouth, he did something that made me laugh really hard, and I was afraid it had popped out. We looked everywhere on the ground and couldn't find it. "Shit! I'm not going to get off," I thought. So I pulled out the other hit and took it, sucking on it for a long time. I wanted to be on the same trip schedule as everyone else and didn't want to wait to see if I'd actually lost the first hit or not.

We went over to somebody's house and joined a bunch of guys drinking champagne and smoking pot, some of whom were on Zodiac. We got ourselves really primed for the party. When we arrived at Andre's, it was packed with high school kids. The disco was dark, with lights spinning and strobing everywhere. We were all like "Whoa! This is great!" I started to trip out hard on the lights and mirrors. The music was really loud and sounded garbled. I couldn't understand what people were saying to me. It was as though time had slowed down.

I got out on the dance floor and just started jumping around. I couldn't determine where the mirrors were, so I was slamming into them and going totally nuts, really getting into it. It's not that I was intentionally slam-dancing. I was just jumping up and down, having a good time, but I was having trouble keeping my balance and gauging boundaries. The dance floor was really crowded. I slammed into a girl in my class who was incredibly snotty. I hated her. Her name was Belinda and she was gorgeous, which increased my enmity, because that's what made her so snobbish. She freaked out and called me an asshole.

"Watch what you're doing. You're so drunk."

"Don't fuck with me, right now!" I hissed at her. "Get out of my face, so help me, you fucking bitch!" It was gratifying to call her that. She'd gotten me all riled up and I was really slamming around. One of my friends came over and pulled me off the dance floor.

"Dude, you gotta settle down, man. You're just terrorizing the place."

I said okay and walked over to a friend who was tripping on Zodiac. I was talking very loudly within earshot of teachers who were chaperoning the dance. I was almost yelling, "Man, this Zodiac is just great! I'm having a great time." My friend said, "Shhhh. Keep it down, man. Mr. MacGregor's over there." He was my algebra teacher, whom I wasn't too fond of either. "I don't give a shit," I said. "Who cares? He doesn't know what 'Zodiac' means anyway. Watch this." I went over to Mr. MacGregor and said, "I'm tripping on two hits of Zodiac." He said, "Charlie, I think you're a little bit drunk. Come with me." He grabbed my arm firmly and at that point, I just lost it. I turned around and decked him. Boom! I laid him out.

The next thing I knew, the principal had me in a bear hug. He was a big guy and I was completely powerless and couldn't move or breathe. "I'm not going to let you go until you promise to settle down," he told me. "Okay, okay. I promise," I gasped. As soon as he put me down, I tried to knock him over and run for it, but he grabbed me again. A juvenile officer from the police department came charging up the stairs. He calmed me down by bringing me over to a corner and sitting me down in a chair. I started crying. He was trying to get me to say what I was on.

"I'm on Zodiac, man!"

"What is Zodiac?"

"It's acid."

He was crouched at my level and he had his hands on me, gently, calming me down. He really knew how to handle the situation. Two girls who were friends of mine and tripping too came over when they saw me crying. They talked to me a while and tried to soothe me. Then Mark came over and really settled me down, which gave him the confidence of the juvenile officer. I trusted Mark and really looked up to him. He was tripping too, of course, and he reminded me not to tell the authorities about the whole gang. I assured him, "I may be totally tripped out, but I'm not going to tell where I got the stuff. I'd never do that."

They took me outside in the cold air on the public sidewalk. I was wearing only a shirt and jeans. The officer sat down next to me. I asked him if I could see my mother and he said, "No. First we have to take you to the hospital to see if you're all right." I figured they wanted to pump my stomach or something. I said, "No, I want to see my mother!" Then I started screaming, "I want to see my mother, the woman who gave birth to me!" I was yelling and crying one moment, then laughing or tripping out on something the next. I was really flipped out.

Finally, the juvenile officer got me calmed down again, and a Saab police car pulled up. They put me in the front seat and buckled me in. I started tripping out on all the blinking lights of all the electronic equipment it was decked out with, touching some of the dials and monitors. With a male police officer in the backseat, a lady cop drove me to the ER at the hospital. There was no staff around, because it was late at night, so they put me in a room with a young, overweight policeman who sat on a chair while I lay on a cot. He tried to keep me occupied while they looked for a doctor to examine me.

He asked me, "What's it like? What are you seeing?" He seemed genuinely curious about what I was going through. Lying prostrate, I looked up at the panel ceiling, which had grooves that looked as though they'd been made by claws. The indentations took on the appearance of multicolored worms moving around. It seemed like a sort of death hallucination. I asked the fat policeman if he'd ever done acid or seen anyone on acid and he said no. He seemed fascinated, though he may have just been trying to smoke information out of me. I thought I'd have some fun with this guy, so I sat up in my cot. There was a mirror and sink in the room.

"You know they say that when you're on acid, you should never look in the mirror."

"Really? Why's that?"

I told him I'd never looked in the mirror on acid before and proceeded to go up to the mirror and look into it. Then I clutched the sink and cried out, "Oh, my God! I see God!" He was bewildered and uncomfortable. Actually I looked purple and pink with some corrosion that made me look burned or melted in places. It wasn't a pretty picture, but it didn't scare me. I was too intent on shocking this cop.

As soon as the doctor came in, I hated him immediately. He gave me a bad vibe. He had no sense of humor. He looked like he didn't want me there, like he hated me. (He probably did.) I felt very rebellious toward this guy. He looked me over, felt around to make sure I was okay, and asked me a bunch of serious questions. Then he gave me a cup and said he wanted me to piss in it. So I went to the bathroom across the hall. He said, "Don't lock the door." I went in, closed the door, and locked it.

I was in my own universe in this bathroom. I took a long look at my face in the mirror, touching it, marveling at the strangeness and the colors. Then I remembered what I was in there for, so I tried to piss in the cup. I looked down at my penis, and it was purple and bubbling with blistery, pussy crawling flesh. It was very grotesque. I looked down at the immaculate porcelain toilet and flushed it over and over and over, tripping out on the water swirling around. Then I heard a faint knock on the door, and voices, though I couldn't tell what they were saying. I didn't answer, since I wasn't sure they were real. I guess they were wondering if I was trying to flush myself down the toilet or something. I tried to pee again and couldn't. I was in there for a long time and finally came out with the empty cup, which pissed off the doctor, who told me to lie down on the cot again.

Around one in the morning, my stepfather showed up. He took the place of the officer who was sitting down with me. He refused to allow the doctor to get a urine sample out of me and was angry at him for asking me to provide one without a parent, guardian or attorney there to represent me. They may very well have been trying to collect evidence for a possible charge against me—not to treat but to indict me. My stepfather had spent a good portion of his college years dosing on psychedelics and was not very trusting of the authorities. I felt comfortable and safe with him there. I asked if he'd ever felt or seen this or that on acid.

"Yeah, yeah," he said. "I know what you're going through. I know what it's like." He was very effective in putting me at ease. He didn't make me feel bad like most parents would have: "You shithead! How could you do that?" He was really cool about it. I didn't feel like I was in trouble and I didn't feel any shame. In fact, my earlier euphoria made a resurgence.

"I really want to listen to music," I kept saying. "I want to hear Jimi Hendrix."

"Okay, we'll listen to some when we get home."

So he signed me out and I got in his jeep and we drove home. I don't know if I imagined it or not, but the best Jimi I'd ever heard came on the radio, maybe one of the long jams on *Electric Ladyland.* When we got home, my mother spoiled my high. She wasn't angry, but freaked out and worried. "I knew you were smoking pot," she cried, "but I didn't know you were tripping. This is serious stuff." Fortunately, my stepfather intervened, saying, "We'll deal with that later. This is not what he needs right now. What he needs is to trip out on something." So he took me upstairs and put me in front of a television tuned to a channel that had shut down for the night, with just the color bars on the screen. I tripped out on that for the rest of the night. The colors flowed into each other and patterns formed behind them. I heard a constant stream of barely audible voices in the other room, but then thought maybe I was hallucinating them, because it didn't seem like the regular pattern of sound.

The consequences of my actions at the disco were a two-day suspension from school. I was lucky not to be expelled, which might have happened at most schools in America due to the stigma of drugs, especially those like LSD. I was also given an in-school suspension for another two days and was told I couldn't come back unless I went to a rehab center. My mother insisted that I go to a therapist instead, and the school agreed.

I was disturbed myself about hitting Mr. MacGregor. It was like my shadow had taken over. I was convinced he wouldn't know what I was talking about, but I was also playing the game of showing how big and in control I was. Maybe I wanted to get caught. I hadn't been violent toward anyone for a very long time, though when I was young, I was extremely violent toward other kids. Before moving in with my mother and my stepfather, I grew up with my father and my stepmother, the latter of whom abused me and my four siblings. It was a rough, working-class household.

I don't regret getting caught, because many good things came of it. I realized what I was doing to myself by being so heedless and self-destructive with drugs. After my early initiations I just didn't have the discipline to use psychedelics on a consistently spiritual or intellectual plane. I think my experience is somewhat parallel to the culture's. It started out with a few conscientious individuals using the materials for spiritual illumination, but then the zealots started pushing it onto the youth, who weren't equipped and started using the stuff as a party drug, with six-packs, joints, coke, Quaaludes, and whatever else.

As I matured, I developed the mental infrastructure for psychedelics. I went on to take mushrooms and Ecstasy, which for me offered considerably more manageable experiences than LSD did. At college, I studied countercultural literature in twentieth-century America, which covered what I call the psychedelic religion. Later I taught a course called Visionary Experience in Literature that featured some of the notable works of this movement.

I believe that we should do more to guide people through intense life experiences and inner journeys—*regardless* of whether they're driven by psychedelics. For this we need to turn away from the acquisitive consumerism that derails the minds of the young, and develop a shamanic tradition suited to the realities of modern culture.

Clark Heinrich

B. 1945

***Writer, poet, ethnobotanical researcher, phenomenologist; author of* Strange Fruit: Alchemy, Religion and Magical Foods: A Speculative History *and the forthcoming* God Without Religion: An Easy Guide to Spiritual Freedom; *coauthor, with Carl A. P. Ruck and Blaise Daniel Staples, of* The Apples of Apollo: Pagan and Christian Mysteries of the Eucharist**

Resides in northern California

Raised in California, Ohio, Colorado, and California in succession

The first narrative presented here, entitled "Heaven," *is an excerpt from Clark's* Strange Fruit: Alchemy, Religion and Magical Foods, *which was published in 1995 by Bloomsbury in the U.K., and subsequently by publishers in Germany and Japan. A companion piece, aptly called* "Hell," *is included in that volume, but not here. The second narrative below is a stand-alone story yet unpublished. Both of Clark's tales here are printed with his permission.*

HEAVEN

My experience with the capricious fly agaric mushroom (*Amanita muscaria*) is long and varied, but I will briefly relate the first of the two most impressive events, both of which occurred in 1977. My friend Michael and I had decided to give the mushroom a good test. After a few nauseating yet somehow uplifting experiences with fresh specimens, we discovered that the mushroom should not be eaten raw. This was fortunate, since Michael thought he was going to die the first night he ate (too many) freshly picked mushrooms, and I became extremely nauseous every time I ate them. After harvesting and drying a sufficient quantity of specimens, we embarked on what was to become a thirty-one-day trial period.

We ate mushrooms every day, usually not very many, but every day. We lost interest in food. We lost interest in work. We were rapidly losing interest in the whole world, and our wives were beginning to think of losing us, i.e., as in "getting rid of." I was reminded of the Siberian folk tale related by Gordon Wasson in *Soma: Divine*

Mushroom of Immortality (1968), in which the men leave their wives during the mushroom season and go off to live with the "Amanita girls." Even so, we continued; the longer we persisted the more we felt divinely inspired to go on.

If the fly agaric really was Soma, the heaven-inducing drink of the ancient Aryans—and every day we were more convinced that it was—then a breakthrough experience might be just around the metaphysical corner. We weren't at all certain we wouldn't die trying, but in our growing dispassion we soon stopped worrying. After all, this was important research, science at its most basic and best. It would be a noble way to die, if it happened, and as a bonus we would avoid old age. We considered it a fair trade-off. Yes, I have to say it, we felt we were on a mission from God. During the first thirty days we experienced many different effects, some consistently, others inconsistently. We felt immense energy, strength and spirituality, occasional sickness or nausea, and frequent euphoria; but passage up into the blissful light eluded us.

The thirty-first day was a full moon. We fasted all day and began nibbling on mushrooms early in the evening. Later, in a nod to tradition, I performed a Vedic fire ceremony, putting a piece of a mushroom cap into the fire as I sang the ancient offertory mantras to Agni, Soma, Rudra, and Indra. Afterward we drove to a nearby bluff and consumed between us about ten more dried caps of different sizes. (I lost track of the exact number: bad science.) I tore each cap in half so we would have the same experience, knowing as I did that potency varied from cap to cap.

At the time, I wasn't aware that fully mature specimens develop more muscimol, the main active chemical, than immature specimens. The mushrooms we ate were the most mature that we had collected, saved for last because they were the least attractive and, we thought, the least potent. For this reason we ate quite a bit more at one time than we had prior to this. They were indeed less virulent than immature mushrooms, but as we were about to find out, far more potent in the qualities for which we had been searching.

We were getting cold, so we went to Michael's house and made a fire. Neither of us had urinated since before we started eating the mushrooms. This was intentional. The active chemicals of the fly agaric pass into the urine unmetabolized, a fact long known to Siberian users. We had planned to test the urine's touted effectiveness, but we'd waited so long to do so that both of us were now ready to burst.

Michael got out two bowls and handed one to me. We looked at each other, laughed nervously, and retired to opposite corners of the room to fill our respective containers. I stress *respective* containers; even seminal research has its limits. We returned to the center of the room and looked at the tinctured water we had wrought. It was glowing with a fiery orange cast. Since we were about to drink it, we first smelled it to see what we were in for, and were surprised at its pleasant odor, or rather, its fragrance.

The phrase "water into wine" redefined itself in my mind as we drank off what we were truly hoping would do something extraordinary to us. If it didn't, we would be more embarrassed than disappointed. We might even be angry, but at least we would know where the phrase "pissed off" originated.

Even before we drank, we were feeling good. Very good. Extremely good. But within minutes after drinking, something amazing started to happen. My body began to feel very light, as though I weighed almost nothing. It felt as if the molecules that made up my body were separating and allowing air to pass through, or that I could feel the space between the atoms. I became aware of tremendous energy at my feet that rose up through my body in wave after wave. "Feeling good" was rapidly changing into the most blissful feelings I had ever known. I looked at Michael and he was radiant, truly radiant. We started laughing and exclaiming in disbelief as the bliss kept increasing. My mind and entire body were in the throes of a kind of meta-orgasm that wouldn't stop—not that I wanted it to.

I had recently been searching through the Bible for clues to possible drug use, so I picked up a copy from the shelf, opened to the Gospel of John and started reading aloud. What I had before considered ridiculously partisan poetry, fiction really, was now revealed in a whole new light. It became for us a fly agaric initiation document, speaking the living truth directly to Michael and me through the mists of the centuries, uncovering layer after layer of meaning artfully hidden in the text. We understood it all: all the references, all the metaphors, all the hidden wisdom. We were completely delirious, of course, but in our delirium we were being initiated *deus ex liber* into an ancient cult of the personified fly agaric. And we couldn't have been happier.

I would read a passage and Michael would exclaim in joy and recognition as we both careened in excitement about the room. After a short while I became so engrossed in the text that I stopped reading aloud, but Michael, who wasn't looking at me, kept responding at the appropriate times. I silently read another line and watched him respond to it. When I realized what was happening, I thought, "Michael," and he turned his grinning head and looked at me, and we experienced simultaneous amazement.

At first we tested ourselves, still without speaking, by mentally requesting a gesture of some kind from the other. It worked. Then for the next short period of time, we carried on the most unusual and effortless conversation of our lives, which wasn't a conversation at all, really; because regardless of whichever of us was having a thought, it instantly became the thought of the other. It sounds confusing, but it wasn't; far from it. As this was happening, the bliss we were experiencing increased still more, which I hadn't thought was possible. Of course, it didn't matter what I thought: I was on a juggernaut, having the ride of my life.

At an unspoken signal, we turned out the light and positioned ourselves on the floor at opposite ends of the living room. I closed my eyes and became very still. The few thoughts that arose in my mind drifted through like enlightening holograms. I was thinking at the preverbal level. I was *seeing*. I had the subtle apprehension that only a few thoughts remained in my mind. These were in the process of passing through and, as it seemed, out of my mind, not to return or be replaced for the time being. The last picture to appear was that of a woman of the Middle East walking down an ancient road, carrying on her head an earthen jar filled with seeds. The seeds were leaking out a hole in the bottom of the jar.

I saw this because I had been troubling over the meaning of a saying attributed to Jesus in the Gospel of Thomas from the Nag Hammadi texts, one of many in which he is answering the question of the unenlightened everywhere: "What is the kingdom of heaven like?" He explained that heaven is like the woman described above, who doesn't know her jar is leaking and continues to walk home. When she arrives at her home, she sets down the jar and it is empty. End of answer.

One can see his audience scratching their heads at this "description" of the heavenly kingdom, just as I had. But in the instant of revelation that was my thought, I understood. The jar is like the head, filled with the seeds of thought and future actions. The woman's only concern is to get home. She is so one-pointed she doesn't even realize she is losing her cargo, and consequently the journey becomes easier the closer she gets to home, because her burden keeps lightening. She realizes it is empty at the same moment she arrives home, and this, says Jesus, is the kingdom of heaven.

As the Indian sage Patanjali said long ago in the *Yoga Sutra*, stopping the flow of thoughts while still retaining awareness causes the individual soul to be absorbed momentarily into the light of the Godhead, and this is the sense in which the parable explained itself to me in that brief vision. The main method prescribed for attaining this state is one-pointed concentration, symbolized in the story by the woman's single-mindedness.

The final part of the seamless vision was that it was *my* last seed, and then there was nothing. Before another thought could arise in my mind, in the midst of a great darkness and a great silence, the heavens opened above my head. In an instant I was flooded with light from above, light of the utmost whiteness and splendor, that quickly dissolved everything in its glory. The bliss I had experienced prior to this new revelation now paled to insignificance in an immensity of light that was also the purest love. As the truth of the situation dawned on me, the word "father" resounded in this heaven of light and I was taken up and absorbed by the unspeakable Godhead. No longer separate, there was neither an enjoyer nor a thing enjoyed. There was union. (Hearing the word "father" may well have been due to my having read from the Bible shortly beforehand; the objectless light, however, was pure, formless, sexless God—of that I have no doubt.)

This is a big claim to make, I know, and the reader may wish to add "suffers from delusions of grandeur" to my other sins. Yet even if this experience existed nowhere but within my own mind and has no reality outside of it, still it remains the single most important event of my life. Nothing at all can be compared to it, yet one feels compelled to make an attempt, however vain.

Some have asked me if this experience could have been "merely" a hallucination and therefore, by implication, unreal. I am forced to answer with a comparison: next to this state, ordinary reality is like a bad imitation, a knockoff, a cheap parlor trick in a grimy hotel, an eternally baited trap for the mind and senses. The Gnostics had this much right: we're trapped in bodies and we can't see our way out. The day-to-day reality we perceive is not an independent reality. It's all done with mirrors.

I have no idea how long I was in that glorious state, because time does not exist there, just as there is no "there" there. I came back to my senses in the morning as I awoke to find myself flat on my back on the hardwood floor. In utter amazement, I reviewed the events of the night just passed. Nearly as incredible as the experience I'd had was the fact that I was still on earth in a human body. Even though I had experienced something for which countless others had spent their whole lives searching and not often finding, in my immaturity I felt cheated. What kind of God, I reasoned in my best anthropomorphic fashion, would lift a person to a state like that only to drop him right back into the dark and cruel world, without so much as a fare-thee-well?

Would You Buy a Used Car from This Man?

The prevailing opinion among those who are most likely to know about such things is that marijuana is neither a psychedelic nor an entheogen, but rather a euphoriant. It certainly is that, but under the proper conditions, with proper concentration and, definitely, proper marijuana, the properties of the other categories can reveal themselves as well.

One fine afternoon in the summer of 1973 I found myself in a friend's living room sitting between two people, neither of whom I wanted to be sitting beside. We were watching a boring tennis match on television and smoking way too much Hawaiian marijuana. I was feeling trapped but was reluctant to leave because I didn't want to hurt the feelings of my host. So I sat there resenting everything.

The TV network broke for a commercial and a local ad came on. It was for an automobile dealership, filmed on location, and it was just awful. Loud, obnoxious, a real assault on the senses. The puffy salesman was standing among rows and rows of cars, pounding fenders and haranguing his viewers. I'd had it. Not having any polite means of escape I retreated inwardly. I closed my eyes and concentrated on the darkness, trying to blot out everything else.

Suddenly I seemed to be looking down into a black pit; nothing at all was visible, yet I had the sensation of depth. At the bottom of the pit a diamond light began to sparkle. It was beautifully white yet somehow clear at the same time, with a bluish tint at the edges. The light started to rise up like a fountain, a fountain of ephemeral diamonds. It was rising up inside of me, and I was watching it happen with utter clarity of vision. This was no daydream—it was more real than the scene I had just shut out.

In seconds the light hit my throat. I say "hit" because I actually felt something hit my throat from the inside. From there it quickly rose and hit my eyes, popping the lids open. Tears streamed down my face. I now found myself staring directly at the pudgy car salesman again, but he had changed. That is an understatement.

Standing in the middle of the car lot, slapping his palm on the fender of a big, shiny automobile, stood . . . a *god.* A genuine, bliss-radiating, jewel-dripping, crown-of-light-wearing, lavender-skinned god was looking right into my tear-streamed eyes and smiling the most beautiful, heart-warming smile imaginable. I'm not a believer in gods, mind you, but there he was, right there on the television. Standing in a used-car lot.

"That's right, I'm what you think I am. And I'm this, too," he said, slapping the fender again. "And I'm this fat guy selling cars. And I'm the two people you don't want to be sitting next to. And I'm the stupid, boring tennis match." His gaze intensified. "And I'm *you.* Don't forget that. And to me, this is all play. So relax, stop worrying about everything and enjoy yourself." Slap!

And that's exactly what I did.

Daniel

B. 1949

Librarian

Resides in Pittsburgh

Born in Newport News, Virginia, and raised in Richmond and Matthews County, Virginia

I Realized I Was Dead

A trip that changed my whole outlook took place during a Christmas ritual in 1969 at the College of William and Mary in Williamsburg, Virginia. I was a twenty-year-old college dropout at the time, visiting some friends there. I was in the throes of a spiritual crisis. Although I'd been raised Methodist, I'd gone through high school as a confirmed atheist. In college I found friends who shared my view, and we made it our mission to pull people away from Christianity to straighten them out. We actually pursued this with zeal.

About a week before this trip, it had suddenly hit me like a sledgehammer that we were doing exactly the same as we accused Christians of doing, proselytizing and converting. I was at a loss. If there was neither a God nor atheism to believe in, then what was there? The trip occurred right at the crux of this philosophical impasse.

There were six or seven of us hanging out together that evening. We shared some joints and a few of us took some Orange Sunshine, which was especially powerful acid in circulation at the time. After a while, somebody said he was going to the annual yule log ceremony and everyone just tagged along. It was an old traditional English custom in which a big log is burned to celebrate the old year passing and the new year coming in.

This was only the second time I'd ever taken LSD, and I was sliding. The religious issues on my mind were plaguing me and I was feeling nervous about a lot of unsettling things going on in my life. I'd just dropped out of Virginia Commonwealth University in Richmond. Having married when I was eighteen, I was now in the process of getting divorced—as were my parents. Making matters all the more interesting, I'd just come up A-1 for the draft. All of this was flooding in on me as the acid took hold. It may not have been such an opportune time to be experimenting with mind-bending chemicals, but, ironically, acid seemed the only stable force in the world at the time—or so I thought.

One of the guys in the group handed me a piece of silver Christmas tinsel, which enthralled me with the light flashing off of it and the trails when I waved it around. It became my anchor and focal point. We trooped out of the dorm to the ceremony, which was being held in a back hall of the oldest building on campus, the Wren Building, named for its designer, Christopher Wren. We filed in through the rear courtyard and suddenly there were far too many people there. I felt surrounded and very paranoid, as though they all knew what I was doing. I figured the drug was so powerful, they couldn't *not* see all the weird phenomena I was seeing. It just had to register somehow. Shapes were shifting and layers were coming off of things. The street lamps were emitting all manner of color through the dark December air. Everything was moving very, very slowly. Sounds had fallen about half an octave. I was dragged down by this general deceleration of the living universe.

As we'd entered the courtyard, everyone was handed a piece of holly with which we were supposed to touch the log and then throw it onto it when it was burning—a little rite that would bring you luck for the coming year. But instead of the holly, I was going to use my tinsel, which by now had taken on great significance. It was everything. My essence was in that piece of flimsy metallic glitter. It had become *me.* I'd been clutching it in my hand since it was first handed to me.

An electrical charge ran through the crowd as some students marched through with the yule log on their shoulders. As growing numbers of hyped-up students crammed into the courtyard, my agitation mounted. Laurie, a friend I was with, not my girlfriend, became concerned for me. She could see that I was getting very distraught, so she grabbed my other hand and fortunately never let go throughout the whole event.

The Christmas sermon commenced—exactly what I didn't want to hear. To get away from it, Laurie and I went in the back door of one of two halls that protruded into the courtyard. Everyone in the courtyard, which was packed enough, was now jamming into this small room, which was decked with portraits of colonial figures. There were probably two hundred college kids in there, but it seemed like thousands. They'd let far too many of us in. If there'd been a fire warden there, he would have prevented so large a swarm from entering.

Suddenly, the crush of bodies made quarters so tight that Laurie and I no longer had motor control of our own limbs. Our feet slid along as the throng moved us—a scary scenario no matter what condition you're in. People were in high spirits befitting the occasion, letting off steam at the end of the semester, gearing up for the holidays and the winter break. It was very noisy with laughter and shouting. Most of them didn't mind being sandwiched and slid around with no control over their own motion, but I was terrified.

Finally, the flow of the herd turned toward the yule log. People tossed their little holly sprigs onto the flames and then went out through a door at the other end of the room. As the crush moved me toward the log, I could feel the heat before I could see it. Then it was there in front of me. I'd envisioned throwing the tinsel on it and then watching it melt slowly and puddle down like mercury at the base of the fire. But that's not what happened. It vaporized instantly in the flames, and I went with it. I was gone.

There was nothing left inside of me. I absolutely panicked. I had to get out of the room. The crowd was going right, so I took off to the left, yanking Laurie along with me as I fought to get across the room. I could hear myself yelling, "Get me out of here! Get me out of here!" I was hoping there was a door on the other end to let us out, but there wasn't. So we had to go back the other way. We ended up on the porch where the sermon had been held. Then I blacked out. I don't remember what happened for about ten minutes. When I regained consciousness, I was sitting down on a cold brick sidewalk with all my cohorts standing over me, peering down as though to wonder, "What are we going to do with him?" The panic had subsided, but I was still very nervous. I let them take me wherever they were going to take me. I had no willpower to do anything for myself.

They brought me to a dorm room, where they lit up some joints and cigarettes. I sat on a bed, then stretched out and lay back in it. The only source of light was a plastic sphere with a multicolored cylinder inside. When the lightbulb within the cylinder heated up, a blade on the top rotated and bands of color were projected out through the faceted surface. Red, yellow, and blue streaks of light flashed through the room. They put on the first side of the Moody Blues album *In Search of the Lost Chord*, with the song "Legend of a Mind" that goes, "Timothy Leary's dead. Now he's on the outside, looking in." It was the perfect record for the moment. I lay in the bed, totally immobile. Then I suddenly started feeling very cold, and that's when the switch took place. Suddenly everything was okay. Another part of myself kicked in and told me, "It's all right."

At that moment, I noticed I was looking down on myself. I was up on the ceiling, floating above the room. I could see everyone else sitting in a circle on the floor, listening to the music. I saw myself lying on the bed, looking up at myself looking down at myself. It was uncanny. I realized I was dead. There was no other explanation. I was very, very cold. It was scary and strange at first. I was shivering as though I were outdoors in subzero weather without a coat on. I was dressed suitably, so it wasn't the elements that were freezing me. On the one hand, I had the strong physical sensation that I was cold, but on the other, I seemed to be without a physical body at all, which suggested that the coldness had nothing to do with my body, that it was something else altogether.

It was okay to be dead. The light was warm, even though I was feeling cold. I opened my eyes again and I was lying on the bed and everything was normal and all right. I knew then that the whole idea of a bad trip wasn't relevant. It just couldn't happen, because I had this previously untapped ability to disconnect and observe. We stayed for just the one album side, which they'd played expressly to calm me down.

Once I was settled down, we went for food, which I didn't particularly want, but it was fun and adventurous to go out and get it. Then it got late and time to go to bed. I was staying in a room in one of the men's dorms, crashing on the floor with a few blankets. There was no way I was going to go to sleep. My hosts put on all four sides of Pink Floyd's *Ummagumma*, a double album made for tripping, very long and slowly evolving. But what I really wanted to hear was some Bach, whose regularity and rhythmic qualities I craved. Suddenly I was hearing just that. As I drifted off to sleep, I heard the beautiful strains of Bach cantatas coming up through the floor into my brain. To this day, I don't know whether somebody in the dorm was actually playing Bach, or whether I'd conjured his exquisite sound.

I tripped all through the next day at a lower level, and the day after that I was back at work shelving library books. Colors were still shifting, almost forty-eight hours after I'd dropped the acid. I ended up shelving a whole truck of books by color, because I just couldn't read the call numbers.

This was the most transformative trip I've ever experienced. It even anchored my spiritual life by showing me that I had the capacity to remove my ego from harm's way by stepping aside and observing. It also cleared up my theological quandary by suggesting that the truth was much larger than a debate over the existence of a so-called god. The trip imparted the gift of acceptance. From then on, there were no rough rides on acid, and I was able to integrate with my often-glorious surroundings without panicking over the loss of self.

Dennis

B. 1946

Film producer, film-score composer, performing musician, journalist

Resides in Hong Kong

Raised in British Columbia

They Don't Show You All This on the Top of the Mountain Just to Destroy You on Your Way Down

I come from a Plymouth Brethren religious background in Vancouver, and spent some time in the Canadian navy. Both organizations are cut and dry about what's right and wrong and the rewards and penalties. The reason I survived the excesses of the Sixties was that those gears were in the mechanism.

At the height of acid, in 1967, when we were doing it for days at a time, my gang of friends developed a game. The aim was not to act gonzo and off the wall but to keep your cool while your head was out there where the psychic landscape was seriously askew. Like surfing the big waves at Wyomea, finesse and control were the key.

We were arrogant lads. We had long hair, played in a band, fancied ourselves good-looking. To play this game, you had to do the following: You had to get a date with a girl from the right side of town. Then you dropped as much acid as you thought you could handle, and drove over to pick her up. This meant greeting her dad and mom. You had to conduct that awful interview with the family before you took her to the movies, then for a burger and fries, and brought her home. No one was to know you were tripping, not even your date, who was a sort of placebo.

While the carpet may have been moving like a bevy of snakes, you had to deal with that bizarre and extended reality. You'd see flashes. Suddenly her mother's face would look molten. I'd often see people as animals. That's when I developed the animal prism through which I often see people. Looking at their faces, I could see under the skin the outlines of a specific animal they embodied. A lot of Canadian hockey players, for instance, are ox people. There are wolf people, sheep people, fish people, bird people.

The objective of the game was to see if you could a) manage all the decorum and politesse with all the distortion rippling around you, b) get all the way to home base with your date, and c) deliver her back home without her or her family ever having a clue of what your mind state was. If any of the unknowing found out, you lost the game, and, of course, all kinds of shit could happen.

How did we fare at this? Well, nobody exactly won the game. You were lucky if you got to first base with the girl. It was all a sophomoric exercise in manly endurance, really—a macho headtrip. We finally caught on that both the trip and the social interaction worked out much better when you and your date did the acid together.

In Vancouver I knew a beautiful Japanese girl named Shugomi, who worked in the travel industry and whose English was perfect. I really wanted to get at her, but it was a hard go. Finally, one night, I convinced her to go out. The opportunity to do acid came up and to my surprise, she was interested. We dropped it and all of a sudden this prim, conservative girl was wanton, wild, wide open to anything you wanted to do. Suddenly you had this beautiful, diminutive thing willing to do anything with sex, cook for you, whatever it was. I took her up to a canyon with a suspension bridge across it and she said she could see the connection between the moon and fish in the water five hundred feet below. We stocked up and went at it for days.

Soon afterward, she just left her job behind, which was very radical for a Japanese. She'd decided that I was the samurai that was supposed to find her and take her away. Today she's a successful sculptor and painter. She remains meticulous, infinitely polite, quintessentially Japanese, but with a twist, much of which came the night she dropped acid with me.

The one time I was ever shoved willy-nilly through the doors of perception was back in the fall of 1974. I'd come back to Canada from a great summer playing music on the French Riviera and other places in Europe, thinking I'd pick up a job real quick. The bubble economy back then made it possible to drop out and drop back in at will. But the times were changing. These were the days of the oil embargo. It was a grim Canadian fall and I was down to my last few hundred bucks. To my great annoyance, there was no work of any kind, which really surprised me. After a few weeks, it was starting to bite. I was close to thirty. My pack of chums was thinning down to a dowdy few willing to maintain the alternative, artistic lifestyle. Most were bailing out, seeking respectability.

I was at loose ends. The weather was getting cold. Nobody wanted me. I couldn't get a gig playing music or any other job. I wasn't seeing any women. A friend came over one night and offered me some shrooms. "Just leave 'em here." I said. "I don't want to do 'em tonight." A few days later, it was suddenly sunny and as a beautiful a fall day as you can get in North America. I thought, *This is the day.* I had no job interviews to go to. I was feeling a bit grim, but ready for something different, and ready to go it alone. It was always a group thing to trip when I was younger, all of us playing with the same toys. But I'd begun to deeply distrust communal consciousness, which meant nothing more than the lowest common denominator.

I always prepared myself for a trip, because I knew how it could bring me down. I lived in a comfortable but small attic apartment in Vancouver, the ocean in one direction, the mountains in the other. I decided to climb Grouse Mountain. I knew that mushrooms gave you physical energy and that it's great to burn it up and use it, so that your body is being cleansed as you undergo the experience. I fueled up on some good whole wheat bread and yogurt, then chanted *om manny pad may om* for a good hour before taking the shrooms. I really went at it. This was something I was going to do for *me.* It was eight in the morning, not eight at night, a new temporal venue away from the party scene.

An hour and a half later, the room was closing in on me. I can get quite claustrophobic. I used to work on the inside of huge oil burners, but finally had to quit, because it drove me nuts. My apartment was a perfectly friendly place to be, but the guy next door was dying of emphysema and his coughing spelled something ominous, and the wild Iranian girl downstairs was playing heavy metal with the volume all the way up. The bad mood was turning physical, so I decided to head out to Grouse Mountain.

As I was standing at a bus stop, I saw a huge billboard picturing jet-set travelers and inviting you to fly away to all these exotic places. At the foot of it, an old bag lady was pushing her load along the street. I took note of the contrast and thought the fantasy life I was living was the billboard, and reality the one walking. I made a mental note not to forget that these two images represented real extremes—and the likelihood was that the bag-lady reality was the one that would prevail. This wasn't depressing per se but a shot of neutral reality. By now I was feeling good in the fresh air. I boarded the bus that would take me to the foot of the mountain.

I had loads of energy streaming through me, so I hiked straight up. It was a pretty hard haul, but I went at it as though it were a walk in the park, not thinking about provisions and timing and the tricky bits along the way. About halfway up, I turned around to see the city laid out before me and sat down. After a little while, two deer came out through the trees. They looked over toward me and, strangely, walked over for a closer look. This was an odd bit of behavior for these animals, who would normally split right away at the sight of humans. I've spent a lot of time in the wilderness, hunting, camping, and, later, shooting documentaries, and I found this brazen confidence highly peculiar indeed.

Of course, the shrooms gave it cosmic significance. Looking at the deer and then down at the city with all its smoke and belch, I imagined that they were trying to tell me something: that I should never forget this juxtaposition no matter what I did, whatever road I chose. If you can retain this taste of primeval nature and the life force at its most stark and raw, you'll get through all the other shit more or less unscathed.

I kept right on going to the top of the tree line and then to the top of the mountain. By now, it was about four in the afternoon. The sun was westering. The city was way down below. At that altitude, it can get quite cold after dark and you can die of exposure. I took pause and thought, *This is exactly what it's like to be one of those holy men* I'd read about. *Whatever is going down there in the ant world, which every ant thinks is the meaning of it all, what's going on up here is the true meaning of it all and it always has been, if life has* any *meaning at all.*

The vista gave me a compelling perspective on the importance of my dreams and plans. I could see where I fit in the big scheme of things. I didn't mind that it didn't matter much if I succeeded or failed in the conventional success and material terms. This was an unexpected perspective to have, considering that I couldn't find work and was short of money. But I saw that the deer didn't need any money to be okay, nor did the mountain, the wind, or the sun.

Remember those deer, I told myself. *They were doing fine with or without the progress down below. They were doing fine before it even existed, and they'll continue to do fine, all things being equal and if the environment is left alone. These guys are doing fine eating their blueberries; lots of blueberries to eat up on the mountain here.*

The whole load of all my concerns about what I going to do with my life—scoring a job, finding a girlfriend, starting a family, making enough to support it—it all lifted away. In that moment, I also saw through the self-inflated importance of the hippie movement's insistence on *changing* everything, when it was so clear there was so much to leave alone and so much to gain from the act of leaving it alone.

The wind was picking up. I realized I had to get off the mountain. So I took off and literally ran the three or four miles down without stopping. It was like skiing without skis, hopping over the rocks, my balance attuned by the jolt to my consciousness I'd just received. There were some dodgy parts and no path in certain patches, where I grabbed branches and slid down the rocks, but I was incapable of a misstep that day.

No, today I cannot fall. Whatever has shown you this will take care of you all the way down. I was riding down this magic river where I couldn't make a mistake, because I was being held up by the spirit of the life force that had given me the revelation. It was as if the whole mountain face were alive, the rocks, the trees, everything. I understood that for this time frame, I'd be protected as long as I didn't do anything stupid. I felt part of an awesome primal hum, that I had a right to be here. *They don't show you all this up here just to destroy you on the way down.* The point was to get down there and make use of this knowledge, to reenergize my life and get on with things.

I got to the bottom in about forty-five minutes and noticed, to my surprise, that I still had loads of energy. So I kept running. I had a friend who lived over in Kitsalino, another five miles away over a major suspension bridge, and decided to hoof it on over to see him. I have a love of fish and chips, the English dish, that goes back to the days when my grandmother made it for me when I came home from my paper route. To this day, the one thing I can cook, for whatever it's worth, is world-class fish and chips, using her recipe. I had an overwhelming urge for the ancestral food, so I ran to an open-air fish market, bought a couple of flounders, and went over to my friend's place. Then I cooked the whole dinner, and we ate and had a great time playing guitar and talking. Then I went back to my apartment, which had been so enclosing, and fell into one of those beautiful sleeps that you're allowed to fall into at the end of a righteous day.

Oddly enough, the next day, when I went to see about a job in television as a writer and score composer, I got it right away. And getting that gig led to other things. A few weeks later, some friends moved to South America and rented me, for a mere seventy bucks a month, their oriental palace of a house on a five-acre spread. So the claustrophobic room suddenly disappeared. I moved up there and kept horses and hunted with my bow on the property. Soon I picked up the best documentary film work ever, which required living with the Indians for a while. In the course of that film work, I gave myself a little holiday in Hawaii and played some music down there, which led me to a ski resort in Europe, where I met a German competitive skier who ultimately became my wife. Suddenly there was enough money, work, and company.

Perhaps it was all luck, but I think that my awakening on the mountain fine-tuned my balance of energies, which sent out a signal that attracted the objects of my desires and ambitions into sharper focus. Much has happened since: travels all over the planet, divorces, disasters. But because of that mushroom experience, I never forgot what's really important.

Fiona

B. 1969

Ph.D. candidate, sociology; journalist for the musical press

Resides in London

Born and raised in the Cotswolds region of the U.K.

UNBRIDLED

I have a very good friend from Edinburgh named Lachlan. We used to do a lot of drugs together when I lived in Scotland. He's the sort of guy you can tell anything to, a real soul mate. One summer he came to visit me when I was staying in Brighton. One night, we went up clubbing in London at a place where LTJ Bukem was the resident deejay. We took loads of proper Pink Champagne (speed), and arrived back in Brighton at five in the morning. We sat on the beach for a bit and went to sleep for a few hours before getting up in the afternoon and going to a pub.

Lachlan is a bit odd. He's got mad-colored hair, and it seems like weird people attach themselves to him wherever he goes. We were sitting outside the pub and a man came up to us. He could tell we were on a comedown and said, "I've got something that will make you feel better." He had stacks of Ganesha blotter acid, imprinted with the elephant-headed Hindu god. Even though it was the last thing you need when you've been up all night clubbing, we bought some.

Lachlan had seen a television program about some gypsies living in a forest nearby and wanted to go and find them. So we drove over to the forest and took the acid and started walking through the trees until we came to a big chalk hill and sat down. It was boiling hot. This was the scorching summer we had a few years ago.

Lachlan started going on that he felt he didn't know me that well, that I held things back from him. He said that I was closed toward people. He kept chatting on and asking me questions. Half the time I wasn't really concentrating, so I kept saying, "What? Sorry, what did you say?," which got on his nerves. It was as if I were in a bubble and he couldn't get through it. I tried to tell him that I didn't keep things from him, that perhaps he knew all there was to know about me. Perhaps he just wished that there was more to me than what he knew.

"No, you really hold stuff back from me," he maintained. I had an image of myself with barriers built up around me, which made me quite paranoid.

There were some hares playing on a grassy bank nearby. I mentioned there was a lot of symbolism about hares, and he said, "Yeah, what is it about girls and hares?" This started a long discussion about Celtic mythology. Then we noted some rowan trees around us, which also have mythic significance. I think they're supposed to balance energy.

Thinking out loud, I said I wished I had a horse so I could jump over the fences and gallop up the hills. "What is it about girls and horses?" Lachlan asked, and just as he did, everything seemed to slip into place in my mind. The feelings of isolation intensified and took on a vivid context, as I started reliving a slice of my early childhood, as though I were back in my body as a seven-year-old.

I had really bad tonsillitis when I was little, which made me virtually deaf for about a year. I'd forgotten all about it. (I rang my mother later to confirm the veracity of the memory, and she said that during that time I couldn't hear her call me from five feet away.) I was a very serious little girl, always reading and letting my imagination run off. I couldn't make out what the other children were saying, so I didn't play with them. I flashed back to the feeling of being shunned by my classmates—and my grandmother telling me it wasn't polite to say "What?" that I should say "Pardon" instead.

I was horse mad when I was young, eventually buying a wild pony from the mountains in Wales and taming him in a day. When I was ill, I watched a children's television series based on the book *The Moon Stallion* about a blind girl that befriends a beautiful white stallion. The story is set in the Vale of the White Horse, the area in Wiltshire around the Uffington White Horse, a chalk figure of mysterious origin, which was carved out of the hill during the Middle Ages by the Saxons or the Celts. Some believe it relates to the cult of the Celtic horse goddess, Epona, and part of a massive system of zodiac-related markings that can be seen from the sky. The area is riddled with legends, and the moon stallion story takes place at the time of the Beltane Festival, a pagan spring celebration.

Unlike the ploughboys and horse whisperers who trained the horses, the blind girl didn't need a talisman or magic words to control the wild stallion. She had a natural gift with horses and could almost read their minds. I related to her because of her affinity with the animals, and because she was an oddball and excluded, as I'd been when I was deaf. As I was pouring all of this stuff out to Lachlan, I was bawling my eyes out. He just stared at me, unable to take it all in. "How can you forget that you were deaf?" he kept asking.

By this time it felt like hours had passed and it was time to move on. As I stood up, I looked across the valley, and saw that there was a horse carved out of the hill almost directly opposite us, about a mile away. We'd been sitting there for hours and somehow hadn't noticed it. I couldn't work out if it was real or a product of my equine-inspired reverie. Under my acid gaze, it was rearing up and pawing the ground impatiently, making sure I took notice. Lachlan thought I must have subconsciously clocked it and that's why I got on to the topic of horses. I wanted to walk across the valley and see it up close, but it was late in the day and we had to get back.

It had grown quite dark by now. Part of the area was owned by the Forestry Commission, which had planted it with a dark evergreen forest that you can't find your way out of. We kept getting lost. It was like a child's worst nightmare. Still in the regressed state of my childhood flashback, now I was really scared.

There were crows cawing and other noises, and it was pitch-black. I had to hang on to Lachlan, the scared little girl clinging to the big brave man. Eventually we found some steps and stumbled down them. It was very eerie descending into the valley. The air felt cold and damp. At the bottom, we emerged from the trees to find ourselves in the same place we'd been about two hours before. We'd just walked a complete circle. It was like Hansel and Gretel losing their way in the woods, only we hadn't left a breadcrumb trail behind us.

Normally I'm pretty much in control when I do drugs, like the mother checking to make sure that everyone is having a good time. But now I felt completely out of control. We'd done just what you weren't supposed to do on acid: you don't wander round a massive woodland at night. I was afraid we might be eaten by wolves or bears. We walked a couple of miles until we found a wall, which we followed along. Then we heard the sounds of traffic, so we knew we were near a road. Finally we found where we'd started from, and made it back to the car.

A few days later, I went back to the spot and saw that there was indeed a chalk horse in the valley, which has since become a very special place to me. The horse, about fifty meters tall, is on the road that leads to the Long Man of Wilmington, another chalk figure at the head of the Cuckmere Valley in Sussex.

I learned so many things about myself on that trip—not related to the wider world, but all about me and why I am how I am. I can't believe I'd actually forgotten those parts of me that the acid conjured up.

George

B. 1956

Author, editor, researcher

Resides in America

Born in Boston and raised in New Jersey

My Entheogenic Agenda

Psychedelic experiences have been an integral part of my life and work for over two decades. I've taken a range of substances, most of which I consider sacred and which do, in fact, have traditional religious uses. I've pursued an academic and professional career inquiring into the religious properties of these special plants and chemicals, which I prefer to call *entheogens,* a term that indicates their spiritual purpose. In the course of my research, I found that in the mythology of every religious tradition I am aware of, there's some magic plant that talks, heals, mystifies, intoxicates, or turns into fire, that either brings you to God, or gets you in a whole lot of trouble, or both, depending on the context.

Before describing my experiences, however, I'd like to say that I am somewhat reluctant to do so. I once asked a peyote shaman to talk about his visions and he declined, saying. "It would be like talking about making love with your beloved. Visions are private." The word *mystery,* like the word *mystic,* has the Greek root *mystes,* which means "to shut one's senses" or "to be silent about." In a conversation I had with world religion expert Huston Smith, he offered the metaphor of a ball floating in water as instructive of the eternal veil of mystery over entheogenic consciousness. Half of the ball is always submerged in water, no matter what side is up. Perhaps we should just accept that entheogens, to be effective, must remain underground, or kept "secret" to protect their sanctity.

Initiations, Early Breakthroughs

I did not get experientially involved in psychedelics until I was twenty-three, in my third year of college, at Columbia University in New York. In the fall of 1978 I took a course in the history of Indian Buddhism, which touched upon the role of the divine plant/god Soma as the inspiration for the Hindu religion. When it came time to write the take-home final, I had writer's block and decided that this would be a propitious time to have my first psychedelic mushroom experience. If religion can begin with such inspiration, I thought, I might better understand if I ingested myself. The experience, however, was uneventful.

My first real breakthrough occurred on my third trip, when I dropped acid with my girlfriend Kathyrn, who abstained. We went to the beach in Santa Cruz. Although I hadn't gotten off yet, it was really extraordinary playing around in tide pools with sea anemones, observing the way they'd flow with the water moving around them. When Kathryn had to go to class, I returned home with her, still feeling no real alteration of consciousness. She kept checking with me. "Did anything happen yet?" I said, "No, I don't notice anything." I lay down on the couch, where I could hear the water running as she showered.

Prompted by this aquatic audial cue, I remembered the water on the beach, and the next thing I knew—and it happened so quickly I didn't immediately register the change—I had a total identification with a sea anemone. I essentially turned into one. The walls of the apartment swished and swayed like the seaweed we'd seen in the tide pools, and everything was flowing like the ocean water there, to the sound of the shower and the music on the stereo. I was completely caught up in the flow of life that was, just a moment before, a concrete physicality.

Kathryn stuck her head out of the shower. "How ya doing? Anything happened yet?"

"No, not yet."

"What are you experiencing right now?"

"Well, I'm just a sea anemone in this tide pool, and everything is moving around like water." Suddenly I realized what was happening, and it blew me away. I'll never forget the laughter that roiled out of me.

That evening I had one of the most beautiful experiences in my life. I was sitting on the couch and noticed a field of energy with darting splinters of multicolored light around a houseplant. Then, while looking at a candle flame, tiny fragments of light began to sputter off the top like a fountain of fireworks, filling the room with sparkles of resplendent light. It was the first time on psychedelics that I cried for joy. Beholding such beauty, I felt I was being welcomed to an ineffable mystery, as though I'd finally come into contact with a spiritual dimension that gave hope to humanity. I'd been a disciplined student of yoga and meditation for two or three years, yet this was my first real gnosis of mystic reality. The plant's energy field was also around me, a tangible bioelectrical force that seemed to be the very energy of life itself. Was this Eros, orgone, or what is called in Asian philosophies Chi, Shakti, or kundalini?

When Kathryn came back from class, she sat next to me, I held her hand and looked into her face. A parade of visages flowed out, the faces of women from all times, young, old, beautiful, hideous. It's a hallucinatory phenomenon that I've experienced several times since. There are meditation techniques for staring into the face of a partner to trigger this effect, where the face goes through a series of fleeting masks, some recognizable, some imponderably complex in the geometry of intertwining inner cubes and outer space.

I felt a whole new dimension of love and compassion, a bioelectrical energy surrounding me, which was intensified by my interaction with Kathryn and the thought of people I loved. I felt blessed and exalted, both ecstatic and *enstatic. Ecstasy* connotes a separation of the soul from the body, while *enstasy* is an intense concentration in the present moment. Zen practice fosters a kind of enstatic liberation in which you drop all your illusions and petty desires and just be here now, whereas certain shamanic and yogic practices pursue an out-of-stasis, cosmic-travel sort of mysticism. I felt I was alternately undergoing both states. This was a real dawning for me. I was twenty-five.

In June 1981 I finally grokked the mystery of the Grateful Dead, when the Jerry Garcia Band came to Santa Cruz. Prior to that I just didn't get what the fuss and cult following was all about. My friend and I took Om Tabs, little yellow barrels of LSD, which we ingested by crushing them up and snorting them so we'd come on very quickly. We came on as the band was playing "Dear Prudence," which was so stirring, I thought that in five hundred years, it would be known as one of the mantras of our time. Garcia seemed to be watching himself play, as though he were channeling the music from another source. I saw a light coming in through the top of his head and going out through his fingers and through the emanations of his guitar, which created rainbow-colored vibrations that filled the auditorium in the same way my vision of the Roman candle had filled the room with splinters of light. I was transfixed.

A few months later I met a fellow in Brooklyn who had an old stash of acid made by Nick Sand, the Owsley protégé, whom Canadian officials alleged was making LSD "106 percent pure" prior to his arrest up there a few years ago. On September 18, 1981, I decided to pass up the Simon and Garfunkel concert in Central Park to drive up to Vermont and take some of this ultra-clean acid. I went for a walk in the forest.

After a short time, I looked up at a stand of white birch trees and they'd become animated by tree spirits. I don't know what else to call them. Instantly I could see the validity of shamanic ontology—the belief in the existence of spirits—but my first reaction was fear. They looked like those big stones on Easter Island, oblong, anthropomorphic beings with long eyes and long faces, morphing in and out of the trees. I've seen similar images in the Cycladic idols of ancient Crete. The beings seemed to be comprised of the trees' ethereal bodies.

I turned away, embarrassed and frightened. I felt like I was intruding. Then I looked at them again and the trees began to assume a menacing posture. They were horrifying. I looked away again, even more alarmed. I said to myself, *Stay calm. Why would these tree spirits be trying to scare me?* I approached this mystery with a sincere heart. *I know that I've wandered into their dimension uninvited, but I mean no harm, and whatever I learn from this adventure, I will use for the benefit of all.*

I looked back at them and they looked back at me. They looked puzzled too, as though scratching their chins, pondering some peculiar enigma. I turned away again and thought, *This is really strange. First they're trying to terrorize me and now they look as confounded as I am. This is a riot.* I looked up at the trees again and at that moment they started doing a goofy little dance, rocking back and forth and laughing, "Ho, ho, ho!" In that moment I got what I was supposed to get from this encounter: The world responds according to how you approach it. The mind and the world are one. This truth, difficult to discern in this gross dimension of reality, is easy to grok in the pure psychic space I was in. As soon as I comprehended this, I looked at them again and they'd disappeared.

In 1982 I entered the Divinity School at the University of Chicago, equipped with a good quantity of the then-legal and relatively unknown MDMA, which we called Adam. The purity of my supply had been established by a nuclear magnetic resonance test. I'd hoped to continue in the vein of Walter Pahnke's studies at Harvard: to scientifically demonstrate the religious value of psychedelic experiences. I naively thought that the Divinity School, with its purported interest in the nature of religion and in revitalizing the sacred, would be the right setting to explore these mystical states in a safe and controlled setting—and with a *legal* drug. But they're not interested in mystical experience at divinity schools. They're interested only in words and in history. If someone had a mystical vision a safe two thousand years ago and left some record of it, that might interest them. But mystical *experience,* the raw and vital force that gives rise to a religion, is too much for them to cram into their semantic, pseudoscientific endeavor to understand God.

I lost patience with the bureaucratic obstacles and decided to conduct the investigations on my own, without university auspices. I started doing quasi-formal (some more quasi than formal) naturalistic observational research, using MDMA and other entheogens. Using my apartment and the basement of the Episcopal House, my associates and I conducted several psychedelic trips for Divinity School students and other grad students and faculty, who thought they'd gone back in time to the experimental Los Angeles of the Fifties. I asked the experients to write a report, and many breakthrough experiences were recorded.

The university campus is surrounded on three sides by fierce ghettos. Hyde Park is one of the most racially tense places I've ever lived. My colleague and girlfriend was a striking blonde from California. Whenever we ventured outside the borders of the university, to a place called the Point, which juts out into Lake Michigan, she'd have to endure catcalls from the homeboys. It was usually a drag. But one time we walked out there with MDMA in our bloodstreams, and on this day, instead of the jeers our presence usually provoked, we attracted sincere, authentic communication. I'll never forget this afternoon, sitting on a stone wall by the lake. We engaged in more genuine, honest, profound, and meaningful conversations about the soul and the nature of God and joy and suffering than I had in any of my classes. We talked honestly about our own experiences, sharing a three-hour oasis of sanity with African-Americans who at first appeared dangerous, as though they might be Blackstone Rangers or members of another inner-city gang. They'd come over to hassle us, but then sensed our openness and sincerity and instead opened up themselves and had intimate exchanges with us. It was amazing! I believe their reaction was triggered by the fact that we were radiating love, peace, and acceptance—instead of fear, anger, and worry.

The encounter at the Point planted the idea that MDMA could help to improve race relations. With that potential use in mind, we handed it out to some people and went to the blues bars on the South Side, two in particular, Teresa's and the Checkerboard Lounge, where the crime rate is so high you have to be escorted in and out by a bouncer who carries a gun on his hip. You might be the only white person in there, and a lot of fear is generated until the music gets going, which tends to melt it down.

These clubs were our laboratories. We'd go there with people who'd ordinarily be afraid to go to that part of town. There was one fellow from Georgia, Luke, who struggled with the racial fear and animosity he'd inherited from his father, an unabashed bigot. Luke was terrified of going to the blues bars for fear of the locals. I pursuaded him to come one night and he had a breakthrough experience on MDMA. By the end of the night, Luke, myself, and our newfound black friends—all experimental subjects, high as kites—were wading knee-deep in Lake Michigan with our arms around each other, watching the sun rise, telling stories of what we'd learned and what we wished to forget.

What happened to MDMA is a real pity. Large illicit labs had sprung up seeking to capitalize on its not yet illegal status. It became widely known as the "love drug," which it is, but as greed and misinformation grew, this extremely valuable substance was lost to scientific or legal religious uses. Finally it was outlawed and its subtle profundity became obscured by hysteria on both sides. The Drug War really began to rage then, in the mid-Eighties. It was time for all of us who'd tasted such sacraments to lay low or be imprisoned.

Saved by the Belle

One evening in February 1983, I felt a strong urge to take LSD, even though I had an exam and a paper due. My girlfriend Lynn tried to dissuade me, but I insisted, "I really need to do this *tonight*" and took about four hundred micrograms. I followed a method I'd learned from the work of Stan Grof for internalizing the effects. The technique is to wear eye shades and headphones for the duration and to not interact with the outside world. Stan used a sequence of varying types of music, which would begin melodically, rise up to a crescendo with a cacophonous peak, and then gently ease off. These suites of edited sound went on for several hours to facilitate the dissolution of the ego and then a period of reintegration. The role of the sitter is to very gently keep the psychonaut focused on the internal process, which is often very difficult, because of natural resistance.

I came on suprisingly fast. My body began vibrating with an intense energy. I felt a sense of complete oneness with the entire planet, as though I'd experienced everything that ever happened all in one instant. There was an initial flash of unity, which then peeled off into a trip through the collective unconscious. I received images from ancient Egypt, China, and India, then fast-forwarded to modern life and memories of my own history, including a bizarre sequence in which I felt I was reliving my conception. At one point, when Lynn wasn't looking, I managed to get the eye shades off. I looked around and the whole apartment was a sea of green electromagnetic energy. The rug swelled up like a rough sea and at the end of each wave was a serpent looking back at me. I watched this for a while and then had the keenest feeling of being out of my body, floating in field of energy. It was incredibly exhilarating.

Then Lynn came back in and coaxed me back into staying with the eye shades and the music, which returned me into my body. After several hours, I felt oddly clear-headed and took off the eye shades and headphones, noticing that it was almost four in the morning, nine hours after I'd dropped. Lynn was sound asleep on the bed. It was extraordinarily quiet. I felt perfectly clear. *That was some trip,* I said to myself, figuring I'd come down. There was an uncanny stillness and purity of presence in the moment. I lit a candle and sat down on the floor to meditate. After a few moments I felt a tingling at the base of my spine, and in the next moment, my whole body was pulsing with new energy. I relaxed into this orgasmic vitality.

I rose to my feet, my body being moved by the energy into a sort of Indian temple dance similar to Tai Chi movements. Then my hands came up into a *hatha* prayer position, palm to palm in front of my heart. At that instant, the energy became very intense and all of a sudden the candle flame became the same size as me. There before me blazed the purest brightest white light composed of the same energy that was guiding my posture. I cried at the beauty of this vision. I felt so blessed to have seen what I felt was the energy of creation at its purest and highest vibration. This did not seem to be a hallucination, but a vision, a *darshan,* a glimpse of another plane.

As I relaxed and surrendered further, it became more intense and the light grew larger and closer to me. As it was about to engulf me entirely, I paused, thinking if it did, "I" would be gone. For now I felt it was enough just to see and know this light. At that moment, I vowed that my life's work would be to reveal this light to others. This was *the light. Let there be light.* At the moment I declined to be dissolved in it, it shrunk back, yellowing at the edges. Then it went down to about two feet high. I sat down for a few minutes of solemn and joyous meditation.

After a half hour I got up and sat in front of a floor-length mirror and looked at myself. My reflection flashed through a procession of changes I'd only seen happen in the faces of others. This was the first time I'd done it with my own mug. I saw the whole evolutionary history of humanity unfolding. Some images were bizarre, imponderable countenances. All the while my eyes remained constant, looking back at myself peacefully through the succession of faces, until the image in the mirror became a goat. A snout began to form. Horns came out of the head. The eyes yellowed.

There was a pause, as though this were the point of this part of the vision. I looked at the eyes and they were not mine anymore! I'd lost my observational capacity. I was utterly panic-stricken. I thought I'd lost my mind, that I'd gone completely, unexplorably insane forever. I was so terrified, I couldn't breathe. My terror released a torrent of harsh, swirling energy into the room. The nature of this dark force was like the cataclysm unleashed from the Ark of the Covenant in the movie *Raiders of the Lost Ark* at the moment Indiana Jones yells to his companion, "Don't look at it!" in order to keep them anchored to Earth and preserved from being ripped into oblivion. (The word *panic* originally connoted fears attributed to the mischief of the pagan god Pan. As my consciousness was overwhelmed by a kind of primordial power, I'd resonated with the archetype of Pan.)

I thought of screaming for help from my sleeping friend, but I could not muster the language and did not want to freeze the moment and get *really* caught in it. So, remembering the advice of my teachers, I tried to bring my mind to rest on a familiar, comforting image, a small statute of Buddha, which to me symbolized centered mindfulness. I prayed with more conviction than I knew I had to whatever was out there, *Please don't let me go crazy. I'll only be a burden on my family and friends. I'm here to help. Please don't let me go crazy.*

At that moment, there appeared before me a beautiful celestial being, hovering five feet off the floor. It looked like green Tara, a goddess of mercy and compassion comprised of green energy; or Kwan Yin, the Chinese Buddhist incarnation of the Hindu goddess of compassion. Natural-sized and sitting in a lotus position, she looked me right in the eye, smiled the most beatific smile and made a sweeping gesture with her left hand in a *mudra,* index finger and thumb touching lightly. All my fear passed with this blessing, and the terrible energy subsided. Then she made a gesture of acknowledgment for this moment. I returned to a state of crystal lucidity and peace in her presence, with the moonlight, the Buddha, and my sleeping companion enhancing the restfulness in the room. Then she turned her head a little and I saw an infinite row of faces trailing behind it. In a few seconds she was gone. I sobbed tears of joy.

I continue to savor the presence of such an angelic being, which often prompts me to ponder its ontological provenance. Feeling I'd reached a crest in my entheogenic vision guest, I did not take so high a dose of LSD for many years afterward.

Tryptamine Ventures

I turned my attention to botanical entheogens and began an exploration of psilocybin mushrooms and Amazonian ayahuasca. On mushrooms, I'd hear mythical beings, voices inside my head. I'd ask them who they were and they'd answer back teasingly, "We are who you came to see."

"Then show yourselves. I want to see you," I demanded.

"We're not going to show ourselves to you. We want you to remain a human being for a little while longer."

I took DMT a number of times. Once I attended a session for about ten people in Big Sur. When it was my turn, I took the pipe but balked at taking a full hit, and passed out, perhaps too afraid. I came to, and the leader was still there, standing over me. "No, you really need to take a hit," he said. So I did and fell back. My tongue curled up and pushed against the top of my mouth. Many *Pranayama* yoga breathing exercises are done with the tongue in this position. Then my mouth filled with the most exquisite tasting fluid, a sweet ambrosial nectar. The closest thing I've tasted in this reality is royal jelly, a special elixir made by bees to feed the queen bee, which is a real delicacy, very potent in amino and pantothenic acids, and a very expensive little drink. I drank it in, sucking it out of the top of my mouth. I told the leader about it, and he smiled and said, "*Amrita,*" which means in Sanskrit "non-death," referring to a nectar of immortality derived from the secretions of inner essences in occult yogic practice. (I'm not saying that this was *amrita* or that I am immortal; I'm merely reporting that a most delectable fluid filled my mouth. I tasted this ambrosia one other time, during a Tantric practice while I was on LSD.)

During one DMT trip, I had a vision of the state of planetary affairs. According to the cosmology of this revelation, more and more people were becoming aware of the dire state of things, and many would soon wake up to the essential divinity of the human being, but it might be too late. Humanity would wake up at the moment it would become extinct! Those souls who'd attained a certain level of integrity, enlightenment, and right conduct, the ones who lived their lives with respect for the whole of life and not just for their own petty parochial interests, would be transported to a dimension ahead, while the selfish, ignorant, greedy, exclusively materialistic, violent, less evolved ones would become like fodder or compost for a new generation of consciousness.

Of all the entheogens, ayahuasca has been the most somatic for me. You drink this stuff and it winds its way down into your gut like a lazy serpent, churns it all up and spews out the garbage. The native people who use it call it *la purga.* Purge it does. This sacrament won't become popular in dance clubs unless they make vomiting trendy. Often the purge comes out both ends. The puking and shitting will control recreational use better than the DEA ever could. The visions are also part of the purge. You give something up and get a vision in return.

The first time I took it was relatively uneventful except for the wonderfully deep vomiting and subsequent flashes of blue light in my forehead. The first few times, I took it in a circle with about twelve other intrepid explorers. The next day, I returned home and, though I was a novice, defeated an expert dart player two out of three times with my eyes closed. Shortly after that, I won a local golf championship, defeating a guy who'd won the previous eight years in a row.

On one occasion, I gathered with some friends in a circle in a high meadow overlooking the Pacific Ocean and took *pharmahuasca:* pharmaceutical harmine, harmaline, and DMT. This was a delicate first experiment, because you have to get the ratio correct. Too much harmine and harmaline and the nausea can be too intense; not enough and you fail to potentiate the DMT, which isn't active unless the harmaline blocks the MAO. Well, I did get it right and proceeded to lay on my back late at night, gazing at the stars. The entire sky became an enormous black panther, the stars points of light that shimmered like glistening black fur. I broke into a full joyous laughter at the mystery and the beauty of it all. How little we know about the soul's journey. We are so smug in our Western science, while the mystery is perhaps more actively pursued out on mountaintops or in forests by people beating drums and dancing around a fire.

Perhaps the most explicit trip I've had occurred when I smoked some DMT and felt like a rubber band pulled back as far as it could go. Just as it was about to snap, the tension in my head was so strong I thought it was going to explode. But then the rubber band was released and I was fired out of my body through a spinning tunnel. The interior walls were emblazoned with Aztec figures, chattering very fast, and I was rocketing out through them. Then I entered into a vast blackness where I saw many symbols of the world's religions.

A telepathic voice informed me there was an immortal component of the human being. It explained that the deathless soul was continually reborn in many different times and places and in many different bodies on a variety of planets over the course of a vast intergalactic adventure. Earth was, apparently, just one stopover in space, and a lifetime here was just an instant in the limitless span of time over the course of the immense enterprise of the soul's journey. I was quite impressed, and took a moment of reflection. I thought, *Okay, what's the point of all this? What does the soul's journey mean? Why do we keep getting reborn?*

So I posed the question "What's the point of all this?" and got this wonderful answer. Chiding me in a punitive but jocular tone, the voice said, "You idiot. Here I've just shown you that your soul is immortal, that you don't have to worry about dying, that the adventure is immense, and you still want to know what it *means?* It doesn't work like that. There is no meaning that you can put into words. The only thing that means anything is what's happening right now. Stop looking for ultimate meaning. Fix your attention on the present moment."

That was it. I thought it was beautiful, perhaps the key I'd been looking for in my many years of experiments. This trip was a reconciliation of two metaphysical poles. I'd just had an expansive vision of the continuous rebirth of planets and souls in a very big universe, and was then brought back full circle to the Now, which is all there ever really is.

Gregory

B. 1958

Computer consultant, publishing consultant

Resides in New York City

Raised in Los Angeles

Sinister Toys and the Internet of Souls

There have been three basic paths of spiritual discovery for me over the last ten years: psychedelics, psychoanalysis, and live rock 'n' roll music. I can't separate out the effects of these three forces, because they've all worked to inform each other. A psychedelic experience can be a signal to pay heed whether you're bracing yourself for an onslaught or truly allowing yourself to have an authentic, unpredictable emotional experience.

In particular, the tryptamine class of psychedelics has furnished the most downloadable—and worthwhile—data. At the outset, DMT was like another psychedelic merit badge I was keen, after reading McKenna, to test my wings on. In the beginning I didn't really have the right equipment. I was using an old hash-oil pipe, which was long in disuse due to that elixir's scarcity since the Seventies.

I'd tried this arcane device a few times, but never got much effect from the DMT powder I'd sprinkled into it, which was supposed to be heated up just right. Then one night, I was lying on my couch watching *L.A. Law,* a show I tuned into regularly back then. Out of boredom, I casually picked up the pipe, lit it without filling it anew, and took a full-fledged hit. Instantly I got extremely stoned and found myself completely caught up in the drama on the tube. The charge came primarily from the vocal tones of the actors, not the teleplay or the plot itself. Suddenly, the things they were saying to each other were *so* meaningful. For two minutes I was transfixed by the scene, which resonated with such titanic passion and heaviness that it blew me away.

The next time I did DMT, it was more deliberate. I took a hit and laid back on my couch to look at the brick wall in my Manhattan apartment. Suddenly it was no longer vertical but slanted like an Egyptian pyramid. A feeling of great antiquity filled the room. The bricks, no longer red but a tan yellow, elongated as though drawn by computer graphics.

Tryptamines began to literally talk to me shortly after a monumental mushroom trip. I decided that it was time for me to take a heroic dose of psilocybin. So I did it the way McKenna prescribed, five to seven grams, alone in silent darkness. I ate the shrooms at night and lay down on my bed.

After a while I began to see images from the time I was a little kid: jigsaw puzzles and toys and commercial packaging for the objects of early-childhood pop culture. A whole toy chest full of such artifacts flowed through my mind in living, early-Sixties Technicolor: the album cover for a record of cowboy songs, featuring a bunch of cowpokes near a chuck wagon, eating pork and beans round a campfire; board games such as Candyland, which represented a sort of alternative little wonderland; cereal boxes, such as Rice Krispies with the little snap, crackle, and pop elves; and Lucky Charms with their signature leprechauns, and candy, in particular the ribbon candy in my grandmother's candy closet. A large poster I had as a kid was reconstructed on my mindscreen, a drawing of an old-time baseball player writ large with vibrant red and green colors. I hadn't seen that picture since I was twelve or thirteen, and hadn't thought about it or had a mental image of it in twenty years. I'd rediscovered the sort of *Nutcracker Suite* universe of the four-year-old, which I would subsequently return to on a series of tryptamine trips.

I was resolutely inspired by this experience. At the time, I was just beginning to work creatively in my career, striving to figure out what I wanted to do in life. I saw that I didn't need to be in the jungle or any other atavistic environment to have a rich, creative wellspring for professional inspiration. The experience opened the gate to validating the material within my own psyche as the inspiration for my creative work. I knew then that I could take inspiration from the anacondas and jaguars and apparitions of my own subconscious, specifically, the mind of the child before acculturation, which is a trippy world indeed.

Sometime after this watershed moment in my personal development—and after additional forays into the candy-colored landscape of my youth—I was again lying on my couch after a toke on the DMT pipe, looking up at the ceiling, which had wooden beams. Soon there appeared an array of a hundred red-jacketed *Nutcracker Suite*–style wooden soldiers, one by one, kicking up their legs like the Rockettes. I thought, "Is this really as deep as it's going to get for me? Am I so stuck in my childhood, that no matter how intense my trip is, I'm going to see these toys?"

Just as I was thinking that, one of the soldiers in the column turned to face me and said, "What? You think there's more than this? You don't think this is enough? What are you waiting for? You just look at this now. This is what there is to see." I had to crack up at this admonishment. "Hey, you're right. Maybe I shouldn't expect to hallucinate more than a column of toy soldiers and have one of them talk to me. That's pretty good."

After that, I was visited, on my tryptamine excursions, by what I call "sinister toys," like Chucky in the *Child's Play* movies or the doll in the *Twilight Zone* that Telly Savalas tries to kill but which keeps coming back to taunt him. They're not necessarily malevolent, but they're not sweetness and light either. They give your psyche a kick in the ass.

If you could poll people who tripped, you'd probably find that among the top three key insights they've had was the notion/vision that "it's all connected." A butterfly flaps its wings in Malaysia and cities fall in Italy. Everything is related. I once had a mushroom trip in which I really thought I'd had a genuinely profound and original insight into the nature of connectedness and how it relates to human organizational structures, of which I identified two types.

One is modeled on hierarchy, like vegetative root systems and genetics and family trees. It's very useful for social control (in corporations, armies, etc.) to have somebody at the top who's in charge of a bunch of people, and each of those people are in charge of a bunch of people below them.

But then there's a whole other biological organization, the rhizome. Genetically identical mushrooms can grow a mile apart from each other, because they're connected underground through the mycelium, a web of barely visible fibers which grows for miles around. Hence, powerful organizations are around us all the time, though we aren't aware of them (e.g., the CIA, the Freemasons, Deadheads, gays in power), because they're very webby, mycelial, and sub-rosa. The network of people that I know is very powerful in spite of their getting things done in ways that aren't so overt and can't be modeled by strict traditional organizational principles.

So I tried out this thesis on a friend of mine, a whip-smart Yale graduate in deconstructionist literature. He came over to chat one evening and I laid out for him the one genuinely original idea that I had ever had on psychedelics, and he said, "Oh yeah, that's Gilles Deleuze, the French theoretician. He wrote about trees versus rhizomes in *A Thousand Plateaus.*" I'd gone to the trouble to write all this down and here it was already in a book somewhere. I thought that was hilarious. But then I shouldn't have been surprised. There are no original ideas, just fresh opportunities to grok what's already out there.

Networks of computers have always appealed to psychedelic people, because of this idea that "it's all connected." The World Wide Web is like a mushroom science fiction fantasy come true—this idea that some mind is stored in hard disks on computers all over the world, and that making your own connections between them can lead to pathways of knowledge that can't possibly be contained within one brain or one hard disk.

Of course, the original Web of Interconnectedness wasn't created with computers and can't be accessed by them either. During an ayahuasca trip in South America, for which I participated in the week-long preparation of the various botanical components by hand, I felt I'd tapped into the telepathic network of the ancient Mayans. It was if they'd strung their own private network through the atmosphere with invisible wires. The words "The Internet of Souls" came into my head. If the ayahuasceros knew how to type and use the computer, they'd be the most powerful guys on Earth. It's not likely that you're going to access the Logos—the Original Website—by your PC, though. The URL is too hard to find. Essentially, we're all scrambling around looking for that URL, but the Logos is always switching its server, so we're not likely to catch up with it.

While it's great to commune with the Internet of Souls via psychedelics, my belief in the wisdom of doing so alone is more confirmed than ever. Tripping socially can be a mine field. Last year, I did something that I don't like to do. I went on a group trip with six other people, some of whom didn't know some or all of the others. We all went to the weekend home of one of the seven and took huge combined doses of really great acid and Ecstasy. The house was way out in nature, where nobody was going to bother us. No cops or hillbillies were going to turn up around the bend and harsh our scene, so we figured we were safe. But we weren't safe among ourselves.

There was a sauna on the premises, which one of the guys went into. After a while, maybe forty-five minutes, we remembered he was in there and decided that we should go in and see how he was doing, since dehydration is always an issue with MDMA. Not that he was dancing in there—far from it. We opened up the door and saw him sitting there, spun out in a strong psychedelic reverie. We told him that maybe he should come out now. He wasn't responsive, so we pulled him out, and then he went all rubbery on us, declining to use his muscles and bones to hold himself upright. He'd bought into the idea that there was an emergency, but there was really nothing wrong with him. He was holding himself up just fine when we found him, and it wasn't like he'd been in there for over an hour. He picked up on our intense concern, and it turned him into a victim, like he really was a casualty who needed—and wanted—to be rescued.

So it turned into an "emergency," though none of us were in any position to drive him anywhere for help. A hospital would have been more than an hour away over rugged terrain. Nor did anybody really believe he needed any help. He was being a drama queen about the whole thing. The longer it went on, the more he believed that something terrible had transpired.

The host freaked, like "Oh my God, are we going to have some kind of fatality on my property?" He didn't know this guy. The fellow who'd brought him was being very coy and defensive, not wanting to take any responsibility for his friend, because he didn't want to harsh out his own scene. But the rest of us pressured him to intervene and take care of him. It was like *Twelve Angry Men*, an incredible psychodrama, forces of morality marshaled against indifference and countermorality. I just thought of all the time we were wasting, the incredible trip that we could have been having if we were just lying on the grass looking up at the stars.

The guy threw up a few times, but he was fine when the drugs wore off. He's a successful businessman.

The Zen philosophy of detachment holds that when you're meditating and begin to hallucinate, you needn't deny that you're seeing things that aren't there, but that you should recognize that it's a kind of cheap trick and not really the point of it all. It's very tempting to get attached to some psychedelic delusions, when you really ought to laugh at the cosmic joke being played on you and move on.

A good occasion for such advice was an early LSD trip at a Grateful Dead concert at Winterland in San Francisco in 1978. I'd gone with my oldest and best friend in the world, whom I'd known since I was ten. We were separated during the concert and I was by myself in the middle of the crowd, dancing. I thought I saw an attractive girl in front of me dancing sort of with me—as if she were only slyly looking at me, if at all, and performing for my sake. I got it into my head that there was a mutual seduction taking place without our actually looking at each other. I was doing my best to be sexy and hot, using all my best moves.

As the evening went on, I began to think that there were many people in the audience watching me and that I was turning everybody on. It was as though I were one long orgasm that was absolutely, irresistibly attractive to everyone around me. I could do no wrong. I was hot hot hot.

After the show ended, I located my friend, and said to him, "Why don't you just suck my cock, right here, right now?" Neither of us is gay. Neither of us have had any gay experiences. Nobody was going to be sucking anybody's cock. During the concert, he was about forty feet away from me, with hundreds of people between us, but I figured that he, along with throngs of others, had received the radiation of my heat, so deluded was I about my libidinal appeal.

It was only when he looked at me and said, "Maybe we should talk about this," that I realized that perhaps he wasn't so moved by my performance and that perhaps others had missed it as well.

Flower Force Field by Brooks Cole, digital composition,
© 2000, courtesy of the artist.

Henry Bass

B. 1934

Economist, maker of educational videos on labor relations

Resides in suburban Boston

Raised in Hopkinsville, Kentucky

This narrative, which takes place in the spring of 1963 in Cambridge, Massachusetts, was written in 1965 at the invitation of novelist Russell Banks, then editor of the Carolina Quarterly, *the literary magazine at the University of North Carolina, Chapel Hill, who was seeking such works for an issue devoted to LSD that never came to be. The story has been edited for this volume.*

HALLUCINATING THE HORROR OF SOBRIETY

Before I was thrown for a loop by the Big One, I had several psychedelic experiences, first with mescaline and later with "Heavenly Blue" morning glory seeds, over a period of about a year in the early Sixties. At the time I was a Harvard grad student, planning a conventional teaching career. To my friends I'd extolled these earlier experiences as mind-expanding, proudly parading my delusions of hell and freezing blizzards. (One of the reasons we took the drugs was to prove our "mescalinity" or that our minds were as tough and imaginative as the next guy's.)

During these trips, I never really *believed* the hallucinations, always retaining the knowledge of the real world one has when trying to awake from a nightmare. Many of the visual distortions were only slightly more profound than the ones that occur every day without drugs, for instance in the state just before sleep or when first waking, when thrown off balance, fatigued from overwork, or otherwise strained. But there was something extraordinary about some of the sensory aberrations that made them exceedingly more powerful than the everyday. The steady stream in which they came certainly had a subliminal impact. But there is more to it than this: it was the spell behind them. You know that one thing is sure, the psychedelic is in the saddle, not you. Once you've swallowed the potion, the bit is in your mouth and it's damn well going to stay there, come hell, snake pits, or icy snow, until the chemicals finally pass through your system hours later. When you wake up to this realization—time and again—as the drug comes on, it's sort of shattering and maddening.

Nothing remotely prepared me for the force of my final trip. One day, just before noon, I ingested some seeds with several friends, some who also partook and some who were there as observers or caretakers. We were all lounging around the Manor, the ironic name we'd given to a seedy but spacious apartment near Harvard's Dunster House. After a while, I became sick and vomited so copiously I worried that the effect might be lost. I went to my bedroom and lay down and relaxed with my nausea. Soon I found myself completely recovered, looking at a vast aquarium in the bottom of a glass of water. I remained fascinated with this for about an hour and then suddenly realized that what I was seeing had none of the attributes of a hallucination or dream. What I saw was indistinguishable from reality.

Excited, I ran into the kitchen and saw that someone had replaced my white Japanese lamp shades with bright red ones. This really shook me up, since it was *not* a hallucination. This was real, man! I felt completely sober and alert, while so many things around me had changed. My companions rushed in to see what all the ruckus was about, and I pointed out the red lamp shades, the wooden table that had become quartzlike, and all the new luster and colors that various things had taken on. I could see from the expressions on the faces around me that they did not see any metamorphosis in the lamp shades and moreover, didn't *want* to. A sour note! They were terribly disturbed at my insistence that everything had changed, that this time the drug had accomplished more than a dream. I could see they had no intention of joining me.

But I couldn't care less. Exuberant and overjoyed, I ran from the house, down the front steps, out into the street, flashed over three blocks in a matter of seconds, vaulted a fence, made a tremendously sprightly crossing of the highway—during which it seemed that traffic slowed and stopped so I could make my way—and ran over to the riverbank of the Charles to work out my ecstasy with somersaults on the grass.

I'd never experienced anything such as this. Even the insects sang for me in a multitudinous chorus. The range of my vision was vastly expanded. I could see hundreds and hundreds of miles into the heavens and tier upon tier of cumulus clouds. After an hour of such unbounded bliss, I was totally exhausted from the mad runnings of my mind, as it vaulted head over heels beyond the limits of ordinary human thought. I grew too tired to think. Indeed, I have never been more enervated. After a long day's mountain climb, I always had a reserve charge of energy to make the final scramble over the last few rocks to the summit. But now I was completely drained.

I struggled home and when I arrived, my companions greeted me with silence and dismay. I didn't have the tuck to follow their aimless conversation, but one of the fellows said something that disturbed me: "But what if he goes into a period of depression?" shaking his head in a sour, knowing way. It was getting dark out by now. Everyone looked glum and scared to death—they really thought I'd gone off my rocker. A dream gone bad, that was all right, but actually going over to the Other World, losing control over one's delusions, that was just a little too much for them. Looking back, if you'll permit me to interject a personal beef, they all seemed colossally square.

Those who had not taken the seeds started arguing over who should stay around and look after those who were high. Two women who'd taken the seeds, one of whom was my future wife, Sue, tried to convince us they were sober and could look after the rest of us. But I was hip to their tricks and wouldn't believe their story for a minute, though I learned later that I'd actually outsmarted myself—they actually *were* sober, having signed on as observers from the beginning.

I'd become depressed and scared by now. Someone had whispered the word "paranoid" and I became more so than I already was. I began to realize that I was losing my mind. The hallucinations had stopped long before. There were no more red lamp shades or quartz table or anything so wonderful or terrible. I knew exactly where I was. The ordinary world was all about me again and it was unbelievably pedestrian and sordid. On the phone, my friend David, an engineer, convinced me that my earlier notions of heaven-penetrating, heightened acuity were completely delusional.

My mind became ambiguous and disconnected. The more I tried to be logical, the more my thoughts raced wildly around, first this way and then that, in terrible confusion, scuffling their way long in the endless winding labyrinth of mental darkness. Definitions had lost their grasp. I simply could not connect one thing with another. Could I ever climb out of this chaos? No, I concluded. Of course not. How can one lose knowledge? How can you forget naked horror? Once unleashed it could never be conveniently suppressed again. I tossed angrily on the floor, frightened and disgusted at my fall from sanity.

Rational thought, practical functioning and living in the real world were all too dependent on simple common sense, which had vanished. I couldn't organize my thoughts and so I began to believe that I wouldn't even be able to solve the most elementary problems. How could I get up, even ever so slowly, walk into the kitchen, get a glass from the rack, turn on the faucet, pour myself a drink and lift the thirst-quenching water ever so slowly to my lips? How could I ever again walk to the john, carefully unbutton the fly on my Levi's, and piss into the toilet? Those Heavenly Blues were mind-expanding, all right. They had so broadened my consciousness that I was helpless in the most simple physical tasks. I honestly thought I was ready for the insane asylum.

But I had an even more dreadful and immediate concern. How could I ever get the moral courage to get through the night? I just didn't have the guts to face this naked abomination in the darkness until daybreak. If Sue had not agreed to stay with me until I got to sleep, I don't know how I would have made it. Even so, I didn't think I was going to endure it. There seemed to be no way out. I couldn't even give in. In facing the horror, you are not allowed failure or death. That is why it is Hell.

When one is insane, one cannot imagine being sane again. In the vast deserts of emptiness, one cannot visualize a gentle rain ever falling to the ground again. When your mind races madly in a thousand directions at once, you cannot imagine it ever becoming constrained enough to go from one small mental step to the next. The unconscious, once laid bare so blatantly, seems just too big for anyone to have any hope of getting a grip on it, least of all its now-former owner.

The conscious mind, however, is not as weak as it seems when it has been tied and etherized by the drug. You don't realize it at the time, but when it recovers its normal strength, it will deal with the unconscious only too well. The wild powers of the unconscious must be controlled to some extent, of course, but in this the conscious mind poses the danger of overkill in the execution of its duties.

By evening the next day I was by no means sober or happy, but I knew that I was going to be all right. By the third day, all the lit-upness and tumult I'd undergone was past history. In fact, too much of the spray I'd caught from the upswelling of my unconscious had been spilled and already evaporated.

I draw no moral from the experience. Psychedelics, I think, are dangerous. But I would not presume to tell another not to live dangerously. As a friend, I would caution him about the pitfalls, but I'd still harbor the secret wish that he would be enough of a daredevil to ignore my warning. I'd never invite anyone to risk his life climbing Everest without oxygen, though I would take cheer at the achievement of the feat. In the end, however, the psychedelics' threat to sanity may not be so great after all. Let's not sell the old conscious mind short in its ability to suppress both the beauty and the fury of the unconscious.

Herbie Greene

B. 1942

Rock-music-scene photographer; unofficial Grateful Dead photographer whose images of the band are collected in the book* Dead Days*; photographer for album covers of the Grateful Dead, the Jefferson Airplane, and other Bay Area rock bands

Resides in the San Francisco area

Born and raised on the West Coast

RIDE THE SNAKE AND BREAK ON THROUGH *OR* CRASHING THE SNAKE DANCE

When I was a kid, I read an article about peyote in *True,* an outdoorsman's magazine, which really stuck in my head and stirred my interest in mind-expanding drugs. Soon after I came to San Francisco in 1960 to study photography at City College, I was inspired by word jazz to turn on and emulate the beatniks. A while later, my communications professor was advocating the use of LSD in the classroom, saying it was great for your birthday, Christmas, any special occasion, making it even more of a holiday. Getting real acid was not so easy yet, though. There was some stuff around that was supposed to be acid, but it was actually belladonna on sugar cubes.

I finally got access to LSD soon after Leary came to town promoting all these environmental specifications you had to adhere to. He had us jumping through hoops, evolving through several bardo planes, and finally achieving clear white light, whatever *that* was. Most of us had no idea. Did a lightbulb turn on? I took acid about once a week for a while, trying to figure out why I wasn't attaining these heavily advertised higher states.

When the rock 'n' roll scene was just beginning to blossom in the Bay Area, I was a staff photographer at Joseph Magnin, a very kicky department store that was a purveyor of all the happening Carnaby Street fashion apparel. I started shooting all the major bands and personalities. I did the first Grateful Dead album cover and the covers for the first Airplane album and *Surrealistic Pillow*. In a collection for a traveling exhibition I compiled called *The Acid Age of San Francisco Rock,* you can see in the eyes that LSD was the common denominator. The Bay Area rock bands and the circle of artists around them constituted a small community. Without really knowing it at the time, we were fairly powerful people. Later I came to think of us as the role models for the Woodstock generation. We were having a really good time, making money and influencing people, and frequently taking acid.

My most memorable trip occurred on the day of the Human Be-in, a huge event in January 1967 that was held in the polo field in Golden Gate Park. It was a beautiful, clear blue day. All of a sudden, you looked around and there were twenty thousand jaunty fellow travelers around you. We had no idea there were so many of us. Ginsberg, Gary Snyder, Michael McClure, Leary, the Airplane, the Dead, and Big Brother showed up. It was a major cultural event, a real Gathering of the Tribes, as it had been billed.

I'd dropped some acid before heading over with two medium-format cameras. I had some trouble reading the light meter, but my pictures that day turned out great. Owsley had cooked up this White lightning acid with which he basically dosed the crowd. They were passing it out to virtually everyone. The ethos of LSD made a larger ripple through the universe that day. Chet Helms told me there were people showing up at the Avalon Ballroom that night who should not or ordinarily would not have been there. Their curiosity had been piqued by the acid and the day's events, and they'd come wandering in to see what the new scene was all about.

That evening, my wife, Maruska, and I had dinner with Albert, the manager of a notable rock band, who held out a handful of White Lightning and said, "Here, try these." When he left, Maruska and I headed up to our bedroom, a superstructure like a little railroad car at the top of the house, which was made of redwood and had an arched roof.

At the time, I was plagued by a series of car accidents in my life that I was thinking about constantly. During the same period I was also conscious of all this literature and lore about snakes, especially cobras. I'd read a short story about snakes in India, how they come around during floods and trap people in the hills and kill them; and also a piece in *National Geographic* about a village in the same country where betrothed girls must enter a cave and kiss a cobra to prove their fidelity. Apparently, most of the brides-to-be survived this, though many farmers in the region are fatally bitten by cobras while tending the fields. I equated the incidence of death by snakebite in India with car accident fatalities here in America, making the connection that stepping on a cobra there was an environmental danger parallel to getting hit by a car or smashing one up over here. These themes were always on the back burner of my mind in those days.

We went up the stairs and dropped the acid, and it came on immediately. I barely had time to light the incense and the candle, turn on the electric blanket, put Ravi Shankar on the turntable, get out of my clothes, and climb into bed with Maruska. All of a sudden, the room looked like an enchanted, glowing red cave. I leaned over and kissed Maruska and she became a cobra. That instant, I heard the screeching of car brakes and saw a shattered windshield before me. I went right through the ceiling. It was like I'd died and was transported somewhere else beyond. My spirit went straight up and one self died and I became my original self again. It was remarkable that in this single moment I simultaneously confronted the two thorns in my psyche that had been gnawing at me. I felt liberated and refreshed. I've never experienced anything like it.

Jack

B. 1947

College graduate, published author

Resides in America and abroad

Born in Manhattan

The Pinball Machine I Could Play without Feeding It Coins

In 1964 I'd smoked marijuana and knew about LSD but didn't know where to find it. You couldn't just go to the corner store and say, "Two hits of your best LSD, please." So I drove with a couple of friends up to Tim Leary's lair at Millbrook and tried to get admitted to the inner sanctum. After we'd been knocking on the front door for some time, Leary himself came down and told us that unless we brought some girls, we weren't going to get inside. I've always wondered if he told us that because he wanted our girls or because he didn't want us taking his. Anyway, there was no LSD for us that day, so I let it go for a while. Out of sight, out of mind.

In September 1965, I went off to a small university in eastern Pennsylvania to study pre-law. I was eighteen and out of place there. I identified with the subculture of discontents, the youth culture that was starting to flower. I wore Beatle boots and was one of the only guys with long hair, so I was threatened by the wrestlers and other jocks who hated "long-hairs," as we were called in the pre-hippie days. After a few weeks, I met the only two other people there who had any experience with drugs. One was a junior named Dan, a psych major, and the other was Malcolm, a freshman like me, who was a musician from Washington, D.C.

I met Malcolm first, and one day he and I bumped into Dan and we all went to the psych lab, where we got very stoned on pot in the surreal environment of all the rats and scientific equipment. Malcolm said he was going home for the weekend and would bring back some LSD. Sure enough, he came back with these tiny sugar cubes laced with two hundred fifty mics of LSD, which were covered in very fine aluminum foil. He said they'd come straight from the Neo-American Church, the Millbrook-based outfit launched by "Chief Boo Hoo" Art

Kleps, a former school psychologist. The cubes were about the size of a thumbnail, a distinctive trait that told you it was the genuine article.

I took acid about forty or fifty times, but more than half the time, there was little if any LSD in what I'd taken. It was usually speed or some other stuff. Only a few trips were rocketship rides, and my first was one of those.

Malcolm and I took these cubes on a warm Friday evening in early October, a really lush and lovely day with mostly clear skies. After an hour, as we strolled across campus to the university bookstore to get some Cokes, my vision all of a sudden became hypermagnified. Things that were really far away came right up in my face. Even though it was now getting dark, the grass was an unearthly shade of green. I could see each leaf on a tree, the remaining light of the dusk bouncing off of the various shapes in my visual field. We enjoyed this play of light and shadow for a couple of hours, at times convulsed with laughter, at other times deep inside our own psyches.

We walked into a college dance and it was totally absurd, completely strung out with weird social and mating games. We couldn't stay there, so we walked around campus some more. Then, I don't know if it was my idea or Malcolm's, but there was a water tower right in the center of the university, and we decided to climb it. It was about four or five stories high.

Now, I'm fairly acrophobic. Some people love the roller coaster. I'll go on it, but it's not my idea of a fun time. I don't particularly like heights, but I felt very brave under the influence of lysergic 25. So we climbed up all the way to the top of the water tower, which had a peaked roof, and lay down on our backs and looked at the clouds, the stars, the sky, and the universe.

I was totally transfixed. I felt like my body was down here while my mind was flying around in the universe, like I was traveling with the stars, that my energy was somehow merged with the universe, just by looking at it. I was captivated by the blackness of space and also by the light. At times the stars and the moon were so bright I thought it was daylight outside, but then I'd find it very, very dark. I wasn't capable of speaking, but we were probably telecommunicating with each other. I was totally conscious of all the mechanics of the physical world. I knew that if I wasn't careful, I could roll off and kill myself.

It got late and we wanted to leave, but we were both so high that we couldn't navigate the way. It was like opening the bay door of a jet plane in flight. The distance down was humongous. The ladder was enclosed in a girding, but we'd lost the ability to maneuver very well. We just weren't physically adept enough to get onto the damned ladder and then turn ourselves around to go down it. So we camped out up there for a significant amount of time.

The drug had made us feel warm for a while, but then, as the hours went on, we started to get cold, since we were dressed only for the afternoon temperatures. I was shivering. I knew that I had to leave, but I couldn't. It was horrific, but as soon as I let go of the urge to leave, I was perfectly content to sit up there and then I didn't feel cold or nervous or out of control. But then the wave would return—*Gee, it's getting late and we really should leave. It's kind of kind of weird being up here.* It wasn't that we had to worry about being caught and getting in trouble. Nobody knew that we were tripping, and we were so high up that nobody could see us. It's just that we didn't want to stay up there *forever.*

There were times when the connection of the mind to the physic was lost. (I remember peeing on acid and not being able to feel it, having to put my hand there.) We wanted to get back down to earth. It seemed like hours passed. The moments of pleasure dwindled and the moments of being scared about loss of control increased. I was becoming frustrated and upset. Finally, I crawled to the ladder and Malcolm followed, but we went down face first! It seemed like it took us hours to get down, though it may have been just five or ten minutes.

When we finally got down to the ground, I hugged and kissed the earth, feeling like *Oh, my god, I fucking did it. I'm back to Earth!* We stayed at the foot of the ladder until daylight. I slept there until it started to get light and then went back to my dorm room.

I smoked DMT only once, in 1967, and it was the most sensorially explosive experience I've ever had in my life.

I'd driven to Brooklyn from Pennsylvania with a friend named Jeffrey to visit someone who lived in a little commune. In one room there was a bunch of people playing music and in another they were passing around what I thought was a hash pipe. Jeffrey and I walked in and sat down in the circle and the pipe came up to me and I took a big hit. It tasted like plastic, like I was smoking a phonograph record. "This ain't hash," I thought. I passed the pipe along and asked what it was.

"DMT."

I asked what that was.

"Haven't you heard of DMT?"

"Isn't that the smokable stuff like short-acting acid?"

The pipe came around again and this time I took a smaller hit, but I was already having mild sensations. I passed the pipe to the person sitting next to me and then all of a sudden I looked down at my feet and my legs extended and opened out like a telescope as I was propelled upward. As my body started rising, my feet got smaller and smaller.

I went through the ceiling of the apartment and into the apartment above us, saw the people there, went through that ceiling, then through the roof of the building, all the while able to see my feet, which extended way down below me. I continued rising up and the building got smaller and smaller. Finally I lost sight of my feet and saw the Earth below and then the classic camera-eye view from the early satellite launchings with the various stages of the spacecraft decoupling and segments dropping off, as the Earth continued getting smaller. I was going up up up up up up up up into the stars, and then I saw the planets and the whole deal. I was blissful.

Then Jeffrey said, "Come on, come on, we gotta go."

"Where?"

"We're going into Manhattan."

"Who's driving?"

"I am," he said.

"Did you smoke any of that shit?"

"No, man, I didn't smoke any of that shit. They told me it was DMT."

So I got into the passenger seat of his Volvo, and my friend Carl, a black guy, got in the back. We drove across the Manhattan Bridge, which is enclosed with girders. I felt as if I were in a tube: back in telescope mode, but this time moving downward. I just held on to my seat, too afraid to say anything, thinking that we were headed straight down into a pit.

After a little while I got concerned and asked Jeffrey, "Are you all right driving?"

"Oh yeah, fine."

I thought, "How the fuck could this guy be driving? We're going straight down." We made it across the bridge and drove around on the streets of New York. I was very quiet, completely lost inside this DMT experience. When we got to our destination, I had trouble walking. My feet felt alternately leaden and bouncy. I must have been a peculiar sight. Jeffrey and Carl were looking at me like I was nuts. I didn't know where we were going or what was happening.

We went to an apartment on the top floor of a big building on the Upper West Side, the sort I call "grandma buildings," because they smell like the little old ladies that used to live there. We opened up the door and as soon as I walked in, the light hit me and I got perfectly straight and everything returned to normal.

My final acid trip, in May 1967, was the only one in which I lost the ability to know the difference between what was real and what was induced hallucination.

By this time, I'd been thrown out of school and was living with a girl named Emily, who ran a coffeehouse where famous folksingers often performed from 1965 to 1967. The university kicked me out when I was in my sophomore year for being a nutcase and not studying. It was like "You're fired/I quit." Emily had a nice apartment and she ironed my shirts and took good care of me, so I moved in with her.

I had some Sandoz acid in 125-mic vials. We used to split them. That's how strong this shit was. We'd take 62½ mics of the real stuff and get a great ride from it, much better than from the 250- or 500-mic double-O gelatin caps. Sometimes we got five 100-mic vials for about twenty-five bucks each and split them between a bunch of people. They came in little glass vials with two pieces of plastic at the top, which you'd snap off without breaking the glass in order to drink the liquid.

I had a friend named Bill who worked on the printing press of a newspaper. He had some friends who were going to Ocean Beach, Maryland, for the weekend, so we decided to drive there to meet up with them when he got off work just after midnight. Bill picked me up in his Austin Healy 3000 and we left Pennsylvania around one in the morning. I'd packed two 125-mic vials and some pot with me. He was ready to down the acid right away, but I said, "No way. We're not doing anything until we get there." I was smart enough to realize that if we got stoned here, we weren't going to make it there.

We arrived in Ocean Beach at around four in the morning, but we couldn't find the people we were supposed to hook up with, so we found an all-night diner and sat down. We were hungry, so we ordered some breakfast. While we were sitting there, some other freaks came around, two couples with the look and the garb: obvious stoners. In those days, there were still very few people who had long hair, so you could spot a freak instantly. They sat down near us and we started talking.

"Do you have anywhere to stay?" one of them asked.

"No."

"You're welcome to come back to our house and stay there."

So we went back to their house and slept on the floor. We got up around nine and went down to the beach to try to reconnoiter the whereabouts of Bill's friends. Bill kept pestering me, "Let's take the acid, let's take the acid." But I said, "Listen, Bill. Just hang on. Let's find your friends first. You're the guy who's supposedly leading us around here, so let me dose myself and then, when you find them, you're welcome to take yours." I knew that if we didn't find these people, I'd need someone to lead me around. I had a feeling that this was going to be a major experience, and that's probably why it was. I opened up my vial and swallowed the whole thing. It was the only time I ever took a whole vial myself.

We walked around on the beach. It was midmorning, starting to get warm. We sat down on a blanket by the ocean, and the acid started coming on very heavily. Still no sign of Bill's friends. He kept bugging me. "Here, smoke a joint." I threw him a bone. "I'm not giving you nothing more until we know that we have a place to stay." So I let him get high on the pot I'd brought, which he eagerly toked up.

All of a sudden I was transported to never-never land, a deep dark place where everybody was a bug with insect faces, antennae coming out of their heads and all this dripping and masticating going on with their mouths. I looked at a clock and it turned into a Magritte painting. Buildings were flowing into other buildings. I started raving, going nuts. Bill continued to bother me for the acid, but I still wouldn't give it to him. I knew that I was getting too far out and that I needed somebody to mind the store and get us to our ultimate destination. By now I wanted to get back to Pennsylvania. The sun was hot. It was about seventy-five but felt like a zillion degrees.

I went up on the boardwalk and into an amusement arcade. I didn't have to put any money in the pinball machine; it played anyway. Everywhere I looked it was either heaven or hell. People were either angels or fairy-god people, or they were gruesome things out of Dante's *Inferno,* snakes, beetles, spiders, crawly things of all kinds. Everybody looked like an invertebrate: Bill and all the tourists on the beach and on the boardwalk. The angelic ones were nice insects such as ladybugs, while others were horrid things with loads of spindly hairy legs. Snakeheads were bobbing around every corner.

I was *gone.* It was about three hours of grisly horror. I was so distracted by the ghastliness of it all that I didn't have time to notice how scared I was. I thought this metamorphosed world was the reality. I was screaming and yelling and jumping around while Bill tried to maintain me.

Strangely enough, considering the state *I* was in, he still wanted the acid I had in my pocket. I guess he figured that just because I was flipping out didn't mean that he would, since, after all, the acid's quality wasn't in question. Finally I said, "Okay, get me back home and I'll let you get high." So we got into the car and started driving back and got stuck in a big construction-related traffic jam trying to leave Ocean City. By now, it was about one in the afternoon.

His car was old and the carpeting was very disheveled, so I was seeing snakes on the floor and all the dials across the dashboard were turning into little bugs. I was yelling and struggling to jump out of the car. Bill buckled me in, but I kept getting loose and jumping out until he figured out a way to tie me in that I couldn't figure a way out of.

The traffic finally started flowing and we started driving. The top was down and my eyes were burning up from the brightness of the sun. I'd forgotten my fucking sunglasses. "Look, I can't take it." I said. "I'm going blind. I gotta get it dark, gotta get it dark." So Bill stopped the car and pulled up the top and started driving again. But he hadn't secured it properly and just as he reached sixty-five miles an hour, it flew off—gone, finished, down the highway. I screamed.

The drive back to Pennsylvania was one of the most gruesome experiences I can ever remember. Bill was mad at me because I still wouldn't dose him. It was hot. The wind was blowing in my face. The light was stinging my eyes. I was out of my mind, horrified by these hideous visions I kept seeing. Sometimes the trip would get very mellow and I'd see very blissful things. I'd imagine that everything was fine and teleport myself back to high school in New York, my first trip with Malcolm, home in Pennsylvania. Then it would switch back to the bug people and the horror. It was really a miserable, miserable experience.

When we got back to town, Bill dropped me off and I crawled up the stairs to Emily's apartment, which was full of people. Often she'd pick people up off the street and feed them and take care of them for a while. Everyone took a gander at me. I looked like I was from outer space, frazzled and sunburned, my curly hair sticking out of my head.

"Put me in the bathtub," I said, and headed off to the bathroom. I took baths to bring myself down or calm myself when I needed to. I took off all my clothes and got into the water and stayed there for three hours until I got myself back together. When I got out of the tub, it was ten at night, about twelve hours after I'd dropped. I looked at my eyes in the mirror and saw that there was no color in them. The pupils were still huge and the irises were white from all the sun I'd absorbed. The brown didn't return to my irises until days later. I had to wear sunglasses even at night for a while.

At that time in my life, I was much more inclined to see the dark side of humanity than experience the cosmic consciousness I did during the good trips I'd had earlier. After leaving school, I felt like an outsider. When I was still enrolled, I was a discontent, but I belonged to SDS and various subversive enterprises. Now I didn't belong to anything. I'd stepped away from my family and lost a lot of friends. I went off into the abyss because I was disconnected, on the road to nowhere.

I never took LSD again. I decided, "Okay, fine. I've done what I wanted to do." I'd finally had the trip I'd always wanted to take, one with authentic, sustained hallucinations. I'd seen flashes of this and that, but I'd never had that ultimate experience of seeing things that weren't there and not knowing the difference.

James

B. 1946

International civil servant

Resides in Southeast Asia

Born and raised in Australia

Tripping Down Under

I tripped for the first time in Sydney when I was twenty-three, in 1969. I was working as a teacher at the time, having just completed an M.A. in English literature. I was turned on at a youth retreat set up by a famous liberal pastor, which, for all its wholesome programs and good intentions, gradually became a drug den. One night a guy walked in with a basket full of tickets: 250-mic dots of LSD on blotting paper. I went with two friends to King's Cross to drop the acid and bop around to the clubs and bars. We were freaks with hair down to our shoulders, sandals, bright shirts, and outrageous gear from op (opportunity or thrift) shops.

The university bars were more tolerant than your average Australian poofter-bashing (*poofter* is pejorative Down Under for homosexual) bars, where, if you walked in looking like a long-haired hippie, you'd probably get picked on by the time you'd ordered your first beer, if not before. Naturally enough, it was the gay bars that became the most reliable respite from that. You might have to contend with aging queers who were chasing the boys, but if you weren't into that, they would leave you alone and you could still move comfortably in this hip milieu. Moreover, the gay blokes were quite good fun. They tended to be very social and know a lot about things, being in the *demimonde,* so they were nonjudgmental and often into grass and acid.

I had my first hallucinations that night. Cars were stretching in long, colorful streaks. As they drove past, perfectly normal automobiles would appear like crumpled wrecks, or as though their bodies were out of alignment with their chassis. Then there were the facial distortions on people whose outstanding features would balloon completely out of natural proportion. If a chap had a slightly prominent forehead, it would go totally primitive and he'd start to look like something from Easter Island. Somebody with a slightly stooped back would take on the manner of Quasimodo.

People's eyes struck me. When there was eye contact, it was as though my own eyes were imprinted with an indelible frame of that person's glance. When you're walking on the street you see a lot of people, but you usually come out of it like you haven't really seen anybody. You can mark an encounter, however, by exchanging what I call one frame of eye contact, like "I've got you, you've got me." For me this sort of connection on acid through a mutually acknowledged look was a way of walking in a godly space. In those brief flashes I could establish everything about the person. It was very communicative, and it confirmed for me that no encounter was accidental. Ever since then, I've had a deep sensitivity for fleeting exchanges of soul matter through this sort of laser-stream eye contact. If you trusted the people you were tripping with, it usually put you on an ice cream kind of trip that was breathtakingly sensual. You could look into the face of your friend and get this flickering gleam of interlocking rapport that moved the friendship to a higher level.

That first LSD trip ended beatifically. We soared all night, gazing out over the Lane Cove part of the harbor from a friend's apartment behind King's Cross, watching the sun come up and listening to Crosby, Stills and Nash, and Van Morrison's "Brand New Day" from the *Moondance* album.

Those first trips in Sydney evoked "Itchycoo Park," the psychedelic wonderland celebrated in the Small Faces' song. Nine-to-five reality could start to drip like a Salvador Dali clock or exude colors that you hadn't noticed before. In the beginning, there was a delight in the surreal, no shock. I'd see, say, a whole facial embossment in a billowing curtain, and exclaim, "Wow! Do *you* see that?"

Then there were the auditory hallucinations. I'd hear a line from the voice of my brother in Melbourne, or a snatch of a joke, voices with no acoustical reality. In the midst of the crack, I'd recount these extremely apposite bits of mad or brilliant sayings for my mates and get a new reaction to the quip, which would set off new cycles of laughter and delight.

There was this tremendous sense that amid all these squares out there laboring along, immersed in their conventional reality, you had this bloody gold mine of a million realities in each grain of sand—Blake's grain of sand. Acid's ability to zap you into that was like uncovering a secret revelation or discovering the Holy Grail. I was grateful for it. It would have been terrible to have missed out on this! You look at ordinary things, like a tree in a park, and it would stand there and just declare itself to you. Acid imbued all things natural with an awesome sanctity.

Back in the early Seventies, it became a regular number to get together on weekends in the summertime and get ripped by the sea. On

Friday nights, a group of us would go down to the Hundred Mile Beach in eastern Victoria, close to the southeast corner of the Australian continent, looking out upon the Pacific Ocean to one side and the Southern Ocean to the other. There were cliffs and beaches with nobody around. We'd drive along the sand dunes, pull up into a cozy lee shore, and lug loads of food, coffee, and good booze, and set them down on blankets on the beach. Then we'd light a big fire and drop acid, running off to swim or explore the shoreline.

We got together in jam sessions, playing guitars, flutes, violins, and Christ knows what. I played a guitar and once when I strummed the strings, I looked up in the sky and saw that the stars were dancing in vibration to the sound. It was like watching the graphic display monitor on a soundboard in a recording studio. The stars were literally moving in direct resonance to the chords I was strumming and the notes I was picking.

It was really something going into rock pools and looking at starfish and periwinkles and such in the summertime with the sunlight so bright, the sky like a strip of blue plastic billowing in the wind, and the water so alive and sparkling. My peripheral vision on acid often made reality flutter, while the details of things, like seashells, would seem to be in microscopic focus.

One moonlit night the sea was a multitude of beings, semiaquatic creatures somewhere between natural beasts like penguins, and semimonsters from Greek mythology—those half-men, half-fish, Poseidon-type characters. The moonlight and waves built up an undulating oceanic quilt over the surface of the sea. I looked around at the rocks in the moonlight and then out to sea again, and there they were, millions of these creatures teeming in the surf. I turned to my friend Roger and asked, "Can you see those creatures in the sea?" He nodded and whispered, "There are millions of them, man. I hope they haven't noticed us," and we started giggling softly.

It was a beautiful feeling, the pulsations of the natural world. Nothing *wasn't* alive, even rocks. I'd press them in my hand and they'd feel only faintly solid, as though covered in a skin, not a cold dead thing at all, but something with a bit of give in it. At times I could even feel them humming, purring. It was the same with picking up sand and letting it run through your hands. Sand normally seems utterly inanimate, but in this state, it seemed to possess some kind of power, as though it weren't just falling but alive and in motion.

On acid it was possible to have an extraterrestrial level of engagement. If you start to relate to someone, the ego defenses can fall away completely. If it goes the other way, you can build a wall that's ridiculously high. But when the walls came down, it was a joyous thing. There'd be a shock of recognition on each other's faces for the karmic connection that went beyond the moment, beyond instantiation, right back to the rocks and the molecules dancing inside them. Acid made it possible to feel total love and generosity and tolerance, and the appreciation that these things could arise, that you could enthrall yourself in being.

There was one trip in Melbourne with my wife-to-be, Mary, and George, a friend who'd just come in from South Africa, which demonstrated acid's soul-connecting properties. George hit it off really well with Mary, who was normally much more reluctant than I was to make new friends. If the vibes are right, I can make friends with someone in the first two sentences of exchange. She was much more cautious, even paranoid, on acid.

It was a winter's night and we had a fire going. After a while, I witnessed this band of colors bringing Mary and George together. It was very tangible, a palpable field of mutual reciprocity. It was such an affirmation to me that people, through the agency of this drug, could immerse themselves in each other so deeply. I was delighted that such a rapport between human beings was possible, particularly between people who were close to me. It was a bit like the scene in Roger Vadim's *Barbarella* in which Jane Fonda's sex-bomb character soared to transcarnal heights of interpersonal communication when she touched palms with a handsome young man from an advanced civilization.

When I took acid with my good friends, we swam, we had baths together, we sat around nude, and there'd be the occasional screw. It was fine and acceptable whether it was right there in the room or elsewhere. It wasn't like bolting into a room and banging away. The vibrations would be flowing, people would feel good toward each other, sometimes a guy and his wife or girlfriend, sometimes someone else's wife or girlfriend. It wasn't a regular feature, but an unconventional occasional outcome when the vibrations were good in the group as a whole.

A couple would be doing a bit of kissing and petting and we'd all get into something else and then look around and find them at it. That was fine. We didn't stand there gawking at them. We felt discreet and got on with what we were doing. There were no hang-up reactions like "We don't fuck in public." If people were happy and really into each other, it was like a God-given gift that they should do it then and there. "So Sally and Tom are getting it on. Great, something's worked out." Getting laid wasn't the goal of the trip, but when it occurred it was usually for good sweet reason.

Of course there were some bad trips. I didn't have any worth remembering, but I'd witnessed several bummers, when somebody got into bad waters, which could be potentially destructive to the group dynamic, not to mention the raw, tender psyches of the trippers. It was hard work to keep the bad tripper from getting into a complete mess and upsetting everyone else. That's the mixed blessing of doing it in groups. At least when you trip alone, you've only got yourself to deal with.

On one trip, Julie, the wife of Gary, a buddy of mine, thought she was going to chew her teeth out. It was Gary and Julie's first trip and I was there with them along with a mutual friend named Alan. She had false teeth and felt that she couldn't get her bite right. She got into this rather morbid depression about it, and it was very difficult to distract her out of it. Then she wouldn't talk to anyone, because she adamantly believed we were all trying to deceive her that she *hadn't* eaten her teeth, ground them to nothing. She became increasingly distressed and psychotic, which made the rest of us feel very uneasy.

Alan was trying to hold her hand and pull her out of it. Eventually she responded to this by going into one of those total love trips. She expected him to screw her, and he didn't want to in part because she was married to his friend. Getting all this attention from Alan, she thought she really loved *him* and that Gary wasn't doing enough to come to her rescue, but Gary was on his first trip too, desperately struggling to stay afloat himself. He was doing all right, but didn't know how to deal with all this. So Alan, being more experienced, got pulled in to helping out, and this led to a love overture that he couldn't reciprocate, either morally or physically. She wanted the cosmic orgasm. "Let's do it, Alan. Let's embrace each other."

When Alan didn't respond as she wanted, she turned on him, all betrayed. "You don't want me. I'm not attractive to you." That led to another twist in the path, in which she felt rejected and didn't want to talk to anybody. She wasn't going to eat or move from the spot. She was just going to stand there until Hell's gate opened. It was a pretty exasperating trip for all concerned.

Hell's Den and Pan's Glen

I was visiting my parents' place in Melbourne a couple of weeks while I lined up an apartment, staying in a bungalow at the back of the house that my brother and I used to share until we left home. I had some trips [hits] with me that I planned to take with my sweetheart Mary, and I also had these tablets called Romilar, reportedly an opium-based prescription drug. A friend told me that if you took one of these with a ticket of acid, it would really kick it on.

So one afternoon after lunch, I dropped some of the acid, though I knew I shouldn't be doing it at home, where I'd be too close to the folks and other people coming and going. For years, I'd had an up-and-down relationship with my parents, particularly with my father.

Nothing tragic, just the usual smart-ass son versus the poor oppressed old man who's desperately trying to retain authority.

The acid seemed to take an awfully long time to come on. I figured it'd gone off or something, so in a very cavalier way, I pulled out the packet of Romilar. There must have been about a dozen tablets. *Oh, fuck it,* I figured. *I'll drop all of 'em.* When the acid did come on a few minutes later, it was a very big load.

I had music on, but was endeavoring to keep it down, as I was paranoid about aggravating my mother and father up in the house and having them come down. I really wanted to avoid dealing with them, because I could sense that an extremely heavy trip was coming on. The earth was quaking and the thunder was rolling through my head. It felt as though it might have been as much as 350 mics.

After a while I began to get tied up into a knot of concern about getting busted by the parents coming in and catching me tripping. I also felt guilty that I hadn't tripped with someone else, that I'd been a greedy bastard not waiting for Mary to get off with me. I heard her voice, "You couldn't wait, could you, James?" and my mother: "James is taking drugs and going mad out there." My mind was flashing wildly, projecting all these horrific scenarios. I realized that I shouldn't have dropped those Romilar, which had apparently stripped away all my defenses.

I started to get really uptight. *Shit! I'm going to lose my marbles.* It was slowly but surely getting heavier and heavier as evening drew on. I wanted to listen to music, but couldn't make up my mind and kept putting LPs on the turntable, then ripping them off. I started to eat one of the bananas I'd bought for the trip, but had to stop. Its slimy texture was repulsive and I couldn't swallow. I just couldn't relax into the trip and was regretting having dropped. I was aware that my negativity was bringing me a lot of grief, but I couldn't get out of it. As the day rolled on, I found myself lying on the bed, desperately trying to stop thinking, to turn off the chatter in my head.

There were these enormous casks of guilt on my chest, the Catholic burden of sin and punishment and fear about Heaven and Hell and disgracing your parents. I'd been devoted to the Church from the age of seven and dumped the whole thing when I was about thirteen. This was one of the bones of contention between me and my parents. Not only was I not a Catholic, I was vocally *anti*-Catholic and couldn't resist an opportunity to have a swipe at the pope—a typical university-age rejection of one's familial roots and values.

I built up a series of catastrophic scenarios in my mind over the course of the afternoon, all of which led to all sorts of problems for me, for all my loved ones, and for everyone who'd ever known me—scenarios like: *I'm going to crack up. I'm going to be taken out of here in a fucking straitjacket. The police are on the way. The neighbors have heard the music—that last track was up way too loud—and now they're up in arms.* I could hear them telling my parents, "He's gone mad." The whole world was focusing on me. "Get Swenson [my surname]. Bring him in."

I tried various distractions to escape from the horrid specter of isolation and ruin, the fear of going crazy. *You've destroyed yourself. You're never going to put yourself together again. You can't even scratch your ass, you're so fucked.* I pulled out a book of poetry, read a line, and that sent me to another level of hopelessness. *Here's this fantastic poetry, and you can't put together two words.* Whatever stimuli I experienced reinforced my fear that I'd gone round the bend.

I was lying in a state of terrible agitation, and then the whole Catholic dread of eternal torment came over me. *You've lost your faith!* They'd taught me that if you'd lost your faith, you'd never be able to get it back again. *You blatantly scoffed at believing in anything, and look at you now! Sure, you don't believe in anything—you're completely lost!* Church doctrine was working its voodoo on me, but exacerbating this was my own belief that you can't go back to being innocent once you've cracked through the naïveté of your original faith. It's just not recoverable once the illusion is broken. It's just impossible to put it together again and pretend you believe in it.

I started to hear croaky noises, probably my own choked-up sputterings, and then the voice of God uttering judgmental pronouncements. "You're damned. You've had it." I felt a tremendous physical weight, like I was being squashed against the bed. I tried to lift my head up and look out into the room over my shoulder. The room was dimly lit and in the shadows I saw these damned fucking devils, these feral black fiends, batlike creatures full of ferocity and horror, with faces and bodies more animal than human, more monster than anthropoid. Their countenances reflected my concerns about Hell and the nature of punishment. And the soundtrack to this hideous scene was composed of these croaky groans of divine judgment I was hearing.

To escape I turned over to lie facedown, but this childlike state of cosmic terror went on for about three hours. The corners of the room were like nests of demons, and these vile beasts of torment crouching in the shadowy nooks wanted to tear my fucking throat out. The ghastly buggers looked like the phantasmic creeps in the paintings of Aubrey Beardsley, like nineteenth-century pen-and-ink drawings of succubi and other horrid apparitions, and the gory, red-mouthed abominations you'd find in Hieronymous Bosch's works. There was a steady stream of monstrosities—with no repetition. The imagery was always metamorphosing, with new nuances branching out of every form. I'd lose one creature when I saw a color on a particular part of its body, and then be greeted by a new and ever more loathsome associated monstrosity. The details of one hallucination kept setting me off onto another.

Around six in the evening, the spell was broken by the worst possible thing, a knock on the door. It was my mother. I'd had the music blaring—Bob Dylan, Pink Floyd or something. I heard her banging on the door, which I'd bolted. "Your father tells you to turn the music down! What are you doing in there?" She may have been less urgently inquiring and more nonchalant than I was thinking she was at that moment, but I was projecting my manic state on everything and everyone. *What am I* up *to? I'm out of my frigging mind!*

She persisted in knocking, so I had to get off the bed. This pulled me right back into reality. I staggered across the room and opened the door. It was a moonlit evening out in the garden. There's my dear mum and she looks *dreadful.* She looked fine, actually, but she was worried, and my mother wore a lot of worry in her face, as a lot of maternal figures do. She was about fifty-five and a wee distraught about my carrying-on and deranged appearance.

"What on earth is the matter, James?" I was obviously flying. My hair must have been extremely tousled. My eyes must have looked fairly zapped, and I had a very strange tone in my voice, which was saying: "It's all right, Mum. Just leave me alone."

"You're taking drugs again, aren't you?"

"No, I'm not. Just get out of here!"

It was kind of a shock—for both of us, I reckon. I was pretty brusque to her, but I couldn't have handled more conversation at that point. I would have come more and more undone, and that would have worried her more. So in a sense, it was with a sort of gruff grace that I got her out of there. I shut the door and sat back down on the bed and turned the music down. Then I "heard" her say to my father, "Dad, James's definitely gone insane. You'd better call the police."

I thought, "Shit, I'd better get my shoes and socks on and get the hell out of here." Then I "heard" the phone ring, though there wasn't one in the bungalow. This led to a series of distractions that, however vexatious, at least got me out of the purgatory I was in before. I figured that it was better to wrestle with the devil you knew—the parents—than the biblical bastard.

My younger brother Tim had been drafted and was serving in the Australian army in Vietnam at the time. We were extremely close; still are. He was calling out to me for help, which was devastating. I wanted to ring somebody to find out how to reach whomever it was that could pull him out of harm's way. Then I realized that I couldn't go inside to the telephone, because Mum and Dad were there and I didn't want to have to deal with them. If *Mum* looked bad, the old man must have looked *ab*-solutely horrific. I was really analyzing my options carefully, and, delusional as I was, this was much more constructive and active-minded than the earlier terror session. *Should I go out to the corner telephone booth? Nah. Who knows* who *I'd meet.*

So I got into music, a Vivaldi violin concerto, and that brought me to a very, very nice mood. *Ahh. The music's there. Nobody's coming. The old lady's okay. I'm going to come down. I'll be all right. It's going to be fine.*

I get my courage up. *Shit, it's a beautiful moonlit night. I'll go out in the garden.* So I walked out of the bungalow and around into the main backyard, where there were a lot of trees and plants. The moon is shining. I look at the willow tree in the garden, a very special tree. To my amazement, I see that the trunk is composed of a group of devas and sprites, sylvan creatures like Pan, nature's brood all knotted together in an orgiastic revelry. The tree was alive with them, shimmering in the moonlight. I'd read about places such as Findtorn in Scotland, where lore has it that nature spirits tend to the agriculture. Now I was actually *seeing* these mythical keepers of the botanic realm. They were gorgeous, very sensual, with pointed ears—male and female sylphs, Puck and his gang!

I dropped to my knees and looked up at the moonlight and at the tree, groaning in a sort of copulatory rapture and awe. This was one of the most exquisitely beautiful encounters I've ever had in my life. You can call it a hallucination, but this was a vision of the hidden life forces, a manifestation of the life within that was commonly only talked or read about. And it was there, right before me! I was creaming my tweeds, not literally, but nevertheless experiencing a sort of orgasmic bliss.

I felt a lovely rustle of nerves in my spine, perhaps from the kneeling position, which was reminiscent of the sort of stretching and contorting I did as a child. That sensual feeling was there. Then I started aping the postures of the creatures in the tree. The branches were writhing as these exquisite creatures dangled and interlocked in brazen postures to form the nape of the tree. It was like walking into Hobbitland or some enchanted, magical forest kingdom. It was palpable, not a mere smear of the mind's brush, or a play of shadows. They were just doing their thing, not for my sake; I was just witnessing it. The energy coming off of the tree was extremely erotic and procreative, though I didn't have a desire to screw any of the pretty little tree nymphs. I was out there groaning and writhing before the tree for a couple of hours.

And wouldn't you know it, my mother and father *were* watching me and indeed *had* thought I'd gone crackers. My mother had apparently peered out the kitchen window, which looked out on the back garden. Around that time every night it would be time for tea by the telly and the cups would come out and the water put on the boil. We swilled tea like drunkards in Australia in this period. Every hour and a half, it was "Let's have a cup of tea." She'd gone out to the kitchen to make up a pot and seen me out there gawking at the tree, and then gone and called the old man.

My father happened to be a cop. When he moved to Melbourne from the country, he worked for a time in a factory and then joined the police force at age forty. He was always rather authoritarian with me and his being a law officer made my behavior doubly complicated for him. His position on getting high was "Anybody who takes drugs is a bloody idiot and should be put in jail." Twenty years later, I tried to get him to have a joint, and even though he'd long been retired, he could never drop that attitude. "You'll go bloody mad!" he'd say, echoing the Australian fear of anything outside the tea and beer reality we lived in, that this is heaven and any fool that dares stray from it was apostate.

I must have looked perfectly dreadful to them, and they were getting pretty panicky already anyway after my mother'd been by. So around 9:30 they came out and interrupted my reverie. By this time, I'd been completely mellowed out by the good vibes. *All that other shit you've worried about—whether you're going to go to Hell, whether they'll put you in jail, whether they don't love you—forget that. Now you know about* this! The vision in the tree was an affirmation of something much bigger and more important than the trivial hang-ups of our sordid lives.

I got up off my knees and walked over to meet them, knowing that this time I really had to deal with them. I felt like I could handle it, though the old man was a bit of a worry. Mum I could reassure that I was just enjoying nature. Her tune was "What's the matter, love?" compassionate-like, but my dad was demanding to know "What the hell have you been taking?" I led them away from the tree in order to get rid of them so I could go back to enjoying it later. I knew I had to join them in the house for a while.

My mother insisted that I eat something. "You've been lying in that room and haven't eaten anything all day." I told her I'd eaten half a banana, but before I knew it she'd set before me a plate with meat, potatoes, and corn, the last of which was gleaming metalurgically. I couldn't eat. One of the reasons I became a vegetarian later was because when I looked at meat on acid, it would throb on the plate. I had to make a token effort to eat, though. Eating the corn was like chewing on rubbery kelp from the sea. I could hardly swallow. I took a little bit and got rid of the plate. I had a beer with my father as a reconciliation gesture. "Let's have a beer, Dad." He was always very happy to quaff a brew.

It was going all right, a reasonable discussion. I told them I was fine, just playing around, doing some meditation, this sort of bullshit. Their facial and verbal expressions were hitting me in a very special way. I could predict their next phrases, which came out like they were puppets and I was their ventriloquist. I knew exactly what the old man was going to say, and then he'd say it. The same with my mother. I knew what the riposte would be. My prescience about their side of the dialogue was uncanny. I had to suppress the impulse to laugh or say out loud what I knew they were going to say—or make fun of them, which I would have done if my brother were there. We would have started to send them up, and they probably would have enjoyed it. But in my current condition, it wasn't safe ground.

I was a bit off-line in the conventionality of my speech. Some of the sentences I let go just didn't hang right at all. You're trying to make lighthearted, pleasant conversation, and you start off on something and you don't sound like yourself and you don't have the structure or the pitch right. And all the while you wonder whether the next thing you say is going to give away that, in their terms, you're cuckoo.

I think the old man definitely thought I was doped up. My mother has spoken about this incident over the years, asking every so often, "You were on drugs that day, weren't you?" I say, "Sure, Mum, I was. Funny it's taken you all this time to realize." But it was hard to be short with them in this state. They had me in a very vulnerable condition. They were a little gentle with me, far milder than they would have been if I were boisterous and drunk with a few of my friends around. They were probably a bit concerned at my odd behavior. I was too meek and considerate by their lights.

I eventually broke free and went back outside and had a few slugs of crème de cacao or some liqueur, figuring it was good to come down with a bit of booze. The sylvan chimera in the willow tree was sealed over in its customary bark skin, so I went back to the bungalow and looked in the mirror, one of the trippiest things you can do on acid. I could see both my mother's and my father's faces in my own, which I could mentally split in half. Up at the house I'd been studying their faces so intently that they were now inhabiting me. I could see that I bore a strong resemblance to both of them. It was profoundly clear that these were the people who had begotten me. *Whatever you are, you are of them.* It was a new threshold of awareness that I was sprung from their DNA, a replicated version of them. The trip ended quite happily. I went to sleep sometime early the next morning.

Jarl

B. 1936

Designer, poet

Resides on an island in Europe, and in New York City

Born and raised in Sweden

An Early Absolution

I took acid for the first time in 1966, at age thirty, when I was living in Australia. LSD has been a liberating force in my life, helping me to break out of the turrets and labyrinths of the patrician duty I was born into as a member of the upper class. Since I was a child, I'd wanted to go into an artistic line of work, but the family had other ideas. When I was twenty-two, they sent me to Australia to study business, but while I was Down Under I escaped and got involved in my true passion, design. I stayed in Sydney for over a decade, eventually taking over a design firm.

I am bisexual and each of the two women I've married has been aware of this prior to wedding me. Sean, an Aussie man for whom I divorced my first wife, was studying medicine at a university in Melbourne, where he was researching the medical effects of various psychedelics, preparing for a career in psychiatry. He read all the literature on LSD and became fascinated. He'd come home all excited about his work and got me interested.

So we prepared ourselves for doing the drug properly, stocking the fridge with trips (hits) on blotting paper from the university, as well as some purported "antidotes." There were five of us at a flat in a colonial house in Melbourne. The paper was blotted with a dark grayish brown circle, about the size of a nipple. Around nine o'clock one evening, we stuck the paper on our tongues, pushing it against the roofs of our mouths. Three of us stayed sober and two tripped, but it was only I who really got off that time, after taking a second dose. After three hours with no effect from the first, I took another.

Around 1:30 in the morning, I was sitting on the toilet, comfortable and relaxed, doing my business, and noticed that when I pressed to shit, the corners of the squares on the chessboard tile floor wavered. I pressed more, pushing blood to my head, and saw more visual phenomena as I did so. When I was finished, I decided to sit down and stay a while to admire the floor. It had beautiful old tiles with a nice patina and depth, which were dancing about and floating. I'd heard that if you looked at a wall on acid, it might collapse, so I pressed on it, but it didn't give but a few decimeters. I returned to the living room and informed the others that my second dose was beginning to work. "Oh, tell us everything you're experiencing!," they chimed. I was their guinea pig for the evening.

As the sun came up, I looked out a window through the leaves of a tree which were dancing in the wind, and saw a fantasy alcazar and surrounding estate in the morning sky. It evoked my childhood home in Sweden, with a high castlelike wall and a road on which carriages drove up to the gates. I was brought up in a country manor, but in this vision it was a sort of a maze that I saw from above. The wall had about seven different meanings in the back of my mind, conjuring a variety of glimpses from my youth. I could jump over this wall, but others were hindered by it. I felt I was accessing the fourth dimension, that I had an extrasensory vantage point on the outside looking in on various people in the manor house and in the maze.

When these freshly tinted glimpses of my early domestic life evaporated, I turned my gaze to an encyclopedia on the floor. It was opened to a photograph of an empty stage as seen from a balcony in an architecturally distinctive Moorish theater or opera house. Robert, my tripping companion that evening, was sitting on the other side of the book. Suddenly I was sitting next to him in that theater, awaiting the start of a performance. The photograph had expanded into an entire three-dimensional playhouse! Only the two of us were in the audience, but I could hear the din of a whole auditorium full of people talking during the minutes before the lights were to be lowered and the curtains to rise. (All my life the theater has been hugely important to me and my family, where it's been a tradition since olden times.)

"I'm sitting in that theater with you, Robert. Are you there too?"

"Suddenly I just was," he said. So his trip had finally begun to work. The illusion lasted for about three minutes, but it could have been a mere three seconds, time was so distorted.

Around ten in the morning I got hungry and went out to the kitchen to see what there was. Everyone but the host was in bed. I loved cornflakes back then and asked him for some. I poured myself a bowl with a little milk and sat down to eat, gulping automatically, thinking it marvelous and lovely. After three spoonfuls, I suddenly felt as if there were a mountain of cornflakes before me. So I stopped the hasty shoveling to satisfy my gluttony, and realized that I'd already had enough. I put the spoon down. Then I reconsidered. *That milk is still very cold. Before it gets warm, I'd like to have a little bit more of these cornflakes.* So I put three more flakes on the spoon and into my mouth, and at least two of those flakes were too many. I felt suddenly filled up. *Excuse me, I can't eat this.*

Then it struck me that if every human, including myself, stopped swilling down his food and was satisfied with just a third of what he usually took, everyone on the whole globe could eat. It wasn't a new thought. I already had a disapproving attitude toward what I saw as the greed of the United States and its acting out in Vietnam. I'd been conscious of Europe's starving millions during the Second World War and later of the deprivations in Africa and Asia. But this came as a flash of "Aha" commonsense logic.

At the end of the trip, I felt I'd had a very pleasant shower of my mind. I felt clean, washed, as though my oil had been changed and I'd turned the page to a fresh new chapter.

While I was visiting my parents' home in Sweden in 1969 to attend to some family business, I launched into a tripping state after smoking a joint and was visited by a vision of my lover Sean, who was back in Australia at the time. The ceiling lifted away and he descended into my bedroom like an angel, hovering about a half-meter above me. He was as vivid as could be, cinemascopically and stereophonically, in all the colors of reality. He came down slowly, and I didn't dare to recognize him at first. *It really can't be . . . It looks as if it's Sean!* Then, as he got closer, I could see that it was indeed him. He was wearing shorts and an open red singlet. He smiled and laughed just as I was going to say, "This is just incredible, Sean. How on *earth* did you do it?"

The sight of him was so astoundingly *real* that I was thrown out of my bed in awe, kneeling for the Lord. The whole thing was too much, so I asked the Lord for forgiveness and wept in gratitude for such a welcome sight, however hallucinatory. It was so Lutheran of me, asking forgiveness for my sins, a reflexive *excuse me.*

I had been missing Sean ridiculously while being caught up in Sweden to settle some family affairs. Now I just wanted to get out of there and go back to Sean and do my design work. I knew that at that time, down in the southern part of the globe, he was taking psychedelics too. I felt that this full-channel telekinesis was a kind of religious transmogrification. From then on, my life was fundamentally changed, as I was now aware that we are far from alone, that things happen beyond our wildest expectations. It was a puissant revelation, and once I accepted its credibility, it was even relaxing in its naturalness and sense of belonging.

For my ego to survive the social stricture within the peerage of my family, I'd already shown all the cards in my deck, including the joker. Now I decided to inform them of what I'd been through, and went first to my father. I had a very close relationship with him and his second wife. He already knew everything about my divorce and Sean, and had never reproached me for any of it. He was rather appalled, though, that my vision was of Sean and not of Jesus. The rest of my family, while generally tolerant of my personal affairs, was quite shocked about this "religious" vision or "soul transit" as I called it. Here I was in the middle of conducting all this important family business, who was going to sit on what board, who would sell what to whom, when I dropped this little bombshell on them.

My mother used to say, "Father has God on a pedestal, but I have Him in bed. I do talk to God when I go to bed. We sort of snooze together." Our family history has bishops and archbishops and priests, and some visionaries too, especially among the women. My mother and grandmother had a good rapport with the realm of the unseen. They were often visited by the spirits of ancestors and once saw one of the family matriarchs coming in the door, though she'd been dead for hundreds of years.

I felt such humility for the vision of Sean coming through the ceiling that I had to believe in something higher than our human selves. After this spiritual epiphany, I felt I had to go through purgatory. At the time, I was staying in a wing of the gardener's house, which had just one room with an open fireplace. I was smoking hashish from Pakistan now and then. I decided I had to get rid of my own psychical muck. I envisaged a large stone well of great depth, with a little bit of air at the top, some water, and under that, more shit than you'd ever seen in all your bloody life. It was all the muck of my life and my personality: my family, my hang-ups and neuroses, my obligations. Just as it is in any old well, over the centuries a lot of crap accumulates. And I had to get it out. That was the order of the Lord: *You must clean your well. Otherwise, you can't get any further. The water you can throw to the flowers, and the rest you must cast away as far as you can.*

I was in that well, scraping up the muck, buckets upon buckets, for some eight months. When I finally thought I'd gotten it nearly clean, I came out of it and thought, *Now I need only to hose down the walls and then vacuum out the rest.* But the well would always refill, just as the rock of Sisyphus would always roll down the hill. I'd look back and see the enormity of the dung heap that had grown.

One day, I took some LSD with a pipe full of hashish. Suddenly I transformed into a butterfly and hopped up on top of the heap. I said to God, "Well, this is all my shit. There is still more, but only a little." Then the Lord Himself appeared, about five kilometers tall. He looked like the most ordinary five-kilometer-tall chap you could imagine. He stood relaxed, leaning on an old-fashioned broom made of birch branches tied together, used for getting horse or cow shit out of the stables.

"It's okay, Jarl," he said, and then this huge otherwordly creature, looking totally human, benevolent, and sweet, put his index finger down to me. "Jump onto my finger," he said. I looked up at this vision as though I hadn't heard correctly. "Yes," he said. "Do it." So I jumped onto his finger. He bent it, and I sat on top of the knuckle. He lifted me up and put me on his shoulder, and then he took his broom and with three strokes he wiped it to oblivion.

I whispered in his ear, "Is this true?"

"Yes," he whispered back.

I contacted a psychic named Astrid Gillmark, who was very in in Scandinavia at the time. She'd written three books, *I See, I Hear,* and *I Know,* which I had read. I wrote her a letter and told her my story, and she agreed to a meeting. I traveled up to where she lived in Uppsala, north of Stockholm. She assured me I was sane and assessed my experience. "You've had a true experience of the Lord, of your sins' forgiveness. You've gone from cocoon to chrysalis and you managed to do that while you're here alive. I congratulate you." She told me I was out of my time, that she saw me as a sixteenth-century English knight. The meeting concluded with a visit to the grave of Dag Hammarskjöld, whose book *Markings* we both held dear. Later on I met with her in Paris, on my way to Morocco.

After this, I went to the family bishop and got assurance that I was in the right way with God. I was unsure of myself, because this sort of visionary business was considered a bit weird in secular, late-twentieth-century Sweden. I resolved to sever myself from traditional obligations. I decided not to go back into commercial business, and I couldn't work for the family, because they couldn't really understand me. So I felt I just had to go out into the world. And off I went, living off the interest on my inheritance for the next fifteen years.

I traveled to the States, then to Morocco. Tangier was one of the way stations hippies would stop in on their way to India or Nepal, or on their way back from Afghanistan. I rented a little house in the Casbah on and off for a couple of years. Once, high on acid, I was standing on the roof, looking out at stars and the clouds in the African night sky, and noticed I could stop a cloud from moving. I knew it was taboo theologically to control nature, but I could "visually" stop a cloud for three-quarters of a minute without interfering with the rest of the sky. The cloud would stay totally still in the sky while the other ones kept drifting. Eventually, this bit of meteorological mischief must have touched my fundamentally Protestant bone, and I stopped, thinking it was naughty.

One year I was staying in a hotel near the Casbah, and a little fellow came up and sold me a trip, saying I should take it straightaway so that when I walked about the city later I wouldn't have anything on me. Though available, drugs were strictly *verboten,* of course, in this Muslim country. As if to mirror this fact, the guys selling the acid and hash in Tangiers looked like frightened, gnarled little creatures. As instructed, I popped this LSD as soon as I returned to my hotel room.

After a bit, I felt terribly out of sorts, so I lay down on a mattress on the cement floor. I felt far from home, in a strange land, where strange things are being hustled at you. I felt vulnerable to being knifed and robbed right there in these cramped quarters among these totally alien wheelers and dealers, beggars and thieves.

I must have drifted off or fallen asleep for a while. The next moment, I was beyond Earth, looking down, awake and totally comfortable. I asked myself, *Do you have your body with you?* I answered, *Yes, I was up there looking at the pearl that we have (our planet).* Of course one gets religious when seeing things like that. I questioned why there had to be so much blood spilling on our planet when there was enough that flowed already from women's menstruation. I wept and prayed for the sanity of peace for all of us.

Over the years, I had LSD in the form of crystals from a university laboratory—star windows, printed Donald Ducks. Some of the experiences confirmed the relativity of time. I'd fall in love with a chord or a note and prolong it, so it felt as if time had slowed or stopped, though the music continued playing. Time just expanded to accommodate the full psychic breadth of the music. And when I released my rapt ear-grasp, the music moved right along according to its original pace, without any discontinuity. This could happen with chamber music, Glenn Gould on the piano, *Sgt. Pepper's.* There were Jefferson Airplane records that lifted me off the globe.

In order to achieve such disjunctions of time, I believe that the mind must move faster than light, at least in certain planes of thought. Once, in a sober state with an American friend, I saw three UFOs in coordinated movement outside Stockholm. Seeing how they moved across great distances instantly and flew out of sight at mind-boggling speed, I drew a comparison to the relativity of sight and sound on LSD. While under the influence, I've seen people disappear from the street. When I turned around to look again, they were back, prompting me to wonder, *What were they thinking about just then? Is there a part of ourselves that actually can time travel irrespective of the perceived rules of humanity, which is really only in diapers?*

I've tripped about 160 times, most recently in 1995. Almost every trip has been like a cleansing shower. We have to go through our own shit, one way or another—our megalomanias, inferiority complexes. If you haven't got a positive mind, or a soul that is basically trying to love existence, then, of course, a trip can be hell.

My LSD episodes have opened my mind and enabled me to look upon life with new eyes. After all my travels, my design career, and my personal developments, I try to be as generous and loving as I can. Today my work often involves helping people, lending a hand to counsel youth or assist the disabled. I also write poems filled with word play that concern the metaphysical issues I'm intrigued with. I keep a notebook at my side, where I record my thoughts in both Swedish and English. Part of every summer is spent reading my poetry to friends and other groups of people. Mostly I'm content to study and to write and be with the souls I feel close to, living in a sixteenth-century house I've restored from ruins.

Jason

B. 1955

Adventure traveler, licensed solar-heating-installation contractor, importer and wholesaler of African and Southeast Asian handicrafts

Resides in New England

Raised in New England

The Shining Ones

Between semesters of my senior year at a small liberal arts college in Connecticut, I had the most profound experience of my life on an acid trip. I was living off-campus, sharing a house with an ocean view at Crescent Beach in Niantic, about a minute's walk to the shore. It was mid-December 1978. Exams were over and Christmas break had just begun. The house was empty except for me and my best friend, Mark. Free of academic obligations, we wanted to blow off some steam, so we decided it would be a good time for a trip. So midmorning on a clear winter's day, we split a hit of four-way Windowpane.

To get the juices flowing, I pounded on some congas in the living room, while Mark drove off on a quick errand. It usually takes an hour or so to get off, but this acid came on in forty-five minutes. Mark came back giggling and reported that he'd had a little trouble driving back because he'd gotten off much sooner than he'd expected. We were both very excited, looking into each other's eyes; jumping up and down. There was a great feeling of anticipation.

We went upstairs to his room and put on a record. I realized that this trip was going to be something different by the intensity of the high coming on, which was first manifested in the music. It sounded so weird, I was transfixed. I'll never forget this piece of music, Colin Wolcott's *Grazing Dreams,* a solo album by the percussionist in the band Oregon that sounds unearthly even when you're not tripping. The music was doing something to me, entering my spine and expanding my consciousness. The walls were vibrating and the air was becoming three-dimensional with psychedelic trails and energy patterns moving through it. Everything was coming alive with psychedelic energy.

Then I started looking at Mark's face. I stared at him and he stared at me, and this is where it started to get strange. His whole face was shifting around, except for one of his eyes, which I fixed upon as the only stable feature. At first I saw other faces in the rearrangements of the energy patterns: an old woman's, a child's, a girl's. Then the faces got distorted and not really human, like masks. If I hadn't had any psychedelic experiences under my belt already, I might have been afraid at this point. But I was open to this. This to me was exciting.

Then I noticed something else. The transmutation taking place within his face spread to my entire visual field, which had become a fluid plastic swirl flowing out of his eye. It got more and more abstract. First his face lost all form, then his body, then the whole room, until it seemed as if all of reality were coming out of his eye in wavy streams. Everything distinct was merging into this one energy form, a flow of thick viscous substance. I had to make an effort to not close myself off to this. I remember wondering if Mark was seeing the same thing in my face. I had the feeling he was. I asked him, "Are you seeing what I'm seeing?" and he replied with an emphatic "Yes!" At this point, I felt our respective consciousnesses were linked.

Then I began to get revelations, piercingly powerful thoughts that came into my mind like a clarion call. It was as though a veil had been stripped away and certain things had become suddenly self-evident. I realized that there was just one force in the universe. *There is only one energy and that is consciousness. And there is only one consciousness, one mind. Human consciousness is part of this mind, and we are, in fact, one with this, which means we are all one.* I felt this was a revelation of the true nature of reality. Materiality had dissolved before my eyes and had resolved into its truer form, consciousness. I saw that I, like everyone, was linked to this one mind and that it was beautiful.

I thought I could "feel" Mark's mind, that he was having the same revelation and that we were mutually astounded by it. *We're all one consciousness. We're not our bodies. That's an illusion. Our physical forms are just a temporary condensation of consciousness in material form. This one consciousness is our true identity. And we all know this deep within us: I know that you know that we all know that we are one. We're all just playing this game. In ordinary reality, we've deliberately gone to sleep on this knowledge.* I saw this as funny, absurd. *It's not just a metaphor. Our minds are all linked, yet we've made this consensual agreement to pretend that we don't know it. We'll just play out this game of creating different forms and names and individualities.* All this seemed to echo from Mark's mind as well.

Then, I could feel him rebelling. I heard him say, "Wait a minute. Can this really be it?"

"Yes."

"It seems so weird, it doesn't seem, well, American, rooted in our culture."

Telepathically, I picked up that he found this mystic vision too "oriental" to his taste, not in harmony with his conditioning and preconceived notions of spirituality. He got agitated.

"I can't deal with this. I have to go. I have to go." He left the house to wander outside.

I was a little surprised that he suddenly backed out. Then I figured, "I understand. He just can't deal with this." But I could, in part because of my reading on Eastern and esoteric religions. It was a beautiful feeling, a verification of what I hoped would be the ultimate truth and a hopeful view of creation: *Don't worry about your body or about dying. That's an illusion. Consciousness cannot die.* To me, this was mind-shattering, the ultimate revelation in my life up to then. I'd read about various concepts of the universal mind, such as nirvana, the Buddhist state of enlightenment, and *samadhi,* the highest level of yoga meditation. I'd always hoped intuitively and intellectually that these things were true.

I kept going with it, concentrating on this mantra, which I was reciting mentally or picking up automatically: "Oneness, oneness, oneness . . ." I started to hear a sound. At first, it was a dull roar, then like the drone of an engine, then like the sound of the ocean, waves in the distance. It grew louder and more penetrating. I couldn't tell where it was coming from. The sound was coming from everywhere. "It's the Om!" I realized, the primal sound of creation, the sound of God's engines. It was pealing out of everything. The celestial chord set off an ecstatic mood and then served as the soundtrack for the peak portions of the trip.

I had a deep-seated notion I could become even more open and focused to the present moment, that I could go completely inside the Now and expand into it. I felt time slow down as I dove into the moment. I trained my focus down to the smallest unit of the Now, which I termed a *chronon,* a word that just came to me. I learned later that there is such a word and it means precisely what I'd applied it to. I felt I was experiencing a single chronon of time. Viewing time as an infinite number of dots in a line, if you draw a line through it, the intersection is the present, while the past is on one side and the future on the other. I was straining to get inside the core of that intersection, the pulse of the Now.

My effort to burrow inside the tiniest subatomic particle of time seemed to stop its flow and enable me to slip right into the kernel of the Now. Then I realized, "My God, every single second is really eternity." I felt I'd dipped into eternity and was experiencing a glimpse of it along with a hint of its vastness. I was blown away by the enormity of these revelations. By now I was flying so high, I felt I was in an exalted state, that I was having a mystical experience of the highest order, something I'd always dreamed of. Whenever I'd taken LSD, I'd always sought a revelation of the sacred. Now I was in the midst of one. It was a great honor, a blessing, and I felt very humble.

The next astounding thing that happened is the hardest for other people to accept. I looked out the window. It was about one or two in the afternoon. The sun was in the sky, but I saw it as a silver disk, not the bright object from which we must avert our eyes. I could gaze upon this orb with no pain. It took me a while to realize, "Wait a minute. That's the sun. But hmm, that's not the way I normally see it, with blinding rays coming out." It occurred to me, instinctively, that I wasn't supposed to be able to do this, so I didn't stare at it for long and I didn't fetishize the image, as I knew that this was not in itself a mystical experience, but rather a manifestation that I was in a higher state.

I may have looked into the sun for thirty seconds before looking away, glancing back now and again. I sustained no damage from this. I don't believe I was simply numb to the pain. I believe that my nervous system had adapted to enable me to incorporate much more sensory input without being harmed. Science cannot yet fully explain how a change in consciousness can alter one's physiology, but there's a whole body of literature on the phenomenon of people temporarily possessing supernatural powers, particularly tribal peoples who use psychedelic substances. For example, there are individuals in Siberian tribes who've taken the *Amanita* mushroom and been able to lift objects that normally couldn't be lifted by five men. And there are cases of Tibetans who go into a trance to invite possession by guardian spirits, which enables them to perform miraculous feats of physical strength. I thought—and still think—that I was in such a heightened state that my visual capacity had been transformed along with my consciousness.

What unfolded next constituted the zenith of this peak experience, if not my entire life. I became increasingly cognizant of the sacredness of the experience I was undergoing and felt an expansion of consciousness beyond the confines of my head and my body. It was as if my consciousness were a huge hot-air balloon and my body was the gondola, a small appendage. I felt I was ascending and passing into a new dimension, that I was expanding upward as well as outward into an astral plane, a higher sphere of creation.

As I entered this realm, I started to hear celestial sounds (not coming from the turntable) like little synthesizer riffs. As this bubble of my soaring consciousness expanded within this new dimension, I became aware of energy forms descending from higher up. It didn't matter if my eyes were open or closed. I could feel another reality superimposed. Consistent with my expanded consciousness was an extended field of vision. I seemed to have 360-degree wraparound vision, as though my eyesight were liberated from the confines of its socket-based axis and could now behold all of ocular space as a dome.

There was a humming sound as the forms on high descended. I immediately intuited that they were beings. I could sense another consciousness coming into contact with me, an assembly of minds. I strained to see these forms, which at first were just indistinct blobs of light and energy. Then they took on vaguely humanoid outlines, like glowing silhouettes of yogis in the lotus posture. I knew they were not physically in the room, but in my mind. The forms I was seeing were not hallucinations per se, but diffuse mental images, visual impressions of something extrasensory to furnish my mind with a way to incorporate their presence.

I realized that these were higher beings, angelic hosts from a spiritual dimension that I had now accessed. They were enlightened beings working for the good of creation, blessing me with a visitation. They were calling to me telepathically, linking me with their consciousness. I could distinguish individual voices.

I was so moved by this that my cup runneth over. This is what I'd been seeking, communion with a higher reality. They were touching my mind, beaming thoughts at me in an ecstatic chorus, saying, "Jason, it's beautiful. Come join us. Be one with us." I reached up to touch them, not with my physical but my astral-form arms. All of their hands reached down and touched my hands, clutching them as their voices repeated, "It's beautiful. You're one with us." Tears were streaming down my face. It was the peak moment of my life. It wasn't like communion with another human being, where you wonder where you're really situated in the other person's mind. There was no question here. Our souls were touching. I felt so blessed and humbled that these higher forms would deign to reach out to me.

I stayed in this state as long as I could, but slowly the angelic hosts began to pull away. I redoubled my efforts to contact them, but they were fading. "No, no, no. Don't go! Don't go!" I was receding out of the astral dimension and it was becoming darker. I couldn't hold on. I fought against it, but faded from this radiant plane.

As I got up and walked around in a slow-motion haze, my next conscious thoughts were "Okay, what do I do with the rest of my life? I'm totally transformed." I couldn't visualize what I was going to do, how I would incorporate the knowledge of this sacred dimension, and the fact that I'd been living just one small part of the total spectrum of reality. *So what do I do now?*

Eventually Mark returned. It turned out he'd been so bewildered, he'd jumped into the icy Atlantic to shock himself into reality. A bit dangerous perhaps, but he was a strapping young man and he said it did him good. I didn't bother trying to tell him what had happened, though I gave him a rough outline a few days later.

For the next week, I was in an altered state, a blissful residue of the trip staying with me. The afterglow faded in intensity over the coming weeks, but the experience still feels very real on a certain level, and I'm still blown away by it, though it's been somewhat difficult to assimilate into my life. The challenge has been how to fulfill the lofty call of the shining ones to join with them, and how to share the experience with others.

In the weeks following the experience, I thought of leaving school, gathering some people together to live close to nature and pursue the spiritual life. That didn't happen. I went on to graduate and then to join, for a while, the ranks of the employed. And though I've done interesting work, traveled extensively, and maintained a spiritual outlook on life, I sometimes criticize myself for not living up to the promise of the revelation that I haven't tried hard enough to attain that sacred realm again. I'd love to experience that communion once more, but if it doesn't happen, I'm still forever grateful that I was blessed by the shining ones.

What Would Happen If I Touched It?

In January of 1979, finally free from school, I organized a rendezvous of several friends in Arizona at the home of a classmate. I'd never been to the Southwest and was eager to take in the spirituality of the desert. So a caravan of chums, including Rickster, Marcus, and Phoenix, headed from various points East to the latter's home in the city by that name.

One of our first adventures out there was a hike into the beautiful and mysterious Canyon De Chelly, on the Navajo reservation. On the night of a full moon we heard a coyote on the canyon rim above us, and then listened in amazement as the howl changed into a screaming human voice. Our native guide, hunched close to the campfire, informed us that the phenomenon was the work of a Navajo shaman shape-shifter, the likes of which live in the canyons of the area and are both respected and feared by the locals.

Thus primed for mystery, the four of us decided to go out into the desert wilderness and have a sacred peyote ritual. We were able to acquire some peyote buttons, but not in sufficient quantity. I therefore proposed that we supplement these with dried *Psilocybe cubensis* mushrooms, which we obtained from a college campus after wandering a couple of dorms. We planned to brew a tea combining the two, even though, at the time, I'd never heard of anyone else doing this.

Most of the planning of the ritual was done by Phoenix and myself, as we had the greatest interest in this sort of thing. He was a very knowledgeable guy, with a particular interest in Western magic and alchemy, and with a keen sense of ceremony. I'd studied Eastern mysticism, and also had a strong interest in shamanism. Rickster was into yoga and meditation, and Marcus was interested in the kabbalah. Whereas I was already well versed in sacred medicines, Marcus and Rickster had never taken any psychedelic before, and Phoenix had only one experience under his belt. At this time in our lives, in our early twenties, we were still somewhat naive but very sincere, which is, in part, why we went on to have a successful vision quest: we were full of the faith that we could really have a magical experience in the desert, that it was out there waiting for us and all we had to do was open the door to it.

We ended up with a ritual based mainly on a Native American vision quest model. One important source was from the book *Seven Arrows* by Hyemeyohsts Storm, which had drawings of medicine wheels. A medicine wheel is a symbolic representation of spiritual forces, consisting of a circle with the cardinal points denoted and assigned special attributes. We decided to assign each point a color, an animal, and one of the four elements. At the ritual site, we would simply draw a circle in the dirt, sit at the four directions, and invoke the spirits, using these totems. To enhance the ceremony, Phoenix sculpted from clay various ritual objects. He made small figures of each of the four sacred animals, and to represent the four elements he made small vessels to hold earth, fire, water, and incense (for air).

On Phoenix's recommendation, we decided that the site for our ritual would be in the Superstition Mountains near Apache Junction southeast of Phoenix, where the terrain is rugged, mountainous desert with few hikers about, especially in winter. There's a famous legend about the area. The Lost Dutchman's Mine is said to be situated somewhere in the Superstitions. According to the story, an old prospector, actually German, emerged from the desert one day with a large pouch of gold nuggets, proclaiming he'd struck it rich. He cashed in his gold and went back out to the desert and was never heard from again. To this day, prospectors are still marching around the area in search of the Lost Dutchman's mother lode or staking new claims. We saw one, in fact, who had a donkey with a pick and shovel and a rifle strapped to its back. Backpackers are cautioned to watch their step in the area, because some of these cranky prospectors have been known to take potshots at hikers who get too close to their claims.

So we drove down there and backpacked in, hiking all day until we came to a huge rock spire called Weaver's Needle. We walked a short ways up a ridge next to the spire and found a small plateau that seemed like the perfect site for our ritual. We set up our tents just below it and waited until nightfall. At Phoenix's behest, we set up a trail of *luminarios,* little paper bags with candles inside planted in sand—poor man's lanterns after a technique from Old Mexico—that lit the way from our tents to the ritual site.

To begin the ceremony, we became solemn and created a sacred circle to sanctify the site and to provide protection from ill winds and foul forces. In a special rite combining Native American with Western magic, we opened the circle, entered within it, and then closed it around us. We invoked the higher powers, praying that only good energy be allowed to enter the circle, and that negative spirits would be turned away.

Each of us sat at one of the points of the compass, facing inward, assembling the ritual objects related to their respective points. Using a pot over a little fire in the center, we brewed a medicine tea of the dried peyote buttons and mushrooms, boiling and simmering the stuff, then chugging it and forcing down some of the dregs. I'd taken both substances separately before and knew that they're basically similar, though peyote is somewhat more electric and closer to acid than mushrooms are. I figured the blend would complement each other, though I was concerned that the dosage was just barely adequate, so I told the others beforehand, "This will put us in a magical mood, but don't expect to get blown away."

After we drank the brew, we began our invocations, which went something like this:

"O spirits of the North, of the color black and embodied by the bear, you who make the winter and the darkness come over the earth, we invite you to come into our circle to teach us the essence of your knowledge and your power. Come into our circle. Bring us your positive energy."

"Spirits of the East, of the color yellow and embodied by the eagle, realm of the rising sun, the dawn of life, you who provide the awakening energy, come within our circle. Show us your sacred ways. Be with us now, and bless us."

"O spirits of the South, of the color green and embodied by the buffalo, land of the noonday sun that nurtures all living things and brings forth the bounty of the earth, come to us with your blessed power. Be with us now and help us learn and grow."

"Spirits of the West, of the color red and embodied by the coyote, you that represent the realm of the setting sun, come be with us now and bring your spiritual power to teach us and bless us."

We invoked the spirits of the earth and the sky and all the forces of nature to show us a sign, some manifestation of their presence. It was the best ritual I've ever participated in in my life. We weren't merely aping a Native American ritual, but had carefully selected symbols, prayers, and talismans that were genuinely meaningful to us, so it was very heartfelt and focused, and it resonated with us on a profound level. After all four of us had finished our invocations, we sat back and waited in silence.

It was a moonless night with a lot of stars. After a half hour I looked up at the sky and noticed that the stars were much brighter than before, twinkling, pulsating more strongly and distinctly. We maintained silence for a little while longer, then the strong feeling of anticipation led to a restlessness that hit us all at once. We looked at each other and decided it was time to move out of the circle. So we ritualistically opened it up to leave its protection, uttering a closing invocation to thank the spirits for giving us the sacred space, and proceeded out into the world. Without discussion, we all wandered off on our own. We each had a separate path to walk.

I hiked up to a small ridge a little above us, losing sight of my comrades. It was quite dark, so it wasn't particularly safe to be wandering around unaware. There were a lot of hazards to look out for, sharp pointy things like cholla cactus, shrubs with spines and needles, and rough terrain. I walked very slowly and deliberately. Gradually my night vision improved and when I reached another ridge I sat down and looked carefully at the plants and stones around me, feeling a wave of gentleness and sensitivity suffusing through me. I felt the life in the earth and said a prayer of thanksgiving to it and to all life. A subtle transformation of my emotional nature had taken place. I was solemnly reflective, open-pored, and acutely receptive to the emanations of nature.

At one point, as if prompted by something, I turned to look up in the sky, and saw something amazing. There before me was a sphere of light of a very bright silvery color. "What is that?" I wondered. In the split second that I tried to identify it I could sense my mind trying to match a formerly seen image with what I was now seeing: the moon, an airplane, an alien spacecraft? But nothing matched. *That's nothing I've ever seen before. That's the unknown!*

The orb, about three or four feet in diameter, was moving slowly across the sky from my left to right, about fifty feet up in the air above the ridge I was on, and about a 150 feet away from me. The sphere did not look like an object with a hard surface. Rather, it had a soft, organic appearance to it, as if composed of something slightly fluid or gel-like. It seemed to subtly quiver, like water sloshing in a balloon. Likewise, the luminosity changed in intensity, ever so slightly pulsating, as it moved silently through the desert night air. It looked like something alive.

And it was definitely real. No, this was absolutely not a hallucination. I never doubted for an instant that I was seeing something really out there externally, something registering on my senses and not just in my mind. If I had a camera, I'm sure I could have taken a picture of it. So I watched with rapt attention as this luminous entity continued to move slowly through the night sky in a slight arc until it reached Weaver's Needle, a good thousand feet away from me, and disappeared behind it.

I don't know why I didn't go running down the hill, shouting to my comrades. I guess I didn't want to break the spell. I felt surprisingly calm. I knew I was witnessing something sublime and amazing and I just wanted to experience it with open acceptance, without making a big scene. I was grateful to be in the presence of the supernatural. It felt like a blessing, which I took as a response to the invocations of our ritual. We'd asked for a sign from the spiritual realm, and here it was.

About half an hour after I'd last seen the luminous entity, I had another urge to look up in the sky, and to my surprise, there it was again! But now it was almost a thousand feet away from Weaver's Needle and moving in the opposite direction, from my right to left, again toward Weaver's Needle. This was quite odd, for it meant it had somehow jumped by invisible means to the opposite part of the sky. Once more, I watched spellbound as it moved slowly across the sky, tracing a half circle above our encampment. As before, when it reached Weaver's Needle, it didn't come out the other side, seeming to be absorbed by it.

After a while I started to feel restless and felt an urge to walk up to a higher ridge, though it was difficult navigating the steep terrain. It was as if I were being called. On top of the ridge there was a big stone that was so flat it almost looked like a man-made altar. I sat down on it and all of a sudden began to feel a very strong vibrational humming. I lay down on the rock and it soon overwhelmed me with its intensity. I could feel my entire body resonating with this force, as though enveloped by a powerful energy field. I was losing control over my body, feeling almost paralyzed.

And my mind also felt jammed; I couldn't form thoughts. Then a voice jumped into my mind: "You are experiencing sacred energy." I let the feeling flow through me. I could sense it was purifying me in some way, but the intensity was hard to take. I wanted to regain my equilibrium, and struggled to sit up. My head was buzzing and I was a little disoriented. It was difficult to take in my surroundings. Then I saw a bright light off in the distance, swirling a little. *Wait a minute! It's the luminous being!* It had landed on the ground some distance away from me. I had trouble focusing my eyesight, but I could make out that the shape of the luminous being had changed, now looking more rectangular than spherical. The light was broken up by something in front of it, a bush or a rock on the ground. It was pulsating, now a very bright, white-blue color. I felt it drawing me to it with an intense attraction. I realized that I might be able to walk right up to it if I wanted to, but that thought really scared me. *Oh my God, what if I touched it and just combusted!*

It appeared to be on a neighboring ridge, about a hundred yards away, but there seemed to be a deep ravine between us. I was frightened that it might draw me to my death, like a Siren. Then I screwed up my courage. *Don't chicken out. Go ahead, walk to it.* The vibration intensified, "Wonnnnnng. Wonnnnnnnnggggg. Wonnngggggg." I felt I had an opportunity to have some sort of communion with this entity, but at the same time, it seemed more alien than ever. *This is just way too much for me. I have to get out of here!*

I struggled to my feet and started to crawl my way down the mountain, my heart pumping wildly. After about fifteen minutes, I got a third of the way down, to a grouping of boulders. I sat down on one of them to catch my breath and noticed immediately that the vibration had stopped. All was quiet but for the normal rustling of the desert night winds. I started to calm down, and thought, *What on earth happened up there?* I rested for about ten minutes to catch my breath.

I then turned my head to the left and saw a shocking sight: It was the luminous entity rounding the ridge and floating down the hill directly toward me. It was spherical once again, very bright, and now only about fifty feet away. I called out to it, raising my hand, saying, "I am your friend!" though my bravado was fake. I was actually terrified. But the moment I had the pang of fear, it stopped moving toward me, as if it had instantly picked up on it and didn't want to upset me. Then it rose toward the sky, assuming the same altitude as when I'd first seen it, moving steadily in a wide circle from my left to right.

As I watched it, the colors changed, going from an intense white to yellow, then losing its luster, to an orange, then a dull red. Finally, it flickered out and disappeared, and that was the last I saw of it. By now, late into the night, I felt I had to get down to earth, to familiar territory. I worked my way down to the campsite aided by the comforting sight of the still-burning *luminarios.*

When I got down to the campsite, I saw that everyone was in his sleeping bag. I didn't say much and just crawled into my own bag and dozed off. When we woke up a few hours later, I asked the group, "Did anybody see a ball of light in the sky last night?"

"Yes, I saw a light in the sky," replied Phoenix. "I saw it moving for a while and then it disappeared." He had no explanation for what it was. Rickster had spent most of the night in meditation with his eyes closed. At one point, he said, he opened his eyes and saw a light in the sky. He thought to himself, "Hmm, a UFO," and promptly shut his eyes again and continued his meditation. It didn't really interest him that much. Marcus, it turned out, had had a bum trip the entire night. He'd felt out of sorts soon after we left the circle, and crawled into his sleeping bag quite early. Interestingly enough, he reported that at one point late at night he'd woken up and seen a strange light in the sky, but he was quite groggy and didn't think much of it, and simply went back to sleep.

We packed up and hiked out. I didn't share many details of what I'd seen, for some reason feeling I should keep it private. I didn't talk to anyone about it for a long time.

But it had a huge effect on me. I felt it was proof that there are things that exist in the world that are just not known or understood. Most people ask, "How do you know you weren't hallucinating?" My answer is, I know the difference between a psychedelic hallucination and something real. What I saw was nothing like a perceptual distortion or an internal vision. Remember that it wasn't a heavy trip dose.

I see the luminous being as a sort of bridge between the physical and the spiritual worlds. Obviously this was something not known to science, but some sort of spirit or life form that lived in or on the earth, that is normally invisible and for some reason had made itself visible to us. I feel that it was something real, albeit obscure, that we'd invoked by our ritual, a manifestation of an earth spirit that belonged to the desert and mountains of that part of the world. Though it's conceivable that someone who conducted the same sort of ceremony without the medicine might have had the same results, the peyote/shroom brew had put us all in the mood for awakening and opened us up to the possibilities of the magic that ensued—a critical element.

In the late 1980s, I made the acquaintance of a Mexican shaman who officiated a Lakota Sioux sun dance I was privileged to attend, and with whom I later did a vision quest (sans any medicine) in Mexico. I told him this story through an interpreter and he listened very carefully. I asked him, "What do you think I saw?" He looked at me solemnly and said, "You saw a spirit. I have seen something like that myself."

Then I asked, "What do you think would have happened if I'd actually walked up to it?" To this day, I feel a slight sense of regret that I didn't have the guts to approach it "face-to-face" to engage or communicate with it somehow. "There's no way of knowing what would have happened," he replied. "You might have died instantly or you might have received some secret knowledge."

I would like to go back to Weaver's Needle someday and perform another ritual to see what would happen. If I was again graced with the presence of the luminous being, I wonder what I would do.

The Orgasm Death Dance

On the Fourth of July, 1983, I had a watershed acid trip at the annual National Rainbow Gathering convened that year in the woods of Upper Peninsula, Michigan.

Every first week of July, a diverse flock of alternative lifestyle folk, many of whom call themselves Rainbow People or members of the Rainbow Tribe or Family, sets up a communal village in an American national forest. The order of the day is celebration, cooperative living, and the sharing of ideas and information that run the gamut from herbal healing to holistic technologies. Activities include workshops for yoga, Native American sweat lodges, and massage. Families are encouraged to come. A Kids' Village is erected with daycare services and children's activities. The basic theme of these congregations is to honor Mother Earth and to utilize the wilderness to recondition ourselves and advance a new way of living in harmony with nature and with our fellow people.

The Rainbow Tribe is comprised of aging and neo-hippies, anarchists, pagans, vegetarians, back-to-the-earth people. Most participants have long hair and dress in tribal raiment, festive clothing such as tie-dyed, Guatemalan, or Native American shawls. Some are yuppies with serious professions, who take the trouble once a year to get back to their roots and recharge their psychic batteries. Those who live the Rainbow lifestyle year-round are probably in the minority.

The sacred day of every Rainbow Gathering is the Fourth of July, which is celebrated as *Inter*dependence Day. A twist on the patriotic tradition, this holiday extols communal values of sharing, belonging, and mutual support. On this July Fourth, a beautiful summer day, I joined a throng who'd begun gathering at dawn in a circle in a big meadow, maintaining silence until noon, when a peace prayer was scheduled. Among the multitude were a significant number who were taking sacred substances to induce a heightened state for greater reception to the day's meaning.

I took a double dose of LSD around ten and sat down on an outer edge of the circle. People were flowing in in small groups or by themselves, sitting on the grass in mute solemnity. Soon there were hundreds of people in total silence, which grew pregnant with pathos and intensity. I sensed a communal vibration of emotion spreading through me and everyone. As noontime approached, I felt a great heart-rending yearning rising from the depths of my soul, indefinable at first. Then I comprehended clearly. It was a plea for peace, for love to appear in the hearts of humankind, for our sufferings to be healed, for the earth to be restored.

My eyes were closed, but I felt it was coming from us all. I felt the heartaches of humankind, how we hurt each other—that's the worst—the torments of war, how we get sick and die. I opened my eyes to an amazing sight. Everyone was experiencing the same wave of emotion. All around me, people were sobbing and hugging each other, running into each other's arms, even those of strangers. The feeling was sweeping through everyone. I've never experienced anything quite so overwhelming in my whole life. I became aware that I too had been weeping as I sat there in the lotus position. I felt we all shared the suffering. The anguish was so intense that it was ripping through us as though we were one great wounded heart.

Then after a while I heard a cry, a voice rising from the center of the gathered hundreds, breaking the silence. It was a man's voice, a soulful prayer beseeching the Creator to hear our supplications for an end to suffering. It was the most sincere and humble prayer I've ever heard. I felt he was speaking for all of us, praying for God to bring love and peace into the hearts of all people. He was not a speaker scheduled to break the silence, but an anonymous person who'd been spontaneously moved to speak, a voice emanating from the communal soul. Others added their voices to prayer, crying out for divine intervention to help awaken us. The emotion was acute, a sustained pang for the suffering of humanity and of the wounded earth.

After a time I grew concerned that we were trapped in the depths of negativity and pain. I worried that we were never going to get out of this, that we were just stuck in grief, the long-pent-up feelings of despair we normally don't want to face, which we'd now conjured up en masse. *Is everything really hopeless?* I wondered. Then in the distance I heard something. A drumbeat. Then I heard music and then singing, growing louder. It was children's voices and laughter. The Children's Pageant was coming our way, a traditional ceremony on the day of the peace prayer. Dressed in festive clothing with painted faces, the children cantered into the meadow led by a band of adult musicians. At the head of the group, some men were playing a beautiful, uplifting melody led by a soprano saxophone.

Suddenly, cathartically, the somber mood of despair was changed to one of joy. "Of course there's hope! There are the children, the future. We can still work to make the world a better place." The children reawakened us to the innate joy and playfulness that is also part of life. A great release could be felt throughout the whole circle, a dramatic shift. The wave of emotion that now passed through us changed our tears of sadness to tears of joy. This was a signal for celebration to break loose. Soon more musical instruments appeared and a great jam was happening. People started dancing to the music of a pickup ensemble of accordion, a trombone or trumpet, tenor and soprano saxes, and hand-drumming on congas and African *jimbes.*

I started dancing vigorously in place, joy bursting from my heart. Never had I felt such a sweeping communal vibration, all of this happening so spontaneously. I felt a charge of energy, as though I'd been infused with pure electricity from a bolt of lightning. It went right through my whole body and out through my arms, seeming to burn my hands. I looked down at them and they appeared slightly swollen and distorted. The energy was coming from some normally untapped source. A barrier had been removed and I was opening up.

I looked up in the sky and saw patterns in the shape of the *dorje,* the Tibetan sign of the thunderbolt, comprised of a short double trident, which symbolizes the invincible power of the Buddha and the dharma. I took this as a sign that cosmic forces were present. Throughout the circle, bodies were in motion, dancing with exuberance. Birds soared overhead. I looked at the trees and they were pulsing with life; they too were dancing with us. Then the lead musicians and dancers wended through the circle right to me, suddenly surrounding me. It was as though I'd drawn them to me or, at the very least, I was fated to be in the center. It felt as though the energy were coming through a group of about two dozen of us who were manifesting an enormous amount of it. We formed a vortex of the most vibrant people, around which wider circles formed.

My delirium continued to climb. I felt that something very special was happening here, that this was sacred celebration energy, the very lifeblood of Creation itself. Everyone looked so beautiful dancing and making music in their festive clothing. *This is the epitome of living,* I thought. *We're expressing the highest level of life energy, the joy of creation.* Somewhere at the center of the universe, I envisaged, the gods were celebrating. They would look just like us in their half-naked bodies, rainbow-colored clothes, long flowing hair, beads and jewels. They would be dancing and celebrating like this on a high astral plane and transmitting their energy to us.

Suddenly it occurred to me, *Wait a minute.* This *is it! We're the holy spirits and the gods at the center of the universe. We're creating the energy. There's nothing else but this celebration. This is all there is and I'm going to give it everything I've got.* The revelation lofted me on another wave of jubilation. I looked around and dozens of people, about a quarter of the throng, were taking off their clothes. Many wore only shorts or loincloths, while those who remained dressed were festooned in colored robes, Navajo blankets, African dashikis, or resplendent homemade garments. Many of the faces were painted. The whole scene was very tribal.

I lost track of past and future and committed myself to the present moment, certain it was the path to something transcendental. I was determined to go with this celebration completely. I saw this moment as an archetypal crossroads in time, ripe with revelatory meaning and building up to something supremely special. I made my decision. *Yes, I want to be free, totally free.* I knew I had to take my clothes off, so I disrobed and felt much better. Then I thought, *Wait a minute. I'm not totally naked yet. I still have my glasses on.* I'm nearsighted, and without my glasses everything's a blur beyond ten feet. I then performed a symbolic act of self-liberation that was a sign I was completely free of any conditioning.

I removed my glasses and flung them way up in the air, watching them turn, end over end, in slow motion, like the bone that transforms into a space station in the film *2001: A Space Odyssey.* I heard myself laughing, not even bothering to see where they fell. It was an amazing act of letting go. It astounds me that I did this, because I'm so protective of my glasses. It was completely out of character, but it was destiny. I rejoined the circle stark raving naked. People were laughing and forming a tight circle with their arms around each other's shoulders, passing jugs of water. I had a tremendous urge to drum and muscled in on a conga I was drawn to. The owner backed off and I wailed away.

The next shift in my consciousness was my realization that all this elated exertion was burning a tremendous amount of energy. It was hard work and I was getting tired. *Wait a minute,* I thought. *What does that mean? We're the gods of this universe. How can we get tired? Will the energy run out? What will happen to us?* The day was elapsing and the hours were passing. The sky was softening its colors as the sun was starting to go down. I'd been dancing naked for three or four hours. *How can I be fading? It must fit into the scheme.* I concluded that we were coming up to some glorious climax and that I should just give this energy my all until I had nothing left.

Then I had visions that maybe I was going to die! I wasn't sure how that would happen, but it concerned me. *Something has to happen. Some great end is coming.* I comprehended that physical vigor was finite, but I felt that this magical charge had to expire in a more meaningful way than with my body's just collapsing in exhaustion. I noticed a lot of couples were pairing off, like mitosis or some cosmically programmed drawing together of complementary elements. *Men and women must come together. That completes the harmony. I too must find a mate!*

It became clear that we were all going to match up and there was going to be a joyous merging. It had to be a sexual union. *That makes sense! Yes! All the celebratory energy will come to its logical conclusion with man and women literally coming together in orgasm.* A transformational event would take place. We would all have this consummate orgasm and merge in a flash of light, forming a luminous sphere of pure energy: the "orgasm death," to borrow a phrase from William Burroughs. I fixated on this erotic-apocalyptic image. What it meant, of course, was that I had to find my mate right away.

I started to cast about, and what do I see but this beautiful naked young woman dancing in the center of the circle. She was absolutely gorgeous, my dream image: exquisite long black hair, slender but incredibly shapely. She had this euphoric energy in her, smiling and laughing and dancing. It was clear. *This must be my mate.* I seemed to be pushed forward and there I was: just her and me dancing in the center. It was the mating dance and she was my chosen one. I tried to hug her. She gently disengaged herself, holding me at arm's length while still gyrating. I was completely in love with this woman.

The next thing I remember was being on my knees, my face at her crotch, inhaling the musky scent. She was laughing and gently extricating herself from me, wriggling discretely, ever so gracefully, away. She led me back to the edge of the circle and the others pulled me back. *Why are they pulling me away?* I wondered. *She's my chosen one.* I went back to her. Then people came out and, very subtly, took my arm and danced me around the circle and back into the edge. I wrested myself free and went back into the center to approach her again. Once again, somebody, in a very sensitive way, guided me back to the sidelines. *What is going on here?* People were doing things to me that did not fit into the vision. I had my first moment of doubt. I'd been deterred in my attempt to merge with this luscious woman and now felt trapped and frustrated just watching her from the rim.

Then a serious-looking face bobbed into view right before me. "Are you okay?" It was very strange. I didn't know what he meant. I muttered "Yeah, I'm okay." After a few moments, his face appeared again. "Are you all right?"

"I don't know." Then this terrible, bizarre feeling struck me. *Wait a minute, where am I? What's happening here?* It was as though a veil had been lifted. The ecstatic energy drained out of me very quickly. I became conscious of my body being tired and weak. The sun was now low on the horizon. I was in a mental haze. A voice like a conscience invaded. *What have you been doing?* A horrible realization came over me, a childlike tremor at the consequences of transgression. *Have I been doing something I shouldn't? Have I been bad?* I told this guy, "I'm wasted. I've got to sit down."

As soon as I left the circle, I was crushed with fatigue and confusion. I sat down and looked at my body and was shocked at how scrawny and weak it appeared. I felt naked and devoid of energy and wanted to cover up right away. This fellow who'd inquired about my state, Bill, stayed on to help me get reoriented, which began with a search for my clothes. I'd never met him before, but he turned out to be my savior during this sudden crash. He was about my age, late twenties, and had driven out from California to the gathering. We managed to find my clothes in a heap, but not my glasses.

I've never experienced such a dramatic loss of joy and plunged so rapidly into the depths of mental and physical exhaustion and self-estrangement. I now had to extricate myself from the elaborate mythology I'd created, a soaring delusion that I'd woven for myself while I was blitzed. Very quickly, it came flooding into my skull what I'd been doing. I'd never ever lost my grip on reality like this before—and haven't since.

I was appalled at my behavior and felt terribly embarrassed and ashamed. I started to feel guilty, like a chastened child. I'd just crashed through almost every social conditioning and now, suddenly, felt as if I'd been cast out of paradise. All my conditioning cascaded back like an incoming tide dragging along all these Freudian and biblical totems. I felt naked and ashamed of my nakedness. I was concerned I may have made others uncomfortable. When you see a fellow with a faraway look in his eyes hopping about in a state of exhilaration, that was okay, but when you see a stranger on his knees with his nose in the crotch of an innocent female reveler, that was unusual, even for a Rainbow Gathering.

But everyone handled it admirably, gently shepherding me away from the virtuous damsel. I want to say for the record how beautiful those people were to know intuitively that I was being a little far-out and to refrain from condemning me. If I'd done this in the middle of downtown America, the police would have been called and I would have been hauled away and branded a criminal and an insane one at that. But at the Rainbow Gathering, my brothers and sisters knew how to handle me and I want to thank them for that.

It turned out that Bill had picked up on my confusion arising from my thwarted union with my "chosen one," in part because he'd dosed himself, which made him exceedingly empathetic. In fact, he was the most empathetic person I've ever met in my life. I was extremely fortunate to meet him. He sat me down and said, "Look, don't worry about it. What you did out there was beautiful. You have nothing to be ashamed of. First of all, everything you did was basically appropriate. Maybe you were a little confused at the end, but you were ecstatic and that energy was beautiful." He was fantastic at comforting and reassuring me. He suggested we wash up and get something to eat, so he took me to my tent to get a towel. We went down to the river and bathed and then went to get something to eat.

I started to get bummed out about losing it so far out in my own metaphysical space. That had never happened to me before. I considered myself an experienced psychedelic traveler. I'd been in even stranger states of consciousness and still been able to see them as strange. I'd never been in an alternate state and thought it was "reality."

After getting a bite, we tried to hunt down my glasses. Even though there wasn't much hope, it was important to look. We tried the rumor control center and the lost and found without success. I felt bad about losing my spectacles. It was symbolic of the whole transgression. "How stupid! How could I have lost my glasses?" We heard that people who found glasses had brought them to the MASH tent where the medical clinic was. Surprisingly, there was a table there with about ten pairs, so maybe there were others like me who'd cast them off into oblivion! Amazingly, I found my glasses there, a little bent out of shape, but functional: no permanent damage. I felt better.

Bill stayed with me most of the night, until I finally drifted off into sleep. He met me the next morning and we continued discussing the whole situation. I felt a need to apologize to the woman I'd ravaged. Here again, Bill helped me out immeasurably. He ran into her and her boyfriend, who'd also been in the circle. In fact, he was a guy I'd been dancing with at one point. Her name was Sonya and his was Miguel. Bill explained that I'd been tripped out, that I had not wanted to offend them, and that I wished to thank them for handling me so delicately. He reported back to me that everything was cool; Sonya was in no way offended. Amends had all been made. It turned out they were leaving the Gathering that day, so if Bill hadn't run into them, there would never have been the redemption and closure there was. I recovered, and the last couple days of the event I was back dancing again.

Seven years later, at the 1990 Rainbow Gathering, I saw a woman who looked like Sonya, dancing in the center of the circle again. I didn't introduce myself.

This experience made me take stock of myself and my use of psychedelic drugs. Here I'd constructed this visceral myth that I was at the center of the universe with the energy of a god coming through me. The force was so strong I felt I was beyond human. I'd been totally confident that I was advancing toward a final orgasm resulting in a death that would transform my material form into pure cosmic energy. When I was suddenly yanked from this Garden of Eden by the hideous dawning that I was a scrawny mortal coming off a chemically induced psychosis, it felt like a terrible rejection of the sacred. I'd come alone to the gathering and was fortunate to have found such a compassionate friend as Bill to get me through the comedown.

This was the toughest trip of all to incorporate afterward. It was especially remarkable that I'd so "lost it" because I have a strong measure of psychological control and a methodical sense of order in my life. In fact, my friends often tease me for having things so planned and structured. I also possess some knowledge of classic mystical experiences (yogic, shamanic, and tribal), and some understanding of altered states, which I usually structure around a ritualized framework. It was humbling that the checks and balances hadn't worked this time.

I can look back and say the experience was a success in that I really did break through. I let go as I never have before or since, giving myself over completely to celebratory energy. Most people don't ever get a taste of something like this. I went all the way, as far as I was allowed to go. You have to pay a price when you go so far, though. You have to expect some kind of negative jolt when the bubble bursts, unless you jump off a cliff while you're still in the exalted state. Maybe that's why a handful of people have done just that, thinking, "Why await the agony of reassimilation?"

So this is a cautionary tale that lends new meaning to the term "overjoyed." There's a danger of letting go too much or in the wrong way, like Icarus soaring to the sun and melting his wings of wax. Although I cherish the memory of the ecstatic energy, I've never let go like that again.

Jeremy

B. 1941

Audio engineer

Resides in northern New England

Raised in New Jersey

The narrator can be contacted at Trippingjeremy@hotmail.com.

THE *SCHLOMUS*: THE PRICE OF A MOMENT'S DOUBT

It's been decades since I've told the story of my monumental acid trip and its profound long-term impact on my life. I've steadfastly avoided doing so because of the dangers of reliving the trip yet again. I've had several flashbacks related to this single episode, which took place on October 13, 1969.

I'd been living on East 81st Street near York Avenue in New York City since 1963, working as an audio technician at a historical library. Although I lived in the city, I spent a great deal of time at a house in Sussex County in northwest New Jersey, near Branchville—a place that was owned by the parents of a friend of mine named Stephen. Many in our crowd of friends considered it our second house. Stephen's parents were away most of the time, so we could use it any time we wanted. It was a magic gift of a place, where we'd often go for weekends and holidays. Eventually, I moved out there, living there from 1973 to 1978.

On the day of the trip, it was bright and sunny, golden and warm. There were three people at the Branchville house: me, Stephen, and a peripheral friend of his called Gary, whom I'd never met. Gary abstained while Stephen and I took some acid I'd gotten from a friend named Bill. We waited an hour, then the three of us went on a walk. We took our traditional route along Mattison Road, past a couple of farms, and then on a trail off to the right and up the mountain. It was about a mile to the top of the Kittatinny Mountain Ridge, which is where the Appalachian Trail runs through New Jersey. On top of that ridge, if you look back east toward the house, you see farm country, fields dotted with cattle. In the other direction is Stokes State Forest.

We got partway up the mountain and the insects were screaming and the sun was hot, so we stopped in an open place to rest for a while. The acid wasn't hitting yet, so Stephen and I both took another hit. When Bill found out later that we'd each taken two tabs of this acid, he went white, knowing how strong it was.

After our rest, the three of us proceeded up the path, which went north toward High Point parallel to the Delaware River. The river valley is on one side, and the broad valley with all the farmland is on the other, stretching all the way to Hamburg Mountain in the distance. As we eased our way up the ridge, the acid began to kick in.

The first significant effect for me was a preoccupation with how I intellectualize everything—how I compulsively put everything into words. I am often down on myself about that, and for not being in touch with my feelings enough. But then I thought, *It's part of the pattern of my existence,* which was a way for me to accept that that was the way I was. I soared higher by letting that burden go.

We proceeded up the mountain until we got to a place that was not quite the top. There was a break in the trees on the right-hand side of the trail, so we could see the view over the farmland. We always stopped there because it's a very beautiful spot. We sat down and enjoyed the view of the countryside: a patchwork of farms and small areas of woods. The trees were sparkling with gold.

A moment of great warmth passed between Stephen and me. We'd been friends since 1963, though our friendship had been rocky from several cycles of losing and regaining trust. We were both gay, though never lovers. We went out dancing and explored things in the gay world together. Being able to trust Stephen at this point in our relationship enabled me to abandon all of the usual restraints on my mind. I let go as I'd never let go before or since. I was sitting down, gazing out at the gleaming bucolic scene, and made the conscious decision to let go, to trust completely. It was as though peels of an onion were coming off and masks were being cast off at breakneck speed. The masks fell away faster and faster, and I got higher and higher at an ever-accelerating rate. There was a tremendous brightness. I felt enormously exhilarated.

As I experienced one rush after another, I was saying aloud, "Oh, God. Oh, God. Oh, God." Then, in a flash of insight, I changed the emphasis in those words: "Ohhh: *God!* Ohhh . . . *God!*" repeating it over and over as I recognized that the unspeakable, unbounded joy I now felt was what we call God. I also became aware of an overwhelming feeling of déjà vu. I realized that I'd been here in this consciousness many times before—that in some way I'd been here all of my life—that this was *that* place, and I'd forgotten about it.

That struck me as the funniest thing I'd ever thought of. It was utterly hysterical that I'd forgotten this wonderful place that was right there all the time. *Isn't that absurd: I'd forgotten!* I remembered that the holy men are always laughing about something, and I knew that what they're laughing about is that the secret of the universe isn't a secret. It's right there all the time, and we forget about it. Then one day we walk up the mountain and we *remember* and think, *Ah, isn't that silly? I'd forgotten.* Then we forget again, and that's okay, because someday later, when we're least expecting it, we'll remember and then think again, *Isn't that silly? I'd forgotten again!*

This epiphany established my religious philosophy for the rest of my life. I believe that the nature of the universe is intrinsically joyous and that it is literally true that "God is love." The two words are different names for the same thing, and both describe the nature of the universe. I feel fortunate to have experienced this directly in my adult life. I am sure that I experienced it many times as a child. After all, this place is where we all come from.

Back on the mountainside, I was virtually slapping my thighs with amusement over having forgotten this joyous place. It occurred to me that laughing was something that only humans do, that it's our intrinsically human sound, as a whinny is a horse's and a bray is a donkey's. This thought added to my exhilaration. I felt fully human and stood tall in a posture I do not normally assume. I reveled in my humanness. "I'm laughing," I bellowed at full voice. "I'm laaaaaaughhhingggg."

Then it occurred to me for the first time that there were other people with me. I felt it was important that Stephen, too, be in this place. I'd gotten to this place through trusting him, and I felt that there would be something wrong if he were not here with me. It became urgently important to me to remind him of this joyous place that he'd forgotten. Words came into my mind and I started saying them. They were not English words, but I knew them very, very well. They described the place I was in. I spoke them aloud to Stephen in great earnestness, so that he would remember. I didn't know anything about speaking in tongues, but that is how people who heard me at that moment would have described it. It sounded to Stephen like gibberish. For the rest of the day, words cascaded ceaselessly through my mind like a waterfall.

So here I am, looking Stephen full in the face, with titanic ardor, spouting babble into his ear. From my vantage point, I was pronouncing words that would form the key to releasing the ever-present joy he had locked away in his heart, so he could join me in this ecstatic state I'd stumbled (back) into. He put up with it for a while. Remember, he was also tripping his brains out.

"Jeremy, how are you feeling?" he asks. This question had a specific meaning to us. We had both been in individual and group therapy with the same psychologist, and within that scene the credo was that the best thing you could do was to express your feelings—lash out, scream with rage, cry, get in touch, and express directly. So for

Stephen to say, "How are you feeling?" was asking me to do just that.

My response was "Yes, yes, yes, yes. All of that, but . . ." and then I let loose with another torrent of my fiery, alien verbiage. From where I was, emotions as we understood them in the regular world were all very well and part of the drama of life, but this God consciousness had nothing to do with that. It wasn't about crying or rage or emotional turmoil. It could be described only by the words I was speaking to him.

Another interesting dimension of my mind-set at this moment was that I felt that the coming together of Stephen, Gary, and me on this mountainside was a meeting of the representatives of our respective clans, that we were engaged in a solemn ur-meeting of critical significance, a primal gathering of three tribal chiefs. I felt I was representing the Jewish race from its inception, while Stephen was performing a parallel role for Italians, and Gary for perhaps another European tribe.

Many of the words I was spouting sounded Hebrew, though they weren't Hebrew words that I knew. I went to Yeshiva as a kid, so I knew the language pretty well. The one word that I remember best today is the one I use to name the cataclysm that was about to happen. That word is *schlomus.* (I've not said that word out loud since 1976.)

Stephen couldn't take it anymore. He felt he really had to stop me from continuing like this. It was scaring the shit out of him. "Jeremy, I don't know what you're doing, but stop!" At that moment I was stricken on a colossal scale. I suddenly understood that I had not had a religious experience at all, but, rather, I had gone mad. And because I'd let go so fully and surrendered so entirely to what I thought was God consciousness, there was no way I could transport myself out of it back to so-called reality. I had fully accepted a reality that I now knew was madness, and was now, unalterably, mad.

I continued to feel, all this while, a powerful sense of déjà vu. I recognized that this change from unbounded joy to a cataclysmic, cosmic feeling of wrongness was utterly familiar to me. The words that expressed this state were spilling through my head, over and over and over. I was silent for the rest of the trip. There was nothing for me to say. After that scene, there was no question of going farther to the Appalachian Trail and completing our walk. We turned around and went back down the way we'd come.

I walked between Stephen and Gary, feeling like a huge wounded animal—wounded on a cosmic scale—crippled, maimed, mad, rent. I felt as though I needed physical support, and I held on to them as we went down the mountain. The words continued to spill inside my head, but I said absolutely nothing about the state I was in. None of us spoke on the way down.

It occurred to me that it was quite possible that my entire life up to that point had been a fantasy in my mind, that I was actually in a mental hospital the whole time, and I was now back at the beginning of a cycle at the end of which I would take this tumble from the tower. The sense of déjà vu was absolute. There was no question that I'd been through this exact experience many times before.

The joyous déjà vu of earlier didn't have this cyclical feeling. Rather, it had the feeling that from time to time one would remember this place and then forget it again, and then maybe later, owing to serendipity, one would remember it again and be filled with joy—and then forget it again, etc. It was utterly familiar, but there was a gentleness and grace about it, with no internal pressure to either remember or forget. By contrast, the *schlomus*—being stricken by a thunderbolt into cosmic wrongness—was like an ineluctable cycle that was fated and cataclysmic, as though I were condemned because of this wound to reenact the cycle forever. I recognized that everything I think of as myself, everything I present to the world and to myself as the person who is me—my ego—I'd constructed specifically to avoid this very experience.

As a kid, each of us is taught, directly and indirectly, that you've got to keep yourself under control, that you've got to "behave," that you can't be in touch with the true nature of the universe all the time, that you can't bellow every time you feel like bellowing, pee every time you feel like peeing, scream every time you feel like screaming. Your parents, by word, action, or facial expression, give you to understand that you may not be who you really are, that you have to pull it together. I think the ego forms in this way: in order to behave in a way that is acceptable to your parents, you—by necessity—suppress your intuitive reality. You behave as though you believe that your reality is what your parents believe it is.

This loss of grace, this cutting ourselves off from the direct experience of God, is what is commemorated in the myth of the Fall. This is the human condition: our connection with the true nature of the universe has been severed, though not entirely (or we would die); so our lives are a balance between keeping ourselves under control and allowing ourselves glimpses of God. We all experience in varying degrees the pain of having to build an ego, which, in some paradoxical way, is built to protect us from the horrible pain of wrenching ourselves away from God.

The spiritual paths help us safely make touch with God, without getting scared and feeling as though we must slam on the brakes. That's what doubt is. When we get too close to God, we may feel, *Uh-oh. This is too much. I'm going mad.* But the Buddha is always saying, "Trust. This is it. This enlightenment of which I speak, which you are now catching a glimpse of, is the same that all of the Buddhas of all times, past and future, are preaching. Have no doubt. This is the Buddha-knowledge." Then, if you believe that, and trust, you can enjoy larger portions of such knowledge. Jesus says, "Put your faith in me. Be as a little child. If you put your faith in me entirely, then the kingdom of God will be yours."

Jesus and the Buddha are both trying to help us make spiritual progress without falling into the pit of doubt and setting ourselves back on the path. Progress should be gradual. As you trust more and more, you're able to experience more and more of the exhilaration and vastness of the mystical experience. LSD, for good or ill, puts you there whether you want to be or not. At least it did for me. So I got what I wanted, but then I paid the price for it, because I doubted.

The enormity of my pain as we were walking down the mountain cannot be conveyed. It was as though the entire universe were filled with woundedness, brokenness, wrongness. As we approached the house, I was able to recall enough of my old fantasy of reality, the one that Stephen and Gary subscribed to, to behave as though I still believed in it. I started talking again, but voicing only quotidian concerns such as "What's for supper?" The next morning, I'd forgotten entirely what had taken place on the mountain. I remembered that something huge had happened, but I didn't recall what it was. In the years that followed, there would be an intense struggle to remember, and there were flashbacks.

Over the next few weeks, I had a constant headache. My friends, who had similar maladies, called them "acid headaches." They are caused, I believe, by blocking from consciousness something that had taken place during a trip. In subsequent years I met quite a number of people who had, in one way or another, gone through *that* trip, a trip that mirrored the Fall. There was a huge drive within me to remember what had happened up on the mountain. The first inkling that broke through to my consciousness was that it had been about God. "That's right! It was about God!" I thought that was wonderful. I continued to explore, and the furthest I went chemically was to do acid again. I did a smaller amount with a friend named Denny, who was much younger than I was and not such a good source of support.

We took the acid about two months after the big trip, around Christmas, 1969. My aim was to get back to that place on Kittatinny Mountain and to remember what had happened. I went right back to the moment of strickenness. I started writing down the words as I went through the experience all over again. Though I didn't re-experience the initial affirmative part of the original trip, I did recall it. So the whole trip was there in my memory. Later I decided that I had to destroy all the words I'd recorded, in order to rid myself of the link to this place, which had been, during this follow-up trip, exactly the same in every detail, and just as distressing the second time around.

Now I felt I needed help, to talk to someone who understood these things, to get a handle on it, even if it meant reliving it. This was without question the most significant experience of my adult life. I felt I couldn't talk to Stephen about it, because I thought that would be to plunge right back into the pit, since he was the one who had set it off when he told me to stop. I'd been banished from therapy with Frederick, the man whom Stephen and I had both been meeting with, both individually and in group therapy. After I'd worked with him very successfully for several years, an incident occurred that made me feel that I'd been manipulated by him and then betrayed. I was so furious, I was taking up the entire hour of group to rant at him; so he kicked me out.

I don't know where I got the courage or folly to phone Frederick, but I called him because I knew he'd done acid and I respected his wisdom. I told him I'd just been through a calamitous acid trip and wanted to have one session with him. He replied, "I never want to see you again and I mean that."

So I started calling upon everyone who might be able to shed some light on the trip. I saw Rollo May, who referred me to somebody else. I saw a bunch of therapists and told my story, hoping one of them would say yes, I've been through this, or I've had patients who've been through this, and these are things you might do to reconcile and integrate. Every professional I talked to said after hearing my story that they now understood much more about such phenomena than they did before—that I was very articulate in my descriptions—and they thanked me for increasing their understanding. But they had nothing for me. The ones who in my mind had more integrity didn't bill me. The bigger-name therapists did bill me, and I thought it was a bit outrageous that they'd gotten so much while I got only the pleasure of recounting the trip again at great peril.

I saw a couple of prominent spiritual people. Ephrem Weissman put me in touch with a woman named Charlotte Selver, who ran something called the Selver-Brooks Studio with her husband, Charles Brooks. They did physical exercises that she called "experiments" which Ephrem thought would be good for grounding me in my body. I was introduced to Hilda Charlton, a guru in her own right, who's made a reputation for herself since those days. She was so good as to commend me to the protection of her guru, who might have been Sai Baba, though I can't recall for sure. She also gave me a packet of dust that he'd purportedly made to materialize, recommending that I put a bit of the stuff on the tip of my tongue when I needed strength and protection. I've done so over the years at critical times, more in the several years following the trip than afterward. I still have some, and, in fact, put some on the tip of my tongue this morning in preparation for relating this story, to help me get through it.

Apart from feeling the trappings of the trip just a hairsbreadth outside my consciousness, with words from it hovering in my skull, another long-term effect of the trip was that I was far less able to manage the ordinary activities of life. I'd be paralyzed by a pile of paperwork at work. Cleaning the house seemed like a formidable task.

I nearly cut short a vacation in the south of England when I found that I couldn't function in the absence of the familiar things of my life in New York. I thought it would help to visit my friend Aaron in Cambridge, but, to my horror, when I told him about the trip, he discredited the entire experience because it had been induced by a chemical. I returned home, feeling out of place, abandoned, and misunderstood.

My physician, who also had a degree in psychiatry, experimented with various drug prescriptions for me. I found that a little bit of Preludin, a popular diet pill back then, would pull me right together. My ego would feel the way it did in the old days. While on Preludin, I was no longer living in terror, as though I were on the verge of tripping my brains out. After a couple of months, I decided I didn't want to be on this or any pill for the rest of my life, so I just stopped. Coming off of the drug was a bit scary. It felt dangerous, close to the edge.

My doctor also prescribed Thorazine, which makes you stupid, so I was reluctant to take it. But I needed something to keep the trip experience from taking me over, so I started taking fifty milligrams—fast-acting—twice a day, not the sort of dose you'd take as a patient in a mental hospital, but enough to make it difficult for me to make connections. It worked. My mind stopped making the connections between the trip and everyday reality whether I wanted it to or not. During the period I was on Thorazine, I was really dull-witted. I could speak and hear only simple sentences. My colleagues at the library were very patient with me; bless their souls. They knew about my troubles, as my life was an open book.

Eventually I went off Thorazine. I was tired of being brain-dead. I noticed that I was at my weakest in the late afternoon, so the time I was most vulnerable to attacks would be on the drive home from work to Branchville, where I'd been living since 1973. So I told my doctor that if I could take five milligrams of Valium just to get me home every late afternoon, then I'd be able to handle the rest of it straight. He bought it, and gave me a prescription that I used for that purpose.

For New Year's Eve, 1973, my friend Dennis and I drove up to Guilford, Vermont, to visit some friends at a commune at Packers' Corners. There was a big party that was held in a huge auditorium-sized room with a stage at one end. Many people, knowing it was going to be a show as well as a party, had prepared acts. One of them consisted of this guy playing sexy music on a clarinet and a woman who was nude but for paper hearts over her breasts and crotch. One by one, she put on her clothes in a reverse striptease. People in the audience were yelling. "Put it on! Put it on!"

Somebody had put some hash in the food and I didn't know about it. As the show began, I started getting really, really high. I didn't have any pills to counter it, so I just had to go with it. At some point in the evening, I went into the *schlomus.* I told Dennis what was happening and he told me that he was also tripping out. We held each other's hands and from time to time said wise things to each other like "I guess that's it." That's how I got through it. This was the easiest of the flashbacks I had, in part because I knew that Dennis was going through something too.

As we drove back to Branchville the next morning, with tears streaming from my eyes, we recited Eliot's "Four Quartets." Everywhere I go I carry a copy of this amazing poetry. When I discovered it again after the trip, I couldn't believe Eliot knew about this stuff. I'm particularly moved by some lines from "Burnt Norton" in which he observes that the burden of memory and anticipation upon our frail physiology "Protects mankind from heaven and damnation / Which flesh cannot endure."

In the fall of 1974, I drove with my friend John, an ex-lover, in fact my first, to look at a piece of property on Hamburg Mountain I was thinking of buying with friends. We smoked joints on the way up. At a particular point on Route 23, just past Lake Gerard, I started to trip. I went back to that place on the mountaintop, the blue of Stephen's clothes, the orange of the leaves, the screaming of the insects, the cascading of words in my head, and the stricken, wounded-animal feeling. It was a full-blown *schlomus.* I was tripping my brains out.

John and I were soul mates, and I could intuit that I dare not tell him what was happening in my head, because if I did, he would go off himself in a sort of sympathetic response. So I showed him the patch of land and drove out to Branchville, all the while behaving as though nothing were wrong. When I told him about it afterward, he thanked me, because he said that I was right, that if at that moment he had thought I was tripping, he would have blown it. I was pleased that I'd done John that favor, but it was also at considerable expense to myself, as it was doubly hard to both relive the trip and stay zipped up about it.

An important turning point was meeting Don in 1974. He was the first person with whom I had a sexual relationship with whom I was able to cry. He was very understanding, not frightened of my tears. He'd kiss my eyes and tell me that I was beautiful. That was one of the greatest gifts I've ever received. As a result of my trust in Don, I began to pull myself out of the depths. I began to feel more competent, more able to take care of the details of my life, more like the self I was before the trip.

A guru came in August 1976. A friend told me about Dr. Kaushek, who came from India, and had a loyal following in the West. He was going to appear for a week at a temporary ashram set up at a farm outside Woodstock, New York. I decided to go. My hope was that Dr. Kaushek would agree to an interview and that perhaps he, being a holy man, could shed some light on what had happened to me. Dr. Kaushek's visit was to culminate with a lecture at a church in Woodstock on Saturday. I had to work at the library that day, so I planned to be at the ashram Monday through Friday and to return to Branchville Friday night. I took the week off from work and went up to Woodstock. When the doctor took a walk in the morning, pausing from time to time to talk to the group, I went along to listen.

Eventually I spoke with him and hastily told him my story. He offered to allow me to relive my trip in his presence. This was a daunting prospect, and I had to decide whether I was up to it. I spent the rest of the week at this wonderful farm/ashram, which was abuzz with buoyant, wholesome spirituality. Everyone there had come with great reverence. During my time there it came to me that I felt a special affinity for the narrator of the first Psalm. I felt that that believer was the person I most hoped to emulate.

I didn't feel I had the courage to go through the trip in Dr. Kaushek's presence, and I let him know my decision. In the course of a lecture that day, he made reference to a person who was in prison and chose to remain there, even though it was possible to open the door and escape. I knew he meant me, and he did. He was looking right at me.

When Dr. Kaushek left the building after that lecture, I felt terrible. There was a kid named Isaac at the ashram, around ten, whose mother was an adherent. He was always persuading people to play games with him. I had had very little contact with the others, but I had agreed to play a couple of games with Isaac. He was running around this terraced area and happened upon me in the room. He took one look at me and said, "He hurt you very much, didn't he?" It just blew me away that this kid could see it and would say something to me.

On Friday evening I left the ashram, in my mind in failure and disgrace, and returned to Branchville. When I got to the house, my friend Stephanie was there, and we drove together back to the city on Saturday morning. On the way, I was telling her about my experience at the ashram: how wonderful the people were, what Dr. Kaushek had said, Isaac's compassion. My story came to a pinnacle on the George Washington Bridge. We were a third of the way across when I started to trip. It was a *schlomus.* I went right back to that place at the top of the mountain. I don't know how I drove, but I was able to say to Stephanie, "It's happening," and she knew what I was talking about. That helped compose me.

I got off at the nearest exit on the Manhattan side, pulled over on Fort Washington Avenue and stopped the car. It struck me that if I was going to have this trip commuting to work on the George Washington Bridge, then I may as well go through it with Dr. Kaushek. So I called the farm in Woodstock from a phone booth and asked if Dr. Kaushek could see me after all. They said they didn't know, but that he was going to be giving a lecture in the church that evening and I could talk to him then. Then I called work and told them I wasn't coming in, that I had to go to Woodstock, that this might be the most important thing I'd ever done. They were furious, but there was no question that I would pass up this opportunity. If I lost my job, I lost my job. This was my chance to have this settled. I called my friend Jim and asked if he'd accompany me on the way back so that I'd have a friend to support me. He said sure.

We drove back to Woodstock right away, arriving at the church while the lecture was in progress. I sat in the back and listened, and when it was over I ran to the front of the church, got Dr. Kaushek's attention, and asked him if he'd still be willing to let me go through the trip with him. He said yes, we could do it the following morning.

That night I had a dream in which Dr. Kaushek identified various disparate aspects of my world as a Volkswagen, the car I drove. When I awoke, I interpreted the dream to mean that he would be there with me as I went through the trip, holding my hand, identifying aspects of the trip as aspects of my self. I thought that with his gentle encouragement, I'd accept each part of the experience as a part of myself and make my peace with it.

I went to Dr. Kaushek's office for our appointment. He said, "Okay, do your experience." There I am, on the spot. I have to start tripping in front of him. I don't know how to do it. So I start to chant, "It's a *schlomus.* It's a *schlomus,*" figuring that would do it, but it didn't. My ace in the hole was that someone had given me a joint. I lit it up and started to get high and then proceeded to whiz past the trappings of the trip to a place that was just black. Never mind the mountaintop and the flashbacks. This place was just black.

I screamed at the top of my lungs and screamed again and again, as loud and as long as I could, perhaps fifteen minutes, taking time between convulsions only to take a hasty breath before howling some more. I cried out, I recognized later, in the way that infants abandoned by their parents do. Jim was off in the woods and he heard it and knew immediately what it was.

I finally stopped screaming, though there was much more to do: I felt as though it were endless. My ego was ripped to shreds. This was not at all what I'd hoped. I just sat there before Dr. Kaushek. He was completely unmoved, not horrified. After a while, he tried to help me rebuild my ego by explaining the nature of reality by his lights. I would say, "No," and he would respond, "If you don't trust me, I can't help you." This held the terrifying threat of abandonment, so I pretended that I trusted him and listened to his reconstruction. Though it didn't correspond to what I believed, I could see that he was doing his best to try to reconstruct my ego. After I'd come down to a degree, he told me he had work to do and said I could stay in his office for as long as I needed to. I stayed for a while and eventually got up and walked out. Later I overheard him explain my screaming to a concerned adherent: "He saw the void and was afraid."

I ran into Isaac's mother, a very sweet woman, who told me, "Right now, it's all up here," touching my head. "If you can make it come down to here," touching my heart, "it should be easier."

I left. Jim and I drove back to Branchville, arriving Sunday afternoon. Some friends were there. I thought, *I can't do this anymore; I can't keep trying to reconcile by getting back to the crux of the trip and make it right. I can't live on the edge like this anymore. Okay, I'll make a bargain with the Devil. I promise that I won't try to go back, and in return you'll protect me.* And I took a Thorazine.

I slumped back. *I'm giving up my connection with God. I'm giving up my intent to be on a spiritual path and to make right a mysterious, wondrous experience that went horribly wrong, in return for protection from going through the nightmare again and again.* But I had to. It was too much. I simply had to protect my ego from further ravaging, and I needed time to mend. The path to the mountaintop had been blasted in my mind so many times, it was now a six-lane interstate highway. The slightest exhilaration could send me right back there. So I gave up heaven to stave off hell. I just couldn't take it anymore. I felt tremendous resignation and sadness.

In 1978 I moved to northern New England. My nightmare immediately receded into the background. My life became about survival, getting used to a new place and a new job at a radio station. The trip became a memory. The decision to move was initiated by a series of Ouija board sessions I had with a bunch of friends.

Just before my move, I had another Ouija board session with a friend I was having an affair with at the time, Robert, and his friend Gerard. Both Robert and Gerard were very good spirit channelers. Robert used to commune on a regular basis with this marquis from the time of Marie Antoinette. It seemed peculiar to me, but he'd accept this stuff like it was perfectly normal. On this occasion, Robert and Gerard got out the board and summoned my "spirit guide," whom I'd never contacted before. My first question was "What about the words?" Speaking through Gerard, the spirit guide asked, "What words?"

"The words from the trip."

"The words are in a language long dead that you spoke in a former life. The translation is as follows: 'O great spirit of the One, life is a blessing beyond description, and I am ceaselessly grateful to you for bestowing it on me.' " I've since adopted that as my favorite prayer. I love it with all my heart. When I'm in situations where I share it, it confers more power if I tell a little bit of the story behind it.

Now, who knows if Gerard made that up, if there was a spirit guide or not. But in my mind, the prayer is powerful and beautiful regardless of its origin. And it's believable that those are the words I was speaking to Stephen that day on the mountaintop, to make him understand.

I have stopped doing mind-expanding drugs of any kind. So that is one way in which I am, in fact, keeping my end of my pact with the Devil. Over the years, I've assumed that if I did not resolve this matter during my lifetime, I would have to go there at the moment of my death. I have reason to believe now that that may not be necessary: that if I'm in the company of people whom I trust, it's quite possible that I will pass peacefully to God without having to face the dragons on the mountain.

John Perry Barlow

B. 1947

Vice chairman and cofounder of the Electronic Frontier Foundation; Berkman Fellow at the Harvard Law School; former Grateful Dead lyricist and cattle rancher; father of three teenage girls

Resides in Wyoming

Born and raised in Wyoming

My First Trip

In a sense, there is only one real trip, the first one. After that, it's merely confirming what has already been revealed. I've probably taken psychedelic substances of one kind or another more than a thousand times. But I was permanently rewired—my sense of the universe was forever changed—the first time I ingested LSD.

I did this sometime in late 1966 at Wesleyan University in Middletown, Connecticut, where I was then a student. The school had a distinguished world music program that brought in Ravi Shankar, Ali Akbar Khan, and others of their caliber, as fellows. Every Friday evening there would be a concert and curry dinner in a converted farmhouse outside of town.

There was a guy I'll call Ben who frequently attended these concerts. I always regarded Ben as a darkly magical character. He was a true prankster, one of the last Dada artists. On one of these curry concert evenings, he approached me and said, "I have a feeling you're interested in psychedelics." Indeed I was.

Not long before, I'd read about the celebrated Good Friday Experiment of Walter Pahnke and was impressed with psilocybin's apparent capacity to steer ideation toward the Divine. I was very eager to establish contact with the Holy Who Knows. I'd been, at one time in my life, a fairly devout Mormon, but I'd traded my faith for juvenile delinquency and had been unable to get it back. I missed it. While I didn't miss some of the behavioral constraints that went along with being a Mormon, I did long to feel connected again to the huge and invisible. Because of the surprisingly Christian angle of the Good Friday Experiment, I thought that I might find in LSD something that might restore my connection with the God of the Bible.

I'd never actually seen any psychedelics up to that point, so I jumped at the chance. Ben handed me a capsule. I took it and sat down to listen to the music. I think Ali Akbar Khan was playing that night. About half an hour into the concert, I started to feel like I could literally feel the music on my skin. Shortly it seemed I could taste it and smell it as well. All of my senses were fusing into one. I also had the strong perception that with every beat of the tabla, a splash of what I now recognize to be fractal webbing would leap from that area of the room and sparkle across the walls.

When I say fractal webbing, I mean the lacy latticework that you see if you map certain chaotic mathematical realities like the Mandelbrot Set to a computer screen. When you use computation to visualize and magnify the "edges" of the Mandelbrot Set, you will see on your monitor exactly the same images that seemed to be exploding from the drum beats that night. It was a moiré of multicolored threads that seemed to connect everything in the room.

The interesting thing is that when I first beheld the fractal webs layering themselves upon the walls of that room, no one had ever seen them on a computer screen. It would be another eleven years before Mandelbrot would discover fractal geometry. But of course, the lack of modeling system hardly meant that the reality wasn't there. Indeed, it is now thought that the brief formulae of chaos math are actually the underlying algorithms of nature. All natural things, whether clouds, trees, river tributaries, blood vessels, or nervous dendrites, derive their structure from the recursive iteration of these very simple little rules.

Seeing those fractals and feeling them in the music, I sensed the complete connectedness of everything. It was obvious to me that all of the separateness I ordinarily perceived was, in fact, an artifact of cultural conditioning, and was indeed less "real" than what I was supposedly hallucinating. At that moment, I knew that I was, for the first time, experiencing things as they are, utterly continuous. There is no discontinuity. There is not one thing and another thing. It is all the same thing, the Holy Thing.

The Holy Thing I experienced that night didn't seem related to God as I had thought of deity before, a separate, invisible, all-powerful, all-knowing entity that was only a greatly enhanced version of something like me. Rather it seemed that God was all the universe, that we were God, that it was God, that everything was all holy.

I had taken a fairly large dose and was disoriented enough that I couldn't speak at the end of the concert. Ben and a couple of friends took me back to the place I was staying. There we lit some candles, put on other music, and sat and listened all night without attempting to say very much. I seemed able to let everything go through my mind without straining the system, as though my awareness were dilated to an aperture that could accommodate the passage of the universe through it without causing me any grave discomfort.

I subsequently had trips where that same kind of opening felt terrifying. On those occasions, I couldn't sustain enough of conventional reality to feel safely myself. There was also on those occasions the terrible feeling that my self had become so fragmented that its bits and pieces would never reassemble into something recognizably "me." I've learned to be grateful for these horrors too, in that they instruct me on my own fragile miracle.

But the first time I tripped, it didn't feel like "I" went away. There was still a me there somewhere—mostly as the point around which my fragments orbited, but that "me" felt like an integral part of everything else. It was more a matter of realizing that I was it. I didn't go away. I just got much, much larger. I went someplace overwhelmingly different that night, and, to a large extent, stayed there for the rest of my life. My transformation didn't go through phases. I was simply somebody different after that.

As many times as I revisited the vision of interrelatedness I had that evening, I don't think I ever felt that quite so strongly again, because, as I say, my settings had already been recalibrated. From that point forward, I could always feel the natural connection of everything, despite living in a world where the illusion of separateness is impossible to resist.

Of course some of that illusion is an operating necessity. Navigating the world of normal consciousness, one has to believe that if you pick up a rock and drop it on your foot, it will be separate enough to hurt you. If you walk off a balcony, you will be separate enough to fall. And yet I know that, on some deeper level, even falling to one's death is a kind of illusion. Nothing dies, it merely moves into another manifestation of the whole.

My sense of time changed that evening. While it is also necessary and practical to go on perceiving time as being an irreversible sequence from past to future, there is a part of me that somehow "knows" that everything is actually happening once and that only the limitations of human consciousness make it appear otherwise.

Another thing that happened to me that night was that I began believing again, for the first time since I was about fourteen, that the universe has a purpose, that no matter what happens in one's own infinitesimal vicinity, the universe is working fine. I don't believe that the meaning or direction or shape of that purpose can ever be understood by us, but it is possible to have faith in it without knowing any of those things. Subsequent to the experience, I've felt reaffirmations of that purpose, and my place in it, in a lot of different ways, primarily through the intervention of the countless meaningful coincidences—or synchronicities—that have become the dominant factor in plotting the crooked course of my life.

There have been improbable encounters at propitious moments, doors that strangely opened to me, little miracles. I think these are there for everyone, but psychedelics make it easier to see and accept aspects of reality that one can't rationally explain. Of course, one can reach this state of awareness without them. Consider the great quantum physicist Niels Bohr, who, when asked if he believed in superstition, responded, "I don't have to believe in it. It works anyway."

The essence of what I received that night was a recognition that reality, in its totality, is something much larger and more complex than will ever fit through the tiny keyhole of human perception. Human perception, even enhanced by all the tools of technological amplification we might invent, will never begin to encompass It. We will always be limited by the filters of consciousness. Consciousness, I now believe, is more about what we don't experience than what we do. Thus, reality, as most people experience it in the objective, scientifically reproducible, Western sense, is really an opinion based on what little we can perceive of the Thing itself.

With the possible exception of having children, taking that trip was the most important thing I ever did. In terms of creating the person I am and how I approach the world, why I do what I do, and what I think it's all about, no other experience in my life has been so transforming. When you know that everything is invisibly connected, it alters everything you do, from the way you treat "other" people to the way you treat "yourself." It certainly changed the focus of my intellectual interests.

Up to that point, I'd been preparing myself to master in physics. Suddenly my focus was much more diffuse but oriented more toward the general vicinity of religion, especially those philosophical traditions, most of them Eastern, that seemed to describe the insights I was given that night. I also read mystical literature from other traditions, including the fairly slender body of it that exists in the Western world, seers such as Meister Eckeart, St. John of the Cross, and Saint Teresa of Avila.

Another thing that happened to me at the time of this first trip was being assigned Teillhard de Chardin for a philosophy course I was taking. I hadn't quite been getting what he was on about, but after the trip, I knew that he had somehow seen what I had seen. He wrote that evolution was reaching a level of complexity where it could become aware of itself, creating a collective organism of mind capable of keeping God company. Understanding his vision and adopting it drives much of my efforts today. I'm trying to spread electronic communications systems in order to hook up the nervous system of that organism.

Engaged in the politics necessary to wire the world, I encounter many people in positions of influence and visibility—politicians, corporate leaders, scientists, engineers, writers, academics—who are motivated by the same mystical drive that propels me. They are acidheads, but nearly all of them are afraid to admit it. It's as though the future were being created by a secret cult. And even though it's my secret cult, I'm not crazy about secrecy or cults, and I'm certainly not keen on having them design the rest of society.

I think it's time to be brave and honest. I know that if everybody who'd ever taken a major psychedelic stood up and said, "Yeah, I did that and this is how it changed my life," the world would be a better place the next day.

Julian

B. 1952

Inventor, entrepreneur

Resides in London

Born and raised in the U.K.

An Awakening from Within

My first experiences with LSD were quite inspirational. In fact, my vocation today as an inventor is a direct outcome of my acid-derived revelations some twenty-eight years ago. Translating the cosmic consciousness I tapped into on acid into a healing force useful to society is my raison d'être.

In 1972 I'd just returned to London from Syria, where I was working as an artist on an archaeological dig in the Euphrates Valley. I was twenty and feeling like my creative potential was not being realized, totally frustrated that here I was back in England and still just spinning my wheels, with no understanding of what my purpose really was. I was staying in two places in Clapham North, south London, looking after my brother's flat and that of a friend.

I got involved in a band, just some friends who got together and banged away. I was the drummer. The subtleties of playing and listening to music on cannabis aroused my curiosity about the possibilities of discovering even more levels of consciousness via LSD. I managed to get a friend to procure me a couple tabs of Yellow Microdot and set them aside for when the time was right.

One day before band practice, I said to myself, *I'll get really nicely stoned with this LSD before the band comes 'round for practice and then I'll be in there with that rhythm and really going for it.* I took one to begin with, then thought, *Well, they're a bit small. I'll take the other one too.* Nothing was really happening. I waited for the band to come. Twenty minutes later, they still hadn't arrived, so I started playing. The beat got faster, the pitch got higher, and I began to hallucinate.

The little marks where the sticks had been hitting the snare drum over the life of the skin were turning into tiny African faces with purple eyes and mouths moving very, very fast. I could make these little faces move faster by increasing the speed of my drumming. I suppose the African features reflected my association of rhythm with that culture.

Time seemed to be stepping on its brakes as I went through these intense physiological and psychological sensations that felt overwhelming and unstoppable, like a riptide. It became tremendously fearsome. I'd taken the precaution of buying a tube of effervescent vitamin C to have on hand in case of a bad turn, so when these overpowering sensations accelerated to the pace of knots, I got a pint mug as fast as I could, filled it with water and dumped in the entire tube. Before it had finished fizzing, I'd already drunk it all.

This feeling—that I was a first-stage rocket taking off—was temporarily relieved, but a few minutes later I was once again feeling overwhelmed. I looked down at my body as though for the first time, and wondered, *Who's looking at my body?* It was as though I were a discorporate being looking down at this "other" body. It was terrifying, especially because of the tremendous body rushes, which made me feel even less in possession of my corporeal self.

My friends had still not arrived, but by that time I wasn't thinking about them anymore. I realized that I needed to get some help quickly, that I should get out of the house and get some more vitamin C. I wanted to get to a park with some trees, somewhere I could feel at ease with myself and my environment. I decided to go to Clapham Common. I remembered there was a chemist on the way, but when I got there, I wasn't *compus mentis* enough to go in and inquire after a tube of vitamin C. I didn't even have any money! So I just rushed over to the common and got there in five minutes, out of breath. But then I realized that this wasn't the place either. It wasn't remote enough. There were plenty of trees but too many people around.

I was sweating profusely and felt my eyes were sticking out like stalks. I was sure people would know I was overdosing or that something highly irregular or illegal was going on with me. I thought I *had* overdosed and that it was imperative to find someone to rectify my poisoned, discombobulated self. I was frantic, and figured my condition was drastic enough to require the whole rescue squad: ambulance, police, fire engine, the works.

I remembered there was a hospital near the common and made a beeline for it. I got inside the front door, only to find that it was not a general hospital but a women's hospital with no outpatient clinic or emergency facility. There was a quiet reception room and a hole in the wall with a sliding-glass window, where I summoned the attention of a girl sitting there. I blurted out that I'd overdosed on LSD and someone's got to help me right away! She placed a quick phone call, eyeing me as though I were a lunatic.

A matron emerged. She sized up the situation and organized things. She said an ambulance was going to come and take me to St. James, a general hospital, and she told me to sit down in a chair in the lobby and try to sleep. Here I was taking off like a first-stage rocket and she wanted me to sleep! Sure enough, an ambulance arrived in due time and I was taken to the emergency unit at St. James, where I was put in a cubicle behind closed curtains. In the cubicle next to mine was someone who'd been brought in from a car accident. There was lots of screaming and crying and rushing about.

A doctor stepped through the curtains. I gave him my story and started to calm down a bit. Then I broke into tears. It was such a relief that someone was going to sort this out, that I could tell somebody about it and it was going to be all right from now on. I cried my eyes out. He instructed me to lie down and try to go to sleep. Again, there was no way I was going to doze off. He went off, and shortly thereafter a bobby came in.

By now I was cruising into much more gentle, second-stage rushes, and I was hallucinating. He had a ruddy complexion with a heavy beard that a razor could barely suppress. His face was forming all these wild paisley patterns. He demanded to know where I'd got the acid. By then I was fearless. I gave him some story about how I'd gotten it at a party. He was persistent and I was persistent back at him. He left knowing he wasn't going to get any joy from me.

I must have been there over an hour and there was still all this screaming and crying next door. It came to me, *I'm in the wrong place. Somebody else needs this space. I don't. Emergency services have obviously done its job for me already.* So I walked out, didn't sign out or say good-bye to anyone, and nobody tried to stop me.

I headed home and the walk back was amazing. I started having cosmic revelations about myself, the trees and the wind, the streets and the cars, life, the universe. *It's all amazing and I'm part of it and I'm okay.* When I got home, I sat down, had a cup of tea and just enjoyed the rest of the ride. Insights came to me like comets flashing across the dome of my consciousness. In the evening, I went over to see my band mates, who lived in a fluctuating house full of Australians, New Zealanders, Canadians, Americans, Turks, all sorts of people. A lot of them were experimenting with LSD, hashish, and marijuana on a regular basis. I ended up moving in.

In the next six months, I took LSD between fifty and a hundred times. Never again after my big-bang start did I experience a bad trip. Over this period, acid awakened something in me like a waiting genius that I knew was there. Although it was a rough launch, this half-year, self-administered course of LSD changed my character completely and set me on a path that would change the rest of my life. What I am today, all of my thinking and endeavors, is a result of that time. It was the most profound thing that had ever happened to me, an awakening from within. I needed something special to satisfy my craving for personal insight and to bridge the void in my formal training. School had been a nightmare for me, perhaps because I'm slightly dyslexic. I left when I was fifteen, not knowing how to read or write.

My acid regime was not about "looning" or partying all night long, but about staying in and communing with higher reality. If I needed to go out to get tea, coffee, and bread and stuff, that was fine, as long as I wasn't in the first stages of trajectory. As soon as you get into orbit, it was serenity, very similar to the way the astronauts talk about going into space.

I found long episodes tiring, especially if I had to work the next day, so I learned to take the right amount so that the intense period would last only an hour. Eventually I did it mostly by myself, as the revelations weren't as intense when I did it with others. I would set the scene so that I wouldn't be disturbed for four hours or longer. I put on some mood-enhancing music, burned some incense, and laid out crystals and various other things. I'd sit in one place in a lotus position with a pad of paper and a pen and write down things that came to me, concepts relevant to the work I saw emerging for myself, directions for me to go. I'd ask a question and wait for the answer.

When I refined my pursuits, I set up an optical mirror and behind that a red strobe with a dimmer. During the trip I'd manipulate the speed and pulse frequencies simultaneously, so that it would dim and pulse at the same time. When I looked at the red strobe, I'd see almost every other color but red, plus all these archetypal hallucinogenic patterns. I set this strobe apparatus behind the mirror and looked into a reflection of my upper body. Big changes would go on in my face: woman, old man, beard, frightening, serene. Each mask was a vehicle for discovery, not a "self-portrait" to get hung up on. I had visions of pure mathematical forms, like a torus, a doughnut-shaped figure generated by a circle or eclipse. I would look through a geometrical tube, watching the outside skin turn inside out, folding in upon itself and exposing new layers of reality.

Acid awakened me to the correlation between the subatomic realm and the heavenly bodies of the astronomical universe. It made me vividly and vitally aware that the self was an integral part of the cosmos. I felt an electrifying sense of belonging and interconnectedness and a profound bliss at the realization that we all have an innate purpose as links in the cosmic chain. I decided that my task was to use these positive revelations to make the best contribution to mankind I could make.

I wanted to bring something back from the cosmic space that acid brought me to, to access that consciousness somehow and carry it back onto terra firma before it "melted," to produce a manifestation that made sense of it all. So I invented a visual-effects concept that explained it quite beautifully. It was like a mandala. When you looked into it, you saw an amazing illusionary space that you believed was there. It's like the Tardis on *Dr. Who,* the British sci-fi TV series from the 1970s. From the outside it's just a phone booth, but once he's inside and closes the door, it's a huge time machine and laboratory.

I designed a piece of technology called the Cosmoscope that has this same feeling about it. It's a very believable expansive space inside a very small one, constructed with fiber optics, lightbulbs, mirrors, and a color wheel. It creates the illusion of a huge sphere with other spheres inside, expanding and contracting with color. It's very restful and peaceful to look at. The spheres are glass balls that look very sensual. You want to fondle them.

The effect produced by this apparatus, an image of a basic structure like the atom or the planets in our galaxy, is called "primordial viewing." When you look into it, you have this compelling feeling of being drawn in, and it just takes over, like a form of hypnosis. The Cosmoscope grew out of an acid-inspired understanding I developed of the affinity between the micro- and macrocosms and between the visible and the invisible, and the notion that the universe is comprised more of energy frequencies than of matter.

At the end of this six-month period, I realized that I had to stop taking LSD. I could feel the beginning of a sort of psychosis setting in. I'd learned enough from acid, and now it was time to cast what I'd learned into material reality. Having brought something back from the psychedelic realm, the scheme for the Cosmoscope, I then went through an evolution in my conception of its purpose.

I went to work with my doctor, a practitioner of natural medicine, including homeopathy, osteopathy, naturopathy, and acupuncture. He hired me to tend the organic garden at his estate in Suffolk, where he'd transformed a Georgian rectory into a therapeutic center. There we built a sensory stimulation tank, then an orgone accumulator, and a pyramid-shaped sensory isolation tank for water immersion. The center provided therapy for terminally or seriously ill people, who underwent a whole regime of treatments that might include acupuncture, a mono-fruit diet, and three sessions a week in the isolation tank.

Working in this therapeutic environment got me going in the direction of healing people, which is not precisely how I envisaged myself in the beginning. I'd always thought of using the Cosmoscope and the sensory isolation and stimulation tanks for more personal pursuits, but this therapeutic angle gave it a new, more solid foundation.

In 1991 I got all the necessary gear together and proved that the Cosmoscope actually alters brain-wave activity. When you look into it, it actually sends you into alpha, theta, and delta states, which are highly meditative. I did an experiment live on the Thames News (ITV, Channel 3 in Britain). I wired up a woman with an electroencephalograph and measured the left and right hemispheres of her brain at very deep levels of consciousness and demonstrated that almost instantaneously after looking into the Cosmoscope, the left and right hemispheres came into coherence.

After the broadcast, I received loads of telephone calls, including one from a mental hospital in Sussex, which expressed interest in using it for their patients with hyperactivity, catatonia, learning difficulties, and other disorders. It was used there for a year without actual clinical trials, but the anecdotal evidence indicated positive results. Some patients who'd been catatonic for many years would suddenly speak after a regime of Cosmoscope treatments.

I believe that it's best to introduce such medicine as the Cosmoscope (and LSD, for that matter) slowly and preferably on the basis of sound scientific evidence. You have to be careful not to flaunt it and invite a challenge. It must be brought into being through a remedial or therapeutic medium, such as helping people with life-threatening illnesses.

I've been given tremendous mileage on my quest for meaning by the few transitory glimpses LSD has given me of the cosmic mesh that stitches the universe together. Like the small quantity of dry fuel in a rocket ship that propels it millions of miles into space, a little has taken me a long way indeed. Now I want to carry through my ideas and refine certain technologies, using renewable energies, to take people into empowering states of self-understanding and holistic health.

Kate Coleman

B. 1942

Journalist, veteran of 1960s political movements

Resides in Berkeley, California

Raised in several parts of the United States, including Syracuse, New York; Miami Beach, Florida; and Los Angeles, California

THEN THE EMOTIONS STARTED HAPPENING

As an idealistic left-wing activist at Berkeley in the early Sixties, I thought there was something deranged about drugs. The hippie culture of self-gratification was anathema to me at first. Roaming my own inner space wasn't conducive to ideological discipline and socialistic obligations to community. I graduated in 1965 without even smoking pot, though I had gotten drunk.

With my B.A. in English lit, I scored a job with *Newsweek* in New York, where I relaxed my strictures and finally got high. I never really loved marijuana, though I was a heavy tobacco smoker for years. At the magazine I was the house lefty and somewhat notorious, in part because of my appearance in a documentary about the Berkeley Free Speech Movement called *The Berkeley Rebels,* in which I rode on the back of a motorcycle, wore miniskirts, and looked alienated like the actress Monica Vitti from Antonioni's flicks. In fact, my nickname among CBS crew was Monica. My look was very boho: short black skirt, black sweater, boots, long straight black hair. When I moved to New York, I cut off my hair in a Peggy Moffet/Sassoon style, sort of Joan-of-Arc.

I took acid for the first time on a visit back to Berkeley in 1967. I was helping the education editor, a pal of mine, on the radical scene there, and introduced him to a lot of activists who'd become druggies. That first acid trip was a big deal. I got together with three old friends, a girlfriend and two guys, all of whom are still good friends of mine. Both guys were hetero at the time and are now gay. We planned out every detail of the trip, lining up art books with Expressionistic stuff like Gorky and Kandinsky, art paper and oil-base *craypa* crayons to draw with, music we wanted to hear (mostly classical), and fruit to eat. We even had contingency plans in the event any of us went awry.

We were uptight little people organizing for ultimate safety and aesthetics.

Our zookeeper was a friend named Marcus who lived on the top floor of a John Maybeck house on Virginia Street. Maybeck came out of the Arts and Crafts Movement and was an influence on Frank Lloyd Wright, so the apartment matched our aesthetic criteria nicely with a beautiful balcony, where we could see the architectonic lines of the house. Marcus was a brilliant grad student who was always playing lowball in the cheap poker parlors in Emeryville and studying the counting system for blackjack. So we all showed up at Marcus's place and took eight hundred mikes of acid in pill form, very formal and ritualized. We got very playful. It was never scary—or sexual, for that matter, though I never did take acid with somebody I was *schtupping.*

I felt I'd set down my soul in this Kandinskyesque *craypa* I did. It was a colorful Expressionistic version of Señor Winces, the guy on *The Ed Sullivan Show* who made a puppet character with his hand. There was a mouth and some amorphous shape that could have been a hand. It was a jolly, cartoony, babylike character in bright colors and blobs of colors bleeding. My sister is a painter and I really loved art, but was afraid to make art around her, so the acid trip was a freeing of the inner wannabe artist.

After about six hours, we went outside and Marcus drove us around. We went to a store for snacks and got the giggles. That first trip and another with the same cast were ultra-cautious, aesthetic, and sweet. We were very respectful and mindful of potential mine fields.

Back in New York I lived a sort of double life. I'd look chic and respectable at the magazine, and then be a screaming meemie in the streets, demonstrating against the war. One afternoon in 1968, my worlds collided when Vice President Humphrey came to *Newsweek* and I encountered him in the lobby. I refused to shake his hand as he worked the small crowd, and then said, "Mr. Humphrey, you are a war criminal and a murderer." I almost lost my job for that one. Katharine Graham and then-editor Oz Elliot were horrified.

As a Yippie leader I helped organize some demonstrations in New York and was personally approached by Tom Hayden to infiltrate the Humphrey campaign in the months prior to the '68 Democratic Convention in Chicago. He wanted me positioned to provide intelligence and to get passes out in order to disrupt the floor of the Convention, but I declined, because I didn't want to give up my personal life.

By now I was convinced that psychedelics were worth exploring, but didn't plot out my trips in New York as I had those first trips in Berkeley. I lived in the West Village in a little walk-up on Fourth Street between Tenth and Charles. There I had a memorable acid experience with my friend Chris, a quivering designer fag who decorated the windows at Lord and Taylor's.

We did a huge dose of Owsley acid. (I think all the acid I've ever done was Owsley. I knew his girlfriend for years. She was in my English lit class at Berkeley.) I was very protective toward Chris and I figured it would be safe for us to hang out in the garden adjoining the basement apartment of my neighbor, the reclusive abstract painter Robert Goodenough, then in his sixties. I'd asked his permission and he'd said, "Fine, go ahead and use it."

The other basement apartment belonged to my dear friend Jim, a flea-bitten songwriter who used to own the Fat Black Pussycat, where Dylan played before the place went into decline. Jim and I were close. We played honeymoon bridge all the time and once developed a neighborhood sitcom called "Stoop Trek." He's still in New York writing music and very poor, bless his heart.

A well-known female recording artist I'll call Susan was a personal friend of his. She was seeing this very mod journalist named Mitch, who's now a screenwriter. Susan was Miss Sixties, at the peak of her fame. She decided to visit Jim that day with Mitch in tow. He and I got along because I was also a journalist and was fresh and saucy, so she also made nice noises toward me. She was careful with me because I was media and very political, much further out than she was.

For some reason Jim told them, "Oh, Kate and her friend are over in the garden, tripping." So they sauntered over. Mitch asked me, "How you doin'?" and then she was all over us trying to give love and suck up some of the vibes vicariously, because she'd never in a million years have the nerve to take acid. She was too chickenshit.

Roald Dahl wrote this hilarious story about a guy at a party who flips out at the social advances of a gushy woman. She comes over to talk to him and opens her mouth so wide, he can see her tonsils, which appear to him as a bunny rabbit coming to eat him. He completely loses it over her overwhelmingness and ends up in a padded cell. Well, Susan did that to Chris, and he went into a bad trip. She started emoting, "Oh, you beautiful people . . ." She was so saccharine and effusive, full of love and giving and Lady Bountiful. I looked at her like "Oh, give me a break." She was so phony, it was disgusting. Who could take this? Chris started shrinking like Shrinking Violet. He turned to me in horror, "Heh . . . Ehh . . ." He started to cry and got very quiet.

I leaned in toward him. "Okay, what's the matter?"

"I can't stand this . . ."

"All right, you want to go back to my apartment and it'll just be the two of us?"

"Yesss . . ."

Susan meant well, of course. She was trying to be friendly, but it was too much. No one could take this shit. It was ridiculous. There's only one thing worse than a star with her head stuck in the sky, and that's a star trying to be your friend for no reason.

I made our excuses. "Chris isn't feeling very well," I told everybody, and I took him upstairs to my apartment and held him and tried to cheer him up. After he was reasonably calmed, I went to the bathroom and looked in the mirror, which I'd never done on earlier trips. I started seeing *everybody:* me as a child, my family, everyone I ever knew, and more. When you look in the mirror with eight hundred mikes of acid in tow, everyone shows up at the dance. I think I even saw Eleanor Roosevelt, for Christ's sake. Because of the suggestibility of the lines and the shadows, I also saw blood streaming and death's heads, because you're not just seeing the immediate family; you're seeing the whole tautology.

On acid, the features of the faces are like stria or the dots and lines of a cartoon cel or a Roy Lichtenstein painting, which vibrate and dance and gather into new particularized forms. The iteration of dots and lines is conducive to seeing visions within the focal image, which you then personalize. I grappled with my sister's image for a while, wondering if I was losing my ego to her. She's a powerful figure, the elder sibling I loved and struggled with. I watched as my face kept changing, eventually into people I didn't know. At first I was fascinated by the progression. *Whoa, this is great! Look at all these people who are in me!* I saw myself as beautiful, then ugly, then as a baby. It was so fast, nothing lasted.

When the uglies took over, I was still transfixed. *Wow, this is wild.* It was a motion picture. I saw myself bleeding—blood gushing all over the place—and that scared me. Then I started seeing skeletons, snakes, leering faces, masks. I made some grimaces to see what it would look like—to interact and contribute to the shapes of things. But it all eventually turned to death's heads in one way or another.

I reasoned with the whole thing, half-detached. *Now what are you seeing? Oh, that's a scary one. Oh, there's your sister. Hah hah! Well, she's part of you too.* There was a running commentary inside my head, rationalizing what I saw. Then, when it got really, really hideous, I told myself: *You could go into a nightmare and freak out, but really you're just being shown the whole* mishigoss, *and of course, it's going to turn scary at one point. Your unconscious is deliberately trying to scare you, and it's doing a very good job.*

I stood there and argued with myself over these monstrous visions, but finally realized, *You know, you can take this up at a later date. You don't have to stand there anymore. Besides, Chris needs you more, because he's doing worse than you are right now.* I'd been in there about ten minutes. I concluded that the narrative of faces was telling me something about all being one, that here was everything in my universe, from hell to high water, my family, my friends, my enemies—everything. When I came out, Chris was lying in a heap, still very frightened, and I tended to him. He was really having a bad trip. I started talking to him, engaging him, slowly cheering him up, and we sojourned on.

It was a great boon to me psychologically to realize how strong I was mentally. I saw how people could flip out from the frightful sights, but I gained strength and confidence under acid. I felt very sturdy.

Back on the antiwar front, I helped organize the demonstrations in Chicago, but then decided not to go, because I'd been busted for rioting on the Lower East Side, and didn't want to risk additional legal hassles my fellow Yippies were sure to incite—and did—at the convention. At my trial in the fall of '68, the judge did a double take at my uptown mien (suit, stockings, hair pulled pack) and dismissed charges. So I was free to leave on a trip around the world I'd planned with my boyfriend Phil, a rock record producer. I figured that with Nixon coming in that this would be my last chance to have a good time before we had to get busy smashing the state.

Phil and I went to England, France, and Spain, then Ibiza, where we rented a little peasant *finca* and gathered driftwood to keep warm every night. The weather was just like Berkeley in the winter: brilliant sun in the daytime and freezing the minute the sun dropped. My girlfriend Janis, whom I'd tripped with my first time back in Berkeley, came to visit us. Phil and I weren't getting along. He was impatient and angry and didn't travel well, and then he started falling for Janis, which didn't help, though she did nothing to encourage him. She was very beautiful, with a big head of hair—all these wiry curls she'd suppressed when we were in school. She was a little neurotic, always carrying her umbrella around. Phil soon decided she was a little old lady and started being nasty to her. At first I was quite jealous and then I was protective of her. All she wanted was a refuge with friends.

I took some acid alone at the height of this threatening love triangle, and sat on the rocks high up so I couldn't hear the waves. I looked at the Mediterranean for hours, and saw *apsara,* the heavenly nymphs of Hindu tradition, beautiful Indian women dancing in the waves, row upon row of them—a frenetic frieze of small-waisted exotic dancers with big bosoms and rounded hips and thighs, swaying endlessly. My eyes got fried by staring at the sea all day. No matter where I looked in the sea, I saw these *apsara* undulating to the rhythm of the waves. It started to get boring. I couldn't see anything else. If I look at waves today, I still see those fuckin' Hindu chorus girls. It's my only acid recall.

But while these visuals were going on, I worked out my jealousy. I realized I couldn't betray my friend just because I was jealous. I was in misery over the fear prompted by the jealousy. It should have been a moment of triumph that he didn't like her, but I liked him better when he liked her, because I loved her. He fell in love with her for the wrong reasons and then he rejected her for all the wrong reasons. Phil and I broke up in Egypt. Then he started hustling my friend, an Africa-based journalist, behind my back. He was later busted and went to jail for dealing.

My last acid trip abroad took place in Nepal in the summer of 1969. I was experiencing the grandeur of the Himalaya and beginning to shed some of my New York armor. Almost everyone I met was a seeker and a moron. I was getting more friendly and into the hippie thing, though I was still very political. I'd found a little community I liked, in a little village west of Kathmandu called Swayambhu, named for the Monkey Temple there.

I was traveling alone and would meet people and travel with them for a while. I'd just trekked up the Jomson Trail, flown to Pokhara, and then set out on a new trek with this hippie pretty boy named Bill, whom I shacked up with for a while. We got a little farther than Birethanti, but I was getting wiped out, so we came back to Pokhara after about a week on the trail. Pokhara is like a bowl, a lake surrounded by mountains, including the majestic Annapurna. Bill took off and then Richard, an old friend, showed up and we took some acid in a room we'd rented in a small hotel.

He had his acid and I had mine, the same Owsley I'd packed in tin foil eight months before. His was bunk and he fell asleep. I'd been weakened by diarrhea and coughing from all the trekking, but here I was, wide-awake and about as far out as I could get. The whole experience reminds me of Paul Bowles's *The Sheltering Sky.*

At about four in the morning, the first light started back lighting Annapurna. For two hours before the sun broke above this beautiful snow-capped mountain, the snow took on all the colors of the light refracted behind it. This was color like you'll never see in your life. It was the most gorgeous thing I've ever seen. I was moaning. *I can't believe I'm seeing this.* The shape of Annapurna was outlined in light and the snow that covered it captured every hue, while the sky turned from purple to blue.

In back of the hotel were farms where families lived in close quarters with their chickens and little patches of hardscrabble vegetable garden and carved-out rice fields of atomic green and deep, dark purple. Annapurna was scarlet and magenta and fire and red and pink and purple. There was no white, because it had been completely suffused by the light of the rising sun. The beauty of this display was natural enough, but the acid deepened my appreciation of it, making the darker colors throb and everything shimmer.

Then the emotions started happening. This was a religious experience. I'd never seen anything so beautiful in my life. I'd been watching the mountain go from inky black-blue to indigo to cobalt to lilac to lavender, all these gradations of every color of the spectrum. When it was at the lilac stage and I could finally see the deep chartreuse green of the rice, the locals suddenly began waking up to their daily routines, letting the chickens out from beneath the baskets they were using to pen them: I lowered my gaze from the mountain to the activities on the ground and saw a bandy rooster hopping on the chickens, going "zizzet, zizzet."

Here is everything, I thought, *from the banal to the divine. Look at this stupid cock running around, fucking for two seconds in his lousy display of sex, and then the brilliant splendor on the mountain.* I thought I'd seen it all, from the sublime to the ridiculous, from the planet's peaks and all their gorgeous colors, on down to the mindless *schtupping* animals. After two hours of spectacular back lighting, the sun finally popped over Annapurna and gave its own true rays, and you could see what was really going on on this earth.

Richard woke up and we flew back to Kathmandu, and then I took a cab to my basement room in Swayambhu. I discovered there was a huge rat that had taken up residence. I was so freaked that Richard said I should come stay with him in his rented rooms behind a Hindu monastery and just above the night quarters of the cows.

I still hadn't come down from my high in Pokhara. Every day at sunset, drumming rituals were held overlooking the rice fields. My hallucinations would really come alive at dusk, amid all the hashish smoke and the insistent rhythms banged out by a gaggle of Western hippies in rags. I was completely softened. All my hard edges had been worn down. I hadn't taken much truck with this spiritual shit and I was always cynical, always the tough guy, and some people really disliked me, while still others wanted to prove something to me. No matter how far out I'd gotten, I'd been a conservative little old lady underneath everything I did, but now I was opening up like a tender flower.

I got higher and higher and higher every night at these sunsets. I was fevered and rushed and beatific and rambling and still on this high from Pokhara. I'd finally experienced something like an ego death. I accepted all the wackiness and heartbreaking humanity of what was happening around me. The humble native Nepalese and the transplanted youth culture from the West ran together in one crazy pageant. I was breaking down. I was manic and hyperemotional. I'd start crying at the slightest hint of poignancy. I would melt and thaw into a dew.

It wasn't so much the poverty that got to me. I was moved by any vignette of anything touching. A dumb animal could get me crying. So could the local tea shop proprietor, "Moti man," who revealed his secret Mao sympathies to me, serving his greasy rice and fighting the monkeys off when they tried to steal the pilgrims' food. Every little village or animal shtick would get to me and I would weep copiously. I was also filled with joy. All of my cynicism had lifted and I was extremely vulnerable.

Every night as the sun went down, I'd get more manic and crazed. I'd go into these rants, and everyone was so stupid they'd listen to me. Finally, one of them took a close look at me and said, "You know, you're sick." So I went out and got checked and sure enough, I had hepatitis. I had a fever every day, which would spike, and I'd go out of my mind. I'd actually been sick before the acid trip, which just launched me into a higher delirium.

I don't know how I got sick exactly. The Peace Corps' dictum to boil water for twenty minutes was impossible, but I always drank boiled tea and ate cooked food. That wasn't enough, though. I'd been weakened by bouts of diarrhea for months on the road. I don't know how I dragged my ass up those mountains.

I took a long cab ride to the missionary hospital on the other side of Kathmandu. I was falling down all the time and couldn't have made it on foot. I was still flying and hallucinating five days after the trip in Pokhara. I thought it was so wonderful that I'd slid from ecstasy into disease, and that the disease was every bit as interesting.

Keely Stahl

B. 1951

Information coordinator for World Harmonic Unified Ministers (WHUM), a nonprofit organization with a Website at www.wayimmune.org, *which shows people how to raise their immunity physically, emotionally, and spiritually; former copyeditor for* Time *and* Life *magazines*

Resides in Philadelphia

Raised in the Bronx

The Menacing Orgasm That Almost Melted Me Away

As an eighteen-year-old at Fairleigh Dickinson University in Teaneck, New Jersey, I often hung out with a group of students who got together on weekends to trip and smoke pot. At one such gathering, I decided to try mescaline for the first time. I'd already taken acid about a dozen times. Although I was mostly carried away in musical reveries on these occasions, I tended to conjure cellular images of my own body, envisioning the blood flowing through my veins.

I took the mescaline with about ten other people around eight in the evening at a friend's apartment. The trip started out delightfully enough, with cars on the street taking on a cartoon cast and trees assuming a beautiful glow. I was so happy to finally hallucinate, having even envied people who had. But then I suddenly began to feel waves of physical sensations flowing through my body. The feelings got increasingly intense as the trip seemed to take on a "physical" as opposed to "mental" tone, which seemed startlingly odd.

This phase began with a gradual melting that flowed from the top of my body down. It was as though my body had become pure sensation, vibrant and glowing, no longer comprised of bones, fibers, and cells. It seemed that this magical electrical energy was dissipating my form. My body was streaming with rushes, at first pleasurable and even ecstatic, but it was so new and foreign to me that I couldn't let it last. I felt I was losing control. The melting suggested that I would have to breathe intentionally rather than reflexively, and I was now afraid that I wouldn't remember to do it!

As my body was rocked with wave after wave, I lost contact with my feet and my legs. I began to experience a total identification with nature, as though my body were merging with the earth, like a tree with roots in the ground. But the notion of becoming vegetative and planted in the dirt was actually very alien and scary. I tried to rally to hold on to my body, to my place in *this* world. I kept seeing a picture of a tree with thick roots running deep into the earth and thought that I'd be dead in some way if I took such form.

The suddenness of the physical feelings was alarming, even more so when they became sharp, as intense feelings abruptly flooded into one area of my body after another. Acute pangs moved out from my chest to my limbs and up to my head. The pains in my chest felt sharp because they'd come on so quickly. I recalled my grandfather's account of stabbing feelings in his chest during a heart attack.

None of my companions could relate to what I was going through. Nobody came forward to say, "Oh yeah, I've gone through that. Don't worry. It's normal." So I started to think there was something terribly wrong with me, that I might have taken something poisonous. I described what was happening and someone asked, "What does it feel like?"

"I don't know. It's scary. It hurts."

"Well, does it feel like knives?"

And I thought, "Yeah! it feels like knives!" and I'd start to feel as though I were being stuck with hard steel.

"Does it feel hot?"

"Yes, it's hot!"

"Does it burn?"

"Yes, it burns!" I'd start to feel whatever sensation they suggested.

Eventually it got so excruciating that I started to lose it. I held on to somebody and fell to my knees, screaming at the top of my lungs until I couldn't breathe anymore. Then I took another breath and held on to him, dragging him down to the floor with me, and wailed loudly and raspily again. With each rush that came through my body, I kept screaming as loud as I could. I thought I was going to melt away or die.

We got word that a couple of friends at another party were having a bad trip and were on their way over. By the time they arrived and found me in my state, they forgot all about their troubles. Eventually my cohorts had to get me out of the building, because someone in the neighborhood had called the police.

I went for a walk outside with my best friend Joia, whom I idolized. The trees looked organic and, holding fast to the soil, long connected to the planet, which looked both enchanting and foreboding to me. Joia tells me today that the mescaline's grip was broken when she told me soothingly, over and over, "I'm the angel. I'm the angel. I'm here and you're here. You can do anything."

Then I went for a ride in a car and somebody gave me a hit off a joint and somebody else, a tranquilizer, which helped a lot. The waves came less frequently and less intensely. I let them happen and they just passed through, sometimes feeling sort of nice, but I was still afraid. Gradually it all died down and I was eventually calm enough to go back to my dorm room. When my exhaustion finally drove me to sleep, I didn't know if I was going to wake up.

When I did awake the next morning, I saw that nothing harmful had happened to me, that I hadn't had a heart attack and died at the tender age of eighteen. I felt good throughout the day, buoyed by the sense that I'd survived an ordeal. But I also felt disappointed, alone, confused, and resentful toward my friends, because no one had been there to guide me out of my predicament.

I really could have used somebody putting his or her arm around me and saying, "Hey, this is what happens. Stop worrying. See if you can relax into it and have a new experience of yourself." Had that happened, I might have become a different person. It could have been a wonderful, ecstatic trip. I'd been looking for a total cleansing physical experience to take over me. The event now loomed as a mystery for me to solve. No one else who was tripping on the same material experienced anything remotely like what I went through. *Why did it happen to me and no one else? Did it mean something good or something bad? Was there something wrong with me?*

I quit college and went into Reichian therapy in 1970, concerned about blockages of energy in my body. As I understand today, the mescaline had initially dissolved these obstructions, but my fear reaction restored them with a vengeance. Under therapy, I gradually surmised that the disconnect between my mind and my body had been the cause of the horrific episode. At the time of the trip, I was just waking up to my body, having only recently lost my virginity. I was still struggling with my sexuality and my body identity. I'd never given myself license to have the feelings, or, conversely, to *not* have the feelings I was *not* having.

The physical phenomena of the trip had been a delayed wake-up call from my body. Most people experience this in puberty and adolescence, but I hadn't. My family was loving and affectionate, but they hadn't given me much guidance about my body. I'd been interested in boys and I was dating and making out and I got my period and all that, but I never felt any real changes in my body, except for gaining weight. I didn't have an orgasm until I was nineteen, about a year after the mescaline debacle, at which time I didn't know what an orgasm was. The initial waves of pleasure I felt during the trip might very well be thought of as surrogate orgasmic rushes. But I was not able to let go and instead had a kind of anti-reaction to the desire for release.

As I came to understand later, pain can be a psychosomatic manifestation of an anxiety about what may or will happen. My mescaline trip could have been the kind of experience that everybody is looking for, but my mind ruined it for my body. I was too afraid of letting my bodily sensations "get away." I could have had a merging with the cosmos and physical ecstasy, a sort of mutual orgasm without sex or self-manipulation, but it didn't turn out that way.

Keith

B. 1950

Webmaster for hire, former director of operations at a gaming institution

Resides somewhere in the western United States

Born and raised in suburban Chicago

First Communion with Life

I had my first experience with LSD in the summer of 1965 in La Jolla, California. Around that time Tom Wolfe was doing background work for *The Pump House Gang* at Wind and Sea Beach, where I was surfing and hanging out a lot. Acid seemed to just materialize that summer, which was a time of big change. People went from being drunk and belligerent to having their intellects tickled. The music changed from good-time "Louie Louie" stuff to lyrics with much more intellectual content and rhythms that seemed both more sophisticated and more primitive.

I was fourteen, hanging out at a coffeehouse called The Pearl on Pearl Street, which had folk music entertainment. One night I was there with a couple of friends. We'd been trying unsuccessfully to score some liquor at a local package store, when another friend showed up and asked us if we wanted to try something that was better than alcohol, longer lasting, and cheaper by the high. We were sold on the economic merits alone, so we forked over a few bucks apiece, downed the medicine, and went over to someone's house and listened to music for a while.

When we really started coming on, around ten P.M., we wandered the streets and spent a couple hours just watching the stoplights turn colors, marveling at the "whispering libido" effect, the hallucinated streaks left by car headlights and other moving things. It seems like a misnomer now, but that was the term in circulation for psychedelic trails back then. I spent the night at a friend's and came home the following morning about nine, changed inside forever.

That first trip was a good goof, a jounce to my sensibilities. I was struck that there was a lot more clarity to life than I'd seen up to then. I hadn't smoked pot yet, but certainly, this drug was much better than alcohol. It awoke interest in simple little things that you overlooked all the time, shadow images that evoked new descriptions. It was like reading poetry and picking out nuances and deeper meanings. I suddenly saw that there was much more to life than what I'd expected up to then. I could see that life was a continual learning process that should be experienced fully—both the "good" and the "bad"—instead of in the narrow range espoused by my parents.

During my early trips I noticed that the body sensations were distinctly oceanic. The rushes were like waves and it seemed to make self-evident the principle that everything in the universe was comprised of waves of energy at varying frequencies. Inspired as well by my surfer's bent, I was always building posters in my mind of waves curling at the beach.

Acid helped me tune into music by showing that the rhythmic hooks had synchronistic meanings in the subconscious, that the bass and drum patterns which evoke the heartbeat provided the keys to concepts that might not be fully understood or accepted if heard as words alone. I was listening to something by Ray Charles or Aretha Franklin when this realization hit me. It was so subtle, it overwhelmed me at the time.

I started to take notice how the culture had begun to trade in the subterranean subtlety of psychedelic consciousness. Country Joe and the Fish, for instance, had lyrics that were imperceptible to the ear unless you were loaded on acid. There's a song on the *I Feel Like I'm Fixin' to Die* album, "Colors for Susan," I think, the last track, in which you can hear them whisper, "Acid is sweet and so are you." That blew me away when I first caught that.

Over the second half of the Sixties, I tripped frequently, with nary a thought about set and setting. From December 1968 through the whole of 1969, there was hardly a week that I didn't drop. For one two-month period, when I was working in the music business, I could be found walking around the studio with a plastic glass filled with Coke and ice cubes with crushed tabs of acid dissolved in it. Quantitatively speaking, I was quite experienced. I'd never had a trip that I couldn't handle, and I thought I knew what to expect from LSD.

As the decade turned, I got to know some people involved in the Brotherhood of Eternal Love, the smuggling outfit based in Laguna Canyon, which had forged a strong tie with Leary and contributed to his defense fund. A couple of guys I knew became merchant-marine types in order to work in the Brotherhood's import operation in Thailand, the first to bring real Thai sticks into this country. I had an old friend named Russell who was telling me all about Orange Sunshine, a distributed product of the Brotherhood. As I learned more about Leary's approach to the "sacrament" of LSD, the pranksterish, zany-spontaneous mode of my life ended.

One night in November 1970, Russell and I went to a Rod Stewart concert and dropped some blotter acid that came through the Brotherhood. The music was fabulous. Stewart was doing songs from *Every Picture Tells a Story* backed by Ron Wood and the rest of the Faces. I'd never experienced this kind of a high before. It was as though I were a third person watching myself along with the concert. The staging and lighting were more advanced than I'd seen at previous shows, and there was an internal light from this acid that was alien to my experience.

It was the cleanest acid I'd ever taken, though it didn't have the hard rushes of most of the stuff I'd known or the flats that the Peace acid had. I kept getting higher and higher and couldn't get a grip. It felt like I wasn't ever going to come down, which really threw me. I was losing touch with reality. I thought I'd been poisoned and was dying. Finally, I said to Russell that I had to get out of there. I was freaking out.

We left the concert hall, and Russell drove me, feeling very agitated, up to his house on top of Kenner Canyon in west Los Angeles. The setting in his bedroom was very conducive to the experience that ensued. He had an Indian tapestry strung up like a tent that came to a pinnacle in the center of the ceiling. There was one tiny Christmas tree light at the very center of the mandala—just bright enough that you could see it was there. It allowed for one's consciousness to flow over the tapestry and up to the peak. There were two beds on either side of a nice coffee table, where there was a candle about six inches high and two inches thick, which Russell ceremoniously lit.

"Maybe I should go to the hospital," I said. He tried to settle me down. "No, no. Just cool out." He was also tripping on the same dose, but handling the whole thing a lot better. He lit up a joint, and I said, "Whoa, are you kidding? I'm high enough! I don't need this." He said, "No, have a couple of hits." I did so, reluctantly, and then he handed me a book, *Psychedelic Prayers,* Leary's interpretation of the *Tao Te Ching.* I'd had no prior contact with Eastern religion.

"I want you to read this," he said.

"But I can't focus on anything."

"Believe me, once you start reading this, you'll be able to focus. But *listen* to the words. Don't just look at 'em."

So I started reading, and suddenly I was captivated by the meanings. I finished a page and was suddenly stuck by the horrible thought that I was physically dying. I turned to Russell and said, "I think I'm dying," and he said, "Part of you is." He told me to look into the candle, and so I stared at it flickering in the darkened room. As I concentrated on the flame, I found that I could actually hold it still with my gaze or intent. Just as the flame stood fixed in space, I felt my whole consciousness rush down into the light and then blow open on the Other Side. I was instantly transported to a totally spiritual world, where I saw myself in three phases: as a child, as a young adult, and as a form I couldn't see clearly at first.

I looked across the flame to Russell for a few moments, and suddenly he had my face. It was the visage I perceived as my real self, unfettered by ego or materialism, a godly image with all of my features and long hair, wearing a cream-colored shirt embroidered on the collar and the sleeves. There was a look of absolute serenity on the face. I recognized it as the pivotal essence of my personality, my soul. An intense sense of oneness came over me. The realizations about what I was seeing hit me like waves.

I kept calling Russell "Father," and he said, "No, I'm not your father."

"Russell, you don't understand. I'm going through a godhead experience right now."

We listened to the first Jefferson Starship album, *Blows Against the Empire*, which has a passage with enormous whooshing engine sound effects, like a huge rocketship blasting off into space, which is quite dramatic and somatically affecting. I melded into the music and allowed myself to leave my body. I still felt as though I were dying, but when that feeling was most acute, I suddenly heard a heartbeat and the sounds of body fluids and motions around me. As I focused on the pinnacle of the mandala, I felt my body was being squeezed as though by the contractions of labor. I was in space looking down on what appeared to be the Milky Way, beholding this white light, a light comprised of all colors. Within that light, which was Life, I saw that my own consciousness was coming into the seed of a new life cycle, as if I'd been thrown out of one body until the next one became available to bring me back in. Encapsulated in this comfortable room, my consciousness trained on the "star" in the ceiling, I was transported back to the womb, where I was getting my last-minute send-off instructions.

When I realized that I was being born again, that life goes on and on and on, the feeling was overwhelming. I was filled with confidence that it was okay to die, because the consciousness that inhabits the flesh has a higher destiny. It never began and it won't end. It just keeps going.

Then I was struck with wave after wave of value wisdom, as though the force behind human spirituality were hitting me for the first time. When I realized that I'd spent most of my life hidden from those values that should be the stones we walk on, I had to weep. I thought I'd blown it up to then, wasting a lot of time, moving in an undefined direction. The *Tao Te Ching* was very clear that if you were going to fight the current, you were going to waste a lot of time, because the river still ends up in the sea. I recognized things I'd done that were wrong or incompatible with the true soul I'd now found. I saw myself as overly given to selfish desires. We all want to live in comfort, but the pursuit of it rarely leads one to the higher meanings of life. This revelation was more primordial than an encounter with Freudian guilt or Original Sin. It was as though I'd come face-to-face with a timeless version of my aboriginal and innately moral self.

Russell stood up and asked me if I wanted to go into the other room. I said, "No, Father, I'm not worthy," which weirded him out. He'd meant the living room, but I had the impression he was inviting me into Heaven. The circle between life, death, and rebirth may seem like a long throw in our conscious daily minds, but having just experienced a psychic rebirth, it wasn't such a leap to believe I might simply terminate a corporeal enterprise to move on to a higher realm.

I realized that the seed of life is consciousness and that, as such, life essentially never ends. Everything material around us has an energy frequency slower than consciousness. If we had the ability, as I did on acid, to freeze the flame for just a single brief moment that feels like an eternity, then perhaps we could learn the energy properties of a wall and then move right through it. It dawned on me that all the building blocks of the social structure were really nothing but an imposing veneer that kept you from being godlike, and that as soon as we knew the true potential of our own energy frequencies to overcome or pass through the artificial walls, the human spirit could be liberated.

If I were to classify the experience, I'd say it was my first communion with Life. I'd gone through Holy Communion and been confirmed in an Episcopal Church, but until I'd "snapped" on acid, I never really felt religious. This *clear-light experience,* as Leary termed it, was a true communion of the soul. I felt as if my consciousness and entire being had broken up with the brittleness of linear ego thought, while the person that filled the vacuum bore the same body of experience with a totally new vitality and an understanding of life's true value.

My intellect was seriously tweaked. I learned how much I didn't know. The values that I'd been brought up to believe in were absolutely shattered. I had a palpable, intuitive sense of life after death as Christ had spoken of it, which was now no longer a mere platitude. I also had a clearer understanding of the Word of Judeo-Christian tradition as well as that of other bodies of accumulated human wisdom. Leary's interpretation of the *Tao Te Ching* made absolutely crystal-clear sense: The easiest path is to stay in the middle of the river of life or as close to it as possible. It's not that you should always strive to avoid doing anything that runs afoul of the Ten Commandments or the natural rules of life. You have to experience all of life. The river may meander, as it's not a straight line.

I subsequently had about five clear-light experiences, in which I ostensibly passed through the flame to my mirror image. That reflection is so pure, it inspires the belief that it represents the person you'll ultimately be, no matter how many times around the wheel you'll have to go.

Kenny

B. 1958

Farmer, hunter, carpenter, electrician, plumber, avid chess player

Resides in South Kona, Big Island of Hawaii

Born and raised in Philadelphia

How Do I Die If I'm Not Here?

I've separated from my body a number of times on various substances. My body usually goes limp and just lies on the ground, while my mind goes off to amazing places. But on a few occasions, my body behaved in strikingly bizarre ways, according to my companions who saw.

One such instance occurred while I was on 5-MeO DMT. The people administering it had a stopwatch and a notebook, using me as a guinea pig for a sort of experiment. I got two good hits off of a pipe. After the second, I told them that it felt very much like garden-variety DMT, but right after I said that, the back of my head exploded visually. I got sucked out through the hole into an amazing trip. The weirdest thing about it was what my body did. I knew what was happening outside my body, but had to rely later on the test administrators' accounts of what the body itself was doing.

According to them, right after the explosion I looked straight up in the air with a stupid look on my face, fell back, then sat up again and started looking around in a panic. Then they panicked themselves for some twenty minutes, because "Kenny" was gone, leaving only his nervous, bewildered body behind. "Kenny" had never left like that before. When I first heard "him" leave, I wondered, *Is "Kenny" coming back? Oh, my God! Am I dead if he doesn't?* My body tried to run, but it had no equilibrium and couldn't even stand up. I was almost crying. *How do I die if "Kenny" isn't here?*

Then I had an out-of-body experience very much like the one I had on ketamine, when I felt as though I'd been thrown into a boiling vat of murky white liquid, where I wasn't sure I had a physical body. As the bubbles in the liquid, passed by my skin, they grazed my consciousness with emotions and memories. I was able to have eight or ten memories at once, depending on how many bubbles were touching me. After that, it was like an interstellar ride, a satellite buzzing through the cosmos.

When I was back in my body I was sitting on my sofa, asking the test administrators, "How do I know if I've smoked this? Have I smoked enough to get high?" They wrote that down and asked, "How did you get on the sofa?" I'd smoked it on the floor. I stopped and thought about it for a second, and right then, everything I did outside the body came rushing in.

I once got hold of four hits of *Salvinorin alpha*—the ultra-powerful extract of *Salvia divinorum*—each of which was about the size of a grain of sand. The portions were so small, we thought our supplier had messed up. There were five of us sitting in a circle in my yard here in South Kona, so we drew straws to determine who'd partake.

The first of the four of us who drew the longest straws smoked one of the alpha grains, but he put it on some marijuana and, not being a pot smoker, evidently coughed it up or otherwise missed it. The next in line tried smoking his hit through the bong, but coughed some of it out and didn't get off. We decided to join the last two hits together, but the only one of us left who was still game to do 'em up was me.

We put the two granules in aluminum foil with a little straw, and they both lit up. There was only a faint dry taste. About twenty seconds later, I started seeing little balloons float in the air, turn into dots, explode out a couple inches, and then shrink back down again. There were six or eight of them blinking off and on. As they opened up, I could see scenes like animated cartoons inside, a different vignette in each balloon.

When I'm on acid by myself and focus on the left side of things, I tap into a greater understanding or concentration of power. I focused leftward as the bubbles became increasingly prolific, until my visual screen literally stopped and I found myself in a three-foot-wide hallway with a black wall. As I looked down the hallway, I noticed that my visual screen was like a sheet of celluloid, and that there were millions of sheets lined up in this black hall, as far down as I could see. I stepped back before the first sheet and saw that it was comprised of common things I was used to seeing, while the action changed speeds in the sheets behind it. That was fun, but I get bored quickly with mere toys of this nature.

So I went back into the hallway again to see if I could slide between a couple of frames. It worked. I could walk as far as I wanted to in the space between the frames, but I didn't go far, because I wanted to stay in the area where everything seemed to be happening. The next frame seemed only a slight temporal distance away from the first one. The action in the second one hadn't happened yet, so it was like a glimpse into the immediate future.

I noticed myriad black circles of various shades on the wall. Being nosy, I stuck my head through one of the holes and was totally blown away. There was a completely different reality on the other side. As my head popped out the other side, I saw a room that was hospital antiseptic, though not just white but gold and silver, a sort of heavenly operating room. I looked across the room and saw two tall and thin, blue-hued humanoid women coming toward me. The energy they were putting out was powerful but intentionally very calming.

I noticed they were walking on the ceiling, but then saw that they actually weren't. Everything on the inside of the hole was upside down, so I was looking up, which was disorienting. I pulled my head out, saw the same black hallway, and stuck my head back through again. The blue women were still there waiting. They rushed over to me and one cradled my head, conveying a warm welcoming feeling like they were glad I was there. "What took you so long?" they communicated telepathically. "It's going to be okay." They were extremely loving, emanating a selfless attitude like "Don't worry about how we feel. Come on, it's all right."

They began tugging on my head and shoulders, trying to pull me through the hole. *Wow, this is like a birthing thing.* I thought. *Cool!* I started trying to help them, but I hadn't yet seen that there was a membrane that hampered my access. I had my right arm and shoulder all the way in, and half my chest in. I looked back and saw other black holes in the wall, through which I saw the other four folks with whom I'd convened to do up the *Salvinorin,* sitting on my lawn and looking at me.

I deduced that if I could get through these holes, my friends could. The heavenly women said, "It's okay. They're coming too." I squeezed out of the hole back into the hallway and returned to the celluloid frames. I found myself sitting on the lawn in a circle with my friends, trying to explain to them how to get to this wall. They told me afterward that all that came out of my mouth was pure blather with no recognizable words.

I got agitated with their incomprehension. I was waving my hands all over, trying to convince them to join me in the hallway of black holes. Suddenly I was caught by what I saw. I looked down at my right hand and could no longer speak. Around my wrist was a tight, black shiny wristband. Beyond the band my hand was liquid glass, with gracefully movable pointed fingers and prismed light shimmering through. I saw that my arm had transformed into a marvelous work of engineering made up of millions of itty-bitty diamonds, all perfectly smoothed in and glistening light. My whole body was a wet suit with zippers up and down my arms and legs. The jeweled right arm—the one that had gotten through the hole into the heavenly delivery room—had slipped out of the wet suit and was waving around, gesticulating, while the flesh-and-blood left arm lay limp and wet-suited on my lap.

I tried to relate this impressive development to my friends, but could feel their confusion and wonderment *on my right arm,* which had become uncannily receptive to emotions. As the breeze blew across the arm, rather than feel the moisture and temperature of the air, I felt my friends' perplexity and their sense of wanting to be there with me. Once I realized that I couldn't get them to understand what I was saying—I had no idea I wasn't speaking English—I thought, *Okay, the heck with this. I'm going to go back to the hallway and through the hole into the birthing room.*

So I headed back out the side of the celluloid strips, but by now, because time was passing, I was way down the hallway. I popped out of the celluloid strips and realized I was way down the hallway and headed back toward the area I'd originally been in. Evidently the hyperspace of the celluloid corridor had not stayed on the same axis as the standard dimension my friends were in, so they saw me getting up to walk around, then all of sudden crawling on my hands and knees, slamming my head into the ground, trying to reach the wall. I could see it, but couldn't get close to it. It had moved, merging with the plane of the ground.

I came to as my friends grabbed me by the arms and tried to soothe me, saying, "It's okay, it's okay." I was crawling around with tears in my eyes, slamming my head into the ground, trying to get back into this hole. Fortunately, it was a grassy lawn, so I wasn't injuring myself.

My feeling is that I'd stumbled upon this birthing room prematurely, before I was expected. As for what I'd be born into and the notion of a realm beyond this one, I believe that there's something out there, but that the explanations of existing religions have defined it too rigidly. Perhaps there are fifty million races in the universe. We may be only a mold for another race altogether, or maybe we're all inside one embryo, the child of a deity race waiting to be born.

The second time I took *Salvinorin alpha* was the most religious trip I've ever had. I was sitting out on my lawn in South Kona with a couple of friends. This time it began like the first, with the appearance of the balloons, but then, before I could focus left, there was suddenly a clean-cut church boy about eight years old behind me yelling and tapping me on the shoulder: "Come on! Let's go! Hurry up! It's time!" I'd only caught a glimpse of him, but he was right off the cover of *The Watchtower,* the broadsheet of the Jehovah's Witnesses.

I tried to turn around and pull backward, but my physical body stayed in place. It was as if there were no air hole to let me out of my body, so I was being sucked back into it. I pulled against the suction, but it seemed that the only way I could have gotten out is to have stabbed a hole in my leg to let the air in. Every time I looked behind me, the boy ran to the other side, yelling, "Come on, come on! Let's go, let's go!" I spent about ten minutes trying to pull myself out, then rested for a minute and felt myself being sucked back in, tight inside my skin.

A couple of minutes later, the boy ran behind a tree, yelling, "Come on, it's going to be too late. We've got to go! We've got to go!" Just then three feral turkeys on my property flew overhead, but the *Salvinorin* translated this piece of sensory information into a vision of the boy sprouting wings and taking off with a bunch of other people who'd been waiting around the tree he'd run behind. He'd wanted me to catch up to this group with him so we could all fly off together to wherever they were in such a hurry to go. When they flew off, I jumped up and went looking around the corner and couldn't find them. My friends said I was running around the yard, flapping my arms as though they were wings.

I liken this little boy to an angel, and I interpret the vision as an invitation—like the heavenly delivery room—to a higher realm, not the heaven of Christianity but a higher goal-oriented plane.

When I was twenty and enlisted in one of the branches of the armed forces, I used to get together once or twice a week and trip with some military buddies. We'd sit around and do things like "Let's see if we can get that marble to roll . . . Let's see if we can get the clock to stop for a couple of seconds." We played like this for several years, to the point that we could each understand what the other was thinking.

One time, four buddies and our respective wives or girlfriends went up in the Sequoia Forest in California for a three-day weekend. We had a bonfire going the whole time. On the second day, the five of us guys were sitting around the fire in a circle, nude and quite high on acid. We had a way of not talking for hours, but still understanding each other. We usually tripped to try to figure things out, not just to joke and have fun, though we did that at times also.

This time we posed the question "Just how in charge are we of our bodies?" Through the "group mind" we created a higher being that the five of us could talk to together. The higher being told us, "You're covered. *You* are in charge." We asked, "What do you mean 'in charge'?" We thought about it for a minute, and the idea that popped up was "Let's see if we can control pain." The group said, "Okay, that's a good one." We threw that at the voice, which said, "It's done. You've done it." We said, "That's too easy. How do we know?" to which the voice said, "That's up to you."

"Someone stick a hand in the fire," the group decided, so one of us thrust his hand right into the flame, holding it in there for nearly a minute, and then pulled it out. It was all blistery, but there was no pain. We thought about this for a while, and went back to the voice and said, "That's fine, but then again we've all stubbed our toe and ignored it." The voice laughed and said, "It's your game." So we decided to go further. Another guy stuck his hand in, this time for a couple of minutes, and when he pulled it out, it was all puffy and black with stuff dripping off it, but there was still no problem with pain. "No, this isn't good enough," we challenged the voice. "It has to go a little further."

Then I, being the one who was picked, stood up and jumped straight in the air and landed totally naked on my back in the bonfire. I just stretched out there, laughing. Apparently, without knowing it, I'd let out a blood-curdling scream as I leapt in the air that was heard two and a half miles away by the forest ranger, who called an ambulance at three in the morning. My buddies looked at me lying there in the fire and talked to me. I was cackling with laughter, saying, "It feels like someone's pouring ice water all over me." All the women, who'd been sleeping in the tents, were awakened by the scream, and came over to the bonfire. They immediately freaked out and moved quickly to drag me off the flames.

I'd been a nondrinker for several years, and my mates thought quickly and reasoned that I had to furnish a reason for "falling" into the fire at three in the morning, so they got me drunk. Being on the wagon for so long, I quickly got very drunk on the shot after shot the women plied me with. The ambulance arrived and we told them I'd drunkenly stumbled into the fire and off I went to the emergency room at the nearest hospital, where I spent the next eight days.

I ended up burning some sixty percent of my body, third-degree in some parts. The hands were burned the worst. I was scrubbed like hell with stiff-bristle brushes twice a day, which was extremely painful. While in the hospital, I couldn't contend with the pain, so I had friends bring me Quaaludes every second day.

The guys all believed that I wouldn't have sustained any burn injuries if the women hadn't pulled me out of the fire. The theory was that once we were sufficiently convinced that the "group mind" could conquer pain, I would have gotten out and just resumed our chatter around the campfire. They blamed my scars and slowness to heal on the fact that I'd been polluted with drink and thus lost my link to the "group mind." I too believe I would have been untouched if the girls hadn't interceded. When I was lying in the fire, I was totally conscious, undistracted by the heat.

I'm a firm believer in the body's ability to regenerate itself. I've experienced it and I've helped other people experience it. I think it's possible for the mind to transcend the limits of the body with group reinforcement—especially when the group is tight and knows each other as well as the five of us did. We believe that after all our years of tripping together, my jumping bare-assed on our communal fire would have been covered if the "group mind" we'd fused together with acid and friendship hadn't been undone by liquor and hyperrationalism in the excitement of the moment.

Kevin

B. 1953

Psychology professor at a small liberal arts college in a large northeastern state

Resides in a large northeastern state

Raised in Wisconsin and Indiana

To Either Die or Come

Much of my undergraduate career at Indiana University in Bloomington was a kind of psychedelic search for God, supported by studies in philosophy, religion, anthropology, and my ultimate career choice, psychology. Tripping at least once a month, I finally had the breakthrough I'd been seeking in my junior year. From intimate relations to career directions to religious belief, its impact on my life has been profound.

I had a couple of friends, a pair of intellectual geeks I tripped with. Don was pre-med, and Stuart was working toward an Ivy League archaeology degree. The three of us decided to take a hit apiece of the blotter named eponymously for the slogan printed on it: Love Saves, which was more powerful, perhaps a thousand mics, and more pure, than anything we'd ever had. You didn't want to take half, because that meant tearing the heart in half, so we each did a whole.

It was a Friday afternoon in mid-autumn. I said good-bye to my girlfriend Peg, who was going home to visit her family for the weekend, and then downed my hit with a glass of orange juice. I sat in my room, waiting to get off, knowing that I'd meet Don and Stuart a little later to see how the evening unfolded.

The acid came on very strong. I was lying in my bed, but I'd lost track of where I was in space. It felt erotic and sexual, but I didn't know what to do with that energy. I was feeling a sort of masturbatory guilt. I wasn't having sex often enough with Peg and was also having carnal longings toward other women. Though I partly relished the freedom to explore such impulses, Peg's leaving for the weekend stripped away a sense of tentative security. I was frightened that I might do something sexually weird and inappropriate.

Sex was, naturally, a major theme in my young adult life. I'd been inspired by *The Harrad Experiment,* the Robert Rimmer book in which Harvard and Radcliffe kids read to each other while fornicating. Peg and I had delved into Tantric Buddhism, and once, on acid, tried the *yab-yum* position, which involves being sexually coupled while sitting almost motionless in a lotus position. The man is erect and inside her, staying that way by the smallest of movements. We lasted for a couple of minutes before moving into regular, animated intercourse.

Now I didn't know what to do with all the sexual energy without my girlfriend around. I got extremely agitated and nervous and ran down to a friend's room in another part of the building, but he wasn't in. I panicked, by now feeling that my body might lose its coherence or dissolve. I went back to my room and lay back on my bed, trying to convince myself that I'd be okay if I just stayed in bed.

Suddenly there was a knock on the door. It was Peg! She knew that I'd be tripping and later meeting up with her brother Alton, who was a friend of mine. She could be rather ESPish at times. She said she'd stopped to say good-bye to her friend Melanie and just had this thought that I needed her. I felt like I was saved, that the name of the acid had been echoed, its wisdom verified. She asked if I was okay, and I replied, "I am now." We held each other for a while and then she left to catch her ride.

After she left, I went to Don's apartment to meet the fellows. Alton went off to hang out with some other folks, so Don, Stuart and I got down to talking about God, as the acid came on like gangbusters. Sitting at the kitchen table, we asked each other whether we believed in God. Don replied, "Of course!" and turned his face and his hands up to the light from the lamp, which beamed down on his face like a beam from Above. Ironic as his gesture was—"Isn't it obvious that God exists and is everywhere?"—it came across as a beatific expression of mystic truth, which took my breath away.

Don then lay down on the floor in a placid reverie with his eyes closed, basking in the feeling of God's presence, while Stuart and I circled around him as though he were carrion, flapping our arms and squawking like malevolent, vulturelike crows.

Then Melanie showed up. She'd come just to say hello and see how we were doing, but she was linked in my mind to Peg, whom I thought might have sent her over to check on my welfare. When she appeared at the door, I looked past her and called out for Peg, then ran right past her and out to her car outside, thinking that somehow Peg was going to be there. I ran down the street exuberantly, eventually slowing down and walking back, feeling ridiculous. Of course Peg wasn't there; she'd left for the weekend.

Melanie's arrival had heightened the erotic undertone of the trip. There was always the chance that she'd come because she was romantically interested in one of the three of us, and for me, she was a connection to a sense of security—albeit not necessarily satisfaction—about sex. Melanie, however, wasn't up to all this. She got weirded out by my behavior and split shortly after I returned from my mad dash out to her car.

After she was gone the three of us quieted down and listened to some music. I was lying on the floor, feeling like I was going to die or come, I wasn't sure which, right then and there. The carnal electricity in my body was so strong, I thought it would kill me. I was consumed with dread that I would have an erection, an ejaculation, or some uncontrollable sexual paroxysm right there in front of my friends.

Finally I gave myself up to this tension, assuring myself that I was, after all, among trusted friends, and that whatever happened was okay, even leaving this existence entirely. And then I did just that, drifting toward a narrow, erotically tinged beam of light that shone from beneath everything. All there was was this beam of life, the primal energy in the universe, and the darkness that surrounded it. I became a part of that light, returning to the source of all creation through a process I understood as death.

I must have been "out" for a while. Stuart was shaking me to come out of it, but it took me an extended time to resurface to consciousness and return to my body. As I saw where I was heading, it felt almost arbitrary that I was coming back to my own body and not, say, Stuart's or Don's; that my personality—my form and appearance, my knowledge, memory, emotions, and sexuality—was an accident or mere contingency, and that the only thing that was essential and true was the white light of God that I'd just communed with. By surrendering my anxieties and fears over losing my bodily integrity, I'd "died" and become one with this light, which was the fuse of the life force, the beam that runs through and unifies us all. I was terrified to let the tension go, but once I did, it felt great.

It was reassuring to return to my body with the security of touching the source of life's energy, the erotic undercurrent that lights creation. Ever since this revelation, I've experienced intense sexual experiences as a kind of reunion of two people's cosmic energies. (The most intensely erotic part of sex is the razor's edge where you get as close as you can to the brink of orgasm without going over it, for as long as possible. Orgasm, of course, dissipates the energy.)

Interestingly, the feeling of being about to dissolve or lose bodily coherence resonated years later, when I broke up with a lover with whom I'd had an incredibly passionate affair. To contend with my distress, I just walked and walked, and finally felt like I needed to do something or my body would just float away. I picked up a hand ax–sized rock and held it close to my solar plexus, not caring who saw me in such a state. Gradually, the tactile, earthen pressure on my chest eased my feelings of insecurity. I still have that rock.

Lena

B. early 1960s

Health-care professional

Resides in America

Born and raised in America

I've Definitely Been Psychotic

My earliest experiences with psychedelics, when I was in high school and college, gave me insights into the human mind that lay the groundwork for my career in the care of the mentally disturbed.

My first window on psychosis was provided by a hit of PCP when I was fifteen. I'd didn't know it was PCP, which I'd never knowingly take. It was called Purple Microdot mescaline and it looked like a minuscule piece of candy. I discovered later that someone else who'd taken it had wound up in the hospital and tested positive for PCP.

I dropped the tiny lozenge at home with two girlfriends in my hometown of Stonington, Connecticut. At one point, I walked a few blocks to a friend's house to get some cigarettes. Everything was slanted and skewed, including myself. I felt taller than the telephone poles, which struck me as hilarious. When I reached my friend's house, she had a friend of hers visiting. I felt as if they were performing some kind of a play for my benefit and I was in the audience trying to figure out what it was about. I couldn't grasp what was going on. They seemed to be communicating in some secret language.

When I got back home, my boyfriend Joshua was there unexpectedly. He didn't like my taking drugs and wanted me to stop. It was good timing actually, as I wasn't faring well. When a Jimi Hendrix song played on the radio I was convinced I was going to die. I knew that he'd died from an overdose of drugs, and since he was being broadcast to me right then, that meant that I was going to die. I lay down on the couch, murmuring to Joshua, "Don't go. Don't let me die."

It was nearing midnight and his mother was waiting outside in the car. Finally, he went out to give her some excuse and she drove off.

The next day, he made me promise not to trip anymore, but a few days later some friends came over to my table in the school cafeteria and said, "We're going to trip this weekend. You want to join us?" I said, "Well I'm going to take a couple of weeks off." Joshua was sitting right there.

"What do you mean a couple of weeks off? You said you were going to quit."

The PCP had shaken me up, but it was as fascinating to me as seeing a flame for the first time. I was drawn to its mystery and power. I respected the damage it could do, but I wanted to try to master it. It turned out to be a formative experience. I discovered that the ideas of reference I'd experienced—thinking the Hendrix song was played for me, and believing that my friends were speaking in a code I couldn't decipher—were features of psychosis. So began my strange empathy for the disassociation and torment that schizophrenics go through.

While I was still in high school, I got very interested in mental illness and the chemistry of the brain. I took a subscription to *Psychology Today* and read as much as I could about it. I eventually got a degree for a profession that enables me to tend to the mentally sick. My primary motivation and guiding force is an empathy for people who are psychotic, having been there myself.

Of course, my interest in psychedelics has not been purely clinical. When I was a sophomore at Penn, I took five grams of mushrooms with some of my best friends, most of whom were boys I grew up with. We went to a dark cabin on a mountain in New Hampshire and we all had a profound experience in which we ultimately felt like we were each gods of our own universe. At one point we were playing with a pile of dirt as though we could make a man out of it.

At the outset of the trip, I felt I had to be cautious where I stepped, as though I were traversing a forest of glass and crystal shards. I said to my friends, "Be careful, you guys. It's very fragile out here," and one of them shot back, "No, it's not fragile out here. Maybe it is right now for your trip, but don't make that our trip." He was dancing around, exuberant. I was struck by that and realized that I'd tried to warn them away from fears that were my own private domain.

So I abandoned the journey I was on and sought out the relaxed euphoria that he was experiencing. Then I slowly slipped into a void in which I felt like I knew what it was like to cease to exist. In contrast to the dying sensation in the PCP trip, this was not scary at all. I emerged into a white light. I felt as though my soul had just been spread all over the universe, as though I'd slid down the shelf of my self into a pool of trip joy, the pure psychical water at the center of all things. We described the trip later as "tripping our brains out," which was apt, because I felt like I'd left my body. I was no longer a person, but pure energy. At the time, I was not aware that I was having a prototypical experience of cosmic oneness as recounted by mystics.

When I read about such visionary states later, I felt especially grateful for my experience, because it seemed that much more authentic and because it gave me a window on the knowledge of the sages.

Even now, years later, I don't really fear death, because I feel like I experienced it. At least I hope that's what death is like, because it was ecstatic and epiphanous and relaxing. I embraced it and it embraced me. I'm afraid of physical pain, but I'm not afraid of not being anymore. I experienced what it was like to completely dissolve and be dispersed, to no longer be one coherent entity, and it was very affirming. In retrospect, I could see that the PCP trip had been an incomplete ego disintegration that had been aborted by fear.

My exploration of the psychedelic pharmacopoeia broadened. My experiences with the phenelethylamines MDMA and 2C-B have been revelatory for their empathetic power and for unlocking doors to my own psychological makeup. Some people describe the effects of 2C-B as a cross between MDMA and LSD. It's a relatively new, totally synthetic concoction, which you used to be able to buy with a credit card in Amsterdam. I describe the sensation of 2C-B in two different ways.

One is analogous to the maxim If you don't like the weather in Boston, stick around, it'll change. That's what 2C-B is like. Every few minutes, you're in a different place. You're happy, you're sad. You're scared, you're intrepid. You're needy, you're replenished. Everything's fine, everything's horrible. You're laughing, you're crying. It's very roller-coastery. The other way I describe it is that if MDMA is a shovel that helps you dig and uncover the repressed shit in your life, then 2C-B is a jackhammer. It's a very powerful psychotherapeutic tool that, like it or not, enables all your neuroses, thorns, and hang-ups to bubble up and confront you. Tremendous insights are just delivered to you.

MDMA is like a big house with all the lights on and all the doors open. You can walk into any room you want and look around. Becalmed, you can dig around to see what's going on in your psyche. The first time I took MDMA, in 1985, when I was nineteen, I wrote out thirty-six pages of self-analysis, front and back, looking at many aspects of myself for the first time. The nice thing about MDMA is that you don't have to go swimming in it. You can look at what you've repressed and pick and choose what you want to work on. But with 2C-B, things are tossed up at you, thrown into your consciousness, things that you didn't necessarily dig for but you just have to see in order to catch onto your own act. Some realizations I've received from 2C-B have brought me to my knees.

When I was twenty-seven I had a major revelation on 2C-B that changed my whole life perspective. Both my parents wanted sons. One wanted three, one wanted six, but they got three girls. I always knew that, being the youngest, I was their last chance to have a boy. They even had a boy's name picked out for me. Part of me always knew that I was a disappointment. I was very tomboyish as a young girl, to the point that people didn't always know my gender until puberty. Even then, I carried extra weight on me as a way to defer my puberty and womanliness. A lot of my self-destruction and self-hatred derive from knowing that I'd disappointed my parents. But in the middle of this trip I suddenly realized, *It's not my fault!* It struck me that I wasn't responsible for disappointing my parents. I didn't pick my gender. It's my father's fault that they had three girls. He's the one who donated the x or y chromosome. The revelation took a tremendous weight off of me. I don't carry the blame anymore. *It's not my fault that I'm a girl.*

Later during that same trip, I looked around and asked myself, *Why do I have so much stuff (clothes, books, recorded music)?*

Because you're afraid of wanting for anything, being in a state of need. You were rejected in a state of need as a child and now you refuse to be in that state again.

Oh!

It was such a profound insight that I went through my closet and filled three big bags full of clothes I really didn't need and took them to a church up the street. It dawned on me that I'd spent so much time trying to make sure that everyone else wasn't lacking for anything, when I was really trying to help myself.

I'm very big on empathy. I see MDMA as an empathogen with some minor psychedelic properties. With acid and other psychedelics, by default you gaze into the big picture, thinking about the cosmos and how everything's connected. MDMA is much more personal, with more narrowly defined parameters.

When I do MDMA on my own and look at what's on my mind, to see what I'm carrying around and what's weighing me down, I'm not distracted by the cosmos and the unified energy field and how we're all connected. It's just me. Tripping is seeing the infinite within or without, it's not clear which. You just ride the waves where they go. But I appreciate the illuminated control that MDMA confers. I'd rather have the power and the glory of God within me rather than project it onto an external being.

The last psychedelic experience I had demonstrated how elusive that power is. My trip on 5-MeO DMT, the most potent psychoactive substance I'm aware of, was an explosion that lit up my being and then sent a shadow through it. I would have preferred to start with plain old garden-variety DMT, but I didn't have any. I knew the stuff I had was pure, because it came from a reliable source, so I kept it for a year in a box in my drawer, waiting for the right day. I thought about it a lot, but it felt like TNT in a safe. A glass pipe is required to vaporize, then smoke, the powder; since I didn't own a crack pipe, I was held up for a while.

Plus, the more I heard about it, the more I realized that this was one substance I did not want to do on my own, as had become my customary modus operandi with other psychedelics. I'm independent and I push people away if there's something freaky going on. I want to be scared by myself. But this stuff was different. I approached it with caution. Finally, sometime in 1996, I met a guy named Phil who had a lot of experience with tryptamines. He said that he would teach me how to smoke the 5-MeO and sit with me during the trip. He had a good energy and I knew I'd be comfortable around him.

So I got hold of a glass pipe and Phil helped me hold the flame far enough away from the powder so that the powder didn't bubble and boil but turned directly from a solid to a gas. You're supposed to use a propane flame, but we used a regular butane lighter to see whether it was vaporizing properly. I took a huge hit of smoke in my lungs and thought, *Oh, this is going to be big.* I felt like I was at the top of a roller-coaster ride about to go down, like the ride of a lifetime was impending. I lay back on the couch and the next thing I remember, I woke up and it was thirty minutes later. I heard this industrial vacuum zzzhoooom! sound, the sort that accompanies a change of dimension in *Star Trek,* and opened my eyes.

Phil and my future husband, Paul, were holding me on to the couch. Paul had a look of concern in his eyes. I was afraid for him when I saw that look. The first thing I thought was that I'd been out cold and they'd already called 911 and were waiting for the ambulance to arrive. I tried to get the words out, "Take my pulse." I didn't know if I was physically okay. I'd never passed out before. Finally, I said, "I'm all right. Physically, I'm fine." I kept saying this over and over, and Phil asked, "How about *meta*physically?" His face was plaid and shifting. "How about spiritually? How are *you*? Are *you* all right?" I returned to normal two minutes later. It was a little scary coming out of it. And because of that fear, I had to struggle to recall where I'd been for thirty minutes.

The first thing I remembered was this tremendous euphoria. They'd been holding me onto the couch because I was squirming around and they thought I was going to fall off the couch. Paul said, "You were sailing and soaring. You were milking it. You had this look of pure ecstasy on your face." Then it started coming back to me, that I had, at least for part of the thirty minutes, been in a tremendously happy state, as though everything had come together and everything made perfect sense: the biggest "Aha!" that you could have. The whole of my being and the world's existence and history had suddenly made complete sense to me.

In images more conceptual than graphic I envisaged a sea of humanoid creatures like stick figures with happy faces. Above them was a sunlike icon, which they worshiped and prayed to. Then a moonlike image, the sun's opposite number, came along. For lack of precise terms for these icons, let's just say the moon came into the sky, and the moon and sun combined to become something larger than the sum of the two, like the two hemispheres of the yin/yang symbol. The people affirmed that the union was right and went wild with jubilation.

"Now we get it! The sun has found her moon!" They decided to hold a party to celebrate the union and designated a day for the festivities. When I woke up and tried to explain all this to Paul and Phil, I realized that I was talking about the wedding I anticipated between me and Paul. I'd been bugging him lately: "When are we going to get married?" I'd been fine on my own, but had realized that I'd found someone whose presence in my life creates a greater whole, so I wanted to celebrate our union. Later I thought that the vision was more primal and person-specific than that, that perhaps I'd reexperienced my own conception, the egg and sperm uniting to create me, and that the celebration had been for the day of my birth.

But this was only the first part of the trip, which lasted but a few minutes. The greater part of it was much harder to access. The more I thought about it, the more I remembered scary things. At one point, there was some sort of Techno music playing, and as the beat slowed down, everything decelerated accordingly until it finally stopped. Then everything, including me, ceased to exist. I told myself, *This time you've gone too far.*

The next day, borders were undulating and things seemed like they were breathing, which made me nervous. In the days that followed, little things would trigger the tiniest insight into what had happened during those missing minutes of the 5-MeO trip. I'd never had a panic attack before, but I started to feel very anxious, almost paralyzed with fear. I was in the bathroom, washing my hands, thinking about it, and felt suddenly transported to the scary place again. A wave of eerie adrenaline washed through me.

For a couple of months after that trip, I got paranoid when I smoked pot, which echoed the trippy feeling and the driving Techno beat that preceded the cessation of all things during the dark side of the episode. A fellow I talked to who did a lot of DMT said that it changes your hardwiring, making it easier to permeate the membrane between ordinary waking consciousness and psychedelic consciousness, so that one can move between the two with relative expedience. If that's true, I consider it a downside to tryptamines. I like to have complete control of when I go over to the Other Side. I don't necessarily want the two sides to touch and meet so easily.

I've tried to tap into the anxiety at the heart of the trip, and for its own part, segments of that underlit hemisphere are still trying to come to the surface to be processed. When I saw the movie *Contact,* the protagonist (Jodie Foster) travels through both time and space in a trippy scene for which the soundtrack and lighting are very spooky. She's rushing headlong alone into unknown territory far from Earth. At one point, she's scared, but keeps saying she's "Okay to go" ahead with the mission, "Okay to go," which reminded me of when I kept repeating, "Physically, I'm all right."

Jodie Foster goes into a strange part of space for several hours according to her own sense of time, but she's only gone a few seconds in real time. Like her, I have some lost time to account for. I wonder, *What happened?* Perhaps it's contradictory, but I want to have control over the psychotomimetic or entheogenic dimensions of my trips.

In spite of the nice union synergy at the outset, I took away more dread than euphoria from my 5-MeO DMT experience. For thirty minutes my body moaned and writhed and stretched and rolled around, but I wasn't there for most of that. I don't know where I went. I find this especially disconcerting, because most people I know who've done DMT tell me they can remember everything from their trips. I can only conclude that my trepidation is shielding me from something potentially cataclysmic that I'm afraid to see.

So I think I may need to take DMT again—this time the normal-strength variety—to go back in there to see if I can pick up where I left off or otherwise explore what had happened to me. If I have something to teach myself, I want to learn it. When something powerful happens to you, if you can render it into words it gets smaller and holds a less mythic power over you. I want to know what happened and then to learn from it and be able to tell my friends about it.

Someone likened a 5-MeO trip to taking a thousand peak-LSD experiences and putting them on the head of a pin. Part of me feels proud that I went on such a high-octane, industrial-strength tryptamine voyage into the depths of my own psychic hyperspace. But I haven't taken any psychedelic since.

Leonard Gibson

B. 1943

Teacher of transpersonal psychology at Burlington College in Vermont; president of the Association of Holotropic Breathwork International; chair of the Rutland, Vermont, Regional Planning Commission; Ph.D. in psychology, Ph.D. in philosophy; father of two children

Resides in Pawlet, Vermont

Raised in Waltham, Massachusetts

Portals of Flame, Petals of the Lotus Blossom

During the fall of 1965, during my first semester as a grad student in philosophy at Claremont College in Southern California, I began what became an eighteen-month regimen of taking high-grade LSD every week or two. I obtained a small bottle filled with blue powder from a street source who said it contained seventy thousand micrograms of pure acid. I measured it out into about two hundred doses. The material was potent and devoid of side effects, as was corroborated by others.

I'd been studying philosophy as an extension of a deep desire to *know* going back to some inchoate time in my childhood. LSD served to concentrate my search and my sense that there was some basic paradigm that revealed the nature of things. However, although I wasn't conscious of it at the time, I was hampered by a fear of authority that prevented me from fully realizing my visions and made my spiritual progress fitful and sporadic for most of my early adult life.

I had revelations on LSD that put me in touch with the themes Plato addressed in his most profound work. But this ironically distanced me from the academic program, where Plato's intellectual structure was a higher concern than his profundity. As it was with Plato, it was the experiential dimension of philosophy that captivated me, and that was most resonant, to my mind, in Eastern thought. I was intrigued by Alan Watts's works, *Psychotherapy East and West* and *The Joyous Cosmology,* his first overtly psychedelic work.

Mathematics was another avenue to mystical consciousness. I'd read a story about a prisoner of the Germans in the Second World

War, who kept his mind together by scratching mathematical formulae on the walls of his cell, and then found himself at the end of long proofs going off into mystical experiences. I was inspired by Alfred North Whitehead, who wrote, with his student Bertrand Russell, *Principia Mathematica,* the culminating work in the history of formal mathematics. Whitehead was brought to the extremities of his mind by his fervent pursuit of mathematical logic and universal algebra. Some of the world's greatest minds—those of Pythagoras and Buckminster Fuller, for instance—conceived the universe as a mathematical construct.

My ontological engines were stoked to a new intensity when I was visited by the spirit of a departed friend at the end of one of my LSD sessions. One night I got a call from Gene, the younger brother of my best friend, Ted, informing me that the latter had just died in Mexico in tragic circumstances. Ted was a very brainy and inquisitive classmate of mine when I was an undergrad back East at Williams College. He'd dropped out of school and gone down to Mexico with Gene, a mechanic not so given to abstraction and intellectual matters.

Gene came to visit me at the small cabin I was living in out in a canyon, and related the full story of what had happened. He said they'd been out in the countryside and Ted had developed a numbness in his arm, which he shrugged off. When it got worse, they went to the nearest hospital. By the time they reached the small-town medical center, his condition had progressed so much that the doctors said they weren't equipped to help him and that his only hope rested in getting to a major city like Los Angeles.

So they booked a flight on a commuter airline, but when they got to the bay door of the plane, the stewardess wouldn't permit Ted on the aircraft, because he was *borracho* (drunk). He was fluent in Spanish, but his affliction had rendered him unable to speak at all. Gene, with only rudimentary Spanish, was unable to convince the stewardess to change her mind. He brought Ted back to the same hospital and he died that evening. Gene said that part of the reason Ted died so quickly was that his hope had been dashed. He knew exactly what was going on, but couldn't do anything about it. It was eventually determined that Ted's illness was either meningitis or a virulent form of polio. He might well have survived had he reached L.A.

One night after midnight, Gene and I were talking about Ted. I was in the final hours of an acid trip, all the storm and fury past, clear and mellow and open. Up to that point, Gene hadn't yet broached how he felt about losing his brother, discussing only the circumstances of his death. He pulled a carton of yogurt from the fridge, took a few spoonfuls, and told me of his reaction to his brother's ordeal and death. For the first time, the force of the emotional dimension came through. As if to underscore our mutual love for Ted, a flame burst alight in the space between us, the way a sheet of paper does when a match is held beneath it. Just as the flame ignited, Gene erupted, "That's what I was trying to tell you!" The shared intensity of feeling, embodied in the flame I was seeing, had suddenly struck home with him.

Gene had been aware of his feeling for his brother as you might be aware of a stone in your shoe. You don't notice it until all of a sudden, when you step down particularly hard, you can identify the cause of the subliminal annoyance. Gene's love for his brother and grief at his loss, which had been sitting latently in his psyche as an indistinct feeling, finally burst forth.

The flame was oval-shaped, pointed at the top and bottom. From the center out to the edges, a spectrum ran from the greens into the purples. It was iridescent, like the old-fashioned Christmas lights with bubbles in them (which are unlikely to garner UL approval today). It filled the room with an orgasmic emotion that circulated through the two of us. The spirit of Ted was present with us. Instantly, I could see that Gene was acting as a messenger for Ted, bringing me something Ted had left behind with which to show me the dimension beyond. It had been buried in Gene's consciousness, which had borne it until a medium—our magnified mutual emotion and my acid-heightened sensitivity—was available to bring it into my awareness.

Loosed from Gene, it revealed Ted's experience standing at the portal between life and death. One cannot simply impart such information directly to someone else. In his *Seventh Letter,* Plato wrote that such a manifestation comes only after long study and close attention, when like a blaze kindled by a leaping spark, it springs to light in the soul and becomes self-sustaining.

I identified the spirit force imparted by the flame as the "mind seal" that Bodhidharma brought to China when he brought Buddhism—a rendition of the ceremonial transmission of *prajna,* the immutable life energy, from master to disciple. (Bodhidharma is the twenty-eighth patriarch in the Indian Buddhist tradition, considered the founder of Zen in China and thus the first patriarch of the Zen tradition.) I believe the flame erupted to show us there was something beyond the corporeal realm, just as the three dimensions of the flame transcend the two of a sheet of paper. The vision of this holy fire burned through the veil of the mundane to the realm of the divine.

A while later I was married in a hippie wedding to my girlfriend Jane. We were both into psychedelics, though her interest was more recreational. I was ingesting LSD more intensively and having some very profound experiences, but they tended to culminate in an uncomfortable contradiction. I'd get to a point where I'd wonder if I'd gone permanently insane, and then finally break through to a sense of mystic clarity and certainty. At that paradoxical flashpoint, my consciousness was flushed to a state of ultimacy.

I became increasingly charismatic over the first year of the marriage. When I'd do acid, dozens of people would show up to listen in and catch the heat. I was really good at describing what was going on in my mind, and my delivery became so compelling, even some of my professors got sucked in. They'd invite me for dinner parties as entertainment, much to their chagrin later, when some of them got censured or fired as the campus's tight-knit social order started blowing apart under the mounting impact of LSD.

One dinner party became a scandal at the college. On the day of the party, I was tripping and the damned phone was ringing all afternoon. I couldn't get away from it. (I was unwilling to take the receiver off the hook, and this is in the days before modular phones that you could unplug from the wall.) At the time, my mother was having a hysterectomy, and I thought it might be my father calling to tell me how she was doing. But I didn't want to talk to him in my state, so I just let it ring, again and again. The neurotic nature of this avoidance was underscored later, when we reached the dinner party. It turned out that it was the host who'd been calling, to tell us to come an hour later.

After all the guests arrived and we sat down to dinner, I was talking to a woman seated on my left, and we really got into it. The conversation came to an incredible emotional fullness, which put her in tears. I turned to the woman on my right, the companion of a Southern Baptist minister named Daniel, and engaged her in a discussion that also got intense. Daniel thought I was bearing down too hard on her and took exception. "You're just making up problems," he said.

"Okay, I have a real problem," I said. "I'm having experiences with LSD which reveal the most precious things that one can understand. But at the same time, I'm so neurotic, I won't even answer the telephone and deal with my parents." Daniel asked me to define these two personas, and I did as follows: one that experienced tremendous revelation through LSD-facilitated consciousness, and one that was afraid to speak of this to his parents.

He held up two fingers. "You have two selves," he said, "but the two are one." He closed down his middle finger and held up his index finger. When I saw that single digit upheld like the staff of mystic union, the universe burst open. The kundalini moved from the base of my spine all the way up, bursting out the top of my head into what's described in Buddhist terminology as the thousand-petal lotus blossom. Chimes went off. I was totally transported. I was so overwhelmed, in fact, that I thought I might be having a heart attack. I rested a while and went home.

By the winter of 1967 I was sleeping only an hour a day, but that was all I needed. I could run for twenty-three hours full-tilt, sleep an hour, and be up and at it again. I was in a permanent psychedelic state. I'd take some acid every week or two, but it never seemed to actually quit. There were peaks and valleys, but I basically remained at the same lofty altitude. I was driving Jane nuts with behavior that would be clinically described as manic. Finally, one night, very late, she told me, "Look. If you wake me up one more time, that's it."

I was lying in bed and had to pee, but I was terrified that I might jostle her awake as I got out of bed. I was getting into a paranoid state and began to fear that if I didn't get up to relieve myself, the amplitude of my bladder would put a stress on my system and I'd have a heart attack. I was absolutely stumped by this paradoxical mental state that translated into a physiological quandary.

I finally screwed up the courage to get out of bed, and as I came to the door out of the bedroom, it dawned on me that *I knew too much,* and that there were fascist vigilantes waiting in the next room who would shoot me the moment I emerged. *Do I step out of the room and get shot, or stand here and die of a heart attack?* I finally worked up the fortitude to step out. As I did, a fire leapt up in the corner of the room, a larger version of the flame I saw with Gene. It was the Burning Bush that Moses saw on Mount Sinai, and I was right there with him, staring into the fire that burns but does not consume (Exodus 3.2). The separation of time and space between Moses and me had vanished. I was seeing the flame with the same eyes he used.

I experienced this flame as a portal through which I could pass to leave this world forever. Heaven was on the other side, and all I had to do was step through to attain such unimaginable bliss, you couldn't want more. I stood on this side of the portal, hesitating, feeling intimations of the bliss on the other side, the *Satchittananda* or being-consciousness-bliss. My sense was that I wouldn't have been literally *burned to* death by the flame, but if I went through it, my wife would have had a corpse to deal with. I thought about it for a while, and, attractive though it was, I decided it really wouldn't be fair to my wife, my family, and my friends. There'd be no explanation, plus it would put psychedelics in a bad light, and I didn't want that. I pulled back from the portal.

I was in a lot of emotional pain, out of sync with my body, my marriage, and my social surroundings. For the next few months, I was totally *gone* I was so high. Whenever a dialogue heated up, this psychic flame would burst upon the scene. My charismatic powers heightened accordingly. People would come around and tune into my wavelength and bask in the sacred fire I was combusting. But I was burning my candle at both ends. My marriage was falling apart and my ability to ground myself had all but disappeared.

Finally I met a wall. I was walking into a class on Plotinus, whose work is collected into the *Enneads* (from the Greek word *enna,* meaning "nine"). The professor was discussing the numerological organization of these works. Plotinus's disciple, Porphyry, had gathered them into a book of eighty-one lectures, nine groups of nine, a structure which spoke to the Hellenistic penchant for magic. I knew about the unique arithmetical properties of the number nine, that if you multiply anything by it and add up the digits, the sum will always be nine. Before computers, accountants checked sums by "casting out nines."

Suddenly, the heavenly charm of numbers struck me like a thunderbolt. I started fulminating and running on about the divine properties of the number nine, and the professor looked at me like "Whoa, man. Where's this guy coming from?" I realized then and there that I was over the edge, that if I carried on like that, I'd be in trouble. It's one thing to talk about the majesty of numbers, but when you're really seeing and feeling the magic, you sound wacko.

My marriage continued to crumble. I took the scores of remaining LSD doses I had stored in the fridge and dumped them all down the drain. But it was too late. Jane had had enough of my indefatigably mantic antics. Everything fell apart and I fled back to Boston under the apprehension that the whole state of California was about to suffer a huge earthquake and fall into the ocean. Nothing in my training or in the culture had prepared me for the scale of revelations and ecstatic visions which I'd had in abundance over the previous year and a half. I needed a totally safe space to be held and protected, and nothing like that existed for me.

Back in Boston I found they were looking for hippies to serve in the vanguard of the new cultural revolution. I helped start the city's first underground newspaper, *The Avatar,* and got involved in Mel Lyman's group, a cult based in the Fort Hill section of Roxbury. It took me six months to descend from the euphoric heights of California to utter depression in a cold-water flat in Roxbury, and then gradually get it back together enough to head back to school in California and finish my dissertation.

After I got my degree, I worked at an Oklahoma university for about six years. I remarried in 1972 and decided that psychology offered more meaningful work, so I quit that job and moved to Austin, Texas, to enter the counseling and clinical psychology program at the University of Texas. I did my internship up at a Boston hospital, where I had trouble fitting in, so much so that they threatened to throw me out, because I was smiling too much and getting along too well with the patients.

While working at the hospital, a catalog from the Esalen Institute was dropped into my mailbox. In it was an advertisement for a workshop by Stanislav Grof. I'd been reading his books since 1976, when I was writing an article on a Whiteheadian interpretation of the LSD experience. In that piece, I referred to acid as a magnifier of the mind, and in *Realms of the Human Unconscious,* Stan refers to it as "a nonspecific amplifier of mental experience." At my wife's urging, I went to Esalen for a week in January 1981 and met Stan.

It was like coming home. I broached my experiences of the sacred flame to him, and his response was upbeat and reassuring. "Oh, many strange things happen," he said. Using his framework, I identified my crisis in 1967 as a "spiritual emergency" the likes of which he'd treated successfully numerous times.

I finished my internship but got stuck on my dissertation. It had taken me only six months to write my philosophy dissertation at Claremont, because I just wrote up what I'd learned from my psychedelic experiences and wove it together with classical and modern texts that spoke to the same issues. But I spent years and years on my psychology thesis, because I was expected to write about something other than my own experience.

I decided, *To hell with it.* I'd blow the degree and get into Holotropic Breathwork, a practice launched by Grof in the mid-Seventies in part because the avenue for legal psychedelic psychotherapy had been closed. The method is to lie on a mat, do some relaxation exercises, and then to breathe rapidly and deeply. To stimulate the process, intense, evocative music is played. This could be indigenous music; sacred music ranging from Gregorian chants to Sufi dervish and Qawali music to Middle Eastern trance music; or contemporary music by composers such as Vangelis, Jarre, and Homer, and groups like Dead Can Dance, Enigma, and Tangerine Dream. For millennia, tribal peoples have focused their powers by gathering in circles to chant, drum, or dance. The !Kung of the Kalahari Desert, for instance, say they dance until the *num* rises. The term *num* embodies their concept of "medicine" and "good" and other benign forces.

I signed up for a workshop and on the first day, felt a magnification of power through the exercises, and eagerly returned for another, where I learned that Grof and Jack Kornfield, the Buddhist teacher and scholar, were holding a weeklong, residential workshop in Poultney, Vermont. I signed up and went.

Between sessions I went home for a while and among my mail was a letter from my dissertation adviser. "It's just as well that you didn't send me your proposal yet," he wrote, explaining that he'd suffered a detached and bleeding retina. I was shocked. What would happen if he became disabled, and I had to find a new adviser? I'd already applied for one extension after another, pushing the time limits of the academic bureaucracy. Reading on, I saw that the few sketchy ideas I did present to him had not been well received. He just didn't see what I saw. *Didn't see!* The metaphor hit me square in my psychical eye. That evening I returned to the workshop, haunted by my age-old difficulty in satisfying the demands of my elders.

The next day, I lay down on my mat and started breathing. The music intensified, faster and faster, as I quickened my breathing. Strong sensations of buzzing energy began to build, then concentrated in my hands. The feeling became increasingly powerful, and I felt compelled to call for pressure on my hands. The compulsion developed by some internal logic I didn't understand but felt driven to heed, to the point where I had my facilitator and my sitter on either side of me, each pressing a thumb into the centers of my palms with all his weight.

I lay faceup, trying to push back with my pinned palms, to intensify the pressure. In an ordinary state, I would have felt pain, but in this one I wanted even more pressure and only at a specific point on each palm—not a hair's deviation from it. Suddenly, I realized I was being crucified. With that revelation the sacred flame burst upon me. The face of God and the intensity of His being shone upon me. It was the same God that appeared to me in the Burning Bush: the purple-green iridescence that burns with emotional resilience through body and soul. But now the blaze of energy surged more powerfully by orders of magnitude than any other feeling I have ever experienced. It was not the God of any theological dogma or moralistic authority—just love and omniscience and the force of a million suns. Today I'm reluctant to attribute a gender to God, as I now understand that "He" appears in many forms, but my vision clearly manifested the sort of powerful kindliness that I deeply wanted a father to show me.

Then I heard a voice within my mind speak to me: *God loves you, but you are afraid of Him. Your father loves you, but you are afraid of him. Stan loves you, but you are afraid of him.* (I'd tried to speak to Stan earlier in the week, but my awe of him had rendered me a babbling idiot.) *All your teachers and mentors love you, but you are afraid of them.*

In that instant, I realized the major neurotic bind of my life. All my life I'd had powerful religious feelings, and yet I was fearful of power and disdainful of all citadels of conventional authority. I realized that I was worthy after all of the love of my father, my teachers and mentors, Stan Grof, and God Himself. My heart dissolved. I lay on my mat, flowing in tears, empty. Where my heart had been in my chest, a vast openness now extended to the ends of the universe. I gathered up my courage and asked my sitter to bring Stan over to me as soon as he was free. When he arrived at my mat, I told him how I'd been afraid, and he gave me a great big hug. He understood.

This breakthrough was the turning point of my life. I could finally see a way through. I bent to academic discipline and produced a dissertation of unadorned behavioral science without any philosophical speculation. My revelations also dissolved the subliminal fear that my psychedelic revelations were only the by-product of a drug. I determined that LSD was not the actual source of my visions, but only a powerful but incidental provocation for them. Breathwork too could bring them about.

But if I'd never had those acid experiences, would I ever have been able to open up so much as I had by the Breathwork exercises? Who knows? I've seen some people open up in Breathwork sessions without ever having had a psychedelic experience, while I've seen others, who *have* had profound tripping episodes, huff and puff to no result.

"No million, free sugar-cube acid mystics," my first wife Jane once inscribed in my journal as I was coming down from a whirling, manic, megalomaniac trip back in 1967. She was right. Psychedelics are indeed no easy freeway to divine consciousness for the masses.

Leonard Mercado

B. 1960

Cofounder and president of the Peyote Foundation, a nonprofit, educational conservatory and religious organization; partner in ceremonial incense supply business; father of four

Resides in Kearny, Arizona

Raised in Arizona

Psychedelic Terra Firma

When you're on peyote, Jesus has a way of always crashing the party, no matter where it might be, including the NAC tepee. When you're in there worshiping with peyote, honoring it as a medicine, you're accepting the guidance of the divine architect for which Jesus is really only an overused name. Bowing down to the original instructions is what first attracted me to the idea of peyote as the sacrament.

What got me launched on this path was an initiation into the divine at age eighteen on a material promoted as "the peyote of Asia," Hawaiian baby woodrose. Though I hadn't even smoked grass yet at the time, I'd already developed a fascination with peyote. Being well-versed in Eastern meditation techniques, I wanted to start with a substance that came out of the ancient mystical traditions of the Orient. So I sent away for some woodrose seeds to a botanical mail-order company that had an ad in *High Times.* They wrote me back that my purchase had been back-ordered for six months because the seeds were out of season, so I shelved the idea in the back of my mind.

A few months later, I had a dream that signaled that the seeds had arrived. I asked my parents for the combination to our P.O. box and my mom gave it to me half-amused, wondering why I suddenly wanted it since I'd never picked up the mail before. I went down to the post office and opened up our box and sure enough, the package was there.

I was so excited about this coincidence that I took the seeds at the earliest opportunity—as it turned out, while at work at my job at a local copper mine, where I was earning about fourteen bucks an hour managing the afternoon shift. It was a decent job but a rough social environment in which to maintain a divine spark of energy in one's heart while bullshitting with the hard-hat boys about who was getting laid and all the town gossip. There was a very entrenched mind-set at the mine, with nepotism in force over five generations. (The supervisor's kids were supervisors; the hard-core muck drivers were the same family, two generations later.) Even in such a constrictive scene, there was a lot of acid being dropped on shift, though I was never party to that.

On the day I did the woodrose, I had a very heavy physical workload. The day crew had left me the chore of shoveling about three tons of copper muck into a steel bin, which I then raised on a crane. I sweated through the first two hours of the trip, working through the initial nausea. Fortunately, I was the only guy at the plant that afternoon. Slowly I was overcome by a buildup of energy that felt like a catastrophe in the making. I didn't know how many seeds I was supposed to eat (they came with no instructions), but I'd apparently consumed enough to cause a complete cosmic meltdown of my reality. Ironically, I'd OD'd on naturally occurring lysergic acid amides that weren't far from what the acidheads on the blasting crew were doing.

In spite of all the concentration and energy I'd just summoned for my job responsibilities, I couldn't shake the feeling that I was about to completely vanish off the face of the Earth. No matter how good I was at running the plant, I was now withering away to nothing. It was so alien and overwhelming that I thought I must be dying. I felt all my systems shutting down.

I'd been practicing meditation quite rigidly every day to shut off my mind. So I decided to meditate and go out that way. I knelt in a praying position in a quiet corner of the plant, and concentrated on the exercises. As soon as I turned off my internal dialogue I felt a lot better. Suddenly I had a hope of one last act worth doing: to die an honorable death. As soon as I gave up trying to hang on, the trip turned increasingly wonderful. When I came back into possession of myself, I was keenly aware that every little sparrow that flew had a beautiful song to sing that meant something.

The experience gave me a kind of perpetual inner smile. I felt that a key to understanding was laid in every corner of existence, that no matter how bad the situation was, there was always an answer to be found. I knew beyond the shadow of any doubt that there was a divine spirit behind all creation. I felt confident that God's architecture was in place, but unsure of how my life fit into it.

I began to play guitar and bass at Pentecostal revivals, where I was a sort of spy on the lookout for people who'd had experiences similar to mine. I witnessed speaking in tongues, apparent miraculous events, and lifesavings, but I didn't see much personal salvation that was experiential, from the spirit within. Most of the meaning derived from the meetings was based on the shared group experience of the music, which was hypnotizing.

I decided to investigate psychedelic consciousness from the perspective of faith, and subjected myself to a plethora of such chemicals from age twenty-two on. I ate a lot of LSD and Ecstasy, did my share of tryptamines, including plenty of mushrooms, tried some *Salvia divinorum,* and dosed myself with as many of Shulgin's mescaline analogues as I could. After a while, it was grating to take on all the hyper-data I was picking up. Ultimately I found that most psychedelic experiences were external to my life.

My ketamine experience is a good case in point. I did it just once, as a favor for a friend. "You could teach me something about this stuff," he said. "I know you don't like needles, but that's the best way to do it." So he gave me an injection and I lay back to see what would happen. Within a few seconds, I left my body and my selfhood completely behind. The feeling of being in the void without a body was so strongly internalized that I could not relate it to the cause and effect of taking a substance. For about forty Earth minutes I assumed that I'd always been this way. Then I started recalling particular aspects of my personality and details that I loved on Earth, and, step by step, traced my way back. *Hmm, Earth. that's right, Arizona. Little valley of the Hila. Nice little family I have. My wife, Raven, her beautiful feet, the way that she* sings . . .

Then it hit me. *Holy cow! These aren't just ideas, but actual realities I'm physically involved with.* I remembered that I had a body and a whole other life than this drifting in the void. Out in the astral world I recalled the whole process leading up to the administration of the drug. I remembered that my friend had flown over from California and told me he had this drug he wanted me to check out. I recalled lying down, my arm being swabbed with alcohol, and then the damn needle going in. It took me that long (forty minutes) to trace back that I'd received an intramuscular injection of ketamine. It was like following Hansel and Gretel's breadcrumbs to find my way back to my own body and identity.

When I finally realized that I'd submitted willingly to this voyage, I was suddenly very impressed and ready to travel around in its unique orbit to see what was going on. Prior to that, I was like pure awareness unattached to a distinct personality. I was conscious of a swirling void, blue alternating with black, with pockets of light that were loci of information that had once been people. I became aware that we belonged to a vast population of souls that were turning on a huge cosmic wheel. Part of the rotating mass was a manifestation of bodies, but most of it was like the iceberg under the ocean's surface that you don't see, which was comprised of the souls that aren't currently alive on Earth. Being with-body myself, I was out on the outer rim of this big blue swirling doughnut, which was the core of all humanity of which only certain elements inhabited bodies at any given time. I could swim in and out of this Big Blue Swirly like a tadpole going in an out of an egg, with the added advantage and pleasure of being able to remanifest in a body.

As the drug wore off, I was able to work my way down the chain of cognition to the awareness of myself lying on the bed. "Yep, still breathing," I'd note and then run back out to interact with the wheel of incarnation. The biggest turn-on wasn't the astral flight but activating a human body and getting involved in the game of time and life that we play on ourselves—just a teeny sliver of the Big Blue Swirly, but that's where I wanted to be. This trip was fantastical, but it didn't leave me with the desire to do ketamine again. In fact, I won't do K again. I just love sitting here on the stoop with my beautiful wife in this particular dimension of quotidian time and space. I love it *here!*

The baby woodrose showed me that there is a God. The other psychedelics showed me that God is tolerant, and then peyote showed me that God is right where I'm sitting. Prior to concentrating on peyote, God was standing back, somewhat amused with me. "There he goes, tripping again." I honor and appreciate those experiences, but peyote was the agent that psychedelicized my actual life. Peyote grounds me, showing me where the work is, putting me in touch with who I am and who I really want to be.

Once you use peyote as a sacrament, it's hard to pick out a particular episode as remarkable, because there's something timeless and continuous about the peyote experience, as though all your experience becomes one. It's almost like a *Twilight Zone* show in which you get much more than you bargained for. Here you expect the trip to last just eight or twelve hours, and it becomes your life. Peyote has, in effect, said to me, *Hey, you want that trip? Here it is.*

Working in the order of occupancy, peyote retunes your physicality first, so that the basis of your experience gets the workout it needs before you take off psychically. A typical experience goes like this: I ingest a large amount of this terribly bitter tasting cactus, which my body tells me I shouldn't be swallowing. Even on some of my best experiences, I ask myself at the outset, *Gawd! What are you doing? Grow up. You don't need to be doing this. You could be drinking hot chocolate, doing anything you want, and here you are doing this.*

Generally, my body will go through an adjustment that entails lethargy, nausea, and mild to acute depression, something akin to what a diabetic must feel going through a severe insulin crisis. Sometimes it takes me on a bad-feeling tour: *There you go. Remember that?* This stage is often brief, just five minutes or so, for which I'm always very thankful, but sometimes it lasts three or four hours.

The more I eat peyote, the more honest I am with it, and, in turn, the less it needs to treat me that way. When I keep it out of my body for a while and then finally eat it again, it says, *Look, we were just saving all this stuff (scenes, lessons) up for you. If you waste all that time without putting us in your body, well, you'll just have to pay for it the next time you do it.* It's like an additive formula. If I take it into my body consistently, it hardly scolds me for avoiding the truths it wants me to see.

Like many people, I often throw up at the peak, which functions as a bioelectrical purging of all the tension I have. It's funny, because throwing up in most civil settings is the last thing we like to do. If you're sitting in church, all dressed up and listening to all the pretty songs, the last thing you want to do is lean over and gork in front of God and everybody. But when you're in the tepee and you throw up, it does you well to actually see the stuff coming out of you. You feel as though the bits in the puke are shreds of the nasty thoughts you were thinking, and sure enough, when it's out of your gut it's no longer in your mind.

Peyote is a very just plant, which tends to give you a round-trip on your journey. While other psychedelics often rub your nose in your troubles, peyote gives your heart strength, so there's no question that the scenes you've just witnessed are resolvable, that there's a reason for the pain in life, and that it's overcome-able.

I first discovered the power of my chosen sacrament when I was twenty. In those days, I couldn't get enough of it down my gullet, so I created a fine powder out of about twenty-five dried buttons and packed it into triple-O gel caps, the biggest I could find. I used a little plunger to compact the powder so I could consume as much as possible in each capsule. I swallowed a few dozen and waited.

While listening to the double-LP collection *This is the Moody Blues,* I concluded that my turntable must have been broken, because the music had slowed down as though the record were spinning at only 16 RPM. The turntable was equipped with a strobe unit to calibrate speed. So I got up to check it out and the strobe indicated that it was running at exactly 33.3 RPM. But I knew that couldn't be. There had to be something wrong with the strobe and/or the turntable, or with my ears. I had a friend come in to check it out, and he said, "No. It's perfectly fine."

"Come on, you're kidding," I said. Then I started wondering, *Wait a minute. What's going on here?* Suddenly, I was punched with the worst nausea I've ever had in my life. I visualized all the capsules opening up in my stomach and the powder rehydrating. I felt so sick and so leaden with lethargy that I could barely get up and make my way to the bathroom. I threw up all the powder, which had turned into a mush. But when I lifted my head out of the toilet bowl, I noticed that all the lights in my head had come on, every single one of them. There was no light left unswitched. It was as though my brain were finally working at a hundred percent.

I walked straight back to the living room, where the music was playing, now at the right speed, and sat down. I felt perfectly fine and the music sounded really good. I proceeded to use my mind to do anything I could imagine. Scenes in my mind appeared as real places, not mere images. It was like an ultimate lucid dream, in which I was actually in the place I was thinking of, able to examine things and receive accurate information I'd have no way of getting on my own.

It felt so sweet and heartening and it gave me so much hope for the possibilities of my mind and a clean body and a pure heart. At the peak of my excitement, I could get up from the most colorful vision, answer the phone and have a conversation or make a cup of tea, then sit back down and take off again, traveling back out of my body into visionary worlds.

Some of the landscapes I can still remember vividly. There's a mountain nearby called Teapot, a local landmark I've admired since I took hikes around it when I was a kid. Now with my eyes closed, facing in the direction of Teapot, I could see the mountain right through the walls. There were arcs of extremely brilliant colors and energy swirling around it, starting at the base and coming out in a large open vortex. I felt I was seeing the real Teapot, the reason why I'd always loved it. The peyote was showing me the place's unique energy, the quality that makes it more than just dirt and stone, which you can't see with everyday eyes.

Several years later a cathartic peyote vision prompted a watershed visit to the Huichol holy land near Wirikuta in the Chihuahua Desert of Mexico, where I first met Raven, who was to be my second wife. The ceremony at which I experienced this vision was very trying, because I was facing things about myself that I didn't want to look at. I had a strong feeling of hopelessness. Like the guy crying out, "Mr. Wizard!" in the *Rocky and Bullwinkle Show,* I needed to know there was a way to personal salvation, which I believe in in the Protestant, even revivalist sense. For a long time I'd been vainly pondering, *Is there a magic ship that will spirit a human being out of this mundane, desire-driven world?*

I'd just rejected an airplane ticket to Mexico given to me the previous night by a teacher named Prem Das, an American author and yogi who'd married into the Huichol tribe and was serving as an apprentice to the late Huichol shaman Don José Matsuwa Ríos. I'd offered it to a woman named Isabella who lived in an artist community in Linda Vista. "Please go to Mexico for me," I implored her. She hesitated, but finally accepted.

During the ceremony, I wondered why I was going through all the pains and rituals again, sitting up all night in the tepee, listening to the water drum and singing the songs. I was tired of looking for things and not finding them, knowing there was a God but unaware of a way to make Him manifest. I wanted to go home to bed.

But then I had a vision, which I hadn't expected, because in my despair I'd given up asking for help. I broke through to a place beyond myself and saw a little baby all alone in the middle of nowhere, crying. Then I noticed, *Hey, that's me!* and felt somewhat grateful for a sympathetic image of myself. A silvery white eagle swooped down, apparently to attack this piece of prime meat, to snatch it up in its talons and carry it off to tear apart and devour. *Well, thank God.* I thought. *Put the thing out of its misery.*

But then it landed on my shoulder and I saw that it was there to help, not to kill me. When the eagle touched me, a great warmth spread through me and I became totally ecstatic as I realized what it meant. My astonishment that it was compassionate jolted me into the realization that maybe there was something out there that cares for somebody else. I felt healed, as though I were suddenly touched by God. I saw clearly that the interaction I was undergoing was my personal salvation, and that I'd actually feared it as much as I'd feared my extinction.

Right away I consciously accepted the flow of life and stopped resisting change. It was like dying (on the woodrose) again. As soon as I felt I could give in to life, I knew that I had to go to Mexico. An inner voice of trust told me, *You've got to go. It's been set up. The medicine is calling you.* I was sobbing, a profound sense of relief washing through me. When I looked up, I saw Isabella on the other side of the fire looking at me intently. The next morning I went over to talk to her.

"Hey, I guess I'm going to Mexico after all," I told her.

"I know!" she said, emphatically.

She asked if I wanted to see what she'd drawn the previous night. "Sure," I said. She opened up her tablet to a picture of me kneeling on the ground with an eagle on my shoulder. She'd been watching me as this scene was occurring in my peyote vision and had somehow telepathically extrapolated it and graphically rendered it.

So I did go to Mexico, where I met Raven and began to integrate my life with the divine consciousness I first tapped into lysergically in the copper mine. The vision changed my life, not just because of the appearance of the eagle or the coincidence of Isabella divining my vision of it—it was the fact that the feeling I received was so true I couldn't deny it.

Now I use peyote religiously—on average, every fortnight. I don't use it to elevate myself into a holy man or saint who's above it all, which is a persona that I fear. I appreciate what God has given me as my life—just the way it is. Peyote gives me the heart to value it while it's happening, not just when I'm sick in bed with a fever, wishing I were healthy, or at a funeral, thinking how good it is to be alive.

Only rarely does peyote take me out of my body, to show me how to be more at home somewhere else and to point things out to help me fix my world. But then it delivers me back. *Here you are, back in your body. Everything's cool, right? Now remember what we showed you.*

Malcolm

B. 1958

Artist, government worker

Resides in New York City

Raised in Detroit

The Psychedelic Is the Creator

When I first encountered psychedelics at age thirteen, I had no real idea of what I was getting into. I was a precocious but melancholy and alienated child, prone to depression; probably not a good risk profile for powerful consciousness-altering drugs. But Detroit was a pretty dismal place that begged for some kind of stimulation. I tried cannabis by the time I was twelve, and loved it. I considered it "natural," and insisted that I wasn't going to take "chemicals," but it wasn't long before I did.

Some friends had been trying various pills, and they finally got me to take a PCP tablet. It was sold as Pink Tab THC, but it was known on the street (well, actually the park outside the school) that it was actually animal tranquilizer. I thought it was great. We always laughed incessantly on it. It was relatively mild and billowy, similar to MDMA, but not speedy. It was a great high but certainly not visionary.

The first visions I saw came from a large pill sold as Chocolate Mescaline. I took one and had a fun time. It didn't seem that much different from the PCP at first, but when I went home and watched TV I started seeing stuff that wasn't there. Curlicues and linear traceries appeared to grow out of the TV image; a face turned devilish, sprouting horns and exaggerated eyebrows. I was highly impressed and felt I was ready for more.

A few months later the chance arrived. It was December 1972. My fourteenth birthday was coming up. Chocolate Mesc was making the rounds again. This time, however, it was a much smaller tablet. With hindsight, I can say that it must have been genuine high-quality LSD, in high-dose tabs, two hundred to five hundred mics each, whereas most pills sold as mesc were actually weak, speedy, poorly synthesized LSD. I was not prepared for the qualitative difference.

I took a tab before going to a local hall where my best friend's band was going to play at a good-bye party for a popular teacher who was leaving our junior high school. In the car on the way over, I felt light and giddy. Everything seemed riotously funny. I was having a great time. Since one hit had barely caused hallucinations last time, I took most of a second tab to ensure effects. I needn't have bothered. As we arrived at the hall, an image of a rocket launch flashed through my head. I was about to take off.

As the band began to play, my high changed. As if a heavy blanket had been thrown over me, my giddiness was replaced by a new state. Visual effects appeared everywhere; motion trails and emanations. Everything seemed heightened and luminous. I became engrossed in the checkerboard pattern of the floor tiles, which began to spin wildly, drawing me in. My perception became infected with a manic energy that seemed to whip up the entire universe into a tumult inside my head. I was bulldozed by the sheer power of it all.

I realized or, as it seemed, was told, that I was a piece of shit. The image of a turd was perhaps derived from the floor tiles, but I was beyond making such connections; I thought it was the truth. Subsequent experience has shown me that the Psychedelic often uses such brutally direct symbolism. By now I was no longer seeing "effects" plastered over reality; instead, I was part of the effect, as though I existed within a movie projected from another dimension. Being a piece of shit, the lowest, most abject form of creation, no doubt reflected my low self-esteem and depressive disposition. Our culture teaches you that you're nothing but shit in a lot of ways, both obvious and subtle. You have to discover for yourself that you're better than that. The Psychedelic can actually help teach this lesson, but it requires guidance and preparation; I had neither.

The scatological turn accelerated the trip in an increasingly nightmarish direction. I began lurching around. I approached the stage, which confused my friends in the band, although some in the audience thought I was part of the show. I tried to put my entire coat into my mouth. Ultimately I believe I left my body, because it went completely out of control. It was in violent motion and could not be restrained. It seemed as if I were watching myself in a movie, as my body, separated from my consciousness, went its own directionless way.

I was "looping," suffering an eternal hell over and over without any progress. There was a voice in my head, my own voice perhaps, psychedelically transformed and separated from self-consciousness. It rode the crest of an inexorable wave, a surging electric current of highly torqued energy that possessed me. It cried out in an incessant stream of repetitious agony: *"WHATAMIWHATISTHISHOWDOISOMEBODYDOSOMETHINGCALLADOCTOR!"*

Of course, the last thing anybody wanted was to involve the authorities. A group of people managed, with difficulty, to get me outside into the parking lot. I was struggling, flailing in all directions and ranting along with the voice in my head. These poor kids, high school age at most, had no idea how to deal with the situation. One of them yelled at me to "Shut up! Straighten up!" as if that would help. I came close to running into a busy street. I shouted out the name of the absent friend who had sold me the mesc, "What did you do to me?"

My parents had gone out for the evening, so a few of my close friends took me home to a flat just a few blocks away. They tried to lay me down and calm me, but it was futile. Pouring orange juice down my throat didn't help. It was a hippie myth that vitamin C was an antidote for bad trips. I continued to unravel, spilling the juice and knocking over the Christmas tree for good measure. It was a losing battle. The landlady heard the commotion; the police were called.

At times it seemed to me that the entire experience happened twice—once to me, and again in a movie that I watched. I viewed from a distance as my tortured self was strapped down and carried out of the house, as if it were happening to someone else. I was taken to a hospital. When I finally regained some degree of sentience, I found myself in a pediatric ward, my arms and legs shackled to the bars of a criblike bed.

What happened between those points is hard to say. Once I was restrained, the trip became more internal. I spent what seemed like forever flowing through hallucinatory realms. I thought that a tape had been triggered in my head, a standard program that plays when you die. Indeed I was dead, or as I heard it "a little bit more than dead." I had had a feeling of utmostness and then some, like being in your own room yet having the urge to go "home," or like lying flat on the ground and then trying to lie a bit lower. It felt like I was going through these repetitions and loops for hours, yet there was much more to the experience and not all of it bad. A turning point occurred when an Escher-like pattern of demonic faces transformed, to my delight, into beautiful feline females.

My return to "reality," however, was far from pleasant. I was alive, after all, but the world (the hospital ward, at least) seemed a mere husk. There was a terrible taste in the bottom of my mouth, and an exhausted, dried-out, deathly feeling about the whole environment. I felt like a discarded tin can with a couple of minute fragments at the bottom rattling around. I had little immediate memory of the events that had brought me there. I didn't really know why I was there; perhaps I'd recently been born?

As I approached "normalcy," my restraints were removed, and I was finally able to register my parents' presence. They were loving and consoling, expressing nothing but concern for my welfare. Outside some cursory questioning, they never pressed me about the matter, then or later. Maybe they thought I'd be gun-shy about tripping after that.

I was, a bit, but I was also amazed and intrigued. I'd learned firsthand how limited our everyday notions of consciousness are. I knew that the experience had touched something very deep in me, at the life-and-death level of being. Despite its phantasmagorical qualities, I recognized a level of reality in the experience that could not be ignored. I wanted to know more, and I was willing to take the risk.

It took me years to really get on track with the Psychedelic, though. After my epic bummer, I found that I could get plenty high on a quarter of a tab, at least with the right acid. I avoided overdosing, but I also avoided deep tripping. As kids, we always wanted to have fun, to use the drug to spice up the quotidian world, but this approach courts problems because it generally entails gauging doses that don't quite obliterate one's ability to function in the "real" world. I had to learn that obliteration was what I was after.

The years went by, and various drugs came and went. Cannabis stayed with me, along with an interest in psychedelic culture, particularly the music. Psychedelics went out of fashion perhaps, but my childhood experience remained a cornerstone in my understanding of the world. It was the late Eighties, the era of "just say no," and I was beginning to think more and more about the nature of saying "yes."

Through fortuitous chance, I had my first encounter with psilocybin mushrooms. It was the first psychedelic I'd taken in ten years. I didn't have a big trip, but it was enough to resurrect my interest, reawakening all the hopes and fears that cluster around these substances. The year was 1987. The media was abuzz with the twentieth anniversary of the Summer of Love. Psychedelics are at the heart of that story, though it's seldom told accurately. I felt I was part of a changing zeitgeist that was beginning to reexamine these things. I began researching the subject, tracking down as much literature and music as I could. I realized that I was part of a growing neo-psychedelic movement. What really catalyzed this was my initiation into true Dionysian ecstasy, at the intersection of me, mushrooms, and the Butthole Surfers.

I'd seen the Buttholes a couple of times, but I hadn't really gotten it. They were known for being scatological and downright weird. Initially they seemed to be an outgrowth of Punk Rock, but as things evolved it became clear that what they were was the preeminent psychedelic band of the era. I found this out definitively at the old Cat Club, a smallish venue on 13th Street in Manhattan, where I went with some friends to trip on psilocybin and enjoy the show.

The band appeared onstage just as I was beginning to feel the shrooms. A few of us wormed our way up toward the front of the tightly packed crowd. The band broke into an incredibly heavy riff and everything erupted into a swirl of sound, bodies, and pure energy. I couldn't help but dance, as the whole room joined in the rhythm of the music. The motion of the crowd was indistinguishable from my own body. I moved as one with the throbbing bottom end, driven by the two drummers.

Everyone seemed to share the same sweaty flesh. I could feel our bones and gristle growing together into a single organism. Incredible sights and sounds flooded my being without pause. Smoke machines and strobe lights bathed the scene. I looked up at the stage, only to see the naked dancing girl pull off her hair (a gorgonesque wig), which blew my mind. Then her maniacal grin revealed tin foil–clad teeth, which also blew me away. Then she simply disappeared, at which point I had no mind to blow; I was just part of the flow.

Maybe it was suggested by the strobe-silhouetted crowd, but I was flashing on newsreel footage of people in the Sixties doing those crazy, whirling-dervish, hippie dances. For the first time, I knew exactly what they were doing. I had never really danced before, other than as a social obligation and even then I was self-conscious. I felt like I didn't know how. But there was no doubt about this dancing; there was nothing to know. I simply joined in with the ecstatic flow of energy that united band, audience, drug, and (it seemed) everything else in the universe.

I was a convert. This was a true watershed experience for me. I finally knew the genuinely ecstatic, suprapersonal side of the Psychedelic. I recognized it as something vital that belonged to everyone, a group that now included me. Alienation seemed like an adolescent indulgence in the face of this inclusive impetus.

After that, I made it a point to see the Buttholes any chance I had. They were always touring in those days; coming to town several times a year. I tripped as often as I could at those shows; indeed I felt like I was backing out of a deal if I didn't. They provided the opportunity and the setting for a special kind of experience. I'm still amazed by how high I was at some of those shows. They usually ended with a few of us wandering speechless, regrouping in a dazed communion.

By now I was committed to the Psychedelic. I even visited a psychedelic church. It was a grungy storefront on 13th Street with an impressive mandala painted on the boarded-up windows, above the slogan The Psychedelic is the Creator. I found it through a flyer handed out at a pro-pot rally. They offered free initiation with their "sacrament," DPT, a short-acting, smokable tryptamine. I was indoctrinated by a classic scraggly hippie type. We had a lengthy discussion, from which I got the idea that the group was a cult that fixated on a mysterious leader said to be the "firstborn of the Psychedelic" and reborn throughout history as Moses, Zoroaster, Jesus, etc. I was dubious, but I didn't feel that I was in immediate danger, so I allowed myself to try their sacrament. I'd heard that one hit of DMT is all it takes, and this stuff was supposed to be similar. The results were anticlimactic; I smoked a big hit in a water pipe, then two more, but it just got me to the edge of really tripping.

I never went back there, but their personification of the Psychedelic, and the use of a religious format, were intriguing to me. I wanted the Psychedelic to be taken that seriously. Presently I encountered the writings of Terence McKenna, which did a lot to convince me that you *could* take it that seriously, without going off the deep end. McKenna was an unabashed psychedelic advocate, which I found inspiring. I'm perhaps an easy target for his kind of omnivorous intellectualism, but I feel that he set a high standard for inspired speculation. Most important, he offered information that actually helped me to trip better.

My first trip after discovering McKenna was one of my most memorable. It was at a Grateful Dead show, which seemed fitting. I was no Deadhead, but I do honor the band. I allowed the mushrooms to lead me on, spending most of the time with my eyes closed, as I received lessons in shamanic hand-dancing, body movements, and meditative themes, which helped to propel and guide the experience along. At one point I saw McKenna's face and understood him as a priestly figure helping to mediate between me and the drug.

I had often seen scrolling fields of patterns or interlocking imagery, but this trip was different. There was a powerful series of centralized images, isolated in the midst of a black space, like spotlit figures on a dark stage. The pictures didn't flow, but changed abruptly, with a sort of snap. I saw a human figure; humanity as such, mounting up what I can only call a stairway to heaven. Then the hand of God extended down in an invitation to union. The hand of Man grasped that of God, but suddenly another, sickly, mechanical hand, or claw, interceded, trying to undo the alliance. The interloping hand then snapped into a hammer and sickle.

The blatancy of this imagery shocked me. I related it to the admonition against Russian communism attributed to the Virgin Mary in the famous visions seen at Fatima, in Portugal. It's easy to explain this kind of thing through simple psychology. I grew up with a vaguely leftist orientation, in a nonreligious home. I learned about religion largely through studying art history. In my psychedelic trance, religion and art (the music) were flowing together in a self-justifying ecstasy. I didn't want any reductive materialism like Marxism interfering. But it was only after the fact that my interpretation came into play. At the time, I experienced the images not as symbolism but as the living truth.

The climax of the trip developed into an increasingly complex diagram of universal life-energy processes in circulation. "What if you fuck up?" I asked. The answer came back like a cosmic shrug: "You try again." Finally, the entire system collapsed back in on itself, snap snap snap, into a perfect golden cube, an alchemical image that epitomized the return to primal unity which I was experiencing.

I was more convinced than ever. Even if one accepts the reductivist premise that psychedelic visions are no more than an agitated condition of your own mind, that they contain no outside input of mystical, or any other, nature, the experience would still have the virtue of displaying possibilities within your mind that have gone unrecognized, or were denied, by your ego. The idea of ego death is a cornerstone of the exegesis that has grown up with the psychedelic community. Often it takes the form of a hallucinatory experience of personal bodily death, typically followed by rebirth into a broadened understanding, in which acceptance of unity displaces the anxiety of separateness. Personal problems are put in cosmic perspective, which tends to minimize them. Experiences of this sort can have a profoundly healing effect, even if it is "all in your mind." Such reductivism only leads to the question of what your mind is "in."

I would say that the mind is not insular, but an interconnected part of a universe of both physical and symbolic substance, whose linkages extend throughout space and time. The Psychedelic has helped me to feel like a part of this continuum. I feel like I have a much greater understanding of non-Western and pre-industrial mind-sets. I used to think that the spiritual worldview developed prior to the Enlightenment had been rendered unavailable by historical developments. But the Psychedelic implants the very breath of primordial awe, opening these things up to contemporary consciousness. I can now understand the psychology of divine inspiration or of magical thinking. When I look at a medieval painting or an alchemical text, it is no longer obscured by its incompatibility with modern thought. Moreover, this understanding does not obviate rationalism; it only broadens the perspective.

If the Psychedelic illuminates the past, it also presages the future. Indeed, my vision of the golden cube seemed to me an augury of the ultimate fate of all things: to return to the original state of unity. This would mean everything in the same place at the same time, the condensation of the universe into a single point; the state immediately preceding the Big Bang. Information technology actually seems to be heading in this direction. The cube I saw might be read as a cosmic computer chip, providing simultaneous access to all information. The physical aspect of such a development is hard to imagine, but the Psychedelic has the characteristic of enabling us to imagine the inconceivable, which is the first step in making it real.

For me, these drugs have played a great role in understanding the accuracy of magical thinking, and conversely, the mythological nature of scientific understanding. In short, they can provide a subjective experience of the unity of dialectical oppositions. Past and future, like life and death, are mutually defining polarities, which are usually experienced as incompatible opposites. The Psychedelic seems to bend the pole into a circle, articulating how it is that these opposites are just differing aspects of the same thing. The recognition of such a "thing" is analogous to the personification of deity practiced by religion, or the positing of theory in science, which brings meaning to what is otherwise just a mass of data.

The great challenge for the psychedelic community is to find ways of bringing these experiences into the everyday world. As an artist, I've found that it's not easy. I made Christmas tree ornaments based on specific hallucinatory images, but simple illustrations don't relate the communicative nature of the visions. More successful were my *Metaphysical Waste Disposal Sites,* a series based on practice, process, and my habitual relationship with cannabis. I smoked pot as a means of inspiration, and then mixed the ashes with acrylic medium to create the paint that was used to make the paintings, which themselves functioned as repositories for the by-product of their own creation. Twenty years after thinking that I was a piece of shit, I had arrived at a more inclusive appreciation of waste.

More recently, my work has moved away from contemporary fine-art modes, toward something more akin to the symbolic devices of Hermeticism and alchemy. This development has been spurred by my exposure to DMT, a particularly potent psychedelic. Psychedelic lore is full of anecdotes of synchronistic convergence. Just after I first encountered DMT, I was told that the street name for the drug was "sparkle." At about the same time, I became reacquainted with an Irish folk song called "Come All Ye" that implores the listener to "trip" upon a "sparkling" green, an invitation to an ecstatic dance. The sparkling is like a hallucinatory rift in everyday reality, which signals an opening into the magic space. I made a floor piece out of marijuana ashes mixed with glitter, or as I referred to it, sparkle. I felt that the ash need no longer be a form of interment, but could be reanimated by the sparkling fragments scattered through it. Not that glitter actually contains light; it reflects light, just as our life is a reflection of the spiritual dimension.

Substances with the kind of power that DMT possesses can be intimidating. I held on to some DMT for a couple of weeks before a friend insisted that we had to try it and I managed to work up the nerve. I inhaled a single hit, and barely had time to lie back before it opened up like a sunburst in the middle of my forehead; a veritable third eye. The sunspot proceeded to reticulate into a complex of luminous circuitry or perhaps a mosaic of organic metal. Somehow I passed through it and found myself in a space that seemed two-dimensional, yet was all around me like a dome or sphere.

A kaleidoscopic array of shifting patterns scrolled across the space. Luminous blue balls circulated around it on a kind of track. Barely distinct from the background, but discernible by a difference in their motions, was a group of cartoonish or playing card–like figures, who were interacting with the balls. I had difficulty grasping the entire scene, as my attention was constantly being drawn to a point that was perfectly central, but I understood as "up." I felt I was being led. Whatever way my mind turned, it was corrected. A voice prompted me, "This is the way, this is the way."

When you eat mushrooms or LSD, it takes a while for the experience to build up to a peak. Often this entry period is the hardest part of the trip to handle; the ego desperately tries to maintain itself. If you can't let go, things can get bad. A brutal experience of death or diminution may occur, my childhood freak-out on Chocolate Mesc being an example. With the DMT, the velocity of the trip was so fast that I was propelled through those levels before they could affect me. I realized that I was dead, and that I was in the place which is the aboriginal base of all existence.

The voice that guided me I attributed to God, although it was the typical psychedelic voice I have always known; my voice really, but attenuated, heightened, and in some sense torqued or spinning. I had no time to doubt or interpret it; I found it completely convincing. As it led me on, the motion became tighter, enfolded. I felt like a rope being tied into a knot of increasing density. The nature of things became clearer and clearer. I felt that all the difficulties of the world must certainly surrender to this understanding. Being dead was not a problem. I was happy to spend eternity in this state.

Then, to my complete surprise, it culminated abruptly. I was tied deeper and deeper into the knot, and then it was as if someone pulled on both ends of the rope and it straightened out, the knot disappearing like a magic trick. Poof! I was released into an empty space of soft grayness. There was no sense of a drug experience that plays out and fades away; it was as if a specific body of information was imparted, and that's all there was to it. I immediately sat up, as if some constraint had been removed, and said, "Yes!" The experience was such that all I could do was agree with it. More than agree, I identified with it, not merely *saying* "yes," but *being* YES. I had felt a truth that I could not distinguish from my own being or from being as such.

Unfortunately, I could not exactly remember what that truth was; not in so many words. My friend seemed to have experienced something similar. "I just wish I could remember where I was just before the end," he said, and I knew what he meant. Materialists may laugh at us if they wish. It's a cliché, the drug user who says, "I knew the secret of existence, but I forgot." After a subsequent trip, I came back saying that it's better to know and to forget than not to know at all. For what's forgotten has left a mark, and may yet be remembered, but ignorance is nothing to be proud of.

Perhaps the Psychedelic reveals something that is simply incompatible with our reality. If you could remember it, it would actually be happening again. This suggests that there is a problem with this reality, something that I believe along with most Western religions, which is embodied in the notion of the Fall. More and more, I have seen my experiences as consonant with the Gnostic shadow side of our spirituality, which seeks to reintegrate the shattered body of God, which is scattered in the form of Creation. As a Psychedelicist, one tries to bring fragments of the other reality back into this one, as building blocks. I believe that all our great life-empowering inventions, language, weaving, baking, money, etc., share this origin. The traditional notion that such things were taught us by the gods is not untrue. We've come a long way from ignorance. If we continue on the path, avoiding the distractions and temptations of this world, we can yet build it into a place that is indistinguishable from the divine world of its inspiration. Then our trip will have reached completion.

Marcel

B. 1951

University sociologist professor

Resides in the eastern United States

Born and raised in California

Is This a Trap or a Welcome?

Back in March 1970, when I was a sophomore studying theater arts at the University of California, Santa Cruz, I picked up a hallucinogenic substance from a guy who'd drift up to campus to sell psychedelics. He said it was acid, and it came in the form of little orange pills the size of saccharine tablets, which were divided into three. I squirreled it away with other goodies, waiting for the appropriate time to drop. I deduced that it might have been PCP some time after I ingested it, when I heard about Peace Pills, which reportedly were hits of PCP in small tabs demarcated into three sections to look like the peace symbol. (I never knowingly took PCP, but I've heard that it's pretty wild.)

A few days prior to my taking one of these orange pills, my friend Derek and I met a freshman girl who called herself Corina, though her given name was Susan. It was common in those days for people to adopt a new name when they came to Santa Cruz, e.g., a guy named Lenny became Sky, a woman named Kelly dubbed herself Tree, and a guy named John assumed the appellation of Patrick Patrick.

Derek, Corina, and I took a walk together, which was a typical way to socialize in Santa Cruz in those days. She was adorable, with blue-jean eyes and long hair. We walked down the hill about four miles from campus into town and then back up again. Soon afterward I learned from Derek that he'd been "seduced" by Corina. I thought, *All right, if this girl is that easy, I want to get to know her better.* So I asked her if she wanted to study together, a proposal tantamount to asking her if she wanted to see my etchings, with the implicit understanding that what I wanted to study was her. She agreed, and lo and behold, I too was seduced. (We had sex.)

We then struck up a relationship, which in that setting was any sort of bond that lasted more than one night. A couple of days into our itemness, I said, "Hey, I have these drugs. Ya wanna drop 'em with me?" She said, "Sure," so we made arrangements to do it the following Saturday.

Saturday came around and she came over. I always liked to eat before I got high, because it was so hard to once I'd gotten off. I tried to eat during a couple of trips, but when I looked at the meat, I saw all the cells moving, which was bizarre and unappetizing. So I'd usually have a hardy meal, drop the drugs, and then not eat again until I started to come down.

Corina did not follow that regimen. She had her own way to get as high as possible as fast as possible, and this entailed not eating. I swallowed my pill on a full stomach, while she dissolved hers under her tongue on an empty one. So she started tripping very shortly afterward, while I was sitting there twiddling my thumbs. Corina decided that I was really out of it and no fun, and that she was going to split to go off and trip by herself. There I was: The drug hadn't even come on and I'd been abandoned. I thought of sticking my fingers down my throat to recall the tab, but then dismissed the impulse as useless and silly. I'd never tripped alone before, having done it either with a guide or with other people who were tripping.

I decided, *To hell with her,* and that I'd go off into the woods, which was always a nice place to trip. Not that I had any choice. I was angry and disappointed and a little frightened. Then I figured, *Hell's bells, there's likely to be at least somebody else tripping on a Saturday. Maybe I'll run into some people who are high.*

I was very controlled the five times I'd tripped previously. I'd let things go only so far, before I'd shake the trip down. I'd shake my head as if to disentangle it, and ground myself and get centered: *Wait a minute. This is drugs.* I was really afraid that if I didn't do that, then I'd just trip off into some other dimension and never come back. So I'd learned to act as my own guide and gotten very good at it, which is why I didn't freak out when Corina split.

I started walking into the woods, and amazingly, the trees opened up before me and then closed behind me, enfolding me in the bosom of the forest. It appeared that there were two stands of trees that parted ranks to widen the space between them so that I could walk through like a veritable VIP. The trunks swayed elastically to the sides as I ambled through, and then closed behind me as I passed. Then I heard tree music, a sort of sylvan pastorale that filled the air, an effusion of the arboreal grandeur of the scene. I would later deem this a synesthesia experience. The aggregate sensory and emotional imprint of being in this forest was manifested into music somewhat like Wagner's pictorial orchestral piece, "Siegfried in the Forest."

I decided that I was not going to shake down this hallucination, that I was going to go with it. The sun was shining down, radiating a dappled light through the leaves. The smell of pine was very strong—as a

Californian, I've always found that an evocative scent. My mother used to pour some kind of pine stuff into my bath when I was a kid. The fragrance always conjures memories of warmth, comfort, and security.

It was so beautiful and enrapturing that I asked myself, "Is this a trap or a welcome?" It could very well have been a trap, some sort of anemone type of organism closing around me. It occurred to me that the trees might not open back up if I turned around and tried to leave. But it didn't feel that way. It felt very harmonious with a fair measure of pomp, as if I were advancing toward something important. It had the tone of the president strutting down the carpet when he comes off *Air Force One,* though not so formal. (I was dressed in only jeans and a T-shirt.)

I felt welcomed, as though I were becoming a part of the forest, as though it were enclosing and caressing me as I moved deeper and deeper into it—like I was arriving at a family reunion and being embraced by the whole brood. There were mythic and fairy-tale overtones along the lines of Alice in Wonderland or Frodo in *The Hobbit* arriving at the Court of the Elf King.

I came to a clearing and thought, *Oh, this is where I've been lead. This is where I'm supposed to go.* I lay down against a rock. The sun beat down on me. I could feel the warmth on my face, a sensation I've always loved. I closed my eyes and held my head up to the magnificent heat-giving light. Then the warmth intensified, as though all of the sunbeams within that clearing were focused right on *me,* and I began to feel warmer and warmer and warmer.

Suddenly, the rays of the sun were magnets pulling on me. I opened my eyes and saw the face of God. He was an Old Testament God high in the sky, with a long beard and flowing hair, benign and loving and all-knowing—right out of Hollywood. He was beautiful and ancient. I had the feeling that this God knew everything about me, every horrible thing I'd ever done, and that He still loved me. He poured down His radiance upon me. There was nothing to hide from Him. He spoke. "Now I can tell you," He said to me. "You are the Sun King." I blinked my eyes and He was gone.

I spent a long time sitting there, puzzling over whether He'd said I was the King of the Sun or the Son of the King. I blew that riff for a while: *Son of the King or King of the Sun? Hmm.* Then I heard an inner voice that said, *You must perform labors.* So it was that only after I completed a series of special tasks would I be duly crowned. I got up and started walking.

There was a little voice in the back of my mind saying, *Don't make so much of this. You're high.* But the ethos of the trip had taken over. It was as though an ancient truth had been revealed to me: that God was omniscient but loving, and that there was nothing to fear from Him. Since then I've come to know other manifestations of God, but this overpowering feeling of His understanding and forgiveness of my foibles is still fundamental to my concept of deity. The face was from Hollywood, but the understanding came from something much deeper and primeval. It kindled my drive to perform labors, and I still take it to heart today, thirty years later.

I went wandering on and came to a road with cars that drove by every so often, rather fast, suggesting to me the speed of light. What came to mind was the shooting gallery in the Magic Theater from Hesse's *Steppenwolf,* in which automobiles are the targets of a frivolous metaphysical carnival game. But that seemed crass or too easy. *My labor can't be to shoot at these cars, but to have the cars shoot at me.* I concluded that I had to play chicken with oncoming vehicles. When I think about this now, it terrifies me. I stood on one side of the road and waited until the last possible instant I could get safely across the road before a car whizzed by, and then darted across to the other side. I bolted across the road barely ahead of passing motorists several times, until I felt I'd done it enough to complete the labor.

I continued hiking along and came to a cliff ledge wide enough to pass on the trail by standing spread-eagled and inching along the side. It was a drop-off of some twenty-five feet, not necessarily lethal, but I'm deathly afraid of heights, and therein was an impediment to overcome. *I must conquer this fear. This labor is to walk along this ledge.* There I was, high as a kite, inching my way on a ledge that I'd never set foot upon even when I was straight, while rocks were falling out from under my feet. *This is really exciting!* I made it across, pleased to have another labor under my belt.

I decided I'd completed about half the labors, and that what I really ought to do at this juncture was to masturbate to clear my mind. So I did that in the sunshine, which was really nice. I considered it a reward for labors done and a little break before moving on to the next ones.

Finally, I'd finished what I thought were all but one of the labors. I don't remember what the others were, but they were probably acts of risk-taking, the unifying theme of the ones I do remember. This is ironic or fitting, as I'm a very risk-aversive person. I'm a religious seat-belt wearer, I won't start the car until everyone is buckled up, and I rag on my kid to wear his bike helmet and soccer pads and so on. In fact, I've done studies of drunk and risky drivers, and I've been an advocate for stricter traffic laws. I'm Mr. Safety himself.

The final labor was to gather my disciples around me. Now, six hours into the trip, I was standing very tall, feeling very good indeed. I glided down the mountain, moving gracefully and effortlessly, and started my search for disciples. I spotted my friend Harry, a freshman. Derek and I were serious, ritualistic drug users, but Harry and his younger crowd were recreational users who got high all the time. They were actually more sophisticated than we were, because they'd had more experience. They'd even taught us some stuff about the psychedelic headspace.

I ran over to him and said, "Harry, I am the Sun King, and you are my disciple." He said, "You're stoned out of your mind, man." I said, "No, really, Harry. I'm the Sun King, and you're my disciple." He began to look a little worried and said, "Let's go inside" and ushered me into his dorm room, where he proceeded to explain to me, in the way you'd explain to a child, that if I went around campus anointing disciples, I was going to get in a lot of trouble. He suggested that perhaps what I ought to do was to come down first and *then* decide if I still wanted to fulfill my mission. "Wouldn't it be nice to listen to some music and drink a little wine and smoke a few cigarettes?" Well, I had to agree with him, and we did just that.

Harry used to tease me all the time about being the Sun King, but I was enormously grateful that I'd run into him as my first disciple and not the provost, the head faculty at the university, or the chancellor. But for many months after the trip, I felt there was a fundamental validity and reality to the experience, that maybe I really was the Sun King. I spent a lot of time puzzling over what that really meant.

It had been a real epiphany, a revelation of God, and—now, this may sound psychotic—that I was a Chosen One of God. I never believed that I was the *only* Chosen One, but that it wasn't everybody that was Chosen and that I had been graced with some kind of divine recognition—let's say as one of the Select Few or Many—and that gave me great comfort.

That was the end of my relationship with Corina. If she'd stayed with me that day, she probably would have been my first disciple, and I wouldn't have had to masturbate. I think that, given a choice, I would have preferred running around naked with her to the controlled terror I underwent. But there was a unique imperative being played out. After that I tripped no more.

The Collapsible Disk

Back when I was a sophomore at Santa Cruz, Simon and Garfunkel released "The Boxer" as a single. People went apeshit over this song. There were no copies of the record in Santa Cruz at Thanksgiving time. I went down to L.A. for the holiday and brought back a copy, and suddenly I was the most popular guy in the dorm. Everyone wanted to borrow my copy of "The Boxer."

One time I was tripping on acid with some dorm mates and someone said, "Marcel, go get 'The Boxer.' We have to hear it." You don't argue with people who are tripping. I remember a story about some guys from Santa Cruz who went down to San Jose to see Kubrick's *2001* while high on acid. The movie boggled them. They didn't get it at all. After the show was over, they cornered the popcorn guy and demanded that he explain it to them. At first, the hapless vendor, a mere kid of sixteen, said he didn't understand it either and he wanted to go home. But the look in their eyes and the fact that they kept inching toward him convinced him that he better try. So there was this poor movie theater employee with a bunch of wacked-out college students gathered around him on the floor like a nursery school class while he tried to explain what the fetus in orbit was all about.

So I ran off to my room in another part of the building to get "The Boxer." As I was walking back to the party room with it, it became rubbery in my hands, so I started playing with it, and it became jelly-like. I wondered, *Can I fold this record into an envelope?* I have a vivid memory of folding this seven-inch vinyl disk into a little envelope.

I folded the top down, the bottom up, and the two sides over, making it into a pocket-sized two-by-two-inch packet. I continued on and arrived at the party-room door. I was about to walk in and show everybody what I'd done, but then stopped myself with the thought *There are people in there who aren't high. If one of them sees this, it's going to shatter, because it's just not possible.* I was convinced that the only people who could see the folded-up record were people who were high.

I reasoned that I'd better unfold it before showing the entire group, so I flattened it out against the wall like you do with a dollar bill to put in a vending machine or an automatic ticket dispenser in the BART. I got it all unfolded so that it looked right, and then walked in and handed it to somebody who put it on a KLH model 11 turntable and played it.

I remember this as clearly as if it were yesterday. I wish that I'd walked into that room without unfolding it, so that there would have been witnesses to my compacting it. But I didn't want to risk shattering this coveted 45-rpm disk, which was the only copy on campus. I have no explanation for why it didn't break when I folded it up.

Mark

B. 1974

Musician

Resides in Brooklyn, New York

Born and raised in Buffalo, New York

Sounding the Black Box of the Subconscious

The most significant and unsettling psychedelic experience I ever had occurred when I combined Syrian rue and psilocybin mushrooms and subsequently experienced a complete whitewash of consciousness: a meltdown of my ego, memory, and sensory and cognitive processes.

In 1996 I was living alone in an apartment in Ann Arbor, Michigan, where I was going to school. One night I steeped a half-ounce of mushrooms in a jasmine tea, letting it steam for about two hours while I extracted the harmala alkaloids from some *Peganum harmala* seeds, which I'd read could, as an MAO inhibitor, potentiate the effects of psilocybin.

My extraction procedure was inaccurate, so I'm not sure how much I really took. I'd read that at the end you were supposed to have a small amount of red-gold crystal, but what I came up with was a swampy, tarry goo. I figured it was less condensed than the crystal would have been, so I took a teaspoon, a good globule, chasing it down with honey because it tasted terrible. Fifteen minutes later I drank a cup and a half of the mushroom tea, and sat down and waited.

Within about five minutes I began to feel the effects. After twenty I was tripping about as hard as I ever did on acid or mushrooms. I realized that it was going to be an intense trip, so I locked the door, unplugged the phone, pulled down the blinds, and turned out the lights. (I hated dealing with phone calls under the influence, when there's nothing worse than when I attract a sober person. Once on acid I had to entertain an uninebriated girl all night—a very unpleasant experience.)

About forty minutes after drinking the tea, microamnesia set in, an effect I usually see on my trips, but much more pronounced this time, especially considering the short amount of time that had elapsed. My memory span shrank exponentially. I was sitting on the couch and kept looking up at the clock, having repeatedly forgotten the time in less than a minute. I laughed aloud at my confusion.

When it really began to hit, I figured it would be over in six hours, so I registered the time I thought it would be over: about four in the morning, which I'd hoped would be an anchor point in reality. *When the numbers represent that time, I'll be coming out of this.* But I gradually lost the ability to decipher the clock. I strained to remember why I wanted to remember those numbers. (It's amazing that I remember not remembering. There was still some vague cache of consciousness to process what was happening.) But it wasn't a matter of the memory being pushed out of place by an avalanche of sensory phenomena. There were no visual associations beyond a hazy blurriness that comprised a two-dimensional plane, and even listening to music, a favorite pastime, was drowned in the murkiness.

I compose music myself, so I usually find it quite easy to listen to it on hallucinogens, when I like to play a lot of dark Ambient music, such as Coil, Brian Lustmord, Robert Rich, Mick Harris, and Thomas Koner. It's labeled "dark" because it's often suggestive of caverns, sewers, ducts, and crawl spaces, with drippy, echoey crypt noises throughout. But I had to turn off the music. I couldn't comprehend it. My attention span waned so quickly that I couldn't follow the progression. I couldn't place what I'd heard twenty seconds before in the context of the present moment.

I felt the need to lie down and went to the bedroom, spiraling inward rapidly. I couldn't place the sounds of traffic outside or my neighbors in the adjoining halls and rooms. The acoustical register of these presences came in ripply and had a strange, panned effect. The aperture of my attention narrowed to a small black hole. It was as though I were rushing toward a chasm and had reached the point just before falling. I began to feel agitation.

As I lay in my blackened bedroom and looked at the blanket, I saw swirling amorphous bloblike effects, but my consciousness was departing so quickly that I was incapable of being entertained by such minor visual hallucinations. I don't remember when I closed my eyes. I lost the capacity of sight in the sense that I wasn't able to interpret the ocular messages my brain was receiving. I had no concept of a past life or a continuum of existence.

The walls seemed to have receded, and I felt no pressure, as though I were weightless. I was floating in a vast emptiness, though it wasn't a void per se, because that would suggest that I knew there was stimulus somewhere else, which I didn't. It was as though I'd been shot into a formless expanse, a space without planets and stars, where I drifted in a languid progression. I'd lost so much memory and sensitivity that I didn't even feel a sense of morbidity or loss about what I was undergoing. All of my subjectivity had left me.

I was writhing a little, quite distressed, but unable to process it as such. I had no grasp of who I was, no knowledge of my name, no concept of being born. I couldn't fathom my sexuality, what my penis was for, for example. I'd lost the capacity to count, and time was utterly obliterated.

The envelope of desensitivity was like a womb without the snugness or comfort. I had only a dim awareness that there was something going on. It was as though a minimal default mental process were at work, like the black box on an aircraft that makes a record of all its activities in the event the pilot and/or the plane is lost. Through the data logs of that fail-safe mechanism, I can now conjure some of what I was able to cognitize during the trip, but I wouldn't have been able to at the time, even if I'd needed to save myself from a peril.

I knew that I was distressed, that I'd put scratch marks on my body, little red lines that faded within a few hours (no broken skin), but I had no reference points for my condition, so I couldn't do anything. I didn't know that there could be anything else. I didn't know I was alive. If somebody had seen me in that condition, they would probably have been afraid for my health and called the paramedics.

If I'd been informed that I was a frog, I wouldn't have known what that was, but would have happily accepted that I had any existence at all, even one that comprised just a pond in which I was supposed to hop around and eat flies.

The nadir of the trip, which lasted about a half hour, was a complete whitewash of consciousness. I couldn't move or even look across the room to analyze what was there, let alone put two feet in front of me, one at a time. I wouldn't have been able to process danger, let alone react to it, because I couldn't access my residual knowledge of harm or death. If I were on top of a building, I could have fallen off the edge and hardly have known. I wouldn't even have thought, *Oh God, what did I just do, fall off this building?* but just continued being amorphously *non compos* until I splattered on the ground.

As the chemicals wore off, the microamnesia slackened and my attention span expanded gradually. At the nadir, I was basically fetal in my state of utter ignorance. Slowly I relearned the basic concepts of my existence. *Oh yeah, I have parents. What are their names again? My own name? I'm actually an independent individual, not an amorphous blob.*

The differences between the sexes and the relationships people have with one another struck me as amusing and perplexing. From a sort of third-person perspective, I tried to call up what my life had contained up to that moment. The turning point was when I was able to look across the room, up at the ceiling, and back across the room again and know that it would still be there. *Hey, it's still there, and for some reason I'm not sure of yet, that's good.*

I regained the ability to analyze my short-term memory. Amazingly, the black box of the subconscious had processed a lot of what I'd undergone, but I was able to crank it open only after I'd landed. It was like stepping out of a swimming pool and onto dry land. Finally able to rise, I got up and walked to my kitchen to get a glass of water, though I had to sit down immediately after I poured it. I was able to receive more and more stimuli and understand their context. One of my first footholds in reality was the sense that I could tell time again.

The drug had taken away what I'd been taking for granted and then slowly handed it back to me. The way back was illuminating, a revelation of everything that comprised the quotidian yet essential functions of living. It's appropriate that this, the first really powerful psychedelic experience I ever had, was a rebirth of sorts. Ecstatically happy that I'd made it through to morning, I called a close friend, who was still half-asleep and told me to call her back.

I intend to repeat the dosages again. I feel I've taken the first step in and now want to go the next one.

Mark Fischer

B. 1952

Natural-food-industry consultant, nature lover, navigator of the psychic landscapes

Resides in Tempe, Arizona

Raised in Parsippany and Lake Hiawatha, New Jersey

Over the Spillway

I'd been curious about mind-altering substances since I was a pubescent kid in 1964, when I'd first heard about LSD. There was a Sandoz Laboratories in the town I lived in, Parsippany, New Jersey. My friend Jack's mother worked there and he was able through some connections to come up with about thirty tablets of pure LSD with the Sandoz label on them. My first acid trips, in 1968, were taken with these 250-microgram tabs.

At the time, we didn't know how precious this stuff was. As the drug scene matured, the market was flooded with suspicious substances purported to be LSD and mescaline. Moreover, many of my friends were drawn toward heroin, which really disturbed me, being a tripping fool. That was one of the factors that eventually drove me away from the Northeast.

My most memorable trip occurred in August 1969, when about five of us decided to do these Orange Barrels that had come along. We knew they were good, but we didn't know how potent they were. I learned afterward that they were a thousand mics each. Each of us took a whole tab and we drove to the reservoir in Lake Hiawatha, the town where my family had moved the previous year.

The social mix wasn't good. My companions had a real attitude and a prankster mentality, like they could do whatever they wanted when they were tripping. They planned to shoot heroin at the end of the trip to come down. These guys were just too cool for me, and I suspected that some of them didn't like me, though I'd known them for a while. Maybe the hostility was all in my head.

There were a lot of weird currents running through my life at the time, problems I wanted to rectify and barriers I wanted to break through. I'd just split up with my girlfriend Barbara, with whom I'd discovered eye-lock intimacy and the hilarity of sex on LSD some months before. I was bothered by the lack of intergenerational communication, especially between me and my parents, whom I really cared about. And I didn't like the urban-decadent direction some of my friends had turned. I discovered later that I was confronting a whole series of walls, each as thin as an onionskin.

As we arrived at the reservoir, everything seemed to be on the verge, brimming with potential for something—what, I didn't know. There'd been a lot of rain recently and the water was just about to go over the spillway as we climbed to the top of it. The sun was about to sink below the horizon, and the drug was coming on very strong and would soon show its full power. The moment reached a cusp when I leaped down a succession of huge concrete blocks that fit together like a giant's playground, an activity which involved a lot of energy and precipitated rushes from the drug. I looked back and saw my companions unmoved, walking away from me. One of them gave me a look I didn't like, which made me really paranoid. There was a bad vibe in the air, so, on a whim, I took off on my own. I just left them behind and decided to walk through town and go home. As I heard later, water started flowing over the spillway just after I left it.

As I walked through town, I really began to get off. Lake Hiawatha is a funky Italian and Jewish working- and middle-class community. The streets were melting and churning and people looked like they were drawn from a *Zap* comic book. I came around the bend to a damped-down field with a muddy path through it like Van Gogh's final work, which depicts crows over a wheat field. Everything in my field of vision looked slabbed on, like one of his paintings.

I came upon the house of the Rosens, a really cool family I was close to. There were eight kids, two of whom were about my age. The father was paraplegic and worked for *The New York Times,* and the mother was a Harvard graduate in psychology. I decided to drop in on them, hoping they would provide me a little sanctuary for a few hours, since I didn't feel comfortable going home. I walked in the door and they all looked up from the meal table in their big common room, which was connected to the kitchen. "Oh, hi Mark. What's going on?" Mr. and Mrs. Rosen and a couple of the kids were just hanging out.

"I'm flipping out on acid." It reverberated in my mind: "Flip flip flip . . . out out out . . ."

"Huh? Oh, Mark!"

Then I thought, *Oh, now I'm in a situation.* They were looking at me like I was crazy. "Let me take a shower," I said. We were on familiar enough terms that I could ask them that. So I jumped in the shower stall and, much to the befuddlement of my poor confused mind, it was set up for a paraplegic. I turned on hot and got cold. I couldn't figure it out. Meanwhile, the acid continued coming on, building up.

When I came out, the room was changed. It was darker and there was an overhead lamp like a spotlight over the table.

"All right, Mark, what's going on now?"

I sat down across the table from Mr. and Mrs. Rosen and they prodded me gently about how I was doing, what I was going through. Then my mom and dad, who'd been summoned earlier unbeknownst to me, arrived. My parents and the Rosens became one symbolic family, and the whole house became symbolic of my universe. Everything in it seemed to represent something to my unconscious mind.

A bit of an oedipal drama was being played out too. Mrs. Rosen took on the vibration of a mother/lover. I found myself reaching out for some level of intimacy with her. She was working it too. As a psychologist, she knew the dynamics of the situation, though one of the mistakes she and the other three made was agreeing with almost everything I said. They were puffing up my ego. I got suspicious and, from time to time, ran to the door and yelled out for the Rosen kids who were my age, "Where the hell *are* you guys?!"

At one point I dashed out of the house, thinking I could fly. I went running down the street and stubbed my toe hard. When I did that, I was suddenly crystal-clear straight. *What am I doing? This is ridiculous.* I went limping back to the house, but as soon I got back there, the whirlwind began again. Soon I was racing around the house with their big Saint Bernard chasing me, so they decided to put me in a small room, which made me feel like they were trying to keep me down or imprison me. It took on the symbolism of just another confining space—either psychical or physical—where an adult stuffs an uppity, independent-minded kid. So I threw a chair through the window and fled.

It was a very weird thing for me to do, which still puzzles me. I'm not a violent person, though it wasn't an act of violence so much as one of desperation, like *Get me the fuck out of here!* I was trying to assert myself, to show them the limits of what I would take. I felt I'd already gone more than halfway toward meeting them on their terms. *I put myself in a jam and I entrusted myself to you. I know it's not your fault that you didn't know how to handle it, but don't put me in a box.*

So I split the Rosens' and headed for my house, about three blocks away. Along the way, I shed all of my clothes. It was just an impulse to be free and unencumbered. All I knew was that naked felt good, and I was doing what felt right. *See, you can't contain me.* So there I was naked, marching down the public street with keen intent: *I'm going home.*

My parents had a police-band radio in their car, because they were paramedics in a volunteer ambulance squad. As they were driving home, they heard, "There's a naked ten [cop code for "person"] walking down Pawnee Avenue." As I got to my lawn, my dad and mom pulled up in their station wagon just as a fire truck pulled up with all its lights flashing. The crew had been in the neighborhood pumping rainwater out of cellars. They'd heard on their radio that there was a naked guy walking down the street and, out of boredom, decided to check it out.

My dad grabbed me and pulled me into the front seat of his car, then got out to dismiss the firemen, "Everything's okay, I've got it under control." But then I jumped out of the car and, still bare-nekkid, started dancing on the lawn. The fire crew grabbed me and threw a blanket over me as my dad called an ambulance. They all agreed they had to take me *somewhere.* I sat wrapped in the blanket in the front seat of my parents' car. The acid was coursing strong.

The ambulance arrived, its red light flashing through the late-summer dusk. They put me onto a stretcher, tied me down, and slid me into the back. I felt like I was physically dying and being slipped into a coffin. The life force seemed to run out of me, as though I were bleeding from every pore of my body. My parents helped them load me up and then drove over separately to Morristown Memorial Hospital. Nobody I knew rode with me in the back of the ambulance.

I blacked out the external world and became gradually conscious of a greater being that emerged slowly as a drone that built up like a million voices saying, "Everything is everything. Everything is everything . . ." Then I felt as if I'd unified with a being of planetary scale with eyes that pointed in every direction. I could sense energies coming in from outer space and going out from the Earth. Then I received a vision of ecological health, like a message across the sky: *Get your inner self lined up. The outer worlds are only as reasonable or understandable as your inner world is.* Then I found myself naked with my ex-girlfriend Barbara in a beautiful Edenic natural landscape. I realized that beauty must first be found within before it could be projected into the external, social, or political worlds.

The ambulance workers wheeled me into the emergency room, where I was shot up with Thorazine, which brought me right down. Then, still tied up, I was checked into a psych ward. I screamed in resistance for a long time, the loudest person that had come through that loony bin in a long time. My dad came in to see how I was. Noting that I was in the hands of "competent authorities," he leaned over me where I lay, strapped down flat to the bed, and said, "Mark, we're going to have to leave you here for a while." I yelled in protest, but he continued out the door

I woke up the next morning feeling normal. Fortunately, they didn't do anything to me—no drugs or electroshock therapy, but they did keep me under observation for ten days. I was stuck in there with a bunch of housewives who were having nervous breakdowns.

The court charged me with indecent exposure and ordered me to see a psychiatrist for six months. At the end of that term, the shrink phoned my mother to say, "Mrs. Fischer, your son is probably one of the better-adjusted people I've ever met."

Matthew S. Kent

B. 1952

President, Peyote Way Church of God

Resides in Aravaipa Valley, Klondyke, Arizona

Raised in southeast Pennsylvania

Maha Maya: The V in My Path

There have been three times in my life when I've cast my burden upon the Lord. The first was back in 1972, when I quit school in search of a more authentic life. I was at Temple University on a scholarship to sing in the concert choir, majoring in Victorian poetry. I'd also enrolled in college to defer combat duty. I had no intention of ever killing anyone for political reasons.

When two of my friends were murdered on the streets of Philadelphia in separate incidents, I suddenly noticed there was a war raging right under my nose and that I'd been living in a surreal, sheltered environment. The day after Nixon and (Philadelphia mayor, Frank) Rizzo were reelected, I decided to get out of Philly and leave my privileged, college-kid comfort behind. (I hedged my bet by disobeying the instruction not to "fold, spindle, or mutilate" my college record card, so the Selective Service Board was never duly informed that I'd left.) Hoping to make a living as a musician or actor, I went out to San Francisco and worked in a drama theater in the Mission District for a while.

For my twenty-first birthday in the summer of 1973, my parents gave me a round-trip ticket to London with the hope that I'd go to a Shakespearean acting school there. But when I arrived in England, I realized that all I had to do was cross the channel to the Eurasian landmass and I could go to China if I wanted. I'd saved a couple of thousand dollars from a summer job laying pipe, so I had the means to get across the globe.

I went to Edinburgh to visit the family of a wartime friend of my dad's, and met some Bahais who introduced me to the *I Ching*. I threw coins in a pattern they interpreted as an indication I was going to the Southeast. But it wasn't Dover I was bound for; it was India. So I started hitchhiking my way to Asia. My third ride, a big Leyland bus, pulled up with a French couple wearing Afghan coats and vests. They asked me where I was going, and I said, "Dover to Belgium to Istanbul to India."

"That's where we're going," they said. "*Allons*. Let's go."

"Roll up for the Magical Mystery Tour," I sang as I climbed in. We crossed the channel and in Istanbul I transferred to another bus that took me all the way to India by way of Ankara, Tabriz, Mashhad, Herat, Kandahar, Kabul, Lahore, Rawalpindi, and Amritsar, before finally disembarking in New Delhi. From there I took a train to Bombay and then a boat to Goa, the former Portuguese colony, where I first saw white people who'd gone native.

I decided to get away from the cantina, where Westerners hung out drinking Coca-Cola and coffee, so I walked as far down the beach as a I could go, and set up camp right by the water with no lights in sight. In a week or so, I met some Brits who had plans to go all the way to New Zealand and start an alternative lifestyle colony on North Island. After getting to know me, they invited me to come along. The idea of launching a community of spiritually minded people appealed to me, so I readily accepted and made plans to wend my way to the site, way out across the Pacific Ocean.

One day, François, the French girlfriend of Colin, one of my British friends, showed up with datura seeds which she'd gotten up the coast from some French junkies who had an enclave in north Panjim. My knowledge of datura at the time was derived solely from reading *The Teachings of Don Juan* by Carlos Castañeda. Datura is known as jimsonweed in the United States and *rena la noche* south of the border. European witches used the root along with henbane and other toxic herbs to make "flying ointment," which was applied to the mucus membranes. The flying, of course, would not be on a broom, but in the mind.

François gave me a hundred seeds and I ate twenty-five of them, expecting a knockdown experience, but nothing happened, I assumed because it was submerged by all the cannabis in my system. After a few weeks in India, I was living and breathing hashish. Before I woke up, the chillum was loaded, and before my feet hit the sand, I was already blasted on some very good Mazar Sharif (Afghan) hash you could buy at government shops in Benares and elsewhere.

After a couple months in Goa, I was ready to hitchhike across the rest of India to Madras, to get a boat to Panang, to go down the Indonesian archipelago to Sumatra, from there to Timor to Darwin, Australia, to Sydney to Wellington, New Zealand, to North Island. But I only made part of that journey. Colin and François recommended that I visit a sacred place called Vijayanagar (now called Hampi) in Karnataka in southern India. They said they'd meet up with me down there and we could go the rest of the way to North Island together.

So I hitched down and arrived with blisters all over my feet from a new pair of sandals. I needed to stay put for a while to do some yoga and get healed up, and Vijayanagar was a stunning location to do so. Throughout the area were ruins of the capital of the largest Hindu empire that had ever existed, which was overrun by the Moguls in the sixteenth century. Exotic structures such as elephant baths abounded. Every rock seemed to be carved. There were ruins of temples on the top of each hill on all four points of the compass, and a big temple right in the middle of the whole complex. The River Tungabadra ran through the village, then bent and turned a corner. I went away from town and down by the river to camp.

During the day, I watched the sadhus, with their dreadlocks and saffron robes and bodies streaked with chalk marks, traverse from an abandoned temple to a tunnel carved through the rocks. They begged in the shady corner, then made their way around the riverbank to the next temple, which was perched at the top of a stack of boulders twelve feet in diameter.

I decided to fast for three days before taking another dose of the sacred herb datura. As the sun went down on the third day, I ate the remaining seventy-five seeds, chewing them one at a time rather than gulping them down as I had the first batch. They tasted lousy. After a while I shrugged and figured the seeds were duds once again and went over to the chai shop near the temple. I ordered some tea and by the time it came around, I couldn't focus my eyes. I was reeling from dizziness, and my legs felt very rubbery. I thought I'd better get back to base camp before something else happened, so I started walking back, and then buckled to the ground and had to crawl the rest of the way.

I wasn't worried about making a spectacle of myself. I couldn't have flipped out anybody in southern India by any "odd" behavior. They've seen it all. We're talking about a part of the world where it's said that people purposely malform their children so that they'll have a living begging. As the night progressed, I entered a realm so deep in the spirit world that my psyche adopted it as completely normal, forgetting that I was tripping and had to suspend judgment. I went down to the edge of the river and dug a hole to take a crap. As I was squatting there, dropping a load, I looked to my right and there between the rocks and the water was a half-decayed corpse. We started to chat, just as naturally as any two living people would converse.

I sensed that there were entities living among the boulders, and they began to materialize, standing astride the huge rocks like guardians. They were humanoid but faceless, very dark and extremely mysterious, like Darth Vader with a stone cape. I felt like an intruder in their midst. I learned later that I'd camped on a burial ground. A sadhu explained that bodies of people were brought to the river there to purify them before their souls left this plane.

The next morning I started to have peekaboo experiences. I'd see somebody in perfect three-dimensional vision, turn away, and when I looked back again he or she'd be gone. Up to then, I'd never had a psychedelic experience that lasted more than eight hours.

That night Colin and François arrived, but I wasn't quite up to entertaining them. I said, "Look, I'm tripping. I'll be together in the morning. Why don't you guys camp right down here and I'll come and see you in the morning?" My last image of them is crawling into a sleeping bag to sleep like spoons between three big boulders by the river. I went back to my own encampment to ride out the rest of the datura. Just before sundown I saw one of the rock spirits turn into a huge shadow of a figure in ancient priest garb, extending from the river all the way to the temple at the top of the mountain. It looked like a giant scrambling up a hill. When it reached the summit, it was—whoosh!—sucked into the temple.

When the sun came up the next morning, I thought, *I'm straight now. Let's go see Colin and François.* But when I reached their campsite, they were gone and there was no sign of their gear. The only indication they'd been there was a mound of dirt. I dropped down and put my ear to it, and darn if I didn't hear breathing and two sets of heartbeats. One part of me said, "This isn't happening. This is the effects of the datura." But the other part of me was convinced they were in there. I inferred that they'd been buried alive by the eidolon that the temple had inhaled the night before. This was the most poignant moment in my life, the V in my path, where I went one way and left the other.

I challenged myself. *Are you going to be so convinced by your cynical mind of what's real and what isn't that you won't go to the lengths of digging up that dirt and look weird doing so, to find out the truth?* I started tearing away at that mound, which had the approximate mass of two people lying in a sleeping bag. I used my bare hands at first, then I grabbed some rocks and carved away at the pile, which was shape-shifting right in front of me, into a lion, then a cobra, then a wolf. I put my ear to the ground, and the beating pulse had grown faster and the breathing more faint. I was desperate. I had to try to save Colin's and François's lives!

I called out for help and a Western couple showed up. I told the woman what I was doing, that my friends were buried by an entity up in the temple. Her partner looked at me like I was a real maniac. I must have looked totally berserk. My hands were bleeding. I had long hair and the beginnings of a beard. She said, "Maybe you're dealing with something beyond your understanding," and they left.

One by one, the heartbeats faded. When I heard the last percussive throb dwindle to nothing, I sat down and wept. That was the beginning of my letting go of propriety, all the mannered behavior that I'd built up as a middle-class Anglo-American of the day. Finally I stood up and wrapped my hands with some rags and went into the village to have a cup of chai to sit and think about all that had transpired.

A native came along with a big banana hoe. In sign language, I convinced him to come with me to do a little work for the price of my new sandals, the ones that had torn up my feet. He followed me down to the mound by the river where I'd last seen Colin and François. I asked him to finish the excavation. He dug down a couple feet and I could see there wasn't anybody in there. So I was convinced that the evidence they'd been buried alive was all an illusion.

I'd read about *maya,* the concept that the manifold reality we see is illusion, but now I felt that I really understood what that meant, that our senses deceive us. As the sun set, I watched a group of about twenty sadhus walk single file through the rocks to the abandoned temple behind the hill. That night, I got in line with them and followed them back to their place. These guys were followers of Shiva, the Lord of the Dance, the Creator and the Destroyer.

I said to one of them, "*Maha maya* [great illusion]," and from that moment on, I didn't speak for a full moon. I listened, and I helped the sadhus with whatever they needed. If somebody wanted water, I'd run and get some. I found the *chillum baba* in the village, and for five bucks, I bought a kilo of ganja and administered it to the sadhus as they wanted it, thus sparing them the need to purchase their sacrament piecemeal. These were not local boys, but itinerant holy men who traveled from temple to temple all across the subcontinent. They could have been speaking Tamil, Urdu, or Kannada. I didn't know.

After a month I started to feel comfortable with them and they with me. I ate what they ate. I went with them when they went to beg, sitting in the background. I tightened up with one of the brothers, Ram Swami, who showed me where I could buy a translation of the *Bhagavad-Gita* with transliteration and commentary. I studied the Gita and did Shivite chants with him.

Ram Swami had only one eye, and most of his toes had gangrenously fallen off, but he'd walked the subcontinent three times, from Rishikesh down to the very tip, to Trivandrum. Each of them was twenty years older than he looked. Some had eyes that just wouldn't quit, eyes that had the depth of eternity. I was struck by their sincerity, by the fact that they were living their religion every day, not just on Sunday, and I was also impressed by their poverty. Being a sadhu is to cast your burden upon the Lord and to travel, as it says in the Bible, without script or an extra pair of sandals.

Vijayanagar was a pilgrimage site for Brahmin Hindus for whom it was a sacred act to give alms to the sadhus. A twenty-five paise (quarter rupee) coin was typically given to each sadhu. But when they got to me, they'd pull out a whole rupee. One time, a woman gave us a ten-rupee note, and then she got down and kissed my feet. But I didn't want that kind of attention. I felt, *Wait a minute. These are the guys who've made the renunciation. I'm here to learn about it.*

Before the sadhus drank the chai, they'd stick a finger in, then make a circle in the ground around the cup, say a prayer, and shake the droplet onto the earth in recognition of its source. After they'd beg for food, we'd prepare it communally back at the temple. We'd all sit down, lay the food and rice out on banana leaves and then the boys would start chanting the names of the deities. We poured a little water as an oblation over the food, then picked up a handful, blessed it and got up to walk outside to put it on the ground or at the foot of an idol, where a monkey or a bird could eat it. The ritual acknowledged that we were both receiving and giving, keeping the circle going.

Each of us was eating only a quarter kilo of boiled rice and some chutney every day, but after a while, it became very hard for me to hold it down. I started losing weight and falling apart physically. At the same time, as I continued reading the *Gita* and chanted with the sadhus, I was spiritually robust. I was encouraged by the sadhus to take a pilgrimage to an ashram dedicated to a fellow named Kumaraswami. I hitched and hoofed my way all the way and never had to sleep out alone on the road, as renunciates were usually forced to do. Somebody always approached, saying, "Please. Stay with me tonight," I reckon because I was a white person following the path of the Hindu holy man.

I got sicker and sicker, going down to 95 pounds from the 145 I'd carried to London. I couldn't keep anything down and could feel the food course right through my internal organs. While I'd never been higher spiritually, I knew that physically I had only fifteen more pounds to go before I was off of this sphere. I really had to think. *What was more important? Which way did I want to go?* The idea of coming back to the United States and facing a Richard Nixon reality was, while sitting by a campfire in India with my sadhu brethren, a very hard thing to imagine. On the other hand, remaining in India to possibly die at the unfledged age of twenty-one seemed imprudent.

Ram Swami told me about a Shivananda ashram in Rishikesh, the holy city at the source of the Ganges, where the climate was more temperate. I could take the train up north, live up there and get well, and continue to learn. I took him up on it and made the arrangements. I was advised to get a second-class ticket, but a big rail strike had downgraded second class to third, so my accommodation bought me passage in a cattle car with a drove of humanity. I spent the first day and night with two arms on the ceiling, one leg on the floor and another leg precariously propped on a woman who was crouched on the floor. Some passengers were literally thrown on and off the train at each station stop.

The train stopped in New Delhi, where I used the last twenty rupees I had left to get a room, a very unsadhulike thing to do. When I woke up the next morning and stood up, I saw myself in a mirror on the wall. It was the first time I'd seen myself for six months. What I saw was a seventy-year-old man. I remembered myself as a supple

Anglo-American in pretty good shape and now saw a gaunt, starved-out sadhu in the mirror. *That's you, guy.* It shook me up to see myself so much further on in life. I felt that I shouldn't be looking like that at twenty-one. Later on, yes, but not now.

That morning in a bookstore in Connaught Circus, my eye was caught by a book called *Spiritual Communities* by Kryananda, a Westerner in Oregon who'd assumed a yogic name and started up a modern religious enclave, parallel to what the Mormons and Amish had done a century earlier. The idea blasted me right there. *That's it! To find a place for me to live, I've got to create a spiritual community.* Toward that end, I decided to go back to Scotland to regain my health and then to find a middle path between Eastern wisdom and Western knowledge before finding a place for my dream of a spiritual community in the Nixonian reality back home. As soon as I made that decision, all paths opened up for me.

A Hindu businessman at the hotel asked me to tell his fortune. I'd observed other sadhus reading palms to earn a little money, so I read this guy's palm. I looked at how he was dressed and how his body was set and told him what physical problems he had and other things about his life. He was impressed and asked me what I wanted in compensation. I said, "A pair of pants, a shirt, and a pair of shoes, and I'd like to know where I can get a cheap ticket back to Europe." He led me to a travel agency and soon I was holding an Air France ticket to London.

When I arrived in London I went to the squatters' digs in Kentish Town. I phoned the Hospital of Tropical Diseases. A woman picked up and informed me, "The doctor's on holiday and won't be back for two weeks." I replied, "I don't think I've got two weeks." So I started hitchhiking up to Edinburgh, where a physician recommended by my father's friend diagnosed my condition as tropical sprue and prescribed the B vitamin, folic acid, for me. I gained my weight back over the next few months and stayed on in Scotland, attending classes at the Edinburgh Divinity School.

After a year, I returned to Philly, where I met my future wife, Annie. The two of us had an adventure in Costa Rica, which landed me in jail, and then a mental hospital, for confronting the local *jefe.* Shortly after my deportation to the United States, Annie and I serendipitously stumbled upon the church where we now serve as clergy.

My experience on datura was the formative psychedelic experience that put me on the spiritual path that led to my involvement in the Peyote Way Church of God. A decade later, I had another momentous trip, which has shaped my theology.

Sometime in 1988 I wanted to take a spirit walk with the medicine. Annie was six months pregnant with Tristan, our third-born, and not up to having any (peyote) tea, but she decided to sit up with me and accompany me on my journey. I drank a fifteen-button tea and we began doing a Tantric eye practice in which you inhale as your partner exhales. We synchronized our breathing this way, sitting in an *asana* (yoga) position with folded legs, and looked steadily into each other's eyes.

All of a sudden, Annie's face transformed into a succession of different animal heads. While remaining a pregnant human female from the neck down, her head changed into that of a lion, then a wolf, and so on. When the head metamorphosed, the skin, then the muscles on down to the bone, peeled away, and then it grew up again into another animal head. The eyes stayed the same, filled with a tranquil, awesome glory that was so beautiful. But around the eyes it was always changing and so horrible at times that I had to break the meditation. I literally fell over in disbelief at certain manifestations.

I struggled to understand what was happening. Finally, it filtered through that this isn't something you're supposed to understand. This is the Goddess. This is female deity. This is *maya.* This is where all form and shape come from, both horrible and beautiful, all at the same time. Prior to that, I'd been reading Joseph Campbell and intellectualizing the concept of female deity, but this was it. Whack! Right through the middle of my head. My vision of deity had breasts and could carry a child.

It was as if the last piece of the puzzle had been put in place. The yin and the yang were united and comprehendible. I'd been singing to a male god, thinking of God in male terms, and then bang, the vision I have of God is a pregnant woman with an animal's head. What I saw was unmistakable. It was the alpha and the omega. As it is embodied in Kali, the Hindu goddess of sex and death who wears skulls on her belt, what has brought you here will also take you out. Because you have sex, you have life, and because you have life, you have death; your spirit will be slit from your body.

This vision brought me full circle to my origins, which are in northern Europe with hairy folks who ran around in the woods worshiping trees and animals—not in Christianity, which was imposed on the European tribes from Rome, but in the nativist peoples who believed in earth spirits, who venerated the female as the beginning of life. I realized who I was working for, that peyote had a female dimension that is just as strong and as balanced as the male one. I believe now that deity is male and female, so I use the gender-neutral pronoun "It" to avoid confusion.

After my vision of the Goddess, I started painting representations of female deities, usually dancing in the desert. Every now and then I stumble on some woman who's done some research and has come up with these old designs, and sure enough, they look a lot like what I've been painting. These are childbearing women, not Twiggy models. My Goddess creatures are squat and big-breasted with long hair, a symbol of wisdom. In one of my works, she's drawing down the moon and in another she's dancing with a snake—the symbol of transformation—in her hands. These images come out of the archetypal self that's connected me to every woman all the way back to Eve.

Skull Flower by Jon A. Bell, digital composition, © 2000, courtesy of the artist.

Megan

B. 1971

Public relations manager

Resides in a city in Southeast Asia

Raised in Glasgow, Scotland

A Blink of Rabbit Fur

In the Manchester Summer of Love of 1988, I was seventeen and just graduated from high school. I took the whole next year off and did nothing but take drugs and run around and misbehave. I was really into the Glasgow club scene, doing a lot of speed three or four nights a week.

I had a boyfriend of a couple of months, whom I'd met at a big rave in Glasgow. He was a deejay, which was a big thing in my crowd. I wasn't getting on very well with him, but he had a car, and that made up for some of the deficit. He had a poofy name, Leslie, and was probably the ugliest guy I've ever gone out with. He had a huge nose, so massive that it really annoyed me. For a while, I saw past it for the brand-new BMW his wealthy parents up in Stirling had bought him.

Shortly after he got it, he drove down to Glasgow and said, "Let's take 'er for a run." We decided to go down to Manchester, about five hours away, so we could go to the Hacienda, a big rave club owned by Factory Records and associated with the band New Order. Leslie brought his friend Jim along, and I brought my friends Kara and Angela. I started to hate Leslie right at the start of the trip, because he wouldn't let me smoke in the car. He also lied, saying he had friends down there we could stay with, but when we arrived in the afternoon, it turned out that he did have a Manchester mate, a fellow named Clark, but he stayed with his mother and wasn't even expecting us.

So the word was that Leslie and Jim, being guys, could stay in the house, but that us girls would have to sleep in the car, since we didn't have the money to go to a hotel. I was furious. If there were ten things Leslie could have done to piss me off, he was systematically going through each one, starting with his nose, then not allowing me to smoke in his car, and now this bit. Kara and Angela quite liked Leslie and felt rather sorry for him because I was sniping at him constantly.

He truly irritated me, because he gave me no reaction. When I screamed, "What do you mean we've got nowhere to stay?" he just shrugged, real dippy like, and went off to sort out drugs for us.

Nights started early in Manchester, because the clubs closed at one, two hours before they did in Glasgow. The local authorities were trying to limit clubbing, because a teenage girl had died after taking Ecstasy. She'd been dancing in the Hacienda and gone outside, where she collapsed and died. It turned out she had a heart complaint she didn't know she had. The exertion and dehydration spurred by the E had apparently exacerbated a genetic defect. The media attention made the Hacienda all the more glamorous, of course. I was dying to go there.

Clark acceded and allowed the girls to get changed in his house while his mum was out. We got into our club gear and went to a pub to pass some time, then to the Hacienda to stand in the queue. There was a lot more vigilance about age and drugs in Manchester. The bouncers were these huge daunting black guys who checked you thoroughly at the door. These blokes were big and mean, six foot four *wide,* never mind tall. I was underage, which I never had to worry about in Glasgow, where it didn't really bother anybody. But we managed to get in with no problem—along with the drugs. Our connection had worked out a funny system with his cigarette packet.

Once inside, the boys and girls split off, because I wasn't talking to Leslie. I'd never been to a club like the Hacienda. It was massive with all sorts of chill-out rooms, which I'd never heard of. In Glasgow we had this tiny hovel with a ceiling just above your head, a deejay's box, and that was it. There was a huge stage just above head height, then another big round stage in the middle, where people would dance and blow whistles at each other. They sold alcohol at the bar, but very little, since people on E don't really booze it up. They sold bottles of Evian at the same price as beer and make a fortune.

We all went to one of the chill-out rooms and took one E each. I'd already taken a hit of speed I'd brought down. Things just got instantly better. I was no longer so angry at Leslie, who went off somewhere where I couldn't see him for the rest of the night. I went up on the big stage with Kara and Angela, and we danced ourselves silly. I nearly fainted at one point. It's so easy to forget about time when you're in that hyper dance mode. It was really intense, a fantastic time. After a few hours we went outside, soaking with sweat, our clothes sticking to us, looking dreadful, not that we cared. You care about it when you're drunk, but when you're on drugs, you're like *Ah, fuck it. We all look the same.* We were talking about how great things were.

At half twelve we looked for Leslie. He knew where we were because he could see us on the stage, so he came down and got us and we drove off to a field at some altitude outside the city. We had no intention of going home. What home? Go back to the car and sleep? We decided to stay awake as long as we could. There was supposed to be a full eclipse of the moon that night. The sky was very clear.

There were about five cars that converged at this field, all friends of friends of Clark's. They parked in a circle facing each other with the headlights on and got a sound system going. I split another E with Kara. Back then, Es were twenty quid a pill and now they're seven or ten, but they were also far more powerful, for sure. We were spending all this money, but it was worth it.

Everybody was just dancing about, really uninhibited, not caring about how they looked in front of others. On Ecstasy you're very comfortable with who you are, not worried about how you present yourself. You're telling the person next to you that he's the greatest thing you've met that night. Conversations take on so much more meaning. Even the dullest person has something valid to say. I'm quite a bolshy person, and if someone doesn't cut it quickly, I'll be off. Not on E, though. I'm laid-back and tolerant with that stuff in me.

I made eye contact with this guy who'd driven one of the cars in our little caravan. He was a bit older, about twenty-three. Leslie was off taking to somebody. The girls were talking to some guys, and this fellow came over and started talking to me. The questions were typically drug-centered: "What did you take? How do you feel?" I was starting to feel a bit weird after taking another half, and it was all a bit much. I was grinning madly and chewing the back of my mouth, a reaction to the speed, which always makes me want to chew gum.

I don't know this guy's name. I never asked him and he never told me, and I never told him mine. After a few minutes he asked me to go for a walk. I felt comfortable with him, so off we went. I don't think Leslie saw me leave. We went over to the trees at the end of the field. It was very dark. I was feeling fervid, not speaking much. He said nice things to me, like "I find you very attractive," which is always a good way to get me into bed. Amazingly I wasn't embarrassed, as I'd usually be. Normally I'd squirm and go bright pink or not know what to say. Fortified by the E, I suddenly felt a surge of confidence and deserved worthiness. *Well, great, I'm glad you do.* We leaned up against a tree.

He was a nice, disarming bloke. I knew he was interested and that it was going to happen when he asked me to go for a walk with him. If he didn't initiate it, then I probably would have. I was also having revenge thoughts about Leslie. I don't normally two-time my boyfriends, but I was really annoyed by him not paying me any attention and suggesting I sleep in a fucking car.

I was focusing on my heartbeat for what seemed like a long time. I thought I was going to explode, and had to consciously not think about it, which was nearly impossible. I was horribly aware of everything inside me. Then he kissed me and I closed my eyes, and when I opened them, he'd changed. It was dark, so I couldn't see everything, but I was fully aware that his face had changed into John Cameron, a boyfriend of my mother's from years before.

My father died when I was fifteen, but I never knew him and don't even have a recollection of him. My mum left him when I was two. They were married when she was pregnant with my older brother. In those days a Scottish woman would leave her man only if he were a wife beater, an alcoholic, or both, which is what my dad was. My mother threatened him with death if he tried to contact us. The day we left, she hit him over the head with a pair of Victorian fire irons. She thought she'd killed him and actually hoped she had.

John Cameron was the first boyfriend my mother had that I was aware of. I couldn't believe it when she pulled this one in. He was a really nice man. We moved in with him when I was nine, staying a couple of years until he took a nervous breakdown. There was never a man in the house except those years we lived with John Cameron. He was the only father figure I ever had.

He was very wealthy and bright, a chartered accountant ten years older than my mum, who was thirty-four when we moved in. He was a real dashing figure with a lot of power and energy about him, even though he was just five foot four, which seemed about a foot shorter than my mother. His face had strong features and a mustache, and he had thick, long, iron-gray silver hair with a big flick, a swath in the front, which was swept back. (Princess Diana had this hairstyle for a time.)

He was a typical bachelor, a real man's man and a big drinker who smoked cigars a foot long. He looked fantastic behind the wheel of one of his five cars, including a Porsche, a Range Rover, and a couple of ancient MGs. He wore three-piece suits and huge full-length rabbit-fur coats, which cut quite an unusual figure. You have to have real attitude to do that. He had three hanging in the hallway that you had to walk past to get to the bathroom. When I was feeling down, I used to shove my face into them to inhale the cigar smoke and the smell of fur.

My mother thought he looked like a bit of a twit or a Glaswegian gangster—"not the most fitting escort for a schoolteacher"—but she clearly enjoyed it. She was tall and busty with a ton of black frizzy hair. I'm sure they made quite a diverting couple, swanning about and throwing whiskey down their necks.

John had a very characteristic fragrance about him, which I still smell every now and again. He used Imperial Leather soap, which I now use myself. The adverts back then featured a rich macho guy with a layer cut and a flick, just like John's. He'd be sitting in a bathrobe, his hairy chest exposed in an omate bath with gold taps, drinking champagne with a chick lying by in a nylon sexy housecoat number. If there was ever an advertising campaign that reached its target market, it was Cussons' for Imperial Leather, because it got John. He was very much that man in the robe and the flick.

In the morning, he used to walk around the house completely naked, and he had the longest and largest willy I've ever seen, to this day. This was the first time I'd ever seen my mother as a sexual being and not just me mum. Suddenly she was paying much more attention to herself. They had an active social life and a very active sex life, which I could hear on occasion. My mother was bloody loud, which I was really embarrassed about, at that age. She said he was sex mad. They were shagging all the time and obviously enjoying it. I started to become more sexually aware in this environment.

John was under a lot of pressure from his family and work, and he couldn't sleep at night. He eventually caved under the stress. When John and Mum broke up, we kids were shipped off to Northern Ireland for a holiday and when we came back, it wasn't to his place but back to our old flat. My mum is pretty hard-bitten and doesn't really fall for anybody. She claims she's never told anybody she loved him, ever. Bur her sister tells me that my mother was in a state when she left John Cameron. His house was not far from where I hung out. Kara lived right around the corner from him. I'd always go over to see his cars, which all had private number plates. From age fifteen I started having sexual fantasies about him, and still do. I saw him only once after we moved out. He walked past a flat we were staying in temporarily, and asked where my mum was. I said, "She's at work," and he went away, and I never saw him again.

When my granddad died recently, in 1998, I flew back to Scotland and my mum and I started talking about John Cameron. She phoned a friend who told her he'd died just three weeks before. Coincidentally, I'd just had a startingly vivid dream about going to his apartment and trying to break in to steal photographs of my family when we lived there. He came in and asked me what I was doing. I told him what I was after and he gave them to me. I woke up marveling at how lucid it all seemed. I pieced it together, and I'm sure he died the day I had this dream.

This bloke I was kissing, leaning against a tree somewhere in a field outside Manchester, was a pleasant-looking guy with dark brown hair, and he didn't have a big nose, which I was happy about. But when I opened my eyes, he had John Cameron's gray-silver hair. I put my hands on his face and started thinking about rabbits, which was probably a mixture of being in the woods, seeing John Cameron's silvery gray hair, and the subliminal memory of his rabbit-fur coat. I wasn't saying anything to this guy about all this.

"Would you like to have sex?" he asked me.

"Yes, please," I responded. I was thinking, "I always wanted to have sex with John Cameron." I don't know how I managed to conjure him at that moment. I suppose he was back in a cupboard ready to be brought out, and this was the time and the catalyst—the E—that did it.

We started to kiss again and I thought to myself, "If I close my eyes, John'll go away." I didn't want that to happen, so I was trying my damnedest to keep my eyes open. I felt completely uninhibited. I didn't have sex outdoors often. I hadn't even had sex in a car.

For guys, sex at seventeen is like "Fuckin' yes! She said 'yes'! I've got a shag!" There's no real tenderness. It's much more about achievement. So you've got this guy pressing on you. I never had loving feelings for anyone I had sex with back then. I was always very embarrassed and covering up by pretending not to give a shit. Half the time I was terrified about what I was about to embark upon, but still went ahead. I'm afraid I don't know how to say "no." I'm a "yeah, sure, all right then" kinda girl.

This interaction, however, was quite different from any teenage sex encounter I ever had. He was being quite slow, drawing out the process and expanding the intimacy. He was looking at me and I was looking at him, rather intently, in fact, in order to keep my eyes open to sustain the illusion of John Cameron. He was looking at me as he unbuttoned my blouse. Aside from my thrill at the sudden materialization (and subsequent coming) of John Cameron, I was also enjoying the experience because I didn't feel the sort of common dread that I normally felt at the prospect of a one-night stand in which I had to go through the motions.

He wore a dark, long-sleeved T-shirt, which I took off his lanky torso. We lay down and he peeled off my tights, which would normally embarrass me. I never go barelegged because of the "fireside tartan" you get from sitting close to electric fires in Scotland. Normally all the fumbling around would distract me, but everything was very fluid and unrehearsed, with no "mistakes" or anything to jolt me out of the mood. I had no inkling of our mates, though I could still hear the music and see the lights.

I usually have to talk to somebody for four hours before I can get them to go to bed with me, but this was like Erica Jong's zipless fuck. I had no interest in getting to know this guy or even pretending to, as I'd done with other guys. It was sort of nice to just do what we wanted to do. So we did.

He took off my panties and pushed up my short black skirt, and went down on me: giving me what we call in Scotland a good "lick-oot"—a rather indelicate term for the practice. Usually I hated being the object of such overtures. I'll give a guy a blowjob at the drop of a hat, but when the guy returns the favor, I tend to assume he's got ulterior motives. I panic—"Jesus Christ, what's he doing down there? Just get this over with quickly, because nothing will come of it and I don't know why you're down there." But this time it was different. I didn't mind at all. In fact, it was great.

It was nice having really good oral sex for *me,* and it was very erotic, him being down there and me watching him, and he seemed to enjoy it too. I'd never look at a guy licking me, but I had to this time in order to keep John Cameron from dissolving. I had my hands in his hair, running them through it. I was being quite forward, pulling him against me, which I would never do.

I got pretty excited and told him I wanted him inside me. He unbuckled himself and I closed my eyes as he entered me. I came after a while, which I'd never done through penetrative sex. In fact, I've only come that way a few times *since.* It was fantastic. Orgasms for me only happen when I either do it myself or from a guy giving a bit of extra attention with his hands—"poking" as it's called in Glasgow. In high school, we used to ask each other, "Have you been poked yet?" Of course, a lot of seventeen-year-old girls don't get close to having an orgasm through sex with a guy. For that matter, my mother has friends who still haven't managed.

A small explosion was taking place. I was being very loud, another thing I'd never do. I thought back on all the noise my mother used to make with John Cameron, a low-pitched, growly animal, intensely carnal sound. I could now understand what she was all agitated about. He came too, inside me, and we stopped moving as he just lay on me for a while. When I opened my eyes, he was the bloke I'd met in the field. John Cameron was gone.

Throughout the experience I felt that he (John) was doing it right. I'd been wanting to make love to him for a long time and I just took the opportunity to make the fantasy real. Until I opened my eyes, it was as though I were awake in my own dream. Normally, you have a dream and it just evaporates in the ether, and you can only vaguely remember it. But I was there for this one, touching and seeing everything.

I grew increasingly aware of where I was and what I was doing, and figured that Leslie would be looking for me. I said, "We'd better get back." The guy stood up and did himself up, then pulled me up. I straightened myself up, but left my tights off. As we walked back, he said, "That was really nice," to which I cheerily replied, "Thank you."

My response to Leslie would be dictated by what I saw on his face. If he was looking for me, I'd make up a story, but he hadn't noticed I was gone, and neither had the girls. He was busy talking to somebody and Kara and Angela were still dancing furiously. We were all soaking since the Hacienda, so I already looked disheveled. Heroin chic was coming in, and the boys especially looked like they hadn't washed their hair in weeks. I didn't let on to anybody in the group about where I'd just been.

The tryst with my anonymous and phantasmic lover was enormously exhilarating, gratifying an ancient urge while also building my confidence for the long term. It gave me a taste of adult sexuality, which I didn't achieve again until I was much older.

Untitled by Maurice Tani, digital composition, © 2000, courtesy of the artist.

Paul Devereux

B. 1945

Author of **The Long Trip: A Prehistory of Psychedelia; Shamanism and the Mystery Lines; The Lucid Dreaming Kit** ***(with Charla Devereux);*** **The Illustrated Encyclopedia of Ancient Earth Mysteries;** ***and several other books; Website address:*** **www.acemake.com/PaulDevereux**

Resides in Cotswolds, England

Born and raised in Leicester, England

Do I Want to Be Seeing This?

One dimension of the unseen that psychedelics, particularly LSD, made manifest to me was "evidence" of the occult. On my first acid experience, while a college student at a London art school in 1966, I saw a person's aura, an envelope of moving light around him. At the time, I had no belief in clairvoyance or any desire to see such testimony of the supernatural, yet I could see that it was more than the figment of Edgar Cayce's imagination, but a real hyper-visual phenomenon made visible to me by the alteration of my perception. Later on, on rare occasions, I was able to see a person's aura without the use of any mind-altering substance.

The following year, during an acid trip in south London, I glanced down at my reclining body and, to my shock, saw a vortex of orange light. It looked like a fiery gas emerging from my solar plexus and opening out into a revolving cone that radiated out, about eighteen inches from my body. *What the hell is that?* I thought. Then I realized I could be visualizing a chakra energy center. It was quite vivid, silently swirling away over my chest. I realized that the old occult traditions really must have a basis in reality after all. It's one thing to say you believe in auras or chakras, but seeing them before your eyes is like taking in their organic reality.

Being dosed on a chemical, there's always the question of whether you're having a hallucination, or whether your doors of perception have been cleansed and you're seeing something that's real on a level other than can be normally perceived. If I saw a hobgoblin scamper across the floor, I'd take it as a hallucination, though it might be a manifestation of something real yet unseen—fear, for example. But in this case, the chakra cone was quite prosaic. It seemed like a standard feature, an ordinary part of the picture, like my big toe; it was part of me.

My reaction was, *Hmm . . . I don't know if I want to be seeing this.* This was no wish fulfillment; quite the opposite, in fact. I found it disquieting, because it indicated that aspects of the occult were true despite their being excluded from our modern mainstream model of reality. *If this is real, then what else might be?* I wondered. *Spirit possession? Black magic?*

I believe that one of the wise uses of psychedelics could be for use by trained clinical psychologists to explore whether some of the most ancient beliefs about the human energy system could be integrated into modern medicine, in the way that a magnetic imaging device, for instance, helps doctors see things within the body beyond normal perception.

On another LSD trip in the late Sixties, I tapped into the Zen appreciation for the paring away of all time and space to the here and now. During a rather challenging segment of the trip, I had the sense that things only existed when I looked at them. It was like being in a totally dark room, with my perception being like a beam of light shining out from my eyes as they moved over my environment. There seemed to be a huge black void behind my head that only filled up when I turned to look at it. This was the literal perceptual truth, of course, but I didn't like it.

The here and now is a very specific, finite point in our experience, though essentially, it's all there is. Everything else is in our heads and does not otherwise exist. We fill in our lives with memories and projections and plans and assumptions that give us the illusion of a causal chain running through our lives. We do it in time—*I've come from somewhere, I saw somebody yesterday. I'll see them tomorrow*—and we do it in space—*I'm going to walk out of this building and know that it's still there behind me.* Such distraction can be so acute that you can bang your car into the one in front of you during rush hour, because you're thinking about something else besides the road before you. The acid had temporarily stopped the void-filling process, stripping away reality to the sight I was seeing at that moment alone.

I began to see the Zen rationale that this moment now is it, eternity. The acid was acting as a cleansing agent, a literal acid, dissolving away all the woolly stuff that got in the way of my direct perception of the here/now. Behind my head was blackness in the sense that there was nothing there until I turned my head and looked at it—until the flashlight of my perception, my vision, lit it up.

The experience reminded me of an old story about a venerable Zen master who'd just come indoors after collecting water and chopping wood. One of his students said to him, "Master, you really shouldn't be doing that. That's not the thing for a great patriarch to be doing." And the master replied, "Collecting water, chopping wood—this is a miracle!" Throughout most of our lives we're anticipating something or regretting something; meanwhile, the moment in which we're actually living passes by us.

Under another mind-altering substance, one from the opiate family, I had a series of unexpected altered perceptions. I was visiting a friend at his home and found myself sitting on the bathroom floor, taking a private moment to get hold of myself. Suddenly, a purple mist gushed out of the skirting boards, covering the entire floor and then rising up my seated body. My feet were enveloped, and then the stuff started creeping up my knees. I didn't want it to submerge my head, so I got up and walked out, leaving behind a vivid violet mist, two feet deep.

A little later, I was sitting alone in a room that suddenly seemed to fill with people. After a few seconds, the place was mobbed! I blinked my eyes and they all disappeared. I realized that I'd been looking down a corridor of time—down the temporal as well as the spatial axis of the room. The figures weren't all there at one time. It was as if all the people who'd ever been in the room had somehow left an imprint of themselves on the space they'd occupied in that room, and I'd been privy to that composite snapshot.

In that same room later that evening, I was lying down, feeling fairly odd. A friend put his head around the door in a curious way, with his hands gripping its edge, and asked, "Are you okay?" I said, "Yeah, sure." Then he vanished into thin air, an apparent hallucination. But half an hour later, this person actually did come to the door, sticking his head around the door in exactly the bizarre, jocular fashion that I'd seen him do earlier. In this instance I'd been precognitive—looking ahead along the time axis.

I was surprised that such perceptions were possible via a poppy derivative, but then I recalled the seership that opium accorded to the poet Coleridge. One of the overriding values of these altered states is that they bestow direct experience of phenomena usually apprehended only in abstraction.

Some people don't mind the marginalized, illegal status of most psychedelic substances in our culture. In fact, some actually enjoy belonging to a subculture. But I personally don't. I want such experiences to be mainstream and properly conducted in a safe, legal context. I want to be able to say, *I'm going to blow my mind today,* and then proceed to the local accredited Mind-blowing Center in town, where there will be people who understand the substances and the nature of the experiences involved, and how to guide me.

Until such an enabling environment is created, there are plenty of discoveries to be made with legal substances. I'm currently researching the lucid dream state, which is likened to awakening within a dream. In the hopes of undergoing such a state myself, I once took a bit of nutmeg (somewhat more than your usual eggnog-flavoring pinch) shortly before retiring for the evening. After a little while, my skin felt very dry, as if it were burning. *Oh, God,* I thought. *I've OD'd on nutmeg!*

I fell asleep and entered a dream in which I saw an open doorway and ran through it, finding myself in a dark tunnel, which looked like an underground car park, but was actually a tunnel beneath an Egyptian temple. Then a spark of clear, wakeful awareness flashed in my dreaming mind. I thought, *Ah, the tunnel of the near death experience (NDE).* This tunnel is a cortical patterning effect called an entoptic image, which can occur in other altered mind states as well as in the NDE. (The exact nature of the neurological processes that produce the effect of the tunnel are not known precisely, because entoptic patterns originate in processes reaching from the retina to deep within the visual cortex. But the effect is cross-cultural, experienced by people in certain trance states everywhere.)

As soon as I registered this, I was suddenly jogging along in brilliant sunlit countryside. Ahead of me was a huge trilithon, two upright stones with a third across the top (like the structures at Stonehenge and the cromlech scattered across Ireland), made of the most beautiful colored marble. There was a long row of these things, one behind the other, forming a kind of open corridor, another version of the entoptic tunnel pattern. (In the visionary state the "tunnel" can appear in many guises.) I ran toward the first trilithon, going faster and faster and faster and then I took off, flying Superman style between the uprights of all the trilithons.

With the sun shining to my left, every time I flashed through a trilithon, the left-hand upright threw a shadow across me, which had a strobe effect: black shadow/brilliant sunshine, black shadow/brilliant sunshine in rapid succession. The frequency of this sequence increased to a crescendo, and I soared out at the far end of this avenue of trilithons. By now fully conscious, I flew up into the most perfect vault of blue sky imaginable, and proceeded to cartwheel, somersault, and loop the loop. It felt totally and physically real. I could feel the air passing over the surface of my skin.

If someone were monitoring me, he would have seen all the physiological signs of sleep. (Actually, people who learn how to become conscious within the dream state can now send signals with their eye muscles, which are not paralyzed in dreaming sleep, as most muscle groups are. While physiologically asleep, they move their eyes in such a way that leaves traces on the polygraph.) I was fully conscious, even though I was still inside the dream. In this condition, the dream takes on a totally real quality, as though all five of your senses are working as sharply as they do while you're awake.

Unlike normal dream imagery, the view had an absolute three-dimensional authenticity. When I passed over trees, for instance, my perspective changed along with my angle of vision, and the appearance of the branches and twigs, and the ground farther below, changed accordingly, staying in true parallax. As I floated past some trees, I grabbed hold of the leaves and felt their waxy texture. When I pulled on the branches, I felt them spring back out of my hand.

I found myself flying over an undulating landscape rather like Herefordshire in England, with blue hills in the far distance. Hovering above the treetops, I saw people moving around below. They looked like normal human beings, though decidedly out of fashion, wearing one-piece sage-green tunics. The technology of this society, which included bicycles, seemed familiar, yet slightly weird and different at the same time.

I thought I ought to return, so I flew back and noticed that the geography was the same I'd just covered. I recognized all the topographical details, certain hills and tracks I'd flown over. I found my way back to the point that I'd first emerged in this landscape, but there was no sign of the trilithons or the Egyptian temple, only a curious, symmetrical green hill, which I took as my point of entry into this dimension, wherever and whatever it was.

I'd really like to get back to normality now, I thought, so I flew headfirst into the hill. I experienced a fleeting blackness, the merest moment of blacking out, and opened my eyes, "waking" up. But it wasn't like waking up at all, but more like changing channels on the television. Being in my bed was no more or less real than the lucid dream I'd just inhabited.

I don't recommend nutmeg as a regular practice, because it's a rough old drug and if you take too much, you can damage your kidneys. But as an occasional experiment for exploring the unconsciousness of sleep, a big pinch in your evening meal can give your dream machinery a boost.

Another legal drug I use for my lucid-dream research is a minor psychedelic called *Calea zacatechichi* (bitter grass), which is used by the Chontal Indians in Mexico for dream divination. I've taken quite heavy doses of the drug, which extends, deepens, and slows the hypnogogic phase between waking and sleeping (characterized by "dreamlets" and flashes of images and sounds).

In this enriched hypnogogic state, I've many times visited fabulous rocky landscapes, where orange-red colors prevail. The very first time I took it, I found myself on my back on a bed of some kind, while looking down at me, with a mixture of gravity and amusement, were three Indians in bright-colored garments, one wearing a hat. I felt I was actually present with these chaps for a few moments, before I soared off again at the speed of an express train. I'd undergone so much traveling in my dreams that night that I was exhausted the next day.

If we can develop secure methods of inducing lucid dreaming, it could become the favored way to explore our minds—that is, until they make dreaming illegal, of course.

Peter

B. 1966

Father, transcriber of legal proceedings, entrepreneur

Resides in Massachusetts

Raised in New Jersey and Massachusetts

I Wasn't Worried That I'd Done This to Myself

One night in the late 1980s I took eight double-dip hits of acid, about sixteen hundred to two thousand mics, at a Pink Floyd concert in Foxboro, Massachusetts. It was a great concert and the drug enhanced my joy of it. When I got home, I figured I was sober, at least done with any kind of hallucinating. I lay down in my bed, and soon the ceiling melted away and flew off into space, replaced by a rich infinite blackness with no stars. Then I started hearing a peculiar mesmerizing music inside my head, a sort of fusion of metal xylophone and the chimes you play with your fingers or a small mallet.

It wasn't echoing the concert I'd just heard. It wasn't Floydish at all, but more like Michael Oldfield's *Tubular Bells* or Tibetan music. It was real, honest-to-God music that I'd never heard before. I was totally enthralled by it and lay in bed and listened to it for hours.

By four in the morning, I still hadn't gotten any sleep yet and I had to go to work the next morning. *This must be it,* I thought. *I've taken one hit too many and snapped my brain.* It was twelve hours after I'd dropped. I'd never been high for longer than eight before. I'd also never experienced auditory hallucinations.

I was getting myself prepared to knock on my parents' door and inform them, "By the way, you might as well check me into an institution, because I'm going to be hearing music inside my head for the rest of my life." I wasn't worried that I'd done this to myself. I was more concerned about how they were going to take it. As far as I was concerned, this was a great way to live. The music was constantly changing. Back then when I was in my early twenties, my whole life revolved around great music. I loved going out to hear great improvised music and here it was in my head—I didn't have to go anywhere.

It was a spiritual sound, more open-ended than religious music is. I felt I'd tapped into the rhythm all around us, the music of the spheres, the intonations of the Earth mother and the father universe. I thought I'd achieved what a lot of people strove for, to *be there,* to be connected: not just to know it's there, but to actually hear it.

It eventually petered out and I fell sleep and woke up and went to work. I was disappointed that I'd lost this spiritual wavelength that had been transmitted into my head, that I'd tuned into the cosmic harmony and had lost the frequency.

Everything You Always Thought We Could Be

My most memorable trip was an experience in Landover, Maryland, in the fall of 1988 or '89, when I was following the Grateful Dead around the country. The Dead had already done one in a series of three shows in Landover, and I was hanging out with friends on a layover day before they did two more.

A drug dealer on tour had become smitten with a friend of mine and loved trying to impress her. She and I were sitting around talking about how much fun it would be to get a bunch of people together for a mushroom party. This guy came by on his bicycle, looked at us, and said, "Hold on." He rode off and came right back with a large Ziploc bag full of psilocybin mushrooms. He took out handfuls and threw them at us, and it turned into a gigantic pile.

We called over all our friends to partake in this bonanza. There were seven or eight of us that had made the trip, coming from all parts of the country. We just dove into it with no real thought as to how much we were eating. It was kind of like opening up a bag of potato chips for people with the munchies. I think we all overindulged.

One of the reasons the experience that unfolded was so remarkable was its humble setting. At that time, they still allowed you to camp out for the shows in the stadium parking lots. The spot the stadium had set up for us was a dirt lot strewn with large-pebbled gravel. It was very difficult to set up a tent or sleep on this surface. That scared away most people, who went to motel rooms. On top of that, it rained. So the folks that remained were the real tourheads, the ones who followed the Dead from city to city and did nothing but that. I'd been to a hundred Dead concerts by that point and was a full-blown "drug addict."

Tourheads often travel in a group that calls itself a family. The people in my particular family had parked their cars in a circle to create a home base. One of us had a van, and every time he parked for a concert, he'd set up a canopy and a living room with a couple of beach chairs and ice coolers to sit on.

He was one of the best musicians I've ever heard. He loved to get people together to bang on pots or pick up a guitar or kazoo or harmonica, whether they knew how to play or not. He could make it sound good, no matter what you played. Just as I was starting to trip, I asked him to play something for me. He said, "Sure," grabbed his guitar and started to play. Pretty soon he'd attracted a flock of musicians who sat around him in a circle. I was soon surrounded by guitars and drums and harmonicas and instruments of all kinds.

I was starting to get off in a big way. Music was hitting me from all directions. I was sitting about five feet from this maestro, in the center of a circle of strummers, bangers, and blowers making phenomenal music. It was free play, jammin', folky pickin' kind of stuff, with each taking a turn on lead. I was the only audience for a while, sitting in a lawn chair and soaking it all in for maybe an hour and a half.

As I got higher, the music became tangible. Every surface of my skin could feel it. It felt like it was touching me in a physical way, like a breeze with thought surrounding my head. It was taking away some of the weight I was feeling, counteracting the force of gravity. I felt lighter because of this lift the music was giving me.

Eventually I had to go to the bathroom, so I got up and excused myself. We'd started late in the afternoon and now it was dark out with no moon but many stars. I was a bit chilled, so I was torn between heading to the port-a-johns and getting my sweater from the trunk of my car. I knew that either one was going to be a chore, in my condition. I decided to go get my sweater. There was no light in the trunk, so when I opened it up, I had no idea where anything was.

Whenever I trip, especially in the dark, I see multicolored spiderweb patterns, an interlacing of glowing lines sort of like those laser stickers that change colors when you move them in the light. They were like spiderwebs that had been well used and no longer had perfect configurations because they were wet with dew or had holes in them. Sometimes I thought they were lines of energy that interconnected the world. These patterns would shimmer and I had to swim my way through the things to get anything accomplished.

I was seeing more Technicolor spiderwebs than I could clothing, so I decided to give up on the sweater and go to the bathroom. I got halfway there and thought, *No, I really need the sweater,* so I turned around and went back and wrestled with the darkness and the spiderwebs all over again. I still had the same problem between my not being able to concentrate and all these glimmering webs in my way.

I must have gone through this exercise three or four times. I was in awe at how silly I was, trying to perform this function I could have done in a minute even in the dark, had I not been tripping so strongly. It had now taken me a half hour between walking halfway to the john and back, standing there and scratching my head, and sticking my hand in the trunk in the hope it would land on a sweater. I was amused at how ludicrous it must have been to anyone watching this scene. Eventually I got the sweater and relieved myself and went back to the group.

The only people in the lot were the true-blue tourheads. I recognized the majority of the group, because I'd been touring for years. I'd gotten to know the faces, if not the names and the people themselves. Tourheads saw themselves as an extended family. Everyone was always welcome at whatever activity anyone was doing in public. You shared your entertainment, whatever it was, with others, and they shared theirs with you.

One group with a huge recreational vehicle and another with a converted school bus pulled their respective wheels together into a V formation and built a bonfire out of tree-sized logs in the opening. They kept feeding this fire, so the flames were as high as the top of the bus. This sort of thing happened at these events, but I'd never seen a bonfire that big. Naturally, it attracted a crowd.

There was a bunch on tour who called themselves the Drummers, who really enjoyed tribal drumming on big congas with straps over their shoulders. So the Drummers and others playing bongos and assorted percussion instruments formed a ring around this roaring bonfire, two or three deep in some places. And around this ring of ragtag musicians gathered all the people who danced. I always loved to dance in these drum circles. They had the flavor of American Indian or African rhythms and they're a heck of a lot of fun to dance to.

Eventually, it seemed like everyone in the parking lot wound up around the fire. There had to be five hundred people there, maybe more. For the next four hours, I experienced an amazing sense of community with all these people. It went on long into the night. I didn't run into one person who was not giving something to someone, helping someone in some way, being a plain generous human being.

People were sharing their food, their water, or their clothing. It seemed like everybody was on mushrooms and on the same wavelength. There was communication beyond the spoken word. Everybody was happy. I didn't run into anyone who was not only in a good mood but an excellent one. I was having the best time of my life. I don't think I've ever experienced a feeling of joy that great. And it was because so many other people were in this same mood and enjoying themselves to the same extent. No one wanted it to end.

As drummers got thirsty, people went up to them and poured water in their mouths so they didn't have to stop playing. They'd be drinking from someone else's hand, likely a stranger's. I know I did it for people I didn't know.

When people from the family I'd come with ran into each other, we'd catch each other up on the amazing things we'd been doing or seen. You would run into people who could do astounding things. There was a guy on six-foot stilts walking around the fire, dancing to the drums. There was a guy on a unicycle, a guy juggling flaming sticks or twelve balls at a time. It was like a Renaissance fair, a banquet in King Arthur's court, or a bacchanalian feast: human beings enjoying human beings to the utmost in a carnival atmosphere, with costumes and performers, music, dancing, food, and drink. The flames threw fantastic shadows and flickered off of all these bodies huddled together, gyrating about. The campsite was huge but we all congregated in one place to be with each other.

There was an abundance of love flowing around. I was amazed that the human race could get along like this, that we really could get together and have an experience with no negative feelings whatsoever. There was a lot of hugging, brotherly and sisterly love, not the romantic sort. It was one of the rare times I've ever seen human beings get together and be everything you've always thought we could be as a race.

I was allowing the music to do with me what it wanted, the kind of free-dancing you see at Dead concerts. When I stopped, I talked to many people, friends, strangers, and people who became friends.

That night I took only the mushrooms and water, lots and lots of water. Before I went on tour, I'd always fill up a lot of milk jugs with water, because you never knew when you'd run into water again. There aren't many parking lots with faucets. If you didn't have water stored away, a lot of times you went thirsty.

I got into a memorable conversation about water when I offered this one guy a drink from my jug. I had my jug and he had his. His contained well water from somewhere in the Midwest and mine had water from my parents' well in Massachusetts. I loved that water. To me it was phenomenal. We discussed the qualities of both of our waters. He claimed he was a connoisseur and could tell me where my water came from. It helped that I'd told him before he made this claim, but he tasted some and confirmed, "Yep, that's definitely well water from Massachusetts."

We talked about how spectacular water was, how life-giving and smooth and cooling it felt as it glided down your throat. We were throwing adjectives at each other, being proud of my water, his water, each other's water, all water. We didn't exchange names and I never saw him again, but wherever he is today, I bet he remembers our conversation too.

I came down slowly and eventually got tired. A lot of people had gone to bed by the time I did. When I woke up the next morning, the fire was in embers and there were still a few drummers and people gathered around. Some people congregated to make breakfast for everybody.

We wished we could carry that feeling beyond that place and time, but then the rest of the world flooded back in on us, the wetness of the parking lot after the rain, the stones we were sleeping on, the fact that you had to get a ticket for the show, and you still had to eat today, and where were you going to get the money for that? All those real-life concerns came back. The feeling had gone.

When I talked to my friends on the phone in the days afterward, they all expressed the same amazement that we'd all shared this sense of humanity, of love and caring and sharing, that the world can be good, if not perfect. For about a year afterward, it bothered me that I'd achieved a peak that I'd never reach again. It hadn't dawned on me that maybe later I'd fall in love and have a baby, that there was life outside my drug experiences.

Since that time, so much has happened that I've realized there are different kinds of peaks. Catching my daughter as she was born, being the first to touch her, was another kind of intense joy. I can't equate the two kinds, because they flowed from different realms of experience, but both were peak-experiences of everlasting value to me. And I know there's more to come.

Everything Else Was Normal

The last time I ever tripped, I experienced some of my biggest hallucinations and also the impetus to stop using psychedelics.

It was 1989 in Milford, Massachusetts, when I was still living with my parents. A friend came over and convinced me to take some LSD with him. It was blotter, Lucky Charm double-dip. Printed on the paper were the familiar clovers, hearts, and diamonds in the popular breakfast cereal. We took four each, about eight hundred mics. Forty-five minutes later we weren't satisfied with how high we were, so we took more, upwards of sixteen hundred mics each altogether.

We had an uneventful, slightly paranoid time in the woods, hiking through acres of undeveloped land with no trails. It was ridiculous to think somebody could be behind the next tree, but I had that feeling for a while. My friend finally caught on to my uneasiness. He was not having that type of time, so he finally said, "I'll be going now," and took off. I was much more at ease after he left.

I went back home and, around nine in the evening, called my friend Michelle, a frequent tripping partner, from the phone in the kitchen, which was dark. Most of my hallucinations come in the dark. The wallpaper in the kitchen had a pattern of blue-and-white stripes inlaid with flowers and vines. As I sat talking with Michelle, the vines started growing off the wallpaper, eventually stretching from one wall to the other. There was no escaping this vine garden all around me.

I laughed because it was extremely humorous that the wallpaper would be doing this. This was why I took LSD, to see this type of phenomenon, contemplate it, and wonder how my brain selected these images for projection. The illusion was dispelled only when I inevitably had to get up and turn on the light.

My mother had seen me earlier that night and knew that I was high. She told me to stay to myself, because it upset her to see me in that condition. So after I wound up the call with Michelle, I avoided that part of the house and went up to my room.

A branch from a tree outside my window started doing what the wallpaper vine had done, except it grew right through the glass. I got up and examined it from several angles and would have sworn I could have grabbed it and swung on it, it appeared that tangible. The branch appeared to have elongated rather than sprouting new fiber and foliage.

After the branch retracted out the window again, I had occasion to look in the mirror. I thought I was almost sober again, but as I looked at my face, it transformed into that of a baboon. My face grew hair, elongated, and took on that baboon look all the way down to the shape of the eye socket and the bluish skin. My hair turned into a mane that grew down my neck and outward all around. It amazed me, because I looked around the room and everything else was normal. The cups were the cups, the curtains looked like the curtains, the TV, the bed, everything was a hundred percent normal. This was strange, because usually when I hallucinated, for instance, when the tree came through the window, I could look at the furniture and it would be a little wavy. I could always tell when I was in a hallucinatory mode.

I felt I wasn't under the influence anymore, yet here I was werewolfing into a baboon in the mirror. My body outside the mirror looked entirely regular, so the mirror seemed to confine the illusion. Only within its frame was the drug in effect, while my reality consciousness was out in the room with me. I was normal in here, distorted in there, like Jekyll and Hyde.

I was disappointed it was a baboon that had shown up in my reflection. I would much rather it was a werewolf or something like that, anything but a baboon. Even a gorilla would have been better. A baboon is the ugliest of all monkeys, in my opinion, colored in strange places that I don't want to be. It was extremely vivid, though I never became a hundred percent baboon or returned to the hundred percent Peter face while the illusion persisted. To switch off the imagery, I just stopped looking in the mirror and was back to normal for the most part.

But the trip had gone sour, and I decided I'd had enough of that sort of thing. Actually, just before this trip, I'd more or less promised myself that I'd never take acid again. Now, as I descended into the familiar hopeless, paranoid feeling I typically had during the waning hours of a trip, my decision was cinched. I realized that I'd learned what I could from psychedelics, that I'd gotten to the last page and there was no longer any need to go back and reread the book.

Philip Cooper

(also known as Bond on the adventure travel circuit—
"It's been said that I can be in two places at once.")

B. 1969

***Hypnotherapist,* karmachanic**

Currently based in the Cotswolds, but living a nomadic life, traveling in South America, Asia, and elsewhere

Born in London, raised in Europe

The Cathedral of San Pedro the Divine

In 1995 I traveled to Chile for the solar eclipse and stayed on in South America for a series of psychedelic adventures. My experiences with ayahuasca and San Pedro stand out in particular.

At the end of an intense ayahuasca ceremony with six other Westerners, the shaman made a "hole" in our crown chakras and then blew some tobacco smoke, representing his spirit, down into our heads, through our spinal columns and all the way down to our toes, sinking a little bit into the ground and gathering up some Mother Earth energy. Then he sucked it out and "covered" the hole back over. The end. Trip over. We'd been casting about in hyperspace for eight hours and that brought us right out. We were instantly back to normal.

My next psychedelic encounter led to the most profound and moving experience of my life. From Peru I went to a sacred place in Ecuador called Vilcabamba, known as the Valley of Longevity. Inca kings journeyed there near the Peruvian border east of Quinca to take the sacred cactus San Pedro. It's on the freak or adventure travel circuit today, so there are a lot of eighteen-year-old kids going there and getting seriously switched on.

I bought some San Pedro from the local tourist information officer. The provincial lore is that if you sell the sacred cactus, you can't conceive children. There were two San Pedro vendors in this village, and neither of them could produce offspring. The spirits of San Pedro are known to dwell in this valley. To prepare the cactus for ingestion, you peel off the skin and then cut off the strip beneath the skin between the meaty, hard part. Then you take the green mulch and boil it for thirty-six hours and make it into a drink.

I walked up the mountain, and when I reached the top and threw up, it started taking effect. I was blown away by the scale of the experience. There was no difference between the inside and the outside, no boundaries between the mountain and me. I was in a beautiful valley system, so I could see vast spaces with myriad color tones and shadows. The mountains breathed. Birds glided through the air. I summoned one to me by thinking the thought and saying it out loud. An eagle came around and hovered directly above me. Afterward, I vowed to do the sacred cactus with even more intent.

I prepared for my second trip by studying Tai Chi for a month and changing my diet, as I didn't want to throw up again. I wanted to keep the medicine inside me. On the morning of a full moon, I drank the brew with two Ecuadorian fellows I'd just met. I sat cross-legged by a river, and observed the medicine traveling through my system. After a while, my intestines felt like they'd been wrung out, and then the medicine, staying inside me, moved up to my mind.

I lifted up my arm, but the limb itself remained on my leg. I leaned forward left and turned my head right to look at myself. *My God,* I marveled, *I'm looking at myself out of my body.* Then I saw myself sitting down, then rising in a fraction of a second, prompting me to wonder, *Which one am I?* I sat down into myself and as I closed my eyes, I saw masses of white light everywhere.

Then I did Tai Chi for a spell, practicing all my newfound knowledge of the art. I did it like I was a master, like I'd never done it before or since. It was beautiful. The sensations were perfect. I didn't have to think about the exercises. When I was pushing out, I was breathing correctly, naturally. I was moving the Chi around through the charged atmosphere. It spread out from my body to my surroundings and beyond, to the cosmos. I grew to an enormous size, in camaraderie with the mountains around me.

I decided that it was time for something to happen. I connected with one of the Ecuadorian guys, Tomás, a wealthy, educated Mestizo in his mid-thirties who owned a bar. He'd brought his two Alsatians with him for the trip. We decided to go up the sacred, pyramid-shaped mountain together. To inaugurate our quest, we sat down and meditated together. Soon we were totally tuned into each other, and ecstatic. We looked at each other at the same time and knew that we were about to go off and have an epic adventure together. As we climbed the mountain, we began to communicate psychically with each other without any effort. He spoke but a few words of English and I but a few words of Spanish, but we didn't have to converse about what we were going to do. It just fell in.

I felt I was experiencing my true nature with everything around me. My consciousness was taking everything in on an elemental, prelingual basis. There was no distraction. It was pure, complete truthfulness and understanding between me and Tomás. I couldn't lie, and he knew he couldn't lie either. I could see then there was no difference between him and me.

When we reached the summit, Tomás suggested that we do yoga headstands. We sunk our centers of gravity down into the mountain, falling, rooting ourselves loosely and naturally into it. My legs were swaying from the winds that blew up from the valley, but I was so implanted, I had no problem maintaining the stance comfortably. We became the mountain. Tomás's dogs acted as our guardians, wedging us in and protecting us as we maintained our rather dodgy positions on the mountain peak.

We looked across the valley to a promontory called the Cathedral about three kilometers away. The mountain there looked like a woman lying on her back. At the tip of her nose was a rock structure called the Nose, which is a sacred place used by the shamans for entering the Cathedral via San Pedro. Upside down we could clearly see a portico with a doorway into the Cathedral, which actually seemed more like a majestic church. The local terrain, at the confluence of three rivers, seemed to move and flow toward this formation, where one could have a 360-degree view of the entire magnificent valley. From the spot we'd chosen it was said that those who take the sacred cactus can feel the intention of the Cathedral.

We lifted ourselves out of our bodies and floated over the valley across the sky to the Cathedral, holding hands telepathically and playing, being very mischievous and silly, like schoolboys. The ground below was a moving mass. No words were spoken between us. I could think a thought to my companion and it was conveyed. When I closed my eyes I saw animal totems, most prominently the eagle. I felt like I'd arrived at my true self. There was no need to examine myself, my motives, my conscience, the whys or wherefores of my life and personality. The moment was endless.

Then we flew inside the psychical door of the Cathedral. (There was no physical entrance.) There was a little hesitation before we surrendered and entered. Inside, there was a swirling mass of spirits and a sort of flowing solid, like Softee ice cream in various shades of gray. I found my place in it. There was no gravity, no gap between anything. The "church" seemed to be enclosed, but I couldn't see any walls or boundaries. It was like a very long concrete well in which I could hear my voice shout and resonate.

The spirits were not humanoid but of the deeper earth, the aura of the rock. A powerful emotion emanated from the primordial core of this place. I felt humble and reverent in the way that the ancient Incas must have felt. As we were making contact and wordlessly communicating with these spirits, I felt a profound sense of unconditional love.

The Cathedral began to open out and reveal more of itself, becoming more like an actual church inside. I may have been projecting a familiar form onto the ineffable place in order to protect myself, which could well be the reason why we abruptly popped out—or were expelled—and returned to our bodies. We hadn't consciously willed our exit, but perhaps an inner guardian had. Darkness was coming on, so we headed back, taking a very calming post-peak hike down the mountainside.

By the campfire, I reviewed the day's events with my partner, through an American guy who acted as interpreter. The moments of sinking into the mountain and entering the Cathedral were the same for both of us. He too had seen the swirling grayness inside and reemerged at the same moment I had. We beamed at each other and hugged to salute our fraternity of the spirit. There was complete mutual understanding and respect for each other. We'd both had a profound experience up there on the mountain. He'd given it to me, and I'd given it to him.

I had a puff of some marijuana and became rather therapistic with my cohorts, who, I could see so very clearly, were projecting their traps and troubles onto me. I trusted myself fully and the others recognized this trust and responded to it. I could see their auras and also the patterns in their psyches, the things that helped them and the things that were holding them back. I was able to choose exactly the right word to alleviate a given problem for that particular moment.

I joined an Israeli girl for a walk through sugarcane fields to a café a kilometer away. She'd taken the cactus at the foot of the mountain with some others. I was trying to bring her into the moment. The wind was blowing through the vegetation. I felt very loving, at ease, like I do on MDMA. We were totally honest with each other and had an intimate talk. Then I had an evening meal and went to sleep around eleven at night, waking up the next morning and remembering everything very clearly.

Today I use my San Pedro experience as a framework for an exercise in my hypnotherapy in which I encourage people to listen to the sounds within, then the sounds without, then the smells, and so on, ultimately creating a multilayered composite of the dynamic incomplete totality of consciousness.

Ever since this trip, I've tried to understand and rediscover my "true nature" as I conceived it. I saw that my life was entirely up to my own imagination. To me, that's what the gurus up in Rishikesh (India) are saying: Do what you would do prior to phrasing it into language. Before I arrived in Vilcabamba, transcendental states were just hearsay or only accessible through so much meditation and hard work. On the San Pedro, I was suddenly there.

Reverend Marianne

B. 1967

Priest in an Orthodox church

Resides in central California

Born and raised in a West European country

THE VISION MADE IT REAL

For me there is no moral barrier to doing an entheogen in church. If you have any spiritual discipline at all, you're going to be in an altered state no matter what, whether it's through fasting, self-renunciation, or some other means of achieving higher consciousness. Three trips in particular have been transformational landmarks in my spiritual journey.

The first of these was the first time I took LSD. I was still in seminary school at Harvard Divinity School, where I went on to earn a Masters of Divinity. Andrew, a friend and classmate, gathered a group of us to commemorate the famed Good Friday Experiment by Walter Pahnke. In 1962, Pahnke, a medical doctor turned Harvard doctoral candidate in religion, ran an experiment with seminary students of various denominations from Andover-Newton. On Good Friday, he brought them to Marsh Chapel at Boston University, where he administered psilocybin tablets and placebos and conducted a blind survey of the participants. Most of those who took the psilocybin reported having profound spiritual awakenings, while those who took placebos did not.

So at ten in the morning of Good Friday in 1994, a group of us from the divinity school ingested a low dose of LSD and made a pilgrimage on foot to B.U. from Cambridge. It took about an hour, and we arrived right in time for Marsh Chapel's service, which lasted three hours. We went to the small chapel downstairs to contemplate the atmosphere of the experiment site. We found a rose on the altar there and went back up to the main church. The sermon was not particularly moving, so I sat and meditated, gazing around the nave.

The reredos behind the altar was a huge carved wooden panel of Jesus with two evangelists at each side. The wood was a gorgeous, rich golden color. I looked at the statue of Saint John, whose Gospel is my favorite. *Ah, that's a lovely work of craftsmanship,* I thought. I shifted my focus to a beautiful statue of Jesus, which started moving and then began talking to me. "Look at me," He said. "Look at what they've done to me. I am the living Word and they've turned me into this dead still statue. They've killed me."

I was like *Whoa! Wait a minute.* His voice was very soft and gentle, His face filled with despair. "I want you to go out and be the Word that I embody," he continued, "because I can't do anything here. It's up to you." I snapped out of it and thought, *Wow, this is interesting.*

This vision of Christ was a formative moment in my life. I wasn't yet ordained, and didn't know what I was going to do with my seminary training. It was just what I needed at that time in my life, giving me the strength to continue and eventually become a parish priest. The acid vision made Christ a reality for me, whereas before He'd been just an intellectual process. When I saw Him moving on the reredos, I knew that it was real, that there is a Christ. The vision deepened my own personal faith and also gave me focus in my calling as a priest. As a member of the clergy, it's important that you have your own theology. Still, I wondered how I'd respond to the supplication I'd received. I'm not an evangelical. I was raised Episcopalian, and we don't go around spreading the Word.

Three years later I was living in central California, serving in the parish where I serve now, a small Orthodox church in the apostolic succession of Thomas the Apostle. One of my fellow ministers, a woman, was praying and prophesying for me, and she came up with something that echoed the Jesus of my Good Friday vision: "You are the Word incarnated."

Oh, my God, I realized. *Here is corroboration of my entheogenic experience. This is serious.* I knew that many people had experiences like mine but most pushed them aside because they were apparently the product of the drug. But here my entheogenic-inspired revelation was being reaffirmed by a minister in my own church!

I felt that the Jesus I'd seen had implored me to carry forth the concept of God's incarnation, that God lives in the flesh, as Jesus himself was an incarnation of God, and was now incarnated in me and in each of us. Unless we go out and share the spirit of Christ, that incarnation is irrelevant.

The vision deepened my appreciation for the theology of the fourteenth-century mystic Meister Eckehart, who was condemned as a heretic by the Church for his conception of *imago Dei,* man created in God's image. Today Eckehart is fashionable among clergy, many of whom are reading about him in Matthew Fox's book *Western Spirituality.* Fox's "creation spirituality" borrows much from Eckehart's conception of the incarnation of God in each person's soul, which is scripturally based on the Gospel of St. John. Now that I'd tasted firsthand the sort of revelation of God's incarnation in man that Eckehart wrote about, I felt I could go out and preach about it. I don't proselytize about taking entheogens, but I do give sermons about my vision and the principle of God living within each of us.

I prefer to take entheogens in religious settings to enhance the spirituality of the experience, but on one LSD trip, I stayed home. I rested on the bed, closed my eyes, and marveled as a parade of lovely tableaux flooded my brain. They were fun, but I soon got bored by the unceasing succession of pretty colors and melting images. I suppose it's okay to let one's mind wander, but when I got stuck in a bubbly pastel scene featuring Barbie dolls sitting on marshmallow clouds and My Little Pony and his fluffy, bright purple tail floating around in the air, I felt it was time to move on to something less trivial and cute.

I knew that more focus was desperately needed if I was going to apprehend the sacramental power of this wonderful entheogen. I decided to drop the concept "God" into the effervescent pool of wisdom in the far reaches of my mind, to see what would happen. I saw a beautiful iridescent sphere resting above an onyx sea, slowly rotating on a north-south axis. Drops of clear blue water rose up from this sea, midway through the dark air and back down, as if from an invisible fountain. I felt like the breath of God hovering over the face of the deep (i.e., the *ruach*) in Genesis 1.

I moved closer toward the sphere to see what was in it. I saw a carousel with white wooden horses, but as soon as I approached, it gave way to the Christ of the Book of Revelation (Chapter 1, Verse 16), white-robed among the seven candles, though there was no two-edged sword coming out of his mouth.

The scene changed when I blinked. I was lost for a while until I found myself inside a shiny, gilded room surrounded by the Egyptian pantheon. Clad in lapis, emerald, and gold, the gods and goddesses of ancient Egypt—*inter alia,* Anibus, Horus, and the semidivine pharaohs—were stunningly beautiful. I was talking to them, admiring them. The colors were sumptuous, rich, and bright, like a Fifties Technicolor movie. It was very vivid and I was quite comfortable beholding such splendor—that is until I remembered what I was there for: "God."

I turned to one of the deities and excused myself. I had to leave. I was mortified: I'd asked the entheogen for a revelation of the true god and then diverged from the path and wound up at a pagan palace that was a sensory playground! God was going to be real pissed off at me now, I knew it! But the Egyptian deity from whom I was taking leave looked at me and smiled. "Don't you know?" he asked. "We're all the same!" And then I realized that he was telling the truth: It didn't matter what shape or form I assigned to God. There was no god that would be cross with me for "misconceiving" his image. There was just the Great Divine, ineffable yet tangible, incorporeal yet manifest. I opened my eyes.

(I've since made peace with world religions. I'd known intellectually that there was an equality among the various creeds of faith, but now I knew it in the flesh, realizing that all aspects and faces of God are equal. This vision sharpened and refined my theology, because it was a lived experience.)

A while later I dropped the word "incarnation" into the same mind pool. I soon found myself hovering over a sort of *Alice in Wonderland* landscape with a fellow with a top hat like Uncle Sam standing before me. He doffed his hat and I could see into his head, but inside it wasn't skull and brains but the sum total of his life: his memories, his feelings, his hopes, everything that constitutes a life. All of these elements were escaping from his skull, floating away into the great void.

I knew somehow that this figure was God and that I was watching the whole process of creation take place before my eyes. Then he looked up at me and asked me, "If you were to bring back one thing from an acid trip to someone who'd never had one, what would it be?" I thought the question a bit odd, coming from God, but after a moment I answered, "A rainbow." He asked why and I said, "Because it is the perfect symbol of light." I pondered the image and realized how pale a single image was in conveying the full force and meaning of the Divine. And then it hit me that the incarnation is only an icon of the mind of God, that it is not the totality but only an archetypal expression of deity. You cannot know the power of the incarnation until you actually commune with God Himself.

I hope to write a book about Maria Sabina, the Mexican shaman who introduced Gordon Wasson to psilocybin. After experiencing its prophetic power myself, I became especially intrigued by that dimension of the sacred mushroom.

One Sunday I officiated the Eucharist, laying the wafers on the tongues of the congregation. (I take the high Anglican view of communion: the Eucharist *is* the body of Christ. I have no problems with the theological veracity of transubstantiation.) Then, during the singing in advance of the sermon, I took some mushrooms. I was finished with my part of the service—or so I thought—and no longer had to worry about performing. I'd expected to just sit back and take in my colleague's sermon and the rest of the service.

Our church is somewhat unusual in its inclusion of both the Eucharist and prophecy in its service. When the sermon is over, ministers may exercise prophecy if they're so inclined and also so moved on the occasion. Prophesying in this context is praying about somebody, receiving thoughts or images about that person, and then sharing them with the person before the whole congregation. Two of our ministers have this gift or penchant, which is not really my thing due to my Episcopalian background. I do the Eucharist; that's my job. I'd never prophesied in my life. But as soon as the sermon was over, I had this urge to prophesy to a woman a few pews away whom I really didn't know and about whom I did not have any concrete feelings prior to that moment.

I saw things about her that I would not have thought possible to know. She's an occasional member of the church, a middle-aged African-American woman who has her own "ministry" on the side. She'd always worn a collar to church, even though she's not ordained. People tended to regard her as a bit odd. I'd never spoken to her before. I was astonished that she of all the parishioners was the one my prophecy had focused on. If the choice had been mine, I would not have picked her as the object of my first prophecy.

I was in a trance. I'd closed my eyes and was totally out in space. I heard this voice: "You need to talk to her, and this is what you should tell her. . . ." It was *that* clear. "No, I'm not going to tell her that," I responded. "I'd make a fool out of myself." But the voice insisted, like it knew what it was talking about and had a good purpose for the whole thing. So I thought, "Ooo kay, here goes." I stood up and called her up to the front. She looked a little nervous and uncertain as she came forward. I'm sure she would have felt as though she were in better hands with either of the other two ministers, who made it a business to prophesy.

Technically, in terms of the formal service structure, it was all right for me to step up. Anyone so moved is allowed to step up and prophesy, but my four colleagues (all in their thirties) had never seen me come forward for this, so they were surprised. They looked up at me like "You want to say something?!" It wasn't really me talking. It was as though somebody else were talking through me. Sitting in the choir stalls on the side of the altar, I went on for about fifteen minutes, knowing what I was saying, but not consciously saying it.

The first thing I did was to rip the collar off her neck. It was kind of abrupt. I told her, "Turn around," and snapped it off and cast it aside. "You are ordained by God," I told her, "but you are not ordained by man. You must be recognized by man before you can wear this." She looked stricken when I defrocked her. "However," I went on, "your call is not invalid. You don't need to wear the collar in order to be a minister for the work you want to do." Then I told her that she needed to find her African roots, because she was trapped.

She's a very strong woman, but she's trapped in a man's world, the African-American man's world to be precise. She really needed to focus on being an African-American *woman,* the prophecy continued. I told her she needed to regain her roots, and that if that involved some paganism, that was fine. I said she had a genuine ministry and shouldn't be caught up in the false one symbolized by the collar she hadn't earned. I finished by giving her a prayer and a blessing. It went over fine. We wrapped up the service and everyone left.

I haven't seen her in church much lately, but when she does come in, she's not wearing the collar anymore. She's sort of hanging in the background, though I know she's in touch with some of the parishioners. I hear she's trying to start her own church. We'll have to see if she follows up on my counsel and delves into her heritage. I'm sure it was humbling and embarrassing for her, but I'd built up my preachment to her as an urging to go after the truth. Many parishioners came up to me and said, "I'm glad you said something to her. Something needed to be said." I replied, "I don't know if it needed to be said or not. It just came to me and that's what prophecy is about."

The rest of the clergy had a problem with that. Unfortunately, in many churches that exercise prophecy, it's used for the preacher's own advantage. That's what had bothered me about prophecy until the moment I'd prophesied myself and realized that it actually could be genuine. The trouble is that it's hard to tell the difference between fake and sincere prophecy. Much of the time, even when God is not urging a minister to speak out, a minister will say something that he or she thinks will work for the person chosen as the focus of the prophecy. But that was definitely not the case with mine. What I'd told her was most certainly *not* what she wanted to hear.

I realized that Maria Sabina was right, that what you say in this way must come naturally. You say what you say and if it happens to cause a bit of discomfort, that's the breaks. Controlled prophecy is telling people what they want to hear, which is utterly useless, in my opinion. Unfortunately, much of the prophetic movement is about saying nice things to people in an insincere format. I was disappointed that prophecy is so misused, which was really underscored by the spontaneity and nonpremeditated quality of my own prophecy. I'd wanted to say something nice but I really couldn't, since that wasn't the true voice I was hearing within me. I wish I could have told her good news: "You're going to get a new car next week!" But that's not the way it works. I'm sure there *are* genuine prophecies that are upbeat, but if you look at the Old Testament, the prophets aren't bearing glad tidings most of the time.

This event was another step in my growth as a minister, but I'm not sure I want to exercise my prophetic voice again. It's kind of scary, because you can't stop it. It just happens. I'm going to give mushrooms (and prophecy) a rest in church. I'll try MDMA next time.

[Note: Since this story was narrated, the church discontinued the practice of prophecy in its services.]

I used MDMA as the sacrament of an "entheogen-compatible service" that was held during a two-day conference on psychology, religion, and drugs, back in 1995. We began the service with a half hour of silence, giving the drug time to take effect. Then there was a chant to announce that the sacraments had kicked in. The service was directed, but we had to leave it open so that anyone could stand up and share his sentiments with the congregation. MDMA tends to prompt people to share of themselves.

In the middle of the service I spoke up. "The whole point of liturgy is the remembrance of a mythology. We gather to remember the life and death of Christ. In this service, we don't have a deity but the whole history of the entheogen movement to celebrate. So we need to remember our forefathers in this movement through music." And then I played "Purple Haze" on a huge boombox.

Everybody got up and started dancing. There were ministers, psychologists, psychiatrists, and professors, some in their seventies or eighties, including some towering figures in the psychedelic community, as well as some younger "kids" like me. It was so beautiful, all the generations coming together, unified by the music and dancing, which underscored the commemorative spirit we'd come to conjure.

Robert Bell

B. 1953

Librarian, editor, journalist; author of short stories, a guide to surnames in the Province of Ulster, Ireland, and a chronology of the Troubles in Northern Ireland

Resides in Denmark

Raised in Northern Ireland

Black Like I Never Saw Black Before

In 1972 Belfast, there were very few "freaks" like me, dressed like John Mayall on the cover of the *Blues from Laurel Canyon* album. That was the year I took acid for the first time, when I was nineteen. For the past three years, I'd been working for the British army in a civilian office, on an auditing team that went onto the bases to count up the guns, tanks, munitions, and stuff and check the paperwork. I was a clerical officer, a rank in the civil service equivalent to lieutenant in the army. So when I came to call at the barracks, they had to give me the respect due a lieutenant and salute me. I had hair halfway down my back, frayed jeans, love beads, the whole business, so it drove them fucking crazy. They hated it.

I'd just moved away from home and gotten my own apartment in the university area of Belfast, the only part of town where Protestants and Catholics could mix. Students and nurses, people from up-country, anyone who didn't like what was happening in the ghettos would gravitate there. It was the one sane district in Belfast during a period of terrible sectarian violence, and there were lots of cheap flats in converted Victorian houses.

I shared the apartment with Keith and George, two brothers from England who were schoolmates and very dear friends of mine. In the flat above us were two girls who were university students. We soon had common cause with these girls, so much so that I lost my virginity to one of them, Meg, pretty early on. After leaving home, everything started to happen at the same time. Meg was a middle-class hippie girl who'd been brought up in a liberal environment. The other girl, Katie, was from just over the border with the Republic of Ireland. She'd escaped from a little hick town and she was wild for anything. It was highly unusual for a Protestant, Meg, and a Catholic, Katie, to be living together, especially so for a girl coming from up-country, who'd be expected to stay with "people," family or close family friends. But Katie didn't pay any mind to that. She moved right in with Meg. They were like souls, very independent.

I'd moved out of my parents' because I wanted a place to bring girls and to use mind-altering substances. The flat was a pretty rough place with three blokes living in it, though. The wall decorations were cut out of magazines, and we had a brown, six-month-old Christmas tree decked with sundry bottle caps, playing cards, broken toys, and dirty socks. It was the worst sort of setting you'd want to start taking drugs in, if you were considering an idyllic environment a criterion.

One night in June, six of us were hanging out: myself, George, Katie and Meg, and two other friends, Harold and Bertrand. Harold was a strange guy with an explosive intelligence that goes in all sorts of directions. Bertrand was a public- (private in American terminology) school boy, handsome and well dressed. He was just sixteen but a total "head," much more experienced in the underground culture we were interested in.

"Why don't we get some acid?" Katie proposed. We were all virgins to drugs, though Bertrand was using a lot of marijuana. Everyone said, "Yeah, grih-ate," so she disappeared into the night and came back with five tabs of Purple Microdot which cost about a pound each, a lot of money at the time. A couple of us were on the dole, getting just six pounds a week.

Because there were five tabs and six of us, we naively determined, "somebody can't have one," not realizing we could have split them up into equal shares with a razor after a routine arithmetical calculation. But Harold volunteered, "No problem. I've heard that you should have someone to look after you, anyway. I'll look after you. I'll just get drunk." So the rest of us popped the tabs down with no qualms.

I was keen to try it. I felt we were in a trusting environment. We knew each other well, or thought we did. The bad-trip stories about people thinking they were Batman and trying to fly were very much the buzz, so we were glad to have this extra protection of Harold playing nursey in case anything went wrong. While we were waiting to get off, we listened to Joni Mitchell's latest album, *Blue,* which we all loved and played to death.

Bertrand, who works for Island Records now, knew a lot about music and he'd brought over a compilation of rock bands doing country stuff. There was a big "roots" thing happening at the time, spearheaded by Gram Parsons in California. On the cover of this record was a cowboy boot composed of flowers with roots growing under the soles. I stared at this cover, from time to time, throughout the evening.

After a while, we wondered, "Have we been ripped off? Is this not LSD after all? If not, what the hell is it?" Then I began to notice something. If you think of acid as a tool, the first useful job it did for me was to awaken me to the intrinsic worth of my own body. I was staring at my hand resting on the knee of my faded blue jeans and I realized, *I've got nice hands.* I'd never paid any attention to my hands before, but I've got big hands with long fingers. They're a notable feature.

Everyone was coming on in their own introspective way. It was strong acid. We weren't hallucinating everywhere, but things had definitely taken on a new look. So I studied my hand, the veins, the hairs, the nails, the whole entity. It looked so beautiful. Part of it was that on acid, anything can look lovely. It has a way of making a still-life painting out of whatever the hell you're looking at. It can help your mind see how perfect and self-contained any scene you look at is. It was the first time I'd really looked at my hand or any part of my body. So I was sitting there feeling terribly proud of my hand. From my sights, the view of my hand on my knee against the background of the rough and dirty carpet, accompanied by the astounding sounds of Joni Mitchell, was a complete and beautiful picture.

One of the things I learned from acid is to look at things in ways in which you wouldn't otherwise have looked, to *really* look. Today in my garden, I have a meditative vantage point where I sit and drink my coffee, which has been the axis around which the whole landscaping scheme has progressed. Acid showed me how to find that perspective.

Now, I said we all knew each other, but we didn't know each other from shit. We'd only known each other a few months. Katie started going off in directions. Suddenly, she was complaining, "Get this shit music off. I can't stand this fucking music, man." Everyone else was getting carried away on the music somewhere or another. And Katie *loved* Joni Mitchell, but she'd had enough, so, muttering, "I can't have this," she took it upon herself to pluck the LP off the turntable. She put on the Faces or some other pop rock. As far as I was concerned, that was great too. "The Faces? Okay, I'll go for that." Then she sat down cross-legged in front of the record player, standing sentry for any interloper.

We were all minding our own business, and from time to time, she would look up with a start. Of course, with the motion of her doing that, everyone else looked up at her. "What are you looking at me for?" she complained. *Hold on a minute, here,* I made note. *We're going to have to watch this girl.* Here she was high on acid for the first time and off on a self-fulfilling paranoia exercise.

It was kind of anxiety-producing. I wanted to get away from it. Our flat was four floors up and we had a little balcony where I wanted to go to get a clear vista and cool out. There was a beautiful view of the city and the mountains beyond. When a bomb would go off in Belfast, you could see the smoke cloud rise from there. But my companions were full of these Batman stories and they thought I was going to try to fly or something. An argument ensued with me saying, "Will you get a grip? I am *not* going to fly. I do not *want* to fly. I want to sit out there and get some peace."

Finally, I had to lay down the law. "Number one, it's my flat. Number two, it's my fucking balcony. Number three, it's my record player. Number four, it's my record. I'm taking this speaker and you can have that one. We'll switch it to mono. I'm going out on the balcony and I'm going to sit there until you get your heads together because I can't hack it." And I did.

This was great. It was a starry night, around midnight. The bars were closing and drunks were emptying out on the street, singing. I loved it out there, really drinking it up. When I went back inside, Katie'd split. I turned to Harold. "Where the hell is she? You were supposed to be looking after her."

"She said she was going. She was causing so much trouble, I didn't give a shit."

"But you were supposed to be looking out for her. Now we'll have to go out looking for her. Anything could be happening, with all the drunks out there."

Belfast was a hairy city anyway. Katie was a Catholic girl and Catholics were getting "assassinated" back in those days. So we put our jackets on and headed out in a search party. As we descended the stairs, the building's entry door banged shut and Katie bounded up with a big armful of yellow flowers, blossoms from a laburnum tree from the grounds of a church up the street. "I wanted to brighten up your flat," she announced.

So Katie was back in order again. As she was putting them out, she said, "I just want to point out that these are poison." She just wanted us to know that she was bringing danger into our haven along with the beauty. We thought, *Okay, Katie's fucking with our heads, but that's all right.*

We were all getting on fine together, having a good trippy time talking bullshit. But having all these flowers around was like an invitation to the outdoors. Everything in the room was dead and these flowers were so beautiful, so we all thought, *Let's get out of the city. Let's fuck off.*

Harold had a beat-up old Austin mini, the wee British hip car of the Sixties, a cheap square box really, but extremely powerful. He was drunk, so I said I'd drive. "No way. You're tripping out of your skull! You're not driving my car," Harold resisted. I convinced him that if we were stopped by the cops, it was better for me to deal with them while I was tripping than him drunk. We were all determined to go into the countryside, to get out of the city. Harold, who'd drained plenty of Harp by then, agreed.

The mini couldn't seat four comfortably and there were six of us pried into this tiny motorcar totally scrunched in, stuck up against the windows with the doors forced shut. We took off for the Giants' Ring, a prehistoric site about five miles out of town. To get there, we drove a twisty country road like a tunnel carved through the trees, like Dingley Dell from an illustrated children's fantasy or cartoon. There was no radio or tape player in the car, but everyone was singing. Driving this little car was fantastic fun, an echo of Loudon Wainwright's "Acid Song" about the breezy ease of driving on acid, so long as you kept your eyes on the highway and didn't laugh, fart, or sneeze. It was diddly-dee, dinkey toy time for us silly-billy kids. We were all still kids really, not that far from children's books and stuff.

The Giants' Ring is a circle of earthworks, four or five thousand years old, which form an amphitheater about two or three hundred yards across. In the middle of a huge shallow bowl are these ancient grave markers called cromlech, which are comprised of three big vertical rocks with another laid over the top. When we arrived, it was about two in the morning and deserted. It was a beautiful night in May or June with a full moon, as warm as it ever gets in Ireland. Standing on this ancient ancestral spot, you can feel the power of the place coming up your feet. I'm not a spiritual person, but the feeling there is very strong. You just sense it.

We wandered over the hills and ended up congregating at the big cromlech in the center, all of us but Harold, that is. He started running around the rim of the Ring, about half a mile around, up and down the hill and dale, drunk. Then he just vanished over that edge of the world.

From about a half-mile away, we saw car headlights coming up the road that leads only to the site. There were just a couple of minutes before it would get to us. In that short time, we remembered that the Giants' Ring was a dumping ground for assassinated bodies. There'd been several battered-up corpses disposed there by the paramilitaries. Informant suspects had been tied hand and foot with a hood over their heads, interrogated, and then shot, right there where we were tripping! All these stories came flooding back to us.

At the time, the IRA were the big bogeymen, though looking back on it later, it was more likely that Loyalist terrorists had been leaving bodies there, since it was closer to their stomping grounds. But the IRA were the ones we were scared of, since we were all Protestant, except Katie. We started freaking out. *Jesus Christ, who the hell is it? What do we do now?* We were at the base of the bowl, about a hundred fifty yards from the entrance, which is a little dip in the circular hill that formed the Ring. The car stopped in the car park. We couldn't see it, but we heard two car doors close.

The next thing we see is two guys in civilian clothes come in through the dip, in crouched positions with guns in their hands. They knew someone was in the Ring because our car was parked outside. It scared the shit out of us. We couldn't tell what the fuck they were. They were just two guys about forty in leather jackets. They could have been anybody: military, intelligence, police, IRA, Loyalist. We knew enough to know they were all bad bastards.

They moved forward one at a time, like Starsky and Hutch, covering each other. Pointing their guns at us in crouched positions, they shouted, "Freeze! Get away from the rock!" From the sound of their voices, we knew they were Irish, which meant they could have been almost anybody. If their voices were English, we would have assumed they were British army or intelligence. The acid made the gun in the hand of the lead guy look massive, like a fucking cannon, and ***black,*** black like I never saw black before, Arthur C. Clarke black-block-absorbing-all-light black, black-hole black. It looked huge even from 150 yards away. My whole mind was focused on this gun, the kind that has a clip in the handle.

"Put your hands on your heads. Move slowly," they screamed. We tried to assure them we were harmless. "It's okay! It's no hassle!" The one with the gun covered us while the other guy came across the field to us, zigzagging low to the ground, and snooped around, looking for people in hiding, weapons, whatever. These guys were jumpy as hell, though they were obviously professionals. If one of us made a wrong move, the consequences could have been horrible. *Jesus,* I remembered, *Harold's running around out there drunk as a skunk!*

The guy who'd put his gun away approached and identified himself and his partner. "Special Branch," he said, referring to the Special Branch of the Royal Ulster Constabulary, the antiterrorist wing of the Northern Ireland police. It became plain they were undercover antiterrorist agents on a routine patrol of a site known to have terrorist activity. It calmed us down that they were only the police. But then we thought, *Oh shit, we're tripping! We're not dead but we're still fucked.*

I tried to cast myself as a responsible fellow and started talking to this guy. "Look, there's a friend of ours here somewhere who's drunk and he's out running about over the hills."

"Don't worry about your friend."

"But he's drunk and you've got these guns . . ."

"Don't worry," he said, real calm and firm.

They didn't give their names or show any identification. The Special Branch wouldn't deign to show you anything. They're superior bastards. These guys looked like Starsky and Hutch from a distance, but when they got up close, they looked like the bad guys Starsky and Hutch would chase. They were real thugs: bad skin, brown leather jackets, turtleneck sweaters.

They wanted to see some IDs, so the guy with the gun hung back to keep an eye on the whole scene, while the other one examined our photo-embossed driver's licenses, which served government identification purposes. For exactly such occasions as this, Northern Ireland is the only U.K. province that requires photographs on the licenses. My mates were relieved not to speak, glad that I was handling that function. They just kept a low profile, saying nothing. But we were an unusual little contingent. We were clearly hippies, wearing beads and bones and beards, Frank Zappa mustaches: the little patch under the lip. The girls were wearing long Indian skirts, loose tops, and no bras.

It was obvious these guys knew we were drugged up. LSD was a Class A drug and there was a minimum seven years in prison for possession. Drugs have never really been a problem in Northern Ireland, partly because there's been so much military and paramilitary activity imposing on privacy and personal liberties. But as they inspected our IDs and asked a few cursory questions, it became clear they didn't give a shit that we were whacked out of our skulls. There was nothing in this for them. They were antiterrorist boys. They didn't know who the hell we were when they came in. The IRA had been using a wide range of disguises, so the police and military had to be cautious. Once, during a student parade, where everybody's in costume, an IRA assassin dressed as an Arab with a machine gun under his kaftan, came out of the crowd, killed a cop, then slipped back in and disappeared. They were very inventive.

It was evident enough that we weren't IRA or anybody up to any sectarian tricks, so they left after giving us a little lecture, that we should be careful where we go, that this was a disposal site for victims of paramilitary terrorism and infighting, and there were people tortured on this very spot on which we were fooling about. They saw us as upper-middle-class college kids, which we weren't. We were working-class hippies, for the most part. We didn't know much about the real world.

We had to stay another half hour until Harold stumbled back. He'd been away for an hour and a half, the bastard. And *he* was supposed to be looking after *us.* Class guy! "Where the fuck were you?" we demanded, then related our encounter with the Special Branch. He just stood there looking cool, but I could tell he was just a wee bit jealous.

We felt good but a bit foolish. Any dumb motherfucker looking for a safe place to trip would never in a million years have gone to the Giants' Ring in the dead of night during this period. It was the middle of the "tit-for-tat war," which went on for about three years. "If you kill one of ours, we kill one of yours." There were two or three assassinations a day. People were shit-scared. Nobody moved outside their sectors. We just didn't think about the danger of this spot that night. It was remote, not private property, so it was convenient for the paramilitaries' uses. There were no official rules against trespassing, but there were unwritten laws we should have observed.

We went back to the flat and began to come down. The whole thing gave us all a story to tell. It would be interesting to hear what my buddies' stories are today. They're probably all the ones who took charge and did the talking.

I Had a *Theory* Who I Was

A few months later, I moved with some friends into a big, beautiful house out in the country in the County Down, about twelve miles outside Belfast. The parents of a friend were away in Kenya, so they rented the house to me and five of my mates. It had beautiful gardens and fields, a barn, and some sheds. It was 1973 and all of us were on the dole. We just lived simply, having a good time. It was a fantastic year we spent there, one of the nicest of my life.

I'd been corresponding with two friends, Stephanie and Mick, a married couple living in Morecambe in Lancashire, England. They were politicos, he an anarchist and she a radical feminist. They were sharing a house with a girl named Helen, whom Stephanie had decided was my soul mate. She wrote me about Helen and was telling Helen all about me, building up this powerful matchmaking scenario. I was between girlfriends, because Meg, the girl I'd been shacking up with, had left my bed one day for that of Harold, another housemate.

According to Stephanie, Helen was sixteen and a hundred percent hippie, living her own life in her own room in Stephanie's house, working sometimes between Social Security benefits. She was from a broken home and had lived in foster homes in the heart of Lancashire, the birthplace of the Satanic mills. In terms of things I was interested in, she was very advanced for her age. She had a fantastic record collection, for instance, which included the complete Allman Brothers, whom I'd only just heard of.

So I made a trip to England to visit her. I couldn't do anything else. I was dying to see this woman. It had all been set up for months, so our springs were coiled for each other. I took the ferry across to Scotland and then a bus down to Morecambe, a seaside retirement community on the northwest coast of England. There are so many old folks there that it's said that when people die in Morecambe in Lancashire, they don't bury them, they just prop them up in bus shelters.

When Helen and I saw each other, we went boom! and went for it straight off. She was beautiful in a gypsy, ragamuffin sort of way. She didn't know what her origins were, but she could have been half-caste Arab, Turkish, or Greek. She was very small, less than five feet tall, while I'm six-six. We spent the day just buzzing on each other, talking, going out for walks by the seashore all wrapped up for the winter weather. She had short black wavy hair tussled all over the place, a beautiful girl, fantastic fun, great sense of humor.

We went to the nearby town of Lancaster, a university town where we'd arranged to meet Stephanie and Mick at a pub. There was a jukebox there, which was novel for me because few Irish bars had them back then. I played the Temptations' "Papa Was a Rollin' Stone" and "Knockin' on Heaven's Door" by Bob Dylan, both hits at the time. Then Helen asked, "Should I get some acid?" She was more experienced than I was at tripping, though I'd been coming on as fast as I could in recent months. I thought, *Shit, I just met this girl and she's ready for anything.*

"Yeah, great," I told her. She went off and came back with this blotter acid, which we decided to take the following day. In the evening, we went back to the house in Morecambe and slept together but didn't have sex. We were just into each other in a nice way. The next morning, I went out and brought coffee back to her room. We dropped the acid first thing: breakfast.

She'd been told that this acid wasn't strong, but she was misinformed. It was far and away the strongest acid I'd ever taken or have taken since. But that was okay, because she was so nice and I felt comfortable with her. She had a superior sound system and a record collection that extended half a wall. I still couldn't get over her being only sixteen. She was dipping into her albums and playing this fantastic music. She had a real far-out pad that she'd done herself. The walls were a washed red and the doors, skirting boards, and window frames were painted bright green.

There wasn't a lót to do in town, being wintertime. We had a little fire going, but it wasn't hot enough to heat the room. So we spent the morning in bed, our heads back on the pillows, touching and talking. Most of the morning was just her face in front of me, this gorgeous, impish face laughing and telling me things. We were tripping very heavily and hallucinating. As I looked into her beautiful, dark brown eyes, the streaks in her irises divided them into orangelike segments, each of which took on a different color of the spectrum. This rainbow pattern was drifting off into infinity like a psychedelic light-show image broken up into dissolving fragments, or the special graphics in a televised sporting match, when a freeze-frame shatters into bits that trail off the screen. There was a sparkling effect over everything, like "Lucy in the Sky with Diamonds." All that was in my frame of vision was a pair of ravishing female eyes and psychedelic color—you know, "the girl with kaleidoscope eyes."

After a couple of hours of this wonderful communion and visual entertainment, I started to doubt. I didn't know who I was. I had a *theory* that I lived in the countryside outside Belfast and that I was called Robert and that I had come over the previous day on a boat and then a bus to England, where I'd never been before, and had met this incredible woman. And that's where it all started to fall apart. I discounted this theory. *This is bullshit. These things don't happen.*

I went back to having fun. Then I started wondering, *Who am I?*

What is real? What is going on? I went over my theory again and it just didn't fit. It wasn't convincing. The whole situation and this girl were too good to be true. I looked around the room and it was doing all sorts of things, changing shape, size, and color. Paintings were becoming windows. I was seeing things that weren't there.

In a deep existential sense, I couldn't reconcile myself to what was happening. I couldn't make the match. And this really freaked me. I was covering it up on the surface, so Helen wasn't aware of my inner turmoil, but inside I was falling apart. I realized how fragile sanity was, like a layer of thin ice over a seething sea of passions and appetites. The manner in which perception is aligned plays a big role. A few degrees off can make all the difference. I always had a fair sense of what I deserved, but she was almost *too* special. On some level, it was kind of a shock that it was all set up that we were soul mates from the get-go. She was totally into me immediately, and I was totally into her. And here we were tripping out of our heads.

I started to freak out. I was a-feared of blowing the situation and freaking her out too. I thought, *Shit, we haven't even made love yet.* That was promising to be something. I didn't have to engineer getting into sex, because that appeared to be a matter of course. It looked like we were going into a real relationship. I felt we'd invested something already. I just couldn't believe the situation. I literally didn't believe it. I thought, *Maybe I'm lying in a straitjacket somewhere.* At that point, my entire history was not enough for me to know who I was. I had only a theory as to what had happened and who I was, and that hadn't won me over yet.

She was still cheerful, but our conversation had slowed down. Then I started to doubt her and to fear her. I didn't recognize anything in the room. There was nothing of mine but the clothes I was wearing under the blankets for the cold. Everything else was Helen's, so I was in the heart of her universe. She was the most active part of an environment that I did not recognize, did not know, and did not trust.

The hallucinations started to go bad. As the rock from which I viewed the world got shaky underfoot, so went the world I viewed. Her room, which had looked so fresh and original, now started to look horrible and cheap. In the same way that acid had focused my sights on the beautiful, it now trained my vision into the dark and dusty corners. The smudge on the wall and the dirt under the table started to grow in three dimensions.

I went into a bit of a panic. I didn't know what to do. According to my theory, we were in a house where my good friend Stephanie lived. In theory, she was in her room up the stairs and around the corridor. If I could get up and go see her, it would prove I was who I thought I was. But I hadn't the balls to do it. I was scared shitless to open the door. I was scared of Stephanie not being there and my theory being wrong. What little environment I knew, though it was shitty by now, was this room. If I opened the door, there might be a black hole. Maybe there was nothing there. Maybe I was in a mental hospital.

What I'd do today is say, "Look Helen, no harm to you, but I'm getting a bit freaked out, here. It's all a bit too much for me. Would you mind opening that door to the big black void out there and go get Stephanie and bring her here so we can have a wee talk, maybe for five minutes, and then you and I can resume." I couldn't do that then for fear of breaking the spell between us.

Suddenly, right in the midst of this downward spiral into the netherworld, this guy came into the room. He stood at the base of the bed, badgering Helen, "Are you coming or not?" I figured he was maybe a boyfriend. If he wasn't, he sure wanted to be. He definitely had a proprietary feeling toward her and a corresponding antagonism toward me. He was pissed. She'd made an arrangement to drive with him to some other town, and now she was breaking it. There he was breathing our air, leering over us from the end of the bed we were nestled in, giving her shit. "Well, I'm not going. I'm staying here," she returned. After this unpleasant exchange, he left in a fume of annoyance, slamming the door behind him.

This had really rocked the boat. By this point, I was upset. I started to plummet and felt a fluttering in my chest and throat like I was about to start gibbering and jabbering. I'd lost it. I thought, *Here we go. Bad trip all the way. Where's the vitamin C? Call the hospital.* It was sour enough before the guy came in, but that just knocked it over.

But the miracle was that he hadn't closed the door when he slammed it. It hadn't clicked shut. Beany, Stephanie's dog, came wagging in, a black crossbred Labrador mongrel I'd known since she was a pup in the days Stephanie and I had shared a house. Beany had come shuffling along the corridor, nudged the door open with her nose, and just trotted into the room.

That was all I needed. I was ecstatic. "Beany! Beany! Come over here, come on! Wow, how are you? We're having a great time. This is Helen. Oh, you *know* Helen. . . ." I was back. *It's all right. I'm okay. My theory's right!* The dog absolutely saved me, pulled me right back from the brink. She was the link I needed.

I was still a bit vexed with the room, so this gave me the opportunity to say, "Hey, why don't we take Beany for a walk?" She said, "Yeah, let's go to the Point," a spit of sand jutting out from the shore. So we went upstairs to see Stephanie. She was happy as Larry because she'd been matchmaking us for months and here we were gaga over each other. "Oh yeah," she said, "you kids run along and have a good time and take Beany."

The Point was like Wuthering Heights, with a beautiful sea crashing, a big sky with scuttling clouds, wind blowing our hair. We went back to the house and made love, fantastic fun. Three days later she upped sticks and came back with me to Ireland. We lived together for a year in the big country house in County Down.

Now, if this guy hadn't come in and destabilized the situation entirely, the door wouldn't have been left open and Beany wouldn't have come in. God knows what would have happened then. I could've ended up sputtering and crying and Helen would have had to go and get Stephanie. . . . I might have been a total mess.

The events of this episode were life-changing as far as my history is concerned. It launched this relationship, then nearly dashed it to bits as I almost freaked out. Beany's coming in the slammed-but-not-shut door was a tiny little flicker of fate that made the difference. Helen and I may not have started a full-fledged relationship if I'd ended up thrashing around on the floor yelling that she was a dragon monster or a witch, which she was starting to turn into. Everything that was hers was already looking bad. She was next.

Robert Charles Wilson

B. 1953

Author of science fiction: The Perseids and Other Stories; Bios; Darwinia *(winner, 1999 Aurora Award for Best English-language Canadian Science Fiction);* Mysterium *(winner, 1995 Philip K. Dick Award);* The Harvest; A Bridge of Years; The Divide; Gypsies; Memory Wire; *and* A Hidden Place

Resides in Toronto

Born in Whittier, California; moved to Canada at age nine

THE IMMIGRANT'S LANDING

My second LSD experience, in 1984 when I was thirty-one, was truly useful for overcoming a severe writer's block. At the time, I was having tremendous difficulty finishing anything or being proud of what I did finish. I'd had one short story published four years earlier, and hadn't been able to come up with anything salable since. I was doing the usual struggling-writer thing, working a lot of clerical jobs. It was starting to bother me. I knew there was something askew I had to fix before I could comfortably define myself as a writer.

I'd come to my first acid experience, a few months prior, with a rationalist defense shield. I was not open to what you'd call the spiritual side of myself. There were kaleidoscopic visual effects and distortions of time and space, but the real revelation was a hint of something more profound, the feeling that there were depths that would be difficult and scary yet ultimately rewarding to explore. It was a sensory playground with an overtone of sanity fraying at the edges, a glimpse of what it must be like for those who'd actually lost the ability to get back into the waking world. That was somewhat intimidating for someone who protected himself from doubt and ambiguity with a strict empiricism and disdain for religion.

But I was also enormously intrigued. For a guy who aspired to writing science fiction and fantasy, here was a challenge to either put up or shut up. *If you really want to know what it's like to be in another dimension, well, here's your chance. You can stick your head right in there with the help of this little tab of acid.* I could hardly turn down the dare.

I wondered how I could put the expansiveness and profundity of acid to work for me, so I read an article by Oscar Janiger, and Peter Stafford's book *LSD: The Problem Solving Psychedelic,* which described the drug's role in overcoming emotional problems, and barriers to creativity such as writer's block.

To cinch the deal, I got a generous invitation from some close friends, Lawrence and Margeux, who had access to what they considered pure material. They lived in a comfortable apartment in the leafy North York section of Toronto, with a beautiful view of a park. They encouraged me to come over and undergo an LSD session under their guidance, assuring me, "Don't worry. We'll be with you. If anything goes wrong, we'll take care of it." How could I decline?

I showed up at their apartment early one morning late in the summer. I'd come resolved to take a high dose and to actively work on my writer's block. The three of us took the acid, then ate a modest breakfast. The experience began to evolve as we listened to Jade Warrior, Tangerine Dream, and other Seventies electronica, much of it punctuated by nature sounds. The first thing I noticed was that the music was synesthetic, with tactile qualities, weight, volume, and position, especially when my eyes were closed. The music surrounded me, and its narrative was manifested visually.

Deciding that I was fully under the influence, I concentrated on my writing difficulties, and in a short while, an insight came to me: that I'd been focusing almost entirely on being a "writer," on how my work would reflect upon me, whether it would be seen as the product of a professional or the vainglorious rubbish of an amateur. I realized that this self-consciousness was crippling, that the real question was not how others perceived my writing, but my relationship with the writing process itself and the characters I'd created.

An image of the old RKO logotype flashed into view. RKO movies used to open up with their signature rotating globe with a radio tower standing on it radiating signals like lightning bolts. A dictum entered my head: "Be the signal, not the antenna." Superficial as that may sound, it was exactly the advice I needed. *Stop trying to be a "writer." Immerse yourself in the story itself. Remove yourself from the equation and concentrate on what your characters want to do and say.*

I stored the symbol away, and the trip opened up into an experience of oceanic bliss. The whole architecture of rationalism that I'd built up to defend myself against the threat of a scary external world was completely shattered. As a shy young man, uncertain about himself, I realized that I'd constructed an armor of words which I now felt was cracking apart and falling away.

Then my verbal ability left me entirely. I lost the facility to string sentences together word by word. The procession of words that constituted my waking existence simply drifted off, and, amazingly, it was okay, because I was conscious of a nugget of an inarticulate but mindful self that remained. I should have been terrified, because I defined myself by the verbal chains I produce, link by link, nearly every second of the day. But I was exhilarated and immensely gratified to shed this defensive shell. It was liberating. The armor wasn't "me." There was still a "me" left when all the words were gone.

One hears much about the dissolution of the ego on psychedelics, but this was more like the *discovery* of the ego. The small kernel of self that survived the meltdown was actually much deeper than the wordsmith persona on which I'd prided myself. Before I even learned how to speak, this core had existed, and it persisted now after the apparent loss of that ability. I was content to be that nucleus of personality and to be overwhelmed with the visual imagery that was now erupting behind my closed eyelids.

I resolved to go deeper into myself through the music. I entered an expanding tunnel of constantly evolving faces and shapes which had an underwater quality, like writhing sea anemones and chains of beautiful luminous fish and other forms of ocean life, layer after layer unfolding as I flew through a vast passageway. This gave way to a more ordered and coherent vision of a sort quite unlike the fractal, mosaic type of visuals I've experienced every other time I've tripped. I started to "fly" over a series of majestic, enormously tall snowcapped mountains, one after another. I was reminded of this vista when I flew over the Kluane Glacier in the Yukon recently. The sheer size and scope and endlessness of this landscape gave it a hyperreal quality, like a lucid dream.

I felt utterly free, though I was not motivating the journey, flying the way you'd imagine Superman would jet and steer himself through the air to get somewhere. I was simply floating, but at great speed, over this spectacular landscape, until I came to a cloud-filled valley where there stood four stone totems, hundreds of feet tall, crowned by eagle heads studded with ruby eyes. The totems were arranged in a diamond pattern with their beaks pointed in to converge in the center. At the point of contact, a colossal electrical discharge crackled out.

The intersection of eagle beaks seemed to be where opposites met—light and dark, life and death, good and evil—where all consistently opposing forces came together in a tremendous pulse of energy. Following the great relief of grasping an insight into the wellspring of my creativity, this ultra-vivid dream was the apex of the experience. Although I felt blessed by this vision, it is difficult for me to catalog, as I don't have a context for it. I've never identified with eagles. I'm not a naturalist. I very seldom go hiking in the wilderness. Nonetheless, the vision had intense emotional resonance, and I think of it often.

When I emerged from this trancelike moment, I told Lawrence and Margeux that I was blissful and that I hoped I didn't embarrass myself by weeping in gratitude. I was on the verge of tears, but held them in. The trip then loped back into the usual sensory distortions. It had been an extremely long and eventful morning and afternoon.

There were moments of doubt, of course. I spent a long time looking in a mirror, trying to sort out what this simian-looking creature could be. My reflection wasn't distorted, but I was seeing it the way you might look at a human being if you'd never seen one before and didn't know quite how to interpret its gestures. We've developed an ability to read a great deal of information from faces and interpret their subtlest expressions, but during this part of the trip I lost that facility. *Here's an interesting primate,* I thought. *I wonder what it's thinking.* My curiousity was piqued, as though I were seeing myself anew, but this was also intimidating, as it conjured the question *How do I appear to other people?,* which recalled the self-consciousness I'd jettisoned so briefly and blissfully.

It started to drizzle as we began to come down in the early evening. We went to the park and set off some fireworks in the rain, which was quite magical. I was still seeing church windows in the grass, stained-glass mosaics in every surface. We ran around in the dark with sparklers, as the trip descended lightly from profundity to fun.

Applying the lesson of the trip was the hard part. I learned to sit down at the word processor and set my self aside in a strange mental dodge, to put aside wondering how an editor or reader might look at what I produced, and simply tell the story. It's hard to put into words just how this is done, because it's not a verbal act. It's a tweak of attitude, a retraining of focus as is done by chanting a mantra. I felt as though the inspiration had been given to me, though not by an external entity.

A few months after the trip, I suddenly found that I could finish stories, and when I mailed them off to editors, some of them proved quite salable. As corny as it may seem, the RKO radio tower emblem has been a totem for me. Whenever I come up against a problem in my work, it's been extraordinarily useful to stop what I'm doing and remind myself to cease being the antenna and to be the signal. There's nothing I've written since for which I haven't recalled this quaint icon of the radio tower on the spinning Earth.

My work has been described as "humanistic science fiction." Most of it takes place in a contemporary setting and is less about alien civilizations than about the intrusion of the alien or the unexpected in contemporary life. (I'm actually a "resident alien" myself. My family moved to Canada in the mid-Sixties. With the Vietnam War going, it didn't seem especially wise to head back "home," so I stayed and fell in love with Canada and the city of Toronto, while maintaining my American citizenship.) My first novel is set in a small midwestern town during the Depression. The townspeople come to realize that someone among them is not altogether human, and the question of what defines our humanity and how we extend that to other people and expect, in turn, to be recognized and understood by it, are recurrent themes in my work.

Psychedelics have played naturally into such themes by wiping away preconceptions about reality so I can approach the settings and characters of my stories from new angles. Many of these preconceptions were lashed into my self-image, so it required an agent as powerful as LSD to extricate myself from them. But I don't get the idea for a book from taking a dose of any drug. Above all else, the psychedelic experience is a way to stand apart from yourself in a way you ordinarily cannot, which is very valuable, though not a precondition, for writing science fiction.

This is not to say that tripping is a facile and predictable means of accessing useful new vistas. By the late 1980s I'd gotten cocky with psychedelics and found out, during a terrifying psilocybin trip, that they'll roundly remind you if you forget to treat them with respect. Alone in my house at Christmastime, I swallowed a big bunch of mushrooms that I didn't bother to weigh, figuring there was no such thing as too much. It started as a mirror experience of the big acid trip. My verbal ability and sense of order fell away, but this time, it didn't leave me the glowing ember of true self that the acid had.

It was pleasant enough at first. I stared out the window at the snow and the trees, which seemed like an infinite cathedral of ice and pine needles. At that very moment, a squirrel leapt up onto the window screen, three inches from my face. Here was this hideous, scrawny little animal peering into my eyes, clinging with its claws to the screen. I'm sure it was as startled as I was, but it seemed like the most horrid omen you could imagine. I was plunged into a very dark place where I felt as helpless as I'd ever felt before. Everything seemed intensely ugly.

A terrible doomsday gloom came over me. I pondered the nuclear standoff between the United States and the Soviet Union, and the whole thing seemed so dangerous and insane that you couldn't begin to explain to an objective planetary observer why we'd set up such a nightmarish system. I began to despair, and the sensory distortions became so intense that I could no longer interpret the external world with any reliability.

I walked through the house looking for something familiar to reassure myself, but every room I peered into was filled with menacing shadows. I looked at my digital watch, trying to figure out how much longer the experience would last, and was dismayed to see that the numbers didn't resolve. The two would turn into a four, the eight into a nine. I couldn't make them relate to one another. I couldn't decide which digits designated the hour, minute, and second.

I called up a friend, but then couldn't articulate what the problem was, so I hung up the phone. I turned on the TV to distract myself, but couldn't make sense of anything coming out of it. There was a small girl in a shop and a strange celestial light pouring down onto her, which then began to flood into the room. Voices were utterly incomprehensible. I lost the ability to interpret spoken language. I could hear individual sounds, but they made absolutely no sense whatsoever. It was horrifically frightening.

I tried to imagine how I'd describe the hell I was going through to my friends, which seemed reassuring. *This is bad, but if I can at least tell people about it, it will make an interesting story.* I discovered that so much of myself was simply how I presented myself to others, that I had a thousand façades and false fronts, a thousand verbal defenses, and a thousand ways to interact with people to convince them I was a nice guy or whatever affectation was expedient for me. All of these guises seemed hollow, false, and arbitrary—nothing to do with a living person. Without these distractions, I was nothing but a shriveled, fearful homunculus. This was the shadow side of the armor-shedding experience. I simply couldn't locate the gist of primordial self that had been so reassuring on the pivotal acid trip. I curled into a fetal ball for a few hours and waited for the pandemonium to pass.

For months afterward I got the chills whenever I thought about this harrowing diversion. I seriously considered never taking a psychedelic again. I gradually came to see this episode as a chastening exercise that taught me to respect the power of these substances. As such, it wasn't entirely negative, but a learning experience. I slowly rediscovered the utility of psychedelics, and have since approached them more cautiously.

The potential value of the psychedelic experience is worth risking a repeat of that worst trip. No trip since has been as good as the breakthrough on acid or as bad as the mushroom debacle, but there's always something valuable I take with me when it's over.

Ruth

B. 1956

Preschool director and teacher

Resides in Portland, Oregon

Born and raised in a small town in northeast Illinois

The Apostate's Homecoming

In 1983 I was coming through Boulder, Colorado, and went to a seminar at the Naropa Institute commemorating the twenty-fifth anniversary of the publication of Jack Kerouac's *On the Road.* A number of literary figures were talking about what it was like back in the Beat/psychedelic era of the Fifties and Sixties. A student stepped up and addressed the panel: "Tell me, weren't drugs, particularly hallucinogens, a big part of what you were doing?" And one of them responded, "Well, drugs were a part of it, but only a small one. Those days were mostly about achieving altered states through meditation."

Diane DiPrima, the Beat poet from San Francisco, then stomped up to the stage and took umbrage. "Now, wait a minute. I think that everybody should know that drugs *were* an important part of our experience. To deny that just because it's the Reagan age of 'just say no' is crazy. We were changing consciousness back then and a lot of what we were doing through psychedelics was very positive."

Now that I have kids of my own, age fifteen seems so young to start using psychedelics. Yet, when I look back on my own life, it felt like the perfect time for me to be doing them, because it was a time of questioning reality and pushing the boundaries of my mind. So for me, the psychedelic period was the formative years of high school and college.

I had strict parents who didn't allow me to go out and party much, so I did a fair amount of tripping while in class and study hall during my high school years in Woodstock, Illinois. I'd take a hit of acid in the morning and start getting off in class. Sometimes that worked better than others. Once I had to leave math to go to the nurse's office. I'd taken a hit, not felt much, then took another. The classroom was breathing and things were coming out of the ceiling and swarming around me. I could barely see my own feet.

I excused myself and went to the nurse and told her I didn't feel well and needed to go home. Behind her was a poster of a surfer girl saying, "I don't smoke cigarettes," who suddenly flew out of the poster and surfed around the room. The nurse noticed my eyes wandering around, and asked, "What's going on here? Are you okay? Are you seeing something?" I had to struggle to remind myself that I looked odd peering around like that. Finally she sent me home.

Leaving the stress of the school environment for home, I began to feel anxious about leaping from the pan into the fire. As I walked, I was thinking, *Oh gosh, my mother's going to be very unhappy about this. Act straight!* At that time in my life I didn't think of home as a refuge but as a place where my parents and I fought with each other, a place I wanted to get away from. All that disappeared the moment I walked in. Seeing my mother there was a marvelous feeling I hadn't expected. *Oh, it's my mother!* It changed our relationship.

I could see her aura. There was a yellow, pink, and white light over her head. Everything melted. The walls were almost liquid, the colors swimmingly vibrant. I had the strong sense that the house was a warm, peaceful, wonderful world. On the deeper level, beneath all the teenage squabble, I could see it was a truly comfortable place. Not that it was always peaceful between my parents and me after that, but there was now this heart connection, and that stayed with me.

My acid-using group of friends and I would try to do it in super-controlled circumstances, planning everything. All right, we've got eight hours when parents are out and nobody's going to be home." Though we didn't acknowledge it out loud, we were watching the windows so that nobody jumped out. We'd heard enough stories to fear that someone might flip out and take a leap. But I never had any bad experiences on psychedelics, and I think a big part of that was who I was at the time. I felt comfortable with myself.

One teenage afternoon, my sense of color was profoundly altered at City Park. I'd brought two hits of Windowpane and took one, putting it under my tongue. I waited about an hour and nothing happened, then thought, *Maybe it got lost.* It was very tiny, the size of a pinhead, and transparent, so it was really easy to lose. So I took out the second hit and put it in my eye. In about five minutes the whole world was swirling. The grass grew up high in a thousand shades of green. I saw colors that I'd never experienced before. I couldn't budge for three hours.

A friend said, "All right, you have to go home now," and I said, "Nope, I can't move." I felt that there were more colors in the world than anyone could possibly catalog and that I was discovering a number of them right then and there. The trees were growing faces, dancing and singing. It felt like a Disney movie, an entire cartoon universe. I concluded that all the animation artists must have used LSD to produce such voluptuous and chromatically alive images.

Years later, after I started transcendental meditation, I suddenly realized I could conjure the same sort of extended color range again. I did a visualization workshop with Diane DiPrima, who's also a magic practitioner. We did a whole weekend called "going to level" (a technique she picked up from the Diggers, who appropriated it from Silva Mind Control, which corporations were using to boost performance and sales). She talked us through various visioning scenarios through which we'd find our temple and spirit guide. In the process, I felt as if I'd accessed the same color palette in my brain that LSD had unfurled. All these amazing things I couldn't control would happen internally. I realized that the acid I'd taken as a teenager had merely unleashed a function of the mind I could also access by other means.

But then, there's nothing like the ripeness for experience of adolescence. On the night of the homecoming dance, when I was fifteen, I took some Mellow Yellow acid with my date Stan and a couple of friends. We did it around eight, didn't get off until ten-thirty, and I had to be home by midnight. So we left the dance and walked around outside. It was dark out, so any little bit of light really shone amazingly, the whole color spectrum in rainbows and prisms.

When I got home, Stan warned me, "Now, you're going to be tripping on your own tonight. These are the things you shouldn't do. Number one: Don't look in a mirror. That's the surest way to a bad trip. Don't freak out, now. I'll call you later." I went in the house, and the first thing I did was get out the mirror and look into it. I saw myself change into an old man, then a very young girl, a very old Chinese man, then myself as an old woman with wrinkles and white hair. I was amazed that all these different people were inside of me and how easy it was to transform. Later I thought I'd seen images of how I looked in past lives.

The last face I saw in the mirror was myself as God. *You are God, the most enlightened being.* There was a bright circle of rainbow light around my head, no doubt a Christian allusion from being raised Catholic. And there was a feeling of knowing everything there is to know. I felt in complete comfort with myself and who I was. I tried to capture the experience in writing the next day and showed the results to a guy I knew. He said, "Oh yeah, isn't that great? The drugs made you think you were God." It didn't translate very well, I suppose.

One night around eleven o'clock, when I was sixteen, I was tripping and decided to go into the church where I'd been baptized and received my first Holy Communion. I'd stopped going to Catholic school after eighth grade, and didn't go to church anymore except on big occasions when the whole family got all dressed up. But even then I felt hypocritical. I didn't believe that church was the place where God really lived. I'd begun to rebel against the "Mother Church," which I thought was the most tyrannical thing there was. Among other offenses, the way the Pope and the Vatican hierarchy treat women set me against Catholicism.

The place was dark, and no one else was in there. Suddenly I felt the presence of a strong energy field, as though I were at the center of a vortex of sacred energy with the whispering of ancient voices all around me. When I saw Wim Wenders's *Wings of Desire* years later, the scenes of the angel eavesdropping on the inner thoughts of the mortals reminded me of the voices I heard in the church. I couldn't make out what they were saying, but it was very earnest, animated, and holy-hushed. The air around me was moving. It was like I was swimming through water.

I felt I'd tapped into this energy there before, accessed a deeper level of the place, where all the spirits that are hanging around came alive. I recalled standing in the pews as a child when it was very hot, feeling like I was going to pass out, and seeing things out of the corner of my eye. Now again I was experiencing a similar peripheral visual phenomenon.

When I focused on the stained-glass windows depicting the saints and scenes from the Stations of the Cross, I felt an enormous amount of light and love and a profound sense of well-being pouring down from the windows into me. The church felt like a really warm, wonderful, safe place to be. It was as though I'd disinterred a spirit in the church that had long been lost. My view of the Church in general changed. Suddenly my grievances didn't seem so important to me, and I felt perhaps what the little old lady in the front row saying her rosary might have felt.

Gosh, this is a truly spiritual place, I realized, *a place to connect.* I felt as if something new were coming to me, like I was having a religious experience. From then on I was able to ignore the politics and just connect with the spirit that had given hope and comfort to so many people.

My newfound faith in religion led me to some strange places. Soon after this, I joined a small offshoot of the Catholic Church called the Pentecostal Movement, which had meetings where people would speak in tongues. The third time I went, I started spouting another language—purportedly West African, according to one of the members. But I was very distrustful of this. It was like some strange force had come over me. Perhaps the fear arose from the rather Catholic worry about the *Exorcist* syndrome, being possessed. I grew increasingly uncomfortable and backed off. The Pentecostals put me off even further because they really expected us to give up drugs, even pot. At that time, psychedelic drugs were tied up with who I was, so I left.

One of my last psychedelic forays was on MDA with my future husband, Francis. We took some at a party in Albuquerque, when we were in college there. After a while we looked around and couples were lying together, taking their clothes off and hugging and kissing.

There were people whom I didn't feel particularly close to and didn't even like, but all of their beauty and virtue was somehow shining through on this MDA. I kept turning to Francis and saying, "Aren't they wonderful? Did you ever know they were so wonderful?" I felt like I loved everybody.

We decided to leave and go back to my house. We were making love and I kept seeing lots of faces. Right in the middle of it, I jumped and looked up and said, "Oh, my gosh, we can't do this here. Look at all the people." Francis was surprised, and leaned up to look around. "There aren't any people here." It was a little freaky.

I eventually quit using psychedelics, because I felt much more anxiety as I got older and took on responsibilities, and grew less trusting of letting my mind go.

Sarah

B. 1946

Political science abstractor and indexer; recently resigned from the science and technology department of a library; tapestry weaver

Resides in Pittsburgh

Born and raised in Pittsburgh

Our Lady of the Eastern Star

At the height of my very first acid trip, back in 1975, I was visited by a bizarre specter in the guise of a strange neighbor. It was as though the whole thing had been programmed for my benefit: *Okay, you want to try this; we're going to make sure that you have a memorable time.*

I was nearly thirty and all of my friends had done acid, but I'd held back. Finally they convinced me it was time. "Once you've done it," they said, "you'll never see things exactly the same way again. It will alter your perceptions of things, even after the trip itself is long past." I was eager to experience an alternative consciousness, and finally did it, with my boyfriend Daniel, my future husband, a veteran of many acid trips.

We dropped the acid at 3:30 on a September Saturday afternoon. We were sitting in our apartment in the Squirrel Hill neighborhood of Pittsburgh, where there's a large population of Orthodox Jews, many of whom were followers of the late Rabbi Menachem Schneerson, a man believed by some to have been the messiah to come. I'd just recently returned from three years in Israel, and my language channels were crossed. I'd start a sentence in English, and it would end up in Hebrew. The amalgam had become one language in my mind. At one point I was even trying to convince Daniel it was a real dialect.

Daniel got out two little brown blots on paper, and we each chewed one up and swallowed it. The dining room table was laid out with pads of textured art paper, crayons, Rapidographs, and colored pencils. I was nervous. My fingers were cold, my stomach a little queasy, my lips numb as if with novocaine. It was such an unknown I was embarking upon. Though I trusted Daniel completely, who knew what could happen?

About an hour later the world began to shift and indescribable changes came swirling over me. The lumpy texture of the walls and ceiling appeared like bubbling white lava. Pictures seemed to advance and recede. The skin on Daniel's face took on greater detail, with every pore exaggerated, as though veils were passing across it rhythmically—from ultra-sharp to blurred to ultra-sharp again. Music became indistinguishable from color.

On the drawing paper, I'd become fixated on Hebrew lettering, which came off of my crayon flowing, wild, and interwoven. We were listening to (and seeing) a lot of great music, including Brian Eno, Kraftwerk's *Autobahn,* which was new at the time, electronic music by the German composer Klaus Schultze, the Beatles' *Magical Mystery Tour,* and a wonderful new Ravi Shankar record. I felt so *right,* peaking, flying, and flashing, when suddenly—a knock at the door.

It was startling. I thought, *Oh my God, who would be coming to see me at this moment?* We had a friend who showed up at bad moments and were convinced it was him. Our first impulse was not to answer it, but we had the music on real loud, and whoever was there knew we were in. Daniel opened the door, and there in the hallway stood a woman unlike any human being I have ever seen. Had her arrival been prearranged by someone wishing to freak me out deliberately, the presentation could not have been more affecting. She was an apparition whose corporeal existence I could not even be sure of.

She was very tall, with an old, heavily made up face out of Fellini's *Satyricon,* with powder, rouge, lipstick, false lashes, and eyeliner slightly out of synch with her deeply grooved wrinkles—all of which combined to form a ludicrous mask. Her head was crowned by a pile of wildly curled, false black hair at least six inches high. She wore garish earrings, and sequins and spangles everywhere ascatter upon a theatrical, floor-length gown of screaming red. *Is this possible? What does she want?* Due to my altered perceptions, the lines of her makeup were drifting off the lines of her skin.

She'd come because she'd just painted her fingernails (also shrieking red), and she wanted somebody to zip up the back of her dress. Apparently she lived across the hall, but I'd never seen her before. She was dressing up for a banquet by the Eastern Star, the women's auxiliary to the Masons, which has all kinds of secret ceremonies, and places a great deal of importance on ritual. "Oh great. The Eastern Star," I replied. It somehow fit into my cosmology at the moment.

According to Daniel, I spoke some blend of English and Hebrew to her (I thought I was speaking straight English), and she just smiled at me. Apparently, the words, tone, or spirit of what I uttered to her set her totally at ease and opened up all kinds of possibilities for her. Either that, or she was so intent on getting zipped up, she didn't care who was doing it or what language they spoke. She was happy. With the movement of her smile, her lipstick seemed to be spreading all over her face. She waved her long red talons around, leaving ornate traces in the air. Everything on her was shining and sparkling.

I wasn't wearing anything but panties and a flannel shirt, but that didn't faze her. She was taking the whole thing completely straight, speaking to me as if everything were completely routine and normal, not realizing that she was altering the course of history.

It took Daniel, who was dumbstruck, a while to realize that she didn't want to turn around in mixed company with her dress unzipped. He left the kitchen, leaving her to me. Seeing that my hands were covered with crayon and ink, she registered her disapproval and signaled me to "Please wash your hands" with an unforgettable wrinkling of her caked-on mask, and a squeamish wiggling of her manicured fingers, while traces of her nails, fragrant, fierce, and overpoweringly *red,* wafted off of her. I obliged and went to the kitchen to wash my hands with a damp cloth.

When I came back, she turned around, and I zipped up her dress. She thanked me and walked out the door. After I closed it, I struggled for a handle on what had just transpired. I had to convince myself that she was not a psychedelic hallucination, that this had really happened. Once I assimilated that she was "real," I fell upon the floor and started laughing. It was light out when I began and dark when I finished. The two of us went through spasms going over the ramifications of it all.

Once the door was closed, she no longer existed, but we were convinced that the second we opened it, she'd be there. So we vowed never to open the door again. We wanted to go out, but ruled it out with the logic that *No, she's out there in the hall and she might want something else.*

She was gone from the apartment, but not from our minds—even after we came down from the acid. She'd made an indelible imprint on our lives and altered the entire scheme of human affairs. She blew my mind, like a stone dropped into a well: First there's a loud explosive splash, then ever-widening ripples. I made a whole series of drawings of her, reminiscences in brightly colored chalks, which drifted off the page, fragrantly and laughingly.

She was *it,* the culmination of all events, the meaning and purpose of everything that had occurred before. Everything that had ever happened anywhere had only been leading up to the Coming of the Lady. So I rewrote the story of the world:

10,000 B.C.E..	Iron Age
3,000 B.C.E..	Rise of ancient Greek civilization, Judaism
33 C.E..	Emergence of Jesus and the early Essenes
1000 C.E..	First anticipated end of the world
1066	Normans invade England
1349	Black Plague decimates Europe and Asia

1492	Columbus discovers New World
1520	Suleiman the Magnificent becomes Sultan of the Ottoman Empire
1603	Jamestown settlement
1757	Battle of Plessy
1789	Bastille liberated
1815	Metternich's Vienna Settlement after the Napoleonic Wars
1861	Serfs freed in Russia
1895	Theodore Herzl conceives a Jewish state
1914	Jean Jaures assassinated, World War I starts
1917	Russian Revolution; Raymond Burr and John F. Kennedy born
1929	Great Depression begins
1933	FDR's New Deal launched
1939	World War II begins
1948	Israel's Independence declared
1957	*Sputnik*
1963	Kennedy assassinated
1974	Watergate
September 13, 1975	Visitation of the Lady

I never saw her again, though Daniel did once as he passed her on the stairs, he going down, she going up. "How's your sweetie?" she asked.

Stephen Kessler

B. 1947

Translator:* Save Twilight: Selected Poems of Julio Cortazar; *poet, journalist, literary critic, writer of fiction and essays, editor

Schooled at Beverly Hills High School; University of California, Los Angeles; Bard College; University of California, Santa Cruz

Resides in northern California

Born in Los Angeles, raised in Beverly Hills, California

The story below, edited from an interview transcript with the help of the narrator, is based on true-life experiences that he has described in fictional form in a novel, as yet unpublished.

The Initiate

In 1969 I was a twenty-two-year-old graduate student in literature at the University of California, Santa Cruz. Like many Americans coming of age at the time, I felt the drama in the surrounding social reality, which was somewhat overwhelming in its tumultuousness. As everyone knows, there was a lot of public violence and social disruption in those days, the King and Kennedy assassinations, the Manson murders, the police riot around People's Park in Berkeley. The defining event of the time was the Vietnam War, an ongoing nightmare that infected everything. I was exempt from the draft, but it was still a horrifying presence. I knew some guys from high school who'd gone to the war. I had a good friend, an army medic, who'd left me a footlocker full of pharmaceuticals in the event that something happened to him. He didn't come back.

There was a lot of stress in the air. I dealt with it partly by using marijuana regularly and psychedelics occasionally. Psychedelics were a way to test one's systems, to blow out the cobwebs and experience a psychic catharsis that would clarify. Whenever I took LSD or mescaline, many distractions and things that didn't seem quite real would just fall away. How I really felt and what really mattered would become more defined. On psychedelics, there was no hiding from who you were. If you were worried or scared about something, that would be intensified. If you were clear about who you were and where you stood, you'd become all the more so.

I was in a very immature marriage from which I was trying to escape. We'd gotten married for all the wrong reasons. I'd immediately realized it was a big mistake, even though my wife had been my high school sweetheart. We were both insecure and not ready for a mature partnership. I was also chafing against what academia was trying to turn me into, a Ph.D. scholar or literary critic in a narrow theoretical model. I was distraught, feeling pinned in by these institutions of convention.

In the late fall of 1969, there'd been rumors for weeks about the Rolling Stones coming to northern California to give a free concert. It seemed to me that it would be an event that shouldn't be missed, as it promised to be a major gathering of the tribes, a convocation of all who were hip, conscious, and aware. There was a great sense of anticipation and portentousness about the concert. People were tuning into radios and talking to each other to find out if, when, and where the Stones were coming, as though it were the arrival of the millennium or something. For me, the Stones' arrival, like some kind of psycho-historical earthquake, was infused with mythic power. I thought of Yeats's poem "The Second Coming": Surely some revelation was at hand.

Finally, it was announced that they'd play at the Altamont Racetrack on December 6. The night before the concert, I drove out to the site alone in my Volkswagen van. In my pocket I had a large brown tablet of what was purported to be mescaline, which I'd bought from a virtual stranger at a café in Santa Cruz—not someone I knew well, but perhaps someone who knew somebody I knew. I was looking for some sort of psychedelic substance, and at the time there were positive rumors circulating about this type of tab.

On the morning of the one-day event, I dropped the tab and set out to enjoy the concert. Several groups, including Santana and Jefferson Airplane, played ahead of the Stones, who came on as it started to get dark. From where I was, far from the stage, the music sounded very bizarre. The sound waves coming over the hilly terrain were warped, as though they were coming from another dimension. Throughout the day it was clear from the tone of the performers and the interruptions of the music that weird things were going on around the stage, though most of the crowd couldn't see precisely what. There were a couple of hundred thousand of us gathered in a sort of natural amphitheater in a scrubby wilderness.

I'm claustrophobic by nature and didn't want to be in the middle of the huge crowd, so I left the surrogate family of Santa Cruzians I'd adopted and wandered out to the periphery. My high had leveled off to the streaming phase, the bones in my face gently vibrating in the breeze, muscles humming, body light and relaxed but wired for endurance.

I hooked up with a stranger named Norm, who was obviously a little freaked out himself. We befriended each other and spent the rest of the day just trying to keep it together. I hadn't brought any food, and he shared some oranges he had. As the day got cooler and darker, we went around scrounging for materials such as fence slats and scraps of paper to build fires. People wrapped in shawls and blankets would gather to keep warm, and there would be wine bottles, joints, and hash pipes passed around. Under the circumstances, it seemed normal to take a hit of whatever was passed to you. I have no idea what I really ingested that day. The wine could have been spiked with drugs. It was all part of the communal experience.

We ignited, tended, and abandoned a series of small fires throughout the evening. Around us wandered the lost and the spaced—refugees from the prevailing mood of turmoil. Their faces looked to me disfigured by the ravages of acid—warped visages their mothers wouldn't recognize, foreheads melting in waves of psychic distress, eyes oozing impure anguish, mouths losing their shape, cheekbones drooping like wax.

There was a sense of menace in the air. It seemed like something terrible might happen at any time. Amid the atmosphere of general distress, I was afraid of some kind of assassination or crucifixion. (I found out the next day that there were three deaths at the concert. One guy who was rushing the stage with a gun, apparently to shoot Mick Jagger, was stabbed by a Hell's Angel; someone was run over by a car, and somebody else died somehow. I heard there were a couple of births too.) It was a strange and spooky affair, but Norm and I made it through. Maintaining my equilibrium to keep myself from being freaked out in this mayhem, and finding a companion with whom to nurse each other through this difficult day, were very exhilarating.

I was still high the next morning. When the engine of my VW bus blew out on the way back to the Bay Area en route to my cabin in the Santa Cruz Mountains, it hardly fazed me. I got a tow to Livermore, the nearest town, and left it there. It was a Sunday and nothing was open, so I hitchhiked the rest of the way home.

And I continued to trip. In fact, Altamont would be the point of departure for a trip that really lasted about six months. It wasn't clear where the psychedelic experience ended and where my organically addled condition began. Whatever the precise inspiration, I was certain that the Rolling Stones' arrival had signaled the revolution of consciousness that we were all waiting for. It was my belief that the concert was the launch of an occult guerrilla offensive whereby the consciousness of the society would be transformed into that of a peace- and beauty-extolling tribe of angelic beings. I suspected that everybody was tripping, not just the people who went to Altamont. There were rumors that the Yippies were putting LSD in the reservoirs. I couldn't tell whether the way I felt was the result of drugs or the dawning of a new reality that I was an integral part of.

On campus the following day, I was still sailing on a psychedelic high, which confirmed for me that there was indeed acid in the drinking water and that the time was at hand to fulfill the angelic mission: It was up to people like me, i.e., creative, artistic types, to be the vanguard in incorporating the new expanded consciousness into everyday life. We would lead a pacifistic cultural revolution that would make for peace and love happily ever after. You might say this was a very naive fantasy, but at the time it seemed like the only antidote to the horror of the war and to a society that was disintegrating.

Grad school did not seem the most appropriate theater in which to join this transformative movement. I'd already arranged to take a leave of absence the next quarter. Even though the term wasn't quite up, I left campus that afternoon certain that Harold, one of my teachers, had sent me an occult message to meet him in San Francisco.

He'd said only that he was not going to be on campus that day, and I knew he had a home in the city, so I inferred that he'd gone there to cook something up. Earlier he'd asked me to be the TA (teaching assistant) in his improvisational acting course the following quarter, the one I'd arranged to take off, but no matter: I thought he'd asked me because improvisational acting was a key instrument of the revolution. The new society would be created not by violence or political measures, but by existential acts of creative rebellion. Street and guerrilla theater, be-ins, and happenings were breaking down the walls between the arts and politics. In my delusional, ecstatic state, I felt that Harold, who was not so much an academic but a writer, director, and actor, was suggesting that I assist him in the task of transforming the world.

I decided to head to the city to find Harold, who would give me my instructions and clarify my assignment, as I was not at all certain about my precise role in the revolution. I didn't have wheels, because the van was still at the garage in Livermore, so I hitchhiked off campus. I was living in the San Lorenzo Valley north of Santa Cruz. If you go north on Highway 9, you come to Skyline Boulevard, which will take you up to San Francisco. Hitchhiking seemed the heroic way to go, through the mountains and away from the freeways. It was also the more scenic route, though by the time I left, it was getting dark.

I got a couple of rides up to the summit and then didn't get any for a while. I thought I might have to walk the rest of the way to the city. I was living so much in the moment that I didn't foresee that it was going to get cold and dark and I might get stranded in the middle of the mountains. The only things I had on me were a penknife, some matches, a little money, my Frye boots, corduroy jeans, a white turtleneck sweater, and a split cowhide fringe jacket. Eventually I did find a ride going down into the Santa Clara Valley, the other side of the hill from Santa Cruz, and then, through a series of rides, I found my way to the city. It was around ten at night by the time I got to town, some six hours after I'd left home.

I proceeded on foot toward Harold's house. I knew he lived somewhere on Laguna Street. I'd been dropped off the freeway on a stretch of that street in the Fillmore District, a black neighborhood, still quite a few blocks from his house, which was up toward the marina. So here I was, this long-haired hippie strolling up Laguna Street on a Monday night. Ever elevated in mood, I felt as though I were gliding over the sidewalk. Indeed, I was traveling light. I have a slight build, five-eight, 120 pounds or so at the time, and I had barely eaten anything in the last few days. It hadn't occurred to me to call Harold to tell him I was coming. I felt I was receiving signals in the environment, through the people I met and the license plates and street signs I encountered, which were secretly directing my steps.

But here in the Fillmore I didn't notice any beckoning beams or markers to point me to my destination. All these black people were giving me hostile and suspicious looks. As I passed one doorway, a woman standing there said, "Hi, Zodiac," no doubt alluding to the Zodiac Killer, an astrology freak who was murdering people in San Francisco. At the time, his identity and whereabouts were one of the city's great unsolved mysteries. I didn't stop to ask if she was just kidding. My appearance probably prompted the remark. Being little, with long stringy dark hair and a mustache, I looked something like Charlie Manson, who'd just been on the cover of *Life* magazine.

I continued to get unwelcoming glances from the brothers and sisters on the street. It suddenly occurred to me that maybe I shouldn't walk the twenty remaining blocks to Harold's house. So I turned around and walked back down to Fell Street and hitched a ride out to Golden Gate Park, from where I hiked over the hill and into the Mission District, to the home of a close friend named Saul. I considered him a kind of mentor from our psychedelic trips together. I figured that he must know what was going on. It was around eleven at night. I rang the doorbell of what I was certain was Saul's house, and some young Latinos came to the door.

"You've got the wrong place."

I stayed on the porch and knocked again. "Come on. Don't mess with my mind. I know what's going on here." They didn't look like hippies or the sort of people I thought were my allies, but I was confident Saul was in there.

One of the new rules of engagement I thought I was privy to was the power of some people to change their appearance at will, like the shape-shifters of classical mythology. I was convinced that one of the functions of psychedelics was to enable you to change form at will. I was experiencing something akin to a dream in which certain figures have a dual identity or a person is recognizable even when he looks like someone else. I thought that these Latino dudes were friends or agents of the movement in an unhip guise, that they were actually allies, coconspirators, even though they appeared unfamiliar.

I sat down on the doorstep. I was tired of hiking around and didn't know where to go from there. By this point, I hadn't slept or eaten much in a couple of days. I was also getting very fatigued, having walked several miles that evening. I was sure that I was being put through a test, and that if I just persevered, I'd be rewarded in the end, and my friends would welcome me. (In fact, I was only a block away from Saul's residence. The whole evening might have gone much differently if I'd knocked on the right door.)

Somebody must have called the cops, because two officers came and politely escorted me into their cruiser and took me down to Mission Precinct Police Station. From there I was taken in a paddy wagon with a really fucked-up older man who did not seem to possess the sentience of a visionary for the new age. I was perplexed as to why I was being paired up with this drunk. We were taken to the City Prison in the Hall of Justice, down at Seventh and Bryant.

Aha, a breakthrough! I was sure that this was part of the plan, a benevolent conspiracy to get me to where I needed to go, never mind the circuitous and disorienting route. As things didn't coalesce in a simple or obvious way, it became evident that I was being put through this ordeal as a kind of initiation. I didn't protest, because I assumed that I was being taken care of.

As I was being booked at the Hall of Justice, I saw several cops tapping away at typewriters. I figured they were poets and that I'd been brought to the poet's induction center. *Far out! At the end of all this, they'll give me a credential.* I'd briefly pledged a fraternity as an undergraduate at UCLA, and I knew that you were put through all sorts of ridiculous hardships in order to join. I thought this must be a rite of initiation into a secret society.

I surrendered all my personal effects and was put in a holding cell with a bunch of winos. Feeling it was incumbent under the circumstances, I commenced reciting poetry, my own and that of famous poets: Dylan Thomas, e. e. cummings, Hopkins, Keats, and anyone else whose works I'd memorized. Thomas's "Fern Hill" was one of the poems I read out to the illustrious group of fellow poets and initiates in whose company I now found myself. The content of the poems was less important than the fact that I knew them by heart and could recite them. The drunks looked at me in various strange ways. I was sure that I saw Robert Bly and Charles Bukowski among the group. I presumed that they periodically had to go through this sort of detail, sitting in the drunk tank with a young poet, to initiate him into the poetic order. It was a duty, one of the secret dues one paid to be a poet, which entailed acting like a stinking bum in some kind of underworld.

The fantasy I was weaving was all-encompassing. Anything that happened could be incorporated into my exalted vision of what was taking place. Psychologically, this was no doubt a self-protective mechanism to neutralize the horror of what was actually happening. I assumed that the ordeal was essential to my passage into a benign cabal of poets and my ordination as a guerrilla angel in the new consciousness.

I thought I could persuade my fellow inmates that I was worthy and qualified to be inducted into the new society, by improvising a nonstop stream of poetry. I launched into a monologue, a running commentary on everything at once, what was going on in the room, on the outside, the historic events of the age, the Rolling Stones at Altamont, and my travails through the night. I saw it as a Homeric recitation of the heroic journey I was on, spoken in a sort of Joycean gibberish. Eventually, a cop came and pulled me out. It was very late and I was keeping people from sleep.

I was placed in the Hole, a bare cell with no furniture, a hole in the floor that served as the toilet, a light in the ceiling. I figured it was one step deeper into the rite of passage, and because of the improved acoustics, I thought it was an even better place to broadcast my epic poetic riff. The painted plaster walls began crawling with an arcane mural. Through the purple haze of my psychedelic psychosis, the textured surface of the cell depicted an incredibly suggestive landscape that contained a narrative. I was supposed to interpret this esoteric scripture, these hieroglyphs which I took to be an extension of the monologue I was doing in the drunk tank. So I jabbered all night in a language I later came to call *schizophrenese.* (Schizophrenic people, as I found out in nuthouses in the ensuing months, can be extremely eloquent and poetic in the freedom of their imaginations. If you actually listen to what such a person is saying, it may make no rational sense, but it can be a remarkable kind of rough poetry.) What I read off the walls was a cunning, manic account of my life story, the day's adventures, and my visions of what was going on in the society, with references from the news and recent history—an aural montage of everything that was swimming through my consciousness.

I couldn't sleep, though the strain of my performance was beginning to tire me. I was starting to feel some discomfort by now. Though I was convinced it was all for the best, I'd had almost enough and wanted to get out. But I thought the way out was to be as eloquent as possible, to prove I had the stamina to join this legion of poets and do my part in remaking the world through art. Now if I could just be articulate and imaginative enough, they'd let me out and give me my crown of laurels or whatever reward I'd receive for surviving my ordeal.

Well, it didn't turn out that way. After a sleepless night, they took me out of the cell in the morning and brought me to a courtroom with all the other bums who'd been in the tank with me. As we started filing into the courtroom, I saw a woman I thought was my mother in the gallery. I'd also seen my father as one of the drunks, and had been quite moved that he was going through this with me, as I knew it was not the sort of thing he'd want to participate in. The parade of familial and other familiar faces was like a *This Is Your Life* narrative, a fast-forward screening of my life story at a sort of induction ceremony to welcome me into the inner sanctum of angelic cadres.

But when I saw my mother there, I protested. "This is too much. You shouldn't have brought her all the way up here." (It wasn't my mother. My parents were in L.A.) I was immediately jerked out of line by a cop, then taken to a cell block with junkies and drag queens, where I spent the rest of that day in a resumption of my rant.

The Hall of Justice is a building of several stories with the city prison on one floor, the county jail on another, and courtrooms and administrative offices on the other floors. I felt as though I were in an M. C. Escher print, a labyrinth of galleries and passages in different dimensions, where I'd turn a corner and enter another tier of reality.

I didn't know what I had to do to get out, but I knew that I had to do something, because if I just sat there, they'd never release me. I took off my clothes so that they'd see I had nothing else to hide. I recited more poems in an outrageously theatrical manner. I was told to shut up, but I figured they couldn't possibly mean it, because I was there to prove my eloquence. The inmates must have thought I was entertaining or annoying as hell, or both. One of the trustees (inmates permitted limited freedoms and responsibilities such as delivering food trays) came over and tried to set my hair on fire. Someone threw water in my face. Finally, I was thrown in the Hole again.

I spent the night there, continuing my heroic babble. I was still naked, because they hadn't bothered to gather my clothes when they ripped me out of the cell block. I saw this as shedding all vestiges of my former identity, in order to go through to the other side.

In the morning, the door of the hole opened and I was given a set of army fatigues to put on, a pair of pants and a green shirt with "U.S. Army" emblazoned on it. I thought, *Hmm, U.S. Army. This must be the new army,* the special poetic forces of the new society. The desk sergeant asked me about my personal property and I laughed, thinking he was being facetious. Who was I to have any property? My ass wasn't even my own, much less my so-called property. I walked out, chuckling. (Weeks later, they got the last laugh when I tried without success to retrieve my clothes.)

They put me in a police van and drove to a huge complex of buildings on Potrero Hill, on the south end of town adjacent to the Mission District. They opened the door and beckoned me out, then pointed me in the direction of this colossal structure and drove off. There I was, a barefoot hippie, in an army costume, standing alone on the street before this big institution.

I could see it was an important establishment of some kind. I walked in. There were doctors and nurses and people in wheelchairs going up and down the halls, so apparently it was a hospital. No one greeted me to brief me on what I was supposed to be doing. *Maybe I'm supposed to be a medic,* I surmised. *Maybe my job is to talk to these disoriented people and tell them everything is fine.*

I saw a woman in a wheelchair and put my hand on hers and told her everything was going to be all right. I felt like Walt Whitman during the Civil War, walking up and down the aisles of sickbeds, tending to the wounded troops. I knew my job was to be a healer. I could see that this was a place of refuge for people when they couldn't deal with the outside world. I was there to be trained in how to take care of them. If I stayed long enough, I'd probably come out a doctor.

Finally, a nurse found me in a place I didn't belong and asked me to come with her. I welcomed any kind of guidance. She called the psychiatric ward, and one of the psych techs, a big black guy in a white outfit, came down to pick me up. *Cool, man. This is great!* I was raised by black domestic servants when I was growing up in Beverly Hills. When I was little, I'd hung out a lot with the help. So I felt like I was in good hands. It appeared that almost the entire staff of the psychiatric unit there at San Francisco General was black. I thought I might have stumbled upon the headquarters of the Black Panthers, because there were all these cool black people doing important work.

They put me in an isolation room with a mattress and no other furniture, a locked door and a little grated window through which I could see out into the general ward. They gave me some pork chops and bread on a plate, but no silverware. Suddenly I realized how hungry I was. This was Wednesday afternoon and my last meal had been breakfast Monday. So I devoured this food and waited to find out what they were going to do with me next. It didn't occur to me that I was a patient. I felt great! There was a task I was being prepared for that would soon be revealed to me.

I looked out the window from my new cell about four floors up. It was late afternoon in mid-December. There was a gorgeous crepuscular light in the urban sky. The lights were coming on in the buildings, and the glowing headlights and taillights of the cars moved smoothly through the twilight. From my vantage point, it seemed there was a ballet going on in the street, the graceful movement of the traffic, people coming and going from the buildings, cars going in and out of parking places. It was awesomely beautiful to me. This beauty was partly a manifestation of my imprisonment, which filtered the reality outside through an appealing tint. I was moved by the realization that there was a world still going on out there. It seemed to be a work of art in progress, which tied in with my concept of my new job, to make the culture more beautiful by everyday acts of grace and imagination.

I integrated everything that was happening to and around me, no matter how awful and inconvenient and utterly alien to life as I knew it, and fit it into a grand design. I even took comfort in the way everything seemed to make sense, however weird or surreal. There have been times I've been on acid out in nature and seen the oneness of the universe, but it was counterintuitive to feel such mystical wholeness in the prison and the psych ward. I had no control over what was happening to me, yet I submitted to it as part of the larger pattern of the new order.

Eventually they let me out in the main ward, and I was able to interact with the other inmates in the rows of cots. I took my job to be part wizard, part therapist, and part healer, and sure enough, I was asked to interview with "the Doctor." They called me into the office of a white-smocked administrating physician in his late twenties, who sat behind his desk. He wanted to know who I was and how I got there.

This tipped me off that I wasn't my former self anymore. I'd graduated to a new mode of identification, much less pedestrian than name, rank, and serial number. I'd left behind the person I'd been, in city prison. He asked me what my name was. "Rambling Dill Pickle," I replied, a moniker I'd adopted because I was rambling around a lot and my grandmother used to make pickles—and after all, my new uniform was green. This was the first time I ever used this nom de guerre. He tried to tease out the truth. I said, "Okay, my name is Joe Mann." I thought that was a good generic name. It was the name of a high school friend who was sort of the all-American boy. It was clear to me he was interviewing me for a job as a doctor.

It didn't turn out that way. I stayed there in the hospital for over a week with no identification, no identity. I refused to engage in mundane, rational discourse with anyone, because I thought that was completely beside the point, under the circumstances. Finally, I decided to call Saul. He was amazed to hear from me. My wife and several other people had been looking for me. I'd just dropped off the planet. So Saul came in and signed a form for my release that stated he would take responsibility for me, and off we went.

Wow, this is great! I'm finally getting to where I was supposed to get to in the first place, only I'm completely remade. We went to his house, sat down in the kitchen and I proceeded to explain where I'd been, starting at Altamont. I had tripped with Saul, who was very hip to metaphysical and psychological matters. I knew I could trust him not to freak out if I said something that sounded irrational. He asked me why I hadn't called him sooner, and I said, "I thought if I stayed in there long enough, they'd make me a doctor." That cracked him up; he thought it was hilariously funny.

Saul was in the middle of finals at law school and couldn't drive me home, so we called my wife and he gave me a ride to the bus terminal the following morning. I boarded a bus headed to Santa Cruz. *So the journey continues. Further!* Having read *The Electric Kool-Aid Acid Test* and known about the Merry Pranksters, I was hip to the auspicious status of being "on the bus." You're either on the bus or off the bus and I was on the bus, so wherever it was going was fine with me. I still had my army suit on along with a pair of moccasins I'd picked up in the Mission.

A young woman got on, carrying a copy of a Dostoyevsky novel, *The Idiot* or *The Possessed.* As she sat down next to me, I said, "Are you really reading that or are you just carrying it around to impress people?" This sort of half-playful, half-mocking remark was perfectly appropriate, I felt, for the job of raising consciousness and helping people to blow their minds. She looked at me and said, "Most of the people you see on the street are not impressed by Dostoyevsky." But to my ear, the words "you see" sounded like "UC": University of California. I was currently enrolled at UC, Santa Cruz, and she'd gotten on the bus somewhere on the peninsula near Stanford, so I thought, *Okay, this is one-upmanship. She's saying that UC people wouldn't be impressed by Dostoyevsky, while Stanford students would.* I was reading layers of meanings into anything I encountered. We had a snappy, richly resonant conversation until she got off the bus.

My wife picked me up at the bus station in Santa Cruz. By now it was close to Christmas, around ten days after the concert. I was still very high, but it felt natural to me, because, after all, there was LSD in the drinking water. I felt fine, on top of it. And why not? I'd gotten through Altamont, through jail and the mental hospital, completely unscathed, proof that I had it together and was on the right path.

The question of how my fantasies were related to the drugs I'd been taking or other aspects of my personality and development is hard to answer. The notion that I was a poet with some positive role to play didn't come out of nowhere. I *was* a poet, though it was unclear to me how I was going to make a life of that. I only knew that I wanted to make a contribution to the culture at large. But it wasn't by merely being a poet that I would make a difference. It was by *being poetry,* moving in the world in a way that would poeticize not only my experience but everyone else's.

My psychosis went on for six months. There were times, especially in certain hospital situations, when I was so uncensored in my discourse that I was really irritating people. There were occasions when my excessive candor put me in physical danger. All the controls were switched off. I felt very nonviolent and peaceful, but I knew it was part of my job to be funny, witty, and spontaneous, and to pierce the veil of appearances by saying what was really going on. Well, they have manners and other means to control such unruly impulses.

At times, I heard voices that I was sure were the thoughts of the staff and the other patients mocking me. Fortunately, I never heard any "orders from on high." Throughout my quest for instruction, the only directions I could find were through my own interpretations of the hidden "texts" I was seeing.

After several months on heavy doses of Thorazine, I was emotionally exhausted. I'd lived an incredible amount in that time and I felt completely emptied. I was never quite climbing the walls, but I was worried at times. I had paranoid fantasies that I'd be assassinated, that I was never going to be let out, that I was being prepared as a sacrificial martyr. My family got involved when they saw how little progress I'd made in abandoning my delusions, and got really worried that I'd be permanently crazy.

During this time I'd been in and out of a series of hospitals and one of the things that sobered me up was seeing people who really seemed destroyed, way further gone than I was. Who knows when they'd come back. When things were clearly not going my way, when I was subject to the rigors and rules of the psychiatric ward and thought I might wind up like these other zombies, I wanted to get out. The whole thing had gone far enough. So I conceived a plan. Instead of acting on every fantasy I had or saying everything that came into my head, I just played it straight, hoping they'd let me out.

It worked. I was eventually released and, for lack of anywhere else to go, I went back to grad school. But I hated being there. The Thorazine had drained and depressed me and made me sexually impotent. It was the closest I ever came to contemplating suicide. Fortunately, I wrote my shrink in L.A. about that and he contacted me in Santa Cruz and encouraged me to come down to see him. That began a yearlong period of intensive psychotherapy during which I began to explore my personal history for the sources of my psychosis and subsequent depression.

It seems so facile to say, "I was mad at my parents." I came from a privileged background, growing up in Beverly Hills. My parents were starting an apparel manufacturing business at the time I was born. The success of the business brought us to Beverly Hills. They were very consumed in their project, and were absent a lot during my childhood. That's why I bonded with the help.

My father was a self-made man who came up from the streets of Seattle and always said to me, "Do whatever you want, as long as you're good at it." My mother's background was more upper middle class. She wanted me to be respectable. She'd have been very happy if I were a doctor or lawyer or professor. That was one of the reasons I was in graduate school.

I harbored a rage for having been neglected by my parents when I was little, and for being so privileged. I was really outraged that I'd grown up so protected and then discovered as I went out in the world that not everyone had such comfort to back them up. To me this was just an unbelievable injustice. Instead of going out and blowing up buildings or organizing antiwar rallies, I decided to be an artist, and then it was somehow decided for me that I would go crazy as a way of shedding my former identity. San Francisco City Prison was my unconscious alternative to professional school and social respectability.

Even during the worst of it, I felt it was a price I was willing to pay to come out at the other end as the person I was hoping to be. In fact, that's what happened. When I became a professional writer, I actually created the life I was looking for, even to the point of playing a prominent role in the Santa Cruz community as a kind of cultural agitator—organizing events, doing radio shows, starting magazines and newspapers, writing columns. I tried to integrate my somewhat eccentric skills and diverse interests into a way of life where I could do journalism, poetry, literary writing, and translating in a way that would contribute in some small way to the local community and the larger world. I don't know if I can credit psychedelics with having pushed me over that edge, to dare to do that, but they were certainly a contributing factor to the madness that brought me there. My psychosis was a crash course in the revolutionary aesthetic consciousness I sought in order to become an artist. If I hadn't had poetic instincts, who knows what would have become of me? Literature was the real safety net, I suppose.

I feel very lucky that I was able to live through this psychotic episode and emerge from it without being destroyed. My circuits had been fried and so profoundly modified that people around me didn't know whether I'd ever rejoin the ranks of the normal. But I came out of it actually treasuring the experience. Somehow I got through this extended strangeness relatively unscathed. I didn't get killed or maimed or go permanently insane. Instead of the devastating breakdown it could have been, the psychosis became a breakthrough into the life I wanted to live.

My aspirations for an angelic mission were in the tradition of Joseph Campbell's *Hero with a Thousand Faces,* which shows a consistent pattern through various hero myths in several cultures: The initiate goes to the wilderness, is completely cut off from society, goes through illness or other physical ordeals, has visions, and then rejoins the community as a wiser person with special knowledge and powers. He may become a leader, priest, or healer.

Although I can't make any grandiose claims for subsequent shamanic accomplishments, I do feel that I underwent a similar odyssey over those six months. My sojourns to the depths of the unconscious were analogous to a wilderness initiation rite in which you wander in the desert for a while. All I really lost in the process was the desire to have a respectable occupation, to fit in and conform, and to do something my mother could be proud to tell her friends about.

I still believe I was participating in a mythic initiation. I'm not a bit less convinced of this now than I was then. It wasn't exactly what I thought it was at the time, a transformation of the whole society, which changed a lot less than we hoped it would. But in many ways I still haven't shed those delusions. I still subscribe to that vision of the artist's job.

Steve Silberman

B. 1957

Co-author of Skeleton Key: A Dictionary for Deadheads; *senior culture writer,* Wired News; *reachable at* digaman@well.com *and Website,* www.levity.com/digaland.

Residcs in San Francisco

Born in Ithaca, New York; raised in Edison, New Jersey

THE ORGANISMIC DISPLAY MONITOR

In the summer of 1977, between my sophomore and junior years at Oberlin College, I was a student of Allen Ginsberg's at the Jack Kerouac School of Disembodied Poetics in Boulder, Colorado, where Allen taught during the summers. I was there for three months, working with him almost every day, transcribing his journals and dealing with many of the daily tasks he needed done.

While I was there I made the acquaintance of one of his boyfriends at the time, a guy about my age, nineteen. We can call him Jake. Jake told me he had some fresh psilocybin, which I was very keen to do, because I grew up in New Jersey, where the only psychedelics I had access to were bad blotter and stomach-churning microdot—terrible bathtub acid.

By the time I made it through high school and a couple of years at Oberlin, I'd taken acid about fifty times. I always had really heavy experiences. My first ten to fifteen excursions were "bad trips" in the sense that I was filled with dread and self-doubt and intense feelings of alienation and isolation. But one of the things I learned eventually is that there is no bad trip; there's the trip that you're having, and if you interpret it as bad, you're in hell. If your reaction is more like *Wow, this is intense, but I'm not going to be destroyed by it or terrified into a panic state,* then you can work with the energy.

As it turned out, Jake's "fresh" psilocybin was actually frozen. In fact, it was slimy, icy goop, because when you freeze mushrooms, the ice crystals break down the cell walls, so it turns into black slime. So the stuff Jake proffered me was like a black, fishy-tasting popsicle. I ate way too much probably, then walked up into the foothills of the Rockies and had a fairly standard psychedelic experience up there. At one point, I got kind of scared and thought death was a bear in the mountains that was watching me. I was up there for the sunset and then figured I ought to hike back down to town.

After having what felt like an interesting and full psychedelic experience of several hours, I came back down to Boulder, where I was staying in a sorority house. It was probably about two A.M., and I thought that I should probably get to sleep. I lay down in my bed, and of course, I couldn't sleep, because mushrooms, like all psychedelics, exert a wakeful influence.

So there I was, tossing and turning. *Maybe if I smoke some pot I'll get sleepy,* I thought. That had worked with acid in the past. So I took a few tokes. What I didn't know, though, was that apparently—I read this somewhere and I'm not certain if it's true—pot potentiates the action of psilocybin even more so than it does for LSD. While cannabis had brought back the visuals of acid when I was coming down, it did help to unwind the trip a bit.

Not so with shrooms. All of a sudden, I was really, really high again. *What am I going to do?* I thought. *I really have to go to sleep.* My roommates were all crashed out in the other room. I remembered that several weeks before, I'd discovered something curious, that as I was going to sleep, if I listened in the right place in my skull, I could hear a kind of white noise that was probably the sound of the blood rushing through my head. If it was really, really quiet, and if I listened in just the right way, I could hear a very low level, barely perceptible hissing sound.

I thought I'd tune into that, and maybe it would calm me down enough so I could go to sleep. So I started listening for the sound with my eyes closed, and then all of a sudden, a very distinct display of lights came into focus in my mind's eye. I couldn't figure out what it was at first. It looked like L.A. at night from an airplane, myriad points of light of different colors over a vast expanse of terrain. It was as though I were looking out at a huge, ornate Indian carpet, a tapestry woven of lights of many hues.

Wow, what's that? I thought. I kept looking at it, and then I noticed that areas of the display were changing color, as if pulses of energy were occurring in certain areas of the display. Then I noticed that some of the changes were rhythmic, which made me wonder. I noticed that right when I was about to take a breath, discrete areas of the tapestry would change, and when my heart was about to beat, there would be a burst of activity in another area of the field.

I came to feel that I was seeing a display of the activity of my nervous system, both conscious and autonomic. My stomach was a little upset by the mushrooms, and I noticed that a fraction of a second before I felt little gurglings in my stomach, there'd be a burst of activity in the display. Thoughts would cause changes in other areas. It was an enormous, slightly three-dimensional, fantastically intricate, visually enthralling tapestry of light. It didn't have a machinelike quality, exactly. It seemed more biomechanical. It felt organic and alive, but there was also something uncannily precise about it.

I'd seen typical acid visuals, and knew that mushroom-generated ones could also have a fractal quality, like infinitely repeated faces or infinite moiré patterns or crystalline lattices. But this hallucination did not have the selfsame, infinite repeating quality that is distinctive of many psychedelic visuals. Every part of what I was looking at was different. What I was seeing was huge, though completely inside my mind.

I tried fooling around with it. *What if I moved my arm?* As soon as I issued the "move arm" command, there was an energy pulse shooting through the weave, a burst of neurological activity. It didn't take any effort to sustain the vision of the tapestry. It was simply there. And I didn't try to break it. I was seeing something practically more spectacular than the Crab Nebula, right inside my own skull! It took my breath away.

I'm not normally given to elaborate abstract constructs about psychedelic visuals, but this was supernaturally alien, spectacular. I was unnerved, but I didn't freak out, like *Ayeee! I have to go to the hospital!* I thought that if I hadn't taken acid so many times before, I'd be thinking that I'd gone completely insane. It was my accumulated experience with psychedelics that allowed me to be comfortable in that place.

I began to feel a little pride, along the lines of *I've tripped so much, nothing will freak me out.* But I don't want to say that. Within the rules of psychedelic engagement, it almost seems like bad luck, like saying it's not going to rain on your day off. But if you've crossed the Sahara five times, you're not going to be freaked out by a little sand. I was able to *witness* what I was seeing.

Allen used to say that kids should be trained in meditation before they take psychedelics, so that they can appreciate the experience in the spirit of what an Indian guru told him: "If you see anything beautiful, don't cling to it. If you see anything horrible, don't cling to it." Simply witness what you see. The ability to witness is a key fruition of psychedelic training. I sustained the vision for about an hour, and then I gradually drifted off to sleep.

A book that was very useful to me for understanding the psychedelic experience was John Lilly's *Programming and Meta-Programming in the Human Biocomputer,* in which he wrote that psychedelics inject white noise into the system of the human mind. Because the mind is a pattern-recognition machine, the psychedelic experience is not perceived as random but comes organized by all of the patterning structures that perform the job of the human biocomputer. He said that psychedelics bring certain normally unconscious, subliminal, under-the-threshold experiences into awareness, because the added white noise makes them louder, boosting all the signals.

By such reasoning, I wonder if there is some kind of subliminal control center in the mind that we're normally not aware of, but which I conjured into visibility that night by means of the psilocybin, the pot, and my focus on the sound of the blood in my head. And I wonder what medicinal powers—both curative and preventive—it could wield if I were able to gain access to it all the time.

Peaches and Scream

I fell to a particularly rank order of the living during a trip at a Dead show at Frost Amphitheater at Stanford University in the mid-Eighties. I'd taken mushrooms for the second day in a row, the first of two times I've ever taken psychedelics on successive days. I've since decided that I don't like doing that.

It was an outdoor show and it was very, very hot. I was sunburned and dehydrated. My friend and I were surrounded by burnouts who inhabited clouds of pungent marijuana smoke. Their skin looked gray, and everybody seemed to be hacking up this green bong paste. It was one of those pockets of decay, a lower circle in the Inferno of a big sprawling Dead concert scene.

The Dead were debuting "Picasso Moon," a song about being trapped in a hellish mental place, which showed up on the album *Built to Last.* I'd never heard it before. Whatever joy was in my trip up to that point went right down the ol' cosmic toilet when they played this song. I became aware that I was roasting in the sun like meat on a spit, surrounded by sickly, unglamorous human flotsam. Even this guy who I thought was beautiful and boyish, looked, with his shirt off, all skinny and parched, old before his time. I was in a really dreadful place.

What brought my trip to its absolute nadir was this guy next to me, probably trying to be helpful, who kept asking me a question. I was in a state of linguistic discombobulation, where I had to sift what he was uttering through a couple of layers of sound/meaning recognition filters to translate his English. I finally figured out that he was asking me if I wanted a peach.

I thought, *Oh, a peach! Wet, nourishing, sweet—the fruit of God.* Touched by his timely hospitality, I replied, "Yeah! Thanks!" He handed me something, and I looked at it, and it was not a peach. It was some kind of clotted, disgusting, yellow-matter custard. I looked at it and said, "*That's* not a peach."

"No, no," he replied. "*—quiche.*"

Oh God, I don't want any quiche, I thought, especially in that sunlight. It seemed like salmonella on a spoon. Right then I realized that

I was really having a bad trip. A conscious description of my state flashed up in my mind: *I am in Hell, where every particle of creation curses its creator.* It seemed the essence of Hell, where you have a microscopic awareness that every single molecule is regretting its existence.

What got me out of that place was going with the flow. I witnessed that I was in Hell, and then I realized that I was having a really bad physical sensation, and had been for a while. It was like when you realize you've had a toothache for two weeks. *I feel like shit! What* is *that feeling?* In this case, I really had to pee. So I walked out of the netherworld I was in to the public bathroom, and by the time I got back to my seat, I wasn't in Hell anymore.

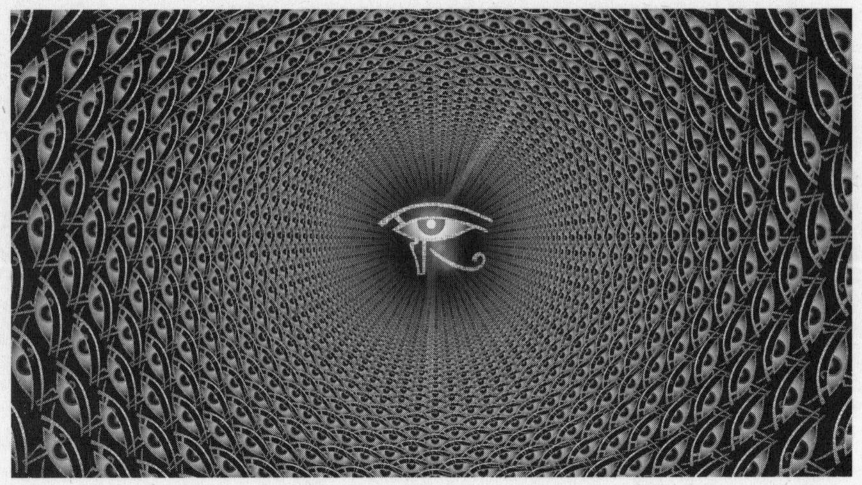

4 March AL 5995 by Brian Moriarty, digital composition, © 1995, courtesy of the artist.

Steven Martin Cohen

B. 1953

Author of the mystery novels **Seven Shades of Black, Becker's Ring, Toy Inventor,** *and* **The Mshenzi Root;** *engineer, toy inventor, artist*

Resides in New York City

Raised on Long Island

A Thousand Cruise Missiles Pointed Straight at My Brain Stem

Life permanently changed for me on September 3, 1970, the first day of my senior year at Lawrence High School on Long Island. Scott, a guy in my Boy Scout troop, had been working on me all summer to break down and smoke pot with him. I refused to try it and had been regurgitating the standard party line: that drugs screwed up your brain and made you stupid. We were home early since this was only a half day of school, so I finally agreed to try his marijuana and put the issue to bed once and for all.

Scott unwrapped some blond hashish from a piece of aluminum foil. I took three hits at three in the afternoon and instantly got high. He put on the record *Don't Crush That Dwarf, Hand Me the Pliers* by Firesign Theater and I soon had a smile plastered across my face I couldn't get rid of. I realized what an ass I'd been for insisting without firsthand knowledge that this state of mind was all psychological. My head had turned inside out and I was watching my brain work in living color.

Up to then I'd had a serious reading disability, which I later learned was called dyslexia. In grade school I was the only kid in both remedial reading and top math, and the education professionals hadn't the faintest idea what was wrong with me. Except for a few stray technical courses in high school, my grades were miserable, and I read so slowly, it was as if I were retarded. I'd be distracted by the spaces between words, and certain letters possessed weird alternative significance based on their shapes and sizes and location on the page.

When I got high I could actually visualize the cause of my reading difficulty and take corrective action. It was as if the words I was reading were chugging along a neurological conveyor belt, then falling off into a traffic circle from which they couldn't exit. In an altered state of mind I could easily patch over this damaged circuitry, and correctly sequence what I was reading, thus avoiding the compulsive pull that would force distracting letters and words in the wrong direction. In the language of servo and control theory, I could now visualize where the electrical-response poles and zeros were in my brain, and navigate accordingly.

Reading repeatedly while high, I was able to improve my reading while straight. At times, my reading speed soared in excess of a thousand words per minute, way up from my usual one hundred or less. Just before the admissions exam for Cooper Union, I smoked some cannabis. Although I had completed about half the math, chemistry, and physics sections, I managed to finish the spatial-relations portion of the test in less than half the allotted time, and my total exam score won me admission at the school.

In the summer of 1971, between high school graduation and my first year at Cooper Union, I traveled with my friend Matt by Greyhound bus across Canada all the way to Vancouver. From there we took the ferry to Vancouver Island and hitchhiked to the west coast of the island and a stretch of Horseshoe Bay called Wreck Bay, so named because thousands of logs had washed up along the shore after the chains lashing them together had broken during a storm. A community of about a thousand hippies was camped out in tents or makeshift structures of logs, some of which were quite elaborate. In a nest of logs, Matt and I built a tepee-shaped tent out of plastic gores we'd taped together.

We stayed at Wreck Bay about a month, meeting lots of friendly people and getting involved in a number of interesting projects, including hoisting a totem pole someone had carved and building a raft we used to paddle out to an island about a mile offshore. Then I met some hippies from New York who were camped near us. One guy had ripply hair over a foot long that looked like a big wavy triangle on a pair of shoulders. We became friends, and he asked if I would like to try some Orange Sunshine LSD. I'd never taken an orange barrel before, and was curious. Four of us would be tripping on this material: my newfound friend with the triangular head, another guy, a girl, and me.

What followed was something like an Abbott and Costello routine, because everyone was smoking dope and seemed to lose track of what kind of acid they had and how much they were taking. They had two-way hits, which were 250 micrograms apiece, and four-way hits, which were 500 micrograms apiece. Both types looked the same, like tiny, orange-colored saccharine tablets. Someone had squashed up four pills in a quart canteen and then forgot there were already four in the mix, and then someone else discovered that they weren't the two-way barrels but the four-way ones. I had one cup of this slurry and it was near the bottom of the canteen, so I probably had at least a thousand mics.

This Orange Sunshine drove me deeper into my head than I'd ever been. It was like a thousand cruise missiles pointed straight at my brain stem, the most extraordinary thing that ever happened to me, both the best and the worst trip I've ever had.

At the first rubbery-lipped signs that I was getting off, I became aware of growing internal activity, as if someone were turning up the brightness control on a movie projector. It started out like looking at a picture frame on which the edges began oscillating like standing waves on four perpendicular ropes. The amplitude of these waves continued growing until the top of the oscillating frame intersected the bottom. Then the frame grew larger and closer to me, until I passed through this wobbling rectangle and became immersed on the other side, with my eyes closed, in the most spectacular animation I've ever seen.

My visual field had effectively expanded hundreds, even thousands, of times in resolution and detail, as though the data density and picture quality of the highest-quality animation had been magnified immeasurably! At times it was like passing through a tunnel of painted walls. Then, in what appeared to be a huge open space within my imagination, I saw enormous spheres made of stained glass with colors brighter than any that I could have seen with my naked eyes.

Imagine an XYZ coordinate system. On the Z axis there was an infinite vertical line of spheres that were separated from one another by thin sticks like drinking straws. Intersecting the grid of the XY horizontal plane I saw hundreds—perhaps thousands—of these vertical axes with spheres on them, each axis moving up and down like horses on a merry-go-round. The imagery on the spheres was changing constantly while their diameters simultaneously expanded and contracted in and out of phase with each other.

I watched the whole spectacle within this three-dimensional universe of expanding resolution while exerting no mental effort to make any of it happen. Just when I thought the resolution could increase no further, it would be multiplied by orders of magnitude in all dimensions, and my bandwidth and grasp seemed boundless.

Then things took a turn for the worse. Night fell and the four of us sat by the fire, listening to the waves break on the beach. My friend Matt was off somewhere drinking screw-top wine, mad that I was taking drugs other than pot. I wasn't very communicative, because I was too busy inside my head, but as the trip developed, I strained to be sociable. It became increasingly apparent that the two other guys and myself were sexually fixated on the woman. Our sexuality seemed to synchronize with the sound of the crashing ocean waves. We all acknowledged there was this great polarity between maleness and femaleness, and there was tremendous sexual energy in the air. Knowing I'd never tripped on this much acid, one guy asked, "Do you feel it?"

I told him I was afraid. I knew I might yield to this primal force and just rape this woman. Being a liberal neurotic Jewish boy from Long Island, I felt that this would have been the most unacceptable thing; if I did it, I'd have to kill myself. But they assured me, "It's okay." She assured me it was okay. I don't know if they meant that it was okay to act upon these sexual feelings or okay to have them. This confusion was causing me a major dilemma. Everything had at least two meanings. I couldn't tell if they were implying we should all have group sex or what. I felt like a huge glandular penis on one single-minded mission to fulfill the genetic imperative. But the thing I feared even more than assaulting this girl was that I was getting closer to losing control. So I announced, "I have to go to sleep."

Of course, falling asleep at that point would be like trying to fall asleep during atmospheric reentry in a space capsule. But I had to get away from there. I didn't want to be around these people anymore. I didn't want any part of whatever it was that we might all be about to do. I escaped to my tent.

Then my spatial perception grew very distorted. I actually got lost in my sleeping bag. I managed to crawl in but couldn't find my way back out! The flashlight was useless. My sense of touch was a more accurate navigational aid than sight, and as long as I avoided acting upon any visual input, I was able to feel my way out of this synthetic cloth nightmare. When I finally extricated myself from the sleeping bag, my vision was completely screwed up. It was as if I were seeing through a pair of telescopes facing backward, my left eye pointed up and to the left and my right eye pointed down and to the right. There was empty black space between what my two eyes were seeing, which was small and far away.

Then I saw the classic "white light" coming toward me. I was terror-stricken, and thought I was going to die. I staggered back to my tripping companions and joined them by the fire, but I just went deeper inside my head. I'd convinced myself that I was dead. Even though I was a devout atheist, I was attempting to convince myself that there was, in fact, a classically conceived god. I had the presence of mind to realize that this was a psychological creation based on the mythology of my youth, but it seemed so true that eventually I thought it was real. Some might have called this a religious epiphany and ran off half-cocked with a Bible and a megaphone. But I still knew something was wrong, that parts of me were playing tricks on other parts, attempting to shatter or challenge every naturally occurring notion that arose. I was resisting this process rather than flowing with it or seeing the humor and irony in it, and this was causing me to have a bad trip.

Some indeterminate amount of time later, I saw myself in a gigantic spiral honeycomb, within which each hexagon-shaped cell contained the soul of a person who'd lived at some time in the past. These were *animate* dead souls—not dead in the sense of being gone or decaying flesh. It was as though every person who'd ever lived were here in this honeycomb, where his soul continued for eternity. I was in a giant hallway with circuitous pathways looking for my eternal place in this enormous honeycomb, as the white light grew closer. Whereas earlier I'd felt my mental facilities were expanding, I now felt they were contracting. Viewing the collective functions of my mind as an army, my men were getting killed off a few at a time, until I was down to just a few guys and me, the head ego. I could feel myself eroding away to nothing.

Exacerbating all this were loose connections between what was going on inside my head and remarks made around the fire, which reinforced all the wrong notions. Apparently, we'd all concluded that we were dead, and this was freaking the shit out of me.

"This can't be!" I cried out.

"Don't worry," someone assured me, "It's okay. We're all dead."

"No," I insisted, "this can't be. If we're dead, we're dead!" I was assured this was okay, and everything was in order and the way it was supposed to be.

"What about my mother?" I asked.

"Your mother doesn't matter anymore," someone replied in that calming conspiratorial voice all paranoids know so well. Great! Just what I needed to hear.

"What about Cooper Union?" I asked, as if this had any greater significance than my mother.

"It doesn't matter. . . . Like, nothing matters." This was the final trigger. I thought my life was over and that I was now going to spend eternity in this honeycomb on the other side of the approaching white light with these crazy people.

I bounced up and ran down the beach, scared to death. As I raced along the shore, I saw sporadic points of light, perhaps campfires or people with flashlights. I must have broken my toe on one of the logs, because in the morning it was very sore and it took a long time to heal. I think some people tried to give me Thorazine, but I don't know whether I took it or whether I was so paranoid, I thought they were trying to kill me. In any event, about four hours of my life are completely unaccounted for. When I again became aware of time, I was with some strangers at another campsite down the beach. They'd apparently recognized my plight and been kind enough to take care of me. The next day I overheard some people say, "Did you hear about that guy who flipped out on the beach last night?" and I knew they were talking about me.

If you have a highly structured, rigidly reinforced sense of internal reality, and something violently assaults it when your defenses are diminished, it could trigger paranoia, panic, or worse, a psychotic episode. The thoughts and images I'd experienced seemed so real and so imposing in their attack on my worldview that it triggered the most fundamental question: *Is it going to kill me or make me live?*

Later I learned how to put the expansiveness of psychedelic consciousness to work for me. During my second year of college, I took some blotter acid that piqued my interest in electronic music. A classmate named Rob was likewise interested, and we'd do drugs, hear extraordinary auditory hallucinations in our heads, and describe them to each other in mathematical terms. We then tried to figure out ways to synthesize these noises, and this led to a whole new phase of my life: digital electronics. Rob and I began to seriously toy around with voltage control oscillators, filters, and the like.

I explained some of my theories to an electrical engineering professor who knew exactly where I was headed with all this, and, in an effort to save me the trouble of reinventing part of this wheel, gave me two data books from National Semiconductor that changed my life—the Linear and Digital catalogs. I ate some psilocybin mushrooms and read both books cover to cover. Immediately I understood what all the integrated circuits did and began designing circuitry using these components. In spite of the fact that I was a mechanical engineering major, I was now quite fluent in digital electronics.

Rob and I then designed some of the same machinery that, had it been built, would have been the direction all of electronic music ultimately went. Without reference to any previous or contemporary work in the field, we developed the theoretical underpinnings of modern digital music synthesis, recursive and nonrecursive digital filters, infinitely variable reverberation generators, harmonizers, and scores of dynamic control philosophies and interface devices, some of which, to this day, have yet to be implemented. We invented all this from scratch, mostly under the influence of psychedelic drugs.

I designed a class of high-speed pipeline processors to implement the real-time accumulation of thousands of sine waves to do what is called a Fourier series synthesis of music. My phase accumulation technique for frequency synthesis ultimately became the basis of a digital toy I designed when I was working as a toy inventor in the mid-Eighties. In fact, it was the basis for a whole class of audio toys that I and others went on to create. I never told my boss that the core algorithm was originally dreamed up during an LSD trip thirteen years earlier, because that surely would have killed the product's credibility along with mine.

I have invented hundreds of things both straight and under the influence of psychedelic drugs. The amplifying effects of these chemicals have influenced the way I think when straight, much like the way smoking pot helped measurably improve my reading back in high school.

I see acid as a sort of jumbling generator or randomizer that can act as a high-speed data reconfigurer. Provided that that data is good, the result can be higher states of order—or lower entropy—which can be used to solve an existing problem or even problems you may not have known existed. This data randomizing in conjunction with other agencies within the mind monitoring that process—parallel processors, so to speak—can enable you to pick out the useful results before they become lost in the neurological noise of thousands of competing signals. If you have disciplined watchdogs watching the process—a controlled randomness, which acid helps facilitate because it increases mental bandwidth—you can see more within a single visual field. By seeing more in one frame, it's easier to make more connections from disparate starting points, thus enabling more connections and tractable intermediate stages between problem and solution.

If you had to move a giant sandpile using a thimble as a scoop, it would take much longer than if you used a shovel or a wheelbarrow for the task. Acid is like temporarily borrowing a wheelbarrow to scoop the drifting sands of fleeting mental images, rather than the more usual thimbles most of us are afflicted with in normal everyday life. If you're a flexible and quick learner, when the time comes to return the wheelbarrow, you may find that the thimble has permanently expanded to the size of a cup or a shovel. Unfortunately—and it's just the luck of the draw—most enter with few tools and leave with even fewer.

Terry

B. 1955

Computer network engineer

Based on the San Francisco peninsula

Born and raised in northeast Ohio

LOOSING THE HOUNDS OF WAR

I attribute a good portion of my ability to handle my Vietnam War–related rage and alienation to LSD and to Mescalito, the spirit of peyote.

I was stationed with the marines in Con Thien, South Vietnam, within a few klicks (four to eight kilometers) of the DMZ, when it was hit in the Easter Offensive of 1972. I'd just turned seventeen, having joined the corps when I was underage. My motive wasn't patriotic duty. It was stupidity.

I was born in northeast Ohio, a very depressed iron—now rust—belt, where there are few jobs. Even at an early age, I knew I didn't want to live there my whole life. So I grabbed the first opportunity to get out, the United States Marine Corps. At that point, in 1971, they'd lost so many marines in Vietnam, they really didn't care about my age. They asked the perfunctory questions.

"Are you?"

"Yes."

"Fine. Sign here." I was sixteen. By age twelve, I was already six-three, two hundred pounds, so I was a big boy.

Of course, another reason I joined the corps was to improve my chances of surviving the war. I thought, *If I go into the army and they send me to Vietnam, I'm going to die.* Since I figured I'd probably be drafted, I wanted to go with as much savvy as possible.

The marine corps was a perfect place for me. They taught me how to survive, and I did very well—while I was there. But I came back with survivor's guilt. *I should have been the one to go. Bobby (a guy I knew in-country who stands for all the Bobbys who didn't come back) died over there and he never did anything wrong in his life. Why did he die, and why was I left to live?* I never understood until much later: It was his time to go. It wasn't mine.

On April 29, 1972, a thousand marines were overrun by twelve thousand NVA (North Vietnamese) soldiers. I lost 115 comrades that day. The North Vietnamese came in waves of several hundred at a time, one right after the other. As soon as one combatant died, the next would come up and take his place. This went on and on, hour after hour after hour.

During the attack, I was hit in the stomach by a B40 rocket, an antitank weapon. It has to spin a certain number of times in order to activate the warhead, and luckily, the person who fired it wasn't far enough away, so I was hit with an unarmed warhead which lifted me up and drove me back in the rice paddy. I woke up in a CH47 double-rotor helicopter. On the way out of the country, we came under ground fire and the chopper took a few rounds of fifty-one-caliber machine-gun bullets through the belly. One of those rounds entered and exited my upper left thigh, taking out my ability to sire kids. It was the third time I was hit, so that was my exit from the war. I'd already been shot in the wrist and the leg, and had shrapnel up my back.

I was interested in getting out on a medical basis, but they did such a good job of fixing me that I was still capable of military service, so after I recovered, they sent me to El Toro Marine Air Station. I would soon be separated from the corps, however, when I struck an officer who was ordering me to do a whole bunch of inane ditch-digging and dirt-moving exercises that had nothing to do with preparing me to fight in the actual fucking war. I refused to do it and when he ordered me to, I put him in the hospital. They gave me two choices, either go to Leavenworth Penitentiary or be mustered out with an Undesirable Discharge by Reason of Request, which is what I accepted. I didn't feel like going to prison. Who in his right mind would? They basically showed me the door and said, "Have a nice day," voiding my rights to veterans' benefits.

After seeing so much death at an early age, I wanted to do whatever it took to let loose the hounds of war from my system and become a normal human being again. I tried to settle down. I stayed in Los Angeles for a little while, but I had a hard time staying indoors and keeping a job. I wasn't capable of dealing with people one on one, and I had a major rage problem. Anything could set me off: a time card I thought was improperly filled out, the way somebody talked to me. Somebody would pull in front of me on the highway and I'd start shrieking at him.

Rather than try to hack it, I gave up and started hitchhiking back and forth across North America. I hitchhiked from L.A. to Key West, Florida, walked along the pier by the Caribbean and took a leak, then hitchhiked to Seattle, Washington, took a leak in Puget Sound, hitchhiked to Maine, took a leak in the Atlantic, and kept moving. The farthest-away place to drain—that was my only goal.

On one such sojourn in 1974 I came to the Bay Area. I got picked up in Berkeley on University Avenue, right on Interstate 80, by an older hippie in his fifties or sixties named Philip, who was driving a big old International Metro delivery van that was outfitted with beds and packed with a bunch of longhairs. They took me into the City (San Francisco), which I'd only seen in pictures.

"We're going to a show. Would you like to join us?" Philip asked me.

"I don't have any money."

"Oh, don't worry about that. Money's not an obstacle."

There was a Bay Area hi-fi dealer called Pacific Stereo which was sponsoring a free concert with the Grateful Dead and other bands at the Cow Palace, where they were also holding a stereo gear expo. They'd given out something like eighty thousand tickets for this event, and the Palace holds only twenty-four thousand.

Philip and his crew had some of these overabundant tickets and, fortunately, we arrived at the Palace hours early and had no trouble getting great seats very close to the stage. Around seven in the evening Philip passed around little pieces of blotter paper with brown dots on them.

"Just put it in your mouth, let it melt on your tongue, and relax."

"Okay." I proceeded to do that. Philip told me that I'd just taken 250 micrograms of 99.8 percent pure LSD-25 manufactured by Sandoz Laboratories in Switzerland. He said he was a doctor of psychology and had acquired these sheets of acid when he requested a supply for research he was conducting. I don't really believe that story, but he did know his acid. He said that the LSD would take about an hour to come on, that after about fifteen minutes, you'd feel pretty buzzed, and after a half an hour, you'd feel like *Whoa, I'm really high!* and then after about forty-five minutes, you'd feel like nothing was happening. Then, after about an hour, you would look at somebody, and his or her face would melt. He said that for the next twenty-four hours there would be wild hallucinations, both auditory and visual. I really didn't believe all that, but I had a certain amount of credence in his voice due to his age and bearing. By this point in my life I hadn't yet done psychedelics, though I'd smoked everything from *sinsemilla* to Mexican ragweed.

We were admiring the stereo components, and sure enough, I started to feel pretty strange. About forty-five minutes later, I felt like I'd taken nothing at all. Somebody said the show was about to start, so we went into the auditorium and I sat in front of a huge pile of speakers at one side of the stage and watched the first act, a band whose name I don't recall. All of a sudden, I started to see musical notation floating out of the speakers: eighth notes and sixteenth notes and G clefs and treble clefs drifting away in the air and then bursting like bubbles. It went on for hours. It was almost like a cartoon.

Then the Dead came on. Back then, Jerry Garcia was playing on the left side of the stage and on the right was Phil Lesh, who had this manic look on his face while staring at his fingers as they moved across the fretboard of his bass guitar. He was plucking away while his eyes were getting wider and wider. I was sure that his eyes were going to pop out of their sockets, and sure enough, they did. The optic nerves and the muscles attached to the back of the eyeballs were dangling out of his head, swinging before his face from left to right in time to the music. It seemed perfectly natural. There was no discomfort on either Phil's part or mine. I thought to myself, *Wow, that's really cool. I wish I could do that.* He just kept playing, getting better and better.

Around midnight, a very frantic lady came up on the stage. "The concert's over. Please go home." They opened up the doors and let us out. On either side of us were lines of cops in riot gear. Apparently all the ticket holders who couldn't get in had gone berserk, overturning cars, smashing storefronts, and trashing whole sections of the street in front of the Cow Palace. It was very ugly, but it had gone on unbeknownst to us inside. It was kind of a bummer to have the concert interrupted and to see all this carnage, but not enough to spoil the trip.

We piled into the van and drove across the peninsula to Ocean Beach, near the Cliff House. The moon was over the ocean and there was this incredible white streak along the tops of the waves, which were like little fingers reaching up and saying, "Hi! How you doing?" The eight of us who'd gone to the concert in Philip's van sat on the beach. Everyone knew each other except for me and another newcomer, a guy about my age named Jonathan.

I was still peaking very strongly, with hallucinations of seagulls and pelicans, which would fly by, turn around on the dime and speak to me. "Hi! How you doing? Are you having a good day? I'm up here floating, having a great time. Having a good trip? Hey, we are too!" And off they'd fly. These were real birds, not cartoon birds, until the moment they talked, of course, when I saw their "lips" move. Sandpipers would come along and look at us, turn their heads to one side and go, "Peep! Peep!" and then scurry off, looking for food.

Dawn broke and we were still out there at the beach. We hadn't eaten anything in quite a while, but we weren't hungry. It was so absolutely gorgeous, the sun rising, the wind blowing. The trees waved at us. "Hi there! How you doing?"—one hallucination after the other. One guy had a long conversation with a hermit crab, kneeling on the beach, discussing Socrates and Aristotle with this rapt crustacean. Apparently, he thought the crab was talking back to him. It didn't run away, at any rate. We were all involved in our own little trips, having a fine time. We stayed on the beach until sundown the day after we'd dropped. It had taken a full day to finally begin coming down. We thought we should find our way back to Philip's house, so we boarded the van and headed there. I knew right then that LSD was something I would do again. The big hallucinations finally stopped after about thirty hours, but I still felt quite high two days later.

There were about eight or nine people living in this commune on Hill Street in the Mission District between 16th and 17th Streets, with Dolores on one end and Valencia on the other end. Philip invited Jonathan and me to stay there for a while, and we did. I would learn to hate all the tofu and vegetarian cooking at the house, but I hung out there because it was free and the marijuana and the drugs were great.

I don't know if Philip was a psychologist or not. He may have had the credentials, but I don't think he was practicing professionally. About a week later, he asked how I felt about doing acid again. I said I'd really like to, but in the daytime rather than at night. So he said, "Tomorrow morning, let's wake up early and take a hit. Then I'll drive you out to Land's End." This was a beautiful spot just a hundred yards north of the Cliff House, where there are places to hang out and explore, such as the ruins of the baths built a century ago by Adolf Sutro. We dropped the acid at about 6:30 as the sun was coming up, and hung out at this spot for most of the day.

When the acid hit, we were sitting on a promontory on the cliff side, watching the rush-hour traffic coming into the city on the Golden Gate Bridge. I peaked very hard and very fast. I was watching waves build up at the entrance to the Golden Gate about three miles away, and one washed over the bridge like a three-hundred-foot tidal wave, so high it crashed over the top of the towers. The bridge started doing a snake act. Trucks and cars were falling off into the ocean or into the entrance to the bay. Off in the distance I could hear people screaming, "I'm dying! I'm dying!" They were laughing uproariously, having a great time on their way to meet their maker. To them this was wonderful! They were like tiny little sticks from where I sat, but I could hear them exclaiming, "Ha ha! This is cool!"

These cries from the "dying" were a real contrast to the anguished sounds of the battle-stricken in Vietnam. The screams of death by violence are horrible. When you hear somebody who's mortally wounded, has lost an arm or a leg, or has a gaping hole in his chest, and he knows he's dying, you not only hear the pain but feel it, psychically. Vietnam for me was a lot of people dying, many of them choking on the jagged, searing impact of the imminence of their premature demise. My acid-induced vision was a way of releasing some of the angst of seeing my buddies die and the inability to do anything about it. By contrast, death in this bizarre LSD hallucination was somehow comforting. "It's okay I'm dying," they were saying. Death was transfigured in such a hilariously unlikely yet spiritually resonant way as to make it easier to assimilate what I had experienced in the war.

All of a sudden the waves stopped their assault on the bridge, and the ocean was perfectly calm. Everything was normal. The wind blew by. Then a bird flew by and said, "Hey, how you doing there? Heh heh heh. Having a good day? I'm having a great day!" He dove down and caught a fish and flew off. I knew then and there that I was going to have a great trip.

Jonathan and I played in the tide pool and then sat for hours, watching the waves come up and hit Seal Rock, which is actually a group of rocks just offshore from the Cliff House. Eventually we could recognize the cycles of the waves, knowing when it was going to be calm, when the waves were going to be big, and when it was going to be calm again. We walked around the tip of the point past Seal Rock to a place just south of there, where you can stand on top of the cliff and see, on the right, Ocean Beach stretching south along the coast and, on the left, Golden Gate Park. The trees in the park were a little darker than those outside of it, creating a checkerboard landscape.

The park wiggled a little bit, then some more, and then it turned into a giant surfboard that jetted out into the ocean. As it went by, a bird flew by and said, "Hey, having a good day? I'm having a great day!" As the park moved away into the ocean, I could see the entire stretch of real estate—the De Young Museum, the Asian Art Museum, the Hall of Science, the Conservatory—rushing past. Jonathan and I ran down to examine the huge hole left in the wake of the giant surfboard.

When we realized the park hadn't gone anywhere, we sat down and laughed, not stopping for two hours. We pissed in our pants, we were laughing so hard. I'd described it vividly enough that Jonathan began seeing what I was seeing. I don't know if it was a shared hallucination or mass hysteria.

We walked through the park and down on to Haight Street, which we strode up and down a few times. Then we walked down to Market Street all the way up to Union Square, then down to Fisherman's Wharf, from there to Union Square, from there to the Mission and back to the house, where we arrived at about five in the morning, just starting to come down. We'd probably walked thirty miles. We slept for a whole day.

After a hitchhiking trip a few months later, I came back to Philip's house and knocked on the door. They said he'd been busted. Apparently, he'd been selling mega quantities of pot. A warehouse full of marijuana, as well as the chemicals and blotter sheets for making LSD, was confiscated. I heard that he fled to Turkey when he was free on bail, and never came back. I never did any research to verify any of this. So much for "Dr." Philip and his amazing LSD, the only acid I ever had with such stupendous vividness of hallucination. With all the other acid I took, if indeed it was LSD, the hallucinations were bland in comparison.

On a hitchhiking trip through the Southwest, I was picked up on Interstate 40 near Flagstaff by a friendly Hopi Indian guy named George.

He saw the guitar I always carried with me, stopped his car, and invited me in. "Come on out and play guitar at my place." The next thing I knew we were talking about drinking tequila and eating peyote. He was about thirty, and I wasn't quite twenty at the time. We drove to a reservation northeast of Flagstaff, where he introduced me to his wife and children, his sister and mother, basically everybody in the valley. There was a big harvest festival going on. I spent a few days on the reservation building fences to earn some money, and drinking and partying at night.

I'd known George and his people less than a week when I was invited to join them in a peyote ceremony. I guess I worked hard enough to earn their acceptance. "Tonight you'll meet Mescalito," they told me. I asked who Mescalito was and they just smiled. "Oh, you'll see."

The ceremony was held in a hut made of logs plastered together with mud. There was a big fire in the middle on which they put juniper bushes, which made it very smoky and hot. The only outlet was a small hole about a foot in diameter. Smoke was everywhere, but I didn't feel claustrophobic. The oldest person there was somewhere between 70 and 120, with wrinkles deeper than the Grand Canyon and deep, deep-set eyes. When he looked at you, he looked straight through you. I don't remember his name, but that night, he showed me how to eat the peyote buttons, which had been dried in the sun.

First you chew on the button for a while, then you spit it out and take a drink of this vile liquid, which tasted a bit like tequila, though it probably wasn't. I'd drunk enough of it to not be bothered by the taste of the buttons, of which I eventually ate nine. There was nausea at the very beginning when it didn't want to stay down. I threw up and was then able to eat as much as I wanted.

The tone of the ceremony was like *We are allowing you to see the way we live. You should have respect for this, because it is a way of knowing your inner self and repairing all the bad things that you've done in your past.* I had no choice but to look reverently at them and listen very carefully.

As I was talking to the old man, I felt a nudge on my left side. I turned and saw that a huge dog was sitting next to me, nuzzling my shoulder. He looked at me, howled at the very top of his lungs, and put his paw on my knee. He was the size of a big Great Dane, about 180 pounds, though he had the face of a German Shepherd, with very large black ears. And he had the biggest golden eyes I've seen in my life. To this day, I remember those radiant eyes, where I saw calm, peace, relaxation. It was Mescalito.

We conferred for hours, covering a lot of ground on the psychic effects the war had had on me, the ability of the human mind to heal those wounds, and how I needed to evolve as a human being. He sat me down and told me, "You have to stop hurting yourself, because one of these days you're going to kill yourself and I don't think you should die yet." This creature knew every evil thought that I'd ever had and every good deed that I'd done for anybody at any time in my life. It was as though he were weighing that good and evil and was pleased with what he saw. That's when he left. He shook his head as though to get a flea out of his ear. Then he got up and walked out of the hut, not parting the curtain, but jauntily walking right through the fabric.

As the night went on I saw shadows and shapes, and I heard things. I heard drums, though none were being played. I heard a high-pitched whistle or flute, though none was being played. Every once in a while, somebody would put a log on the fire and sparks would go up to the ceiling, which I'd see for an hour.

At some point during the night I passed out or fell asleep. The next thing I remember it was morning. When I woke up, there were two or three others curled up in various corners of the hut. The fire was out. I could see bits of sunlight coming through the top. I had a headache like you would not believe. I felt like my head was literally going to split apart and I was going to die.

I got up and walked out. There was an older lady sitting there and she wiped her hand across her face and then handed me a wet rag, indicating I should wash my face with it. Then she gave me something to drink and pointed me to a house. The homes on this reservation weren't mud huts or tepees and wouldn't have looked out of place in Tennessee or Arkansas. There were a couple of cars up on blocks, an old refrigerator in the back, some trash off on one side.

I went into the house and George told me to take a shower and put on some clean clothes. When I came out, he said, "You're very lucky. The old man named you last night."

"What?"

"You got your name last night."

"What's my name?"

"Silver Eagle."

I said okay, that's cool. It was a good name. I liked it. He told me the old man had said that I was the only white man he'd ever seen that was able to fly. He apparently felt that I was worthy of a very powerful name.

I worked a couple more days on the reservation, cleaning up some places, building fences. Then one day George gave me a hundred dollars and took me to the interstate, where I resumed my hitchhiking across the Americas. I hitched from San Francisco to the Panama Canal and back again, then to Alaska and back again. I spent two and a half months wandering in British Columbia without seeing another human for most of that time.

One reason I never had a bad trip on psychedelics is that I'd already seen the worst in Vietnam. I'd heard stories about people on psychedelics who'd turned into animals and started gnawing on children's legs and stuff, but that crap never happened to me. I'd already seen it in real life, so I didn't need to see it again during a trip. Seeing the Golden Gate Bridge doing a snake act didn't frighten me all that much, whereas seeing trucks and tanks detonating in Vietnam really freaked me out.

I can't say psychedelics are going to do it for everybody, but for me they really did a lot. In olden times when sailors at sea experienced a storm, they'd throw oil on the water to calm the raging sea. That's what acid did for me. It calmed my raging waters and enabled me to see inside what I was doing, how I was thinking, and how to translate that into life. After a few trips I realized, *You know, maybe I can handle people. Maybe there is a way to control the rage and frustration. Maybe there's a way around it,* and I was eventually able to find it.

Tim Page

B. 1944

Photographer, journalist, author of **Page after Page: Memoirs of a War-Torn Photographer; Tim Page's Nam; Sri Lanka;** *and* **Ten Years After;** *coeditor of* **Requiem: By the Photographers Who Died in Indochina and Vietnam** *(1997 winner, Robert Capa Gold Medal Award, International Center of Photography Infinity Award for Best Publication, and other awards)*

Resides in Kent, England

Born and raised in Kent, England

Memoirs of an Acid-Salved War Photographer

I can never be sure why my mind is in the condition it is, if it was the European acid I did before I had brain surgery, the prescriptions I took afterward, or the various combinations of substances I've taken, legal and illegal, throughout but especially since.

In the early summer of 1967 I moved to Paris after two and a half years shooting the war in Vietnam and then the Six Day War in Israel. Four women came through my bed one night when I was tripping on acid for the first time. I was in my dirty mood about sex in those days, enjoying a noisy and scratchy fuck. I got up at four in the morning and drove down to St. Tropez with one of the birds for a summer of acid.

The occasion was a production by the happening *artiste* Jean Jaques Lebel of Picasso's only play, *Desire attrappe par la coeu* (Desire caught by the tail), which was performed only once before, in the Forties on French Resistance radio by all the luminaries of underground Paris. This time, Taylor Mead and Ultra Violet put it together with strippers from the Folies Bergère, Julian Beck and Judith Molina's Living Theater (an American avant-garde troupe who'd done *Mysteries in Smaller Pieces*) and with music by the Soft Machine. Mike Rutledge (who started "The Softies") arrived from Switzerland with an old-fashioned fluted apothecary bottle with a glass stopper full of liquid Sandoz LSD-25. It was like carrying nitroglycerin around.

I licked a few droplets off the web of my thumb and forefinger, took a couple of blasts of good Moroccan keef and the whole wobble machine kicked in. It was almost like snorting, a real screaming head, with weird patterns up the sides of my skull. Somebody said, "Let's all go jump in the surf," so we dove about in the waves for a while.

I was driving a group of us in my Volkswagen squareback into town for the performance and started seeing things that weren't there: sheets of light-montage video graphics coming at me like incoming fire, the Jupiter sequence in *2001,* and the trailer for ABC's *Movie of the Week,* the most advanced television graphics of the time. I had to give the steering wheel to someone else, and curled up in the firewall like a Gl in a foxhole. These were my first hallucinations.

The next thing I knew I was in a beautiful villa that belonged to some contessa, taking pictures of a candle burning, with a giant window overlooking a valley, a lava lamp going, LP records scattered, a woman wearing only a bra. Then I found myself walking down a dirt road. I have no idea how I got there. I had two Leicas and two Nikons, a pair of shorts, and a T-shirt. I got in the car and some cohorts took me down the mountain to the main road. But I couldn't handle being in the car again, so I got out and walked, taking odd shots of fields and vineyards. I must have walked ten kilometers back to Gassin outside St. Tropez, where I was staying at this communal house with the cast of the show and all the assorted extras and hangers-on. It was like something out of *Hair.* I had a bed downstairs which was my zone. I spent the whole six weeks on acid, wine, and good food.

When I went back to Saigon in 1968, there was a continuous supply of acid in the flat where I was living, but it never occurred to me to take any. It seemed inappropriate. Vietnam was plenty weird enough, and I was only a moped ride away from the best opium on the planet. A man would come over and lay on my floor with a long pipe filled with the stuff. On weekends I went to a neo-Taoist peace island on the Mekong Delta to meditate or smoke dope, eat macrobiotic, then come back to the madness of Saigon and the war. You didn't meet a lot of people who tripped in Nam, though I did know a chopper pilot that flew on acid, who used to land his gunship and leave his calling card: "The Acid Killer Has Been Here." John Steinbeck Jr., working there as a deejay, did acid sometimes. He got busted for smoking dope, and became a Taoist peace activist, once marching a cat and rat into the foyer of the American Embassy to show people how to live in harmony.

I've never had a really bad freak-out while tripping, where God and mother demand all. Maybe this is because I've been DOA twice and because I've been like the snail on a razor edge described by Kurtz in *Apocalypse Now,* witnessing and even recording the conflict and madness of war. It was the craziness brought on by my injuries that put me about as far out as one would like to get.

The first DOA experience was a 1962 motorcycle accident that split my head open and parted the temporal artery. The second occurred in 1969 in Vietnam, when a 250-pound antitank mine exploded three meters in front of me and I took a piece of shrapnel in the right side of my forehead, which lodged in the back. I recall a complete meltdown of color, a brilliance bled of all chromatics. By the time they opened my head up at a field hospital at Long Binh, the hemorrhage was the size of an orange, two hundred cc's, which they took out. The neurosurgery was done by a guy who happened to be one of America's top brain surgeons when he was drafted. After this blow to the head, I didn't start taking acid again until 1973.

For a year after the initial surgery, I was hemiplegic, with no use of my left side for a year. I walked around with just the scalp pulled over the hole, until the trauma of the skull injury went down. I went to a rehab clinic, then to a hospital for a year to have a second load of plastic surgery. My whole head was rebuilt. It's plastic up on the right side, laid in at the Good Samaritan Hospital in L.A. by the guy who tried to save Bobby Kennedy. I never say "touch wood," but say "touch plastic" instead.

I went off the deep end for a few years when I didn't understand the difference between joie de vivre or madness. I went into a downward spiral of self-abuse, painkillers and other pills, booze, violence to every woman I loved, unemployment, all the worst shit of the Vietnam War veteran. Nothing worked out and no one seemed to understand my case. In Rome I loaded a six-shot .38 special, removed one round, spun it, held it to my face, and pulled the tigger. It came up empty, one chance in six that it would—a breakthrough.

Finally in 1973 I got wrecked on acid, throwing caution to the wind and taking a thousand mics, boosting the high when it slackened. I did it for the *erasia,* the forgetfulness, trying to wipe away the present the way alcoholics and junkies do. I had a complete catharsis in which I careened and cascaded through whole reams of cycles. It could be disputed that it was the best medication under the circumstances, but then who's to judge? The most obsolete word in our vocabulary is "if." I wrote my entire autobiography *(Page After Page)* without using the word until the last line: "There's no ifs and buts. You only go around once."

From 1973 to the end of the Seventies I lived in California, where I hung out with a sordid assortment of journalists, artists, and Vietnam vets. We were all caught up in the postwar whiplash. I lived for a time and did a lot of acid with one of the staff writers at *Rolling Stone.* I catered the Bicentennial Acid Freak Out for *Rolling Stone* in Sonoma. I tried to count the number of trips I'd taken, but I gave up trying to distinguish one from the other. There was one five-month period mid-decade when virtually every day was touched by psychedelics. I don't recall any planning in that time. I didn't make more than a few thousand dollars a year. I lived by the grace of friends.

Acid fused this block of years together. I have a lot of trouble pulling apart a series of experiences and metamorphoses, including getting myself admitted to a psychiatric hospital and being a guinea pig for a number of shrinks, getting deported from the United States, coming back, and winning my court case against Time-Life, for whom I was working when I spilled some of the contents of my cranium in Vietnam.

When I was living in San Francisco, destitute to score a lid, I rang a friend I'll call Tony in Berkeley. Two weeks later I moved in with him, launching some demented days indeed. Tony was one of the original army disk jockeys in Vietnam, doing "Camp Malaria" ads and all this wacky Armed Forces Radio stuff. I stayed on the floor of his apartment up above the campus in a place called Channing Way behind the fraternity and sorority houses. There were a minimum of three people—squatters is perhaps more accurate—per room in this building of eight Sheetrock student flats. I had an affair with a girl upstairs. There was a Swiss mechanic and a gay bookbinder who grew orchids next to the bonfires we always had.

Tony had a yellow Volkswagen he drove around to colleges reading modern stoned poetry out of the back. I took some pictures and painted houses to earn a few bucks. We had a little plastic vial with a cork cap filled with a thousand hits of Windowpane, four hits in each pane. Whenever we dropped, we were always barbecuing on the hibachi, breaking up pallets, and using junk from the streets to feed the fires, because we couldn't afford charcoal. Whenever I've taken acid, I don't care where it's been, I've always had the desire to search for twigs, things combustible. It's the cave mentality. You must have a central point where people can find each other.

Everybody who set foot in the apartment either came or left treed out of their brains. Tony bumped into William Burroughs Jr., fresh out of prison, and brought him over. He eventually stole my Frye boots. When his dad came to visit shortly afterward, I moved in with an anthropologist lady upstairs until we fell to blows. A sign of Bill Sr.'s doings was the plastic swing-top garbage pail in the corner of the kitchen, which had melted down into the linoleum. All that was left were two hypodermic needles.

A neighbor would turn up and participate in the ongoing frenzy. "Have you dropped? You want some?" He'd have a term paper to write or a course to attend. "Well, come back later," we'd tell him, and he would. No sooner had you come down from one trip that you'd start another. We'd do up some acid and drive a '53 Chevy over to Mendocino County, stopping off for a six-pack of Dos Equis and gasoline we'd pay for with food stamps, pulling over again to smoke another joint. It was like a continuous Furry Freak Brothers cartoon. As with an alky, the straight moments were no longer delineated.

I tripped at Death Valley with Tony and my girlfriend Carla. It was magical, desert perfect, like dissolving. I could reach the stars. We started a little fire with some brush and had the tape deck in the car going with Van Morrison singing "Listen to the Lion" from *St. Dom-*

inic's Preview. Tony had made a tape of all our favorite trip music, long tracks by the Doors, Paul Horn inside the Taj Mahal, "Going Home" by the Stones. Then he got all freaked about snakes and religiously got up and drew a circle around us.

The only thing you'd have to worry about out in Death Valley is rattlers, which are heat-seeking. It's not unheard of for them to crawl into sleeping bags. Now, the thought of waking up to a rattler in my sleeping bag in the desert was not the sort of thing you dwell on when you're on acid, because it conjures up all kinds of ghastly, horrible, hell-like pictures. I've watched a snake slither under my knees. You panic and you're fucked. But the snakes didn't come and we took another dose of acid.

In a motel room in Ensenada, Tony and I did twenty-five-hundred mics and started drinking mescal and lots of Dos Equis. Then we went around to the little strip clubs. By four in the morning we were literally crawling down the main street of town. We vaguely came to as the state governor showed up for the unveiling of one of these awful concrete statues of a *presidente.* The pictures I shot that day were very, very weird.

My photography career was treading water. While others were busy building up their archives and businesses in the post-Vietnam years, I was out there screaming at the moon, crawling around deserts on my hands and knees, drooling and spewing in Ensenada, or leaning out of the back of a truck to check out where we'd parked—McDonald's or Pizzaland, California—en route to the ocean or the next party. It seemed kind of fun to be with ten people whose brains are dissolving too, going down the Pacific to find a place like Mont Tamal Pais in Marin County to watch the sunrise on the beach. Central casting would send everybody. There was always some fool there in an Afghan and a flute. The women would sit around blowing bubbles. The children, who all had names like Sunrise and Roach, must have presumed their parents were off their rockers. There was no control. The last thing we would have thought about was the children.

Acid enabled life to go on without regret or remorse. It was like surfing. Over the years, tipping sackfuls of LSD into my system was like putting a Zip drive on my photo library to cram more pictures onto the hard disk. There was a period when I did so much acid that I assimilated more than I could have in a normal existence. It acted as a RAM byte cruncher, like force-feeding geese with information and experience. I used to wish I could jump ahead and come back with all the experiences I would have had in the interim. Acid enables you to take that leap ahead and come back ten years richer, to stand away from the planet and beam into it, to observe it and also be part of it in a new and strange way.

Acid was the devious mad path I snuck down, half-afraid of the medical consequences, but it fortunately acted as a balm and capacitor. It wasn't quite the glue itself that held me together, but it created a reserve current and an auxillary trajectory chamber where I could dump a lot of psychical stuff I could sort later. When it all surfaced eventually, it came out with a clarity that wasn't frightening but revelatory.

The pictures I shot on acid are good, provided it was a good place to shoot in the first place, particularly a frame I shot in Yosemite, which is quite strong, as though I'd tapped into something. I stopped there with Tony on the way back from a trip to Oregon. This was before the park was compromised, when there was still a bit of Ansel Adams left in the place. It was autumn and there were rainbows in the waterfalls.

I'd trained in forestry for a bit, and I like being out in nature, but I hadn't until then experienced a wilderness trip with the same bright revelation or the ability to transcend mere vision, ambience, and feeling, and interface all that into a photograph. There were no people in these pictures. They were of patterns of leaves, mists breaking a bit of water, the themes of classic oil paintings. It could well have been that it was simply time for this to happen. There was a synergy to the whole undertaking. For some reason there was a perfect wind on the roll, so there wasn't even half a frame missing. I even took a picture of an oil spot on the road that could have been a junker, but it too was on the money. I used some of the shots from this series in an exhibition. They continue to earn money for me at the agencies that represent my work.

That day in Yosemite, the acid locked something in, as though a giant switch were thrown deep within my aesthetic consciousness. After that my landscape photography became stronger. It helped me to take pictures with "paint," to use the photographic medium in a more Zen-like way. Rather than doing some demented hippie-trippy bullock through the pastures, I'm able to take the freaky sides and wobbly bits when I'm really peaked out, to take all that fairground spring energy and align it so I can really use it.

Acid wired in an understanding of the Other Side that enabled me to resume my will to live while pointing out that though death is something feared, 'tis better to countenance it with a certain Buddhistic flexibility. By that I don't necessarily mean "faith," though one does have to attune one's psyche to the forces in control. In Thailand, for instance, you can't ignore the *pi,* the spirits. If there's one lesson I've learned from being in Southeast Asia, it's that there are energies that comprise a continuum. So it makes sense to have a *pi* house in your garden to keep them sweet.

Today I'm too old for the uncertainty of LSD. I do enough weird things going off on the road for long periods of time. To minimize the unpredictable, I travel business class on airplanes and stay at nice hotels. Even with the end of the conflict, I just can't take acid in the middle of downtown Cambodia, though I know people who do. The

Indochina I've seen, and can still see through the veil of modernity, was weird enough. Everything you saw in *Apocalypse Now* was real.

Today I meditate before my Buddha each morning. When I find center, when there's nothing to see or touch, I'm in a space that appears to be made of clouds, a marvelous, seamless igloo which is lightly thawed, a sort of inflatable cocoon lined with a plush surface like the long, beautiful white fur I had in my Paris bedroom, which used to be great to fuck on. Then I'm in touch with my missing dead friends to whom the *Requiem* project is dedicated.

All these faces appear to be seated on banquettes in little sentry boxes or Orthodox pews like you find in Baltic graveyards for talking to spirits. I'm standing offstage and they're talking quite audibly. I have remarks to make that are completely out of place as per normal and try to project my voice into this ambience. I seem to be screaming, much as I imagine I did as I woke from the anesthesia after the head surgery, though in reality it is a mere whisper they cannot hear.

Heaven 3 by Jon A. Bell, digital composition, © 2000, courtesy of the artist.

PART III

A Conversation with Terence McKenna

A Conversation with Terence McKenna

Shamanologist, lecturer, and author or coauthor of seven books, including *The Invisible Landscape* (1975), *The Archaic Revival* (1991), and *True Hallucinations* (1993), Terence McKenna (1946–2000) was, arguably, the most eloquent and persuasive spokesman for the psychedelic experience and the plant kingdom from which it emanates that the planet has ever unleashed. The astonishing—and most promising—aspect of McKenna's scholarly and poetic rant is that he actually believed that psychedelics, particularly the serotonergic tryptamines, *mean* something, that there's something *intended* for us within their frontiers, and that we really ought to cautiously but intrepidly cross over and check it out. He wasn't merely suggesting that they offer cool visuals and groovy love vibrations. He was confident that what they impart is *ultimate.* The focus of his quest wasn't so much to manifest the tripper's soul per se but to unveil the ineffable Other, the revelation of which might help put his or her soul in ontological context.

McKenna proclaimed the power of the tryptamines (i.e., psilocybian mushrooms and DMT in its various forms, derived from either nature or a chemistry lab) to purposefully, by a suprahuman Voice, impart the secrets of the eternal Mysteries, the aim of evolution, and the End of History. The very purpose of these plants, he insisted, is to reveal to us the wisdom of the *gnosis,* the esoteric truths held by the Gnostics to be essential to salvation, and the *Logos,* the divine mind at the heart of all Creation.

The psilocybian mushroom, he writes, is "an intelligent organism radiating through the galaxy over millions of years . . . an extraterrestrial intelligence that has seeded our planet with the spores within which lie the pathway to evolutionary intelligence and galactical citizenship." Claiming that the tryptamine could access a "dimensional vortex beyond which seemed to be eternity, the land of the dead, all human history, and the UFOs," he considered the frequent yet officially unconfirmed sightings of flying saucers and "alien spacecraft" an almost erotic tease to prepare us for the advent of extraterrestrial intelligence. This "encounter of the Alien Other," he writes, is "a shockwave generated by an eschatological event at the end of time." Thus, he argued, even the future can be seen via the psychedelic.

McKenna's descriptions of the DMT experience are breathtaking in their beauty and utter weirdness:

> Here is the realm of that which is stranger than we *can* suppose. Here is the mystery, alive, unscathed, still as new for us as when our ancestors lived it fifteen thousand summers ago. The tryptamine entities offer the gift of new language; they sing in pearly voices that rain down as colored petals and flow through the air like hot metal to become toys and such gifts as gods would give their children. The sense of emotional connection is terrifying and intense. The Mysteries revealed are real and if ever fully told will leave no stone upon another in the small world we have gone so ill in.

Strangely enough, much of McKenna's cosmology is actually plausible. He could very well have been right, that the universe *is* composed of language (isn't DNA itself a code or language?), that we must first transcend parochial cultural contexts to truly understand reality, and that the sacred plants could have been placed here by some knowing force to enable us to manifest the translinguistic dimension and make contact with the Alien and Ineffable. Why not? If life beyond this Earth cannot be discounted, and if the Voice within the plants cannot be effectively muzzled or refuted, then McKenna could very well have been onto something. Regardless of whether his theories are proven right by independent sources in our lifetime, coming from perhaps the premier psychonaut of the modern psychedelic age, his dispatches from the Other World are well worth heeding. I know of no other human being who's brought back so many artifacts from the Great Beyond.

Ever partial to tryptamines, McKenna maintained that the psilocybian mushrooms conjure "the greeny engines of Creation" as compared to the psychoanalytic glass house manufactured by LSD. Far beyond the gentle pulsing of color and softness in the soul reported by most mycelial mystics, McKenna described mushroom-related phenomena that are quite literally out of this world. During an Amazon expedition in 1971, described in *True Hallucinations,* McKenna and his brother Dennis discovered (or "intuited," as Dennis told me in a recent correspondence) that the tryptamine in the native *Psilocybe cubensis* mushroom attaches itself to the user's DNA, causing the two strands of the double helix to vibrate intensely. (They took the high-pitched tone they heard as corroboration of this.) The McKennas believed that the tryptamine had sprung loose the secrets of the universe embedded in the DNA, the two spiral staircases of which move in opposite temporal directions, one toward the past, one toward the future.

Upon their return to the United States, McKenna found that the structure of DNA resembles the sixty-four-part sequence of the *I Ching,* so he set about to compute the ancient Chinese divination guide into a huge fractal equation for all human history. The result was his original Novelty Theory and Timewave Zero, which he describes as the score of "the biocosmic symphony, . . . a kind of mathematical mandala describing the organization of time and space . . . a picture of the patterns of energy and intent within DNA." Timewave Zero, recently upgraded to incorporate a noted mathematician's corrections of a minor error, is available as a software program through McKenna's Website. (Interestingly enough, the McKennas aren't alone in fashioning something useful out of a psychedelic-honed fascination with DNA. Kary Mullis, the 1993 Nobel Prize Laureate for Chemistry for his invention of polymerase chain reaction [PCR], a system for multiplying minute amounts of DNA for research, has said that he probably would not have made the discovery if he hadn't taken LSD, which had shown him a way to get "down there . . . with the molecules.")

According to McKenna's intricate mathematical formulations, time will work in an ever-tightening spiral of events toward "maximum ingression or novelty," leading to the final time or *eschaton* on December 22, 2012, a date that happens to coincide with the end of the Mayan calendar. Life on earth, according to the theory, will then transform into a paradise more pagan and Dionysian than the dour salvation conceived by Baptists for the resumption of life after Armageddon.

Consider Stanislav Grof's observation that synchonicity, the acausal chain of related events, is accelerated by the "emergence of archetype," which, in turn, can be effected by the psychedelic. To project this principle on a macrocosmic scale, the psychedelicization of planetary consciousness that McKenna foresaw would compress the spiral of events and hasten the ingression of novelty to a boiling point. As I understand it, once contact with the Main Dynamo is expanded via the ever-widening tear in the Cosmic Veil made by psychedelic consciousness and other manifestations of the Archaic Revival, the flow of synchronistic signals and ensuing interconnections will engulf the human race like an ever-intensifying schedule of beneficent mind-field sorties, filling the human sensorium to capacity the way that Jupiter's black spot filled with monoliths in Arthur C. Clarke's *2010* (1982), after which the cosmos must necessarily burst at the seams to accommodate the new resplendent spheres of consciousness.

Like any prophetic vision of an end time set to occur within its author's presumed lifetime, McKenna's was somewhat ripe and overwrought, by my sights. Never mind the chances for hotwiring a planetwide fusion of spirit, culture, and technology in little more than a decade. It'll be hard enough for high-definition television or the World Trade Organization to coalesce and evolve by the year 2012. Even so, the sheer optimism of McKenna's predictions, and the lyric intensity, effusive mirth, and often self-effacing humor with which he delivered them, confer some cracked measure of hope in their veracity.

McKenna himself has become a *meme,* a replicable code like a gene that has entered the slipstream of the psychedelic "group mind," where he can be conjured like a veritable archetype. A rave promoter I met in London claimed to have received an out-of-the-blue phone call from McKenna, with whom he'd not made prior contact. He'd been trying to sleep after a long night of tripping and clubbing during a visit to San Francisco, when, in the middle of the night, the phone began to ring with an "insistent and incessant" tone. He picked it up, and a distinctive gnomish voice claiming to be Terence McKenna proceeded to relate the promoter's entire evening to him. When I met McKenna a few months later, he said he'd never even heard of the guy, chalking the whole thing up to his (McKenna's) having, by some hilarious quirk of human affairs, made the Big Time, where manifestations of his persona had entered the public domain, capable of being downloaded at will. I have no doubt that now that he's crossed over to the Other Side, some psychedelic explorers will begin to hear *his* singular voice—ever the more insistent—speaking through the plants.

The material presented below is the product of two extended conversations at McKenna's home in South Kona, Big Island of Hawaii, on January 17 and 18, 1998, some sixteen months before he was diagnosed with glioblastoma multiforma, the most malignant of brain tumors, which eventually required him to move to the mainland for treatment. (His doctors assured him there was no causal link between the extremely rare affliction and his decades of illegal drug use.) The modernist eco-dwelling, which generates its own power by solar voltaic cells, is situated about a mile up a rough dirt road through a lush, subtropical rain forest. Spare of furniture, McKenna's jungle nest was well equipped with the staples of his existence, a communications center and two entire walls lined with thousands of books, a pipe lying in an ashtray ready at hand. At one end of the living room was a spiral stairway up to his private chamber, which was illuminated by a domed skylight. On each of the two days, we sat on a mat in the middle of the floor and conversed from morning until well past lunchtime.

When we met by arrangement on the highway the first morning, the elfin Celt immediately put me at ease with his contagious whinny of a laugh about the silliness of consumer culture, political developments, the foolishness of contemporary life. I felt right at home.

"The fact is that, in terms of human evolution, people* not *on psychedelics are not fully human."

On Trips and Tripping

LSD

TM: My very first acid trip took place in the summer of 1965 in San Francisco prior to my enrollment in Berkeley that fall. A friend had gotten the acid and he sat for me. I've actually never had a trip like this since. It was very bizarre.

The universe divided itself into two opposing concept entities which were all there was. One was called the *losteks,* which were profound, the very essence of solidity, meaning, and being. They were not funny, not human, not friendly—they were godly. The spelling is perhaps suggested by that of the Jovian moon. The opposite concept was the *Pinkastares,* which embodied all the silliness that fills in the cracks between the *losteks.* The *Pinkastares* were fragmented, small, jumpy, brightly colored, and trebly. The difference between the two was like the contrast between Wagner and a child's music box.

So I oscillated between these two antipodes. I would announce, "The *losteks,*" and then melt in awe and religious wonder. Then I'd say, ". . . and the *Pinkastares,*" and this would issue gales of laughter and rolling around on the floor. For a couple hours I just pronounced the two words. I was in company, but they were growing restless. Nobody there had ever witnessed anybody in quite this state before.

Finally, about four in the morning, my sitter had had enough. I was in no shape to be turned loose, but he just threw me out, putting me on his front stoop on Green Street. I was vaguely aware that I was supposed to go to my job as a restaurant busboy at noon later that day. I had about thirty blocks of San Francisco between me and my job to traverse over the next eight hours. So I went down to California Street and took the trolley up to Grace Cathedral at Stockton and California, the big Episcopal structure by the Maritime Union. I let myself in and proceeded to have a religious epiphany in the realization that they'd gotten it all wrong—it was the rose window that was God.

I shouldn't have been walking around on my own in that state, but then I went across the street to the Masonic Temple. The great doors stood open and I walked into the immense lobby. I walked into an elevator. There were only five floors. I pushed floor five. The elevator went up to the fifth floor. I stepped out and found myself in the foyer of a theater, a performance space. Nobody seemed to be around, so I walked through these velvet curtains into this vast theater with rows and rows of empty seats down to the proscenium. Hung over the stage was this enormous banner about twenty feet across. Emblazoned on it was the letter *M*, which I instantly understood was for me.

Right then I had the intimation that I had some destiny, though I'm not sure I have one today. I certainly have a reputation I didn't have then, when I was just a spear-carrier at the center of the Sixties revolution. When I saw the letter *M* on that banner, it was like "Aha, I have a destiny!"

CH: And your name in lights! That's what's scary sometimes about acid, the "for me" delusions.

TM: Yes, delusion of reference, when you think something's about you and it isn't. Yes, you've got to watch that. It's a problem with all psychedelics. Speaking of which, at La Chorrera (Columbia) in '71, when my brother Dennis went nuts and had a series of revelations, one of them was "In the future there will be a machine that many, many people will have, and it will be named after us."

"Named after us?" I asked.

"Yes. It will be called 'the Mac.' " And so it came to be. (Yes, I'm a Macintosh user.) Dennis and I had the trip of all trips in the Amazon, described in *True Hallucinations*. More than that I don't hope to have this side of the yawning grave. Anyway, from that revelation at the Masonic Temple I somehow made it back to ordinary reality, but I've never revisited the place in my psyche where the *losteks* and the *Pinkastares* reside. The reason why I've never written about it is because I never reached a conclusion.

CH: Well, that's an interesting trip. It has a bifurcation, dualism, a delusion of reference, a religious epiphany. Our readers will want to know that you were once young and susceptible and had no mastery over the psychedelic mysteries.

TM: I don't feel that I have any great mastery at the moment—perhaps *relative* mastery.

Maybe the reason that psychedelics are such a formative force in my life is that they worked for me as advertised. When talk of LSD first hit, I was growing up Catholic in a small town in western Colorado (Paonia), and I had all kinds of resentments toward my parents and their lifestyle. I was dark, into Jean Genet, Albert Camus—an existential brat. My politics were half-baked Marxism. Later in 1965 I took one of those five-hundred-microgram White Lightning caps from Sandoz, and it was an experience of complete boundary dissolution and love, which had, prior to that, been moved way out of my vocabulary. In a single trip, all my animosity toward my parents, all my ambivalence toward my sexuality, everything was replaced with the force of revelation. Those earlier trips were not ideologically freighted. They were emotional transformations.

LSD Vs. the Tryptamines

TM: It's hard for most people to hallucinate on LSD. An acid hallucination is a little fan-shaped thing on the wall that blips back and forth. Well, a psilocybin hallucination is MGM Grand. The kettledrums roll, the curtain lifts, the high-kicking girls are there, and off we go! DMT is the granddaddy of them all, because it delivers ninety-five percent of what can happen on psychedelics in two and half minutes, and it takes no prisoners.

CH: I would think that something that intense you wouldn't need to do more than a half-dozen times in your life.

TM: If you get it, you don't need to do it more than that. I know people who say it's their favorite drug, who haven't done it since 1968. It's not a drug of abuse. I do it once a year or so. The thing about profound experiences is that if they're too profound, you can't remember them. In other words, if it's too out-of-category other than that you've just been through something that completely threw all your switches, you can't really say much about it.

CH: I had terrible times coming down on acid.

TM: I did too. I find acid difficult, fragile in the sense that you can have a negative thought and it's like a boulder rolling down the hill. It can bring the entire mountain down on you. Acid is somewhat contentless. It's psychologically abrasive, like pouring Drano into your psyche. It just cores out the plumbing and leaves you in a fairly existential place. You may need that.

Acid may do you more good than psilocybin in this respect, but psilocybin is less introspective. It has a message. It wants to tell you its story. It doesn't want to go through your story in high detail. Psilocybin is active at one gram, but you don't hear voices until five grams. I've been interested in certain functions, and I've found that the tryptamines do what I want. Then it's just a matter of standing more, going deeper. There are many psychedelic drugs that I haven't taken. I find that the synthetic ones *seem* synthetic, more like drugs and less like doorways.

MDMA

TM: I've done MDMA a half-dozen times. It's not very interesting to me. I felt real good, but minus the hype, it was just amphetamine. If you study the history of drugs, every one of them at some point travels under the banner of being a "love drug." LSD did that. Psilocybin did. I think it's true in every case. I'm not knocking it. To say that MDMA is the thing for restructuring your relationship, as though taking two hundred mics of acid would be futile, is odd, to my mind.

CH: But MDMA seems to throw open the doors of your psychological house and enable you to calmly, without panicking, examine your own neuroses.

TM: Yeah, but I think on a hundred mics of LSD the same thing would happen. Plus, MDMA has some toxicology issues that need resolving.

Ketamine

TM: I've done ketamine about five times, in fairly light doses, 125 milliliters. A doctor friend was very enthusiastic about it, so he shot me up. My impression is that it's an intrauterine-memory drug. You can't feel your body, which you interpret as weightlessness. And you can't feel your lungs working, so you feel as though you're getting placental oxygen, since the last time you felt like that, you were receiving oxygen through your umbilical cord. It muffles sound, which enhances the strange weightless feeling, and you're also totally relaxed, as a fetus would be.

As it came on in the first five minutes, it was like being embedded in warm shaving cream or Styrofoam. Then there was the sense of open-cage elevators rising. There was a sort of high-pitched dramatic organ tone, like one would hear in a hierophany. This has never happened to me on any other substance. I'm not sure it's a pro or a con, but I'd lost the concept of "high on a drug," so I couldn't figure out what was happening.

What is this? I asked.

Who's asking?

Who cares?

I was grappling with this for a few minutes, and then it hit me. *This is a trip!* And then it all came together. *Oh, right! I'm a human being. I took a drug. This is a psychedelic experience and an interesting one, in fact. Now I'm oriented. Let the trip proceed.* But those few minutes in which I was just lost in the noise were very bizarre, because I just couldn't figure out who or what it was.

One thing I experienced on ketamine, which I remembered from acid trips years ago, was this weird perception that many people have had, which is hard to know what to do with: You have this very strong impression that the world is always like this; we just don't notice. This is an absurd proposition, because hell, if the world were really like this all the time, we would damn sure notice!

CH: It's a way to reward yourself for having traveled so far in your mind. You're calling yourself a discoverer, saying, "This is a little secret we're all keeping from ourselves."

TM: Ketamine is very artificial. There's nothing like it in nature. Also, I don't think you should do drugs that might prevent you from noticing if your house was burning down around you. This stuff puts you down. They could remove your pancreas and you wouldn't bat an eye. Ketamine is dubious.

Salvia divinorum

TM: Before I did *Salvia divinorum* (translated as "the diviner's mint") for the first time a couple years ago in California, I'd heard that it was quite kick-ass, so I had a certain amount of trepidation. The hallucinations came on as little pink bunnies and little blue kitties, like the wallpaper of a child's room. I realized that it was a parody of my fear. It was deliberately insulting me with hallucinations acceptable to a six-year-old. So I addressed it. *I may be chickenshit, but I'm not this chickenshit. You can lift the veil slightly.* Then the trip normalized into the kind of streaming that happens on the first part of an ayahuasca trip.

The next time I took *Salvia* was in a rain forest in Mexico in a tent at night. Then I saw a very specific hallucination. It was as though a pair of invisible hands were, in a very professional manner, dealing and shuffling cards in darkness. I couldn't see the hands. All I could see were these neon-blue cards being shuffled.

I've also taken it out here in South Kona. I took it in a room with a skylight on a moonlit night with silver light pouring through, so there were all these high-contrast black and silver shadows. It was the perfect situation in which to hallucinate on a psychedelic. There were no hallucinations with my eyes open. With my eyes closed, it was like turning on a light, that quick. The hallucinations didn't require any time to form. They were just present, undulating, three-dimensional, spatially convincing, and there was a voice inviting me to "walk into it." I said, "No, I'll conflict with the world I'm in. I'll stumble over furniture."

"No, walk into it."

All you need to get off is a single leaf. You smoke it to get the most efficient results, though I was eating it. No drug that powerful has ever been discovered in nature. The high is challenging. Even DMT test pilots get white-knuckled. People come out of it thrashing and babbling about geometry, about having folded up or unfolded, a lot of talk about folding. What this means is that it's transforming the spatial orientation centers of the brain. Some come back shaking, saying they've been flattened over miles, that they're huge and paper-thin.

Salvia's interesting, because there's no near relative. It's a drug in a family of chemicals never known to contain drugs, so it can't be scheduled easily. The only way it could be properly scheduled is if you adduced medical evidence that there was something wrong with it, but nobody knows the pharmacological dynamics of this stuff yet. Meanwhile, it's still legal. What is the establishment going to do with this? To suppress it will create a drug industry around it. To leave it alone is to admit defeat in the drug war, because it is a powerful hallucinogen. Can they afford to turn their backs on this?

Cannabis

TM: When you first encounter cannabis, it's very psychedelic. I did wonderful things on cannabis in the early days. I could get into these places where I could imitate authors' styles extemporaneously with voice. I would do these long, wandering monologues in the style of Melville, Poe, or Lovecraft. It took me a lot of pot-smoking before I finally realized I was really stoned, but I entertained a lot of people before I got there.

DMT

TM: The best DMT I ever had was made in the laboratory, not from a plant. My favorite plant source is *Psychotria viridis*, the Amazonian bush used to enhance the visions of ayahuasca. In my experience, the hallucinations on 5-MeO DMT are disappointing, not as dramatic as regular DMT by a long shot. It's like an enormous emotion.

My first encounter with DMT was in February 1966. That did it for me. The compass of my life was set. DMT is the thing you've spent your entire life slowly getting used to the idea that it doesn't exist. "Give it up. Get over that." But then, here it is. It's like primal innocence, proof that God loves you, or proof that the world is entirely marvelous, that, if that's possible, anything is.

CH: One of my interview subjects attributed the current rise in circulation of DMT to your public enthusiasm for it.

TM: I'll take credit for it, because for years, I was the only person saying that we've got to look at this. By saying this everywhere for a dozen years, there is some in the underground now. Rick Strassman did a study of DMT (published in the MAPS newsletter) that confirmed my findings. Sixty percent of those who had the full dose saw entities. That's the point I wanted to make. There's something in there. Rarely is a drug so specific as to consistently conjure entities for most who take it.

When you take an oral psychedelic, you negotiate with it on some level. At twenty minutes it's this, at one hour it's this, etc. With DMT, the entire thing unfolds in about twenty-five seconds after you inhale it, and then you're at the peak. Since there's been no sense of travel, it's not like a journey. It's like a place. It's as though you've just transited through the membrane and now you're in this other dimension and you have no idea of the planet you left behind. It's fully realized. A door opens and then you're there.

The other strange thing about DMT is that if you're paying attention, it does not affect your mind. You are exactly who you were when you smoked it. What it affects is what we normally call reality, which is completely replaced by another reality, while you're not. So your challenge is to deal with the change of reality. *Did it kill me? When will it be over? What the fuck is this?*

Here's this drug which is, as far as anybody can tell, perfectly harmless, and yet the experience is so extreme that I would venture that ninety-nine point nine percent of the human race goes to the grave without ever even suspecting something like that is possible. You don't have to go to Africa or climb Mount Everest. It's one fucking hit away. It's a complete confoundment of Western—and Eastern—psychology, religion and science. It's like an alien artifact, like something that fell from a flying saucer.

How can this be? Why isn't this making eight-inch-high headlines in every newspaper on Earth? If it's important what Saddam Hussein is doing, what the government of Australia is doing, then it is certainly important that science has delivered into our hands an easy method to access inhabited alien worlds in two-minute slices.

"Well, it's a hallucination," they say. Well first of all, you don't have to do too much philosophy to figure out that reality is some kind of hallucination. Saying it's a hallucination is not a knockout punch.

If art is a probing of the unknown, then how come human art has not a whisper or a hint of DMT in it? We've had Beccafumi, Pollack, Piero della Francesca, but nobody got near this, not even the Surrealists. Yet, here's this experience that leaves you absolutely quaking. It's like an aesthetic orgasm, a Niagara of beauty, but *alien* beauty. Every atom of it is alien and unpredictable, and all of it is beautiful.

The Otherness of DMT

CH: How and why do you characterize it as "alien"? Why can't this strange and fascinating imagery be a reflection of the inner universe rather than the otherness you ascribe to it, as though it were, as you suggest, a gift from beyond the galaxy?

TM: Because we can't describe it, while we can describe everything else. Analogy fails. You can't say it's like this or that. The truth is it's not. Isn't that what "alien" means—foreign? I'm not saying it's beyond the solar system. I'm saying it's alien.

CH: You've suggested that the psychedelic mushrooms may be a gift from extraterrestrials.

TM: The mushrooms as a life form may be alien. The mushroom experience as well is alien, because it has no context.

CH: What makes you so confident that otherness itself holds something that's meaningful, when it might be finally all boiled down to something that we might comprehend?

TM: Rudolph Otto, the German theologian who died in 1937, defined God as "the wholly other." I associate the transcendent with "the other." It seems natural to me, but this may be a personality trait. I don't put much credence in astrology, but I'm a very extreme case astrologically, a triple Scorpio with a heavy twelfth house.

CH: Isn't the God of Christian America a familiar and approachable figure, like a grandfather with white robes, a guy you can talk to?

TM: In that case, what does the admonition "fear God" mean? This is not to say that God is both bad and good. It means that God is alien.

I've always understood that the way was the weird. If it's weird, stand next to it until something weirder comes along. By that means I navigated myself to India. I was born with this curiosity about the strange. When I was young I was told there were dinosaurs in the hills, that a hundred million years ago this was all ocean. I went out and found the clam and snail shells and the dinosaur bones, and this gave me the sense of deep time.

I've always been interested in nature, specifically color in nature, which is to me the path to psychedelics. When I was a kid I collected gold and silver ores and pyrites and stuff like that. Then I moved on to butterflies, which I've collected all over the world. Then I got into science fiction and rockets. All of these seemed to me as psychedelic as psychedelics themselves. It was the best I could do in 1952. I was teased about being weird and different. I became who I am around the time I was eleven, and I've always been that person ever since. I've added on sexuality and this and that, but basically I'm curious.

CH: My father, for one, would say that there's enough mystery and ambiguity in *this* reality. Why should we analyze, break down, and identify and know this other reality, which you say is tumultuous, volcanic, astonishing, ineffable?

TM: First of all, we need data points. It's a big question whether this is the only reality or not. That's been an issue for thousands of years. DMT settles that: *This is not the only reality. Next question?*

CH: What kind of reality is it?

TM: There's nothing of this reality there. By nothing I don't mean chairs or books. I mean space and time, before and after, up and down. They've eliminated that.

CH: Why should our minds try to embrace something so befuddling?

TM: "Befuddle" implies that it's puzzling, which implies that your mind can get a certain amount of distancing and then no further. That implies a game: How far can your mind go into this and still rationally apprehend what is happening? So it becomes an instantaneously available frontier. I have a friend who says that when he takes mushrooms, his goal each time is to stand more. I know exactly what he means, that it can always trump you in the weirdness department. It can always lead you to a point beyond which you would prefer not to go. And DMT is more confounding than anything.

Now, if your model of the psychedelic experience is that you're going to go into your private unconscious and have creative thoughts or vivid memories or explore heart-blockage issues, then DMT will completely confound you. It does none of that. That's not to say that such inquiry isn't worthwhile on the other psychedelics, but DMT is not a psychoanalytic tool. It's evidence of a trans-human reality. You certainly wouldn't take somebody who's worried about his marriage and say, "Here's evidence of a trans-human reality—this will fix you up." He'd say, "No, no. I want to reconcile with my wife!"

CH: Do you have an interpretation for the machine element of the elves?

TM: I notice now on the Internet that you can search "self-transforming machine elves" on Yahoo and get a page of stuff. But these tend to be flat and low-dimensional descriptions of the entities. All linguistic descriptions of DMT are. It's hard to English what they are. What you're seeing is a brain function that is normally suppressed, a three-dimensional model of your own syntax.

You see language being processed in a way that ordinary serotonin metabolism doesn't support—the assembly, the architecture, and the syntactical constraints. All this stuff that is normally hidden in the active language is suddenly not only available but visibly deployed in three-dimensional space and emotion. You recognize it as intimately of yourself. In a sense you recognize it as your soul. The DMT tykes are keen for us to do this. It's a language lesson. It makes me wonder what the first language was like. Did the plants teach us to talk? If so, they don't talk the way they taught us to.

CH: Why the diminutive? Why the tykish, elfin motif?

TM: Here's one thought I did have on that. From the moment you enter into the DMT experience, you're in a domain that is the idea of somebody really weird of a reassuring environment for a human being. It's warm and comfortable and softly lit. It's domed and enclosed. As I looked at it more and more, I began to realize it's the equivalent of a maternity ward. It's an arrival place, a hatchery built to receive human beings loaded on DMT, and it's designed to control our impressions of that world. They've been waiting for you. They know you're coming.

Weird as it is, every single thing about it is designed for human consumption. The toys they offer, these Fabergé eggs, are in a sense nothing more than the plastic geometric shapes that you would hang over a bassinet to coordinate an infant's color and spatial reflexes. The entities say, "Do not give way to wonder. Do not abandon yourself to astonishment. Pay attention." And then they do this language lesson thing, iterating it over and over, using sound to make objects, or at least visual hallucinations, appear in the air. The entire encounter is never longer than three to six minutes. Then you pull out of that through a series of declensions back to ordinary reality.

DMT's Language Lesson

TM: Everything over there is nonreferential to everything over here. You can't speak about this world in that language, though you can listen to tape recordings of these glossalalias by people spontaneously producing languagelike phenomena on DMT, mouth noises that are clearly under the control of syntax but one released from conventionalized meaning.

CH: Have you published any sayings or phrases in this language?

TM: Well, spelling is an issue . . . It sounds like this: EE kem wye STOK see kee pee PEEN. Vid nim gyo WOKS sid dee mahok a ben dee kee KEK det nen get bikeek teen. Ayus dee viji ZEN GWOT, kay MWON day kwa OK dikee tee teekt. EE vidimee NEEN nenk wah OK sot vay bon wa hagendekt . . .

Stoned on DMT, it's an ecstasy to do this, an absolutely indescribable full-bodied phenomenon. And the sound is accompanied by the meaning, which is visible. You adjust it. You push in and pull out. It's like modeling. You use your voice to model an idea in a hologram. If you analyze language, you can tell that language as we practice it today is unfinished. We're still trying to understand each other's intents, i.e., thoughts.

I take my thought. I consult my dictionary. I choose words from it and put them through an English syntax filter. I acoustically modulate the air coming out of my body with my mouth, throat and lips, and thereby send a signal through the air that enters your ear to your brain, where it's transduced into a phenomenon in your nervous system that you identify as a person speaking. You consult your dictionary. You match up the incoming acoustical signals with the words in your dictionary and then form an assumption, based on the idea that your dictionary and mine are the same, that your interpretation faithfully replicates my original intent. Now if you understand only Chinese, you will not reconstruct the simulacrum of my intention. You'll only hear acoustical noise.

If, in fact, the psychedelics modulated consciousness and introduced consciousness into the human species, then it's reasonable to assume that this process has not slackened or halted, and that maybe we're on the brink of a new modality of language that, through neurological rewiring by experiments with drugs and prosthesis, we're going to be able to process language through the visual cortex rather than through the acoustical centers of the brain. This will give us a universal human mode of communication.

In ayahuasca groups in the Amazon, we'd sit in complete darkness loaded on this plant brew. People would sing. After it was over, I'd hear the old guy next to me say to his wife, "I liked the part with the silver and the orange, but I thought that when it turned into the blue and black striping that it was too understated." But it's one thing to imagine what music might look like. Imagine a synesthesia of spoken language. What would this conversation look like, and what would we learn from it if we could see it that we don't learn by merely listening to it?

The secret that DMT is trying to tell us is either that language is only the tip of the iceberg that we need to discover, or that language is in the process of transforming itself. These entities seem to be syntactical creatures made of language. In that other world, everything has the quality of a brilliant pun. Now, the magic of a pun is not that it means one thing and also another thing; it's that it simultaneously means both things at once. In the ontology of this world, that's impossible. In that world, it's given. To verbalize the way things really are in the DMT reality, you need a language in which every word is a multiple pun. To describe things there using our limited language, you have to destroy at least half of them, and then you're left with only a facet.

Spoken language is something we do because we can. We have the mouth, the glottis, the larynx, and the lungs, but it's not communication as it was meant to be. It's a flattened and depressed and compromised form of media. What the DMT tykes are offering is the opinion that "you shouldn't assign sounds to meaning. You should give it visibility."

CH: To make manifest.

TM: Yes. When they speak, you literally *see* what they mean. There's this fantasy that once we were telepathic and/or that we will be again. If I could hear your thoughts, I'd be telepathic. The DMT experiences have given me a completely different take on this. Telepathy is when I see what you mean, a transduction of intentional meaning into visual space. The DMT entities make objects out of syntax that are themselves somehow imbued with autonomy or life, because they can speak as well. They can make subsets of their own objectiveness. Twenty seconds before, you were sitting in a ratty apartment with your strange friends fiddling with some strange drug. Now that's all gone and you're inside what may as well be a flying-saucer being given an eighteen-dimensional language lesson by these shifting buildings made out of light. They don't say, "We want to trade for fetal tissue" or any of that horseshit. They say, "Do this language thing."

James Joyce and Marshall McLuhan were onto how people, according to their cultural programming, were cued to either sounds or images. There is much to explore in this area. For instance, as I'm speaking, are you seeing pictures or are you hearing words? Whatever the answer is, is that genetically or culturally determined? The DMT creatures want to show us a new ontos of language. If there could be a shared three-dimensional space, then ambiguity would be much diminished, and the social glue of communication would be strengthened. When you think about the fact we have a global civilization knitted together with nothing more than small mouth noises and that we have five hundred human languages with no one fluent in more than ten or so at a time, it's amazing that we've gotten as far as we have. What we need is to eliminate ambiguity and widen the bandwidth of language. I have no idea why these entities locked up in a plant, coming from whatever dimension they're coming, give a shit to hand this on to us, but this seems to be their gift.

The news about the world reaches the surface of your body as a unity of radiation, but your senses each have a take on it. Your eyes take one channel, your nose another, etc. You break down the seamless modality of the exterior world and channel it in these various ways, and then presumably reconstruct it into a sufficiently faithful simulacrum so that you can do your business and stay alive.

Unifying the senses would give an experience of the world not like seeing, not like hearing, not like tasting or smelling, but like all of those and whatever emergent properties come from their combination. I'm talking about the evolution of the human nervous system and sensorium through drugs, prosthesis, and design. We've been building virtual reality since *Ur.* First we used brick, mortar, steel, and glass. Now we use electrons. A city is a virtual reality, a replacement of the natural environment with the constructs of the human mind. It was all in somebody's head once. We live inside these ideas which we excrete. Human beings are the idea-excreting primate. A mollusk can excrete a shell of one genetically specified type for its species. We're epigenetic excreters. We can produce all manner of forms in the physical world that were previously constructs of our imagination. No other animal does anything like that.

Where virtual reality comes in is as a prosthesis to achieve this. If we want to create an environment where you can see what I mean, then first time out, we may need to do some fancy technical fiddling. We need a computer that listens to my speech and assigns a predetermined geometric shape to the various articles of speech and connects everything together in some syntactically acceptable way, so that while I'm talking, this essentially voice-driven sculptural modality will come into being. If you could build an apparatus like that, people would quickly transfer loyalty to the sculptural mode of communication. If you could see what people mean, you would not need a locally learned language. You wouldn't need to learn Japanese to understand what a Japanese person has to say. You could see what he means. I mean in the ocular sense, absolutely.

In English we sense this, because we associate visual clarity with understanding—"I see what you mean." The ontos of language wants to go toward the visual. If I read a paragraph from Proust, we could then spend two hours discussing what the author meant. But if I show you a sculpture by Brancusi, that's what the artist intended.

CH: Do you anticipate DMT becoming a tool of a growing number of people?

TM: It's a benchmark. To animate it, understand it, to explore it, and surpass it are all-important goals. As we dematerialize, and that seems to be what's happening—we're getting ready to decamp from three-dimensional space and time into the imagination, which is as vast as the universe itself. Virtual reality, simulation, showing each other the contents of our minds, taking psychedelic drugs to make these contents more exotic, and then modeling: This is where the human future is headed. We've been doing this for a long time. When people started telling stories around the campfire, they were inventing show business and inviting people to step into the imagination, folks. Let's take a trip down memory lane, somewhere else.

Psychedelics and Religion

CH: Is religion a worthy medium for psychedelic exploration, or are psychedelics good fuel for religion?

TM: Psychedelics are good fuel for religion. Every drug religion or cult I've seen seems to get a large amount of message from a small amount of psychedelic. But I think they should give more drug, less message. I'm very worried about what religion's going to do with psychedelics. For instance, as Christianity moves on to its deathbed, I expect it will reach for drugs to sustain itself.

CH: I had a Christian vision on LSD, an image of the "blood light" that I believe Gerard Manley Hopkins wrote about, a tremendous sense of confidence that this was the love of the Father shining through the flesh of Jesus.

TM: The love of the Father shining through the flesh is not a Christian revelation. "Of Jesus" turns it into a Christian revelation. I've had such visions, though I resist them furiously. I have a Jungian vocabulary, which allows me to steer around such places. *Uh huh, here comes the archetype. It's highly numinous, meaning that people have prayed to it for millennia. It has power, but do not give way.* Once on a mushroom trip at some epiphanous moment I knelt and the voice said, "Get on your fucking feet. You will meet this on your feet."

"Oh, I'm sorry. A moment of reverence." I was feeling a sense of awe. Totally inappropriate, apparently.

I was raised Catholic and I'm very anti-Catholic. I think it's a horrible, horrible institution—the dogma and the social politics. I agree with Suetonius when he said that Christianity is not a religion but a cult of Christ. Religions deal with the great questions of man's origin and fate. Christianity touches none of that. Christianity is a species of Hellenistic Gnosticism, which is built on a foundation of neo-Platonic idealism. There are basically only two religious positions available in the West: dualism and monism. Christianity is a radical form of dualism—mind/body, good/evil, and the eternality of evil, which is pure Manichean dualism—though it denies this. One can have a revelation of dualism and have only the vocabulary of Christianity to wrap it in. So you say, "I'm having a Christian revelation," but if you knew more about Hellenistic religion you might say you were having a Marcionite revelation.

I've thought a lot about Christ on psychedelics. What if we thought of the whole thing as some bizarre crypto-biological experiment that went wrong? Christianity is a cult of physical immortality, which was unheard of in the Hellenistic world. The doctrine of the resurrection of the body, a central dogma of Christianity, is astonishing. The promise is that at the end of the world we will be reunited with our bodies, that graves will open and corpses will animate and everybody whoever lived will be alive in the flesh. In the Apostles' Creed, it's one of the top ten of things you sign on to . . . "the resurrection of the body and life everlasting. . . ."

CH: I'd thought that was specific to the Catholic faith . . .

TM: Are there others? (Laughter) Do you mean, as my father used to call them, "off-brand" religions? Actually, the Apostles' Creed is used throughout institutional Christianity.

There's a wonderful story in the Gospel, in which the three women come to the tomb the morning after the Crucifixion, and the stone has been rolled away. Christ is sitting on the edge of the tomb, alive. They approach him and he says, "Touch me not, for I am not yet completely of the nature of the Father." Here is Christ reborn, resurrected, but saying he's not yet completely transformed. This implies a process that was uncompleted.

The way I understand Christ is as a precursive reflection of the concrescence, in other words, an image of something that lies in the future, perhaps the union of spirit and matter, and this particular person, the son of a Galilean carpenter, just happened to be situated in a place in space and time where it was his fortune, good or bad, to have to act out this precursive reflection. I'll bet that if you can put yourself into Christ's mind as he went about his career, the main question he was asking himself was *Why do I do the things that I do? Why am I compelled to behave this way?* The answer lies deep in the mechanics of the historical continuum.

The mind will generate dramas of psychopompic transformation. This is what gave Jung the key to understanding alchemy, that the mind presented with the unknown, whether through meditation or through the swirling of a chemical vessel, will project a drama of fall and redemption. This is simply the structure of the psyche. We meet this coming at us in the world all the time without recognizing that we create it.

CH: Intense psychedelic experiences have been tough for me personally to incorporate into my life, so I have a kind of dualistic take on so-called religious revelations and the whole phenomenon of psychedelic consciousness.

TM: It is very hard to incorporate it. That's why the "recreational" categorizing of these drugs can wreak havoc. Most people end up scaling down the dose, so that the ego can manage the content of the experience. Well, then you've got a defanged experience. On acid particularly, you can get really spun out and confused on low doses.

Freak-outs

CH: In many of the experiences described to me there was a darkness closing in on the subject and later a release.

TM: If we're going to talk about serious boundary dissolution, you have to talk about erasing the boundary between life and death.

CH: Have you had moments of mortal terror?

TM: How about intense alarm? When you feel like that on a psychedelic, it usually indicates that you need to oxygenate your brain. So sing. Open your mouth and belt out a few bars of "Row row row your boat." The other thing is to have a bomber of cannabis rolled and ready. That's the rudder on your ship, if you get into strange water. Smoke some of that. You may get into different strange water, but it will certainly shift the modality.

CH: Could you describe a moment of psychedelic-induced intense alarm that you experienced?

TM: One that I don't want to visit anytime soon occurred when I took half a dose of ayahuasca and half a dose of mushrooms together. This is probably not a good idea. After a fairly normal trip by myself, sitting in a big chair, I was hit with the notion that "something's wrong." So I came to a state of full alertness, surveyed the situation, discovered nothing was wrong, explained to myself that nothing was wrong, and five seconds later it repeated, "Something's wrong." Five seconds later, the cycle repeated itself and proceeded to again and again.

Later, in analyzing this state, I realized that my short-term memory was being interrupted and was not transcribing into RNA. I knew my whole life story. What I didn't know was the last thirty seconds. This may sound like a minor problem, but it was a huge one. When you can't find it, you keep poking back for it. That's the "something's wrong" impulse. Then you say, "No, nothing is wrong."

"Well, something's wrong."

"Nothing's wrong."

"Yes, something's wrong."

It graduated in intensity, because I was becoming alarmed. I had the image from *2001* of Dave outside the spaceship saying, "Open the pod-bay door, Hal."

"I'm sorry, Dave. I can't do that."

I could almost see the jammed molecular machinery, that the drug molecules were not, for some reason, decoupling from the synapse the way they should. Here we are locked outside the spaceship, can't get the door open, and panic is rising. Finally I held on to the idea that *it's a drug and therefore cannot last forever.* I vowed not to move from the spot until it was over with, no matter how horrible it became. Then I started breathing and waiting and soon—good old pharmacology; drugs don't last forever—I could feel this thing decouple and snap out of place, and forward we went. But had I remained in that place, it was truly madness, truly unbearable. I don't think you could get used to that.

Breathe, breathe, breathe, and the thing will move. It's almost always helpful, unless there's a serious problem, such as you really *were* molested when you were eight and discovering it right at that moment. Buddhist practice is excellent for psychedelics. Americans should learn to sit still and pay attention and analyze what Buddha called the upwelling of causal effect.

Of course, caution is also advised. I've met ayahuasceros in the Amazon, native guys, who said, "I did this for twenty years, and then

I had a trip that so pushed me around that I never went back." It's like mountain climbing. Just because you've climbed the world's ten tallest mountains doesn't mean that you couldn't slip, fall, and be killed on the next assault.

The Relative Dangers of Psychedelic Exploration

CH: Some of my interview subjects have related how they subjected their bodies to ordeals while tripping, in the belief they'd taken on some supernatural invincibility.

TM: People, you should behave as though you're mortal, for God's sake! Be happy if the evidence is to the contrary. Remember the old Russian saying that Reagan used to quote all the time: "Trust but verify." That's the way to proceed with psychedelic explorations. Doing one's homework can be critical.

Do people actually get fucked up from psychedelics? Absolutely, they do. But do they if they take them infrequently and in high doses? I think what they do is take them at low doses frequently and in combination with alcohol and other drugs. This is stupid. The real problem is the wannabe, the person who isn't really interested in psychedelics, but all his friends are, so he takes some and gets anxious and has a panic attack and then turns in his friends, and then there's cascades of karma and hysteria. Most people take drugs because they're the hip thing to do. That's a terrible reason. There's a small percentage, say ten percent, who do their homework.

What would it be like to take DMT without a knowledge of modern art, philosophy, quantum physics? It just gets flatter and flatter until finally it's "a buzz, man!" The drug cannot create information out of nothing. You have to have stuff in your head in order to triangulate that kind of experience.

CH: You're saying in effect that psychedelic drug use should be regulated.

TM: I think it should be regulated to some degree. We don't let people drive cars just because they want to—out of concern for the safety of the rest of us. For crying out loud, turning people loose on the streets with no information about drugs is completely irresponsible. In this respect, we're where sex education was in 1870. We should educate people, even to the point of perhaps, when you're a senior in high school, you go out on a sort of psychedelic field trip. This would require a social revolution and a note from your parents, of course, but people should be informed of how these things work. Then let it go at that. The term "recreational drugs" both trivializes and markets drugs. "This is not important, but it is for sale—and fun." That categorization makes the legal task of suppression easier, of course.

The only constant that I've observed in psychedelics is that they dissolve boundaries. Psychedelics affect each of the personality types differently, because each relates to boundary issues differently. One man's heaven is another man's hell. Psychedelics are definitely not for everyone, but I think they're probably for most people. Who it's not for are people who have trouble maintaining boundaries, people who through traumatic upbringing or genetic predisposition are in danger of floating away anyway.

On Cultural Developments, Science, Technology, the Future, and the End of Time

The Rave Scene

TM: "Re-Evolution," the recording I did with the Shamen [a top-twenty hit in the U.K.] was made when Colin Shaman, the genius of the band, asked me to see them while I was in England, with the idea that maybe we could work on a project. He and I talked on a sound-stage and he later asked if they could use the tape. I said, "Sure."

I was there because the rave scene was looking for elder figures and at fifty I qualified. I was preaching plants and that was a new message to a lot of them. England has a season of mushrooms, a wonderful thing in September when people troop out to Wales and go nuts for days. This is a good thing. The hope and faith of rave is that music can actually affect the human nervous system, though I think there's too much heroin in that scene, which is a very youthful one. Many are there because they're clueless, because their friends are there, because it's the place to be. But on the other hand, some of the most encouraging young people I've met have come out of rave. The music is good too. (You should listen to Coil, Station Rose, Zevulia, for instance.) I go to raves in Australia, South Africa, Germany, everywhere. The culture comes from England, but by now it's spread from Kyoto to Alice Springs. The Australian rave scene, for one, is totally self-sustaining, booming, enormous.

CH: How do you interface with the rave scene?

TM: Somewhat uneasily. Usually I'm there to do something onstage. They're information-starved. They'll stop the music, sit down on the floor and listen to me for an hour at three in the morning, and then go back to the music and the smart drugs. I see it as a sort of magnet for the creative and interesting young people. But then they find themselves in it and redefine themselves. The scene is not based only on Ecstasy. There's a huge amount of acid and a great interest in psychedelics of all sorts.

When you think about it, "the Sixties" were really just about eigh-

eighteen months prior to 1968, which was the turning point, the year of rage with street-fighting, cop-killing, bomb-building. The rave thing has been charging forward full-bore since 1986. It's twelve years old and it rules large sections of the planet. So for them it was almost as though, in this frantic effort to be like the Sixties, they went so far past that era that we don't need to talk about it anymore. Of course, we in the Sixties had that war to contend with. It was more complicated.

The Pagan Scene

TM: I was at this scene in western New York called Starwood, which bills itself as a pagan festival: five days of nudity, cannabis, this and that. On the final night, they piled up dead apple trees two hundred feet high and set them on fire, and six thousand people tore their clothes off and danced all night long around this thing, raising a cloud of red dust in the air a thousand feet high. This was my first trip to the "Midwest." It was so far west in New York that I flew to Cleveland to get there.

I took one look and thought, *No wonder the right wing is alarmed.* I'd never seen anything like this. They were actually *fucking.* In California, "nudity" means you take your clothes off on the beach. To these people, "nudity" meant bondage, leather, tattooing, body piercing, jeweled nipples, perfume, incense, yellow brass, tinkling gongs, trickling water. These were pagans. I love them. As they say of themselves, "We're corpulent," and they certainly are. These naked people are not your sylphlike, tiny-titted fairy girls. These are major human beings moving like summer thunderstorms.

They had this thing called the Temple of Aphrodite, where you just presented yourself to be laid and were escorted in and so it was. I'd never been to any social function where that was going on. I was in a relationship at the time, so I declined the invitation, but I smoked some DMT with some people there.

"Where can we get loaded?" I asked.

"How 'bout the Temple of Aphrodite?"

"Great!"

The pagan community sees itself on one level as the repository of the psychedelic impulse, in part because the mystery rites of Greece were probably psychedelic. It's also where all the people who hate monogamy congregate—the polyamorists, the this and thatists. It's very factionalized. You have the OTO (Ordo Tempo Orientalis: the Aleister Crowley people) and various other "denominations." It's a sexually loose crowd. They love to eat. They love to fuck. They smoke dope. They eat meat. They carry on. I saw S&M stuff, but it didn't seem to dominate the scene. They're into costuming.

CH: Is this sort of paganism part of the evolution of culture you speak of?

TM: This is certainly a manifestation of the Archaic Revival I've written about. The twentieth century has seen a series of manifestations of the archaic impulse: Freud (the discovery of the unconscious), Surrealism (the abandonment of reason), German National Socialism (the call of the blood), jazz, rock 'n' roll, sexual permissiveness, rave culture, obsessions with shamanism and boundary dissolution, new myth-making.

CH: None of this neo-paganism seems to be hurting anybody.

TM: Unless you have a lot of stock in linear, constipated print-culture, in which case at this point you're probably shitting white.

CH: The Satanists are a drag, of course.

TM: But who has ever met someone who said, "Hi, I'm a Satanist. Come join us this Friday. We're going to sacrifice some children. We'll make a place for you." They're out there, but it's largely a projection of the fevered paranoia of the right-wing political imagination. To them we're *all* devil worshipers.

Shamans and Shamanism

CH: Are you a shaman?

TM: No no. I'm a shamanologist. I do shamanic journeying, but I don't cure. From a sociological point of view, the power to cure is all that matters. The fact that he has this rich interior world and mysterious experiences is irrelevant. His social function is to cure. A shaman who cannot cure is a broken shaman.

CH: Isn't shamanism to some degree a shell game, as you say the spiritual culture of India and the East is? Do we need to invest power in the shaman, or should we be shamans ourselves?

TM: In modern civilization we're far away from the sources of shamanic inspiration. It's a very difficult, specialized function, like becoming a neurosurgeon. The initiation rites of aboriginal societies are as close to the shamanistic mysteries as most people get in their lives. When I was much younger, I toured the world looking for doorways into other dimensions, and I found a lot of what I call "wise old man" wisdom embodied in those guys sitting on porches at twilight smoking their opium pipes and gazing off. They can tell you something about how to live, how to have children, how to bury the dead, but they can go to the grave without themselves ever having an inkling of this psychedelic thing. Shamanism operates over a gradient that slowly turns it into priestcraft.

There's also the question of shamanism practiced not in the presence of psychedelics. Is it phony? Is it efficacious by other means? There's a dispute about this among anthropologists. One school says that shamanism achieved with drugs is decadent and one saying that shamanism achieved without them is. It's a question of primacy of tools. I think that the school that opposes drugs is operating under a Victorian value system, looking at it through the white man's lens.

If we lay out the various techniques of ecstasy side by side: intoxication by plant alkaloids, abandonment in the wilderness, flagellation and ordeal, obviously psychedelics are the most effective and the least invasive. If you flagellate people in tropical environments, you get septicemia. You can lose people in the wilderness. You can force shamanic experience, but how many are permanently traumatized or even die in ordeal situations? Every aboriginal culture must access the unconscious, and the fortunate ones are those that have psychedelic plants in their immediate environment that facilitate this.

Shamans are *meme* traders. What genes are to genetics, *memes* are to philosophy, history, and the humanities. A *meme* is the smallest possible unit of an idea. Madonna is a *meme*. Marxism is a *meme*. There are profound ones and short-term ones, and they all compete just like genes. The march out of the animal mind has been accomplished by this trading at the borderland of the Other. Shamans trade with entities in other dimensions, which may be our own nervous system, the Gaian mind, friendly extraterrestrials several dimensions over, God, or a higher mathematical space where there's some kind of an intersection. The Other could be any of these things. We're not in a position, at this point, to sort this out.

CH: But you're leaning toward the friendly-extraterrestrial theory . . .

TM: I'm torn between two pretty possibilities. The extraterrestrial possibility, which, at our present state of scientific knowledge, most people could probably come to terms with, given the amount of faith in unseen extraterrestrials. The other possibility, applying Occam's razor here, is that what we're talking about is dead people. The shamans say, "Didn't we tell you that it's all done through the magic of the ancestors?" "Ancestor" is a pretty sanitized term. "Dead person" brings it home a little more cogently. Is it possible then that the human soul exists autonomously from the human body and that there is no unbridgeable barrier?

CH: Like virtual conferencing across time and the death barrier. The Mayans did that, right?

TM: Yes. The Mayans are the only high civilization who took drugs in the presence of an extensive culture. They had no Egypt, no Moses, no Plato, no Christ, no Rome, none of that to guide them, and yet they produced calendars, philosophy, theater, poetry, mathematics, astronomy, architecture, hydrology.

CH: Shouldn't people, if they do elect to do psychedelics, do them through a shaman or similarly trained guide?

TM: The problem is we have no shamans here. Those who claim to be shamans are the last people you'd want to put confidence in. The closest thing to shamans in our society are psychiatrists who have the guts to work with psychedelics. You have to realize how far out that is, because there's no medical or malpractice insurance that covers such treatment. If something goes wrong, you're just destroyed and taken away to jail. But there are people who have given high doses to hundreds if not thousands of people in a psychiatric setting.

I'd rather see a very practical, hands-on psychiatric approach to psychedelics than turn it over to religions and have it dogmatized, not that a psychiatric school couldn't also become mired in dogma. The psychiatrists that I know are pretty eclectic. If you give people psychedelics you have to keep them reassured and give them permission to go wherever they want the experience to take them. I don't know if you need a lot of method or theory. You just need to be a compassionate human being who's reassuring when that's what's required.

I couldn't do it, because of what Jung calls the danger of transference. All therapists know about this. People who are tripping are guaranteed to try to transfer something to you. You're his father, mother, lover, the guy stalking him, the person he's stalking. It's extremely challenging work of a sort I hate to do. I am not a people kind of guy. I've been in situations where people have come apart on psychedelics. They're okay twelve hours later and I'm a wreck for three months. That's why I do most of my tripping alone, because I find that I go deeper and return clearer than if somebody else's thing is unfurled all around me.

CH: In order to bring about the kind of society you seem to want to breed, don't you need more formal social situations in which to conduct the psychedelic experience? The ayahuasca religions in Brazil, for instance, seem to be a wholesome approach.

TM: They're wholesome but low-dose. They couldn't run a scene like that with real doses of ayahuasca, because then you couldn't maintain a social context. I believe that if you can maintain a social context, you're still inside the cultural game, like sitting in a church with people in uniform, having hymns chanted at you. With the psychedelic you want to go beyond that. I unplug the phone, lock the door, and lie down in a darkened room.

I think people should *begin* their psychedelic exploration with guides. If your first several trips out don't show any major structural flaws in your hull, then you can go it alone. The guide is not really a guide. That's a misnomer. Nobody can guide anybody else. They should be called "reassurers." They're just there to say, "It's okay. You're doing fine."

CH: I could use one of those.

TM: I know! Everybody does. The most important question in the universe at that moment is *Am I doing all right?* And the answer is (usually) *Yes, you're doing fine.*

Novelty Theory and the End of Time

CH: I find your optimism about the state of the world's civilization and the fate of the ecology cheering and heartening, even though I remain pessimistic myself.

TM: It's possible to be an optimist without being a cockeyed optimist. Look what we've done. For fifty years the thermonuclear arsenals were pointed at each other. This is a planet ruled by carnivorous monkeys that have atomic weapons and only used them twice on human populations. That's remarkable.

I believe we're in the garden party before the crunch, the long afternoon before the stormy night. I don't say the future won't be tumultuous and horrifying, but we're going to make it. Most of us. My optimism is inspired in part by something I've developed called Novelty Theory, which takes observations that anyone can make and verify as true and build a case for optimism out of. By "novelty" I mean "density of connection." Hypernovelty or hypercomplexity is the state in which, as more and more things are connected, everything would be moving toward infinite novelty, a system in which every point was what mathematicians call cotangent to every other point.

Fact one: The universe has grown more complex from the very first moments of its existence. This growing toward complexity has not been absolutely smooth. There have been hiccups and setbacks, but the system homeostatically resets itself to always move in the direction of deeper complexity. This phenomenon affects all matter and all energy in the universe. At the moment, human society happens to be the greatest and most complicated form of novelty in the universe.

Fact two: This movement toward complexity occurs faster and faster as you approach the present. It's not a steady process. It's an asymptotic accelerating process. That means that the amount of novelty that the universe could generate in a billion years five billion years ago, it can now generate in just twenty years.

If the business of nature is the creation and conservation of complexity, then we are nature's golden baby. So being a human being is not an existential cosmic accident for which you should give thanks to a Gnostic god who doesn't give a shit anyway (science's position). It turns out that human beings are the cutting edge, the raison d'être, the very purpose of creation. So the idea that the universe values novelty rescues human beings from meaninglessness. Humans therefore exemplify universal values. The universe is trying to produce systems very much like the systems we have. Suddenly God then lies in the future, as mathematician Alfred Whitehead believed. He spoke about an aboriginal god that is growing toward itself through time. Yes, God exists, but is not complete. The very existence of a temporal continuum indicates that God is straining toward some kind of union with itself.

CH: It takes faith to believe that, right?

TM: If God was complete, why is there the phenomenon of temporal enfoldment. This is a problem in many religions. In Buddhism, if a single being achieves enlightenment, all beings do. Buddha achieved enlightenment, the paranirvana. Have we all therefore achieved it? The answer is: Yes, no, maybe, and don't ask the question. The universe exists in two states, a completed state of true being and a state of becoming, which has a petition for true being and seems to be moving toward it through time. Complexity, the generation of connectivity, seems to be the value that is seeking to be maximized.

CH: Is the entire human race participating in this pursuit of novelty?

TM: The Internet has created, on many levels, more connectivity than in the previous history of the Earth. In 1992 it didn't exist except for a few assorted UNIX-wielding geeks. In 1998 everybody's using it and any household can compose in hypertext and put up a Website. There's never been anything like this except, perhaps, the introduction of radio. The Internet ends isolation for people. It is boundary-dissolving the same way a drug is. In fact, say it softly, but the only difference between a drug and a computer is that one is too large to swallow and our best people are working on that problem. There's a migration of these things toward each other.

There was a funny incident a few years ago. A woman who writes a column on cyberspace for a major newspaper was told that the cybernetic revolution was fueled by psychedelics. She thought that was an outrageous claim, so she went to SIGGRAPH (the Association for Computing Machinery [ACM] Special Interest Group on Computer Graphics), and asked about a hundred people what they thought of this opinion. Something like ninety-three agreed, so she dropped her opposition to the concept.

Studies have shown that the growth of science was directly related to the introduction of the international postal union, which created the opportunity for academic colleagues to correspond with one another. What do you think E-mail is doing to the speed of discovery? How many people do you think have stopped reinventing the wheel in a laboratory because they realized that Uri or Suchan or somebody somewhere in the world had already done that work and here's the paper on it. Science is learning how to eliminate redundancy from the research process and pump it out ever faster.

The discoveries that lie on the horizon are unimaginably transformative for human society. Did you follow how a bunch of atoms was teleported recently? *Nature* magazine reported how a bunch of photons was transported twelve feet with zero time loss. Not a fraction of any zero. Absolutely zero. The device is the product of a storm of mathematics from this guy Anton Zelinger at the Institute for Quantum Cryptography in Vienna.

There is an intelligence associated with this planet that is nonhuman, therefore very alien, and from our point of view, capable of doing anything. There is something we share this space/time continuum with that can, when it chooses, take on any form it wishes. It doesn't work like alien abductions. It is not cheesy, lame, dumb, or tacky like that. It has an aesthetic. It totally penetrates all space and time and it can change the texture of your thoughts if it wants to.

Bottom line, there is something very weird going on, something ahead of us, not very far in time, that is extraordinary, the equivalent of time travel, alien contact, and religious revelation rolled into one. And it gives off some kind of distorting radiation, a field that bends ideologies that come into its influence. We've drifted near some kind of cataract, a *chronosynclastic infindibulum* (a phrase from Kurt Vonnegut's novel *The Sirens of Titan*), which means this is a black hole in the narrative and anything can happen.

So as we proceed into the future, more and more people are having peculiarly skewed quasi-revelations of this thing we're approaching, which is complicated by a blurring of memory and dream in modern society, as the print age dies away. One guy announces that the world will end on May 25th. Another announces that the Pleiades space lords are on their way, someone else that if we'd only dig beneath the Great Pyramid, vast reservoirs of knowledge will be found and our true circumstance in the cosmos revealed. People are locking their doors at night so that aliens from other star systems won't perform proctological examinations on them. But why should they want to look up your ass? All these people are getting it wrong. Those Heaven's Gate people who committed suicide were resonating with the concrescence, the thing I talk about that's coming in 2012 or whenever, but they got it wrong. Everybody has it wrong, including me. But they got it *really* wrong.

As an airfoil approaches the speed of sound, Q-forces ("Q" is the symbol for vibration in an airfoil) build up on the leading edge, and if the airfoil isn't designed correctly, the vibrational forces will destroy the wing and the airplane will fail. But if it's designed right, the Q-force reaches its maximum and then begins to drop and you slip smoothly beyond hypersonic flight. The culture can be thought of as an airfoil moving faster and faster through historical time, and the Q-forces, in the form of religious cults, terror cells, renegade scientists, nutty dictators, and mendacious politicians, are shaking the social airfoil to pieces as the acceleration rises. Sometime in the next decade after the turn of the century, we will smash through it or the airfoil will be ripped apart and there will be outbreaks of plagues, and religious nuts will seize control of major governments, and race wars and famine will take place. Or it will right itself. I'm sure it will. I'm not apocalyptic.

Appalling things will happen, of course. Mexico City, the world's largest urban center, could be buried in volcanic ash. There are plenty of pressure points where something could happen. But catastrophe motivates us. When the Three Mile Island disaster happened, I was cheering it on. Can you imagine if they had had to evacuate Washington, D.C., and declare it a no-go zone? If what had happened at Chernobyl had happened at Three Mile Island, we'd be living in a new world, just like the Russians are. The federal district would have had to be evacuated and the appalling nature of what has happened to the social contract would have been laid bare like a sliced-open tumor for all to see. They got it under control, so we don't even remember what happened.

Human beings represent qualities of nature found nowhere else in the world of organic organization. Life runs on genes. We don't. We run on *memes.* We haven't changed much in fifty thousand years, but our cultural *meme* systems are being exchanged every eighteen months. We are ourselves like a canary in a mine or a weather vane in the wind. This planet is moving toward transcendental redefinition of itself. After one and half billion years of evolution, organic organization is reaching some kind of threshold and passing through it.

Biology is a strategy for dimensional conquest, culminating with the cheetah, which is able to run sixty miles an hour, leap thirty-five feet, and see half a mile away. But that's it. It's locked in the moment. Then comes man, who can remember, which means command images of what is *not* going on, in other words replay the past and strategize by watching the movies, and out of that comes language and technology. These are fourth-dimensional strategies, while the evolution that led to the cheetah is about the conquest of three-dimensional space.

If you post guards at the front of the cave, go to the back of the cave where the furs and the fire and the women are and take a lot of drugs, the first boundary that dissolves is this three-dimensional paranoia. It's almost as though the mind has two confirmational geometries, like sulfur, a yellow powder that when heated melts into a black liquid, and if you keep heating it, into a black solid, and keep heating it still, into black liquid again. The ordinary confirmational geometry is for ordinary consciousness, but remove stress and threat and add a lot of alkaloids and perturb the brain and it will unfold into a hyperdimension, a four-dimensional matrix. The psychedelic experience is 4-D perception.

When man began to speak and recall, the conquest of the fourth dimension, time, was under way. All of the uniquely human attributes are time-binding. To bind time we write books, we build myths, we remember genealogies, we predict the future. This planetwide process has been going on since the birth of language, but it's now reaching some kind of culmination. From the point of view of 4-D, next week is as easy to look at as last week, and over there is as easy to look at as right here. In 4-D it's all-present. In 4-D, all books can be read without opening them. All boxes have a door on the side that you can look into without disrupting them. All the "tricks" of shamanism can be explained if you grant that the person is accessing a higher dimension.

So culture is the transition along McLuhanesque lines from the 3-D animal mind to the 4-D posthuman mind. And the human experience is the fractal domain between those two, where you're half in and half out. On Tuesdays you're an angel; on Wednesdays you're a monkey. And this boundary is constantly shifting.

Something has torn loose in one species. Only because we're embedded in it do we not proclaim it God's descent into history. Out of billions and billions of species that have lived and gone extinct on this planet, we are the point species that is the first over the line into this hyperdimensional modality. And we're doing it by building a global image of ourselves, a human mind the size of the planet linked through a symbiotic relationship of intelligence and geology, the latter being the gold, copper, aluminum, steel, and glass that will become the infrastructure for the integrated global technosphere of data transfer—the new prosthesis of humanity.

It's not coming. It's here. If you go to the media lab at MIT or the CERN (the European Laboratory for Particle Physics, in Switzerland), and stand at the nexus of the Internet, you realize that it is already here. It's just a matter of passing the word down the ranks that a new order of being has sprung from the forehead of historical mankind. As Hans Moravic said, when you build an intelligent machine, the first task you set for it is to build a more intelligent machine. The speed at which these iterations are happening is causing a singularity. I think that the singularity is built into the structure of space and time.

There are people who would just laugh at that. They've reached the same conclusions I have but think it's just a human phenomenon. Still, they take the curve of energy release, the curve of the rate of invention, the curve of the rate at which computers are being connected together, and project them all out a decade or two into the future and everything goes to infinity. At an enormous historical momentum, we're slamming into omniscience. We're reaching deeper levels in understanding space, time, matter, and energy than was ever necessary for the prosecution of simple commerce.

The rate of novelty is accelerating so fast that for all practical purposes, it's going to reach humanly unfathomable levels of intensity within our lifetime, not a thousand years in the future or a hundred. That cheerful Newtonian scenario of gradualism has just been canceled by the connectivity, the meltdown, the psychedelicizing, the internationalizing, the globalizing that is going on. Something that big is happening. We're redefining ourselves so fast that we are becoming unrecognizable to ourselves. It's an epiphany, an apotheosis, the end of the world, the beginning of the world. You just can't unfurl enough superlatives and hyperboles to bracket what is happening. This is what this planet was made for.

CH: Who's doing this with any planning in mind?

TM: Nobody. That's the wonderful thing about it. It's built into the dynamics of the system. We're like atoms in a magnetic field, or bees around a hive. Everybody just wants to make some money and move to the suburbs, and that drive alone is sufficient to propel the species and the planetary ecosystem toward this end or beginning. Everybody just needs to do a good job and keep an open mind and not clench. There will be a lot of clenching from fear and anxiety, because the news is that very little of what we recognize and relate to as our world will survive.

Is the planet moving toward some sort of conclusion? Are psychedelics a curiosity or are they central to the unfolding of the immediate human future? I think they must be the latter, because I can't imagine practicing human history for another five hundred years in the same way that we have been. We've painted ourselves into a corner where the only choice is real nightmare—triage, epidemic disease, famine, fascism, the collapse of human rights—or a leap to an entirely different level. We've taken business-as-usual off the menu. Now only the extreme possibilities loom.

My faith is with technology and with psychedelics. Politics aren't going to take us much further. We're awakening as a planet to the very good news that all ideology is parochial and culturally defined, like painting yourself blue or scarifying your penis. A culture is a limited enterprise. How could someone be so naive as to imagine that an ideology, a thought system generated by the monkey mind, would be adequate to explain the universe? That's preposterous. It's like meeting a termite who tells you he's a philosopher. What could you do but smile at the very notion.

There's more change occurring in our lifetime than has occurred in the previous history of the planet, so we're going to see some major speed bumps sweep past us. People are so adaptable that they don't understand what's happening. Think of how we grew up under the threat of the Soviet Union. It's gone! But nobody exalted. People say the Jews and the Arabs will never get it together. It's a done deal. Don't worry. All these things will work out. We're very impatient.

The Internet has remade the world in six years, and most people take it for granted now. It's disturbing that many are retreating from full participation in this new reality, because they can't understand it anymore. They don't know how to talk to people who are transgender, or how to code an HTML document. They're just giving up. They might as well go live in a museum diorama.

CH: How will the great link-up occur (in 2012) if people are dropping out of these developments?

TM: As novelty grows more intense, it concentrates itself in fewer and fewer domains. As we move toward this singularity, more and more people are becoming place holders, because they can't understand what's happening. This has to do with relativism. People believe anything they want, and it no longer matters, because there is somewhere a core of cutting-edge thinkers who are still trying to integrate all this stuff with fact.

The Preeminence of Science

TM: I'm not a believer. I'm not going down the path of sheer revelation. One of the bad things about psychedelics is that they've left us with a legacy of intellectual relativism. If you want to believe the U.S. Air Force is trading fetal tissue with aliens for fiber-optic technology or that the secret of life handed down from Atlantis is under the Great Pyramid, or that Baba-gi so-and-so is God, I'm not supposed to criticize you, because it's all the same, right? This is relativism. I hate this. It's the death of thought, and that's what the New Age rides on. You're not supposed to ask hard questions. In California, people never say, "I think your belief is horseshit!" People are so polite, and everyone seems to disdain science. I hate the fact that America, the land of Jefferson, fills the ashrams of India with ditto-headed seekers. People should not follow leaders. The free-thinking enlightened individual is the highest ideal of humanity that has ever been articulated: responsible, reasoning, compassionate, and definitely not driven by ideology.

My only academic degree is a science degree, a B.S. in Ecology and Conservation of Natural Resources from the University of California at Berkeley. I also studied art history and the philosophy of science. The guy at the workbench who works for a detergent company is not a scientist. That's ridiculous. Those guys rarely study the philosophy of science, so they don't understand what it is epistemologically, what its bottom line is. I'm famous for knocking science, but I knock it as an insider. It's the only human enterprise where you get credit for proving you're wrong. By that *bass-ackward* movement, it's managed to stay open-ended for twenty-five hundred years, while religions have crashed and burned. Inquire of nature, make models, be willing to discard the models, keep the hypotheses simple, use numbers. It's done a marvelous job.

CH: A case can be made that as science advances, humanity desecrates itself.

TM: I don't find that case persuasive. As science advances, it brings change, some good, some bad. Are we to give up inoculation for disease, public health, the telephone? The relevant question is the social policy that deals with the science. How is it put in place? Who does it serve?

The Internet was the greatest unanticipated transfer of technology to the lower classes in human history. By lower classes, I mean that we're all peasants really. When was the last time you spent time with someone who formulates American foreign or social policy? I don't spend time with these people.

CH: I'm trying to remember . . .

TM: Well, peasant (laughter), that was the last time you were up at the castle. We're rich peasants, of course. Don't confuse poverty and peasantry. We're rich peasants, but we're totally in the dark, and the great ones come and go on their sleighs from the castle, and we mark their comings and goings, but we have no idea what's brewing up there. Every once in a while they stumble and we get LSD or the Internet or something else that slips through the cracks. It's impossible to control history and it's so wonderful that so many people are trying, because it makes for such an interesting game.

The Role of Psychedelics in the Evolution of Consciousness

TM: Ultimately, something wants to be communicated through psychedelics. Something wants to be told, and it's not something ditzy like "Love your neighbor as yourself." (Laughter) We know that. That's not news.

CH: But if something so interesting and presumably sophisticated and worth knowing is trying to be communicated to us, why isn't it just posted on a Website so we can all download it?

TM: It's difficult for the human mind to get it. If you're not paying attention, it may appear as if your world is about to end. I believe there's a historical implication for the changes that are taking place, that the introduction of psychedelics caused this surge in the technologies that are shrinking the world and knitting us all together. To what degree is it simply a metaphor that the Internet is a collective nervous system, or *is* it, in fact, a collective nervous system? Has the planet become the womb of a posthuman intelligence of some sort, which we are scurrying around implementing?

Something is moving into the biosystem of this planet and dropping a whole higher order of information, writing, mathematics, music, technology, and we are fabricating this stuff, which is a simulacrum of our brain. And the planet itself is to be the motherboard. We're laying this cable and setting up these antennae and we think it's to push pornography or sell automobiles and beer, but it serves some deeper purpose. We're destroying all our politics and social institutions in the process. Everything has been tossed in the kettle, but we don't care. The main thing driving us is to put these technologies in place. It's almost as though we've hit the main vein of human creativity. Now we can't stop until we're God.

CH: What would that be?

TM: Ultimate power, ultimate knowledge, the ability to travel through time, through space, immortality, transformation of matter into energy, energy into matter. Don't you think we'll be downloading copies of human personalities into software and hardware? Everything you can imagine will be achieved. How about this guy Tiller, who said there's a moral imperative to bring back the dead; if you have the power to do it, how can you not do it?

CH: Fundamentalism about life on the other side of the life cycle from abortion, like the marines' code of not leaving their dead on the battlefield.

TM: Right. In fact, he even went further. Not only must we bring back the dead. We must bring back all possible human beings. Apparently we humans have this Faustian thing built into us. Until we can hold the universe like a screaming marble in the palm of our hand, we will define ourselves as uncompleted.

The psychedelics, by dissolving boundaries, as the Internet does, are allowing all kinds of creative connections to take place, which then push us harder. When you have a quantum physicist talking to a cryptographer and they're both talking to a kitchen designer, you're going to get something that you would never have expected. In one sense, psychedelics are simply enzymes that make the creative process and the process of discovery go faster. Thomas Kuhn's book *The Structure of Scientific Revolutions* shows that all scientific revolutions have had this quality of being revelations. Scientists always try to clean it up and say logically it went like this, but it never went logically. They occur in a situation very similar to psychedelic experiences: dreams and revelations.

A dirty little secret of modern science is that it was founded by an angel. The evening of November 18, 1621, a twenty-two-year-old Frenchman serving in the Habsburg army that had camped in southern Germany has a dream in which an angel appears to him, saying, "The conquest of nature is achieved through measurement and number." This is what he records in his diary. This was René Descartes, the guy who founded modern science. Cartesian rationalism is based on angelic revelation. The great scientists of old couldn't schedule their psychedelic experiences. They had to wait until tension and circumstance created it. Now, basically on demand, people can take these drugs and look at their professional concerns and integrate them in new ways. I know a lot of people in the hard sciences who have made breakthroughs on psychedelics.

CH: Most people are, perhaps narcissistically, focused on the integration, healing, or growth of their own personalities when they take psychedelics, while you seem focused on history, culture, the fate of civilization, the future.

TM: People have two questions: Where did we come from? Where are we going? I think psychedelics provide answers to those two questions. I developed a whole theory of evolution based on psychedelics, saying that the critical factor in moving advanced primates into being primitive human beings was the presence of psilocybin, which improved acuity, thus improving hunting, stimulated sexual appetite, and bifurcating consciousness, offering a choice between the static and a fantasized alternative.

CH: So drugs make you smart.

TM: We wouldn't be here if it weren't for psychedelic drugs. In terms of the role of psilocybin in human evolution on the grasslands of Africa, people not on drugs were behind the curve. The fact is that, in terms of human evolution, people not on psychedelics are not fully human. They've fallen to a lower state, where they're easily programmed, boundary defined, obsessed by sexual possessiveness, which is transferred into fetishism and object obsession. We don't want too many citizens asking where the power and the money really goes. Informed by psychedelics, people might stop saluting. "Take your political party, your job, whatever, and shove it."

Society dissolves as people discover their individuality. The trick is to create a society that honors both the community and the individual without placing one at a disadvantage to the other. America comes close, doing it through mere anarchy, which is how it should be done, to ride as close to the cusp of totally flying to pieces as you can. I love America. The fact that it tolerates me, doesn't bug me, indicates that it's a great, great system.

If psychedelic drugs actually do expand consciousness, as they were originally billed when they entered the stream of Sixties culture, then it is socially irresponsible not to put them into the toolbox. The style of culture we inherited from *Ur* (kingships, cities) is fatal. If we persist in our scripted behavior, we will go extinct. This mushroom, this innocuous-looking thing sitting in the pile of dung, made us human and could make us human again, but we have to say good-bye to all these things. We cannot practice resource extraction, male paternalism, etc., another five hundred years. The planet will not put up with it.

Why I Trip

CH: Why do you still brave these waters?

TM: I should quote George Mallory: "Because it's there." I want to trade *memes* with the Other. We're going to the edge and there we meet these entities. They're unlike us. We're obviously unlike them. This is a situation in which either we have nothing to say to each other or we must trade. That's what you always do when you contact another human group. "Here, we have knives and marbles and matches. What have you got?"

CH: So where are you when this inquiry is finished?

TM: I don't want to leave this world before ordinary people can, by some means, access and walk through DMT hallucinations. In other words, psychedelics should be used to drive art, and technology should be used in the service of this.

CH: And for your own personal quest?

TM: For most people, the early trips are the most narcissistic and the most difficult, because if you have issues with your upbringing or your sexuality or your class, they'll stand in high relief in the first trips, because, unlike psychotherapy, psychedelics work. You can't keep revisiting these things twice a week for thirty years! So then, what's the rest of your psychedelic career to be about? For me it's for spinning abstract hypotheses, for understanding. When you understand something, you are being most uniquely what human beings are. Understanding is the poor man's psychedelic. All a psychedelic can do is accelerate that process. Whitehead said that understanding is the apperception of pattern as such. When you coordinate a pattern, you understand. If you look at a roomful of people and discern the women, that's a pattern; brown eyes, elderly, other patterns.

Well, in any given situation there is an infinite number of patterns to be coordinated. Normally we don't spend hours looking at a scene before we make a move, because the patterns on the surface are sufficient for the coordination of decisions relating to the animal body. But, in fact, one could look at a pebble for days, and in a sufficiently enlightened state of mind, there would always be more to be learned. My brother came up with an apt geometric metaphor: "As the sphere of knowledge expands, the surface area of ignorance grows ever larger." Another way of saying that is "As you build the fire bigger, the greater the darkness that you reveal."

Cultures are very narrow slices of the sum total of the patterns potentially coordinatable by a social system. When people move outside of that, they become bearers of the charge of otherness. These are shamans, priests, scientists. Essentially, a shaman is someone deputized by a culture to go outside the culture. If you think of the culture as a spaceship, then the shamans are the people who do the EVAs (extra vehicular activities), whom you send outside to fix it from outside, because it can't be fixed from inside. Shamans know a dirty little secret about culture, which is that it's show business. Everybody else thinks it's reality. The shaman knows that it's artifice.

In the Amazon, when I was going up these rivers or landing in an airplane, the people would come out, the women with babes at breast and everyone tittering and giggling. They'd want to touch the airplane or the camera. Meanwhile there's a guy standing off at a distance just looking. He's the shaman. He has none of the innocence or simplicity of the others. He knows that people are people in all contexts and he's looking straight past your Gortex and your camera and insect repellent to see who you are.

Psychedelics as an experience of boundary dissolution are half the equation. The other half is what the subject thinks about that. With some people, you dissolve their boundaries and they say, "That's madness. I don't ever want to take that again. I'm ready to go back to my job and my church." We can't live without boundaries, but we need to be aware of them as provisional. A theme of the past year in my raves and talks has been the idea that culture is not your friend. A culture is a set of rules or an operating system that defines boundaries. Psychedelics indiscriminately attack this boundary-building process. A Marxist state, a fascist state, a democracy, and a theocracy can all get together to concur that psychedelics are terrible and have to be suppressed.

The French term for orgasm as a little death (*petite mort*) is an acknowledgment that orgasm is boundary-dissolving. In that sense, sex is the drug most people are able to access. There's a wonderful saying in Italian: "Bed is the poor man's opera." Most people arrange their lives so they can have sex, so they can have this incredibly fleeting, brief moment when it all falls away. Drugs do this same thing and for longer periods, so they gather to themselves the same attitudes and anxieties that surround sex.

So we've talked about the negative effects of psychedelics, how they take something away (boundaries) from culture and order systems. What do they give us? Once boundaries are taken away, wholeness is accessible. Wholeness is the great entity behind all these boundary-defined multiplicities. Suddenly, in the absence of boundary, good and evil, life and death, self and other, youth and old age, male and female, are transcended, and that is the essence of our notion of religiosity: the plenum, the One in neo-Platonic terms, the source from which all comes.

Language fragments reality and gives us multiplistic and manipulable forms that are grist for the cultural mill. When you take psychedelics, you could almost say we become like animals. We are returned to the boundaryless, prelinguistic wholeness, but because we've made this journey into language, we are exalted then by this contact with the seamless, nameless totality of things, the great unspoken silence of the animal mind. When we merge back with it, bringing the experience that history and language have given us, we become ecstatic for some reason.

CH: You're not saying you would like to jettison the teachings of culture.

TM: No, I think the real test of psychedelics is what you do with them when you're not on them, what kind of culture you build, what kind of art, what kind of technologies. The wholeness thing cannot be underestimated. It may sound trivial, but what's lacking in the Western mind is the sense of connectivity and relatedness to the rest of life, the atmosphere, the ecosystem, the past, our children's future. If we were feeling those things, we would not be practicing culture as we are.

It's interesting that the rationalist drive to compile a complete catalog of the inventory of the planet has brought the Trojan horse of psychedelic consciousness inside the city wall. "These quaint aboriginal people; look at them intoxicating themselves on these bizarre plants. Let's unleash our scientists and clinicians and grind this down into a bunch of academic papers and explain what's going on." But it turns out that this cannot be ground down to some academic trivia. This is a real Trojan horse and it's forcefully promulgating values that are as antithetical to the values of modern civilization as mercury is to water. So now a dialogue must take place.

People always ask, "When the mushroom talks to you, how can you tell it isn't your own voice or your own mind?" The answer to that is "Because it surprises you." We identify the other than ourselves by the fact we can't predict its behavior. Psychedelics persist in astonishing.

CH: So psychedelic exploration is like a Chinese box . . .

TM: Right, with one box inside the other. . . .

Untitled by Maurice Tani, digital composition, © 2000, courtesy of the artist.

Appendix: A Concise Index of Psychedelic Substances

Among the drugs considered psychedelic for the purposes of this book are the following groupings, with specific examples of the compounds and substances that belong to them. This is a partial list that relates to substances described in the narratives.

Indoles: An indole is a crystalline heterocyclic (having a ring composed of atoms of more than one kind) compound that is the product of the decomposition of proteins containing tryptophan, an essential amino acid. Made synthetically by distilling a coal tar product obtained from crude petroleum, and also formed as a product of the intestinal putrefaction of proteins, the indole comprises the nucleus of tryptophan and of all the tryptamine alkaloids (see below). (Alkaloids are organic, nitrogen-bearing compounds found in natural sources, especially seed plants. The great majority of so-called psychedelic substances are alkaloids.)

Examples: Lysergic acid, found in LSD (lysergic acid diethylamide, invented in 1938 by the Swiss chemist Albert Hofmann), which is made from the ergot grain (usually rye) fungus *Claviceps purpurea*; and in the Hawaiian woodrose (the *Argyreia* genus; *Argyreia nervosa* being the especially potent Hawaiian baby woodrose) and morning glory plants (*Ipomoea violacea* and *Turbina corymbosa*, among others), particularly in the seeds.

Tryptamines: A tryptamine is a crystalline amine (an amine being an organic compound derived from amonia) produced by a process called decarboxylation (the removal of the carboxylic acid group through the loss of carbon dioxide), from tryptophan. A subgroup of the indoles, tryptamines (e.g., melatonin, a natural brain chemical) are found endogenously in the human body, especially in the pineal gland, hence Hunter S. Thompson's ingestion of a substance he suspected of being human pineal, in *Fear and Loathing in Las Vegas* (1971). Serotonin, a monoamine neurotransmitter, is 5-hydroxy tryptamine (5HT).

Examples: Dimethyltryptamine (DMT), as the name suggests, is a tryptamine, and psilocybin mushrooms and ayahuasca contain tryptamines. DPT (dipropyltryptamine) and DET (diethyltryptamine) are short-acting synthetic tryptamines. Lysergic acid (see above) has a tryptamine structure embedded within it based on the indole nucleus.

Much is made of the fact that DMT is so powerful and yet so quickly metabolized (within minutes) due to its being a tryptamine familiar to the nervous system—thus the inference that this psychonautical boot fits and is meant to be worn. DMT and its more potent cousin, 5-methoxy DMT (5-MeO DMT), are produced in powder form and smoked in a glass pipe. First synthesized in 1931 by the Canadian chemist Richard Manske, DMT is also found in nature: in plants used in ayahuasca brews, which are orally active only in combination with a beta-carboline (see below); in the venom of the *Bufo alvarius* toad, which contains 5-MeO DMT; and in the venom of bufotenine toads, which contain 5-hydroxy DMT (5HO DMT).

Ingested orally, ayahuasca is a mixture of two kinds of plants: the DMT-bearing *Psychotria viridis,* a bush in the coffee family, or occasionally from *Diplopterys cabrerana,* among other plants; and the vine *Banisteriopsis caapi,* which contains tetrahydroharmine and traces of harmaline, members of the family of harmala or beta-carboline alkaloids (also indole derivatives), which act as a monoamine oxidase (MAO) inhibitor to block the action of the MAO in the stomach and permit oral absorption of the DMT in the tryptamines. *Peganum harmala* (Syrian rue), another source of the harmala alkaloid, is also used as an MAO inhibitor in tryptamine brews. An MAO is an enzyme which breaks down amines (e.g., tryptamine, dopamine, histamine) found in the synapses of the brain and in the stomach. An MAO inhibitor blocks that process, availing the amines in the synapses, including the neurotransmitter serotonin, for uptake and reuptake by the receptors.

There are over two hundred species of psilocybin mushroom species worldwide, most of which contain two active ingredients: psilocybin (4 phosphoryloxy DMT), and psilocin (4 hydroxy DMT), which are active when ingested orally *without* beta-carbolines. In the southern part of the United States, the mushroom species most likely to be in use is *Psilocybe cubensis,* the current (correct) name for *Stropharia cubensis.* In more temperate climes, such as the Pacific Northwest, the likely species is *Psilocybe semilanceata,* the so-called Liberty Caps, which are also the most popular ones harvested in the U.K. and Europe. The Pacific Northwest has other much more potent species, but they are rarer. These include *Psilocybe cyanescens,* and *Psilocybe baeocystis,* and a newcomer, *Psilocybe azurescens,* the most potent of all. The species *Panaeolus subbalteatus,* while weak to moderate in potency, is common throughout North America and many parts of the world, and is one of few psilocybians that fruit in the spring. In 1955 R. Gordon Wasson, then vice president at J. P. Morgan, became one of the first whites ever to partake of *Teonanacati,* the divine mushroom of Mexico, when he ingested *Psilocybe caerulescens* in a *velada* (midnight ceremony) lead by *curandera* shaman Maria Sabina. It was the species *Psilocybe mexicana* from which LSD-inventor Albert Hofmann first isolated psilocybin and psilocin at Sandoz Laboratories, publishing the results in 1958 and 1959, respectively.

DENNIS McKENNA ON THE TRYPTAMINES

(How one takes one's "T" may determine the experience's lasting power.)

I think the UDV (the Uniao do Vegetal, a church in Brazil which uses ayahuasca as a sacrament) has it about right. Their model is that* Banisteriopsis caapi *is the "force" and the* chacruna, *the DMT-containing admixture, is the "light." It's the combination of force and light that makes the experience, and you can fine-tune the experience by altering the respective proportions of the two.

I think what is unique about the DMT/beta-carboline combination is that it enables one to experience the "gnosis" of DMT in a more controlled, less overwhelming fashion, and hence, you get more out of it; you learn more. In that sense, the* Banisteriopsis caapi *acts as a channel or a filter. The problem

with DMT alone is that it's so intense and so short; you come back knowing something profound has occurred, but you can hardly comprehend it. Ayahuasca allows you to put it into context and make more sense of it, if only because it's less intense and more prolonged. So there is a coherency there that you don't find with smoked DMT.

Much the same considerations apply to the mushrooms, since the active ingredients—tryptamines closely related to DMT—are also orally active (though without beta-carbolines). Rather than just flooding the receptors all at once, as occurs with smoked DMT, oral activity changes the absorption kinetics; hence the duration and intensity of the experience. After extensive experience with all of these, I've become convinced that the way humans were "meant" to experience tryptamines is in an orally activated form.

[Known for providing a grounded, factual counterpoint to the exotic conjecture of his late older brother Terence, Dennis (b. 1950) is a Ph.D. in botany, and an author, ethnobiologist, and consultant to the natural-products industry.]

Phenethylamines. The end product of phenylalanine, an essential amino acid, in the putrefaction of tissue, a phenethylamine, according to Alexander Shulgin in the frontispiece of his *PiKHAL,* is: "1) A naturally occurring compound found in both the animal and plant kingdoms, an endogenous component of the human brain; 2) any of a series of compounds containing the phenethylamine skeleton, and modified by chemical constituents at appropriate positions in the molecule." The amines dopamine, epinephrine, and norepinephrine, endogenous to primary mammalian metabolism, are considered phenethylamines.

Examples: Mescaline, MDA, MDMA, 2C-B.

Mescaline, first isolated in 1897 by the German chemist Arthur Heffter, is derived from the *Lophophora* genus of peyote cacti and the *Trichocereus* genus, including *pachanoi,* the San Pedro cactus. Contrary to popular belief, no part of the peyote or San Pedro button contains the poison strychnine. In the Seventies, the majority of laboratory-analyzed substances called "mescaline" turned out to be LSD and/or other chemicals, such as PCP, of varying grades of quality and purity.

First concocted in 1910 by the German team of G. Mannish and W. Jacobson, MDA (3,4-methylenedioxyamphetamine, derived from the safrole of nutmeg, the dried seed within the East Indian tree *Myristica fragrans*) and MDMA (3,4-methylenedioxy-N-methylamphetamine, a spin-off, also known as Ecstasy, E, X, and Adam, patented in 1914 by Merck, the German pharmaceutical firm) are both amphetamine as well as phenethylamine derivatives. The *A* in their initials stands for amphetamine, which is a shortening of the term alpha-methyl-phenethylamine.

2C-B (4-bromo-2.5-dimethoxyphenethylamine, also called Venus or Bromo; invented by Shulgin in 1974) is a phenethylamine derivative, but not an amphetamine, as it lacks the alpha methyl substitution.

The phenethylamine family is quite broad. Although mescaline and MDMA both fall under this grouping because they share some basic molecular structure in common, almost any person who has taken both separately would report that they produce decidedly different phenomena, thus underscoring the chemical—as opposed to the botanical or mental effects–related—nature of the classification.

Cannabis: Tetrahydrocannabinol (THC) is the primary psychoactive ingredient in the plants *Cannabis sativa* and *indica,* as well as in the hashish and hash oil derived therefrom. THC is one of some four hundred cannabinols, which are fat-soluble compounds found in the resinous parts of the plant. Cannabinols are rare among so-called psychedelic substances in that they are not alkaloids.

Salvia divinorum: Salvinorin A (also called Divinorin A), the principle psychoactive ingredient in this leafy plant, is a member of a class of natural compounds known as diterpenes, which are derived from the volatile oils of the plant. The traditional method of ingesting *Salvia divinorum* is by chewing the plant, but the leaves are smoked for maximum effect. Almost as potent by weight as the synthetic LSD, *Salvia divinorum* is the most potent psychoactive plant in nature. It is also rare among psychedelic substances in being a nonalkaloid.

***Amanita muscaria* (or Fly Agaric):** A nonpsilocybian mushroom, the psychoactive ingredients of which are currently thought to be ibotenic acid and muscimol. Ibotenic acid, an unusual heterocyclic amino acid, is decarboxylated in the body or upon heating to provide muscimol, an alkaloid that stimulates a type of brain receptor normally acted upon by a neurotransmitter known as gamma-aminobutyric acid (GABA). Thus, distinct among substances considered psychedelic, muscimol is known as a GABA receptor agonist.

Nightshades: Deliriants and hypnotics derived from certain plants in the *Solanaceae* family of over two thousand species, many of which contain the alkaloids atropine and scopolamine, which are used in surgery or medicine as antispasmodics, and also in belladonna-like substances found in the "flying ointments" of witches.

Examples: *Datura stramonium* (jimsonweed), *Datura meteloides, Atropa belladonna.*

Opiates: Painkillers and other medications derived from the latex (the milky stuff, not the "sap" per se) in the opium poppy, *Papaver somniferum.* Physically addictive, opiates are not commonly considered psychedelic, but hallucinatory and visionary experiences of an oneiric nature are known to occur via some opiates.

Examples: Opium, morphine, codeine, and heroin, which is semisynthetic.

Dissociative anesthetics: A class of drugs noted for their common effects, not their common botanical origin or chemical structure.

Examples: ketamine (a children's anesthetic, also called K and Special K), PCP (phencyclidine, an animal tranquilizer, nicknamed Angel Dust), DXM (dextromethorphan, a cough syrup ingredient), nitrous oxide (so-called laughing gas used by dentists to dull the perception of pain).

Considering their function of deadening sensation and their potential dangers, anesthetics occupy a strange chair at the psychedelic table. William James was ardent about the validity of the mystic realms he attained by nitrous oxide, and scientist John Lilly is zealous about the spiritual attributes of the ketamine state. Unlike the classic psychedelic indoles, tryptamines, and phenethylamines, which are serotonergic, interacting with serotonin in the brain, the dissociatives are glutamate antagonists.

***Calea zacatechichi* (Mexican bitter grass):** a plant in the daisy family, which is called *Compositae* or *Asteraceae.* The chemistry of this plant is yet poorly understood, but it is loaded with sesquiterpene lactones (fragrant compounds formed by hydroxy acids), one or two of which are probably responsible for the psychoactivity.

Notes

EPIGRAPH

vii. Blake, William, as cited by Wasson, R. Gordon, in Leary, Timothy, Ralph Metzner, and Gunther M. Weill, eds., p. 35, paraphrased.

PREFACE

xi. *psychedelic states anticipate the dying process.* McKenna, Terence, *The Archaic Revival,* p. 249, paraphrased.
xii. *Feeling that death was close, McKenna told . . . "If psychedelics don't . . . then I don't know what really does."* Martin, Douglas.

THE PSYCHEDELIC [IN] SOCIETY: A BRIEF CULTURAL HISTORY OF TRIPPING

3. *Doors of Perception . . . "as it is, infinite."* Blake, William, "The Marriage of Heaven and Hell, Plate 14," p. 256.
4. *use of psychedelics . . . on the rise.* Travis, Jeremy.
5. *"a holy institution" . . . "for God to enter."* Smith, Huston, in Wasson, R. Gordon, p. 10.
5. *Among notable initiates . . . Homer.* Stafford, Peter, p. 93.
5. *Among notable initiates . . . Socrates.* Ruck, Carl A. P., in Wasson, R. Gordon, p. 15.
5. *A communion between gods and men . . . to claim Persephone, the daughter of the grain goddess Demeter, back from death.* Ruck, Carl A. P., in Wasson, R. Gordon, p. 85.
5. *son she'd conceived there.* Wasson, R. Gordon, p. 62.
5. Ruck, Carl A. P., in Wasson, R. Gordon, p. 59. "the bellowing roar . . . bowels of the earth."
5. *"Even a poet could only say . . . pillar of light."* Ruck, Carl A. P., in Wasson, R. Gordon, p. 47.
5. *A scandal ensued.* Ruck, Carl A. P., in Wasson, R. Gordon, p. 47.
5. *Ruck believes . . . Socrates was tried and condemned.* Ruck, Carl A. P., in Wasson, R. Gordon, p. 15.

6. *"We have drunk the Soma . . . ; we have found the gods."* O'Flaherty, Wendy, p. 134.
6. *Disney (a known cocaine user).* Hughes, James, p. 174.
7. *Disney's chief visualist . . . subject of mescaline experiments by Kurt Beninger.* Stafford, Peter, *Psychedelic Encyclopedia,* Third Expanded Edition, p. 113.
7. *"the founders of the [personal] computer industry were psychedelic-style hippies . . . no question about it."* Forte, Robert, *Timothy Leary: Outside Looking In,* p. 131.
7. *Bob Wallace . . . has said that . . . shareware . . . was psychedelically inspired. Psychedelic Science* documentary.
7. *Mitch Kapor . . . has attributed "recreational chemicals" with enhancing his business acumen.* Davis, Erik, *Techgnosis,* p. 166.
7. *Marshall McLuhan's 1968 observation that "the computer is the LSD of the business world."* Davis, Erik, *Techgnosis,* p. 170.
7. *firms "such as Sun Microsystems . . . recognize the popularity of psychedelics among their employees."* Rushkoff, Douglas, *Cyberia,* p. 37.
9. *Cary Grant . . . admitted taking acid over a hundred times . . . helping him control his boozing and come to terms with unresolved conflicts.* Whalen, John.
9. *Henry Luce reported "chatting up God" . . . Mrs. Luce believed that LSD was . . . not advised for the masses. "We wouldn't want everyone doing too much of a good thing," she is reported as saying.* Whalen, John.
9. *research focused on the use of LSD in treating alcoholism . . . at Hollwood Hospital in British Columbia and Spring Grove State Hospital in Baltimore.* Whalen, John.
9. *William Wilson waxed glowingly about . . . "LSD and some kindred alkaloids."* Forte, Robert, *Timothy Leary: Outside Looking In,* p. 244.
10. *Thirty-four state legislatures and the District of Columbia have passed laws—though in conflict with federal law—recognizing marijuana's medical value.* NORML: "Medical Marijuana, Frequently Asked Questions," furnished in an e-mail message, December 1999.
10. *The FDA has . . . approved new trials for LSD, psilocybin, DMT, MDMA, and ibogaine. Psychedelic Science* documentary, and MAPS Website.
10. *According to Curtis Wright . . . "It's clear that these agents have a role . . . as potential ways to help people." Psychedelic Science* documentary.
11. *it is believed that the number of MDMA "pills" taken every week has increased steadily from one million in 1992.* Saunders, Nicholas, *Ecstasy: Dance, Trance, and Transformation,* p. 85.
12. *R.U. Sirius . . . "You can find it . . . in the American heartland."* Sirius, R. U., pp. 88–89.

BASIC FEATURES OF THE PSYCHEDELIC EXPERIENCE

15. *what . . . Huxley called the "horror of infinity."* Huxley, Aldous, p. 134.
15. *One subject . . . was afraid of falling through the "vast spaces between atoms."* Masters, R. E. L., pp. 72–73.
17. *"bummers can be productive and liberating." . . . Salvador Roguet . . . was a mentor to Richard Yensen, Ph.D., who . . . treated alcoholics . . . at the Maryland Psychiatric Research Center.* Whalen, John.
17. *Yensen had acquired the largest legal supply of LSD in America . . . provided that he revise his research and safety protocols.* Leiby, Richard, and Whalen, John.
17. *"one danger of the mystical path . . . let go of a life-killing accumulation of defenses."* Matthiessen, Peter, *The Snow Leopard,* p. 46.

17. *"catalyst or amplifier of mental processes . . . preexisting matrices or potentials of the human mind."* Grof, Stanislav, *Beyond the Brain,* p. 29.
17. *inner radar that scans the system.* Grof. Stanislav, *Beyond the Brain,* p. 96.
17. *"realm of objective fact."* Huxley, Aldous, p. 16.
18. *Gaskin . . . describes the unspoken interplay between musician Ravi Shankar and his concert audience.* Gaskin, Stephen, pp. 154–58.
19. *"sound was encased in silence . . . the sparkle of sunlight in the waters of a stream."* Devereux, Paul, p. 4.
19. *Huxley replies, "There seems to be plenty of it."* Huxley, Aldous, p. 21.
20. *"I was seeing what Adam had seen . . . The Being of Platonic philosophy.* Huxley, Aldous, p. 17.
21. *"The literature of religious experience . . . some manifestation of the* Mysterium tremendum," Huxley, Aldous, p. 55.
22. "lit-upness" Huxley, Aldous, p. 134.
22. *"In vision . . . 'translucent fruit.' "* Huxley, Aldous, p. 103.
22. *"The landscapes . . . Other World of heaven."* Huxley, Aldous, p. 103.
23. *"hyperdimensional jewel . . . a window into another time, place or world."* McKenna, Terence, *True Hallucinations,* p. 77.
23. *according to Oscar Janiger . . . "You can't manipulate it . . . harder to safely drive an engine and make light."* Whalen, John.
23. *"The LSD experience is an enormous event . . . but those who are unprepared may be fragmented by it," says Sidney Cohen.* Morley, Jefferson.
23. *"I did not understand how one could come back . . . forever thinner than before."* Devereux, Paul, p. 10.
25. *". . . I came loose from the sky," . . . "the chilly hiss of decaying energy."* Kesey, Ken, p. 184.
27. *"an unspeakable sense of gratitude for the privilege of being born in the universe," citing Blake's observation that "Gratitude is heaven itself."* A citation from Aldous Huxley's *Moksha* as edited by Horowitz and Palmer, Stafford, Peter, *Psychedelic Encyclopedia,* Third Expanded Edition, p. 14.
27. *"to discover that we have always been where we ought to be."* Huxley, Aldous, p. 78.
28. *William James . . . points out that* all *mystic experiences have an ephemeral yet indelible quality. . . . he delineates four "marks" of the mystical experience . . . as if the subject were "grasped and held by a superior power." . . . "light of common day . . . inner richness and importance."* James, William, p. 300.
28. *"our normal waking consciousness . . . in the artificial mystic state of mind."* James, William, p. 305.
29. *the monkey in the Buddhist allegory, which hops from window to window.* Kornfield, Jack, in Forte, Robert, *Entheogens and the Future of Religion,* p. 127.
29. *"Lacking the temper of ascetic discipline . . . the experience of the Other."* Matthiessen, Peter, *The Snow Leopard,* p. 47.
29. *Kornfield cautions would-be nirvana seekers . . . to condition the mind for the highest spiritual states.* Kornfield, Jack, in Forte, Robert, *Entheogens and the Future of Religion,* p. 122.
29. *In traditional Buddhist societies . . . instruction starts with* sila, *virtue . . .* prajna, *wisdom through higher insights built on the basis of virtue and discipline.* Kornfield, Jack, in Forte, Robert, *Entheogens and the Future of Religion,* p. 120.
29. *especially arduous training is required . . . only the first openings of consciousness.* Kornfield, Jack, in Forte, Robert, *Entheogens and the Future of Religion,* p. 133.

29. *these states too dissolve. . . . One craves deliverance, but one must let even that go.* Kornfield, Jack, in Forte, Robert, *Entheogens and the Future of Religion,* p. 133.
29. *The "self-shattering point" . . . 'temporary loss of differentiation of the self and the other world.' "* Stevens, Jay, p. 175.
30. *heaven, hell, and archetypal realms . . . have "already been charted by the breadth of Buddhist psychology."* Kornfield, Jack, in Forte, Robert, *Entheogens and the Future of Religion,* p. 131.
30. *Kluver . . . documented "form constants" . . . weblike filigree structures such as honeycombs; the tunnel; and the spiral.* Stafford, Peter, *Psychedelic Encyclopedia,* Third Expanded Edition, pp. 142–43, and Lyttle, Thomas, *Psychedelic Monographs and Essays, Volume Five,* p. 45.
30. *Shulgin's popular six-level system for rating . . . was designed to refer only to intensity, not content.* Shulgin, Alexander, *PIKHAL,* pp. xxxiv–xxxv.
30. *Stanislav Grof's . . . some six thousand subjects of psychedelic sessions.* MAPS Newsletter, Autumn 1998, on its Website, which also stipulates that Grof conducted two-thirds of them himself.
30. *Grof's "formal characteristics of nonordinary consciousness" and Masters and Houston's "psychological effects" of the psychedelic experience.* Grof, Stanislav, *Beyond the Brain,* pp. 31–51, and Masters, R. E. L., p. 5.
31. *four successive levels of psychedelic experience: the* sensory, *the* recollective-analytical, *the* symbolic, *and the* integral. Masters, R. E. L., pp. 142–50.
31. *Grof's four levels of psychedelic experience . . . transcended the limits of time and space.* Grof, Stanislav, *Beyond the Brain,* pp. 37–44.
31. *"universe is seen as an infinite web . . . have been transcended."* Grof, Stanislav, *Beyond the Brain,* p. 51.
35. *not a "toxic psychosis" but a "journey into the unconscious or superconcious mind."* Grof, Stanislav, *Beyond the Brain,* p. 30.
35. *"the relativity . . . consciousness associated with inorganic matter."* Grof, Stanislav, *Beyond the Brain,* p. 44.
35. *patients reported identification with plants . . . and other natural processes.* Grof, Stanislav, *Beyond the Brain,* p. 44.
35. *"Each of us . . . is the whole cosmic network."* Grof, Stanislav, *Beyond the Brain,* p. 45.
35. *The Newtonian-Cartesian model . . . and aboriginal rituals.* Grof, Stanislav, *Beyond the Brain,* p. 29.
36. *holomovement . . . word coined by . . . David Bohm . . . too immense to be seen in true parallax.* Grof, Stanislav, *Beyond the Brain,* p. 83.
38. *At the peak of . . . the LSD "epidemic" . . . most of whom already had a history of psychiatric disorder.* Stevens, Jay, pp. 273–74.
38. *As the media hammered away . . . panic attacks multiplied drastically.* Whalen, John.
39. *"re-experiencing following cessation of use of a hallucinogen of one or more of the perceptual symptoms that were experienced while intoxicated with the hallucinogen."* American Psychiatric Association, pp. 130–31.
39. *Dr. H. D. Abraham claims that "structural damage" . . . "acquired color confusion . . . and trailing phenomena."* Abraham, H., p. 4, as cited in Lyttle, Thomas, *Psychedelic Monographs and Essays,* Volume Five, p. 48.
40. *dissociatives . . . are "extremely toxic to developing fetuses." . . . "carry a real risk of permanent brain damage," in particular Olney's lesions or NNMA Antagonist Neurotoxity.* White, William E.
40. *D. M. Turner . . . troubled by . . . "psychedelic heroin" . . . doesn't "obey the shamanic rules." TRP,* Issue One, Summer 1997, from Website.

METHODOLOGY AND PERSPECTIVES USED IN THE MAKING OF THIS BOOK

43. psychedelic . . . *coined in 1956 by . . . Humphrey Osmond. Oxford English Dictionary,* Second Edition, on CD-ROM.
43. entheogens, *a term coined in 1979 by scholars R. Gordon Wasson, Carl A. P. Ruck, Jonathan Ott, Jeremy Bigwood, and Danny Staples* . . . entactogens . . . *coined by Heffter Research Institute cofounder Dave Nichols.* The Vaults of Erowid Website.
50. *the "shadowy absence that's always present in America, the exterminated native race."* Savage, Jon, in James Nenke and Parke Puterbaugh, p. 193.
53. *"In an effort to integrate" . . . the Council on Spiritual Practices . . . has formulated a "Code of Ethics for Spiritual Guides" . . . certain "primary religious practices."* Forte, Robert, *Entheogens and the Future of Religion,* pp. 174–75.

CHARLES HAYES

97. *(T. S. Eliot's) "significant soil."* Eliot, T. S., last line in "The Dry Salvages," the third of the *Four Quartets,* p. 199.
98. *Baudelaire's "bath of indolence."* Baudelaire, Charles, "The Double Room," p. 5.

CLARK HEINRICH

115. *I performed a Vedic fire ceremony, putting a piece of a mushroom cap into the fire as I sang the ancient offertory mantras to Agni, Soma, Rudra, and Indra.* Clark Heinrich writes: In the ancient Soma ceremony, participants first offered the Soma drink to the gods before drinking it themselves. This was done by pouring some of the drink into the sacrificial fire as priests chanted invitations to the gods to come and drink. It was believed that the rising steam from the offering carried the drink to the gods' "heavenly abode." This is why they were called drinkers of steam.
117. *the Nag Hammadi texts.* Clark Heinrich writes: The Nag Hammadi texts are early Gnostic writings that were discovered in Upper Egypt in 1945. Consisting of fifty-two tractates, comprising twelve books and part of a thirteenth, these works have shed much light on the hitherto largely unknown practices and beliefs of Christian Gnosticism, as well as early Christianity itself. They are a "must read" for anyone interested in Christian origins and Gnosticism.

JEREMY

207. *Protects mankind . . . Which flesh cannot endure.* Eliot, T. S., p. 178.

A CONVERSATION WITH TERENCE McKENNA

412. *"an intelligent organism . . . galactical citizenship."* McKenna, Terence, *True Hallucinations,* p. 209.
412. *"a dimensional vortex . . . the UFOs."* McKenna, Terence, *True Hallucinations,* p. 133.
412. *"encounter of the Alien Other . . . eschatological vent at the end of time."* McKenna, Terence, *True Hallucinations,* p. 194.

412. *"Here is the realm . . . gone so ill in."* McKenna, Terence, *Food of the Gods,* p. 261.
412. *"the greeny engines of Creation."* McKenna, Terence, as quoted in Rushkoff, Douglas, *Cyberia,* p. 68.
413. *The McKennas believed . . . one toward the future.* McKenna, Terence, *True Hallucinations,* p. 194.
413. *The result was . . . the score of "the biocosmic symphony."* McKenna, Terence, *True Hallucinations,* p. 194.
413. *a kind of mathematical mandala describing . . . intent within DNA.* Rushkoff, Douglas, *Cyberia,* pp. 89–90.
413. *Kary Mullis . . . has said that he probably would not have made the discovery if he hadn't taken LSD, which had shown him a way to get "down there . . . with the molecules. Psychedelic Science* documentary.
413. *"maximum ingression or novelty."* McKenna, Terence, *True Hallucinations,* p. 198.
413. *synchonicity . . . is accelerated by the "emergence of archetype."* Grof, Stanislav, *Beyond the Brain,* p. 47.
414. *His doctors assured him there was no causal link . . . illegal drug use.* Davis, Erik, *Wired,* p. 158.

APPENDIX

453. *"end product of phenylalanine in the putrefaction of tissue."* Shulgin, Alexander, *PiHKAL,* p. 815.
453. *"(1) A naturally occurring compound . . . modified by chemical constituents at appropriate positions in the molecule."* Shulgin, Alexander, *PiKHAL,* frontispiece.

Bibliography and Resources

BOOKS

American Psychiatric Association. *Diagnostic Statistical Manual of Mental Disorders.* Washington, D.C.: American Psychiatric Press, 1994. ISBN 0-89042-064-5.

Baudelaire, Charles. *Paris Spleen.* Translated by Louise Varese. New York: New Directions, 1972. ISBN 0811200078.

Blake, William. *The Portable Blake.* Edited by Alfred Kazin. New York: Viking Penguin, 1974. ISBN 0-14-015026-9.

Braden, William. *The Private Sea: LSD and the Search for God.* Chicago: Quadrangle Books, 1967. LC # BL65.D7B7.

Champion, Sarah, ed. *Disco Biscuits.* London: Sceptre/Hodder and Stoughton, 1997. ISBN 0-340-68265-5.

Coleman, Dan. *The Varieties of the Meditative Experiences.* New York: Halsted Press, 1978. ISBN 0470991917.

Davis, Erik. *Techgnosis: Myth, Magic + Mysticism in the Age of Information.* New York: Three Rivers Press, 1998. ISBN 0-609-80474-X.

Davis, Wade. *Shadows in the Sun: Travels to Landscapes of Spirit and Desire.* Washington, D.C.: Island Press, 1998. ISBN 1-5563-354-9.

DeKorne, Jim. *Psychedelic Shamanism: The Cultivation, Preparation and Shamanic Use of Psychotropic Plants.* Port Townsend, Washington: Breakout Productions, 1994. ISBN 1559501103.

Devereux, Paul. *The Long Trip: A Prehistory of Psychedelia.* New York: Penguin Arkana, 1997. ISBN 0-14-019540-8.

Ebin, David. *The Drug Experience: First Person Accounts of Addicts, Writers, Scientists, and Others.* New York: Orin Press, 1961. LC # HV5801.E2.

Eisner, Bruce. *Ecstasy: The MDMA Story.* Berkeley, California: Ronin Publishing, 1989. ISBN 0914171682.

Eliot, T. S. *Collected Poems 1909–1962.* New York: Harcourt, Brace & World, Inc., 1970. LC # 63-21424.

Forte, Robert, ed. *Entheogens and the Future of Religion.* San Francisco: Council on Spiritual Practices, 1997. ISBN 1-889725-01-3.

———. *Timothy Leary, Outside Looking In: Appreciations, Castigations, and Reminiscences.* Rochester, Vermont: Park Street Press division of Inner Traditions, 1999. ISBN 0-89281-786-0.

Gaskin, Stephen. *Amazing Dope Tales and Haight Street Flashbacks.* Summertown, Tennessee: The Book Publishing Company, 1980. ISBN C-913990-29-9.

Gilman, Alfred Goodman, Louis A. Goodman, et al., eds. *Goodman and Gilman's The Pharmacological Basis of Therapeutics.* Seventh Edition. New York: Macmillan, 1985. 0-02-344710-9.

Grof, Stanislav. *Beyond the Brain: Birth, Death and Transcendence in Psychotherapy.* Albany, New York: State University of New York Press, 1985. ISBN 0-87-395-899-3.

———. *Realms of the Human Unconscious: Observations from LSD Research.* London: Souvenir Books, 1975. ISBN 0285648829.

Grof, Stanislav, and Christina Grof. *Spiritual Emergency: When Personal Transformation Becomes a Crisis.* Los Angeles: J. P. Tarcher, 1989. ISBN 0874775388.

Hanna, Jon. *Psychedelic Resource List, Third Edition.* Sacramento, California: Soma Graphics, 2000. ISBN 09654383-2-5.

Heinrich, Clark. *Strange Fruit: Alchemy, Religion and Magical Foods.* London: Bloomsbury Books, 1995. ISBN 0-7475-1548-4.

Hofmann, Albert. *LSD: My Problem Child: Reflections on Sacred Drugs, Mysticism, and Science.* New York: Putnam Publishing Group, 1983. ISBN 0874882567.

Hughes, James. *Altered States: Creativity Under the Influence.* New York: Watson-Guptill Publications, 1999. ISBN 0-78239-0163-6.

Huxley, Aldous. *The Doors of Perception; Heaven and Hell.* New York: Harper and Row, 1990. ISBN 0-06-090007-5.

James, William. *The Varieties of Religious Experience.* New York: Collier Books, 1961. ISBN 0-02-085960-0.

Jay, Mike, ed. *Artificial Paradises.* London: Penguin Books, 1999. ISBN 0-14-118115-X.

Jay, Mike. *Blue Tide: The Search for Soma.* Brooklyn, New York: Autonomedia, 1999. ISBN 1-57027-088-0.

Julien, Robert. *A Primer of Drug Action: A Concise, Nontechnical Guide to the Actions, Uses, and Side Effects of Psychoactive Drugs.* Seventh Edition. San Francisco: W. H. Freeman and Company, 1995. ISBN 071672619X.

Kesey, Ken. *Demon Box.* New York: Penguin Books, 1987. ISBN 0-14-008530-0.

Leary, Timothy, Richard Alpert, and Ralph Metzner. *The Psychedelic Experience: A Manual Based on the Tibetan Book of the Dead.* New York: Citadel Press, 1995. ISBN 0806516526.

Leary, Timothy, and Ralph Metzner. *Psychedelic Prayers and Other Meditations.* Berkeley, California: Ronin Publishing, 1997. ISBN 0914171844.

Leary, Timothy, Ralph Metzner, and Gunther M. Weill, eds. *The Psychedelic Reader: Classic Selections from the Psychedelic Review, the Revolutionary 1960s Forum of Psychopharmacological Substances.* New York: Citadel Press/Carol Publishing, 1997. ISBN 0-8065-1451-5.

Lee, Martin A., and Bruce Shlain. *Acid Dreams: The Complete Social History of LSD: The CIA, the Sixties, and Beyond.* New York: Grove Weidenfeld, 1992. ISBN 1000065655.

Lyttle, Thomas, ed. *Psychedelic Monographs and Essays.* Vol. 5. Boynton Beach, Florida: PM & E Publishing Group, 1991. ISSN 0892-371X.

———. *Psychedelics: A Collection of the Most Exciting New Material on Psychedelic Drugs.* New York, Barricade Books, 1994. ISBN 0-9623032-2-4.

Maslow, Abraham H. *Religions, Values and Peak-Experiences.* New York: Penguin Arkana, 1994. ISBN 0-14-019487-8.

Masello, Robert. *Fallen Angels . . . and Spirits of the Dark.* New York: Perigee Books, 1994. ISBN 0-399-51889-4.

Masters, R. E. L., and Jean Houston. *The Varieties of Psychedelic Experience.* New York: Holt, Rinehart and Winston, 1966. LC # BF207.M3.

Masters, Robert, Ph.D., and Jean Houston, Ph.D. *The Varieties of Psychedelic Experience: The Classic Guide to the Effects of LSD on the Human Psyche.* Rochester, Vermont: Park Street Press division of Inner Traditions, 2000. ISBN 0-89281-897-2.

Matthiessen, Peter. *At Play in the Fields of the Lord.* New York: Vintage Books, 1991. ISBN 0679737413.

———. *The Snow Leopard.* New York: Penguin Books, 1987. ISBN 0-14-010266-3.

McKay, George, *Senseless Acts of Beauty: Cultures of Resistance Since the Sixties.* London: Verso Books, 1996. ISBN 1859840280.

McKenna, Terence. *The Archaic Revival: Speculations on Psychedelic Mushrooms, the Amazon, Virtual Reality, UFOs, Evolution, Shamanism, the Rebirth of the Goddess, and the End of History.* San Francisco: Harper San Francisco, 1991. ISBN 0-06-250613-7.

———. *Food of the Gods: The Search for the Original Tree of Knowledge: A Radical History of Plants, Drugs, and Human Evolution.* New York: Bantam Doubleday Dell, 1993. ISBN 0553371304.

———. *True Hallucinations: Being an Account of the Author's Extraordinary Adventures in the Devil's Paradise.* San Francisco: Harper San Francisco, 1993. ISBN 0-06-250549-9.

McKenna, Terence, Ralph Abraham, and Rupert Sheldrake. *The Evolutionary Mind: Trialogues at the Edge of the Unthinkable.* Santa Cruz, Calif.: Trialogue Press (Dakota Books), 1998. ISBN 0-942344-13-8.

———. *Trialogues at the Edge of the West: Chaos, Creativity, and the Resacralization of the World.* Santa Fe: Bear & Company, 1992. ISBN 7039603205.

McKenna, Terence, and Dennis McKenna. *The Invisible Landscape: Mind, Hallucinogens, and the I Ching.* New York: Seabury Press, 1975. ISBN 7041470333.

———. [Under the pseudonyms O. T. Oss and O. N. Oeric]. *Psilocybin: Magic Mushroom Grower's Guide.* Berkeley: And/Or Press, 1976. ISBN 7046848240.

Merriam Webster's Collegiate Dictionary on CD-ROM. Dallas: Zane Publishing, Inc., 1997.

Mullis, Kary. *Dancing Naked in the Mind Field.* New York: Pantheon, 1998. ISBN 0679442553.

Narby, Jeremy. *The Cosmic Serpent: DNA and the Origins of Knowledge.* New York: J. P. Tarcher, 1998. ISBN 0874779111.

Nenke, James, and Parke Puterbaugh, eds.; texts by Charles Perry, Barry Miles, and Jon Savage. *I Want to Take You Higher: The Psychedelic Era 1965–1969.* San Francisco: Chronicle Books with the Rock and Roll Hall of Fame and Museum, Sarah Lazin Books, and Alexander Isley, Inc., 1997. ISBN 0-9118-1700-8.

O'Flaherty, Wendy, translator. *The Rig Veda.* London: Penguin Books, 1981. ISBN 0140444025.

Ott, Jonathan. *Pharmacotheon: Entheogenic Drugs, Their Plant Sources and History.* Occidental, California: Jonathan Ott Books, 1996. ISBN 0961423498.

Oxford English Dictionary, Second Edition, on CD-ROM. Oxford: Oxford University Press, 1994. ISBN 0198612605.

Perrine, Daniel. *The Chemistry of Mind-Altering Drugs: History, Pharmacology, and Cultural Context.* Washington, D.C.: American Chemical Society Books, 1996. ISBN 0841232539.

Rudgley, Richard. *The Encyclopaedia of Psychoactive Substances,* London: Abacus division of Little, Brown and Company, 1999. ISBN 0-349-11127-9.

Rushkoff, Douglas, *Coercion: Why We Listen to What "They" Say.* New York: Riverhead Books, 1999. ISBN 1-57322-115-5.

———. *Cyberia: Life in the Trenches of Hyperspace.* San Francisco: Harper San Francisco, 1994. ISBN 0-06-251009-6.

Saunders, Nicholas, with Rick Doblin. *Ecstasy: Dance, Trance and Transformation.* Oakland, California: Quick American Archives, 1996. ISBN 0-932551-20-3.

Saunders, Nicholas, Anja Saunders, and Michelle Pauli. *In Search of the Ultimate High: Spiritual Experience Through Psychoactives.* London: Random House/Rider, 2000. ISBN 0-7126-7087-4.

Schultes, Richard Evans, and Albert Hofmann. *The Botany and Chemistry of Hallucinogens.* Second Edition. Springfield, Illinois: Charles C. Thomas Publishers Ltd., 1991 ISBN 0398038635.

Seymour, Richard, and David Smith. *The Physician's Guide to Psychoactive Drugs.* New York: Haworth Press, 1987. ISBN 0866563822.

Shulgin, Alexander, and Ann Shulgin. *PiHKAL: A Chemical Love Story.* Berkeley, California: Transform Press, 1991. ISBN 0-96-30096-0-5.

———. *TiHKAL: The Continuation.* Berkeley, California: Transform Press, 1997. ISBN 0-9630096-9-9.

Smith, Huston. *Cleansing the Doors of Perception: The Religious Significance of Entheogenic Plants and Chemicals.* New York: Tarcher/Penguin Putnam Inc., 2000. ISBN 1585420344.

Snyder, Solomon. *Drugs and the Brain.* New York: Scientific American Library, 1986. ISBN 0716760177.

Stafford, Peter. *Psychedelics Encyclopedia.* Third Expanded Edition. Berkeley, California: Ronin Publishing, 1992. ISBN 0-914171-51-8.

Stafford, Peter, and Bonnie Golightly. *LSD: The Problem-Solving Psychedelic.* New York: Award Books, 1967. ISBN 7027306860.

Stamets, Paul. *Psilocybin Mushrooms of the World: An Identification Guide.* Berkeley, California: Ten Speed Press, 1996. ISBN 0898158397.

Stevens, Jay. *Storming Heaven: LSD and the American Dream.* New York: Perennial Library, Harper & Row, 1988. ISBN 0-06-0097172-X.

Storm, Hyemeyohsts. *Seven Arrows.* New York: Ballantine Books, 1985. ISBN 0345329015.

Strassman, R. J. "Human Psychopharmacology of LSD, Dimethyltryptamine and Related Compounds," article in *50 Years of LSD: Current Status and Perspectives of Hallucinogens: A Symposium of the Swiss Academy of Medical Sciences, Lugano-Agno* (Switzerland). Edited by A. Pletscher and Dieter Ladewig. New York: Parthenon Publishing Group, 1994. ISBN 1850705690.

Tart, Charles T. *On Being Stoned: A Psychological Study of Marijuana Intoxication.* Palo Alto, California: Science and Behavior Books, 1971. ISBN 0-8314-0027-7.

Thompson, Hunter S. *Fear and Loathing in Las Vegas: A Savage Journey to the Heart of the American Dream.* New York: Warner Books, 1971. ISBN 0-446-31393-9.

Travis, Jeremy, Director, National Institute of Justice, U.S. Department of Justice Office of Justice Programs. *Rise in Hallucinogen Use.* Series: National Institute of Justice Research in Brief, October 1997, a paper posted on the Serendipity Website: *www.cia.com.au/serendipity/dmt/166607.html.*

Turner, D. M. *The Essential Psychedelic Guide.* San Francisco: Panther Press, 1994. ISBN 0-9642636-1-0.

Valadez, Meno (paintings), and Susana Valadez (texts). *Huichol Indian Sacred Rituals.* Oakland, California: Amber Lotus division of Dharma Enterprises, 1996, ISBN 09456798806.

Wasson, R. Gordon, et al., with a preface by Huston Smith and an afterword by Albert Hofmann. *The Road to Eleusis: Unveiling the Secret of the Mysteries.* Twentieth Anniversary Edition. Los Angeles: Hermes Press Book, distributed exclusively by William Daley Rare Books. Ltd., 1998. ISBN 0-915418-20-X.

Watts. Alan, *The Joyous Cosmology: Adventures in the Chemistry of Consciousness.* New York: Pantheon Books, 1962. ISBN 0394702999.

Weil, Andrew, and Winifred Rosen. *From Chocolate to Morphine: Everything You Need to Know about Mind-Altering Drugs.* Boston: Houghton Mifflin, 1998. ISBN 0395911524.

White, William E. "This Is Your Brain on Dissociatives: The Bad News Is Finally In, version 0.1," paper posted on the Lycaeum Website, November 1998: *www.lycaeum.org/drugs/DXM/dissociative.brain.damage.h tml.*

Young, Warren, and Joseph Hixson. *LSD on Campus.* New York: Dell, 1966. TM 681510.

Zimmer, Lynn, and John P. Morgan. *Marijuana Myths, Marijuana Facts: A Review of the Scientific Evidence.* New York: The Lindesmith Center, 1997. ISBN 0946156849.

PERIODICALS

The Entheogen Review: The Journal of Unauthorized Research on Visionary Plants and Drugs. Sacramento, California. ISSN 1066-1913.

Festival Eye, Summer 1988, Volume 1, No. 3, London.

Head Magazine, London.

Journal of Psychoactive Drugs (formerly the *Journal of Psychedelic Drugs*). San Francisco, Haight-Ashbury Publications in association with the Haight-Ashbury Free Medical Clinic, San Francisco. ISSNs 0279-1072 and 0022-393X, respectively.

Magical Blend, Chico, California. ISSN 1073-5879.

Mondo 2000, The Guest Designers Issue, Issue 17, Fall/Winter 1997, Berkeley, California. ISSN 74470-77997.

The Nation, special issue: "Beyond Legalization: New Ideas for Ending the War on Drugs." September 20, 1999. ISSN 0027-8378.

Psychedelic Illuminations, Volume 1, Issue 7, Fullerton, California.

Tricycle: The Buddhist Review, Volume 6, No. 1, Fall 1996, Buddhist Ray, Inc., New York. ISSN 1045-484X.

TRP (The Resonance Project); The Journal of Modern Psychedelic Culture. Premier Issue, Summer 1997, Seattle. Website: *www.resproject.com.*

ARTICLES

Abraham, H. "Visual phenomenology of the LSD flashback." *Archives General Psychology:* 40 (1983).

Allen, J. R. F., and B. Holmstedt, "The simple β-carboline alkaloids." *Phytochemistry* 19:1573–82 (1980).

Applebome, Peter. "Carlos Castañeda, mystical and mysterious writer, dies." *New York Times,* June 20, 1998.

Browne, Malcolm W. "5 Quantum theorists share 2 Nobel Prizes in sciences." *New York Times,* October 14, 1998, p. A16.

Cloud, John. "The lure of ecstasy." *Time,* cover story: "What ecstasy does to your brain." June 5, 2000, pp. 62–73.

Davis, Erik. "Terence McKenna's last trip." *Wired,* Volume 8.05, May 2000, pp. 156–68.

Haber, Daniel B. "Buddha's beatnik." *Metro* (Bangkok), May 1998, pp. 20–21.

Leiby, Richard. "The magical mystery cure." *Esquire,* September 1997, pp. 98–103.

Manler, Jeremy. "Caution: Replicating the lifestyle of DNA guru Kary Mullis may be hazardous." *Chicago Tribune,* 1998.

Martin, Douglas. "Terence McKenna, 53, Dies; patron of psychedelic drugs." *New York Times,* April 9, 2000, p. 40.

Morley, Jefferson. "Clare Boothe Luce's acid test: newly released diaries reveal she used drug." *Washington Post,* October 22, 1997, p. D1.

Schone, Mark, and David J. Prince. "Adventures in e-commerce: behind the massive spike in ecstasy use is a global smuggling and distribution system." *Spin,* special dance issue, June 2000, pp. 116–20.

Sirius, R. U. "The new counterculture." *Time,* November 9, 1998, pp. 88–89.

Smith, T. A., "Tryptamine and related compounds in plants." *Phytochemistry* 16: 171 (1977).

Whalen, John, "The Hollywood experiment: LSD studies that could open the door to a new age." *LA Weekly,* July 3, 1998, and *Utne Reader,* December 1998, seen on *Utne Reader* Website: *www.utne.com.*

Wren, Christopher S. "A seductive drug culture flourishes on the Internet." *New York Times,* June 20, 1997, p. A1.

FILMS AND TELEVISION DOCUMENTARIES

Altered States, a film directed by Ken Russell based on the novel by Paddy Chayefksy, 1980, Warner Brothers DVD.

Being John Malkovich, a film directed by Spike Jonze, written by Charlie Kaufman, produced by Michael Stipe et al., featuring performances by John Malkovich, John Cusack, Cameron Diaz, Catherine Keener, and Orson Bean (who looks uncannily like the late Tim Leary), 2000, Universal/USA Home Enterainment DVD.

Chappaqua, a film directed by Conrad Rooks, 1966, Fox Lorber video.

Getting High: A History of LSD, television documentary broadcast on the History Channel, February 1, 2000. Available on video, product no. A&E-42640, from both the History Channel and A&E Websites.

Intrepid Traveler and His Merry Band of Pranksters Look for a Kool Place: The Long-Awaited Film of the Original Bus Trip of 1964, filmed and edited by Ken Kesey and the Merry Pranksters, 2000. Available on video from Ken Kesey's Website, *www.intrepidtrips.com.*

Psychedelic Science, television documentary on psychedelic research, written by Bill Eagles, coproduced by the BBC and A&E, broadcast in the U.K. in 1997 on the Horizon program; also broadcast in 1997 on the Hard Disk program on Danish television with commentary by journalist Alex Frank Larsen. The transcript for the Horizon program is posted on the BBC Website at *bbc.co.uk/horizon/psychedelictran.shtml.*

The Trip, a film directed by Roger Corman, written by Jack Nicholson, featuring performances by Peter Fonda, Bruce Dern, Dennis Hopper,Susan Strassberg, and Peter Bogdanovich, 1967. Video now out of print.

WEBSITES

Association for Holotropic Breathwork International
www.breathwork.com
Website for the method created by Stanislav and Christina Grof for "moving toward wholeness" via concentrated breathing

Bear's Pages
www.thebear.org
Augustus Owsley Stanley III's Website

The Burning Man Project—Official Site
www.burningman.com
Website for the annual Burning Man celebration

Changes: Celebrating Our Growing Consciousness
www.changes.org
Website with psychedelic themes

Council on Spiritual Practices
www.csp.org
Website for the nonprofit organization that advocates the responsible use of entheogens

DanceSafe
www.dancesafe.org
"fact-based drug information" and "harm reduction services" for the "rave and nightclub community"

Deoxy.org: The Deoxyribonucleic Hyperdimension
www.deoxy.org
an on-line anthology of psychedelic literature, images, and links

Ecstasy.org
www.ecstasy.org
Website launched by the late Nicholas Saunders to serve as a resource for various dimensions of MDMA, including dance culture and toxicology issues

Eleusis: Journal of Psychoactive Plants and Compounds
eleusis.lycaeum.org
on-line version of the hardcopy journal

Entheogen Dot
www.entheogen.com/index.html
on-line journal on various dimensions of entheogens, legal, pharmacological, etc.

The Fane of the Psilocybe Mushroom
www.lycaeum.org/~thefane/
Website of the British Columbia–based "fourth way mystical school" that upholds the principle that all psilocybian mushrooms are sacraments

***Head* magazine**
www.headmag.com
Website for the British magazine devoted to psychedelic, spiritual, and erotic themes

Heffter Research Institute
www.heffter.org
Website of the organization devoted to researching the beneficial properties of psychoactive substances; named for the German chemist who first synthesized "mezcalin"

High Times magazine
www.hightimes.com
Website for the magazine with themes related to cannabis, psilocybin, and other psychedelic drugs

Albert Hofmann Foundation
www.hofmann.org
Website for the foundation dedicated to the documentation of the history of psychedelics, named for the Swiss chemist who first synthesized LSD

Hyperreal
www.hyperreal.com
an on-line resource on raves by location, rave music, and psychedelics

Island Foundation
www.island.org
Website for the organization that provides resources on psychedelics, named for the book by Aldous Huxley about a psychedelics-enabled utopia

Intrepid Trips
www.intrepidtrips.com
Ken Kesey's Website

Timothy Leary
www.leary.com
Timothy Leary's Website

Levity
www.levity.com/index.html
an assortment of homepages for artists and authors involved in alternative consciousness, including Terence McKenna's

Lindesmith Center
www.lindesmith.org
Website for the Drug Policy Research Institute, a member of the Soros Foundations Network; includes a searchable database

Lycaeum
www.lycaeum.org
"The world's largest entheogenic library and community"

Magical Blend
www.magicalblend.com
Website for the magazine devoted to alternative consciousness

Terence McKenna
www.levity.com/eschaton/tm.html
Terence McKenna's Website

Terence McKenna Land
deoxy.org/mckenna.htm
An assortment of McKenna-related material, including reviews, interview and lecture transcripts (some in audio), an index of quotes, a bibliography and Website list, and sources for related products, such as video and audio recordings

Medlines
www.chiro.org/places/medlines.shtml
links to several searchable medical databases

Mind Books
www.promind.com
on-line purveyor of books on psychedelic and alternative consciousness, run by Bob Wallace

Multidisciplinary Association for Psychedelic Studies (MAPS)
www.maps.org
Website for the organization devoted to researching the health potentials for psychedelics, with a searchable database of psychedelic research information

NORML
www.norml.org
Website for the National Organization for the Reform of Marijuana Laws

The Peyote Foundation
www.win.net/~peyote
Website for the organization that serves as a resource on the legal, conservation, and religious issues of peyote

Peyote Way Church of God
www.peyoteway.org
Website for "the oldest tax-exempt all-race peyotist church in the United States"

The Peyote Way Church of God, Unofficial Page
www.peyote.net/welcome.html
links to several peyote and San Pedro–related Websites, as well as other psychedelic links

The Psychedelic Library
www.druglibrary.org/schaffer/lsd/lsdmenu.htm
an extensive on-line library of books devoted to psychedelic themes

Pub Med
www.ncbi.nlm.nih.gov/PubMed
the search engine for Medline, the medical database of the National Library of Medicine, National Institutes of Health

The Rainbow Family of Living Light Unofficial Homepage
www.welcomehome.org/rainbow.html
information on Rainbow Gatherings and Rainbow people

Sacred Dance Society
www.sacreddance.org/home.htm
Website for the "nonprofit religious society dedicated to the practice of community dance"

The *Salvia divinorum* Research and Information Center
salvia.lycaeum.org
Website devoted to information about *Salvia divinorum*

Schaffer Library of Drug Policy
www.druglibrary.org/schaffer/index.htm
a comprehensive on-line library of material on drugs and drug policy

Sentient Experientials
www.experientials.prg
Website for an organization devoted to ethnobotanical exploration and discovery

Serendipity
serendipity.magnet.ch
a large resource on psychedelic and related legal matters with mirror Websites in Switzerland and Australia

The Shroomery
www.shroomery.org
information on psychedelic mushrooms

Paul Stamets Website
www.fungi.com
information on mushrooms of all kinds, by the author of *Psilocybin Mushrooms of the World: An Identification Guide*

***Trip* magazine**
www.tripzine.com
Website for *Trip*, formerly *TRP* (*The Resonance Project*), "the mainstream print periodical dedicated to the study of psychedelics, expanded consciousness, and the science of reality and perception"

The Vaults of Erowid
www.erowid.org/entheogens/entheo_def.shtml
an extensive on-line resource with a searchable database on psychedelic issues, created by the nonprofit organization "dedicated to studying and providing information about humanity's never-ending search for meaning and spirit"

HELP

Drug Detoxification Rehabilitation and Aftercare Program
Haight-Ashbury Free Clinic
529 Clayton Street
San Francisco, California 94117
(415) 565-1908
Not a hotline, this clinic offers information and referrals for people with substance abuse problems.

Harm Reduction Coalition
www.harmreduction.org
This organization promotes "harm reduction education, interventions, and community organizing, . . . fosters alternative models to conventional health and human services, . . . [and] provides resources, educational materials and support to health professional and drug users in their communities to address drug-related harm."

Mental Health Association of New York
1-800-LIFENET
The mental health crisis information and referral service for New York City, the MHA of New York is a twenty-four-hour referral service for treatment of substance abuse and mental health problems throughout the five boroughs of New York City. Emergency room and mobile crisis referrals are available. Callers from outside New York are referred to their local Mental Health Association.

National Mental Health Association Information and Referral Service
1-800-969-NMHA or 703-684-7722
Not a hotline, this is the national office of the National Mental Health Association, which can provide referrals for mental health treatment.

Spiritual Emergence Network (SEN at CIIS)
California Institute of Integral Studies
1453 Mission Street
San Francisco, California 94103
(415) 648-2610
Website: *www.ciis.edu/comserv/sen.html*
Founded in 1978 by Stanislav Grof, M.D., and his wife Christina, SEN is now associated with the California Institute of Integral Studies, an accredited graduate school that incorporates knowledge from the world's spiritual traditions into the education of mental health professionals. SEN provides information, referrals and support for individuals who are experiencing crises related to personal transformation, as well as an opportunity for professionals to work with "spiritual emergence" clients and receive education and training leading to licensure.

Substance Abuse Mental Health Services Administration (SAMHSA) of the National Institutes of Health
1-800-662-HELP
www.health.org/phone.htm#phone
Operating twenty-four hours a day, this service provides advice and referrals to individuals about the availability of drug and alcohol treatment services, including referrals to programs in the caller's local area.

Acknowledgments

Heartfelt thanks to:
Helene, my amazing wife, who generously and lovingly created the opportunity for this book to be written;
Sheree Bykofsky, my agent, whose confidence in the project is responsible for spurring me to get it done;
David Stanford, my first editor, for bringing the project in from the cold, for ongoing advice and cheerful inspiration, and for the invaluable service of putting me in touch with his contacts, many of whom became participants;
Paul Slovak, my second editor, for seeing the project home and drawing much better structure, focus, and content out of the original manuscript, having a superb eye for the clutter to cast out and for the holes to fill with literary mortar;
Terence McKenna, wherever you are now, for contributing, with levity and grace, the products of a piquant and provocative conversation;
Brooks Cole, Alex Grey, Brian Moriarty, Maurice Tani, and Jon A. Bell, for their fabulous artwork, which is featured in these pages, and their generosity of spirit in granting me permission to use it; special thanks to Brooks for recruiting and galvanizing the others and gathering it all in (contact Brooks at *brooks@holocosmos.com;* Alex at *info@alexgrey.com* and his Website, *www.alexgrey.com;* Brian at *prof@ludix.com;* Maurice at *mtani@home.com;* and Jon at *joanjon@sirius.com*);
Robert Forte, a true friend of the project, for comradely consultation and editorial guidance, useful referrals and references extended with warmth and professional consideration;
Jonathan, my friend for nearly three decades now, for inspiration and advice and substantial contributions to this project;
Clark Heinrich, for the exotic story he contributed and for being a chum with whom to chew the literary fat;

Robert Bell, for giving me a story when I needed it, when he didn't have to;
Paul W. Morris, for ushering the project in through the first door of the publication process, as David Stanford's assistant, in which capacity he first scrutinized the book proposal and preliminary manuscript and judged them worthy of David's attention, and for being a helpful extra pair of eyes on some of the narratives;
Julie Holland, for her abundant and frequent help in sharing expertise on psychiatric and pharmacology issues;
Kit Bonson, for all the hours she devoted to sharing her knowledge of certain psychopharmacology issues;
Dennis McKenna, for generously taking the time away from more important matters to clear up some scientific issues, and for contributing his perspective on tryptamines;
Sasha Shulgin, for his amiable help in defining chemical concepts;
Dave Nichols, for his color diagram of the indole/tryptamine structure, and other technical information;
Alex Frank Larsen, for providing information about the Danish LSD scandal;
The New York Times Book Review, for running my author's query, which produced numerous responses that resulted in a large number of participants in the project;
MAPS (Multidisciplinary Association for Psychedelic Studies), for running my author's query, which had a response rate that yielded several excellent participants, and also for useful facts and information in response to my queries;
Mark Fischer, my new friend, for so much help in navigating the terrain of the peyote way, and for stitching me into his community in Arizona;
Ruth Mary Anna Wilson Wright, for helping me, with the sweetest disposition imaginable, with information about MDMA usage and rave/dance culture in the U.K.;
Margaret and Richard Sobel, my cousin and her husband, who took such good care of my New York City apartment, for accommodating me there when I was in town, for faithfully forwarding important mail and messages when I was not, and for introducing me to some interesting people who made a valuable contribution to the project;
Stephen and Vincent, who thoroughly instructed me in the ways of rave, sharing their music, their expertise, and their companionship in London and beyond;
Nick Moore, for his solidarity and for his briefings and introductions in London;
Tony Jack, my English cousin, for videotaping the *Psychedelic Science* documentary and for putting me up in London;
Messrs. J & J in Bangkok, for their white-room soirees that provided new contacts and puffings of inspiration;

Dan Levy, for facilitating and for useful information;
Katy Keiffer Weiss, for her emotional support, for her objectivity in making cutting suggestions, and for being a sounding board throughout the process;
Joan and Bob, for putting me up for so long in San Francisco;
Brian Hassett, for pointing my attention in the right direction more than once;
my parents, for their help and support and for putting me up during visits to the Midwest;
Palle and Vibeke, my wife's parents, for positive reinforcement and putting me onto the story of the Danish LSD scandal;
Marion Huyck, my English teacher back in sophomore year of high school, who gave me an A-plus on a paper and thus helped plant the notion that I could really write;
and Carolyn Bennett, for sensitivity and emotional and literary support that kept alive the dream of being a writer during impossibly gloomy and unlikely times.

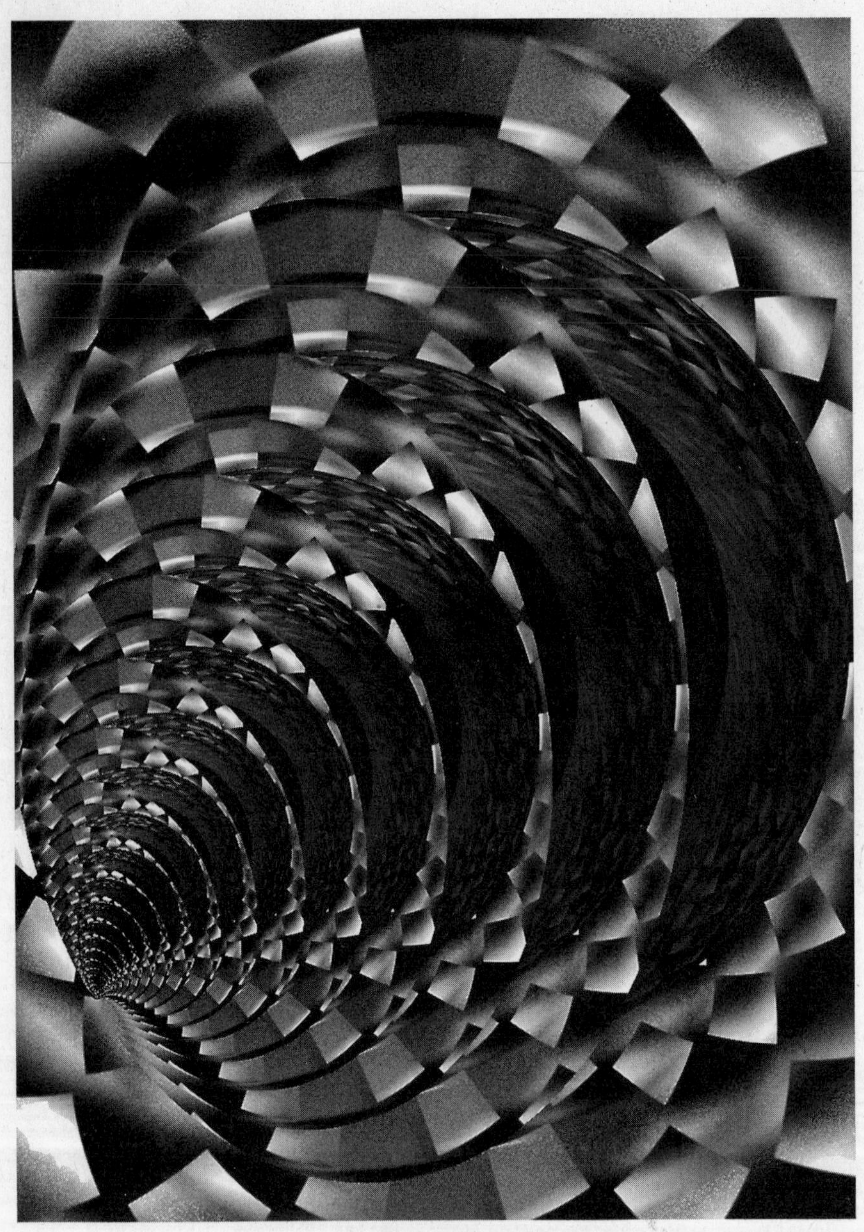

Vortex Closer by Brooks Cole, digital composition,
© 2000, courtesy of the artist.

Index